Envisioning Global
LGBT Human Rights

(Neo)colonialism, Neoliberalism, Resistance and Hope

Envisioning Global LGBT Human Rights

(Neo)colonialism, Neoliberalism, Resistance and Hope

edited by Nancy Nicol, Adrian Jjuuko,
Richard Lusimbo, Nick J. Mulé, Susan Ursel,
Amar Wahab and Phyllis Waugh

HUMAN RIGHTS CONSORTIUM
SCHOOL OF ADVANCED STUDY
UNIVERSITY OF LONDON

ISBN 978-0-9931102-3-8

School of Advanced Study
University of London
Senate House
Malet Street
London WC1E 7HU

Cover images: Envisioning Global LGBT Human Rights. Cover design by Val Fullard.

Contents

Acknowledgements   vii
List of figures and tables   xi
Abbreviations   xv
Notes on contributors   xxi
Foreword   1
Corinne Lennox and Matthew Waites
Overview   9
Nancy Nicol

PART 1. Between empathy and contempt: colonial legacies, neoliberalism and neo-colonialism   41

1   Vacillating between empathy and contempt: the
    Indian judiciary and LGBT rights   43
    Arvind Narrain

2   Expanded criminalisation of consensual same-sex
    relations in Africa: contextualising recent developments   63
    Adrian Jjuuko and Monica Tabengwa

3   Policing borders and sexual/gender identities: queer
    refugees in the years of Canadian neoliberalism and
    homonationalism   97
    Gary Kinsman

4   Queer affirmations: negotiating the possibilities and
    limits of sexual citizenship in Saint Lucia   131
    Amar Wahab

5   Violence and LGBT human rights in Guyana   157
    Pere DeRoy with Namela Baynes Henry

6   Cultural discourse in Africa and the promise of
    human rights based on non-normative sexuality
    and/or gender expression: exploring the intersections,
    challenges and opportunities   177
    Monica Mbaru, Monica Tabengwa and Kim Vance

7   Haven or precarity? The mental health of LGBT asylum seekers and
       refugees in Canada   205
       Nick J. Mulé and Kathleen Gamble

PART 2. Resilience, resistance and hope:
organising for social change   **221**

8   The rise of SOGI: human rights for LGBT people
       at the United Nations   223
       *Kim Vance, Nick J. Mulé, Maryam Khan and
       Cameron McKenzie*

9   Resistance to criminalisation, and social movement
       organising to advance LGBT rights in Belize   247
       Caleb Orozco

10   The multifaceted struggle against the Anti-
       Homosexuality Act in Uganda   269
       Adrian Jjuuko and Fridah Mutesi

11   Emergent momentum for equality: LGBT visibility
       and organising in Kenya   307
       Jane Wothaya Thirikwa

12   *Kuchu* resilience and resistance in Uganda: a history   323
       Richard Lusimbo and Austin Bryan

13   Gender theatre: the politics of exclusion and
       belonging in Kenya   347
       Guillit Amakobe, Kat Dearham and Po Likimani

14   Telling Our Stories: Envisioning participatory
       documentary   371
       Nancy Nicol

       Appendix: Envisioning Global LGBT Human
       Rights participatory documentaries   403

       Index   413

Acknowledgements

Envisioning Global LGBT Human Rights (hereafter Envisioning) was led by an executive team composed of the principal investigator, a knowledge mobilisation coordinator, and the chairs and co-chairs of five research teams. These members were collectively responsible for the overall direction of the research and partner engagement; monitoring and reporting on local, regional and international conditions and developments; and evaluation and assessment of Envisioning's goals and work.

We wish to acknowledge and extend our thanks to those executive team members for their commitment, insights, resourcefulness and contributions to this project:

Principal investigator: Nancy Nicol (School of Arts, Media and Performance, York University, Canada).

Knowledge mobilisation coordinator: Phyllis Waugh (then, Rainbow Health Ontario, hereafter RHO, Canada).

Africa research team chairs: Richard Lusimbo (Sexual Minorities Uganda, hereafter SMUG) and Monica Mbaru (then, Gay and Lesbian Coalition of Kenya, hereafter GALCK).

Canada research team chairs: Nick J. Mulé (School of Social Work, York University, Canada) and Erika Gates-Gasse (then, Ontario Council of Agencies Serving Immigrants, hereafter OCASI).

Caribbean research team chairs: Charmaine Williams (Factor-Inwentash Faculty of Social Work, University of Toronto, Canada) and Kenita Placide (United and Strong, Saint Lucia).

India research team chair: Nancy Nicol (details as above).

Law and human rights mechanisms research team chairs: Douglas Elliott (Cambridge LLP, Canada) and Susan Ursel (Ursel, Phillips, Fellows, Hopkinson LLP, Canada) and Kim Vance (ARC International).

Envisioning would not have been possible without the contributions of its partners, made up of non-governmental organisations, legal collectives and community-based organisations. Partners contributed research, expertise,

Figure 1. Envisioning conference, Toronto, Canada, 24 June 2014. Photo credit: Envisioning Global LGBT Human Rights.

resources, facilities and networking, as well as outreach and knowledge mobilisation of project outcomes. We thank them all:

Africa partners: Lesbians, Gays and Bisexuals of Botswana (LeGaBiBo), Botswana; GALCK, Kenya; SMUG, Uganda.

Canada partners: Africans in Partnership Against AIDS (APAA); Alliance For South Asian AIDS Prevention (ASAAP); Black Coalition for AIDS Prevention (BlackCAP); Centre for Feminist Research (CFR), York University; Egale Canada Human Rights Trust; International Human Rights Program (IHRP), Faculty of Law, University of Toronto; Inside Out Toronto LGBT Film Festival; Mark S. Bonham Centre for Sexual Diversity Studies, University of Toronto; OCASI; Osgoode Hall Law School, York University; Pride Uganda Alliance International (PUAI); Pro Bono Students Canada; RHO; Sexuality Studies, York University; The 519 Church St. Community Centre (The 519); and York University.

Caribbean partners: Jamaican Forum of Lesbians, All-Sexuals and Gays (J-FLAG), Jamaica; United and Strong, Saint Lucia; United Belize Advocacy Movement (UNIBAM), Belize; Society Against Sexual Discrimination (SASOD), Guyana.

India partners: Naz Foundation (India) Trust; Naz Foundation International (NFI) in conjunction with the Maan AIDS Foundation; Sangini India Trust.

International partners: ARC International; International Gay and Lesbian Human Rights Commission (renamed OutRight Action International); International Lesbian Gay Bisexual Trans and Intersex Law Association; and Global Alliance for LGBT Education (GALE), Netherlands.

Thank you to the Ontario Research and Innovation Optical Network (ORION) for technical support and web hosting the research team's internal communications.

In addition to Envisioning partners, we wish to acknowledge and thank the following organisations which contributed the additional expertise and knowledge that informed this research: Alternative Law Forum (ALF), Bangalore, India; Botswana Network on Ethics, Law and HIV/AIDS (BONELA), Gaborone; Coalition of African Lesbians (CAL), Johannesburg, South Africa; Caribbean Forum for Liberation and Acceptance of Genders and Sexualities (CARIFLAGS), Saint Lucia; Centre for Refugee Studies (CRS), York University; Civil Society Coalition on Human Rights and Constitutional Law (CSCHRCL), Kampala, Uganda; Freedom and Roam Uganda (FARUG), Kampala; Human Rights Awareness and Promotion Forum (HRAPF), Kampala; Icebreakers Uganda, Kampala; Lawyers Collective, Delhi, India; National Gay and Lesbian Human Rights Commission (NGLHRC), Nairobi, Kenya; Refugee Law Project (RLP), Kampala; and Women's Health in Women's Hands (WHIWH), Toronto, Canada.

We also wish to express our thanks to a large number of community-based and academic researchers, videographers and undergraduate and graduate students for their hard work, commitment and thoughtful contributions to research and videography. Our gratitude, as well, to the Research at York (RAY) programme, the Centre for Feminist Research (CFR), and York University's School of Gender, Sexuality and Women's Studies for additional support and funding for student research assistants. We also acknowledge and thank Pro-Bono Students Canada in conjunction with Osgoode Hall Law School, York University, and the University of Toronto's law faculty for its support to law students working with Envisioning.

Envisioning was housed at CFR, York University, Canada. We extend our gratitude to CFR directors, Enakshi Dua (2011–15) and Alison Crosby (2016) for providing support and advice to Professor Nicol and the Envisioning team and partners. Much gratitude as well to the Office of Research, York University, for its guidance and assistance, to Envisioning and CFR staff for administrative support. Special thanks to Envisioning staff member, Kaija Siirala, for her contribution to the participatory documentary teams and video editing.

Many people participated in the Envisioning study through interviews and focus groups, including several who spoke about highly traumatic and difficult personal experiences. We wish to acknowledge their courage in sharing their stories and we extend special thanks to all those who took part for their invaluable insights. We hope that their contributions will reinforce efforts towards greater awareness, human rights and social change in the struggle to achieve equality and dignity for all.

We wish to acknowledge and support our funders. From 2011 to 2016 Envisioning received a Community University Research Grant (CURA) from the Social Sciences and Humanities Research Council of Canada (SSHRC), held by principal investigator, Nancy Nicol. Additional funding was contributed by the Law Foundation of Ontario in 2012 and 2015 in support of research reports and knowledge mobilisation outcomes on LGBT refugees in Canada. Although these bodies provided funding, the outcomes of Envisioning's research do not necessarily reflect their views.

Research was conducted in accordance with Canada's Tri-Council Statement on Research Ethics and in accordance with ethics guidelines at Canada's York University and University of Toronto. In addition, the Envisioning executive team developed 'Envisioning guiding principles', which informed and steered the research team and partners' methodology and their work together.

This anthology is dedicated to human rights defenders across the Commonwealth.

List of figures and tables

Figure

1. Envisioning conference, Toronto, Canada, 24 June 2014.
   Photo credit: Envisioning Global LGBT Human Rights.   viii

2. Pride, Delhi, India, 28 November 2011. Photo credit:
   No Easy Walk to Freedom, Envisioning Global LGBT
   Human Rights.   4

3. Caribbean research team, Emancipation Park, Kingston,
   Jamaica, 10 July 2013. Photo credit: Ulleli Verbeke,
   Society Against Sexual Orientation Discrimination and
   Envisioning Global LGBT Human Rights.   15

4. SMUG participatory documentary team, International
   Day Against Homophobia, Nairobi, Kenya, 17 May 2012.
   Photo credit: Envisioning Global LGBT Human Rights.   21

5. United and Strong participatory documentary team,
   International Dialogue, Saint Lucia, 5 February 2012.
   Photo credit: Envisioning Global LGBT Human Rights.   33

6. Envisioning Global LGBT Human Rights research team,
   World Pride, Toronto, Canada, 29 June 2014. Photo credit:
   Envisioning Global LGBT Human Rights.   34

7. Demonstration in front of the High Court, Delhi,
   28 November 2011. Photo credit: *No Easy Walk to Freedom*,
   Envisioning Global LGBT Human Rights.   41

8. Protest against the Supreme Court ruling that reinstated
   Section 377, recriminalising consensual same-sex acts in
   India, Delhi, India, 11 December 2013. Photo credit:
   No Easy Walk to Freedom, Envisioning Global LGBT
   Human Rights.   50

9. Pride, Delhi, India, 28 November 2011. Photo credit:
   No Easy Walk to Freedom, Envisioning Global LGBT
   Human Rights.   56

10.   Demonstration by Rainbow Identity Association and
        Lesbians, Gays and Bisexuals of Botswana, Gaborone,
        Botswana, 2013. Photo credit: *Botho: LGBT Lives in
        Botswana*, LeGaBiBo and Envisioning Global LGBT
        Human Rights.   197

11.   Asylum seekers, Toronto, Canada. Photo credit: Ulelli
        Verbeke, 2014, Society Against Sexual Orientation
        Discrimination and Envisioning Global LGBT Human
        Rights.   206

12.   First Pride march in Uganda, Kampala, Uganda, 6 August
        2012. Photo credit: *And Still We Rise*, Sexual Minorities
        Uganda and Envisioning Global LGBT Human Rights.   221

13.   Dialogue 2012: Focus on Strengthening Caribbean
        Response and Linking Regional and International
        Advocacy around the World, Saint Lucia, 6 February
        2012. Photo credit: ARC International and Envisioning
        Global LGBT Human Rights.   225

14.   Emancipation Park, Kingston, Jamaica, 10 July 2013.
        Photo credit: Ulelli Verbeke, SASOD and Envisioning.   252

15.   Opening of the first Pride in Kampala, Uganda, 6 August
        2012. Photo credit: *And Still We Rise* (2015), SMUG and
        Envisioning.   340

16.   LeGaBiBo participatory documentary team workshop,
        Gaborone, Botswana, 1 May 2012. Photo credit:
        LeGaBiBo and Envisioning.   378

17.   GALCK and SMUG participatory documentary team
        workshop, GALCK Centre, Nairobi, Kenya, 16 May
        2012. Photo credit: Envisioning Global LGBT Human
        Rights.   379

18.   Caribbean team participatory documentary workshop,
        Kingston, Jamaica, 9 July 2013. Photo credit: Envisioning
        Global LGBT Human Rights.   383

19.   International Day Against Homophobia, 17 May 2012,
        Nairobi, Kenya. Photo credit: Envisioning Global LGBT
        Human Rights.   385

20.   Photo credit: *Telling Our Stories*, Envisioning Global
        LGBT Human Rights.   387

21.   *No Easy Walk to Freedom* production team, Delhi, India,
        31 October 2011. Photo credit: Envisioning Global
        LGBT Human Rights.   391

22.   Milan Centre, Naz Foundation (India) Trust outreach
       workers with client, Delhi, India, 29 October 2011.
       Photo credit: *No Easy Walk to Freedom*, Envisioning
       Global LGBT Human Rights.   393

23.   Filming *No Easy Walk to Freedom* in Delhi, India,
       14 November 2011. Photo credit: Envisioning Global
       LGBT Human Rights.   396

24.   Sangama demonstration, Bangalore, India, 19 November
       2011. Photo credit: *No Easy Walk to Freedom*, Envisioning Global
       LGBT Human Rights.   397

Table

1.   Timeline of UN resolutions, joint statements and reports   230

Abbreviations

AAA	Alliance Against AIDS (Belize)
ACHPR	African Commission on Human and Peoples' Rights
ACLJ	American Center for Law and Justice
ADF	Alliance Defending Freedom
AHA	Anti-Homosexuality Act (Uganda)
AHB	Anti-Homosexuality Bill (Uganda)
AFRA	Artists for Recognition and Acceptance (Kenya)
AIDS	Acquired Immunodeficiency Syndrome
ALF	Alternative Law Forum (India)
amfAR	American Foundation for AIDS Research
ANC	African National Congress
APAA	Africans in Partnership Against AIDS (Canada)
APRM	African Peer Review Mechanism
ARC	ARC International
ASAAP	Alliance for South Asian AIDS Prevention (Canada)
AU	African Union
AUC	African Union Commission
AWID	Association for Women's Rights and Economic Change
BOC	Basis of Claim (Canada)
BlackCAP	Black Coalition for AIDS Prevention (Canada)
BONELA	Botswana Network on Ethics, Law and HIV/AIDS
CAL	Coalition of African Lesbians (South Africa)
CCM	Country Coordinating Mechanism (Belize)
Caricom	Caribbean Community and Common Market
CariFLAGS	Caribbean Forum for Liberation and Acceptance of Genders and Sexualities
CEDAW	Convention on the Elimination of all Forms of Discrimination against Women
CEHURD	Centre for Health, Human Rights and Development (Uganda)
CCR	Center for Constitutional Rights (US)
CFR	Centre for Feminist Research (York University, Canada)
C-FAM	Centre for Family and Human Rights
CHOGM	Commonwealth Heads of Government Meeting

CMHA	Canadian Mental Health Association
(the) Consortium	Consortium on Monitoring Violations Based on Sex Determination, Gender Identity and Sexual Orientation (Uganda)
CSCHRCL	Civil Society Coalition on Human Rights and Constitutional Law (Uganda)
CRTA	Caribbean Regional Trans in Action
CSOs	civil society organisations
CTAG	Caribbean Treatment Action Group
CVC	Caribbean Vulnerable Communities coalition
DCO	Designated Country of Origin
DFN	Designated Foreign National
EJE	extrajudicial executions
EACJ	East Africa Court of Justice
EI	Education International
ECOSOC	United Nations Economic and Social Council
FARUG	Freedom and Roam Uganda
FTM	female-to-male
FWI	Family Watch International
GALCK	Gay and Lesbian Coalition of Kenya
GALE	Global Alliance for LGBT Education (Netherlands)
GALZ	Gays and Lesbians of Zimbabwe
GATE	Global Action for Trans* Equality
GII	Gender Inequality Index (UNDP)
GNSWP	Global Network of Sex Work Projects
GTA	Greater Toronto Area
GUYBOW	Guyana Rainbow Coalition
HIV	Human Immunodeficiency Virus
HRAPF	Human Rights Awareness and Promotion Forum (Uganda)
HRC	Human Rights Council
HRW	Human Rights Watch
IAHCR	Inter-American Commission on Human Rights (of the OAS)
IBU	Ice Breakers Uganda
ICCPR	International Covenant on Civil and Political Rights
ICESCR	International Covenant on Economic, Social and Cultural Rights
ICJ	International Commission of Jurists
IDAHO(T)	International Day Against Homophobia (and Transphobia)
IFHP	Interim Federal Health Program (Canada)
IGLHRC	International Gay and Lesbian Human Rights Commission
IHRP	International Human Rights Program (University of Toronto, Canada)

ILGA	International Lesbian, Gay, Bisexual, Trans and Intersex Association
ILO	International Labour Organization
IPC	Indian Penal Code
IRB	Immigration and Refugee Board of Canada
IRCU	Inter Religious Council of Uganda
ISHR	International Service for Human Rights
ITGNC	Intersex, transgender and gender non-conforming
J-FLAG	Jamaican Forum for Lesbians, All-Sexuals and Gays
JCHS	Jamaican Coalition for a Healthy Society
KEMRI	Kenya Medical Research Institute
KHRC	Kenya Human Rights Commission
KNCHR	Kenya National Commission on Human Rights
KNEC	Kenya National Examinations Council
KULHAS	Kuchus Living with HIV/AIDS (Uganda)
LeGaBiBo	Lesbians, Gays and Bisexuals of Botswana
LGBT	lesbian, gay, bisexual, transgender
LGBTI	lesbian, gay, bisexual, transgender, intersex
LGBTTTI	lesbian, gay, bisexual, transvestite, transgender, transsexual and intersex
LGBTTTI Coalition	Latin American and Caribbean Coalition of lesbian, gay, bisexual, transvestite, transgender, transsexual and intersex organisations
MARP	Most at Risk Populations
MARPI	Most at Risk Population Initiative (Uganda)
MSM	men who have sex with men
MUWRP	Makerere University Walter Reed Project (Uganda)
MWA	Minority Women in Action (Kenya)
NACO	National AIDS Control Organisation (India)
NAC	National AIDS Commission (Belize)
NAWG	National Advocacy Working Group (Belize)
Naz India	Naz Foundation (India) Trust
NGLHRC	National Gay and Lesbian Human Rights Commission (Kenya)
NEPAD	New Partnership for African Development
NFI	Naz Foundation International
NGOs	non-governmental organisations
NOII	No One Is Illegal
OAS	Organization of American States
OAU	Organization of African Unity
OCASI	Ontario Council of Agencies Serving Immigrants
OHCHR	Office of the United Nations High Commission for Human Rights

OII	Organization Intersex International
OTHP	Ontario Temporary Health Program (Canada)
OutRight	OutRight Action International
OPEC	Organisation of Petroleum Exporting Countries
PALU	Pan African Lawyers Union
PAR	Participatory Action Research
PEMA	Persons Marginalized and Aggrieved (Kenya)
PIF	Personal Information Form (Canada)
PLWA	people living with AIDS
PRRA	Pre-Removal Risk Assessment (Canada)
PSI	Public Services International
PSMO	Pan American Social Marketing Organization
PUAI	Pride Uganda Alliance International (Canada)
PUP	Peoples United Party (Belize)
RAD	Refugee Appeal Division (Canada)
RCC	Roman Catholic Church
RCMP	Royal Canadian Mounted Police
RHO	Rainbow Health Ontario (Canada)
RLP	Refugee Law Project (Uganda)
SASOD	Society Against Sexual Orientation Discrimination (Guyana)
SMUG	Sexual Minorities Uganda
SOGI	sexual orientation and gender identity
SOGIE	sexual orientation, gender identity and gender expression
SOGIESC	sexual orientation, gender identity, gender expression, and sex characteristics
SRI	Sexual Rights Initiative
SSHRCC	Social Sciences and Humanities Research Council of Canada
STI	sexually transmitted illness
TEA	Transgender Education and Advocacy (Kenya)
The 519	The 519 Church St. Community Centre (Canada)
UDHR	Universal Declaration of Human Rights
UHAI-EASHRI	UHAI–East African Sexual Health and Rights Initiative
ULS	Uganda Law Society
UN	United Nations
UNAIDS	United Nations Programme on HIV/AIDS
UNDP	United Nations Development Programme
UNESCO	United Nations Educational Scientific and Cultural Organisation
UNFPA	United Nations Population Fund
UNGA	United Nations General Assembly
UNHCHR	United Nations High Commission for Human Rights

UNHCR	United Nations High Commission for Refugees
UNHRC	United Nations Human Rights Committee
UNIBAM	United Belize Advocacy Movement
UP	Ushirikiano Panda (Kenya)
UPR	Universal Periodic Review
U-RAP	University of West Indies Rights Advocacy Project
VDPA	Vienna Declaration and Programme of Action
WHO	World Health Organisation
WIN	Women's Issues Network of Belize
WHIWH	Women's Health in Women's Hands (Canada)
WSW	women who have sex with women

Notes on contributors[1]

Guillit Amakobe is a transgender activist and poet. They[2] participated in Envisioning's research and featured in a video portrait in the *Telling Our Stories* series, developed through the participatory documentary work carried out in Kenya. In 2011, Guillit was selected as a fellow, through Fahamu Networks for Social Justice, on the inaugural Pan-African Fellowship Programme, which provided support for the creation of a trans peer support group. This eventually grew into Jinsiangu, a Nairobi-based organisation working to create safe spaces for and increase awareness of intersex, transgender and gender non-conforming Kenyans. Having grown up in Nairobi's notoriously violent Dandora Estate, Guillit is particularly concerned with the intersections between gender identity, economic oppression and violence. Guillit is currently living in Toronto and studying massage therapy with the goal of working with people who would normally feel uncomfortable about massage due to gender dysphoria or other points of struggle with their bodies.

Austin Bryan is a student of Africana studies at North Carolina State University. He was a research assistant at Sexual Minorities Uganda (SMUG), a role which formed part of the ethnographic fieldwork he completed in Kampala (2015–16), studying (as a Roy Park Scholar and Caldwell Fellow) the country's lesbian, gay, bisexual, transgender, intersex (LGBTI) communities. His work has been presented at the University of Cambridge and is published in two edited anthologies. Austin's research interests lie at the intersection of queer theory and African studies.

Kat Dearham, a queer feminist researcher, writer and counsellor in training, is a former member of Envisioning's Africa research team, working for several years with various lesbian, gay, bisexual, transgender, queer (LGBTQ) organisations in Kenya, including the 'None on Record: Stories of Queer Africa' project. Kat

---

1   The anthology editorial team is comprised of Nancy Nicol, Adrian Jjuuko, Richard Lusimbo, Nick J. Mulé, Susan Ursel, Amar Wahab and Phyllis Waugh. For more information on Envisioning Global LGBT Human Rights, and to access its resources, publications and participatory documentary films, please see: www.envisioninglgbt.com.
2   Guillit identifies by the pronouns 'they', 'their' and 'them'.

is currently a social work master's candidate at York University, Toronto, where she is aiming to establish a practice which combines individual approaches to healing with community building. Her main focus is on experiences of trauma and healing in racialised queer and trans communities. She was a co-founding member of Jinsiangu, a group working to create safe spaces for and increase the wellbeing of intersex, transgender and gender non-conforming people in Kenya, and is the co-author of Jinsiangu's *Resilience*, a resource guide for intersex, transgender and gender non-conforming Kenyans. She has also written for the *Queer African Reader* and *MIXD zine #2.*

Pere DeRoy was a graduate student in York University's Faculty of Liberal Arts and Professional Studies, where she completed her MA in Development Studies in 2017. She is starting a PhD in Women, Gender and Sexuality studies at the University of Kansas in 2018. Originally from Guyana, she was an assistant on the Envisioning Caribbean research team, analysing interviews conducted in Guyana and Jamaica on the lives LGBT persons are managing to live, in an environment of homo-bi-transphobia. Pere contributed to a presentation entitled: 'Discourse of Sexuality and Resistance in and from the Global South: a Caribbean Case' on behalf of Envisioning at the 2015 Congress of the Humanities and Social Sciences, Ottawa, Canada. Pere's research interests encompass human trafficking, labour and the global economy, sexual and reproductive health, violence, LGBT and women's advocacy.

Kathleen Gamble is a PhD student in Gender, Sexuality and Women's Studies at York University, and assisted Envisioning's Canada research team. Kathleen contributed to the team's investigations on LGBT asylum in Canada, conducting data analysis and helping to liaise and work with Canadian community partners. Kathleen co-authored (with Mulé, Nicol, Waugh, Jordan and OCASI) the Envisioning research report: 'Envisioning LGBT refugee rights in Canada: is Canada a safe haven?' (2015).

Namela Baynes Henry was a member of Envisioning's Caribbean research team and also a community researcher for the project in Guyana. Namela is a grassroots human rights activist who has worked to advance LGBT rights for more than 20 years at the local, regional, and international levels. She conducted Envisioning's primary interviews in Guyana and contributed to the 2013 participatory documentaries *Sade's Story* and *Homophobia in Guyana.*

Adrian Jjuuko is a lawyer and executive director and founder of the Human Rights Awareness and Promotion Forum (HRAPF), the first and only specialised legal aid service provider for LGBTI persons in Uganda. Adrian was a member of Envisioning's law and human rights mechanisms research team. He was coordinator of the Civil Society Coalition on Human Rights and Constitutional Law Uganda, the Coalition that led the challenge to the Anti-Homosexuality Bill/Act (AHB/AHA). It won the US State Department's Human Rights Defender of the Year Award 2011 during his tenure. He currently chairs the Coalition's legal committee, and in this capacity coordinated and organised the successful legal challenge against the AHA, 2014. He also led HRAPF in its challenge against the passing of the AHA at the East Africa Court of Justice, the first case to dispute legislation criminalising LGBTI people within the African regional framework. He brought a successful challenge before Uganda's Constitutional Court to section 15(6)(d) of Uganda's Equal Opportunities Commission Act, which had prevented the Commission from investigating matters affecting LGBTI persons. In recognition of his courageous work to advance the human rights of sexual and gender minorities in Uganda, Adrian was awarded the Vera Chirwa 2016 award by the Centre for Human Rights, University of Pretoria.

Maryam Khan is a PhD candidate at York University's School of Social Work. She is passionate about carrying out critical research on issues related to LGBTQ policy, race and racialisation, intersectional and transnational feminism, Islam and sexual diversity, gender and sexuality, decolonisation and anticolonial perspectives. For her doctoral research, Maryam focused on LBTQ Muslim women in the Global North. She is a full-time faculty member at Wilfrid Laurier University's Faculty of Social Work.

Gary Kinsman was a member of Envisioning's Canada research team. He is the author of *The Regulation of Desire, Homo and Hetero Sexualities* (Black Rose Books, 1996) on the regulation of sexualities in 'Canada' (contributor's quote marks), co-author (with Patrizia Gentile) of *The Canadian War on Queers, National Security as Sexual Regulation* (UBC Press, 2010), and editor of *Whose National Security? Canadian State Surveillance and the Creation of Enemies* (Between the Lines, 2000) and *Sociology for Changing the World, Social Movements/Social Research* (Fernwood, 2006) as well as numerous book chapters on gender and sexual politics. His current work revolves around the making of the neoliberal queer in the context of neoliberal capitalism and homonationalism. Gary is a long-time queer liberation, anti-poverty, Palestine solidarity, and anti-capitalist activist living on indigenous land. He is also involved in the AIDS Activist History Project, Faculty for Palestine, the We Demand an Apology Network (demanding an apology from the 'Canadian' government for the purge campaigns against lesbians and gay men) and with Queer Trans Community Defense, which is organising against gentrification in downtown Toronto. He currently divides his time between Toronto and Sudbury, where he is a professor emeritus at Laurentian University.

Corinne Lennox is senior lecturer in human rights at the Institute of Commonwealth Studies and associate director of the Human Rights Consortium at the School of Advanced Study, University of London. Her research interests include the human rights of ethnic, religious and linguistic minorities and indigenous peoples, global governance on human rights and civil society mobilisation. She holds a PhD and MSc in international relations from the London School of Economics and Political Science (LSE), an MA in the theory and practice of human rights from the University of Essex, and a BA (Honours) in political science and human rights from McMaster University in Canada. She has worked for many years as a human rights practitioner with various non-governmental organisations (NGOs), including Minority Rights Group International, and has been a trainer and consultant on minority rights for the UN Development Programme and the UN Office of the High Commissioner for Human Rights. She is a trustee of the Dalit Solidarity Network-UK, a fellow at the Human Rights Centre, University of Essex and associate editor of the *International Journal of Human Rights*. Corinne has published widely including in the *International Journal on Minority and Group Rights* and the *Netherlands Quarterly of Human Rights* and is co-editor of the *Handbook of Indigenous Peoples' Rights* (Routledge, 2015) and co-editor of *Human Rights, Sexual Orientation and Gender Identity in the Commonwealth: Struggles for Decriminalisation and Change* (Institute of Commonwealth Studies/Human Rights Consortium, 2013).

Po Likimani is an anti-oppression activist, a farmer and a spoken-word artist. They[3] were a co-founding member of Jinsiangu, a group working to create safe spaces for and enhance the wellbeing of intersex, transgender and gender non-conforming people in Kenya. Their chapter in this volume is a collaborative oral history of the founding and evolution of Jinsiangu. Po identifies as gender non-conforming and works towards a sustainable and just world through teaching, public speaking and community mobilisation and empowerment. They are deeply committed to gender justice and self-determination. Po has been involved in queer, trans and sex-worker liberation movements in East Africa for the past decade and co-authored *Resilience*, a resource guide for intersex, transgender and gender non-conforming Kenyans, published by Jinsiangu.

Richard Lusimbo was the chair of Envisioning's Africa research team from mid 2012 to mid 2016 and a member of the team based in Uganda. He is SMUG's research and documentation manager, based in Kampala, and co-director with Nancy Nicol of the Envisioning/SMUG documentary, *And Still We Rise*. Richard serves as co-chair of Pan Africa ILGA, has been heavily involved in a

---

3   Po identifies by the pronouns 'they', 'their' and 'them'.

range of advocacy and community mobilisation activities in Uganda, Africa and internationally, and is helping to lead PrEP[4] advocacy campaigns in Uganda and regionally. He also has a strong background in science and technology, digital security and documentation tools. In December 2017, Richard graduated with an M.Phil in Human Rights and Democratisation in Africa from the Centre for Human Rights, Faculty of Law, University of Pretoria, South Africa.

Justice Monica Mbaru is a judge at the High Court of Kenya. She contributed to the development of the Africa research team which brought together partners and researchers from Botswana, Uganda and Kenya; and chaired the team from 2011 to mid 2012. Activists, human rights defenders and country-based organisations contributed to the material used in the work. The project benefited from North/South collaboration, which has created a network of researchers and different experts on sexuality, human rights, law and art. Monica's chapter in the book was written in partnership with human rights defenders from Botswana and Canada, who helped assess the work of UN bodies, African regional human rights mechanisms and national legal protections for sexual minorities.

Cameron McKenzie is a PhD candidate in Health Policy and Equity at York University. His research has focused on Indigenous Northern issues, disability and the queer and trans community. His current doctoral research, titled: *Policy in Motion: LGBTQ Health from the Fringes to the Mainstream?*, examines how the sociopolitical climate and economy serves, and has served, to shape responses to LGBTQ population health needs in Canada. Cameron also has a private practice and is a full-time faculty member at Wilfrid Laurier University's Faculty of Social Work.

Nick J. Mulé is an associate professor at York University's School of Social Work and he has been seconded to teach policy, theory and practice at the School of Gender, Sexuality and Women's Studies there. Nick was a co-applicant on Envisioning and a member of its executive team. He was the academic chair of the Canada research team, which studied the experiences of LGBT-identified asylum seekers and refugees who were settling in the Greater Toronto Area (GTA) and their service providers. He was also a member of Envisioning's law and human rights mechanisms team, on which he conducted research regarding the interaction between treaty bodies and LGBT human rights initiatives, including decriminalisation. He publishes and has research interests in the areas of social inclusion/exclusion of gender and sexually diverse populations in social policy and service provision focusing particularly on the

4   Pre-exposure prophylaxis medical intervention to radically reduce the risk of HIV infection.

degree of their recognition as distinct communities in cultural, systemic and structural contexts. He has also undertaken a critical analysis of the LGBT movement and the development of queer liberation theory. A queer activist, Nick is the founder of Queer Ontario. Additionally, he is a psychotherapist in private practice serving gender and sexually diverse populations in Toronto.

Fridah Mutesi is a Ugandan human rights lawyer and an advocate for equality and social justice for women and sexual minorities. As one of the lawyers who challenged the AHA in Uganda's Constitutional Court and in the East African Court of Justice, Fridah co-authored, along with Adrian Jjuuko, the chapter in this volume on the struggle against the AHA. She is the current coordinator of the Civil Society Coalition on Human Rights and Constitutional Law, a coalition of NGOs that was initially founded to challenge the AHB/AHA, and after the law's downfall, continues with joint advocacy and response on human rights issues. She is one of the founding partners of Veritas Advocates, a law firm that provides affordable and pro bono legal services to marginalised and indigent persons, among others. Fridah worked as the head of HRAPF's access to justice department, and on many other cases that target LGBTI and other marginalised persons, including *Adrian Jjuuko v. attorney general* which challenged Section 15 (6)(d) of the Equal Opportunities Commission Act barring the Commission from investigating matters considered immoral and/or socially harmful to the majority in society. The act was declared unconstitutional. Fridah's advocacy work transcends borders. She has advocated and has contributed to reports and papers submitted to various institutional advocacy platforms, including the United Nations Human Rights Council and The African Commission on Human and Peoples' Rights. She was nominated for and participated in the prestigious US state department's international visitor leadership programme.

Arvind Narrain is ARC International's Geneva director. He contributed expertise to Envisioning's India research team, and its law and human rights mechanisms research team. Prior to his ARC International position, Arvind was a founding member of the Alternative Law Forum (Bangalore, India) and was one of the team of lawyers litigating the historic case against section 377, the law criminalising same-sex conduct, in both the Delhi High Court and the Supreme Court of India. Arvind has co-edited three volumes which focus on queer politics in the Indian context: *Because I Have a Voice: Queer Politics in India* (with Gautam Bhan, Yoda Press, 2006); *Law Like Love: Queer Perspectives on Law* (with Alok Gupta, Yoda Press, 2011); and *Nothing to Fix: Medicalisation of Sexual Orientation and Gender Identity* (with Vinay Chandran, Yoda Press and Sage Publications, 2016).

Nancy Nicol was Envisioning's principal investigator and currently is professor emeritus in York University's School of Media, Arts and Performance, where she taught from 1989–2016. Nancy is a documentary filmmaker, writer and activist, whose work probes into issues of human rights, social justice and struggles for social change. Her documentaries explore women and work, reproductive rights, migrant workers' rights, LGBT rights and social movement histories. They include the award-winning series, *From Criminality to Equality*, which traces 40 years of lesbian and gay organising in Canada, from 1969 to 2009. As part of Envisioning's participatory documentary projects, Nancy directed *Sangini* (2016) and *No Easy Walk to Freedom* (2014); and co-directed *And Still We Rise* (2015) with Richard Lusimbo. Her recent publications include: 'Envisioning Global LGBT Human Rights: strategic alliances to advance knowledge and social change' (with Erika Gates-Gasse and Nick J. Mulé), *Scholarly and Research Communication,* 5 (3), 2014; 'Sexual rights and the LGBTI movement in Botswana' (with Monica Tabengwa), in C. Lennox and M. Waites (eds.) *Human Rights, Sexual Orientation and Gender Identity in the Commonwealth: Struggles for Decriminalisation and Change* (Institute of Commonwealth Studies/Human Rights Consortium, 2013); and 'Legal struggles and political resistance: same-sex marriage in Canada and the US' (with Miriam Smith), in A. Crocker, J. Pierceson and S. Schulenberg (eds.) *Same-Sex Marriage in the Americas* (Lexington Books, 2010). In 2017, Nancy donated a large body of her original footage on queer history in Canada filmed between 1994 and 2009, to the Canadian Lesbian and Gay Archives.

Caleb Orozco is an LGBT/human rights advocate in Belize, and a health educator and activist with two decades of experience in the human development sector. He was a member of Envisioning's Caribbean research team. For the past seven years he has worked primarily within the field of HIV and human rights as executive director and founding member of the United Belize Advocacy Movement. Through legislative analysis, litigation and public education, he has worked tirelessly to advocate for a participatory and rights-based approach to health services for HIV-affected and marginalised populations, and for the eradication of discriminatory laws that affect these communities in the Caribbean. He was the principal litigant in the *Caleb Orozco v. attorney general of Belize* case, a constitutional challenge to Section 53 of the Criminal Code (which criminalised same-sex intimacy), that was ruled unconstitutional on 10 August 2016. Caleb is active at the hemispheric level in international and regional organisations, such as the UN and the Organization of American States, in the cause of raising the standard of protection and human rights enforcement for LGBT populations. He is also the author of articles and shadow reports on these issues.

Monica Tabengwa is a lawyer from Botswana and was a member of Envisioning's Africa research team as well as its law and human rights mechanisms research team. Currently working for Pan Africa ILGA as executive director, Monica is a human rights activist and defender with extensive experience in human rights and social justice advocacy, extending to regional and international human rights mechanisms. Monica started her career as a prosecutor with Botswana police, and then joined the women's rights sector, where she provided legal assistance to indigent women and children in Botswana. Subsequently, she left Botswana and joined the Coalition of African Lesbians (CAL) as advocacy adviser, doing regional and international advocacy work on LGBTI rights. Later, she joined Human Rights Watch as LGBTI researcher, including the documentation of human rights violations and specifically focusing on the rights of sexual and gender minorities in Africa. She has extensive experience in gender and rights-based training and strategic litigation. She was one of the early members of Lesbians, Gays and Bisexuals of Botswana (LeGaBiBo) and has continued to provide them with legal support, which contributed to the successful litigation for freedom of association for the organisation in 2015.

Jane Wothaya Thirikwa is a social justice activist with more than eight years' experience in LGBT organising efforts in Kenya. She provided expertise and insights to Envisioning's Africa research team regarding Kenya's LGBT rights movement. Jane was featured in a video portrait in the *Telling Our Stories* series, Envisioning's video portraits of LGBT activists working in the countries involved in the study. She participated in advocacy programmes at both the Gay Kenya Trust and the Gay and Lesbian Coalition of Kenya (GALCK), coordinating grassroots initiatives as well as building partnerships with the wider social justice movement in Kenya. Jane holds a BSc in Communications and Public Relations from Moi University, Kenya and is completing a Gender, Sexuality and Women's Studies programme at York University, Toronto. She is a 2014 Atlas Corps Fellowship alumna and served as a global engagement fellow at the Human Rights Campaign (HRC) in Washington DC. Currently Jane is the global partnerships coordinator at KAIROS Canadian Ecumenical Justice Initiatives, Toronto.

Kim Vance is the executive director of ARC International and was a co-chair of Envisioning's law and human rights mechanisms research team. Prior to co-founding ARC International in 2003, Kim served as president of Egale Canada (Canada's national LGBT organisation), and is a seasoned activist within LGBTI communities at the international, national and local levels. For more than a decade, Kim served on the editorial board of Atlantic Canada's LGBT community newspaper, *Wayves,* and helped found Nova Scotia's provincial LGBT organisation, NSRAP. She has received the Pride Community Service

Award and the Rev. Darlene Young Community Award in her province. Kim secured the first registered domestic partnership in Canada and was a successful litigant in one of the Canadian court challenges to secure equal marriage rights for same-sex couples. She is the very proud mother of two adopted children, Marcus and Patty. Kim founded and chaired an international affairs committee within Egale, and oversaw the organisation's participation in the 2001 World Conference Against Racism, held in Durban, South Africa (including a research project on the intersections of race and sexual orientation). She oversaw the development of the first conference for LGBT activists in the South East Asia region. Kim has also participated in all of the UN Beijing review conferences in New York City, examining advancement and development for women around the world, and has planned numerous international dialogues in locations around the world, including Brazil, South Korea, South Africa, Montréal, Geneva, Argentina, Saint Lucia and Istanbul.

Amar Wahab is associate professor in the School of Gender, Sexuality and Women's Studies at York University. He is a co-investigator with Envisioning and also a member of its Caribbean research team. His research interests include: sexual citizenship in liberal multicultural and postcolonial nation-state formations (mainly related to the Caribbean and Canada); race and queer transnational politics; critiques of queer liberalism; and race, gender and the politics of representation. He is the author of *Colonial Inventions: Landscape, Power and Representation in Nineteenth-Century Trinidad* (Cambridge Scholars Publishing, 2010), which explores the racialised and gendered construction of colonial subjects in the contexts of slavery and indentureship. His work in queer and sexuality studies is published in journals such as *GLQ: Journal of Lesbian and Gay Studies*, *Interventions: Journal of Postcolonial Studies* and the *Journal of Homosexuality*. His current project, funded by the Social Sciences and Humanities Research Council of Canada, is 'Queer Diasporas in Canada: a case study of transnational activism and politics', which focuses on queer anti-racist critiques of homonationalism in Canada.

Matthew Waites is senior lecturer in sociology at the University of Glasgow. He is author of *The Age of Consent: Young People, Sexuality and Citizenship* (Houndmills: Palgrave Macmillan, 2005); and co-editor (with Corinne Lennox) of *Human Rights, Sexual Orientation and Gender Identity in the Commonwealth: Struggles for Decriminalisation and Change* (Institute of Commonwealth Studies/Human Rights Consortium, 2013). He is co-editor, with Patricia Hynes, Michele Lamb and Damien Short, of three special issues on sociology and human rights, including two issues of the *International Journal of Human Rights* in 2010 (14 (6), 'Sociology and human rights: new engagements') and 2012 (16 (8), 'New directions in the sociology of human rights') – both also published as books by Taylor and Francis; and a special issue of *Sociology*, 'The sociology of human rights' (46 (5), 2012). He also co-edited (with Kelly Kollman) 'The global politics of LGBT human rights' special issue of *Contemporary Politics* (15 (1), 2009). He has authored articles in journals including *Sociology*, *Social and Legal Studies*, *Parliamentary Affairs*, *International Journal of Human Rights*, *Contemporary Politics and Sexualities*. A recent article in *Sociological Review* is titled 'LGBTI organisations navigating imperial contexts: the Kaleidoscope Trust, the Commonwealth and the need for a decolonizing, intersectional politics.' As an activist he has supported and worked with LGBT asylum seekers, and he has collaborated with Envisioning on such events as 'LGBTI Human Rights Activism and Film' at the Centre for Contemporary Arts in Glasgow on 15 November 2015.

Foreword

Corinne Lennox and Matthew Waites

Let it be known: that in the period when the global LGBT[1] movement faced its most extreme challenges from the rise of homophobia in many regions, that among all those who rose to the challenges of transnational North/South partnerships between academics and activists, the Envisioning Global LGBT Human Rights project (Envisioning) gave leadership.

From its inception Envisioning was unique and as creative as it was political. The project's name expressed its visionary concept and strength of purpose, while also signifying its highly original combination of participatory action research and documentary filmmaking with more conventional social and legal research. Envisioning was founded in a period, beginning in 2011, which demanded ambitious thinking on a global scale to oppose a new tide of violence and prejudice. In particular, academics in the Global North faced the challenge of rising from their positions in ivory towers to meet, connect with, and support the activists and scholars of the Global South who were fighting for their lives and loved ones. The already-established activist researchers who led Envisioning moved quickly beyond words to action.

This volume presents learning and research from the project. It is a book for activists as much as for academics and will also interest those in governmental or non-governmental organisations (NGOs), policymakers and practitioners of many kinds. Above all, the book presents reports from some of the most fiercely fought battlegrounds of contemporary sexual politics, spearheaded by leading activists. Any activist in the realm of gender, sexuality and human rights can benefit from reading this; and it will be indispensable as a contribution to understanding developments on sexual orientation and gender identity (SOGI)

1   We use the frame 'LGBT' – lesbian, gay, bisexual, transgender (or trans) – to be consistent with the acronym used by Envisioning LGBT Human Rights, both for their project and throughout this volume. However readers should be aware that this terminology has been contested for good reasons and it is usually expanded/ clarified to include such abbreviations as I (intersex), Q (queer) and + (to indicate an open-ended categorisation). Please see Nancy Nicol's 'Note on terminology' at the start of her opening chapter.

C. Lennox and M. Waites (2018) 'Foreword', in N. Nicol et al. (eds.) *Envisioning Global LGBT Human Rights: (Neo)colonialism, Neoliberalism, Resistance and Hope* (London: Human Rights Consortium, Institute of Commonwealth Studies), pp. 1–8.

in the states covered, or at the United Nations. Similarly, the contents will provide specific source material for academics across many interdisciplinary fields and disciplines in terms of gender and sexuality studies; postcolonial, sociological, sociolegal, cultural and film studies; and the fields of politics and social policy.

We have been invited to provide this foreword as editors of an earlier volume to which several Envisioning members contributed: *Human Rights, Sexual Orientation and Gender Identity in the Commonwealth: Struggles for Decriminalisation and Change* (2013), which was also published by the School of Advanced Study, home of the Human Rights Consortium (HRC) at the Institute of Commonwealth Studies (ICWS). Both volumes focus on states of the former British Empire, which are now in the Commonwealth, with an emphasis on challenging imperial criminalisations and power relations still shaped by colonialism. The earlier volume was published open access online, as well as in print, in order to provide a resource for activists worldwide; chapters have since been downloaded 45,000 times in more than 170 countries (as of the end of April 2018). This book is similarly being published open access and in print by the HRC/ICWS. In some ways, it may thus be considered a sister volume, and there are overlaps in the work of authors including Monica Tabengwa, Adrian Jjuuko, Nancy Nicol and Gary Kinsman, as well as in the coverage of states like Uganda. Indeed, Envisioning hosted and filmed a launch for our book in 2013, which can be viewed on video via its website (and also Envisioning's website),[2] thus contributing enormously to its having reached wider publics. However, the Envisioning anthology emerges from a very distinct, far more extensive and ambitious project, and should be approached in its own right.

The Envisioning project involved work across selected states from the four regions represented in this book: Africa, South Asia, the Caribbean and North America. Although titled 'LGBT', the project was also concerned with exploring different societal understandings of sexuality and gender, not always encompassed by Western notions of SOGI. In its central focus on generating understandings from the knowledge and experiences of activists in the Global South, Envisioning thus embodied a transnational imaginary, seeking to address existing power relations forged by colonialism and capitalist economics, not by disconnecting but by forming new connections and collaborative, transformative partnerships in the co-production of knowledge. Crucially, the project emphasised the leadership of Global South partners within specific societies.

---

2   See http://commonwealth.sas.ac.uk/publications/house-publications/lgbt-rights-commonwealth   or   http://envisioninglgbt.blogspot.com/p/conferences.html (both accessed 9 Apr. 2018).

It is important to appreciate the Canadian origins of the project.[3] Although sometimes perceived internationally as such, Canada has not been a liberal oasis (as asylum research in this volume shows), but it can nevertheless be suggested that, in the critical activist and intellectual milieu around Toronto from which the project sprang, there seems to be greater sensitivity to colonialism and decolonial politics than exists in the United Kingdom, at least (from where we write). Hence Envisioning's emergence in Canada rather than in other Western states may perhaps be partly explained – in the long view – by referring to Canada's experience of being a former colony, to the ongoing political claims of indigenous peoples which inspire political engagements, and to the continued embrace of the multiculturalism ethic, which is not a major feature in European states.

This volume contains the fruits of the many partnerships formed, combining contributions to represent and conclude the work done. Envisioning evolved centrally from the participatory action research approach, which is often lauded but rarely executed in such a complete and true fashion. This required a much longer project lifespan, which unfortunately is not often accommodated by conventional funding cycles. Yet the results of this approach have made Envisioning's impact far greater than conventional, top-down scholarship. Research and activism were conceived as intertwined in complex ways, with researching often but not always oriented to political and normative goals shared in activist movements. Most of the researchers involved were themselves activists, often based in NGOs, rather than in university-based academic posts. Their work focuses particularly on documentation, recognising the urgency and educational power of recording the details of struggles both lost and won. This involved research encompassing data collection and analysis for movements to reflect on, including the writing that is presented here. Hence, many of the chapters here focus on the documentation task, recording events and citing extensive primary sources of evidence which include movement statements, newspaper reports and drafts of official legislation, while others provide more conceptually developed analyses. The chapters are bursting with the invaluable first-hand insights of activists at the cutting edge of social struggles, as they reflect on objectives and strategies, making this volume an essential reference point for those who are concerned with the global struggle for LGBT human rights and equality.

As already mentioned, the combination of research and writing about activists with their involvement in participatory documentary video filmmaking made Envisioning distinctive among transnational projects supporting LGBT people. At its heart was the strength of Nancy Nicol's and Phyllis Waugh's

---

3   Funding for the project was granted under the Social Sciences and Humanities Research Council of Canada. Notably, our *Human Rights, Sexual Orientation and Gender Identity in the Commonwealth* (2013) volume also benefited from Canadian funding in the form of a small Canadian Embassy (in London) grant.

partnership. They travelled to locations of contestation, got to know local activists, and invited them into the process of documenting their movements through filmmaking. It was through such partnerships that Envisioning became firmly rooted, growing to enable numerous regional teams to branch out and flourish. Often – if not always – this seems to have borne fruit that came to nourish even some of the most stony grounds of religious bigotry, yielding seeds for potential future harvests, if cultivated. Indeed capacity enhancement, such as through skills training in filmmaking, was central. However, participants were also open to constructive questioning of the project's own framings, as expressed in the chapter on Saint Lucia, and a simultaneous focus on mutual, reciprocal learning.

The number and range of films made by Envisioning across diverse contexts is highly impressive and, when viewed, their significance as social documents and activist tools immediately becomes apparent. We can all benefit from the fact that Envisioning has made public engagement such an important component of its activities, evidenced by the extensive documentation available on its website, and the efforts made to screen the films widely both to audiences directly affected by the topics and to those elsewhere who express solidarity. We are proud to have hosted English and Scottish premières (in London and Glasgow) in November 2015 for two of these – *No Easy Walk to Freedom*, from India; *And Still We Rise*, from Uganda – to bring Envisioning's work to the UK. These events exemplified the way Envisioning gave Southern activist voices prominence in the North, with speakers including Arvind Narrain of Voices Against 377 in India, Richard Lusimbo of Sexual Minorities Uganda (SMUG), and Junic Wambya from Freedom and Roam Uganda.

Figure 2. Pride, Delhi, India, 28 November 2011. Photo credit: *No Easy Walk to Freedom*, Envisioning Global LGBT Human Rights.

Perhaps *And Still We Rise*, made in collaboration with SMUG, will prove to be Envisioning's most outstanding achievement in film. Activists were fully involved in the filmmaking, and the result is a documentary filled with emotion, life and the energy of resistance. Richard Lusimbo and Junic Wambya explained at the UK launches that the film had enabled those in the movement to tell their own true story for the first time. When this is viewed alongside the essential Ugandan activist research in this book, by Adrian Jjuuko and Fridah Mutesi, Richard Lusimbo and Austin Bryan, the project's overall contribution to awareness in Uganda becomes even more impressive. Certainly the contributions in this volume are best appreciated alongside the films, of which many are immediately available online (see Nancy Nicol's concluding chapter 'Telling Our Stories: Envisioning participatory documentary'). It is remarkable and admirable that – as Nicol notes in that chapter – SMUG has submitted both the film *And Still We Rise* and the video interviews supported by the Envisioning project as evidence in the US Federal Court case against anti-gay extremist Scott Lively, who is accused of crimes against humanity.

A clear strength of Envisioning's work, moving beyond efforts described in our earlier volume, is the increased attention it brings to gender identity issues and trans people's experiences. Arvind Narrain's India chapter at the beginning of this book explores a positive recent legal ruling for recognition of a third gender, and uses this to contextualise a negative 2013 Supreme Court ruling which reaffirmed criminalisation of much same-sex sexual behaviour. The attention to trans experiences is particularly valuable, for example, in Pere DeRoy and Namela Baynes Henry's chapter on Guyana, which discusses distinctive law in the Summary Jurisdiction (Offences) Act 1893 that specifically outlaws cross-dressing ('wearing of female attire by a man, wearing of male attire by a woman'), and a related case. It is extremely important to bring this form of explicit criminalisation of cross-dressing and its recent deployment to light internationally, illustrating the fact that the problems associated with criminalisations are certainly not restricted to sexual behaviour alone. DeRoy and Henry highlight a punitive measure that could be replicated if not challenged.

Another important and original structural feature of the Envisioning project and this volume is the focus on connecting struggles in a range of Global South contexts with difficulties over asylum, migration and access to citizenship in the Global North – particularly in Canada. This feature of Envisioning's work certainly deserves praise, in a context of ongoing exclusionary practices – such efforts are described in chapters by Gary Kinsman, and Nick J. Mulé and Kathleen Gamble. This linkage demonstrates a transnational and reflective imaginary built into the project's design, whereby the implications of human rights abuses worldwide were addressed back to the privileged Canadian state, demanding interconnected learning.

It is essential, more generally, to grasp Envisioning's central and distinctive methodological focus on sites of current contestation. That is, Envisioning specifically selected sites of contestation for participation and engagement, yielding a project which has truly been operating at the frontlines of activism and conflict, in contexts such as Uganda, Kenya, India and Belize. This made the research particularly difficult to conduct, record and complete, yet has resulted in great benefits. The project's scope also allows the interactive effects between litigation and social mobilisation as forms of resistance to be seen. The chapters show that these approaches to activism exist on a continuum, with social mobilisation buttressing attempts to use the law, and maintaining momentum when adversaries have successfully challenged judicial decisions.

Readers familiar with global LGBT activist debates, and the contexts where human rights struggles have been most intense will quickly appreciate the originality and value of the contributions here. One chapter that stands out for its perspective on global institutions and discourses, and is of clear importance for a wide readership, is 'The rise of SOGI: human rights for LGBT people at the United Nations', by Kim Vance, Nick J. Mulé, Maryam Khan and Cameron McKenzie. It provides an invaluable chronology of civil society engagements and changes in the positions of UN institutions and presents unique interview data from 12 UN officials, also drawing on observation data and state voting records to develop a distinctive analysis of the present global institutional context. This offers insights for current struggles to move forward, with the mandate of the UN Independent Expert (created by the Human Rights Council in June 2016) to monitor 'violence and discrimination based on sexual orientation and gender identity', but which numerous states seek to remove.

More generally in the volume is collected the work of many inspiring individuals who set the pace and direction of contemporary activism. For example, Arvind Narrain is a leading queer human rights activist, lawyer and scholar from India, who has played a pivotal role in legal cases; Adrian Jjuuko has been similarly pivotal in cases in Uganda as a human rights lawyer and activist; and leading African LGBT+ activist Monica Tabengwa is executive director of Pan Africa ILGA (a regional body within ILGA: the International Lesbian, Gay, Bisexual, Trans and Intersex Association). Jjuuko and Tabengwa offer an authoritative survey of forms of expanded criminalisation by states across the African continent. This is also of value for comparing the practices of various European colonialisms, particularly when combined with the astute strategic reflections in African contexts offered by Monica Mbaru, Monica Tabengwa and Kim Vance and it raises concerns about the limits of strategies focused on the courts. Adrian Jjuuko and Fridah Mutesi, and Richard Lusimbo and Austin Bryan, also provide activist reports from the coalface in Uganda, which – in light of the leading activist roles of Jjuuko, Mutesi and Lusimbo – seem likely to stand as the most detailed and authoritative first-hand narratives of LGBT activist organising in Uganda. Particularly when read together, these chapters represent a powerful documentation embodying collective memory of struggle and resistance.

Caleb Orozco, who formed and led the United Belize Advocacy Movement (UNIBAM), provides a substantial account of that movement's struggles including his own legal case for decriminalisation of same-sex sexual behaviour. This is a case which has vital implications in Latin America and the Caribbean region, and has been reported and debated in global institutional contexts. Orozco has emerged as a groundbreaker in his own society, while in the process, as he reports, suffering many forms of abuse including an assault. It is thus a credit to both himself and to Envisioning that he has been able to find a way to narrate and chronicle his autobiographical history, particularly valuable because it provides first-hand knowledge of strategic choices made, and threats experienced, which only such a pioneer can pass on. He has won global recognition for his leadership including being the 2017 recipient of the David Kato Vision and Voice Award.

The volume also brings to the fore further new research and documentation from contexts less familiar to many international readers concerned with sexualities and genders outside heterosexual norms. For example, it includes significant original work from Guyana, by Pere DeRoy and Namela Baynes Henry, and concerning Saint Lucia by Amar Wahab. In the latter, Wahab uses rich data to explore how queer Saint Lucian voices challenge the limits of intelligibility of the Western gaze to explore how wider contexts of economic globalisation link to social vulnerability, and the consequent effects of poverty on people's lives. This discussion demonstrates a deepening critical analysis of developments, advancing current postcolonial theorisations in relation to economic markets, and greatly assists international readers in disaggregating Caribbean states to understand their specific national histories and trajectories.

This brings us to another valuable feature of Envisioning's work, which is the combining of an insistent focus not only on racism, imperialism, colonialism and their ongoing effects, with attention to the effects of capitalism, specifically in the present era of neoliberalism. Envisioning was concerned to integrate neoliberalism explicitly into its analysis from the outset. Its guiding principles committed researchers to an integrated anti-oppression analysis, and a critical perspective on globalisation and neoliberalism – as Nancy Nicol explains in her opening chapter. The value of such an approach perhaps emerges most clearly in Wahab's contribution on Saint Lucia, which shows the need to understand specific national governmental strategies with reference to the relationships between national and transnational economies. While a mainstream understanding of neoliberalism would associate it with free markets in goods and in persons, an Envisioning author like Kinsman tends to associate neoliberalism with 'tightening borders in the north', suggesting scope for more development of analyses based on specific conceptions. Envisioning's work points in the right direction and keeps the issue in view.

Meanwhile, the chapters from Kenya raise potent questions for those participating in and developing analysis of current movements for change, including how those concerned with sexuality and gender relate to opposing religious movements or wider human rights alliances. Jane Wothaya Thirikwa shows how transnational organised religion plays a crucial part, for example through the work of the American Centre for Law and Justice, and Family Watch International which now have offices in Kenya as well, further promoting prejudice. Religious discourses interplay with health knowledge claims and the arguments of politicians. Furthermore, the chapter by Guillit Amakobe, Kat Dearham and Po Likimani presents a compelling conversation over how funding structures and associated rights-based approaches shape the form of organising. In this instance the community-based group Jinsiangu – for intersex, transgender and gender non-conforming people – has reportedly been forced to sacrifice a participatory focus on psychosocial support in order to meet structural requirements for donor funding. A need for deepening critical intersectional analysis and politics is suggested. This raises issues that will resonate widely in activist debates, and is a resource for taking forward these debates about the politics, effects and governmentality of international funding, and the trends of closing space for civil society in general.

Overall, perhaps one of the most distinctive characteristics of the Envisioning research, in all its diversity and complexity, is the sense of interconnections between multiple levels of societies and of social analysis – with attention to local, national, regional and global levels, each with their own features including social norms, institutions and legal practices. In this volume the Envisioning team contribute towards understanding at all of these levels, with central space for and valuation of grassroots insights and conversations. The visionary politics of transnational collaboration and mutual learning that the project team espoused is well-represented, and stands as an inspiration for all committed to envisioning, and working for, a better future.

Overview

Nancy Nicol

This anthology is one of the outcomes of a five-year (2011–16) international research collaboration entitled Envisioning Global LGBT Human Rights (Envisioning) for which I was the principal investigator. Envisioning was conceived of as a strategic partnership that would enhance connections between geographically dispersed partners which share a common legacy of British colonial laws criminalising same-sex intimacy and gender identity/expression. Envisioning sought to support and enhance links connecting community leaders, researchers, activists, legal experts and human rights defenders so that they might share data and knowledge from different contexts and locations. Its goals were to research and document the experiences of lesbian, gay, bisexual and transgender (LGBT) people, including human rights violations on the grounds of sexual orientation and gender identity (SOGI),[1] and to share knowledge on contemporary struggles to advance decriminalisation, human rights and equality. Working with the Envisioning partners and members of the research team has been an amazing, challenging and transformative journey.

Criminalisation and persecution of LGBT people has increasingly become a focus of international attention, policy and law. Although colonial-era laws

---

1   Note on terminology: the use of terms with regard to sexual orientation or gender identity (SOGI) and expression is complex, with historical, regional, cultural, class and activist implications. The terms lesbian, gay, bisexual, transgender (LGBT) and SOGI are adopted by many activists and human rights workers internationally, and were employed by the Envisioning research team. Our use of LGBT or SOGI is meant to be neither all-embracing nor exclusive. Envisioning researchers and partners also used 'queer', 'sexual minorities', and 'LGBTI' (lesbian, gay, bisexual, transgender, intersex) as well as other terms indigenous to members' and partners' language and region. As our research encompassed many international communities, we acknowledge that terminology differs from place to place or topic to topic. Different cultures and indigenous peoples worldwide use diverse descriptors that predate terms such as lesbian, gay, bisexual, transgender, and such naming often reflects differing concepts of identities and/or practices. Contributors to this anthology deploy a range of terminologies depending on their perspective, location and context.

N. Nicol (2018) 'Overview', in N. Nicol et al. (eds.) *Envisioning Global LGBT Human Rights: (Neo)colonialism, Neoliberalism, Resistance and Hope* (London: Human Rights Consortium, Institute of Commonwealth Studies), pp. 9–39.

have been removed in the West through a process of legal reform and social movement organising, they have been retained in post-independence countries throughout the Commonwealth. As a focus for the study, Envisioning identified regions in the Commonwealth in which strategies to challenge criminal code laws were underway or being considered. In order to research, document and analyse these processes, Envisioning established partnerships in Belize, Botswana, Guyana, India, Jamaica, Kenya and Uganda. We also included United and Strong in Saint Lucia, as a strategic partner in the Caribbean which could contribute knowledge and expertise. Envisioning partners in the Global South include grassroots LGBT groups, human rights groups, and HIV/ AIDS education and prevention non-governmental organisations (NGOs). All of them work to advance awareness and rights on the basis of SOGI and a number of those in the Global South are involved in constitutional challenges to laws which criminalise people on that basis.

Secondly, through our link with ARC International, who work to advance SOGI issues at the UN, Envisioning sought to support connections and collaboration to enhance Global South partner access to international human rights mechanisms. Thirdly, focusing on Canada, Envisioning aimed to gather research on LGBT asylum seekers and refugees in order to better understand the dynamics that lead to forced migration, and to examine refugee policies, practices and settlement services in terms of the impact on and experiences of LGBT asylum seekers in Canada. This research was supported by partners from diverse ethnic communities in the Greater Toronto Area (GTA) who work with LGBT asylum seekers and refugees. Many of them were at the forefront of developing programmes to address the needs of these vulnerable populations during the 1990s, when a number of services were established in the GTA to respond to growing numbers of LGBT refugees seeking asylum in Canada.[2] To inform our understanding of their experiences, we also aimed to foster the sharing of knowledge between Canadian partners, and Global South and international partners.

Although Envisioning focused on researching laws, constitutional provisions, asylum and struggles to advance human rights, the information gathered was not only concerned with laws but, rather, with the ways in which LGBT people's lives intersect with law and what their stories tell us – sometimes in horrifying ways and sometimes in inspiring ways – about their aspirations for a better world of equality, freedom and liberation. The Envisioning research team hoped to gain a better understanding of these processes, share knowledge

---

2   Our study was limited to the GTA, which is Canada's primary immigration and refugee destination, receiving two to three times as many immigrants as Montréal or Vancouver – the second and third Canadian destinations – according to Newbold and DeLuca (2007). Moreover, as Cooney (2007) states, Toronto is known to be the primary destination for LGBT newcomers to Canada.

and resources across the partnership, and contribute outcomes that would enhance awareness of these issues.

During the period of the project's research, the cultural, social, legal and political landscape related to SOGI issues has been highly dynamic: characterised by sharp conflicts, shifting judicial terrain and ongoing human rights violations. At the same time, LGBT rights organising has grown significantly in the Global South and in international forums such as the United Nations (UN). These developments have coincided with dynamic changes in jurisprudence and legislative reforms that have advanced or negatively impacted LGBT rights in different contexts. At the same time, there has been deepening economic, political and environmental crisis, and an assault on civil liberties driven by neoliberal, nationalist and neo-colonialist forces. During this time, a worldwide refugee crisis intensified as people fled violence and persecution, a crisis to which global capitalism contributed through trade and economic policies. In the context of intensified fears in the era post the 9/11 terrorist attacks of 2001, states have stepped up policing of borders to regulate the intake of refugees and immigrants. Among those caught up in this crisis are LGBT asylum seekers, many of whom are stranded in refugee camps, living in highly precarious and dangerous conditions, exacerbated by the hostility they encounter due to their SOGI.

Whether as a result of Trumpism in the US or autocratic powers in Eastern Europe or sub-Saharan Africa, all too often sexual minorities have been in the crosshairs of forces of reaction. A Human Rights Watch report (2016) which examines the politics of fear and the assault on civil liberties notes:

> By closing the political space in which civic groups operate, autocrats are trying to suck the oxygen from organised efforts to challenge or even criticise their self-serving reign ... An increasingly popular method to crack down on civil society is to target organisations of lesbian, gay, bisexual, and transgender (LGBT) people or those that advocate on their behalf. Some repressive governments claim, much like their calls to limit the right to seek foreign funding, that LGBT people are alien to their culture, an imposition from the West (p. 19).

As its name suggests, Envisioning was inspired by a sense of hope and aspiration that reflected developments at the time it was initiated. In particular, in July 2009, a precedent-setting ruling of the High Court of Delhi read down Section 377 of the Indian Penal Code which criminalises 'carnal intercourse against the order of nature'. The ruling was significant for a number of reasons. The colonial roots of criminalisation on the basis of sexual orientation may be traced back to Section 377 of the Indian Penal Code, introduced in 1861 by the British. From India the law spread throughout the British Empire (Gupta, 2002; Baudh, 2008; Human Rights Watch, 2008; Sanders, 2009). Today, this legacy remains accountable for half of the laws in the world that continue to criminalise 'unnatural practices', 'sodomy' or 'buggery' (ibid.). The Delhi High Court ruling in 2009 had implications for cases challenging similar laws across the Commonwealth and inspired hope for change in India and internationally (Narrain and Bhan, 2006; Narrain and Gupta, 2011).[3]

In addition to the Delhi High Court ruling, challenges to colonial-era laws in other Commonwealth countries, coupled with the growth of Global South organising and advances in recognition of SOGI in international human rights forums and jurisprudence, provided a tangible basis on which to develop an international research partnership. Envisioning brought together legal and human rights professionals, academic and community-based researchers, and 31 community partners based in Africa, the English-speaking Caribbean, Canada and India into an arena of mutual learning. Many of the Envisioning contributors, and the authors of this anthology, have been at the forefront of key battles to advance LGBT rights internationally in recent years. Their chapters bring to life critical struggles in Africa, the Caribbean and India. Moreover, Envisioning provided an opportunity to turn a Global South lens on the Global North, a perspective that infuses the pages of this anthology.

Following an introduction to each chapter, I will give an overview of Envisioning's methodology, and examine some of its experiences, challenges and insights. Envisioning also made extensive use of participatory documentary as a way of gathering research and engaging community partners. An overview of the documentary outcomes, and the methodology and challenges of this work are discussed in chapter 14. Envisioning documentaries are also cited in relation to themes discussed in various chapters.

Anthology themes

The authors offer different perspectives reflective of their different contexts, but chapters tend to converge around three key themes: colonial legacies; neoliberalism and neo-colonialism; and resilience, resistance and hope. The term neo-colonialism[4] is used in this volume to describe efforts by Global

---

3 Also explored in the Envisioning documentary *No Easy Walk to Freedom* (2014).

4 It should be noted that our use of the term 'neo-colonialism' runs counter to the way US-based evangelical Christian right bodies employ it. They label LGBT human rights supporters as 'neo-colonialists', contending that those who support LGBT rights are imposing sexual liberationist policies on Global South countries, thus positioning themselves in Africa as defenders of 'African' values, with the argument that homosexuality is 'un-African' (Kaoma, 2012; Van Zyl, 2011; Jjuuko and Tabengwa, ch. 2, this vol.; Mbaru et al., ch. 6, this vol.). US-based religious right groups make a similar argument in opposing LGBT rights in the Caribbean, purporting to defend 'family values' against the international 'gay agenda' (Southern Poverty Law Center, 2013; Orozco, ch. 9, this vol.). Such US-based groups have actively opposed SOGI rights in many Global South countries as well as at the UN (Human Rights Watch, 2017; Norwegian Agency for Development Cooperation, 2013).

North-based Christian right evangelicals and organisations against advances in LGBT people's rights, including efforts to resist decriminalisation of consensual same-sex acts – an effort which Kaoma (2012) describes as 'colonis[ing] African values'. Chapters examine the legacy and impact of British colonial-era laws on SOGI rights, recent legal challenges to this legacy in the Global South, and organising efforts to advance social change and LGBT rights in the Global South and at the UN.

Neoliberalism and neo-colonialism are themes that cut across both parts of the anthology. In part one authors examine the impact of neoliberal policy and neo-colonialist interventions on legal and legislative developments in the Global South, and on policy affecting refugees and asylum in Canada. In part two, they examine the impact of neoliberalism and neo-colonialism on the lives and experiences of LGBT people, human rights defenders and on organising efforts to advance social justice and LGBT rights in Africa, the Caribbean and across the UN. Part two also examines activism and community building in the Global South and at the UN – speaking to the resilience, challenges and aspirations for the future of this dynamic struggle for change.

Challenging the British colonial legacy

The course of legal battles launched against colonial-era laws that criminalise people on the grounds of SOGI has proven to be prolonged and challenging. However between 2011 and 2016, laws that criminalise sexual practices have decreased and legislation that protects LGBT people from discrimination, as well as legislative recognition of same-sex relationships, has expanded (Carroll and Mendos, 2017). Nonetheless, legal developments in parts of Africa took a turn for the worse in 2014, where new laws were enacted that increased penalties for same-sex intimacy and broadened the scope of criminalisation (Carroll and Itaborahy, 2015; various chapters, this volume). Since 2012, five countries worldwide have decriminalised same-sex intimacy: Lesotho in 2012, Palau in 2014, Mozambique in 2015, and the Seychelles and Belize in 2016 (Carroll and Mendos, 2017). In India, the Supreme Court set aside the 2009 Delhi High Court ruling that decriminalised same-sex acts and on 11 December 2013 reinstated Section 377 – that case is still before the courts. At the time of writing, 71 countries still criminalise consensual same-sex acts. This includes 32 in Africa, 23 of which apply to both women and men; ten of the countries that make up the Commonwealth Caribbean (Caricom),[5] of which five apply to both women and men (Carroll and Mendos, 2017).

Intersex, transgender and gender non-conforming (ITGNC) people are also impacted by the use of laws that criminalise 'unnatural offences' or 'sodomy', as

5   The 11 Caricom nations are: Antigua and Barbuda, Barbados, Belize, Dominica, Grenada, Guyana, Jamaica, Saint Kitts and Nevis, Saint Lucia, Saint Vincent and the Grenadines, and Trinidad and Tobago.

well as by vagrancy laws.[6] Moreover, there are specific measures that criminalise transgender persons, such as the colonial-era 'cross-dressing law' in Guyana.[7] Such laws, as well as persecution by state and non-state actors, contribute to high levels of violence and discrimination against ITGNC persons. The Trans Murder Monitoring project (Transgender Europe, 2016) documented 2,016 reported killings of trans and gender-diverse people in 65 countries worldwide from 1 January 2008 to 31 December 2016.

On 10 August 2016, Caleb Orozco (chapter 9) and a coalition of allies celebrated a precedent-setting ruling when the Supreme Court of Belize struck down Section 53 of the Criminal Code, thus decriminalising same-sex intimacy in Belize. The first of its kind in the region, this legal victory was a result of years of community building locally and from across the region. In his chapter, Orozco, a litigant in the case and a founder of UNIBAM, gives a first person account of community organising and the struggle for decriminalisation in Belize. The author provides a window into what became a fiercely contested battle, as religious-based groups led street protests in opposition to decriminalisation. Launched in 2010, the case challenged the constitutionality of Belize's colonial-era Criminal Code statute, Section 53, which bans 'carnal intercourse against the order of nature', punishable by ten years in prison.[8] Orozco's lawyers argued that Section 53 violates the provisions of the Belize Constitution that recognise individual rights to human dignity, freedom from arbitrary or unlawful interference with one's privacy, and equal protection under the law.[9]

The decision in the Orozco case inspired hope for change in other jurisdictions across the Caribbean that have similar colonial-era laws. However, the path forward is highly contested. In Jamaica, the 1864 Offences Against the Person Act criminalises private consensual adult same-sex intimacy between

---

6   For an excellent report on the use of vagrancy laws on LGBT and ITGNC communities, as well as sex workers, the poor and marginalised in Uganda see Jjuuko (2016b).

7   Commonly referred to as the cross-dressing law, Section 153 (1) (xlvii) of the Summary Jurisdiction (Offences) Act of Guyana was enacted in 1893 under the colonial administration.

8   *Caleb Orozco v. attorney general of Belize*, see: www.u-rap.org/web2/index.php/2015-09-29-00-40-03/orozco-v-attorney-general-of-belize (accessed 15 Feb. 2018).

9   The overall responsibility for the case rested with the University of West Indies Faculty of Law Rights Advocacy Project (U-RAP), see: http://u-rap.org/web2/index.php/2015-09-29-00-40-03/orozco-v-attorney-general-of-belize/item/2-caleb-orozco-v-attorney-general-of-belize-and-others (accessed 15 Feb. 2018). Lawyers for Orozco argued that the law contravenes his rights to protection of family life, personal privacy, and human dignity under s 3(c); equality and equal protection before the law under s 6(1); freedom of expression under s 14(1); privacy under s 14(1); and non-discrimination under s 16(1) of the Constitution of Belize.

Figure 3. Caribbean research team, Emancipation Park, Kingston, Jamaica, 10 July 2013. Photo credit: Ulleli Verbeke, Society Against Sexual Orientation Discrimination and Envisioning Global LGBT Human Rights.

men under Articles 76, 77 and 79 of the Criminal Code.[10] In 2011, a challenge to the Jamaican anti-sodomy law was filed at the Inter-American Commission on Human Rights.[11] Several domestic court challenges were filed at the same time. In February 2013, a young outreach worker at Jamaica Forum for Lesbians, All-Sexuals and Gays (J-FLAG) initiated a domestic challenge against the sodomy law of Jamaica, after he was evicted from his home due to his sexual orientation.[12] The case asked the Supreme Court of Jamaica to rule on whether the law violates the claimant's right to privacy under Jamaica's Charter of Fundamental Rights and Freedoms. However, due to threats against him and his family the litigant was forced to withdraw the case. In his affidavit, he told the court: 'Though the cause and the case are noble, I am no longer

10 Art. 76 criminalises 'the abominable crime of buggery' (anal intercourse) subject to being 'imprisoned and kept to hard labour for a term not exceeding ten years.' Art. 77 extends the scope of the law to cover any attempt to commit sodomy, subject to imprisonment 'for a term not exceeding seven years, with or without hard labour.' Art. 79 criminalises 'any act of gross indecency with another male person', subject to two years' imprisonment with or without hard labour, see: http://jflag.org/?s=what+jamaican+law+says+about+homosexuality (accessed 15 Feb. 2018).

11 *A.B., S.H. v. Jamaica* P-1249-11.

12 *Javed Jaghai v. attorney general of Jamaica*, 2013 HCV 00650.

willing to gamble with my life or the lives of my parents and siblings'.[13] Sadly, this outcome demonstrates how violence and intimidation result in denial of access to justice for gay men in Jamaica. J-FLAG documented discrimination and violence affecting LGBT persons in Jamaica, including an interview with the litigant, as part of Envisioning's participatory documentary work: see Nicol (chapter 14).[14]

Pere DeRoy and Namela Baynes Henry (chapter 5) examine LGBT rights in Guyana in the context of the cross-dressing law that imposes a fine on anyone who 'being a man, in any public way or public place, for any improper purpose, appears in female attire; or being a woman, in any public way or public place, for any improper purpose, appears in male attire'. The authors draw on Envisioning research data that found high levels of discrimination and violence towards transgender persons. Henry spoke on the findings at the 2014 World Pride human rights conference in Toronto:[15]

> We had one person who was brutally attacked … when the police came, because she was a transgender person they left her lying on the road. She was taken to the public hospital where she was left unattended for almost eight hours … Because they're excluded from the education and economic aspects of the society, most of the transgender persons end up doing sex work. That's another nightmare … police would come around and pick up the transgender persons and take away their money … they extort money from the client as well as the transgender persons doing the sex work. That is a norm.

In February 2009, following the conviction of seven individuals for violating the cross-dressing law, the Society Against Sexual Orientation Discrimination (SASOD) joined a case challenging the law.[16] The applicants contested the law as unconstitutional on the grounds that it was vague in scope and contravened the prohibition against sex and gender discrimination in the Constitution of Guyana. On 6 September 2013, the court dismissed these claims, finding that the act does not discriminate on the basis of sex, because the prohibition treats both men and women in the same manner. However, Chief Justice Ian Chang stated that, 'cross-dressing in a public place is an offence only if it is done for an improper purpose.' The appellants appealed the decision, seeking greater clarity from the court on the meaning of 'improper purpose', and objecting to

---

13 See http://jflag.org/javed-jaghai-withdraws-from-constitutional-challenge-to-anti-gay-laws/ (accessed 15 Feb. 2018).

14 Litigation against the criminal code provisions in Jamaica is ongoing. On 27 Nov. 2015, Jamaican lawyer Maurice Tomlinson filed a constitutional challenge to the anti-sodomy law, with the support of the Canadian HIV/AIDS Legal Network and AIDS-Free World.

15 During her talk, 'Telling Our Stories: LGBT lives in the Caribbean – Guyana', 27 Jun.

16 *McEwan, Clarke, Fraser, Persaud and SASOD v. attorney general of Guyana.*

the judge's decision to strike out SASOD as a valid litigant in the case.[17] The appeal court upheld the former ruling and unanimously dismissed the appeal. The appellants appealed this ruling to the Caribbean Court of Justice (CCJ).

Despite these challenges recent developments in Latin America and the Caribbean have inspired hope for change. In a landmark decision on 9 January 2018, the Inter-American Court of Human Rights ruled that countries under its jurisdiction must recognise the rights of trans people to change their gender markers and name in all public records and official documents. Further, the court stipulated that the process should be confidential, free, and not require surgery or hormone treatment. The court also ruled that same-sex couples must have rights and legal protections, including the right to civil marriage.

The opinion is legally binding on 20 Latin American and Caribbean countries[18] that are signatories to the American Convention on Human Rights. Of those countries, only five jurisdictions – Argentina, Colombia, Brazil, Uruguay and parts of Mexico – currently recognise same-sex marriage. The ruling is particularly timely in Panama, Chile and Costa Rica where national debates on equal marriage have taken place recently. The most groundbreaking aspect of the opinion is with regard to legal gender recognition, given that most Latin American countries do not currently allow it. Some countries do, but only through complex, costly and time-consuming processes (Berezowsky Ramirez, 2018b).

The decision is a result of activism and work by Latin American-based NGOs and activists, including the work of the LGBTTTI Coalition of Latin America and the Caribbean, working in the context of the Organization of American States (OAS). Turning the court's ruling into a reality will require ongoing work, however, the court's decision has shifted the grounds of the debate throughout the region and has given SOGI rights advocates an important and inspirational resource (Berezowsky Ramirez, 2018a).

Later in 2018, on 12 April, the High Court of Justice in Trinidad and Tobago ruled that laws criminalising same-sex intimacy between consenting adults are unconstitutional. Section 13 of the Sexual Offenses Act of Trinidad and Tobago, a colonial-era law, imposed 25 years in prison for same-sex intercourse. Further, Section 16 imposed up to five years imprisonment on a person who is sexually intimate with a person of the same sex without having intercourse. Following the Belize decision, this case marks the second ruling to

---

17 For more information on the case, see: www.sasod.org.gy/sasod-blog-cross-dressing-appeal-case-judgment-2017 and www.u-rap.org/web2/index.php/2015-09-29-00-40-03/mcewan-others/item/1-mcewan-clarke-fraser-persaud-sasod-v-attorney-general-of-guyana (both accessed 10 Sep. 2017).

18 The case is immediately legally binding on Costa Rica, which brought the case, and on Argentina, Barbados, Bolivia, Brazil, Chile, Colombia, Dominican Republic, Ecuador, El Salvador, Guatemala, Haiti, Honduras, Mexico, Nicaragua, Panama, Paraguay, Peru, Suriname and Uruguay.

strike down such laws in the region. The case was brought by Jason Jones, an openly gay citizen of Trinidad and Tobago, who had left the country because of discrimination on the basis of his sexual orientation. The ruling affirmed that people must be able to make decisions about whom they love and with whom they wish to form a family. Attorney General Faris Al-Rawi said on 13 April that he would appeal the High Court ruling (Human Rights Watch, 2018).

Arvind Narrain (chapter 1) examines five cases under Section 377 in India spanning the period between the first reported use of the law in 1884 and 2014, and contrasts the Delhi High Court ruling of 2009 that struck down Section 377 with the Supreme Court decision of 2013 which overturned the High Court ruling.[19] Narrain argues that the concept of 'constitutional morality'[20] articulated in the Delhi High Court ruling shifted consideration of homosexuality within law from 'tolerated' to 'something that needs to be protected … at the heart of the freedoms guaranteed under the constitution.' This space of dignity however, Narrain continues, was cut all too short by the Supreme Court ruling in 2013 that upheld Section 377, reinstating the nation's ban on same-sex sexual relations. The ruling failed to consider the affidavits of those impacted by the law and sidestepped the constitutional arguments in the case. Further, Narrain examines the Section 377 ruling of the Supreme Court in light of a decision four months later by a different bench of the Supreme Court, on transgender rights.[21] The judges in this case, Narrain writes, 'traced a place for the transgender community in both Indian mythology and history' and opined that the current abject status of *hijra* people[22] is due to 'colonial intervention' which, the author points out, includes

19 In 2009 the Delhi High Court ruling in the case *Naz Foundation v. Government of NCT of Delhi* struck down Section 377 on constitutional grounds. The decision was appealed to the Supreme Court by a range of religious-based organisations and individuals. On 11 Dec. 2013, the Supreme Court ruling in *Suresh Kumar Koushal and another v. Naz Foundation and others* set aside the Delhi High Court ruling and re-instated Section 377, recriminalising same-sex intimacy in India.

20 The concept of constitutional morality was articulated by Dr B.R. Ambedkar, a leader of the Dalit movement in India, in his speech 'The draft Constitution', delivered on 4 Nov. 1948. In striking down Section 377 IPC, the High Court of Delhi drew on Ambedkar stating, 'popular morality or public disapproval of certain acts is not a valid justification for restriction of the fundamental rights under Article 21. Popular morality, as distinct from a constitutional morality derived from constitutional values, is based on shifting and subjective notions of right and wrong. If there is any type of "'morality" that can pass the test of compelling state interest, it must be "constitutional" morality and not public morality', *Naz Foundation v. Government of NCT of Delhi and others*, WP(C) no.7455/2001: para 79, 2 Jul. 2009.

21 In the case, *National Legal Services Authority v. Union of India.*

22 Please see Narrain, ch. 1, for information about the *hijra* community in the Indian context.

the use of Section 377 against transgender persons in the first documented case under Section 377 in 1884. Finally, Narrain notes that the litigation against Section 377 came to 'represent the entire community'. Reaction against the Supreme Court ruling was swift with demonstrators pouring into the streets across India and internationally. The parties supporting the Naz petition filed a 'curative' petition[23] requesting that the Supreme Court review the case.[24] In August 2017, a Supreme Court bench in a separate case declared that the 2013 Supreme Court ruling in *Koushal v. Naz,* had gravely erred in annulling the Delhi High Court verdict and held that 'privacy is a fundamental right', and 'Discrimination against an individual on the basis of sexual orientation is deeply offensive to the dignity and self-worth of the individual'.[25] In the meantime, additional petitions against Section 377 were filed. In January 2018 the Indian Supreme Court decided to re-examine its 2013 decision. Hearings began on 10 July 2018 and a decision is expected by October 2018. Legal experts and activists in India are hopeful that the court will finally now overturn the law. (Jha, 2018; Reuters, 2018). Coupled with developments in Latin America and the Caribbean, should the Indian court strike down Section 377, a critical tipping point in the battle to decriminalise same-sex intimacy will be reached. Nonetheless, the path ahead remains highly contested, particularly in Africa.

Monica Tabengwa and Adrian Jjuuko (chapter 2) write about 'expanded criminalisation'[26] to describe a process in post-independence African countries to further criminalise same-sex conduct across Africa today, a process which the authors argue represents 'a big departure from the status quo in Africa before 1990 where homosexuality was largely not discussed and where arrests for same-sex relations were largely unheard of.' The authors identify three key strategies in the expansion of criminalisation: 1) expanding or reinterpreting existing colonial-era laws, as Uganda revised the law in 1990 to increase the punishment for 'carnal knowledge against the order of nature' from 14 years imprisonment

---

23 Art. 136 of the Constitution of India, 1950, guarantees appeals to judgments passed by courts, including the apex court. The curative petition came into being after a 2002 case, where the Supreme Court may reconsider its judgment/order in order to 'cure gross miscarriage of justice'. See www.firstpost.com/india/rainbow-at-the-end-of-the-tunnel-curative-petition-on-section-377-a-last-legal-remedy-to-toss-draconian-law-out-2605384.html (accessed 15 Feb. 2018).

24 For a summary of the grounds of the curative petition see: Briefing Paper: The Section 377 Curative Petition, International Commission of Jurists, ICJ 2016, available at: http://orinam.net/377/wp-content/uploads/2016/03/India-QA-art-377-Advocacy-Analysis-brief-2016-ENG.pdf (accessed 15 Feb. 2018).

25 *Justice K.S. Puttaswamy (retd.) and ANR v. Union of India and ORS*, Judgment 24 Aug. 2017, para. 126.

26 Thirty-two countries across Africa have laws that criminalise same-sex intimacy, with a variety of punishments ranging from small fines to lengthy prison sentences and, in some jurisdictions, the death penalty (Carroll and Mendos, 2017).

to life; 2) invoking constitutional prohibition, as Uganda introduced a constitutional amendment in 2005 prohibiting same-sex marriages, a trend that rapidly spread to Nigeria, Zimbabwe, Rwanda, the Democratic Republic of Congo, Liberia, Cameroon, Malawi, Kenya, Tanzania and the Gambia; and 3) developing new expanded laws, as with, in 2014, Nigeria's Same-Sex Marriage (Prohibition) Act,[27] other laws in Malawi, Burundi, Cameroon and Uganda, and the criminalising of 'homosexual propaganda' introduced in Algeria, Nigeria, Burundi, Cameroon and Uganda.

The right to form organisations that advocate for LGBT people's human rights has been severely limited or denied in countries where same-sex conduct is criminalised. Mbaru, Tabengwa and Vance (chapter 6) discuss recent litigation and significant incremental gains in case law, based on constitutional protections that guarantee freedom of association in Botswana, Kenya and Uganda. In March 2012, Lesbians, Gays and Bisexuals of Botswana (LeGaBiBo) and the Botswana Network on Ethics, Law and HIV/AIDS (BONELA) launched a constitutional challenge over LeGaBiBo being denied registration under the Societies Act of Botswana. On 17 March 2016, the Appeal Court of Botswana upheld LeGaBiBo's right to register, arguing that to deny it violated the rights to freedom of expression, assembly and association protected by the Botswana Constitution. In this milestone decision, the High Court ruled that 'carrying out political lobbying for equal rights and decriminalization of same-sex relationships is not a crime' and that 'It is also not a crime to be a homosexual'[28] (although the penal code provisions that criminalise same-sex intimacy in Botswana remain in place). In Kenya, the National Gay and Lesbian Human Rights Commission (NGLHRC) pursued a similar strategy to challenge the refusal to register an LGBTI organisation.[29] In April 2015, the Kenya High Court ruled in NGLHRC's favour. See also, Jane Wothaya Thirikwa (chapter 11) on the Kenya case. In Uganda (June 2016), Sexual Minorities Uganda (SMUG) and Human Rights Awareness and Promotion Forum (HRAPF) filed a constitutional challenge against the Uganda Registration Service Bureau, whose registrar had refused to reserve the name, 'Sexual Minorities Uganda'. Authors Mbaru, Tabengwa and Vance (chapter 6) also examine recent case history in Uganda where earlier gains in recognising constitutional protections for LGBT persons were not translated in the 2012 freedom of association case that challenged the actions of the ethics and integrity minister for raiding a workshop on

27 Same-Sex Marriage (Prohibition) Act, Nigeria, 2013, see: www.placng.org/new/laws/Same%20Sex%20Marriage%20(Prohibition)%20Act,%202013.pdf (accessed 15 Feb. 2018).
28 *Thuto Rammoge and others v. attorney general of Botswana.* MAHGB-000 175-13.
29 *Eric Gitari v. Non- Governmental Organisations Co-ordination Board and four others,* 2015, eKLR (accessed 6 Nov. 2017).

Figure 4. SMUG participatory documentary team, International Day Against Homophobia, Nairobi, Kenya, 17 May 2012. Left to right: Richard Lusimbo (research), Nkyooyo Brian and Junic Wambya (videography), with Yoon Jin Jung (MFA, York University) and Phyllis Waugh (Envisioning knowledge mobilisation coordinator). Photo credit: Envisioning Global LGBT Human Rights.

LGBT issues.[30] The High Court in Uganda held that the minister's actions were justified, broadly interpreting the scope of Section 145 of the Penal Code Act, which defines 'unnatural offences'. Finally, the authors note that decriminalisation of homosexuality in Mozambique was expected.[31] That country is one of the three in Africa, including South Africa and Botswana, to provide protection against discrimination based on sexual orientation, a provision that has been in effect there since 2007.

Adrian Jjuuko and Fridah Mutesi (chapter 10) examine resistance to the Anti-Homosexuality Act (AHA) in Uganda and give a first-hand account of the constitutional challenge to the act. Morality codes limiting public discussion have been in force for many years in some countries;[32] however,

30 *Jacqueline Kasha Nabagesera, Frank Mugisha, Julian Pepe Onziema, Geofrey Ogwaro v. attorney general and Rev. Fr. Simon Lokodo*, see: https://globalfreedomofexpression. columbia.edu/wp-content/uploads/2015/06/Judgment.pdf (accessed 24 Oct. 2017).

31 The Criminal Code law in Mozambique was a hangover from Portuguese colonial laws and had not been enforced since independence in 1975.

32 Egypt (1937), Jordan (1962), Iraq (1969), Iran (1986), Kuwait (1960) Lebanon (1943), Libya (1953), Morocco (1962), Qatar (2004), Saudi Arabia (2001), Somalia (1964), Tanzania (1981), Tunisia (1913), Syria (1948) (Carroll and Mendos, 2017, pp. 41–2).

there has been a recent uptick of new laws, like the AHA, criminalising 'promotion' or 'propaganda', or banning the 'promotion of non-traditional sexual relations to minors' (Carroll and Mendos, 2017). Targeting human rights defenders and LGBT rights organising specifically, such laws emerged in Russia in 2006. Recent anti-promotion laws have been passed in the Russian Federation in 2013, in Lithuania (2014), Algeria (2014), Nigeria (2014) and Indonesia (2016). In Uganda similar laws were passed in August 2014 but were rescinded by a constitutional court five months later. The laws, which target media, social media, organisations, public activity or human rights work that seeks to support SOGI rights or to portray homosexual behaviour as 'normal', constitute a profound assault on freedom of association and even on freedom of speech. Violence with impunity against LGBT people spiked in Uganda following the passage of the AHA (SMUG, 2014) and is documented in the SMUG/Envisioning documentary, *And Still We Rise*.

In addition, some countries have recently sought to regulate NGOs to create barriers to the establishment or registration of those that support LGBT rights, thus limiting their ability to access funding and repressing their ability to organise. For example, in Uganda following the constitutional court ruling that struck down the AHA in 2014, the Non-Governmental Organizations Act (NGO Act) was passed and assented to by President Museveni on 30 January 2016.[33] The latter act states that, 'an organisation shall not be registered under this Act, where the objectives of the organisation as specified in its constitution are in contravention of the laws of Uganda'. For a discussion of these developments in terms of resistance to the AHA, see Jjuuko and Mutesi (chapter 10). Following these developments, SMUG and HRAPF initiated a legal challenge to the NGO Act that is currently in process.

For information about Envisioning documentary films dealing with legal challenges and organising, see Nicol (chapter 14). They include: *Botho: LGBT Lives in Botswana* (2013), on LeGaBiBo's constitutional challenge to the penal code in Botswana; *A Short Film on Kenya LGBTI Stories* (2012), on the Gay and Lesbian Coalition of Kenya (GALCK) decriminalisation strategy; *And Still We Rise* (2015), on the impact of and resistance to the AHA in Uganda; and *No Easy Walk to Freedom* (2014), which traces the struggle against Section 377 of the Indian Penal Code.

Neo-colonial and neoliberal impacts on SOGI human rights

Authors in the first section of the anthology provide reflections and insights on globalisation, neoliberalism and neo-colonialism with respect to SOGI issues in the Global South and asylum in Canada. Amar Wahab (chapter 4) argues for the need to address human rights from the perspective of broader struggles for self-determination in the context of neoliberal globalisation, and speaks to the

---

33 For more see Jjuuko (2016a).

need for a reorientation to decolonise queer studies and for 'a return of the gaze northwards from the Global South.' Monica Mbaru, Monica Tabengwa and Kim Vance (chapter 6) examine the debate on 'tradition' in the African context and at the UN. Nick J. Mulé and Kathleen Gamble (chapter 7) offer critical perspectives on neoliberal policy and LGBT refugee issues in Canada, focusing on the refugee determination system and mental health. Gary Kinsman (chapter 3) gives a critical perspective on national identity, border security, and the assimilation and depoliticisation of queer liberation in Canada.

Wahab (chapter 4) notes that 'heterosexuality has been increasingly mobilised by the postcolonial state' as 'crucial to both national solidarity and a sense of sovereignty'. The author argues that homophobia and human rights cannot be separated from the broader tensions of the struggles for self-determination in the context of neoliberal globalisation. Citing studies on the impact of structural adjustment and neoliberal policies, the author provides a critical examination of globalisation with regard to self-determination in post-independence Caribbean countries. Wahab notes that postcolonial states that are marked by legal homophobia, 'are often misrecognised as excessively hetero-normative/homophobic and by default, without histories of non-normative sexualities, intimacies, desires…'

Further, drawing on Puar's (2007) concept of homonationalism and Massad's (2002) critique of 'the gay international', Wahab challenges the dominant discourse of the West and the 'imperialist drive to civilise the Global South.' He contextualises the Envisioning interview data from Saint Lucia, pointing out that it suggests the need to rethink 'homophobia' on the island. Wahab challenges the essentialist construction of Saint Lucia as transhistorically homophobic, which effectively silences the local LGBT subjects, denying their agency in lieu of intervention by Western LGBT human rights advocates. In considering global LGBT human rights discourse, he argues that the presumption of freedom of LGBT subjects as dependent on legalised public visibility has 'grave implications for how we think about the archive of queer history in the Global South', noting that both postcolonial nationals and global LGBT human rights advocates may construct queerness in ways that fail to recognise sexuality and desire which do not conform to Western LGBT subjectivity or 'which are not only about "sexuality" per se.'

Mbaru, Tabengwa and Vance (chapter 6) provide a detailed legal-activist historical overview of the debate on 'traditions' at the African Commission and at the UN through the lens of Africa. The overview explores the intersection of colonial legacies with contemporary influences that oppose decriminalisation across Africa. The authors argue that women's reproductive rights, and SOGI rights, have become a 'cultural and religious battleground', seen by African fundamentalists as an attack on the continent's traditional values and culture. These forces seek to uphold the 'traditional' African family and conservative views on the role of women, and to render homosexuality more visible and marked for exclusion, contempt and violence. The authors explore these battles at the national, regional and international levels, tracing recent activity at the UN, the African Union and the African Commission, and discuss the impact of these processes on LGBT Africans. The contributors note that while traditionalists argue that same-sex sexuality is 'un-African', same-sex intimacy and gender diversity have existed in African cultures for centuries.

Turning the lens on Canada, authors Gary Kinsman (chapter 3) and Nick J. Mulé and Kathleen Gamble (chapter 7) examine neoliberal policies in Canada and their impact on LGBT asylum. During the period of this research (2011–16), the Canadian government introduced significant changes to refugee and immigration policy which made it much more difficult to claim asylum in Canada, with particular negative effects for those doing so on the basis of SOGI.

Mulé and Gamble analyse and discuss data from Envisioning's research with LGBT refugees and service providers, focusing on mental health issues, including the impact on service provision of policies and procedures in the context of a neoliberal environment. The Immigration and Refugee Board (IRB) of Canada, in assessing SOGI refugee claims, requires 'proof' of the claimant's SOGI. That process places the onus on LGBT claimants to produce highly personal evidence to substantiate their SOGI status. Prior to their arrival in Canada, many of the LGBT refugee claimants who participated in this study lived lives of silence and social isolation due to discrimination and fear of persecution. The immigration and refugee regime throws newcomers, grappling with identity issues which may be deeply private, into a highly stressful situation where their SOGI must be demonstrated, often in ways conforming to Western and stereotypical assumptions of LGBT identity (Envisioning, 2015). Mulé and Gamble discuss how the claims process itself can make LGBT refugees feel persecuted and/or threatened and the requirement to prove SOGI identity can trigger painful memories, all of which impacts on the mental health of an already highly traumatised minority. In addition to the refugee claims process, they look at how experiences of escaping violence and later settling in Canada can also affect mental health and wellbeing.

Kinsman analyses border policing, refugee policy and the claims process and raises significant questions with regard to the current asylum regime in Canada, noting that 'who gets to define what queerness is ... can also be part of a new regulatory regime imposing Western hetero/homo-derived classifications and LGBT definitions on the experiences of people coming into Canada.' Kinsman examines how a decidedly neoliberal agenda and changes to refugee and asylum policy in Canada shifted responsibility, including financial responsibility, from state agencies to community organisations, agencies and churches. Moreover, that shift is within the context of tightening borders, intensification of surveillance, detention, deportation and 'normalisation' in the post 9/11 era. Contrasting neoliberalism in the Global South and the

Global North, in its implications for LGBT advocacy, the author argues that 'Neoliberalism in much of the world maintains a moral conservative approach to women, gender and sexual diversity', while 'Non-moral conservative forms of neoliberalism', based on legal equality for queers in countries like Canada, have led to 'the emergence of the neoliberal queer', who has abandoned liberationist perspectives challenging the social relations of exploitation and inequality inherent in capitalism. Rather than a rights approach, Kinsman argues that activists need to address and learn from border struggles and 'interrupt regimes of detention, deportation, surveillance and normalisation.'

Resistance, resilience and hope

Global South organising continues to grow, demonstrating tremendous courage and resilience in the face of discrimination and violence. That spirit infuses the chapters in this second section. Legal obstacles and the absence of human rights protections continue to hamper the work of organisations and human rights defenders. Activists face highly negative public discourse in the media as well as from local politicians, religious leaders and the wider civil society, which in turn places those who advocate for LGBT rights at risk. Yet, despite these challenges, activists and LGBT and human rights organisations continue to pursue strategies to advance LGBT human rights: building community, creating local and regional coalitions, developing civil society allies and pursuing international human rights protections, as well as filing constitutional challenges in the courts.

Authors explore a range of concerns and questions in relation to advocacy and resistance while tracing some key developments in the Global South and at the UN in the advancement of SOGI issues, rights and recognition. They also provide critical perspectives on the impact of religious right evangelical forces (often based in the Global North) that oppose efforts to advance recognition of SOGI issues at the UN and LGBT rights in the Global South. Two studies that are most relevant to these tensions are: a Southern Poverty Law Center report (2013) on the role of the US religious right in the struggle for decriminalisation in Belize, and a study by Kapya John Kaoma (2012) on the influence of the US Christian Right in supporting discriminatory laws and policies in Africa. Orozco cites the Southern Poverty Law Centre report, which identified the prominent Christian legal powerhouse Alliance Defending Freedom's (ADF) support for Belize Action (which led the way in bringing together Catholic, Evangelical and Anglican Churches as interested parties to oppose the challenge to Section 53). Founded in 1994 by 30 prominent Christian leaders in response to what they saw as growing attacks on religious freedom, ADF has an annual budget of more than US$30 million. Adrian Jjuuko and Monica Tabengwa (chapter 2) cite the work of Revd Dr Kapya Kaoma, a noted authority on the ties between US religious leaders and local politicians. He researched the role of the American Center for Law and Justice (ACLJ), Human Life International, and Family Watch International (or The Family), US-based organisations which were, according to Kaoma, 'steadily building political networks and legal infrastructure across Africa, working to renew and expand colonial-era proscriptions on sexual rights; and to impose a decidedly American conservative theological understanding of family values onto Africa' (p. 4). Kaoma highlighted the force with which African politicians and newspapers reframed the human rights struggle of African sexual minorities as an import by Western powers, arguing that decriminalisation of same-sex intimacy is the antithesis of their respective cultures, playing the sovereignty card in their appeal to 'traditional values'. By claiming that homosexuality is 'un-African', neo-colonial religious right conservatives exploit the politics of postcolonial identity that reject Western influences, using the myth of a foreign homosexual conspiracy to discredit opposition parties and divert attention from their own inadequacies, corruption and attacks on the population (ibid.).

Vance, Mulé, Khan and McKenzie (chapter 8) give an overview of SOGI issues at the UN, mapping the progress of SOGI initiatives and the engagement of civil society. Beginning with the efforts of lesbian women in the 1970s and 1980s, the authors trace key developments such as the first resolution on sexual orientation and human rights at the UN Commission on Human Rights in Geneva in 2003, and the first independent trans organisation working at the international level, Global Action for Trans* Equality (GATE), founded in 2010. The contributors discuss key developments such as the Yogyakarta Principles in 2006 and their ongoing relevance and influence,[34] and the adoption of the first resolution on human rights and SOGI by the UN Human Rights Council on 17 June 2011. In September 2016, the Council appointed Vitit Muntarbhorn, as the first ever independent expert on SOGI issues, to study and report annually on the nature and extent of discrimination faced by LGBT persons. The first report was delivered in June 2017.[35]

---

34 The Yogyakarta Principles address a broad range of international human rights standards and their application to SOGI issues. On 10 Nov. 2017 a panel of experts published additional principles expanding on the original document reflecting developments in international human rights law and practice since the 2006 Principles, The Yogyakarta Principles plus 10. The new document also contains 111 'additional state obligations', related to areas such as torture, asylum, privacy, health and the protection of human rights defenders. The full text of the Yogyakarta Principles and the Yogyakarta Principles plus 10 are available at: www.yogyakartaprinciples.org (accessed 20 Nov. 2017). For more information see Narrain (2016).

35 The independent expert's report on 'Protection against violence and discrimination based on sexual orientation and gender identity', seventy-second session is available at: https://static1.squarespace.com/static/55098723e4b011797c300d41/t/59f1f4b4 7131a528acd740a8/1509029045468/IE+2nd+report.pdf (accessed 20 Feb. 2018)).

Caleb Orozco (chapter 9) situates the Section 53 constitutional challenge in Belize within a historical and activist context, arguing that the case was strategic. Orozco details how it built on local, regional and international organising efforts, beginning with the founding of UNIBAM in 2006, and a legal review by the National AIDS Commission that called for repeal of Section 53 in 2008. Speaking of 2013 as 'a time of turmoil in Belize', when the Section 53 case was heard and the Gender Policy, which included sexual orientation, was introduced, Orozco recounts the debate on LGBT rights that rocked Belize. Orozco notes, 'The case against s. 53 in Belize rendered our opponents visible for the first time'. It exposed the role of evangelical Christians who resisted change and coordinated 'constitutional marches' in opposition to decriminalisation.

Intersectional approaches and coalition building are prominent themes from Global South authors in this volume, who contribute insights on building alliances and coalitions. Jjuuko and Mutesi (chapter 10) and Lusimbo and Bryan (chapter 12) discuss their efforts to locate LGBTI rights within the broader human rights agenda, including the formation of the Civil Society Coalition on Human Rights and Constitutional Law which brought together 50 civil society organisations to oppose the AHA, and connected the assault on LGBT rights with a wider attack on civil liberties. Similarly in Kenya, the movement took 'a multi-tiered approach',[36] holding annual consultative meetings in East Africa and partnering with allies such as women's rights organisations. This method was adopted by GALCK, created in 2006 to bring together isolated LGBT groups across Kenya. Kenyan author, Jane Wothaya Thirikwa, writes how mobilising efforts widened their scope to include health, security, an enabling legal environment and quality citizenship. Similarly, Orozco discusses how Caribbean activists formed regional alliances and sought to advance their rights through regional bodies such as the Organization of American States.

Lusimbo and Bryan (chapter 12) challenge overly simplistic perceptions depicting LGBTI lives in Uganda as a 'single story of tragedy' and give a detailed historical and activist history of LGBTI mobilising in Uganda starting from 1999. Beginning with the precolonial history of homosexuality in Uganda, the authors explore Western anti-homosexuality influences from the colonial era to the passage of the AHA in 2014. They trace the growth of organising by LGBTI Ugandans, resulting in their greater public visibility in the country. They also outline regional LGBT organising in East Africa and Southern Africa, and efforts including litigation which initially led to progress being made in Uganda in 2008. The authors note that the introduction of the Anti-Homosexuality Bill (AHB) in 2009, coupled with a surge of homophobic media, forced SMUG to shift priorities in order to focus on stopping the bill

36 M. Kareithi, 17 May 2012, in the documentary *IDAHO* (2012).

from being passed. They recount the growing persecution suffered by the community, and the negative impact on services and organisations in the context of the AHA. Lusimbo and Bryan also emphasise the resilience of the LGBTI movement in Uganda as its organisations continued to build in the face of violence and discrimination.

Jjuuko and Mutesi (chapter 10), lawyers on the team that successfully challenged the AHA, write: 'This was one of the most memorable moments in the history of LGBTI organising in Uganda; people wept, shouted, and danced, and the rainbow flag was triumphantly waved in the courtroom.' The authors detail the key provisions of the law, the arbitrary arrests that ensued, and the mobilising strategies, including the process of building the constitutional challenge. The team of seven lawyers 'risked their careers to stand up for what they believed in.' Ten petitioners joined the case, strategically selected to represent a broad spectrum of society. The contributors show how local, national and international politics played a key part, from the five years it took to get the law in place, to the court case that struck it down in five months.

Thirikwa (chapter 11) examines LGBT activism in Kenya and religious-based opposition to LGBT rights, noting a clampdown on the rights of LGBT people in Kenya, 'fuelled by morality dogmas' and 'by right-wing legislators seeking political mileage' following the introduction of the AHB in Uganda. Thirikwa discusses the influx of heavily funded American Christian evangelicals including the American Center for Law and Justice, which maintains its East African Centre for Law and Justice office in Kenya, and Family Watch International, which has set up a base in Kenya in addition to its work in Uganda. Thirikwa writes that a network of religious groups continue to instigate violence and discrimination against LGBT people by 'purporting that homosexuality is taboo, ungodly, "un-African" and a threat to the "normal" family unit.'

Guillit Amakobe, Kat Dearham and Po Likimani (chapter 13) focus on organising by ITGNC Kenyans, and call for an intersectional approach to community-building. They also speak to the growing militarisation of Kenyan society and targeting of terrorism since the Iraq war, leading to increased surveillance and an assault on civil liberties which impact LGBTI people. Structuring their chapter as a conversation, the authors draw on their experience as co-founders of Jinsiangu, a community-based group focused on the provision of psychosocial aid for ITGNC Kenyans. Reflecting on the tensions and implications that can arise, they analyse the intersections between LGBTI and ITGNC organising, class, exclusion and community-building, and examine the impact on organising of the heavy presence of the development industry, donor dependence, the human rights framework and the rights-based perspective. They argue that these often undermine intersectional approaches which seek to better link LGBTI concerns with other issues. Crucially, they contend that these influences fail to meet the needs of a community ridden with poverty, self-esteem issues, lack of information and limited resources. The contributors argue for an intersectional, culturally more appropriate way of organising that will connect LGBTI matters to those concerned with land rights, labour and economic justice, rather than treating LGBTI matters separately. See also Nicol (chapter 14) on Envisioning documentaries: *And Still We Rise* (2015), on mobilising against the AHA in Uganda and the role of US-based evangelical Christians in Uganda; *No Easy Walk to Freedom* (2014) on intersectional approaches to queer organising in India; and *The Time Has Come* (2013), on SOGI work at the UN.

Envisioning methodology and goals

Integral to Envisioning was the incorporation of perspectives from grassroots partners alongside the aim of supporting international exchange. Envisioning sought to develop global partnerships that respect cultural, economic and social differences, informed by a critical analysis of neoliberalism and the imposition of normalised heterosexuality and minoritised homosexuality on indigenous forms of same-sex eroticism and gender identity and expression. While LGBT identities exist in non-Western countries, terms such as LGBT and SOGI are rooted in Western concepts which inadequately describe the indigenous practices, including gender transfer or third-sex, that exist in the regions covered by this study. Further, colonialism shaped understandings of gender, sexuality, family and women's social position, a process that continues today through capitalist global relations. Policing sexual and gender identities and expressions is entangled with issues of power and inequity inherent in capitalism, racism, colonialism, neoliberalism and imperialism (Drucker, 2000; Gupta, 2002; Reddy, 2006; Human Rights Watch, 2008; Kidwai and Vanita, 2000; Tamale, 2011; Lennox and Waites, 2013; chapters in this volume).[37] Colonial laws contributed to discrimination and violence against people on the basis of SOGI and expression throughout the world.[38] Moreover, during the period of this research, neo-colonial and neoliberal forces, in conjunction with local political and religious-based forces, worked to expand existing laws

37 Also expressed by Saleem Kidwai when interviewed on 16 Nov. 2011 by Nancy Nicol for the documentary, *No Easy Walk to Freedom* (2014).
38 Legal terminology differs in different countries and is complex to interpret. Most criminal code laws do not mention 'homosexuality'. Criminal codes may refer to: 'sodomy', 'buggery', 'the habitual practice of debauchery', 'indecency', 'carnal intercourse against the order of nature', or 'unnatural touching'. Moreover, laws are interpreted through domestic jurisprudence in complex ways. In some jurisdictions laws are unenforced, yet calls for their removal are resisted. In many different jurisdictions, our study found that formal charges were often not laid, but the existence of criminal code provisions led to incidents of police intimidation, extortion, entrapment, imprisonment without trial, and custodial violence and rape.

and introduce new forms of criminalisation of sexual and gender identities and expression.[39]

Envisioning developed an interdisciplinary research methodology, drawing on theory and literature from sociolegal studies, sociology, history, and gender and sexuality studies. Although research was undertaken in multiple sites, the study was not comparative. As conditions in each country are historically produced and geographically specific, a qualitative study probing the antecedents to laws criminalising LGBT people and civil society responses to them must be tailored to each site. The work required sensitivity to cultural differences and a critical stance towards the imposition of Western definitions that fail to engage with the diverse practices and understandings of SOGI in the Global South. This was particularly important given that those opposing LGBT rights in the Global South often appeal to nationalist and anticolonial histories, arguing that homosexuality is a Western import which is contrary to their values.

Setting up the partnership also required a response to structural inequality that would facilitate and encourage equal participation. A number of critiques of North-South partnerships note that imbalances of power and differences of perception consistently undermine initiatives to involve intended beneficiaries and thus fail to generate locally appropriate knowledge (Cooke and Kothari, 2001). Considering imbalances of power from the vantage point of a colonised indigenous Australian, Linda Tuhiwai Smith (1999) speaks eloquently to the challenges of research in a context of structures of inequity and power imbalance:

> The term 'research' is inextricably linked to European imperialism and colonialism. The word itself … is probably one of the dirtiest words in the indigenous world's vocabulary. When mentioned in many indigenous contexts, it stirs up silence, it conjures up bad memories, it raises a smile that is knowing and distrustful (p. 1).

Ugandan law professor Sylvia Tamale (2011) points to unequal relationships in research where it was assumed that only the researcher 'can create legitimate, scholarly knowledge' and that those being investigated were 'naive subjects' (p. 13). In particular, with regard to studies on sexuality, Tamale writes, 'Nowhere were assumptions regarding the "knower", the known, and the "knowable" more taken for granted than in sexuality research conducted on colonised populations such as those found in Africa' (ibid.).

Furthermore, the conditions faced by Global South LGBT organisations, human rights defenders and researchers were particularly difficult. A 2009 Human Rights Watch report found that, 'Global South LGBT organisations are under-resourced and severely isolated'; and 'individual LGBT people and activists face extraordinary levels of abuse, rights violations and violence' (pp.

---

39 See Jjuuko and Tabengwa, ch. 2.

2–5). The report recommended that 'building better networks for support and communication is crucial' (ibid.). In this context the first challenge Envisioning faced was to develop ways of addressing structural inequality and isolation to support the full and equal participation of Global South partners.

Envisioning aimed to address these challenges, a process that required ongoing monitoring and assessment. It took two years of consultation and travel to build a research team and incorporate partner insights and goals into Envisioning's design. That process enriched and clarified the methodology, built relationships, and developed a basis for genuine collaboration. Partners contributed to the development of Envisioning's goals, were signatories on the funding applications, and were directly involved in defining and developing the research and – once Envisioning was underway – in the co-production of knowledge. Envisioning provided funding to support community partner staff time and to create and support research and participatory video staff positions. It also provided resources, equipment, travel and capacity enhancement to Global South community partners. Envisioning's governance structure consisted of five research teams (Africa, Caribbean, India, Canada, and law and human rights mechanisms – the latter provided technical advice to the regionally based teams). An executive team, composed of the principal investigator, the chairs of each research team, and a knowledge mobilisation coordinator, guided the work of the project overall. This structure fostered participation by partners and members from all the regions involved through regular team meetings, sharing of resources, discussion and assessment of changing conditions and developments, and collective decision-making.

In practice, the concept 'nothing about us without us'[40] guided our work. We recognised that, only through Global South partners leading the research in their local area, would Envisioning produce outcomes both appropriate and useful to those particular regions. Through foregrounding the voices of Global South partners, researchers and activists, Envisioning sought to mediate against dominant discourses from the West. Sharing resources and knowledge helped to overcome isolation, strengthen capacity and increase our opportunities to learn from each other through South-South and North-South exchange. During its first year, Envisioning's executive team developed guiding principles that all research team members reviewed and voted upon. These codes committed Envisioning to an integrated anti-oppression analysis and a critical perspective on globalisation and neoliberalism and, in keeping with its community-based collaborative principles, they encouraged co-authorship

---

40 From the Latin *Nihil de nobis, sine nobis*, this is a concept with a long and complex history but, coupled with the goals of participatory action research, we essentially understood that no research, representation or outcome from Envisioning should be done without the full and direct involvement and consent of members of the group being investigated.

by university and community team members. The document also affirmed an expanded definition of authorship beyond formal academic criteria, in order to acknowledge community-based experience as a contribution to authorship, and it called upon research team members to 'respect and appropriately acknowledge the contribution of interviewees to authorship' (Envisioning, 2011, p. 3).

This anthology therefore names and acknowledges, where possible, interview participants' contributions and insights.[41] However, where disclosure of their identity could place a person at risk, they are referred to as 'anonymous'.

Envisioning drew on multi-methods including qualitative interviews, focus groups and participatory documentary, informed by participatory action research (PAR) (Hall, 1979; Kondrat and Julia, 1997; Smith, 1997). The latter builds the development and application of the findings into educative materials to inform public policy and actions, as defined by those who took part (Rutman et al., 2005). Envisioning took a proactive approach, not merely for the sake of knowledge development, but also to apply community development theory to research, a process that merges into practice by benefiting affected participants (St Denis, 2004) and one which arises from the perspective that research has a responsibility to contribute to social knowledge and to effect social change (Lather, 1986). Envisioning merged community-based and academic-based participants in order to produce results that would benefit the particular group around which the investigations were based (Reitsma-Street and Brown, 2004). For more on Envisioning's methodology see Nicol et al. (2014).

Working with Global South partners, Envisioning used participatory documentary extensively in combination with PAR. Through these means and through capacity enhancement, Envisioning worked with community partners to develop research, documentation skills and community-based authorship which would translate first-hand experiences into effective interventions. The data collected contributed significantly to that goal and to a better understanding of the issues affecting LGBT people. The participatory approach also enhanced partner outreach and strengthened community engagement, resulting in outcomes useful to the partners for public awareness and knowledge mobilisation.

Envisioning supported regional and international meetings in Kenya, Saint Lucia, Jamaica and Canada, to facilitate exchange and collaboration. The first of these conferences was the International Dialogue and Training on LGBT Human Rights: Focus on Strengthening the Caribbean Response. Held in Saint Lucia in 2012, it was co-organised by ARC International and United and Strong (Saint Lucia). The dialogue brought together 60 participants from

---

41 All participants gave verbal and written informed consents. The intended use of the
    research data was explained to everyone taking part. Consent forms were translated
    into local languages or translated verbally on site.

Figure 5. United and Strong participatory documentary team, International Dialogue, Saint Lucia, 5 February 2012. Left to right: Kenita Placide (research), Nancy Nicol (Envisioning principal investigator), Avellina Stacy Nelson (videography), Yoon Jin Jung (MFA, York University), Montgomry Dalton (videography), and seated: Bary Hunte (videography). Photo credit: Envisioning Global LGBT Human Rights.

the Caribbean, India, Asia/Pacific, Africa, Europe, the USA and Canada to discuss regional mobilising, international human rights mechanisms, legal and community organising strategies, human rights violations and documentation.[42] In 2014, in conjunction with World Pride in Toronto, Envisioning brought international research team members together. It contributed five panel presentations involving participants from Africa, Canada, the Caribbean and India, at the World Pride Human Rights Conference, University of Toronto, and mounted an exhibition of photography and participatory documentary at the Canadian Lesbian and Gay Archives.[43] Over the lifetime of the project, Envisioning supported research team members from all the regions involved to take part in domestic and international conferences in the areas of law; social-legal studies; women, gender and sexuality studies; LGBT histories of organising; and asylum, immigration and refugee issues. These efforts contributed significantly to knowledge exchange and collaboration across the team.

42 For more information see the final report at: http://arc-international.net/strengthening-capacity/international-dialogues (accessed 21 Feb. 2018).
43 As part of the exhibition, Imaging Home: Resistance, Migration, Contradiction. See https://clga.ca/past-exhibitions/imaging-home-resistance-migration-contradiction/ (accessed 21 Feb. 2018). Video documentation of the exhibition may be found at: http://envisioning-tellingourstories.blogspot.com.

Gathering information on sexuality and gender diversity is highly challenging, complicated by prejudice, violence, fear, shame, trauma, exclusion, isolation, poverty and racism, as well as the fact that to talk about sex is taboo in many cultures. Complicating matters further, local or national discourse or animus with regard to religious, cultural or ethnic minorities also limited partners' and researchers' ability to gain access to populations in working class, impoverished or rural areas. A number of community researchers made groundbreaking efforts to travel to different parts of their country to gather data and reach out to new populations.

Throughout the period of the investigations, researchers and partners in the Global South were working under conditions of criminalisation and discrimination that impacted their organisations and everyone involved. Global South partners and researchers were often forced to negotiate between constraints and societal openings to conduct their work. The safety and security of team members and of participants was a priority that required an ongoing response. In Canada, Envisioning partners working with LGBT asylum seekers were experiencing stresses due to fiscal restraint and decreased funding, coupled with significant changes to refugee and immigration policy in Canada under the then Conservative government (Envisioning, 2015).

Figure 6. Envisioning Global LGBT Human Rights research team, World Pride, Toronto, Canada, 29 June 2014. Photo credit: Envisioning Global LGBT Human Rights.

Conclusion

Envisioning built a collaborative partnership with leadership and involvement from grassroots and international groups, bringing together diverse experiences and contexts. Despite many challenges, a high level of engagement by partners, community researchers and participants was evident over the project's lifetime. Envisioning produced a significant body of research outcomes, including this anthology, which represents a culmination of our work together.

I hope that our work will contribute to awareness and knowledge on SOGI issues and to supporting efforts to advance human rights and social justice. However, drawing on some insights in this anthology, it is clear that more research and analysis is required that will address SOGI issues, while at the same time working to analyse and support intersectional approaches that connect SOGI concerns together and alongside of issues of inequality, racism and exploitation in relation to the broader economic and political impact of global capitalism. More resources are needed to aid the work of human rights defenders in the Global South and to facilitate exchange. And more education is needed to raise awareness of the discrimination that LGBT people face and to acknowledge the tremendous courage and resilience of defenders in the Global South, and well as their leadership and contribution to the worldwide struggle to advance social justice and human rights.

We confront a global system that is in crisis: environmental crisis, economic crisis, refugee crisis. International dialogue and organisation is essential to confront threats to human rights and social justice. Partnerships that incorporate a critical examination of neoliberalism and global capitalist relations are best positioned to expose the workings of the systems that contribute to inequality and exploitation, and thereby to work more effectively to advance social justice and change. The challenges we face are significant, but if we aspire to building a more inclusive world, we must work hard and keep hope alive.

References

Baudh, S. (2008) *Human Rights and the Criminalisation of Consensual Same-Sex Sexual Acts in the Commonwealth, South and Southeast Asia* (New Delhi: South and Southeast Asia Resource Centre on Sexuality).

Berezowsky Ramirez, D. (2018a) 'La Corte Interamericana redirige el debate sobre los derechos LGBT', Proceso 5 Feb., available at: www.proceso.com.mx/521348/la-corte-interamericana-redirige-el-debate-sobre-los-derechos-lgbt (accessed 7 May 2018).

— (2018b) 'Latin America could lead the way for LGBT rights in 2018', Procesco 6 Feb., Human Rights Watch, available at: www.hrw.org/news/2018/02/06/latin-america-could-lead-way-lgbt-rights-2018 (accessed 18 June 2018).

Carroll, A. and L.R. Mendos (2017) *State-Sponsored Homophobia*, 12th edn. (International Lesbian, Gay, Bisexual, Transgender and Intersex Association), May, available at: http://ilga.org/downloads/2017/ILGA_State_Sponsored_Homophobia_2017_WEB.pdf (accessed 21 Feb. 2018).

Cooke, B. and U. Kothari (2001) 'The case for participation as tyranny', in B. Cooke and U. Kothari (eds.) *Participation: the New Tyranny* (London: Zed Books), pp. 1–14.

Drucker, P. (ed.) (2000) *Different Rainbows* (London: Gay Men's Press).

Envisioning Global LGBT Human Rights (2012) 'Envisioning LGBT refugee rights in Canada: exploring asylum issues', available at: http://envisioninglgbt.blogspot.com/p/publicationsresources.html (accessed 21 Feb. 2018).

— (2014) 'Envisioning LGBT refugee rights in Canada: the impact of Canada's new immigration regime', available at: http://envisioninglgbt.blogspot.com/p/publicationsresources.html (accessed 21 Feb. 2018).

— (2015) 'Envisioning LGBT refugee rights in Canada: is Canada a safe haven?', available at: http://envisioninglgbt.blogspot.com/p/publicationsresources.html (accessed 21 Feb. 2018).

Gupta, A. (2002) 'The history and trends in the application of the antisodomy law in the Indian courts', *The Lawyer's Collective* 16 (7): 9.

Hall, B.L. (1979) 'Knowledge as a commodity and participatory research', *Prospects* 9 (4).

Henry, N.B. (2014) 'Telling Our Stories: LGBT lives in the Caribbean – Guyana', talk at the World Pride Human Rights Conference, Toronto, 27 Jun.

Human Rights Watch (2008) 'This alien legacy: the origins of "sodomy" laws in British colonialism' (New York, NY: Human Rights Watch).

— (2009) 'Together, apart: organizing around sexual orientation and gender identity worldwide', available at: www.hrw.org/en/reports/2009/06/10/together-apart, 11 Jun. (accessed 21 Feb. 2018).

— (2016) 'Twin threats: how the politics of fear and crushing of civil society imperil global rights', available at: www.hrw.org/world-report/2016/twin-threats (accessed 17 Feb. 2018).

— (2018) 'Trinidad and Tobago: court overturns same-sex intimacy ban', available at: www.hrw.org/news/2018/04/13/trinidad-and-tobago-court-overturns-same-sex-intimacy-ban (accessed 18 Jun. 2018).

Jha, N. (2018) 'India might finally remove a 157-year old law that criminalizes gay sex', *BuzzFeed*, 10 July, https://www.buzzfeed.com/nishitajha/india-section-377?utm_term=.efVaEnDB3#.coMyXPwgQ (accessed 11 July 2018).

Jjuuko, A. (2013) 'The incremental approach: Uganda's struggle for the decriminalisation of homosexuality', in C. Lennox and M. Waites (eds.) *Human Rights, Sexual Orientation and Gender Identity in the*

Commonwealth, Struggles for Decriminalisation and Change (London: Human Rights Consortium, Institute of Commonwealth Studies), pp. 381–408.

— (2016a) 'Museveni's assent to NGO Act will cost us all', *The Observer*, 26 Feb., www.observer.ug/viewpoint/42802-museveni-s-assent-to-ngo-act-will-cost-us-all (accessed 21 Feb. 2018).

— (2016b) (ed.) 'The implications of the enforcement of "idle and disorderly" laws on the human rights of marginalised groups in Uganda', Human Rights Awareness and Promotion Forum (HRAPF), available at: www.hirschfeld-eddy-stiftung.de/fileadmin/images/laenderberichte/Uganda/16_09_28_HRAPF_Idle_and_Disorderly_Research_Report.pdf (accessed 20 Feb. 2018).

Kaoma, K. (2012) 'Colonizing African values: how the U.S. Christian right is transforming sexual politics in Africa', (Somerville, MA: Political Research Associates), available at: www.politicalresearch.org/resources/reports/full-reports/colonizing-african-values/#sthash.rGmxjIhm.lDKbif9t.dpbs (accessed 17 Feb. 2018).

Kondrat, M.E. and M. Julia (1997) 'Participatory action research: self-reliant research strategies for human development', *Social Development Issues*, 19 (1).

Lather, P. (1986) 'Research as praxis', *Harvard Educational Review*, 56 (3): 257–77.

Lennox, C. and M. Waites (2013) (eds.) *Human Rights, Sexual Orientation and Gender Identity in the Commonwealth, Struggles for Decriminalisation and Change* (London: Human Rights Consortium, Institute of Commonwealth Studies).

Massad, J.A. (2002) 'Re-orienting desire: the gay international and the Arab world', *Public Culture*, 14 (2): 361–85.

Mohanty, S. and S Ravikumar (2018) 'India's LGBTQ community is hopeful as court hears challenge to gay sex ban', Reuters, 10 July, https://www.huffingtonpost.com/entry/india-gay-sex-ban-challenge_us_5b44c3efe4b048036ea2e07e (accessed 11 July 2018).

Narrain, A. (2016) 'The Yogyakarta Principles on sexual orientation and gender identity: marking ten years of SOGI jurisprudence', ARC International, 25 Nov., available at: http://arc-international.net/blog/the-yogyakarta-principles-on-sexual-orientation-and-gender-identity-marking-ten-years-of-sogi-jurisprudence/ (accessed 9 Nov. 2017).

Narrain, A. and G. Bhan (2006) (eds.) *Because I Have a Voice: Queer Politics in India*, (New Delhi: Yoda Press).

Narrain, A. and A. Gupta (2011) (eds.) *Law Like Love: Queer Perspectives on Law* (New Delhi: Yoda Press).

Nicol, N., E. Gates-Gasse and N.J. Mulé (2014) 'Envisioning Global LGBT Human Rights: strategic alliances to advance knowledge and social change', *Scholarly and Research Communication*, 5 (3): 1–16, available at: http://src-online.ca/index.php/src/article/view/165 (accessed 21 Feb. 2018).

Norwegian Agency for Development Cooperation (2013) 'Lobbying for faith and family, a study of religious NGOs at the United Nations', Mar., available at: https://www.norad.no/en/toolspublications/publications/2013/lobbying-for-faith-and-family-a-study-of-religious-ngos-at-the-united-nations/ (accessed 17 Feb. 2018).

Puar, J. (2007) *Terrorist Assemblages: Homonationalism in Queer Times* (Durham, NC: Duke University Press).

Reddy, G. (2006) *With Respect to Sex, Negotiating Hijra Identity in South India* (New Delhi, Yoda Press).

Reitsma-Street, M., and L. Brown (2004) 'Community action research', in W.K. Carroll (ed.) *Critical Strategies for Social Research* (Toronto, ON: Canadian Scholars' Press), pp. 303–19.

Sanders, D.E. (2009) '377 and the unnatural afterlife of British colonialism in Asia', *Asian Journal of Comparative Law* 4 (1): 176–227.

Sexual Minorities Uganda (SMUG) (2014) 'From torment to tyranny: enhanced persecution in Uganda following the passage of the Anti-Homosexuality Act in 2014: 20 December 2013–1 May 2014'.

Smith, S.E. (1997) 'Introduction', in S.E. Smith, D.G. Willms and N.A. Johnson (eds.) *Nurtured by Knowledge: Learning to Do Participatory Action-Research*, (Ottawa, ON: International Development Research Centre).

Smith, T. L. (1999) *Decolonising Methodologies: Research and Indigenous Peoples*, (London: Zed Books).

Southern Poverty Law Center (2013) 'Dangerous liaisons: the American religious right and the criminalisation of homosexuality in Belize', available at: https://www.splcenter.org/20130709/dangerous-liaisons (accessed 21 Feb. 2018).

St. Denis, V. (2004) 'Community-based participatory research: aspects of the concept relevant for practice', in W.K. Carroll (ed.) *Critical Strategies for Social Research* (Toronto, ON: Canadian Scholars' Press), pp. 292–302.

Tabengwa, M. with N. Nicol (2013) 'The development of sexual rights and the LGBT movement in Botswana', in C. Lennox and M. Waites (eds.) *Human Rights, Sexual Orientation and Gender Identity in the Commonwealth, Struggles for Decriminalisation and Change* (London: Human Rights Consortium, Institute of Commonwealth Studies).

Tamale, S. (2011) 'Researching and theorizing sexualities in Africa', in S. Tamale (ed.) *African Sexualities: A Reader* (Cape Town, Dakar, Nairobi and Oxford: Pambazula Press).

Transgender Europe (2016) 'Transgender Day of Visibility 2016 – trans murder monitoring update', 29 Mar. available at: http://transrespect.org/

en/tdov-2016-tmm-update/ (accessed 21 Feb. 2018).

Vanita, R. and S. Kidwai (2000) (eds.) *Same-Sex Love in India, Readings from Literature and History* (New York, NY: Palgrave).

Van Zyl, M. (2011) 'Are same-sex marriages un-African? Same-sex relationships and belonging in post-apartheid South Africa', *Journal of Social Issues*, 67 (2): 335–57.

Documentary films

A Short Film on Kenyan LGBTI Stories (2012) dir. I. Reid, C. Kaara and J. Muthuri (Kenya and Canada: Gay and Lesbian Coalition of Kenya and Envisioning Global LGBT Human Rights), available at: https://vimeo.com/73786260.

And Still We Rise (2015) dir. R. Lusimbo and N. Nicol (Uganda and Canada: Sexual Minorities Uganda and Envisioning Global LGBT Human Rights, available at: https://vimeo.com/178217397.

Botho: LGBT lives in Botswana (2013) dir. N. Nicol (Botswana and Canada: Lesbians, Gays and Bisexuals of Botswana and Envisioning Global LGBT Human Rights), available at: https://vimeo.com/69577157.

IDAHO (2012) dir. N. Nicol (Kenya and Canada: Gay and Lesbian Coalition of Kenya and Envisioning Global LGBT Human Rights), available at: available at: https://vimeo.com/46496713.

No Easy Walk to Freedom (2014) dir. N. Nicol (India and Canada: Naz Foundation (India) Trust, Naz Foundation International and Envisioning Global LGBT Human Rights), available at: https://vimeo.com/87912192. For information and trailer see: www.noeasywalktofreedom.com.

The Time Has Come (2013) dir. K. Vance, J. Fisher and S. Kara (Paris, Brasilia, New York, Nairobi, Kathmandu, Oslo, Geneva and Toronto: ARC International and Envisioning Global LGBT Human Rights), available at: http://vimeo.com/67796115.

PART 1

Between empathy and contempt: colonial legacies, neoliberalism and neo-colonialism

A battle is now taking place between the old criminal law frameworks which shackle LGBT lives and the new constitutional interpretations which seek to confirm the inherent dignity to which LGBT persons are entitled. The rights of these individuals now stand precariously poised between empathy and contempt (Narrain, chapter 1).

Figure 7. Demonstration in front of the High Court, Delhi, 28 November 2011. Photo credit: *No Easy Walk to Freedom*, Envisioning Global LGBT Human Rights.

1

Vacillating between empathy and contempt: the Indian judiciary and LGBT rights

Arvind Narrain

Since the colonial era, laws criminalising same-sex conduct as well as gender expression have sought to curb the right of lesbian, gay, bisexual, transgender (LGBT) persons to freedom. However, recent times have seen a more powerful use of the constitutional framework to articulate, contrary to the criminal law, the rights of LGBT persons to freedom. A battle is now taking place between the old criminal law frameworks which shackle LGBT lives and the new constitutional interpretations which seek to confirm the inherent dignity to which LGBT persons are entitled. The rights of these individuals now stand precariously poised between empathy and contempt.

This chapter will map this oscillation between empathy and contempt by discussing five emblematic cases. Two of them encompass the situation of LGBT people in colonial India, and the remaining three pertain to the contemporary era. They span the period between 1884 and 2014, and the stories hidden within their interstices tell us how the law confines LGBT people in terrifying and tragic ways but also how they challenge those confines in inspiring ways.

Two cases (*Queen Empress v. Khairati*[1] and *Nowshirwan v. Emperor*[2]), which date from India's colonial history, presage patterns of persecution of LGBT persons in present-day India in important ways. They speak to Khairati's and Nowshirwan's aspirations for a better world in terms of the freedoms they sought, but which were denied by the law. The three contemporary cases (*Naz Foundation v. NCT Delhi*;[3] *Suresh Kumar Koushal v. Naz Foundation*;[4]

---

1 I.L.R. 6 All 205.
2 AIR 1934 Sind 206.
3 *Delhi Law Times*, vol. 160 (2009) 277.
4 2013 (15) SCALE 55: MANU/SC/1278/2013.

A. Narrain (2018) 'Vacillating between empathy and contempt: the Indian judiciary and LGBT rights', in N. Nicol et al. (eds.) *Envisioning Global LGBT Human Rights: (Neo)colonialism, Neoliberalism, Resistance and Hope* (London: Human Rights Consortium, Institute of Commonwealth Studies), pp. 43–62.

and *National Legal Services Authority v. Union of India*)[5] are relatively well known and embody the politics of hope for a better future as well as its betrayal.

Khairati and the question of gender identity

The decision of *Queen Empress v. Khairati* in 1884 is the first reported case of the use of Section 377[6] against a person described by the court as a 'eunuch.'[7] The ironically named Justice Straight was called upon to adjudicate whether a person who was arrested by the police on grounds of habitually wearing women's clothes had committed the offence under Section 377. The medical examination of Khairati, according to the judicial record, showed that Khairati had 'syphilis and exhibited signs of a habitual sodomite, had indeed committed the offence of sodomy'.[8] The sessions court judge noted:

> The man is not a eunuch in the literal sense, but he was called for by the police when on a visit to his village, and was found singing dressed as a woman among the women of a certain family. Having been subjected to examination by the Civil Surgeon … he is shown to have the characteristic mark of a habitual catamite – the distortion of the orifice of the anus into the shape of a trumpet and also to be affected with syphilis in the same region in a manner which distinctly points to unnatural intercourse within the last few months.[9]

5 Supreme Court of India, *National Legal Services Authority v. Union of India, and others*, writ petition no. 400 of 2012 with writ petition no. 604 of 2013, judgment 15 Apr. 2014. See http://orinam.net/377/wp-content/uploads/2014/04/Judgement_Nalsa_Transgenderrights.pdf (accessed 13 Mar. 2018).

6 Section 377 of the Indian Penal Code reads: 'Unnatural sexual offences: Whoever voluntarily has carnal intercourse against the order of nature with any man, woman or animal, shall be punished with imprisonment for life, or imprisonment … which may extend to ten years, and shall also be liable to fine. Explanation: Penetration is sufficient to constitute the carnal intercourse necessary to the offence described in this section.'

7 The term 'eunuch' is today seen as a derogatory reference to the transgender section of society known as the *hijra* community. This community in India has a recorded history of more than 4000 years. Most hijras live in groups that are organised into seven *gharanas* (houses), situated mainly in Hyderabad, Pune and Bombay. Each house is headed by a *nayak*, who appoints gurus, spiritual leaders who train their *chelas* (wards) in *badhai* (dancing, singing and blessing), and protect them within and outside the community. The system replicates matriarchy, creating interdependence between the ageing guru and the chela who has been cast out of her family. The nayak and senior gurus acting as lawmakers decide any disputes that take place among the hijras, and administer punishments such as imposing fines and expulsion from the community.

8 *Queen Empress v. Khairati* I.L.R. 6 All 205.

9 Ibid.

Justice Straight decided that while he 'appreciate[d] the desire of the authorities at Moradabad to check these disgusting practices', he was unable to convict Khairati, as 'neither the individual with whom the offence was committed, nor the time of committal nor the place is ascertainable'.[10] Although Khairati was acquitted in the end, the key point to note is the violence to which she was subjected during the entire legal and police process.

One should note the gratuitous violence of arresting a person merely because their gender does not match their biological sex. It can be conjectured that the arrest itself would not have been made with courtesy and civility as Khairati was considered to be a person engaged in what Justice Straight called 'disgusting practices'. This effectively put her outside the 'human pale', and one can only imagine the nature of the arrest. After it, she was subjected to an anal examination by the civil surgeon. The violation of bodily integrity and assault on her dignity emerges vividly.

All in all, the figures of authority were complicit in weaving a discourse based upon an attitude of disgust towards Khairati, who transgressed the norms of gender and sexuality. The civil surgeon's anal examination found that the shape of the anus indicated that sodomy had been committed. The district authorities of Moradabad found the practice of singing dressed as a woman sufficient to arrest Khairati, and Justice Straight, though he acquitted her, supported the authorities' desire to 'check these disgusting practices'. The silence in the judgment is the voice of Khairati herself. It can be inferred that Khairati, though born a man, identified as a woman and lived her life as one. The fact that she never denied having 'dressed and ornamentated as a woman'[11] can be interpreted as an indication of how important her chosen gender was to her. In spite of the fact that Khairati had been arrested, subjected to an anal examination, and found not to be a eunuch but to possess male genitals, her chosen identity survived all her tormentors' efforts to criminalise what to her must have appeared 'natural'. It was her gender transgression that implicated Khairati as a potential criminal under Section 377, a reality that she never denied but continued to stubbornly own. Her insistence on her chosen gender gave Khairati a dignity that was difficult to obliterate.

Khairati's case points to the fact that the person of transgressive gender is largely absent in the colonial legal record. The fragment that records Khairati's travails speaks to the question of a larger absence from history of the lives and stories of those who were persecuted on grounds of their gender identity. Khairati's story also points to the work to be done to find and tell the story of how the law in colonial India was used for persecution based on gender identity.

10 Ibid.
11 Ibid.

Nowshirwan v. Emperor: calling a new world into being[12]

In a 1935 decision from Sind, a province of Pakistan, Nowshirwan Irani, a young Irani shopkeeper, was charged with having committed an offence under Section 377 with a youth aged about 18 called Ratansi. The prosecution story was that Ratansi visited the appellant's hotel and had tea there. Nowshirwan asked Ratansi why he had not come to the hotel for a while, and was told that Ratansi had had no occasion to do so. The latter then went to the pier to take a boat, but on finding he had no money, came back to Masjid Street, where he saw Nowshirwan standing on the road a short distance from the hotel. Nowshirwan asked Ratansi to come to his house, and when he did, he locked the door and started taking liberties with the young man, who did not welcome the overtures and wanted to leave. Nowshirwan removed his trousers, loosened Ratansi's trousers, and made the youth sit on top of his organ. Ratansi got up from his lap, but not before Nowshirwan had spent himself, wiped his organ and put on his pants. The reason this incident came to light was that Solomon, a police officer, and his friend Gulubuddin saw the incident through the keyhole, marched in, and took Ratansi and Nowshirwan to the police station.

The judge was not convinced by the prosecution story that Nowshirwan had forced Ratansi to have carnal intercourse. He believed Ratansi had been made to pose as a complainant and as a result made hopelessly discrepant statements. The judge was not prepared to rely on the evidence of the eyewitnesses, Solomon and Gulubuddin, whose conduct he found strange. Further, the medical evidence could prove neither forcible sexual intercourse (the prosecution story) nor an attempt to commit the act of sodomy. In the judge's opinion, 'as the appellant had not even if we take the worst view against him gone beyond a certain stage of lascivious companionship, I do not think he deserves to be convicted for any of the offences with which he was charged or could have been charged'.[13]

The story of Nowshirwan and Ratansi seems to be one of sexual desire acting itself out between two men of different class backgrounds. The limited material present in the appellate decision gives us a clue that even the judge was convinced the nature of the relationship was consensual. As the judge noted: 'Moreover the medical evidence militates against the story of a forcible connection on the cot [and] the appellant who is a fairly hefty young man having intercourse in the manner stated originally. There is not the slightest symptom of violence on the hind part of the lad.' He concluded: 'If he was in the house of the accused behind locked doors, I have not the slightest hesitation in believing that he had gone there voluntarily'.[14]

12 AIR 1934 Sind 206.
13 Ibid.
14 Ibid.

The story of desire secreted within the judicial narrative seems to be that Nowshirwan and Ratansi knew each other and that the former made the first move on that fateful day. He asked Ratansi why he had not come to the hotel for some time. Ratansi left after finishing his tea, only to come back in the same direction. When he returned, Nowshirwan was waiting on the road and asked him to come to his house. They seemed to have some sort of prearranged code by which they signalled to each other the desire to meet, and subsequently they went to Nowshirwan's room. However, owing to the misfortune of their liaison having been witnessed by an over-zealous policeman or a policeman with a grudge, what should have been an intimate act between two consenting parties in their bedroom became a public scandal.

The prosecution sought to twist a consenting act between two men into a story of Ratansi being forced to have sex with Nowshirwan. The former was coerced by those around him into posing as a complainant against the very person with whom he had earlier had a consenting sexual relationship. The fact that it was consenting did nothing to exculpate Ratansi from becoming a victim of judicial ire. Indeed, the judge reserved particular fury for him.

In the judge's words, Ratansi 'appears to be a despicable specimen of humanity. On his own admission he is addicted to the vice of a catamite. The doctor who has examined him is of the opinion that the lad must have been used frequently for unnatural carnal intercourse.' In the course of appreciating the medical evidence, the judge noted: 'There was not the slightest symptom of violence on the *hind part* of the lad'.[15] Thus, the story of an encounter between two people of the same sex who desired each other, was reduced in the judicial reading to an act of a perverse failed sexual connection. The use of terms like 'animal-like' and 'despicable' placed the sexual act within the framework of moral abhorrence. One has to read between the lines of the judicial text to hazard a guess as to the nature of the intimacy between Nowshirwan and Ratansi. The two knew each other and had possibly met before in Nowshirwan's room, which might possibly have been a space where the coercive heterosexism of the outside world could be forgotten for the brief time that they spent with each other. That short interlude might have been a moment when they imagined a world not yet born and a time yet to come, when their desire would be accepted without a murmur. This imaginative realm of impossible desires was what was rudely interrupted when the policeman, Solomon, spied through the keyhole.

It can be surmised that Solomon had noticed their previous meetings, hence he was on the alert to take action on that eventful day in Sind in 1935. Solomon stands for the compulsory heterosexism of the larger world or what Oscar Wilde would have called the 'unnatural virtue' in which the world abounds, which will give no space for the expression of any intimacy that challenges its own laws.

15 Ibid.

It was this fragile experiment of creating a 'little community of love' (Liang and Narrain, 2009), outside the bounds of law's strictures and societal norms, that society was attacking via Solomon, giving it the judicial imprimatur of a 'failed sexual connection'. The tragic story of Nowshirwan and Ratansi speaks to the absence of a certain vocabulary. The language of love and intimacy, longing and desire, and the expression of spontaneous bodily affection, find no safe habitation within the terms of the law which degrades such experimental creation of new forms of intimacy. Its language has an impoverishing effect as it strips the physical act of the rich emotional connotations of human intimacy and reduces it to a 'perverse failed sexual connection'. By stripping the act of sex of its multiple meanings, it produces Nowshirwan as a subject of the criminal law.

One could look at Nowshirwan and Ratansi as being unwitting frontiersmen in the history of the battle against Section 377 and as being among its first recorded tragic victims. In another register, Nowshirwan and Ratansi stand in for Oscar Wilde and Lord Alfred Douglas, with Ratansi not just forced to become a witness against Nowshirwan but also to deny a part of his own being in terms of his role in creating that 'little community of love'. Just as Oscar Wilde was betrayed by Alfred Douglas, who described his lover as 'the greatest force for evil that has appeared in Europe during the last three hundred and fifty years' (Murray, 2000, p. 221),[16] so too was Nowshirwan, in his hour of greatest need, betrayed by Ratansi who became the complainant against him. Their story exemplifies the perversities of a law that turns lover against lover and converts an act of intimacy into the crime of carnal intercourse.

Nowshirwan's story remains emblematic of the ethical and moral poverty of the judicial discourse, even though it grappled with homosexual expression for more than 158 years. It is important to note that despite the Indian Constitution coming into force with the language of equality, non-discrimination and dignity, the judiciary in the postcolonial era continued to characterise homosexuality with terms such as 'unnatural', 'perversity of mind' and 'immoral'. The ethical language of dignity and rights was never perceived as applying to LGBT persons (see Narrain, 2008).

---

16 Though it should be noted that this statement was made a long time after Oscar Wilde's three trials. During the trial and its immediate aftermath, Lord Alfred Douglas stood by Oscar Wilde. He was the only friend of Oscar Wilde to remain in London during the trial, even though he was under threat of arrest. He also petitioned the authorities to release Oscar Wilde. As Murray notes: 'Unlike Wilde's other friends, Douglas worked for him tirelessly, never giving up hope that he might be able to change if not the sentence, at least other people's attitude to it' (2000, p. 92).

Naz Foundation v. NCT Delhi: **the promise of hope**[17]

The first time the judiciary moved outside the range of responses outlined above was 158 years after the Indian Penal Code came into force and 59 years after the Indian Constitution did so. The social context pertaining in the late 1990s and the beginning of the new century differed dramatically from the one that existed at the time of Nowshirwan's persecution. The norms that straitjacketed Nowshirwan and Ratansi from expressing their sexual identity, and the law that deemed the former a criminal, were beginning to be questioned. This practice of questioning the set ways of the heterosexist world began with the queer struggle's emergence with its insistence on problematising norms of gender and sexuality. It is this context of an emerging LGBT community – one that simply did not exist in Nowshirwan's and Ratansi's day – that underpins any present-day engagement with Section 377. In simple terms, when people like Nowshirwan have been arrested under the law in recent times, people beyond the family and friend network have got involved. Queer people across the country rally together and begin to support those who are subjected to the law's persecution. Thus, any story about those who are arrested under Section 377, be it the arrest of gay men in Lucknow (2006) or the arrest of HIV/AIDS workers in Lucknow (2001), become part of a contemporary history of struggle against Section 377. This stands in stark contrast to the persecution of frontiersmen in earlier struggles against it, such as Nowshirwan and Ratansi.

The bringing together of the stories of Nowshirwan and Ratansi, and those persecuted under the law in contemporary times, has culminated in a legal challenge to that very same law. The Lawyers Collective filed a petition challenging Section 377 on behalf of the Naz Foundation before the Delhi High Court in 2001.[18] It challenged the constitutional validity of Section 377, and made an argument for it to exclude the criminalisation of same-sex acts between consenting adults in private. In technical terms, the petition asked for the statute to be 'read down' to exclude the criminalisation of same-sex acts between consenting adults in private, limiting the use of Section 377 to cases of child sexual abuse.

The important shift that had been made, as compared with the colonial period, was the use of the fundamental rights chapter to test the constitutional validity of the law. In particular, the petition argued that Section 377 violated

---

17 Delhi High Court, 2009, *Naz Foundation v. NCT Delhi*, 160 Delhi Law Times, 277.
18 Materials filed in the Delhi High Court are on file with the Alternative Law Forum (ALF).

Figure 8. Protest against the Supreme Court ruling that reinstated Section 377, recriminalising consensual same-sex acts in India, Delhi, India, 11 December 2013. Photo credit: *No Easy Walk to Freedom*, Envisioning Global LGBT Human Rights.

the right to equality,[19] the right to privacy and dignity,[20] and the right to expression.[21]

The petition itself, though filed by a single non-governmental organisation (NGO), gradually began to represent the entire community. The Lawyers Collective and the Naz Foundation began this process of making a 'public interest litigation' truly 'public' by hosting a series of meetings dealing with different stages of the petition. Over the next seven years, this process of continuous consultation with the community contributed towards Section 377 becoming a more politicised issue, a process that in turn led to Voices Against 377, a Delhi-based coalition of NGOs working for the rights of LGBT persons, women and children, filing an intervention. The petition's key stages included the affidavit filed by the Union of India (home ministry), which indicated that the government would stand by the law; the affidavit filed by the National AIDS Control Organization (NACO), which in effect said that Section 377 impeded HIV/AIDS efforts; and the impleadment of Joint Action Kannur (JACK, an organisation denying that HIV causes AIDS) and of B.P. Singhal (a former Bharatiya Janata Party (BJP) Member of Parliament, who represented the opinion of the Hindu right wing that homosexuality was against Indian culture).

19 Art. 14. The state shall not deny to any person equality before the law or the equal protection of the laws within the territory of India.
20 Art. 21. No person shall be deprived of his life or personal liberty except according to procedure established by law.
21 Art. 19. (1) All citizens shall have the right – (a) to freedom of speech and expression.

Completely new was the chance to challenge the law under which Khairati and Nowshirwan had been prosecuted. The challenge could now be posed in terms of the Indian Constitution, which came into force in 1950, on the basis that the law violates the fundamental rights of LGBT citizens. Even though it is now possible to mount such a challenge, India, especially in the post-liberalisation era, has not been a hospitable space in recent times, and is certainly not a final refuge for those characterised by the Supreme Court as the 'oppressed and the bewildered'.[22] In fact, the Supreme Court has been positively hostile to a whole range of applicants, right from slum dwellers to all sections of organised labour (see Suresh and Narrain, 2015). So it was with trepidation that queer activists awaited the hearing. How would the judges understand the complex issue of sexuality and rights? How indeed would we be able to persuade them that this was a rights issue?

The judiciary has generally been subject to analysis in terms of the reasoned argument and the decided case. In contrast, little attention has been paid to the gamut of other kinds of responses by judges day-to-day in the courts: their questions, their expressions, the tone of their comments, their personal reactions. As Lawrence Liang (2007) noted:

> Witnessing the courts functioning on a day-to-day basis also allows you to uncover another secret archive, an archive of humiliation and power. It is said that seventy per cent of our communication is non-verbal and this must be true of legal communication as well. The secret archive that interests me consists not of well-reasoned judgments or even the unreasonable admonishment of the courts, but the various symbolic signs and gestures that accompany them. An incomplete index of the archive includes the stare, the smirk, the haughty laugh, the raised eyebrow, the indifferent yawn, the disdainful smile and the patronising nod amongst many others.

In this secret archive of what Liang correctly characterises as 'humiliation and power', another category of responses emerged almost as a complete surprise. These can be characterised as representing the quality of judicial empathy. The questions and comments of the judges in the *Naz* case revealed not the intention to humiliate but instead a strong sense of their empathy for the suffering of LGBT persons. Chief Justice Shah communicated this empathy in ample measure and took judicial notice of the social discourse of homophobia by saying that we all know the kind of sneers and mockery this issue attracts in society. To substantiate this point, he narrated the moving instance of a boy mocked for his sexuality and thus unable to take his exam. It was in this context of harassment that the boy approached the court for a chance to do his exam again (Narrain and Eldridge, 2009, p. 49).

During the hearings the judges displayed sensitivity, not only to instances of brutal violence but equally to the more subtle language of discrimination.

22 *State of Rajasthan v. Union of India* (1977) 3 SCC 634 at 70 (per Justice Goswami).

This created a magical space for the brief duration of the court proceedings. Lesbian, gay, bisexual and transgender persons, who were so used to the sneers and jeers of society, suddenly felt that they were not only being heard but also respected. Simply through the art of empathetic listening the judges restored dignity to a section of society upon whom the government seemed intent on pouring nothing but contempt and scorn. The judges involved in the hearings did something unique. They spoke about sex without a sneer, and for the first time in the recorded judicial history of India homosexual sex was discussed within a context of intimacy, love, affection and longing. That discourse became part of the judicial register and displaced the relentless focus on the stripped down homosexual act as a threat to civilisation at its very roots. The conflation of homosexuality with excess, through the focus on group sex, was challenged by the nature of judicial questioning, and the discourse about homosexuality was linked to contexts of emotion and feeling. A new path was being forged in learning to talk about the intimacy that Nowshirwan and Ratansi shared, within the terms of the law. For the first time, it seemed possible to see Nowshirwan and Ratansi and many others like them in terms other than the basely carnal, and for opening up that possibility, one should credit the empathetic listening demonstrated by Chief Justice Shah and Justice Muralidhar.

In such circumstances, the *Naz* judgment could well have been justified in making the argument for the decriminalisation of homosexuality, based on Hart's (1967) position that it was not the law's business to regulate a zone of private morality. Such an understanding would have been sufficient to achieve the result of reading down Section 377 to exclude consensual sex between adults from the ambit of criminalisation. However, the judges chose to tread a more ambitious path. They began their written decision by referencing Dr Ambedkar, who in the Constituent Assembly had noted: 'Constitutional morality is not a natural sentiment. It has to be cultivated. We must realise that our people have yet to learn it. Democracy in India is only a top dressing on an Indian soil which is essentially undemocratic.'[23] They continued:

> Popular morality or public disapproval of certain acts is not a valid justification for restriction of the fundamental rights under Article 21. Popular morality, as distinct from a constitutional morality derived from constitutional values, is based on shifting and subjective notions of right and wrong. If there is any type of 'morality' that can pass the test of compelling state interest, it must be 'constitutional' morality and not public morality.[24]

In addition: 'Moral indignation, howsoever strong, is not a valid basis for overriding individuals' fundamental rights of dignity and privacy. In our

23 *Naz Foundation v. Union of India and others* (para. 79), see https://indiankanoon. org/doc/100472805/ (accessed 27 Feb. 2018).
24 Ibid.

scheme of things, constitutional morality must outweigh the argument of public morality, even if it be the majoritarian view.'[25]

What the judges did, by articulating the notion of constitutional morality, was to change the terms within which the judiciary considered homosexual expression. From the first tentative steps when Hart, as well as the famous Wolfenden Committee Report, had made space within the law for 'private immorality', now homosexual expression was to be seen as not just something that has to be 'tolerated', but rather as something that needs to be protected. This is because protecting the expression of homosexuality goes to the heart of the meaning of the freedoms guaranteed under the Indian Constitution. In a reversal of the terms of the debate, it became 'moral' to protect LGBT rights and 'immoral' to criminalise people on grounds of their sexuality.

Constitutional morality in the judges' reading requires that LGBT persons are treated as equal citizens of India, that they cannot be discriminated against on grounds of their sexual orientation, and that their right to express themselves through their intimate choice of partner must be fully respected. It's only when the dignity of LGBT persons is respected that the Indian Constitution lives up to its foundational promise. Taken one step further, constitutional morality also requires the court to play the role of a counter-majoritarian institution, which takes upon itself the responsibility of protecting constitutionally entrenched rights, regardless of what the majority may believe. In the judges' apt conclusion:

> If there is one constitutional tenet that can be said to be underlying theme of the Indian Constitution, it is that of 'inclusiveness'. This Court believes that the Indian Constitution reflects this value deeply ingrained in Indian society, nurtured over several generations. The inclusiveness that Indian society traditionally displayed, literally in every aspect of life, is manifest in recognising a role in society for everyone. Those perceived by the majority as 'deviants' or 'different' are not on that score excluded or ostracised.[26]

The theme of 'constitutional morality' thus brings about a paradigm shift in the way the law looks at LGBT persons. Protecting their rights is not only about guaranteeing a despised minority their rightful place in the constitutional shade, but it equally speaks to the vision of the kind of country we all want to live in and what it means for the majority.

Indian law seems to have traversed the journey from Nowshirwan to the Naz Foundation, from being persecuted for same-sex intimacy to making some space for the 'little communities of love'. However, the victory in some ways proved fragile, as the decision in 2013 in *Suresh Kumar Koushal v. Naz Foundation*[27] was to show.

25 Ibid., para. 86.
26 Ibid., para. 130.
27 2013 (15) SCALE 55: MANU/SC/1278/2013.

Suresh Kumar Koushal and the failure of citizenship

Suresh Kumar Koushal, an astrologer, was not a party before the Delhi High Court in the *Naz* case. He brought a Special Leave Petition (SLP) challenging the *Naz* decision before the Supreme Court just seven days after the historic Delhi High Court judgment. He was joined subsequently by 14 others from the spectrum of Indian society, comprising all religions, all united by one thing only, opposition to the *Naz* judgment.[28] This vociferous opposition from representatives of all major Indian faiths prompted a response from those in favour of the Delhi High Court judgment. As a result, the parties before that court, Voices Against 377 and Naz Foundation, were joined by 19 parents of LGBT persons, 14 mental health professionals, 11 law teachers, 16 teachers and Shyam Benegal, a public-spirited intellectual, who all filed interventions before the Supreme Court.

The information brought before the court in the *Koushal* petition by those supporting the *Naz* judgment included affidavits testifying to harassment and violence, all inflicted under the shadow of Section 377. However, in its judgment the court chose to disregard the violations it had caused. With infamous logic, the judges concluded:

> A miniscule fraction of the country's population constitute lesbians, gays, bisexuals or transgenders and in last more than 150 years less than 200 persons have been prosecuted (as per the reported orders) for committing offence under Section 377 IPC and this cannot be made sound basis for declaring that section ultra vires the provisions of Articles 14, 15 and 21 of the Constitution.[29]

The decision is best described in Vikram Seth's eloquent words as a 'bad day for law and love' (2013). As an exercise in reasoning, the *Koushal* judgment failed to demonstrate why it reached the conclusion that Section 377 was constitutionally valid. However, the failure of the *Koushal* case goes beyond a mere breakdown in reasoning, to questions that go to the heart of what the

28 *Suresh Kumar Koushal and another v. Naz Foundation and others*, Special Leave Petition (SLP) no. 15436 of 2009 was the first SLP to be filed against the *Naz* judgment. Since then, 15 other parties have also filed SLPs challenging the *Naz* judgment: *Apostolic Churches Alliance through its Bishop v. Naz Foundation; S.K. Tizarawala v. Naz Foundation; Bhim Singh v. Naz Foundation; B. Krishna Bhat v. Naz Foundation; B.P. Singhal v. Naz Foundation; S.D. Pratinidhi Sabha v. Naz Foundation; Delhi Commission for Protection of Child Rights v. Naz Foundation; Ram Murti v. Government of NCT of Delhi; Krantikari Manuvadi Morcha Party v. Naz Foundation; Raza Academy v. Naz Foundation; Tamil Nadu Muslim Munnetra Kazhagam v. Naz Foundation; Utkal Christian Council v. Naz Foundation; Trust Gods Ministry v. Naz Foundation; All India Muslim Personal Law Board v. Naz Foundation; Joint Action Kannur v. Naz Foundation.*

29 *Suresh Kumar Koushal v. Naz Foundation*, 2013 (15) SCALE 55: MANU/SC/1278/2013.

Indian Constitution means (Coalition for Sex Workers and Sexual Minorities' Rights, 2014).

Beyond equality, privacy and dignity, the one concept developed in the *Naz* judgment that has resonated widely is the notion of constitutional morality. In an inspired move, Justice Shah went to the Indian Constituent Assembly Debates. Employing the concept of *constitutional* morality as articulated by noted jurist, economist, politician and social reformer, Dr B.R. Ambedkar, the judge made the point that a notion of *public* morality cannot be used as a basis to deprive a minority of their rights. In other words, if India was a form of democracy based upon majority rule only, then 'any legislative transient majority in tantrums against any minority'[30] could discriminate at will against women, Muslims, Christians and disabled people. Rejecting this notion of majoritarian oppression, the *Naz* court underlined the point that India is a constitutional democracy rooted in a tradition of inclusiveness, and therefore the fundamental rights of all persons of whatever stripe or persuasion are non-negotiable. The *Naz* court applied this notion of constitutional morality derived from Dr Ambedkar, and the notion of inclusiveness as expressed in 1947 by Jawaharlal Nehru,[31] to LGBT persons. The ruling was based on a profound appreciation of the deepest meaning of the Indian Constitution's commitment to protect the fundamental rights of all persons and groups, however 'miniscule' those groups might be.

It is this particular understanding of the Constitutional Court's role that the *Koushal* judgment failed to appreciate. By arguing that it was duty bound to respect the will of parliament, which represented the 'will of the people', it abdicated the responsibility of the judiciary to protect all minorities from the vicissitudes of majority opinion. Its conclusion that a 'miniscule fraction of the country's population constitute lesbians, gays, bisexuals or transgenders', and hence it was unnecessary to adjudicate the

---

30 Concurring opinion of J. Krishna Iyer in *Maneka Gandhi v. Union of India* (1978) I SCC para. 81.

31 In his 'Tryst with destiny' speech, Constituent Assembly, delivered at midnight, 14–15 Aug. 1947, on the eve of independence, available at: http://nehrumemorial. nic.in/en/gift-gallery.html?id=214&tmpl=component (accessed 27 Feb. 2018). Nehru, while introducing the Objectives Resolution, which went on to become the Preamble of the Indian Constitution noted: 'Words are magic things often enough, but even the magic of words sometimes cannot convey the magic of the human spirit and of a Nation's passion [… The Resolution] seeks very feebly to tell the world of what we have thought or dreamt of so long, and what we now hope to achieve in the near future.' The *Naz* judgment read Nehru's aspiration as an aim for inclusiveness. As they put it: 'Where society can display inclusiveness and understanding, such persons can be assured of a life of dignity and non-discrimination. This was the "spirit behind the Resolution" of which Nehru spoke so passionately.' See *Naz Foundation v. NCT Delhi*.

Figure 9. Pride, Delhi, India, 28 November 2011. Photo credit: *No Easy Walk to Freedom*, Envisioning Global LGBT Human Rights.

validity of Section 377, did profound disservice to the very meaning of Indian constitutionalism.[32]

While reason is a key component of the law, emotion is not alien to it either. Judicial decisions at their best are not cold and unfeeling but display a profound empathy for human suffering. A court that is moved by human suffering produces judgments like that for the pavement-dwellers (*Olga Tellis*)[33] and the bonded labourers (*Bandhua Mukti Morcha*).[34] It could be argued that by responding to human suffering, judges embody a form of constitutional compassion that should really be at the heart of the judicial function.

This idea of compassion as central to the very purpose of the constitution finds a place in Jawaharlal Nehru's famous 'Tryst with destiny' Constituent Assembly speech of 1947 to welcome India's independence. Referring to Gandhi, he said: 'The ambition of the greatest man of our generation has been to wipe every tear from every eye. That may be beyond us but as long as there are tears and suffering, so long our work will not be over'. Clearly, from the perspective as articulated by Nehru, constitutional functionaries – such as the judges of the Supreme Court – should bear in mind that they have a great constitutional responsibility to redress the causes of 'tears and suffering'. In *Koushal*, the court turned a blind eye to human suffering. Two affidavits read out in court testify to this wilful blindness. Senior counsel, Mr Shyam Divan,

32 Ibid.
33 *Olga Tellis and others v. Bombay Municipal Corporation and others etc.*, see https://indiankanoon.org/doc/709776/ (accessed 27 Feb. 2018).
34 *Bandhua Muki Morcha v. Union of India and others*, see https://indiankanoon.org/doc/595099/ (accessed 27 Feb. 2018).

read out the one from Kokila, a transgender person who was brutally raped by the police.

> In the police station I was subjected to brutal torture. The police took me to a room inside the police station, stripped me naked and handcuffed my hands to a window. Six policemen all of whom seemed to be drunk, allegedly drunk, hit me with *lathis* and their hands and kicked me with their boots. They abused me using sexually violent language, including the statements: 'we will fuck your mother', 'we will fuck your sister', *khoja* [derogatory word used against transgenders] and *gandu* [one who gets penetrated anally, a derogatory word].

> I suffered severe injuries on my hands, palms, buttocks, shoulder and legs. The police also burned my nipples and *chapdi* [vaginal part of the hijra body] with a burning coir rope. One policeman of the rank of SI [Sub Inspector of Police] positioned his rifle on my chapdi and threatened to shoot me. He also tried pushing the rifle butt and lathi into the chapdi and kept saying, 'Do you have a vagina, can this go inside?' while other policemen were laughing. This was done with the specific purpose of insulting me by insisting that I as a transsexual woman was not a real woman as I was not born with a vagina.[35]

Senior counsel, Mr Ashok Desai, read out the second affidavit from Vijaylaxmi Rai Chaudhari, the mother of a gay man:

> My child is living with the agony and disrespect of being penalised at any point of time under an unjust law. It stopped him from coming out for long. Even after he came out, he always felt insulted since he can't live his life equally celebrated and accepted by the law and the society. The thought that Anis could for no fault of his own be harassed by the state, makes Section 377 totally unacceptable for any otherwise law-abiding, just and self-respecting citizen.[36]

The narratives of rape, torture and harassment suffered by LGBT persons did not move the court, nor did the reports of parents of LGBT persons, who stated that the law induces a profound sense of fear and destroys the ability to enjoy a peaceful family life. As such, the judgment profoundly fails to satisfy constitutional promises. Beyond the question of law, *Koushal* also does disservice to the idea that a place exists where law and love can meet. The right to love was left unspoken in *Naz*. Although *Naz* never used that phrase, the decision did open out judicial horizons to the possibility of a place where law could generously meet love.[37] Until the *Naz* judgment, the lives of LGBT

35 On file with the ALF.
36 On file with the ALF.
37 Justice (retd.) A.P. Shah (2015) noted: 'The Delhi High Court judgment started an important conversation in this country, one that is spiritedly continuing today, and that is compelling a move away from the language of homophobia, towards a vocabulary of choice, personal autonomy, the fundamental right to love, and greater sensitivity towards the "variability of the human kind"'.

persons were understood merely in terms of the desired freedom to perform certain sex acts in the privacy of bedrooms. *Naz* was instrumental in breaking down those closet doors and strongly asserting that 'the sense of gender and sexual orientation of the person are so embedded in the individual that the individual carries this aspect of his or her identity wherever he or she goes'.[38] From this articulation of sexual orientation and gender identity (SOGI) as integral aspects of personhood, the judges continued: 'It is not for the state to choose or to arrange the choice of partner, but for the partners to choose themselves.'[39]

Thus, *Naz* asserted that questions pertaining to SOGI were not really about the freedom to perform sexual acts in private but rather about the identity and personhood that flows from the freedom to form profound intimate attachments with people of your own choosing. It is this right to a form of public expression of an individual's personhood – which goes beyond what they do in their own bedroom – that is deeply imperilled by the *Koushal* judgment. For all those who believe in the right of individuals to express themselves through forming intimate attachments not constrained by the barriers of caste, religion and sexuality, the decision in *Koushal* represents an undeniable setback.

National Legal Services Authority v. Union of India: recognising transgender citizenship

A little over four months since the serious setback suffered by those involved in the *Suresh Kumar Koushal* case, another bench of the Supreme Court delivered a remarkably progressive judgment in *National Legal Services Authority v. Union of India*,[40] this time in the context of transgender rights.

The judges began with a powerful acknowledgement of the wrongs inflicted on the transgender community.

> Our society often ridicules and abuses the Transgender community and in public places like railway stations, bus stands, schools, workplaces, malls, theatres, hospitals, they are side-lined and treated as untouchables, forgetting the fact that the moral failure lies in the society's unwillingness to contain or embrace different gender identities and expressions, a mindset which we have to change.[41]

They then traced out a place for the transgender community in both Indian mythology and history. By referring to its presence in two great epics of India,

---

38 *Naz Foundation v. NCT Delhi.*
39 Ibid.
40 Supreme Court of India, *National Legal Services Authority v. Union of India and others*, writ petition no. 400 of 2012 with writ petition no. 604 of 2013, judgment 15 Apr. 2014. See http://orinam.net/377/wp-content/uploads/2014/04/Judgement_Nalsa_Transgenderrights.pdf (accessed 13 Mar. 2018).
41 Ibid., pp. 1–2.

the *Mahabharata* and *Ramayana*, the judges recognised a cultural sanction to transgender existence. The fact that this section of society was not discriminated against and in fact was a part of the ruling class under the Muslim Mughal rulers was also referenced by the judgment. In the court's opinion, the reasons for the current abject status of the hijra community had to do with colonial intervention. In 1871 the British passed the Criminal Tribes Act under which the very existence of the hijra community was rendered criminal. By referencing the unjust arrest of Khairati,[42] which, as noted above, was the first documented case of the use of Section 377, the judges recognised that using it formed another part of the colonial apparatus that ends up targeting the hijra person. The judgment holds that the denial of rights to the transgender community is a violation of the right to equality (Article 14), the right to non-discrimination (Article 15), the right to affirmative action (Article 16), the right to freedom of expression (Article 19(1)(a)) and the right to dignity (Article 21).

The *National Legal Services Authority* judgment (*NALSA* judgment) is particularly innovative in its understanding of what freedom of expression means. In the judges' opinion:

> Gender identity, therefore, lies at the core of one's personal identity, gender expression and presentation and, therefore, it will have to be protected under Article 19(1)(a) of the Constitution of India. A transgender's personality could be expressed by the transgender's behavior and presentation. State cannot prohibit, restrict or interfere with a transgender's expression of such personality, which reflects that inherent personality.[43]

The judges also read the right to life and personal liberty under Article 21 very broadly: 'Legal recognition of gender identity is, therefore, part of right to dignity and freedom guaranteed under our Constitution ... Self-determination of gender is an integral part of personal autonomy and self-expression and falls within the realm of personal liberty guaranteed under Article 21 of the Constitution of India.'[44] In conclusion, the judges held that:

> Discrimination on the basis of sexual orientation or gender identity includes any discrimination, exclusion, restriction or preference, which has the effect of nullifying or transposing equality by the law or the equal protection of laws guaranteed under our Constitution, and hence we are inclined to give various directions to safeguard the constitutional rights of the members of the TG community.[45]

The *NALSA* judgment was remarkable both for its inclusive language and its range of progressive orders. The state and central governments were directed to

42 *Queen Empress v. Khairati.*
43 Supreme Court of India, *National Legal Services Authority v. Union of India,and others*, as above.
44 Ibid., p. 69.
45 Ibid., p. 73.

implement a spectrum of measures on health, social welfare and combatting stigma. The state was also directed to recognise the self-identified gender of persons, be they male, female or third gender, without surgery being a prerequisite.

The *NALSA* judgment stands in stark contrast to the *Koushal* one. The former implicitly acknowledges the contradiction between the worldviews of the two courts. Though the judges stated that they could not express an opinion on the constitutionality of Section 377 – since that question had already been adjudicated in *Koushal* – they made the important point that Khairati's persecution highlighted the fact that 'even though he was acquitted on appeal, this case would demonstrate that Section 377, though associated with specific sexual acts, highlighted certain identities, including Hijras and was used as an instrument of harassment and physical abuse against Hijras and transgender persons.'[46]

The fact that the *Koushal* and *National Legal Services Authority* cases expressed such contrary opinions on the impact of Section 377 only highlights the need for a larger bench of the Supreme Court to resolve the contradiction.

Towards a conclusion

The stories of Khairati and Nowshirwan illustrate the lack of a language of empathy and a judicial inability to comprehend what Khairati and Nowshirwan experienced. Unfortunately, this lack continues into independent India. Too often it has not been seen fit to apply the language of the Indian Constitution to LGBT persons and their lives. It was only in 2009 that the *Naz* decision cracked open this legal mould. In the decision, the limited legal view that LGBT lives only raise issues of criminal law under Section 377 was broken. Only after this judgement could the courts and the wider public begin to see these issues and these lives through the lens of the rights to equality, dignity and privacy.

The fact that the 2009 decision was overturned in 2013 in *Koushal,* and LGBT persons were denied their constitutional rights, was a setback. The acknowledgement of the discrimination faced by the transgender community and the fact that the people who belong to it are full human beings with rights in *NALSA,* won back part of what was lost through *Koushal.* The Supreme Court has now decided to re-examine *Koushal* through the constitution of a new bench in the curative petition. This has reignited hope that the judgment will be set aside. The Supreme Court, in its order dated 2 February 2016, noted:

> Since the issues sought to be raised are of considerable importance and
> public interest and some of the issues have constitutional dimensions
> including whether the curative petitions qualify for consideration of

46 Ibid., pp. 13–14.

this court in the light of the judgement in Rupa Hurra's case, it will be more appropriate if these petitions are placed before a Constitution bench comprising five Honourable Judges of this Court.[47]

One hopes that the Supreme Court will resolve the contradiction between *Koushal* and *NALSA* in favour of a broader and more encompassing vision of LGBT people as full human beings entitled to all human rights. Such a decision would honour the constitutional promise of full equality for all persons, regardless of SOGI. However, until such time as the court takes a decisive step in favour of LGBT rights, it should be noted that rights are won not only in the courts but also on the streets. The right to expression, as well as the right to love, continues to be asserted in myriad ways, despite the court decision in *Koushal*. The question really is: 'How long will a decision that goes against a right that has been established on the ground continue to stand?'

References

Coalition for Sex Worker and Sexual Minority Rights (2014) 'Dignity first: one year of resistance to re-criminalisation of LGBT lives', Alternative Law Forum, available at: http://altlawforum.org/campaigns/dignity-first-one-year-of-resistance-to-re-criminalisation-of-lgbt-lives/ (accessed 27 Feb. 2018).

Hart, H.L.A. (1967) 'Social solidarity and the enforcement of morality', *University of Chicago Law Review*, 35 (1): 1–13.

Liang, L. (2007) 'Devastating looks: smirks, quirks and judicial authority', *Kafila*, available at: https://kafila.online/author/mingdom/page/16/ (accessed 27 Feb. 2018).

Liang, L. and S. Narrain (2009) 'Magic in the "city of words"', *Himal Southasian*, Aug., available at: http://old.himalmag.com/component/content/article/584-magic-in-the-city-of-words.html (accessed 27 Feb. 2018).

Murray, D. (2000) *Bosie* (London: Sceptre).

Narrain, A. (2008) 'That despicable specimen of humanity: policing of homosexuality in India', in K. Kannaibran and R. Singh (eds.) *Challenging the Rules of Law: Colonialism, Criminal Law and Human Rights in India* (New Delhi: Sage), pp. 48–77.

Narrain, A. and M. Eldridge (eds.) (2009) *The Right That Dares to Speak Its Name* (Bangalore: Alternative Law Forum).

Seth, V. (2013) 'A great day for prejudice and inhumanity, a bad day for law and love', NDTV, 13 Dec., available at: www.ndtv.com/video/news/the-buck-stops-here/bad-day-for-law-and-love-vikram-seth-to-ndtv-on-supreme-court-ruling-on-gay-sex-300992 (accessed 27 Feb. 2018).

47 Order dated 2 Feb. 2016 in curative petition nos. 88–102 of 2014.

Shah, A.P. (2015) 'From hostility and hatred to courage and freedom, Ninth Tarkunde Memorial Lecture', delivered in New Delhi on 12 Dec. Full text available at: https://www.ndtv.com/india-news/justice-shahs-hard-hitting-speech-on-decriminalising-homosexuality-1255624 (accessed 20 Oct. 2017).

Suresh, M. and S. Narrain (2015) *The Shifting Scales of Justice: the Supreme Court in Neo-Liberal India* (New Delhi: Orient Blackswan).

2

Expanded criminalisation of consensual same-sex relations in Africa: contextualising recent developments

Adrian Jjuuko and Monica Tabengwa

For the past two decades in Africa, new and disturbing trends have been developing: post-independence criminalisation and expanded criminalisation of same-sex relations. These have involved expanding the laws inherited through colonialism by means such as: expressly criminalising consensual same-sex relations between adults; extending the application of the laws to women who have sex with other women; applying the laws to persons and organisations doing advocacy or providing services to lesbian, gay, bisexual, transgender (LGBT) people; making the punishments harsher and restricting the rights of such individuals through constitutional amendments.

In 1990, Uganda increased the punishment for 'carnal knowledge against the order of nature' from 14 years' imprisonment to life; in 1998, Botswana expanded the criminalisation of same-sex conduct to apply to women. Then, in 2005, Uganda introduced a constitutional amendment expressly prohibiting same-sex marriages, a recriminalisation trend which rapidly spread to Nigeria, Zimbabwe, Rwanda, the Democratic Republic of Congo, Liberia, Cameroon, Malawi, Kenya, Tanzania and the Gambia. In 2014, both Uganda and Nigeria succeeded in passing their laws, though in the former the Constitutional Court declared the Anti-Homosexuality Act (AHA) to be unconstitutional for having been passed without quorum. Only Rwanda formally dropped its plans to criminalise same-sex conduct while the rest are still formally or informally debating how to expand criminalisation of this conduct effectively. Most of these countries already have colonial laws criminalising same-sex relations. Harassment, violence and other human rights violations continue to escalate with some states actively persecuting lesbian, gay, bisexual, transgender, intersex (LGBTI) persons and their communities. This is a big departure from the status quo in Africa before 1990, where homosexuality was mostly not discussed and arrests for same-sex relations were largely unheard of. What went

A. Jjuuko and M. Tabengwa (2018) 'Expanded criminalisation of consensual same-sex relations in Africa: contextualising recent developments', in N. Nicol et al. (eds.) *Envisioning Global LGBT Human Rights: (Neo)colonialism, Neoliberalism, Resistance and Hope* (London: Human Rights Consortium, Institute of Commonwealth Studies), pp. 63–96.

wrong? What happened to change the status quo? This chapter will attempt to discuss the trends of criminalisation from the precolonial period (the period before imposition of colonial rule in sub-Saharan Africa, specifically preceding 1880) to date. It will then delve into the factors that appear to drive the current wave of homophobia, from the role of conservative US evangelicals to the globalisation and politicisation of the LGBTI struggle and the need to protect and preserve what are regarded as traditional values. Its concluding remarks will provide some recommendations for further consideration.

Expanded criminalisation: definition and the current trends

In this chapter the term 'expanded criminalisation' refers to the process of building on existing laws to further criminalise same-sex conduct by adding to or reinterpreting them. The six different models used to achieve this are: constitutional; strengthening of existing laws; new criminalisation; enforcement of existing criminal laws; enactment of broader laws; and the judicial model.

The constitutional model

This is where a clause prohibiting same-sex marriages or same-gender sexual conduct is expressly included in the constitution or the protection of same-sex relations is deliberately struck out of it. It is by far the most harmful model. The constitution is the supreme law in most countries; inserting a clause prohibiting same-sex marriages or relations into a constitution can be read as having the effect of stopping courts from interpreting it in a way that favours the rights of LGBTI persons. In 1995, Uganda used this model to prohibit same-sex marriages.[1] This provision has not been challenged in its courts partly because currently, the LGBTI movement there is not interested in a battle over same-sex marriages, when they cannot even legally love who they choose to because of the sodomy laws. However, the other reason is that it would be almost impossible to challenge this provision because the principles of constitutional interpretation emphasise the rule of 'harmony' or 'completeness'. These require 'that Constitutional provisions should not be looked at in isolation. Rather, *the Constitution* should be looked at as a whole with no provision destroying another but supporting each other.'[2] As such, no practical way exists to

1   Through inserting the current art. 31(2a), which prohibits same-sex marriages, into the Ugandan Constitution. See Constitution (Amendment) Act, 2005, section 10 (Uganda).

2   Per Barungi Bossa JA/JCC in *Davis Wesley Tusingwire v. attorney general*, Constitutional Petition no. 2 of 2013 (Constitutional Court of Uganda), para. 7. This principle had been established and confirmed by the Supreme Court in earlier cases like *Paul Semogerere v. attorney general*, Constitutional Appeal no. 1 of 2002 and *Attorney general v. Susan Kigula and others*, Constitutional Appeal no. 3 of 2006.

challenge such a provision once it is part of the constitution, except through international mechanisms.[3] During the recent discussion in Uganda of the Constitutional Amendment Act 2015, unsuccessful attempts were made to amend Article 31(2a) to expressly prohibit same-sex practices in addition to same-sex marriages.[4] In Kenya, a member of the drafting team admitted that the protection of LGBTI rights was deliberately left out of the 2010 Draft Constitution (Ringa, 2009).

The constitutional model is the very antithesis of the kind of constitutional protection which countries like South Africa have expressly adopted to protect LGBTI rights – the first country in the world to do so. However, even there traditional leaders agitate to have discrimination on the grounds of sexual orientation removed from its constitution. The House of Traditional Leaders submitted a proposal to the National Assembly's constitutional review committee to amend its section 9 to remove sexual orientation provisions and the review committee has referred the matter to the political parties (Conway-Smith, 2012). Moreover, the Traditional Courts Bill[5] threatens to give powers to interpret customary law to the same traditional leaders who want protection of LGBTI rights to be removed from the Constitution of South Africa (Reid, 2012).

The model through which existing laws are strengthened

Through this model existing laws are deliberately made tougher in terms of same-sex conduct and it is applicable where same-sex relations have previously been criminalised. Two approaches are taken: either a new law is introduced to supplement the existing one, or the existing criminal laws are amended to create new offences or enhance the punishments.

A number of countries have taken the first approach. Uganda's AHA falls into this category as it was a completely new law but one that supplemented the existing penal code provisions. The now nullified AHA introduced the new offences of 'homosexuality' and 'aggravated homosexuality', and did away with the archaic Indian Penal Code language of 'carnal knowledge against the order of nature'.[6] One of the challenges of such language was the lack of a

---

3   E.g., a ruling by the East African Court of Justice would be binding on Uganda under art. 38 of the provisions of the Treaty for the Establishment of the East African Community.

4   See, e.g., submissions made by the Family Life Network (FLN) to the parliamentary legal and parliamentary affairs committee on the Constitutional (amendment) Bill 2015, Kampala, 20 May 2015, available at: http://parliamentwatch.ug/meeting/meeting-family-life-network/ (accessed 27 Feb. 2018).

5   B1-2012 (formerly B15-2008), Republic of South Africa, Traditional Courts Bill, available at: www.parliament.gov.za/storage/app/media/Docs/bill/616525_1.pdf (accessed 27 Feb. 2018).

6   The Anti-Homosexuality Act (AHA), 2014, sections 2 and 3 (Uganda).

clear definition. With the introduction of new all-encompassing definitions for homosexuality which, rather than criminalising acts, criminalised homosexuals' whole existence, nothing could be done around support work and advocacy for equality without it being regarded as a criminal act such as 'aiding and abetting' or promoting homosexuality. The other new offences included criminalisation of 'brothels', the definition of which includes houses belonging to homosexuals and hotels where they can get rooms; criminalising landlords who provide accommodation to LGBTI persons;[7] and criminalising the promotion of homosexuality, which could go as far as covering all advocacy and service provision work around LGBTI rights.[8] Another new law is Nigeria's Prohibition of Same-sex Marriages Act,[9] which criminalises the solemnisation of such marriages,[10] and prohibits the registration of 'gay clubs, societies, their sustenance, processions and meetings'.[11] This model was proposed in Kenya in August 2014. A bill presented before the Kenyan National Assembly by the Republican Liberty Party sought to prohibit all forms of sexual relations between persons of the same sex, introduce the offence of aggravated homosexuality, enhance the punishments for same-sex relations, and condemn foreigners who committed such offences to death by stoning (Mathenga, 2014).

The second approach, whereby existing criminal laws are amended to create new offences or enhance the punishments, is the most commonly used. In the Gambia, the president recently signed a Criminal Code amendment,[12] which contains similar provisions to those that appear in the Ugandan AHA (*Guardian*, 2014). Burundi reviewed its Criminal Code in 2009[13] and added consensual same-sex relations to the offences (Human Rights Watch, 2009; *Pink News*, 2009). And in 2012, Liberia proposed amendments to the Domestic Relations Act and the Penal Code respectively. If these become law, they will penalise any individual who 'seduces, encourages, or promotes another person of the same gender … to engage in sexual activities' (Human Rights Watch, 2013b)[14] in addition to prohibiting same-sex activity and marriages.

In 2006, Zimbabwe amended its Penal Code to define sodomy as: 'Any male person who, with the consent of another male person, knowingly

---

7 Ibid., section 7.
8 Ibid., section 13.
9 Same-sex Marriage (Prohibition) Act, 2013 (Nigeria).
10 Ibid., section 1.
11 Ibid., section 4.
12 Criminal Code (Amendment) *Act*, 2014 (the Gambia).
13 *Loi No. 1/05 du 22 avril 2009 portant révision du code pénal* [Law no. 1/05 of 22 Apr. 2009, Amending the Penal Code], art. 567, see www.wipo.int/wipolex/en/details. jsp?id=13386 (accessed 28 Feb. 2018).
14 For an update on Liberia see: Country Policy and Information Note. Liberia: Sexual orientation and gender identity. Version 2.0. Feb. 2017, available at: www.refworld. org/pdfid/589dd4bc4.pdf (accessed 7 May 2018).

performs with that other person anal sexual intercourse, or any act involving physical contact other than anal sexual intercourse that would be regarded by a reasonable person to be an indecent act'.[15] This extended the criminalisation to consensual intimate contact between two people of the same sex from the simple definition of having practised anal sexual intercourse. Uganda also took this approach in 1990 when it amended the Penal Code to enhance the punishment for carnal knowledge against the order of nature from 14 years' imprisonment to life,[16] stating that it was in response to the HIV pandemic (blamed at the time on homosexuals). Only one country, Mozambique, has recently done the opposite by amending the Penal Code to remove the criminalisation of same-sex conduct (Lopes, 2017).[17]

The new criminalisation model

Some countries which previously never criminalised homosexuality, have proposed new criminal laws. The Democratic Republic of the Congo (DRC) particularly stands out. Homosexuality is not, and never has been, criminalised in the DRC but at least three attempts have been made there since 2010 to pass laws criminalising same-sex relations. Perhaps the most serious one occurred in 2010 when the Sexual Practices Against Nature Bill was presented before Parliament with the aim of criminalising such practices. A Member of Parliament (MP) reintroduced the bill before the National Assembly in 2013 (Bah, 2014). In Rwanda, another country which has never criminalised homosexuality, the National Assembly debated whether to make it a crime, but in the end the government denied that it intended to pass such a law (Musoni, 2009). Until recently, none of the efforts under this model had been successful but, in December 2016, Chad passed a law criminalising same-sex conduct for the first time, joining a long list of African countries with similar laws.

The model through which existing criminal laws are enforced

Under this model, the state suddenly starts vigorously implementing laws criminalising consensual same-sex conduct, some of which have been on the law books in many countries since colonial times but have largely remained dormant. In the past decade, a marked increase has become apparent in the

---

15 Criminal Law (Codification and Reform) Act, Cap. 9:23 (no. 23 of 2004), S.I. 152 of 2006, Supplement to the Zimbabwean Government Gazette (16 Jun. 2006). See the Zimbabwe Legal Information Institute website at: https://www.zimlii.org (accessed 5 Mar. 2018).

16 Penal Code (Amendment) Act, 1990 (Uganda).

17 Mozambique's Parliament adopted a new Penal Code on 28 Nov. 2014, which was subsequently ratified by the Mozambican president and published in the Official Gazette of 31 Dec. 2014. It came into force on 29 June 2015. The law repealed the Mozambican Penal Code that had been in force since 1886.

enforcement of existing laws or the more vigorous enforcement of them. Perhaps the most notorious enforcer of anti-gay laws in sub-Saharan Africa is Cameroon, where stories of arrests of persons suspected of being homosexuals are rife.[18] Uganda is also increasingly enforcing these laws and, since 2009, arrests have taken place every year (Human Rights Awareness and Promotion Forum (HRAPF), 2013). Indeed these numbers have increased, with 46 cases of arrests recorded in 2014 (HRAPF, 2015). Countries like Zimbabwe and Malawi – where the president had to declare a moratorium after two men were apprehended in 2012 – also continue to enforce these laws.

The model through which broader laws are enacted

This model involves the enactment of broader criminal laws which target LGBTI persons and groups without expressly stating so. They usually concern registration and operation of organisations, public order management, control of pornography, and prevention as well as control of HIV/AIDS. The biggest tactical advantage of this model for the state enacting such laws is that, because they can be generally applied and are not specifically targeting LGBTI persons, it is difficult to advance effective legal arguments that they are discriminatory.[19]

Uganda, for example, has enacted laws in the following four areas that affect LGBTI persons and organisations. The first is the Non-Governmental Organisations (NGO) Act of 2016, which the president signed into law on 30 January 2016.[20] The law is generally progressive but has provisions that restrict the registration of organisations whose objectives contravene Ugandan legislation, and it also imposes 'special obligations' on such bodies. Section 44 bars organisations from engaging in activities which are prejudicial to the security and laws and interests of Uganda. These provisions – which are too broad, vague and undefined – would end up restricting the work of human rights defenders including LGBTI persons.[21] Second is the Public Order Management Act of 2013[22] giving powers to the police to stop public gatherings. It may affect meetings of NGOs working on LGBTI issues. The third is the Anti-Pornography Act of 2014[23] with a broad definition of pornography, which would also cover some of the materials used by LGBTI activists engaged in health-related initiatives. Finally, the HIV Prevention and Control Act of

---

18 See, e.g., Human Rights Watch (2013a).
19 Of course it could be argued that these laws have an adverse impact on a particular group but this would require going beyond the text of the law to analyse the implications, as Oloka-Onyango (2015, pp. 473–82) does for the laws recently passed in Uganda.
20 The NGO Act, no. 5, 2016.
21 See Human Rights Awareness and Promotion Forum (HRAPF) (2016). Also see Jjuuko (2016).
22 Public Order Management Act, no. 9 of 2013.
23 Anti-Pornography Act, 2013.

2014,[24] which criminalises intentional transmission of HIV, has presumably led to fewer LGBTI persons undergoing voluntary testing for HIV. Many fear testing, since a seropositive result might be manipulated to convict them of 'intentional transmission', regardless of whether this actually happened.

In the case of Zimbabwe, its NGO Bill[25] would deny local NGOs involved in 'issues of governance' access to foreign funding and prohibit the registration of foreign NGOs engaged in such governance matters. The bill extends the definition of these to include 'the promotion and protection of human rights and political governance issues' (Human Rights Watch, 2004, p. 1). This would certainly have affected LGBTI groups.

The judicial model

Under this model the judiciary interprets existing laws broadly and extends their reach. It therefore differs from the other models in that the primary legal actor is the judiciary rather than the legislature. In many jurisdictions, the judiciary has the final power to interpret the law, including the constitution. Judicial precedents on the reach of the law thus become, in effect, part of the law itself until they are overruled or legislation is enacted which overrides such precedents. Once again, Uganda is the leader in using this model. In the case of *Jacqueline Kasha Nabagesera, Frank Mugisha, Julian Pepe Onziema and Geoffrey Ogwaro v. attorney general and Hon. Rev. Fr Simon Lokodo,*[26] the Ugandan High Court held that a skills training workshop conducted by organisations working on LGBTI rights was illegal since it would amount to aiding a criminal act under Section 145 of the Penal Code Act, which criminalises 'carnal knowledge against the order of nature'. In effect, the court judgment extended the reach of Section 145 from the sexual act itself to advocacy and activism work around legal change, and effectively banned organising to oppose such laws and service provision for LGBTI persons. This decision is under appeal. An earlier one from the same court had limited the reach of section 145 to sexual acts.[27]

The above are the main models facilitating further criminalisation of same-sex conduct in Africa. It is a very worrying trend. Although there have been some apparently positive developments – such as the nullification of Uganda's AHA, the halt in plans to criminalise in Rwanda, and the decriminalisation through legislation in Mozambique – the movement towards expanded criminalisation is by far the strongest.

24 HIV Prevention and Control Act, 2014.
25 NGO Bill, HB 13, 2004 (Zimbabwe). It was passed by the Zimbabwean Parliament but the president never signed it into law.
26 High Court miscellaneous cause no. 33 of 2012 (Uganda).
27 *Kasha Jacqueline and two others v. The Rolling Stone Magazine and Giles Muhame,* High Court misc. app. no. 163/2010.

Criminalisation of homosexuality in precolonial and colonial Africa

Politicians and cultural leaders have made various assertions that homosexuality was never practised in traditional sub-Saharan Africa during precolonial times. Such statements generally suggest that it was imported from outside sub-Saharan Africa with Arabs and colonialists often being blamed for it. Hrdy (1987) asserted that 'homosexuality is not part of traditional societies in Africa'. Similarly, Gelfand (1979) singled out the Shona as having no problems associated with homosexuality. In Buganda, Sir Apollo Kaggwa (1905) claimed that the Arabs introduced the practice. Anthropologist Marc Epprecht (2008, p. 1) refers to these kinds of pronouncements as a 'strange consensus' among anthropologists, historians and politicians. Indeed he goes on to show that this consensus is baseless (ibid).

It has been documented that homosexuality is as indigenous to Africa as heterosexuality. Many practices that occurred across the continent could clearly be regarded as same-sex ones. For example, the Portuguese noted the existence of 'unnatural damnation' in 1558 among the Kongo, and in the 1590s Andrew Battell made observations about same-sex relationships among the Imbalanga, in what is now modern-day Angola (ibid.).

Other accepted same-sex practices include woman to woman marriages, which take place in more than 40 ethnic groups spread across sub-Saharan Africa from South Africa, through Benin and Nigeria, to Kenya and South Sudan.[28] Others that were accepted in some African societies of the past include men treated as women, for example such individuals among the Langi in Uganda might even be allowed to marry men (Tamale, 2003). Ancient paintings and traditional dances and language provide evidence of a history of homosexuality in the continent. For example, a 2,000-year-old cave painting in Zimbabwe depicts same-sex relations (ibid.). In terms of dance, the royal Buganda dance, the *Bakisimba*, is highly erotic and has males acting out female roles and dancing with men in a visibly sensual way (Tamasuza, 2009). Furthermore, many indigenous languages contain words that refer to homosexuality, for example, the Lugandan word *bisiyaga*. It has debatable origins but has been in use at least since the Arabs first came to Buganda during the reign of Kabaka Ssuuna, 1832–56 (ibid.). In the Shona language the words *murumekadzi* and *mukadzirume* can be loosely translated as man-woman and woman-man respectively. The first refers to a man who takes on female roles and the second to a woman who takes on male roles (Epprecht, 2004). This is perhaps a reference to transgender persons. However, these practices may not easily fit within today's description of same-sex relations and tags like 'LGBTI'. They had many different purposes, perhaps the least of which was sexual pleasure. For example, men who took on female roles could sometimes do so

28 See Epprecht (2004), p. 224; and Wieringa (2005), pp. 285–6.

because they were possessed by spirits – that is, they were acting as mediums for female spirits (ibid.). It is important to note that the individuals involved in such practices usually conformed to the dominant heterosexual way of life (ibid.). They went on to marry, have children and be part of heterosexual/heterocentric families. In this sense, such persons were similar to those of today described as 'in the closet'.

It is also important to note that some of these practices were documented more by non-Africans than Africans, usually with highly disparaging language. The heterosexist worldview of these authors perhaps prevented them from studying the practices more thoroughly and thus discerning their real nuance, meaning and significance. For example, the Buganda king, the *Kabaka*, is commonly referred to as *Bbaffe*, which loosely translates as 'our husband'. Used by men and women in reference to the king, the term could easily be mistaken as meaning that the Kabaka was literally a husband to both men and women in the kingdom, and it was acceptable for him to have physical relations with both sexes.

Another vivid example can be found in the Portuguese descriptions regarding the Shona Kingdom of Mutapa and its king, or Mwene Mutapa. The Portuguese described the Mwene Mutapa's advisers as 'women', which was due to a literal translation of the term used for them (Beach, 1980). The implication was that, since they were regarded as women, the king treated them as his wives and could perhaps have sex with them.

These precolonial practices were not necessarily encouraged in these societies, but nor were they necessarily punished. Precolonial African societies 'tended to place an extremely high and prodigiously over determined value on heterosexual marriage and reproduction. Individual sexual desire was largely subsumed to the broad interests of the extended family or lineage' (ibid., p. 37). Despite this, individuals were often given leeway to veer from accepted gender roles and sexual practices, provided they did not affect the broader interests of society. As such, homosexuality – just like celibacy and adultery – was deliberately not encouraged but at the same time it was not suppressed (ibid., p. 37). Such things were simply ignored and hardly discussed.[29] This is perhaps the source of the 'strange consensus' that there was no homosexuality in traditional Africa.

More importantly, these practices were not criminalised. All African societies had established social norms, and deviance was usually punished. For sexual deviants the punishments were particularly heavy, and so, if heterosexuality was one norm from which no deviation was allowed, punishments for homosexuality would have been prescribed. Thus, the fact that there seems to be no designated punishment for same-sex relations points towards tacit

29 Indeed, President Yoweri Museveni of Uganda stated that homosexuality had always existed but had never been encouraged (Njoroge, 2013).

acceptance of these practices, rather than the assertion that they did not exist. Indeed, it could be said that it was colonialists who first introduced criminalisation of homosexuality.[30]

Criminalisation of same-sex relations during colonialism

Western criminalisation of homosexuality was introduced into most of sub-Saharan Africa in colonial times. Territories in that region during the period were purportedly shared between the British, the French, the Germans, the Portuguese and the Belgians. All these colonial nations, apart from Belgium, imposed laws criminalising same-sex relations on their colonies.[31]

Britain had already criminalised same-sex relations and introduced penal laws criminalising same-sex conduct in the colonies it had previously established in India.[32] Thus almost all British colonies in Africa brought in those laws which described such activities as 'carnal knowledge against the order of nature'.[33] The only exceptions were Ghana and South Africa. The laws imposed in Ghana had been developed for Jamaica (Friedland, 1981) while South Africa was the only British colony not to become subject to these laws. Instead, its law was inspired by Roman-Dutch legislation. These laws outlived colonialism, and as they remain in the law books of these African countries, they continue to greatly affect the LGBTI persons living there. A lasting legacy indeed, as Human Rights Watch observes.[34]

Some colonies in French-ruled Africa also suffered the introduction of laws criminalising same-sex relations, despite the fact that homosexuality had been decriminalised in France in 1791 (ibid.). These were: Senegal,[35] Cameroon[36] and Benin.[37] Moreover, these laws still exist to date.

---

30 See Amnesty International (2013).
31 Belgium had decriminalised homosexuality in 1794. Although France had done the same earlier, in some colonies, it was still imposing laws criminalising same-sex relations in 1791.
32 Section 377 of the Indian Penal Code 1860 criminalised carnal intercourse against the order of nature.
33 The African countries affected were: Botswana, Gambia, Kenya, Lesotho, Malawi, Mauritius, Nigeria, Seychelles, Sierra Leone, Somalia, Swaziland, Sudan, Tanzania, Uganda, Zambia and Zimbabwe.
34 See generally, Human Rights Watch (2008).
35 The Penal Code provision currently in force is art. 319 of the Senegalese Penal Code *Loi de base no. 65–60 du 21 juillet 1965 portant Code Pénal du Sénégal* (Basic Law no. 65–60 of 21 Jul. 1965 on the Penal Code of Senegal).
36 The current law is section 347 bis of the Cameroon Penal Code, Chapter 5, Part 3 of Book 1.
37 The current law against homosexuality is art. 88 of Benin's Penal Code of 1996, and until then it relied on the Penal Code of French West Africa adopted by French colonial decree on 6 May 1877.

German law criminalised homosexuality through paragraph 175 – a section of the German Criminal Code between 15 May 1871 and 10 March 1994 – which made homosexual acts between males a crime, among other things. However, as German colonial rule did not last long, with the British and the French taking the colonies over after World War 1, its impact on the colonies' criminal law was minimal (Human Rights Watch, 2008).

The Portuguese introduced criminal laws in their colonies of Mozambique and Angola. The former does not currently criminalise consensual same-sex relations while the latter does.[38]

The fact that the colonialists introduced written laws does not imply that there were no preexisting laws in Africa. The continent had its own system of laws based on unwritten norms and customs. It is quite difficult to find any discussion of punishment for homosexuality in such laws, yet punitive measures for other sexual transgressions are well recorded.[39] The early writers, including African ones who were no doubt imitating the style of their Western teachers, only mentioned in highly disparaging language the existence of the practice. This tends to support the view that, in reality, same-sex relations were not actually punished in Africa before colonialism, despite the apparently negative view held of them. As already seen above, such practices were also not openly embraced and heterosexuality was certainly dominant.

The colonialists, especially the British, took their time in developing laws that were 'suitable' for the conditions in the colonies and did not simply impose existing English laws on them. Although British law was introduced in Africa through the Africa Order in Council, 1890, the colonies (meaning the white representatives of the British government and white settlers) were soon afterwards empowered to make their own laws. Many of them simply adopted laws that had already been developed; India was seen as a good source. That is why we see the language of the Indian Penal Code 1860 – which already contained section 377 criminalising carnal intercourse against the order of nature – incorporated into the laws of most of British Africa.

It could be argued that perhaps the lawmakers were too lazy to review the Indian laws in light of the conditions in each of the colonies, and thus Section 377 was introduced almost inadvertently. However, the fact that when the colonies made their own laws, they chose to leave in the provisions on same-sex relations says a lot about the intention. The 'lazy legislator' theory seems unlikely in light of subsequent events. Uganda, for example, abandoned the Indian Penal Code in 1930 and adopted its own, which was modelled on the Griffith Code that had been adopted by Queensland, Australia in

---

38 Angola criminalises same-sex relations in sections 70 and 71 of the Penal Code.

39 E.g., for girls among the Baganda, adultery was punishable by death, or in cases where the sentence was reduced, they could suffer mutilation and in some cases fines. See Roscoe (1911), pp. 261–3.

1901.[40] Instead of removing the provisions on same-sex relations, they added the provision on 'gross indecency' and enhanced the punishment from ten years' imprisonment to fourteen and corporal punishment. This seems to demonstrate a clear intention to 'deal' with the issue of homosexuality, thus leading to deliberate efforts to further criminalise homosexual behaviours.

The fact that the colonialists introduced criminalisation of homosexuality would seem to contradict the generally prevalent opinion at the time that Africans did not practise it. Why legislate against a behaviour that did not exist? Or, alternatively, if legislation was necessary, then it can be presumed the behaviour existed. On closer scrutiny however, the fact of criminalisation could be said to reinforce the paradigm of the absence of homosexuality among Africans. This is because the laws were not introduced to 'cure' Africans of the practice but rather to deal with European homosexuality. It was criminalised in Britain and largely abhorred; indeed, it has been shown that some of the leading explorers, colonists and missionaries practised it and perhaps left Europe to escape from the restrictive environment.[41] Thus, when the laws were adopted, they were intended more for Europeans than Africans. This was in line with the whole system of colonialism, which was mostly built to serve European interests. Africans were largely out of the picture, and a separate legislative system – customary law – was mainly applied to them. Arguably, therefore, criminalisation of homosexuality served exactly the same purpose as it did in Europe: the control of Europeans' behaviour.

It should also be noted, though, that the laws were rarely enforced during the colonial period. Increasingly, perceptions concerning homosexuality continued to change in Britain and other parts of Europe, all of this occurring at the same time as the anti-colonialism movement between the end of World War II and 1965. By 1967, when homosexuality was decriminalised in Britain, most African countries were already independent. Most former British colonies thus retained these laws at independence and simply adopted them; said laws still form part of the legislation of these countries today.

Criminalisation of homosexuality in post-independence Africa

At independence, perhaps most governments were too preoccupied with the new power – and the trappings that came with it – to give much careful consideration to the nature of the laws that they were inheriting. Ironically, they also coveted the colonial state's power of repression and suppression, against which they had hitherto fought, and deliberately left the laws in place (Prempeh, 2007, p. 479). Many colonies simply adopted new constitutions that were negotiated in London and other capitals of the former colonial

40 1930 Penal Code Ordinance, no.7 of 1930, later Cap 128 of the Laws of Uganda Protectorate, revd. edn. 1935.
41 See generally, Aldrich (2007).

powers. These constitutions gave full powers to the legislatures to make their own laws. In the case of British colonies, the various post-independence laws passed for each colony clearly gave the new state the power to make their own. Somehow, though, the new legislatures found it easier simply to adopt the existing colonial laws. Although many of the independence constitutions were hurriedly amended, ostensibly to remove the last vestiges of colonial rule, the laws made by the colonialists remained deliberately untouched (ibid, p. 502). They continued in force and many still remain so. Some of the most enduring are the penal codes.

Moreover, in the past decade, many African states have taken these laws down from the shelves, dusted them off, and are now actively resurrecting them. Such laws now serve important functions in the modern economic, political and social dialogues between former colonies and former colonial powers

They are being used, for example, to fend off any criticisms of African states in terms of their criminalisation of same-sex relationships and treatment of LGBT citizens by using the argument that the former colonial powers introduced them in the first place. As such criticisms are often levelled at African states in the context of discussions about economic and other forms of aid the Global North is proposing to provide, the origins and existence of these laws allow African leaders to accuse former powers of having a double standard. Indeed, the point of independence was the ideal opportunity for the British to repeal such laws, mirroring their inclusion of human rights provisions – to protect British citizens or nationals who remained in the newly formed states – in the constitutions drawn up following independence.

A corollary purpose of these laws is to reinforce the notion of African state sovereignty. The treatment of African state citizens is asserted to be the concern only of the particular state involved. Sovereignty has of late become the best excuse whenever other countries express concern about the existence of such laws.

Why expanded criminalisation?

Homosexuality has existed in Africa for as long as it has anywhere else in the world. It is part of the human condition. There is evidence, as outlined above, to show that homosexuality existed in precolonial Africa and that, though it was not encouraged, it was mostly not criminalised. As explained above, criminalisation of same-sex practices was introduced to the continent through colonialism. However, at independence, African states adopted those criminalising laws alongside others used to entrench colonialism. After some time, however, these independent states started taking ownership of the laws and Africanising them. Africanisation consisted of – and continues to be accomplished largely through – amendments and expansion of penalties.

The latest wave of legal change, over the last two decades, is concerned with the expanded criminalisation of the LGBT community. New laws are used to buttress existing ones, the punishments for existing ones are expanded, and the statutory wording is changed to clearly define the offences being criminalised.

As discussed above, this was not always the case. Merely describing the trend begs the question: what has led to these legal steps aiming to expand criminalisation? The reasons can be summarised as: the growth of Pan-Africanism; the rise of the LGBT movement globally and in Africa; the role of evangelicals and other religious fundamentalists; the recent changes in constitutionalism in the continent; the threat of the South African experience; the HIV epidemic; political opportunism; and the global culture wars which make African states into proxies.

The growth of Pan-Africanism

One of the main reasons for the protracted battle against homosexuality in Africa is the growth of the Pan-African identity in the continent, with agitation increasing for African solutions to be found for African problems. In its earliest form, Pan-Africanism was about African peoples coming together to oppose colonialism, imperialism and to uphold traditional African values. It has now developed from opposing colonialism to opposing neo-colonialism and all other forms of exploitation within the continent. Championed by pillars like Kwame Nkrumah of Ghana, Sekou Toure of Guinea, Leopold Sedor Senghor of Senegal, and Muammar Gadaffi of Libya, it led to the foundation of the Organisation of African Unity in 1981 followed by the African Union in 2003. The African Charter on Human and Peoples' Rights (ACHPR) uses the language of peoples' group rights and duties, all of which are concepts cherished by Pan-Africanists.[42] More recently leaders, such as Thabo Mvuyelwa Mbeki of South Africa, have championed arrangements like the New Partnership for African Development (NEPAD) and the African Peer Review Mechanism (APRM). Increasingly, African leaders are standing together to solve African problems. At the United Nations level, the strong African Group stands up for African issues.

The connection between this growth of Pan-Africanism and the increased criminalisation of homosexuality, is that African states join together to oppose what they see as another form of Western imperialism: the focus on decriminalisation of homosexuality and acceptance of same-sex relations. The often-expressed justification for this is that African states are sovereign and can therefore determine how to deal with the issue. The real underlying reason is the need to demonstrably stand up to the West in a variety of contexts. This political dynamic also explains why some African presidents, such as Yoweri

---

42 ACHPR, 1981 Chapter 2, arts. 27–9 on duties. For a critical discussion of the language of duties, see, e.g., Mutua (1995).

Museveni of Uganda and the recently ousted Robert Mugabe of Zimbabwe, came out strongly against homosexuals. Increasingly, the West's requirement of support for LGBT rights, especially in the context of aid and other forms of political assistance, is portrayed domestically in these countries as an imposition of Western values on Africans. Political opponents level criticisms along these lines at existing leadership in order to gain advantages in internal and international political struggles. In this political dynamic, the individual rights of LGBTI persons have been sacrificed.

Resistance in the form of basic criminalisation – as well as extending the reach of criminal law against same-sex relations – seems to be the domestic response to increased Western agitation for human rights protections for LGBTI communities in African states. President Museveni made this resistance quite clear when he lashed out at the US and other Western countries during his signing of the AHA on 20 February 2014, saying that: 'There's now an attempt at social imperialism, to impose social values. We're sorry to see that you [the West] live the way you live but we keep quiet about it' (Biryabarema, 2014). This use of the concept of 'social imperialism' fits neatly into the popular view in Africa that homosexuality is a Western import and that it is evidence of how the West is destroying African values and systems. Political leaders adopt this analysis and use it at the national and regional levels, reinforcing the political trend towards expanded criminalisation of same-sex relations.

The rise of the global LGBT movement

The global LGBT movement has grown exponentially in the past two decades so that groups advocating for equality and non-discrimination for LGBT persons can be found in virtually every country or region in the world. The rapid growth of this movement is not just in Africa but everywhere in the world. Bolstered by England and Wales's 1967 decriminalisation of same-sex relations in private for the age group 21 years upwards,[43] the decriminalisation movement gained momentum. Many countries in Europe, as well as Canada, Australia and others, have now eliminated criminal laws against homosexuality and homosexual behaviour. Indeed, these countries have moved on to protect the human rights of LGBT people in positive ways.

In Africa, South Africa became the first country to prohibit discrimination based on sexual orientation and gender identity (SOGI) in its 1996 Constitution.[44] Leading figures in South Africa like Nobel peace prize laureate Archbishop Desmond Tutu have openly supported the cause for LGBT equality. The UN Human Rights Council has passed resolutions protecting the rights of LGBT persons and so have regional human rights bodies including the African Commission on Human and Peoples' Rights (hereafter, African

43 Sexual Offences Act of 1967 (England and Wales).
44 This is under Section 9 of the Constitution of the Republic of South Africa, 1996.

Commission).[45] Since the 1990s, many countries have gone on to legalise same-sex marriages, including Canada and now the United States of America.[46] Protection of LGBT rights is now part of many countries' foreign policy and the former US President Barack Obama was key in ensuring that the US took the lead on this. Even the Pope has, within specific contexts, shown that the church should not discriminate against families with LGBT children (Molloy, 2014). The LGBT movement has, within a few decades, gone from being despised to being a force to reckon with, receiving support from powerful governments and opinion leaders. Those who are opposed to the equality of every person are now in the minority in international politics. At the same time, this rise in influence and capacity to effect change has rendered the LGBT movement vulnerable to attacks, particularly from fundamentalist religious figures and politicians of all stripes. Allegations of a global gay agenda aimed at recruiting children and decimating the traditional family continue to be made, and to be believed, and the emerging power of the LGBT campaign, including its tendency to focus solely on LGBT issues above anything else, makes them all the more believable. Therefore the LGBT movement's growth and gains have provoked a reactionary expansion of the anti-gay movement, which explains why laws are used to curtail the advancement of the campaign for equality.

The role of evangelicals and other religious fundamentalists

These developments have not been lost on the anti-gay religious fundamentalist groups which have successfully enlisted a significant number of prominent African religious leaders and politicians to campaign about restricting LGBT people's human rights. According to Rev. Dr Kapya Kaoma (2009), researcher and noted authority on the ties between US right-wing evangelicals and anti-LGBT legislation in Uganda, powerful US-based Christian fundamentalists, see Africa as virgin ground for promoting their anti-gay and socially conservative agenda. These evangelical groups have lost power – and financial support – in their base, the US, and have now shifted to regions such as sub-Saharan Africa, recruiting clergy and African leaders to further dominate global Christian politics. One way of doing so is to use domestic laws to entrench stigma and discrimination against LGBT rights. The discussion has been particularly enflamed by the 'threat' of gay marriages occurring in the rest of Africa (after being allowed in South Africa), and the false claim that homosexuals are bent

---

45 The first one was passed on 17 Jun. 2011, requesting a study on discrimination and sexual orientation (A/HRC/17/L.9/Rev.1). The second focused on human rights and SOGI (adopted 26 Sep. 2014). A/HRC/RES/27/32 was passed, calling for a report from the Office of the High Commissioner for Human Rights on best practice for combating discrimination based on SOGI.

46 US Supreme Court, *James Obergefell, et al., petitioners v. Richard Hodges, director, Ohio Department of Health, et al.*, 576 US (2015).

on 'recruiting' children into the practice in order to boost their numbers. This has led to many actively resisting LGBT equality efforts.

Another argument evangelicals use is that a 'homosexual agenda' exists to take over the world and erode African cultures and values. This kind of thinking was evident in the Ugandan Anti-Homosexuality Bill (AHB) 2009's memorandum, which clearly articulated the bill's purpose was to safeguard the African traditional family, and to protect children. A direct connection is plain between the rise of the Pentecostal evangelical movement in Africa and the agitation for the increased criminalisation of homosexuality. Waves of evangelism, of all religious stripes, have swept through the continent for centuries, starting with the Arab Muslims' arrival and including the later Catholic and Anglican missionary movements. But it is the most recent Pentecostal evangelical wave that has produced the greatest agitation against homosexuality in the continent. It is thus scarcely surprising that the rise of this movement there has coincided with an expansion in criminalisation of same-sex relations (Campbell, 2014).

The Pentecostal groups are led by the charismatic preachers of a gospel of material prosperity and puritanism. As Kapya Kaoma (2012, p. 3) comments: 'A sympathetic approach to local culture and the retention of certain cultural practices might explain the growth of the prosperity gospel in Africa.' These preachers attract large followings and influence them to extend their beliefs into political actions. Mostly, these teachings have derived support from the generally widespread belief in demons and ancestral witchcraft across Africa. In Uganda, prominent leaders of the Pentecostal movement speak out vehemently against homosexuality. These include Pastor Joseph Sserwadda, its chief leader in Uganda, Pastor Martin Ssempa, who is undoubtedly the most fiery opponent of LGBTI rights in the country,[47] Pastor Solomon Male,[48] and Pastor Stephen Langa of the Family Life Network (FLN). These leaders often

---

47 Pastor Martin Ssempa, a Ugandan pastor and activist and founder of the Makerere Community Church, is a leading anti-gay crusader in the country. In 2012, he was convicted on charges of conspiracy to tarnish Pastor Robert Kayanja's name after accusing him of 'sodomising' youths in his church. Since he is also an American citizen, a subpoena was issued for him to give evidence in *Sexual Minorities Uganda (SMUG) v. Scott Lively* which was ongoing in Massachusetts, US. Since it was issued, he has rarely appeared in public or made comments about LGBT persons, and thus it has never been served on him personally. See *The Kampala Sun* (2016).

48 Pastor Solomon Male, a Ugandan pastor and executive director of Arising for Christ, is one of the country's strong opponent of homosexuality. He was also convicted alongside Ssempa on charges of conspiracy to tarnish Pastor Robert Kayanja's name by accusing him of 'sodomising' youths in his church. He chairs the National Coalition Against Homosexuality and Sexual Abuses in Uganda (NCAHSAU), though he was at one point opposed to the AHB, which he described as 'a waste of time'.

form strategic alliances with US evangelicals who provide them with support and propaganda.[49] The latter frequently fly to Africa and preach directly to the congregations, raising up anti-gay hatred.[50]

Those on the religious right also form important political alliances. In Uganda, the Hon. David Bahati, the MP who tabled the AHB, and Hon. Nsaba Buturo, the then minister of ethics and integrity, as well as President Museveni, are all said to be closely linked to The Family, a powerful evangelical group which is opposed to homosexuality (*Observer*, 2009). In his work on the subject, Kapya Kaoma has documented this connection between evangelicals and the increased agitation for expanded criminalisation of homosexuality in Uganda, Zambia and other parts of Africa (2009, p. 6).

In Uganda, submissions made in litigation surrounding these laws provide clear, direct evidence of the religious right's involvement in anti-LGBTI legislation. The Inter Religious Council of Uganda (IRCU), the FLN and the Uganda Centre for Law and Transformation, all religious right groups, applied to join the case challenging the AHA 2014 as respondents.[51] In their application, they clearly indicate that their efforts were key to the passing of the AHA,[52] a direct admission that these religious groups played an important role in that process.

Recent developments in constitutionalism

Starting in the 1990s, the so-called third wave of constitutionalism (Huntington, 1991) reached Africa. It appeared to embrace democracy and human rights for all (Fombad, 2007) but, as later events have shown, has largely been a mask for imperial presidencies and may yet be a false start until more substantial changes are made (Prempeh, 2007). Long-term dictatorships started to falter and fall, and new leaders came into power in many countries. Infamously labelled the 'new breed of African leaders' by US President Bill Clinton (1993–2001), they included Yoweri Museveni of Uganda, Meles Zenawi of Ethiopia, Paul Kagame of Rwanda, and Isaias Afewerki of Eritrea, who all went on to preside over dictatorships or semi-dictatorships. In East, West and Southern Africa, constitutional discussions began to be held. In East Africa, assemblies were

49 A key example is the alliance between Pastor Stephen Langa's FLN and Scott Lively, which saw the latter coming to Uganda in March 2009 and preaching against homosexuality.

50 E.g., Lou Engle soon followed Scott Lively in visiting Uganda. He held a mass rally at Makerere University which was attended by the AHB's mover, Hon. David Bahati and the then minister of ethics and integrity, Hon. Nsaba Buturo. See Kron (2010).

51 *Inter Religious Council of Uganda (IRCU), the FLN and the Uganda Centre for Law and Transformation v. attorney general of Uganda and ten others*, Miscellaneous Constitutional Application no. 23 of 2014.

52 Ibid.

put together to draft new constitutions – Uganda's was promulgated in 1995, and that of Eritrea in 1997. In francophone West Africa, national conferences bringing together civil society organisations were held in 11 different countries, which in most cases resulted in new constitutions.[53] During the same period, in anglophone West Africa, new constitutions were promulgated: for example, Ghana's in 1992 and Nigeria's in 1999. Moreover, with the end of apartheid in South Africa, a new progressive constitution was implemented in 1996 and around the same time many other Southern African states got new leaders and constitutions.[54]

This wave of constitutionalism was mostly about human rights protection and providing space for political party activity. The debates surrounding human rights did not in most cases lead to a discussion on LGBT rights, but they did lay the ground for every marginalised group to be able to make future claims for inclusion. Only South Africa expressly recognised sexual orientation as a protected ground for non-discrimination.[55] However, sex and gender as grounds for non-discrimination are protected in almost all these constitutions and, at least at the international level, the term 'sex' has been declared to include sexual orientation.[56] The constitutions use highly inclusive phrases like 'all persons', 'all citizens', 'any person', 'every person'. This has allowed marginalised groups such as LGBTI persons to claim their rights in courts. In Uganda, the High Court has ruled in two cases that the constitutional Bill of Rights applies to LGBTI persons equally,[57] despite the majority of the population being opposed to same-sex relations.[58]

This rise in constitutionalism has allowed these marginalised sections of society to claim equal rights. As a result, anti-gay bodies fear that LGBT groups may use the constitutions to make successful claims for other rights, including the right to marry. A consequent political push back has led to constitutions being specifically amended to prohibit same-sex marriages, and to legislation

---

53 These took place between 1990 and 1993, in most of francophone Africa: Benin, Chad, Comoros, Republic of the Congo, Gabon, Mali, Niger, Togo, and Zaire (now Democratic Republic of the Congo).

54 E.g. Zambia in 1996, Namibia in 1990, Malawi in 1995, Angola in 1992 and Mozambique in 1990.

55 Constitution of the Republic of South Africa, Section 9(3).

56 *Toonen v. Australia*, Communication no. 488/1992, U.N. Doc CCPR/C/50/D/488/1992 (1994), para. 7.

57 These were *Victor Mukasa and Yvonne Oyo v. attorney general*, High Court miscellaneous cause no. 247 of 2006 and *Kasha Jacqueline, David Kato Kisuule and Pepe Julian Onziema v. The Rolling Stone Newspaper*, miscellaneous cause no. 163 of 2010.

58 The Pew Research Center (2013) established that the African public are the least accepting of homosexuality worldwide with 96% of Ugandans believing society should not accept it.

being introduced to further prohibit same-sex relations. In Uganda, the fear of LGBT persons claiming the right to marry led to the 2005 amendment of the Constitution's Article 32 (which provides constitutional protection for marriage) firmly restricting it to heterosexual couples.[59] The current efforts to expand criminalisation can also be seen as a reaction to the third wave of constitutionalism opening up many African nations' constitutions to claims for non-discrimination and equality for all.

The threat from South Africa – the recognition of same-sex marriages

South Africa is one of the most influential countries in the continent and its biggest economy. It is a strong pillar of the African Union and the Southern Africa Development Community (SADC). What happens there usually has an effect on the rest of Africa. Its 1996 Constitution prohibits discrimination on the basis of sexual orientation,[60] the first time that a constitution had introduced a prohibition on this ground, not just in Africa but worldwide. In 1998, the Constitutional Court of South Africa in *National Coalition for Gay and Lesbian Equality and another v. minister of justice and others*[61] decriminalised consensual same-sex relations. This was a major step, which paved the way for many other developments, including legalising same-sex marriages[62] and allowing same-sex couples to adopt.[63] These developments, especially in relation to marriage and adoption, horrified many including within South Africa itself. Prior to that, such matters could conveniently be regarded as only happening in the West and never in Africa. Their occurrence in South Africa was a 'game changer' for LGBTI rights, and meant that they were now much closer to home and could not easily be dismissed as Western issues. As a way of insulating themselves against the possibility of legal same-sex marriages, African countries started legislatively prohibiting them and also further criminalised same-sex relations.

The HIV epidemic

Perhaps more than anything else, the HIV epidemic, and the efforts made to counteract it, brought discussions on sexuality to the fore throughout Africa

59 Civil Unions Act 2006 (Uganda).
60 This is under Section 9 of the Constitution of the Republic South Africa, 1996.
61 *National Coalition for Gay and Lesbian Equality and another v. minister of justice and others* (CCT11/98) [1998] ZACC 15; 1999 (1) SA 6; 1998 (12) BCLR 1517 (9 Oct. 1998).
62 *Minister of home affairs and another v. Fourie and another* (CCT 60/04) [2005] ZACC 19; 2006 (3) BCLR 355 (CC); 2006 (1) SA 524 (CC) (1 Dec. 2005); *Lesbian and Gay Equality Project and others v. minister of home affairs and others* [2005] ZACC 19.
63 *Du Toit and another v. minister for welfare and population development and others* [2002] ZACC 20.

and the world. This also opened up discussions about homosexuality and its perceived role in exacerbating the epidemic, and led to the recognition of the category 'men who have sex with men' (MSM) as one of the key populations whose needs must be addressed in order to fight the spread of the disease. However, anti-gay groups have used these same studies to blame and demonise homosexuals, leading to calls for expanded criminalisation of homosexual behaviour.

When HIV was first diagnosed in the US, it was initially described as an epidemic among gay men and for a long time AIDS was described as a disease of gay men only. In Uganda, this perception drove the amendment of the criminal law in 1990 to increase the punishment for homosexuality from imprisonment for 14 years to life.[64] This same reasoning is still used today in the quest to further criminalise homosexuality, based on the false premise that criminalisation will stop the practice, and thus stop HIV from being spread through same-sex relations.

Political capital purposes

The current expanded criminalisation efforts are also mainly about politicians creating political capital for themselves. As established and long-lived political leaders are increasingly seen as more dictatorial and less democratic, with consequent loss of popular support, they resort to any issue that can help them regain their lost popularity and perceived legitimacy. Anti-homosexuality discourse and legal measures promise to provide such an opportunity for renewing these leaders' political popularity, due to the widespread opposition to homosexuality as promoted not just by the politicians but by religious leaders.

This dynamic was clearly played out during the five years of the AHB, later the AHA, in Uganda. David Bahati, the obscure politician who tabled the bill in 2009, went on to win the next election in 2011 unopposed in his constituency, and thence to become vice chair of the ruling party caucus in parliament. He is now a minister in President Museveni's government. Speaker of Parliament, Rebecca Kadaga, who insisted on passing the bill, despite obvious procedural deficiencies in its introduction,[65] was popularised in the Ugandan press and maintained her position in the next parliament. When she lashed out at John Baird, the Canadian foreign minister, over his negative comments about the bill, the popular media hailed her as a Ugandan hero (*Chimp Reports*, 2012).

---

64 Penal Code (amendment) Act, 1990 (Uganda).
65 Indeed, during the AHA case the Constitutional Court criticised her actions which were partly the basis on which the AHA was nullified. See *Professor J. Oloka-Onyango, Hon. Fox Odoi-Owyelowo, Professor Morris Ogenga-Latigo, Andrew M. Mwenda, Dr Paul Semugoma, Jacqueline Kasha Nabagesera, Julian Pepe Onziema, Frank Mugisha, HRAPF and the Centre for Health, Human Rights and Development (CEHURD) v. attorney general*, Constitutional Petition no. 8 of 2014, p. 26.

President Museveni, who signed the bill into law, was voted into power for a fifth term in a controversial election in February 2016. He was congratulated when he signed the law and a huge thanksgiving party was organised for him (Hodes, 2014). It is clear that the popular support and political rewards they receive is the reason why politicians want to be associated with the passing of such laws.

Export of other countries' culture wars to Africa

Culture wars, which are said to exist in every country, could also be described as clashes of values and value systems. One of the issues at their centre is same-sex relations. The dominant view in the past was that such relationships were immoral and non-religious. Nowadays, a general move internationally towards acceptance of same-sex relations is evident. Nevertheless, the changes are only happening due to LGBT communities' constant engagement and struggles with the dominant cultures.

In the US, Canada and some countries in Western Europe such as the UK, France and Germany, it is these efforts that have made progress possible: legal protection has been achieved for LGBT persons, with some laws including recognition of same-sex union and marriage. As expected, the positive changes have, in many cases, not been fully accepted and conservative groups are working to reverse them. This means that, with legal protections and a foreseeable continuation of such gains in some jurisdictions, anti-gay organisations have refocused their efforts to stop such measures happening elsewhere. Africa provides an easy ground for the fighting of these wars. In the same vein, liberal groups also struggle to make recognition of LGBT persons a global reality and have extended their activities to lobby their governments or friendly foundations to work globally to protect LGBT rights, including in Africa. That is why, for example, different US foundations fund various bodies in Uganda, Zambia and other African countries which work in this area. The financial support given to anti-gay groups is used to advocate for such purposes as legislation aimed at further criminalising homosexuality (Kaoma, 2009), while funding given to pro-LGBT groups is used to oppose such legislation.

The way forward: suggestions on how to stem the tide

In the last decade negative rhetoric against minority groups has risen across the world, especially that which targets sexual and reproductive health freedoms of women and LGBT people. This trend, particularly virulent in Africa, has largely been driven by US conservative religious groups and their agents who use their extensive resources throughout the continent in a bid to regain their lost relevance as custodians of human morality and family values in the West (ibid.). Political leaders have also taken advantage of this trend to denounce, demonise and vilify LGBT persons for political gains. They use negative populist views to distract attention from their own deficiencies while inviting support from wealthy powerful religious leaders overseas, especially right-wing evangelicals from the US. Ironically, given the colonial origins of anti-homosexual criminal laws, these political leaders justify their denunciation of homosexuality as being 'neo-colonial' and 'un-African', and therefore Western impositions which are contrary to African culture and religion. We suggest the following measures for stemming this tide:

Responding squarely and respectfully to the falsehoods

It is crucial for the LGBT community and their allies to engage directly with the falsehoods being peddled by anti-gay groups. The talk of a 'gay agenda' – to take over the world, decimate African values, reduce African populations, or to recruit all children into homosexuality and eventually turn the whole world gay – may seem ridiculous, but in the domestic politics of many African countries these ideas are taken very seriously. Such false information needs to be combated with clear, scientific and supported narratives that reveal it for what it is: a web of lies. More evidence-based studies need to be done on these common myths, and the findings widely disseminated. There is also a need for more space in the media to discuss these myths. Furthermore, the work and organising of pro-LGBT organisations needs to be more transparent and visible in order to do away with the thinking that a secretive 'gay agenda' exists to make the whole world gay. These anti-gay myths are sometimes 'confirmed' in the eyes of those opposed to LGBT rights when gay-rights groups are seen as employing so-called aggressive and antagonistic behaviour in their fight for rights. Although it is vital that such characterisations are not uncritically accepted, we must at the same time be precise in our public awareness work. For example, it may not always be useful to label someone opposed to homosexuality – or the methods employed by anti-gay activists – as homophobic. It is essential to unpack this term and employ it only where it really fits. Sometimes, it is important to understand the views espoused by the opposing side and respond in a respectful way in order to build bridges and create social space for dialogue to take place. Change takes time and takes different forms; the successes achieved in some parts of the Global North in terms of protection of LGBT persons have demonstrated this. Africa therefore needs to tackle the issue at its own pace, but emphasising protection of human dignity and human lives. In the next few decades, a clear and marked change will be detectable as has been the case in some parts of the Global North.

Holding accountable those responsible for spreading hate

Whereas African countries may not yet be willing to hold accountable their citizens who promote hate under the guise of protecting morals or religion, other countries can hold their own citizens to account. The use of religion to dominate and persecute is nothing new, of course. However, the current spread of criminal laws against same-sex conduct, as well as other limits imposed on bodily integrity – such as Uganda's Anti-Pornography Act of 2014[66] – are challenges that must be addressed immediately. In many African countries LGBT persons can be both direct targets and 'collateral damage' as a result of persecution and imprisonment. Much of the damage has already been done through the passage of new and/or expanded laws, which directly persecute LGBT persons and those defending their rights. In addition, a variety of laws – such as the NGO Act in Uganda[67] – narrow and control advocacy and stifle minority groups' dissenting voices in many African countries; these include Nigeria,[68] Kenya[69] and Zimbabwe.[70] Even though some of this harm may not be undone at this time, in some circumstances it is possible to hold accountable those responsible.

The attention and publicity around the AHB in Uganda brought about much-needed international scrutiny of ongoing human rights violations based on gender, sexual orientation, and gender identity and expression in the country. This scrutiny brought into the open the connection between US conservative right-wing Christian campaigners and Ugandan political and religious leaders, as already discussed above. This kind of exposure created a context for LGBT activists in Uganda to begin strategising about how to hold those campaigning for expanded criminal laws responsible for hate crimes against LGBT Ugandan citizens. The impetus for action gained ground in the country from 2012 onwards, with LGBT activists taking on the anti-gay US religious crusader Scott Lively using the US Alien Torts Statute.[71] Although the case against him was ultimately lost in the US courts due to the first amendment protections that he enjoyed as a US citizen, the court made it clear that his actions of promoting hate against homosexuals outside the US would constitute persecution under international law. This forced Lively to appeal, an evident sign that the strategy had worked. In Uganda, the case has already had an impact, with reduced numbers of US evangelicals coming to the country and actively speaking out against homosexuality in public.

In order to export these anti-gay endeavours into Africa, US stakeholders rely on finding willing local champions. American missionaries mentored and sponsored domestic politician David Bahati and the religious leader, Pastor Martin Ssempa so that they could launch their careers in Uganda, and they

66 Anti-Pornography Act, 2014 Republic of Uganda.
67 NGO Act, 2016.
68 Bill to Regulate the Acceptance and Utilisation of Financial/Material Contribution of Donor Agencies to Voluntary Organisations, Jun. 2014 (Nigeria).
69 NGO Coordination Act proposed amendment, 2011 (Kenya).
70 NGO Bill, 2004 (Zimbabwe).
71 During *SMUG v. Scott Lively.* Case 3:12- Civ-30051 MAP 2012 where SMUG is represented by the Center for Constitutional Rights (CCR).

provided the platforms from which they preached hatred. In 2008, Pastor Rick Warren[72] travelled to Uganda and partnered with Ssempa in running an anti-gay campaign. It is therefore also essential that such collaborations are exposed, and that the participants are held accountable together with their sponsors. For example, when the fact that Warren favoured Ssempa's work was exposed, he was forced to denounce that support (Ethington-Boden, 2014). Having originally refused to condemn the extreme bill, Warren – much criticised following suspicions of having backed it – finally relented and released a statement to correct certain 'untruths'. He even urged Ugandan pastors not to support the law as it was 'unjust, extreme and unchristian towards homosexuals' (*ShadowProof*, 2009). Indeed, after this exposure, Ssempa appeared to have lost much of his drive in advocating for anti-homosexual legal measures. Moreover, since the Massachusetts court issued the subpoena on him in May 2015, as part of the *Lively* litigation, he has rarely commented on or discussed LGBTI issues and is said to be in hiding (*Kampala Sun*, 2016). Such strategies therefore work, and make those who are minded to support and export homophobia accountable for their actions.

Taking advantage of the opportunities presented by expanded criminalisation

Opportunities are present in every situation, however unpleasant. Activists for LGBTI rights need to take advantage of these even in light of heightened hostility and expanded criminalisation. A case in point is the tabling of the AHA in Uganda. This law exacerbated an already dangerous environment for LGBTI people in that country, but activists were able to use its existence to expose homophobia, increase organising efforts, and forge partnerships domestically and internationally that had hitherto been difficult to achieve. They gained support in this way and were consequently able to bring a legal action to have the law nullified. Such efforts open up the space and enable dialogue and debate, which helps to change perceptions and expose the violations suffered by LGBT groups.

Non-Africans respecting and valuing African solutions for African problems

The rest of the world has a lot of experience and expertise to offer Africa on how to deal with homophobia. However, this advice loses its value if it is paternalistic and domineering. It is essential to respect, value and support homegrown movements. African countries will not and cannot decriminalise in exactly the same way as the US or the UK have done, or any other country for that matter. The specific sociopolitical contexts of each country always intervene, so that the techniques which worked in one may not necessarily be applicable elsewhere.

One that may not work is confrontation, which involves making demands for immediate equality and change. It is, rather, negotiation, mutual respect

---

72 Rick Warren, the founder and senior pastor of the Saddleback Church in California, US, is an influential conservative preacher and author.

and understanding that are the hallmarks of African engagements. Allies should support these African initiatives and attempt to gain insight into approaches used by the African LGBTI communities; it is not helpful to impose a particular model of how the work should be done.

It must be acknowledged that many communities in Africa never sanctioned violence against people based on their sexuality; rather, the spirit of *ubuntu*[73] and general tolerance are more common. The proliferation of anti-same-sex conduct, criminal laws and intolerance came with Western colonisation, and in particular with British colonialism. These laws, by and large, were rarely enforced until recently. In Botswana, for example, no one was known to have been prosecuted for 'carnal knowledge against the order of nature' until the Kanane case in 1995,[74] in Zambia until two men were arrested in 2013 (Karimi, 2013), and in Malawi until the prosecution of Tiwonge Chimbalanga and Steven Monjeza after an engagement ceremony in 2009 (BBC News, 2009). In Uganda a full trial of a person under these offences has never taken place, and it is only in relatively recent times that arrests have been made (HRAPF and The Civil Society Coalition on Human Rights and Constitutional Law, 2013). Accordingly, to demand immediate decriminalisation may not be the most effective or useful path for African groups to take. Their priority, rather, is to develop understanding and respect for LGBT persons within the community.

It is important to respect and value locally generated ideas, views and strategies and allow LGBT and other supportive groups in Africa to take charge of their destiny. Western allies' interventionist and paternalistic approaches have tended to stoke the fire of negative rhetoric against LGBTI rights. Concepts such as 'aid conditionality'[75] and international sanctions for human rights violations as tools to promote human rights for LGBT persons, can jeopardise the same people they are designed to protect. In Liberia, a speech by former British Prime Minister David Cameron about cutting aid to countries that violated citizens' rights, including those of the LGBT community, resulted not only in LGBT people being blamed for all manner of social ills in Liberia, but gave impetus to more laws being passed to impose harsher sentences for same-sex conduct.[76] Similar views were expressed across sub-Saharan Africa, in Ghana, Malawi, Zambia and other states which are mainly dependent on foreign aid, and resulted in many local citizens blaming and vilifying LGBTI groups for their woes.[77] Supporting Africa-led initiatives

---

73 Loosely translated as 'I am because we are', it means that communities are a sum of their many individuals, coexisting and supporting families and each other.

74 *Kanane v. the state*, 2003 (2) BLR 67 (CA).

75 See Anguita (2012).

76 See Human Rights Watch (2013b).

77 See, e.g., Canning (2011).

instead would negate the rhetoric that LGBT NGOs are fronts for Western allies intent on spreading homosexuality and same-sex marriage.[78]

Maintaining visibility and presence

For a long time, LGBTI people in most of Africa have lived closeted lives and the few who have openly come out were only able to do so in recent times. It is therefore crucial to maintain the visibility and presence of the community and to keep LGBT concerns alive, regardless of the sacrifice. It is important to reinforce the message that even the most homophobic and intolerant cannot legally or morally condone violence against people on the basis of perceived or actual SOGI status. The testimonies of systemic discriminatory conduct by state and non-state agents, and the continuous rejection, displacement and undue violence imposed on the bodies of LGBT persons in Africa are impossible to ignore. Even the African Commission finally had to acknowledge the existence of these facts. At its 56th Session from 21 April to 7 May 2015 in Banjul, Gambia, it finally relented and voted to grant the Coalition of African Lesbians (CAL) observer status (Asiimwe, 2015). This vote followed a resolution which had been passed at the previous session condemning violence and discrimination against individuals based on 'real or imputed SOGI status'.[79] The granting of observer status not only legitimised and recognised CAL as an important and deserving contributor to the African human rights framework, but also gave voice to the thousands of LGBTI Africans who are denied the same rights in their own countries and societies.

Exposing the real intentions of these laws and how they affect civic space

Through the politicisation of sexual and reproductive health and rights, political, religious and other community leaders have sought to isolate LGBTI persons, activists and supporters, criticising them for trying to create 'special' rights and protections. It is vital that this is realised and resisted as being a ruse deliberately constructed to obscure and eliminate voices of dissent, and limit civil society actions that criticise government for violation of citizen rights and/ or failure to adequately provide them. A case in point is Nigeria's Same-sex Marriage (Prohibition) Act of 2013, which criminalises such marriages and also the registration and operation of NGOs and clubs supporting LGBT

---

78 For a more detailed discussion of the role of international solidarity and the pitfalls to avoid while engaging on issues like the AHB in Uganda, see Jjuuko (2016).

79 The African Commission's 'Resolution on the Protection against Violence and other Human Rights Violations against Persons on the Basis of their Real or Imputed Sexual Orientation or Gender Identity', adopted at the meeting of the African Commission at its 55th Ordinary Session held in Luanda, Angola between 28 Apr. and 12 May 2014, see www.achpr.org/sessions/55th/resolutions/275/ (accessed 28 Feb. 2018).

issues.[80] This law affects not just LGBTI organisations but all which provide services to key populations, including HIV-related services. LGBT issues must not be addressed in isolation but must be integrated into mainstream human rights campaigns such as violence against women and other sexual and reproductive rights. In Uganda, the AHA of 2014 was defeated by a group of ten petitioners, only four of whom were openly gay.[81] This was only possible because the act had been understood to impact on a wider section of the public, not only LGBT persons and groups. Non-LGBT civil society organisations and individuals were also affected who were either related to, in contact with, or known to LGBTI groups or individuals. According to clause 14 of the original bill, parents, friends, work colleagues and everyone in contact with or knowing of LGBTI persons were expected to report them to the police.[82] And any NGO that provided a service to a known homosexual was also to be sanctioned by the law.[83] The reach and destructive impact of such a law needs to be further exposed and rejected.

LGBTI persons/groups supporting other equality causes – intersectionality

All human beings live multiple and layered identities, all of which are a direct result of social relations, history and the operation of power structures. We belong to and identify ourselves as members of various groups at the same time and can therefore simultaneously experience both oppression and privilege. For instance, a university professor who is otherwise privileged due to the job he holds, but who identifies as transgender, can experience workplace discrimination because of his gender identity.

Intersectionality is defined as a tool of analysis that 'aims to reveal multiple identities, exposing the different types of discrimination and disadvantage that occur as a consequence of the combination of identities ... It takes account of historical, social and political contexts and also recognises unique individual experiences resulting from the coming together of different types of identity' (Association for Women's Rights in Development, 2004, p. 2).

---

80 Section 4(1) (Nigeria).
81 The Petition is officially cited as *Professor J. Oloka-Onyango, Hon. Fox Odoi-Owyelowo, Professor Morris Ogenga-Latigo, Andrew M. Mwenda, Dr Paul Semugoma, Jacqueline Kasha Nabagesera, Julian Pepe Onziema, Frank Mugisha, HRAPF and CEHURD v. attorney general*, Constitutional Petition no. 8 of 2014. In respective order, the petitioners are: a law professor, one of the MPs who authored the minority report on the AHB, a former leader of the opposition in the last parliament, a journalist and media company owner, an HIV activist for MSM, a lesbian activist, a trans activist, a gay activist, an organisation offering legal aid services to marginalised groups, and an organisation working on health issues.
82 AHB, no. 18 of 2009.
83 Ibid., clause 13.

Discrimination is experienced by LGBTI persons on the basis of multiple factors including gender, sexual orientation, economic status, age, health status, race, ethnicity, gender identity and nationality. It is impossible to separate the different types of discrimination and oppressions because they intersect to create, sustain and exacerbate vulnerabilities. Focusing on one cause obscures other sources of oppression and discrimination and can result in partial solutions. Awareness of these multiple factors must be considered and integrated into intervention strategies that support programmes and policies.

For instance, MSM do not form a homogeneous group. The concept of MSM is in itself problematic because it focuses only on a sexual behaviour. It fails to encompass the broader social context that defines and shapes the daily experiences of LGBT persons as members of communities who may hold different social locations and identities, and have different lived experiences determined and shaped by various factors. It is therefore important to acknowledge that homophobia is not necessarily the only cause of oppression and persecution, and that many different factors converge and intersect to make LGBT people vulnerable.

It follows from this intersectional analysis that LGBT groups should also be involved in supporting causes and movements for social and political change generally. This creates the opportunity to gain assistance from allies and also helps others to recognise that the human rights campaign is one big movement and that no one is seeking special rights or undermining other people's rights.

Conclusion

Laws seeking to further criminalise same-sex relations in Africa are now commonplace. These retrogressive and dangerous laws threaten the very existence of LGBT persons and work to deny them support from other groups in society. The reasons for them are many and varied but what is clear is that both religious and political leaders benefit from this state of affairs. These actors paint the gay rights movement in a negative light and feed the largely conservative African populations with falsehoods. The laws are used as a tool to dominate and suppress, quite reminiscent of apartheid and other forms of exclusionary politics. They are also used for reasons completely unrelated to the circumstances of LGBT people, that is, to advance the interests of politicians and others in acquiring and maintaining power. To deal with this trend, there must be concerted and deliberate efforts to address the issues raised and also to seek acceptance and understanding from the rest of the population. The struggle is long-term. It is work that must be done with a distinct appreciation for local conditions and cannot be done in isolation. It is a struggle that involves uplifting everyone. It is essential that the global human rights movement appreciates and incorporates these basic facts. The faster this occurs, the easier it will be to advocate for the reform of such laws in Africa. It remains clear that this trend is not irreversible; on the contrary, it is unsustainable since it is counter-productive to subject part of the population to violence and exclusion simply on the basis of their SOGI.

References

Aldrich, R. (2002) *Colonialism and Homosexuality,* (Oxon: Routledge).

Amnesty International (2013) 'Making love a crime: criminalisation of same-sex conduct in sub-Saharan Africa', 25 Jun., available at: www.amnesty.org/en/documents/AFR01/001/2013/en/ (accessed 6 Mar. 2018).

Anguita, L.A. (2012) 'Aid conditionality and respect for LGBT people's rights', *Sexuality Policy Watch*, 9 Mar., available at: http://sxpolitics.org/we-recommend-134/7369 (accessed 6 Mar. 2018).

Asiimwe, D. (2015) 'African Union rights agency gives gay lobby observer status', *The East African,* 2 May, available at: www.theeastafrican.co.ke/news/African-Union-rights-agency-gives-gay-lobby-observer-status-/2558-2703782-opip1w/ (accessed 6 Mar. 2018).

Association for Women's Rights in Development (AWID) (2004) 'Intersectionality: a tool for gender and economic justice', *Women's Rights and Economic Change*, 9 (8), available at: https://lgbtq.unc.edu/sites/lgbtq.unc.edu/files/documents/intersectionality_en.pdf (accessed 6 Mar. 2018).

Bah, V. (2014) 'DRC looks to follow in Uganda's footsteps with anti-gay bill', *Think Africa Press*, 17 Mar., available at: http://allafrica.com/stories/201403111646.html (accessed 6 Mar. 2018).

BBC News (2009) 'Malawi gay couple to face court after engagement', 29 Dec., available at: http://news.bbc.co.uk/2/hi/africa/8433640.stm (accessed 28 Feb. 2018).

Beach, D. (1980) 'The Marquis de Sade: first Zimbabwean novelist', *Zambezia*, 8 (1): 53–61, available at: http://pdfproc.lib.msu.edu/?file=/DMC/African%20Journals/pdfs/Journal%20of%20the%20University%20of%20Zimbabwe/vol8n1/juz008001007.pdf (accessed 6 Mar. 2018).

Biryabarema, E. (2014) 'Ugandan president signs anti-gay bill, defying the West', *Reuters*, 24 Feb., available at: www.reuters.com/article/2014/02/24/us-uganda-gaybill-idUSBREA1N05S20140224 (accessed 6 Mar. 2018).

Burgess Carter, J. (2012) 'Senate passes "No same-sex marriage" bill', *The Daily Observer*, 21 Jul.

Campbell, H.G. (2014) 'Museveni and reconstruction of homophobic colonial legacy in Africa: which way progressives?', *Pambazuka News*, 11 Mar., available at: https://www.pambazuka.org/global-south/museveni-and-reconstruction-homophobic-colonial-legacy-africa-which-way-progressives (accessed 6 Mar. 2018).

Canning, P. (2011) 'In Malawi, more scapegoating as riots erupt', *LGBT Asylum News*, 20 Jul., available at: http://anti-wycliffite.rssing.com/chan-1375744/all_p64.html (accessed 19 Jul. 2017).

Chimp Reports (2012) 'Kadaga gets hero's welcome: vows to consider anti-gay bill', 30 Oct., available at: www.chimpreports.com/6690-kadaga-gets-heroic-welcome-vows-to-consider-anti-gay-bill/ (accessed 28 Feb. 2018).

Conway-Smith, E. (2012) 'South Africa's traditional leaders want gay rights constitution clause changed', *Global Post*, 6 May, available at: www.globalpost.com/dispatch/news/regions/africa/south-africa/120506/traditional-leaders-oppose-gay-rights-constitution-clause (accessed 6 Mar. 2018).

Epprecht, M. (2004) *Hungochani: the History of a Dissident Sexuality in Southern Africa* (Montréal, QC and Kingston, ON: McGill-Queen's University Press).

— (2008) *Heterosexual Africa? The history of an idea from the age of exploration to the age of AIDS* (Durban: University of Kwazulu Natal Press).

Ethington-Boden, E. (2014) 'Scott Lively and Rick Warren: the PR campaign to whitewash the right's anti-gay Uganda history', *Political Research Associates*, 6 Mar., available at: www.politicalresearch.org/2014/03/06/scott-lively-rick-warren-the-pr-campaign-to-whitewash-the-rights-anti-gay-uganda-history/#sthash.A3pvIk5O.dpbs (accessed 6 Mar. 2018).

Fombad, C.M. (2007) 'Challenges to constitutionalism and constitutional rights in Africa and the enabling role of political parties: lessons from Southern Africa', *The American Journal of Comparative Law*, 55 (1): 1–45.

Friedland, M.L. (1981) 'R.S. Wright's model criminal code: a forgotten chapter in the history of the criminal law', *Oxford Journal of Legal Studies*, 1 (3): 307–46.

Gelfand, M.E. (1979) 'The infrequency of homosexuality in traditional Shona society', *Central African Journal of Medicine*, 25 (9): 201–2.

Guardian, The (2014) 'Gambia leader approves new anti-gay law', 21 Nov., available at: www.theguardian.com/world/2014/nov/21/gambian-leader-approves-anti-gay-law (accessed 28 Feb. 2018).

Hodes, R. (2014) 'Uganda throws party to celebrate passing of anti-gay law', *The Guardian*, 2 Apr., available at: www.theguardian.com/world/2014/apr/02/uganda-celebrates-anti-gay-law (accessed 6 Mar. 2018).

Hrdy, D.B. (1987) 'Cultural practices contributing to the transmission of human immunodeficiency virus in Africa', *Reviews of Infectious Diseases* 9 (6): 1109–19, available at: www.cirp.org/library/disease/HIV/hrdy1/#n49 (accessed 28 Feb. 2018).

Human Rights Awareness and Promotion Forum (HRAPF) (2015) 'Annual Report 2014', available at: http://hrapf.org/wp-content/uploads/2016/09/annualreportfortheyear2014.pdf (accessed 6 Mar. 2018).

— (2016) 'Position paper on the Non-Governmental Organisations Act, 2016', available at: http://hrapf.org/publications/legal-analyses/ (accessed 5 April 2016).

HRAPF and The Civil Society Coalition on Human Rights and Constitutional Law (2013) 'Protecting "morals" by dehumanising suspected LGBTI persons: a critique of the enforcement of the laws criminalising same sex conduct in Uganda', available at: http://hrapf.org/?mdocs-file=1619&mdocs-url=false (accessed 29 Sep. 2017).

Human Rights Watch (2004) 'Zimbabwe's Non-Governmental Organisations Bill: out of sync with SADC principles and a threat to civil society groups', available at: https://www.hrw.org/legacy/backgrounder/africa/zimbabwe/2004/12/zimbabwe1204.pdf (accessed 6 Mar. 2018).

— (2008) 'This alien legacy: the origins of "sodomy" laws in British colonialism', 17 Dec., available at: www.hrw.org/report/2008/12/17/alien-legacy/origins-sodomy-laws-british-colonialism (accessed 6 Mar. 2018).

— (2009) 'Forbidden: institutionalizing discrimination against gays and lesbians in Burundi', 29 Jul., available at: www.hrw.org/report/2009/07/29/forbidden/institutionalizing-discrimination-against-gays-and-lesbians-burundi (accessed 6 Mar. 2018).

— (2013a) 'Guilty by association: human rights violations in the enforcement of Cameroon's anti-homosexuality law', 21 Mar., available at: https://www.hrw.org/report/2013/03/21/guilty-association/human-rights-violations-enforcement-cameroons-anti (accessed 6 Mar. 2018).

— (2013b) 'It's nature, not a crime: discriminatory laws and LGBT people in Liberia', 3 Dec., available at: https://www.hrw.org/report/2013/12/03/its-nature-not-crime/discriminatory-laws-and-lgbt-people-liberia (accessed 11 Sep. 2017).

Huntington, S. (1991) *The Third Wave: Democratization in the Late Twentieth Century* (Norman, OK: University of Oklahoma Press).

Jjuuko, A. (2016) 'International solidarity and its role in the fight against Uganda's Anti-Homosexuality Act', in K. Laror, E. Mills, A. Sanchez and P. Haste (eds.) *Gender, Sexuality and Social Justice: What's Law Got to Do with It?* (Brighton: Institute of Development Studies), pp. 126–34.

— (2016) 'Museveni's assent to NGO Act will cost us all', *The Observer*, 26 Feb., available at: www.observer.ug/viewpoint/42802-museveni-s-assent-to-ngo-act-will-cost-us-all (accessed 6 Mar. 2018).

Kaggwa, Sir Apollo (1905) *Ekitabo Ky'empisa Z'abaganda: the Customs of the Baganda in the Luganda Language* (Kampala: New Era Printers & Stationers).

Kampala Sun, The (2016) 'Fellow pastors hide Pastor Sempa from USA court', 8 Mar., available at: http://kampalasun.co.ug/2016/03/08/fellow-pastors-hide-pastor-sempa-from-usa-court/ (accessed 28 Feb. 2018).

Kaoma, K. (2009) 'Globalising the culture wars: US conservatives, African churches and homophobia', *Political Research Associates*, available at:

www.politicalresearch.org/2009/12/01/globalizing-the-culture-wars-u-s-conservatives-african-churches-homophobia/#sthash.mNy0e22i.dpuf (accessed 6 Mar. 2018).
— (2012) 'Colonizing African values: how the U.S. Christian right is transforming sexual politics in Africa', *Political Research Associates*, available at: www.politicalresearch.org/wp-content/uploads/downloads/2012/10/Colonizing-African-Values.pdf (accessed 6 Mar. 2018).
— (2014) 'How anti-gay Christians evangelize hate abroad', *Los Angeles Times*, 23 Mar., available at: www.latimes.com/opinion/op-ed/la-oe-kaoma-uganda-gays-american-ministers-20140323-story.html (accessed 6 Mar. 2018).
Karimi, F. (2013) 'Zambian men arrested over alleged homosexual acts', CNN.com, 8 May, available at: http://edition.cnn.com/2013/05/09/world/africa/zambia-gay-arrest/ (accessed 6 Mar. 2018).
Kron, J. (2010) 'In Uganda, push to curb gays draws US guest', *The New York Times*, 2 May, available at: www.nytimes.com/2010/05/03/world/africa/03uganda.html (accessed 7 Mar. 2018).
Lopes, E. (2017) 'The legal status of sexual minorities in Mozambique', in S. Namwase and A. Jjuuko (eds.) *Protecting the Sexual Minorities in Contemporary Africa* (Pretoria: Pretoria University Law Press), pp. 183–9.
Mathenga, O. (2014) 'Kenya: new bill wants gays stoned in public', *The Star*, 12 Aug., available at: http://allafrica.com/stories/201408120968.html (accessed 6 Mar. 2018).
Molloy, A. (2014) 'Pope Francis says the Catholic Church should support families with gay children – but that same-sex marriage has "not crossed our minds"', *The Independent*, 8 Dec., available at: www.independent.co.uk/news/people/pope-francis-says-the-catholic-church-should-support-families-with-gay-children--but-that-samesex-marriage-has-not-crossed-our-minds-9909727.html (accessed 6 Mar. 2018).
Musoni, E. (2009) 'Rwanda: govt cannot criminalise homosexuality – minister', *The New Times*, 19 Dec., available at: http://allafrica.com/stories/200912190017.html (accessed 6 Mar. 2018).
Mutua, M. (1995) 'The Banjul Charter and the African cultural fingerprint: an evaluation of the language of duties', *Virginia Journal of International Law*, 35: 339–80.
Njoroge, J. (2013) 'No killing, marginalisation of sexual minorities in Uganda; Museveni', *Daily Monitor*, 19 Mar., available at: www.monitor.co.ug/News/National/Uganda-does-not-kill-or-marginalise-sexual-minorities/-/688334/1724870/-/6bdtyk/-/ (accessed 6 Mar. 2018).

Observer, The (2009) 'Museveni, Bahati named in US "cult"', 25 Nov., available at: www.observer.ug/component/content/article?id=6187 (accessed 11 Sep. 2017).

Oloka-Onyango, J. (2015) 'Of mice and farmers' wives: unveiling the broader picture behind recent legislation in Uganda', in J. Oloka-Onyango *Battling Over Human Rights: Twenty Essays on Law, Politics and Governance* (Oxford: African Books Collective), pp. 473–82.

Pew Research Center (2013) 'The global divide on homosexuality: greater acceptance in more secular and affluent countries', available at: www.pewglobal.org/files/2013/06/Pew-Global-Attitudes-Homosexuality-Report-FINAL-JUNE-4-2013.pdf (accessed 6 Mar. 2018).

Pink News (2009) 'Burundi outlaws homosexuality', 27 Apr., available at: www.pinknews.co.uk/2009/04/27/burundi-outlaws-homosexuality/ (accessed 28 Feb. 2018).

Prempeh, K. (2007) 'Africa's "constitutionalism revival": false start or new dawn?', *International Journal of Constitutional Review* 5 (3): 469–87.

Reid, G. (2012) 'Traditional courts bill threatens LGBT South Africans', Human Rights Watch, available at: www.hrw.org/news/2012/05/29/traditional-courts-bill-threatens-lgbt-south-africans (accessed 6 Mar. 2018).

Ringa, M. (2009) 'Kenya: law experts rule out rights for homosexuals', *Daily Nation*, 18 Oct., available at: http://allafrica.com/stories/200910190050.html (accessed 6 Mar. 2018).

Roscoe, J. (1911) '*The Baganda; an Account of Their Native Customs and Beliefs*, (London: Macmillan & Co), pp. 261–3.

ShadowProof (2009) 'Truth wins out: Rick Warren speaks out against anti-gay Uganda bill', 10 Dec., available at: https://shadowproof.com/2009/12/10/truth-wins-out-rick-warren-speaks-out-against-antigay-uganda-bill/ (accessed 28 Feb. 2018).

Tamale, S. (2003) 'Out of the closet: unveiling sexuality discourses in Uganda', *Feminist Africa*, 2, available at: www.agi.ac.za/sites/default/files/image_tool/images/429/feminist_africa_journals/archive/02/fa_2_standpoint_3.pdf (accessed 6 Mar. 2018).

Tamusuza, S. N. (2003) *Baakisimba, Gender in the Music and Dance of the Baganda People of Uganda* (London: Routledge).

Wieringa, S. (2005) 'Women marriages and other same-sex practices: historical reflections on African women's same-sex relations', in E. Morgan and S. Wieringa, *Tommy Boys, Lesbian Men and Ancestral Wives: Female Same-sex Practices in Africa* (Johannesburg: Jacana Media).

3

Policing borders and sexual/gender identities: queer refugees in the years of Canadian[1] neoliberalism and homonationalism

Gary Kinsman

Who needs to know who is 'really gay'?

At a round-table discussion with Toronto-based social agencies addressing LGBT[2] refugee concerns in Canada, held on 22 February 2012 and sponsored by the Envisioning Global LGBT Human Rights research project (Envisioning), a member of a group involved in sponsoring queer refugees asked a question of those present. Could anyone – especially individuals from countries that LGBT refugees are arriving from – assist them in determining whether claimants were

1   I write this on indigenous land, and all work on refugee rights must recognise this. Everyone aside from the original indigenous peoples has come from somewhere else, and this is further complicated by histories of slavery and indentured servitude; even among indigenous people there has been migration. In doing this work and research it is important to develop a firm anti-colonial and anti-racist approach that 'troubles' Canadian borders and immigration/refugee/citizenship policies (Walia, 2013). I thank Cynthia Wright for the stimulating conversations and suggestions informing this chapter.

2   Throughout this chapter I use 'queer' and 'LGBT' (lesbian, gay, bisexual, transgender) interchangeably to refer to people engaged in diverse erotic and gendered practices. At the same time I stress that these are not adequate terms, are Western- and Northern-derived and cannot even fully make sense of sexual/gender experiences in the West and North. Even though 'queer' is often an attempt to capture a wider range of sexual and gender encounters, it is still coded in a Western fashion. The diverse sex and gender practices in which people engage in many parts of the Global South cannot be understood through these classifications. Many indigenous erotic and gendered practices in these societies cannot be understood simply through hetero/homo or male/female binaries (Massad, 2007; Drucker, 2000; 2015).

G. Kinsman (2018) 'Policing borders and sexual/gender identities: queer refugees in the years of Canadian neoliberalism and homonationalism', in N. Nicol et al. (eds.) *Envisioning Global LGBT Human Rights: (Neo)colonialism, Neoliberalism, Resistance and Hope* (London: Human Rights Consortium, Institute of Commonwealth Studies), pp. 97–129.

'really gay', and therefore valid refugees to sponsor (Envisioning, 2012). This person also asked if LGBT groups based in these applicants' countries of origin could be enlisted to provide this kind of sexual and gender identification. The Envisioning research network challenged this position both at that event and in later meetings.

I was taken aback by the above person's request. First of all, I recalled my historical work on national security campaigns and the identification of homosexuals. During these years, the Royal Canadian Mounted Police (RCMP) moved people from 'suspected' to 'confirmed' homosexuals so they could be purged from the public service; and interrogations were conducted in the military with a focus on engagement in same-gender sexual practices to determine if individuals were 'real' homosexuals and therefore could be purged from the military (Kinsman and Gentile, 2010). The current refugee sponsorship process occurs in a different social and historical context and rests on struggles for LGBT rights, but it still raises important concerns in terms of who might be the recipients of this knowledge? What power/knowledge relations is this bound up with? What social standpoint was being taken up with this question? How is it that groups rooted in the LGBT community are involved in trying to establish who is really LGBT?

On investigation it became clear that this comment came as a result of the regulations that the sponsoring group has to negotiate vis-à-vis Canadian state refugee policies, where, if it wants to participate, it must take responsibility for sponsored refugees and feels mandated to protect national space. This gets taken up within state text-mediated relations through which the sponsored LGBT refugee is discursively constructed. As Dorothy Smith points out in her critical feminist sociological approach, ruling in this society is often coordinated by people through official texts (Smith, 1990; Smith and Turner, 2014), and this includes the refugee approval and rejection process. Later in the chapter I will sketch these text-mediated relations into the picture.

Moreover, in a neoliberal twist, these sponsored refugees are now accepted in a context where responsibility (including financial) is shifted from state agencies to community organisations, agencies and churches. As Rohan Sajnani (Envisioning, 2014) suggests: 'The government has used the resettlement framework to off-load its responsibility to asylum seekers onto community organizations. This tactic has effectively reduced grants for asylum and government sponsorship', allowing the government 'to off-load their responsibility for refugee protection onto civil society' (ibid., pp. 24, 27).

A pilot project for sponsoring LGBT refugees was announced in 2011 by immigration minister Jason Kenney and has since been renewed. Groups can sponsor refugees and the federal government will step up with funding for their first three months in Canada. These funds are accessible only through a state-regulated process for refugees who have already been approved by the United Nations High Commissioner for Refugees (UNHCR) and often have to endure long waits and processing times.[3] These private sponsors must commit to supporting the refugee for the first year they are in Canada, including food, accommodation, and assistance with orientation and settlement. The sponsoring group also takes on part of the regulatory work of establishing who is really gay and really a refugee. Only relatively small numbers of LGBT refugees have entered Canada this way, since few are in a financial position to engage in this sponsorship. However, this allowed the federal government to claim that it was making LGBT refugees a priority while the number of refugees generally being accepted and settled was cut back after 2012 (Envisioning, 2015, p. 11).

The truth of people's sexual orientation or gender identity (SOGI) is also decided in the decisions of the Immigration and Refugee Board (IRB) for non-sponsored refugees in Western terms, based on essentialist theories of differences in SOGI. This perspective views LGBT characteristics as innate, essential and often as physiologically based (Kinsman, 2003). If the person has no same-gender girlfriend/boyfriend, has children, is married to a member of the other gender, is not publicly 'out', or their story seems inconsistent with essentialist theories of sexuality and gender identification since their experience has been more fluid than fixed (Rehaag, 2008), they have been rejected, even if these decisions have sometimes been overturned on appeal.

Given that sexualities and genders are culturally and historically made and can shift in people's life experiences (Kinsman, 2003), this approach does not lead to an adequate grasping of these social experiences. It also raises questions about who gets to define what queerness is, or whose definition of LGBT it is that asylum seekers have to fit into. It can lead to the denial of other social practices of gender and eroticism. Some of the problems with these decisions that impose a definition of LGBT on to the experiences of people from the Global South will be detailed later in this chapter.

This identification process also points to an involvement of some LGBT agencies in the new regulatory regimes that asylum seekers face. It is based on refugee claimants having to perform to state officials and sponsoring groups that they are really LGBT. This is difficult to prove, given the situations they have come from. It also may make little sense in terms of people's sexual and gender practices and the social organisation of gender and sexual relations in the countries or communities they are fleeing from. While creating important possibilities for those fleeing sexual and gender oppression, this can also be part of a new regulatory regime imposing Western hetero/homo-derived classifications and LGBT definitions on to the experiences of people coming into Canada.

This regulatory project is one of making 'good' refugees, 'responsible' LGBT people, and 'proper' citizens and national subjects. There are similarities

---

3   For instance, Kenya has an approximate wait time of over four years, and no country has a wait time of less than one year (Envisioning, 2014, p. 26). This creates highly unsafe situations for LGBT asylum seekers.

here with other forms of settlement work (including multicultural forms) for immigrants and refugees that makes them into 'proper' refugees, permanent residents and especially citizens in the context of Canadian state and capitalist social relations. This is also why it is important to be able to operate simultaneously and dialectically *within, against and beyond* (Holloway, 2005; 2016) current refugee and border regulations. Despite claims that limitations are needed because there are strains on Canadian infrastructure, the regulations must be used and stretched to provide entry and support for as many people with need as possible, through direct action support work and campaigns, to organise against restrictive regulations that deny status to many people, and push beyond them for an alternative that permits all who need to enter and stay in Canada.

At times, accepting refugees is viewed within Canadian LGBT community formation as 'saving' these people from backward homophobic cultures. Sometimes they are viewed in a normalising gaze as children in need of proper socialisation to become adult LGBT people like those in the West. This approach can carry with it important 'civilisational' aspects, when imposing Global North constructions of what is civilised on to people of colour from the Global South. Orientalist forms of homonationalism (Gentile and Kinsman, 2015; Dryden and Lenon, 2015; Said, 1979; Puar, 2007) inform this perspective, constructing people from Muslim and Arab backgrounds and other people from the Global South as coming from 'bad' homophobic cultures.

There are two different but related ways this is deployed. One is in an overtly racist fashion, arguing that these people's cultures and societies – and by implication these individuals – are backward and homophobic, compared to those of the civilised West. At the same time, many of them do encounter heterosexism and anti-trans practices in their own communities and in the broader society. This racist response blends into racism towards people of colour more generally, including that which exists in LGBT community formation against people of colour. As one round-table participant put it: 'There is rampant racism in the LGBT community' (Envisioning, 2012, p. 11), and it is important to remember that the pervasive racism faced by LGBT refugees and migrants of colour is also generated within LGBT communities. Himani Bannerji (1995) also points out that these more extreme and overt forms of racialisation rest on more common-sense forms. And often what appears to be a well-intentioned 'missionary' approach of trying to save LGBT refugees from their bad cultures also rests on a common-sense racism that constructs them as passive victims, denying them agency and subjectivity. Although different from the more extreme racist response, this is also a form of racism.

This chapter explores the policing and bordering of LGBT refugees by sketching out these developing relations while raising questions that need to be pursued further. The aim is not to provide definitive answers but to open up a broader conversation about these matters.[4] It investigates a major contradiction between the formal right of LGBT people to claim asylum in Canada and the obstacles which deny that claim to many. Formal right of acceptance of LGBT refugees occurs at the very same time that neoliberalism is tightening borders in the North against poorer people of colour from the Global South, and making it less possible for them to claim asylum. So although Canada is a safe haven for LGBT refugees on a formal level, is it so in practice? As we shall see, for the vast majority of refugees and migrants – including those denied status – Canada is not a safe haven.

This investigation brings together insights from the Envisioning Canada research team (Envisioning, 2012, 2014, 2015) and critical studies of immigration, refugee and migration policies (Wright, 2006, 2017; Anderson et al., 2012; Balibar, 2004; Nyers and Rygiel, 2012; Mezzadra and Neilson, 2013), including work on queer migration (Luibhéid, 2008; Luibhéid and Cantú Jr, 2005) alongside my work on the making of the neoliberal queer (2016, 2017a), and accounts of the neoliberal transformation of state and social relations globally and within Canadian state and social formation (Sears, 2003; McNally, 2006). The social relations of neoliberalism have reshaped immigration, refugee and border policies, which organise this contradiction between formal rights and the *actual* obstacles and barriers produced through administrative practices.

External and internal border barriers

Envisioning provides a global context for looking at the refugee determination process, including from the social standpoints of those in the Global South and refugee camps. Major barriers stop people from ever getting to Canada. Material circumstances and social possibilities prevent people from being able to afford to get to Canada or to apply for and receive visas. People are also unaware that they can claim asylum in Canada as an LGBT person facing harassment and discrimination. Barriers include the conditions in refugee camps, the lack of Canadian government offices and officials in many parts of the world (some were closed down or their operations were reduced, and some files were closed under the Harper government), and the difficulties in getting accepted as refugees by Canadian officials.

For instance, Envisioning Africa research team member Eric Gitari, executive director of the National Gay and Lesbian Human Rights Commission

---

4   This chapter was initially written prior to the Liberal government taking office in Nov. 2015 and, although it has been updated, it cannot fully address the limited changes this government is bringing about in immigration and refugee policies. On some of these changes and proposals, see Nerenberg (2016). Also see the frequent updates on the Canadian Council for Refugees site at: http://ccrweb.ca/en/home (accessed 6 Mar. 2018).

in Kenya, reported on conditions in refugee camps in Kenya – where he has done support work and research – for those fleeing anti-LGBT laws and discrimination in Uganda. He described homophobia in the asylum regime, including police harassment and the denial of confidentiality, which leads to identification and violence (Envisioning, 2015), and also how, for many LGBT asylum seekers, the excessive documentation required by the Canadian government effectively makes resettlement in Canada very difficult. As he points out: 'The lived reality on the ground, and the policy by your government are very disconnected' (2014, pp. 16–17). The Canadian government often falls short of meeting its pledges because its standards are too high, there are many administrative barriers and it is notorious for taking a long time to resettle people (ibid., p. 17).

At the same time, there are major internal barriers for those who are able to get to Canada. These include the refugee regulations themselves, the need to demonstrate they are really LGBT, racism, difficulties in getting social assistance, housing and employment (when many employers require 'Canadian experience'), living in poverty, cuts to services, concerns about safety and personal security, and problems in accessing health services (Envisioning, 2015). Asylum seekers who are LGBT also face all the problems that refugee applicants face with the tightening of Canadian border policing. Although much of this chapter focuses more on these internal barriers, they are also informed by pervasive external barriers. Whether internal or external they have a mediated or mutually determined character, which combine to make things more difficult for all asylum seekers not just LGBT ones.

Racialisation, formal rights and the tightening of border regimes

While neoliberalism allows capital to move around the world freely (McNally, 2006), it leads to a tightening of borders for people of colour from the Global South. This causes an intensification of state formation in relation to border regimes, including surveillance, detention, deportation and normalisation. The dilemma is that the achievement of formal rights and neoliberal attacks occur at the same time with the former having been enacted in the context of neoliberal tightening of borders against people of colour. Although neoliberal border regimes can provide formal rights, which is a step forward, they do not provide a substantive right. For instance, we all have the same formal right to stay in the most expensive hotel in the city, but in reality we don't because many of us simply can't afford it. Regarding asylum seekers, although all LGBT people may have the same formal right to claim asylum in Canada, in practice, most are denied that possibility because of their material and social circumstances and because of the barriers built into the regulations. Formal rights remain trapped within the current social form[5] of border regimes.

5   On the Marxist use of social form, see Holloway (2005) and Corrigan and Sayer

As Dean Spade (2011) points out, it is important to focus on the administrative law and regulations through which substantive barriers are constructed. They affect different groups of people differentially, including the social variation between those who have the resources to obtain a visa and get to Canada on their own, and those who do not. As one round-table participant put it: 'People who are poor have a disproportionate experience of harm because of their orientation, and these are the people who cannot get here because they don't have the assets. The situation is only going to get worse' (Envisioning, 2012, p. 6). A visa is required for residents of most countries, but is difficult to obtain. People with financial resources and connections can get into Canada, but many can only make it across the border into adjoining countries, end up in refugee camps, and are far less likely to be selected by Canadian officials as refugees. This situation has shifted somewhat recently as the Canadian Liberal government has been accepting thousands of Syrians from refugee camps.

In the Canadian context, as Cynthia Wright (2017) points out, Western LGBT organisations have undertaken the fight for legal equality in the immigration system at the same moment that many states are transforming the post-World War Two immigration and refugee regime informed by neoliberalism. Many LGBT immigration and refugee activists see this struggle in narrow LGBT terms, because for many it developed through support for formal equality rights within general acceptance of the social form of state immigration and refugee policy. These struggles won some acceptance in some countries, including Canada, starting in the early 1990s. Some of those fleeing their countries of origin because of gender and sexual oppression can now claim LGBT status as refugees in Canada and 41 other countries (Envisioning, 2015, p. 11).

The contradiction is that, although there is a focus on immigration and refugee rights for LGBT people, immigration and refugee status more generally is increasingly precarious, as more people have their applications denied and live without status. As a result of these changes including Bill C-31, which will be addressed later, there was a 20 per cent decrease in family class immigrants (from 2006 to 2011), a 30 per cent drop in accepted refugees, and a 50 per cent drop in refugee claims (from 2006 to 2012). In the period 2006–14 there were 87,317 detentions and 117,531 deportations (Never Home: No One Is Illegal – Vancouver, 2015). Asylum claims went from 20,500 in 2012, to 10,380 in 2013, to 13,450 in 2014 (UNHCR, 2015). All of these changes have an impact on LGBT immigrants, refugees and migrants. But until recently there was little critical analysis of this development among queer activists.

A narrow and limited rights politics cannot address the complexity of border regimes. We cannot simply fit into neoliberal shifts in immigration and

---

(1985). Moving beyond the 'natural' appearance of these forms, this stresses that they are always historical and social in character and can therefore be socially transformed.

refugee policy and attempt to modify them, which those supporting formal equality sometimes seem to do. Refugee politics must also address the needs of those whose applications are refused and those without status. This group is growing and includes many queers.[6] Even the granting of 'status' from state agencies is far too limited since it is entirely reliant on state bureaucratic processes and a move beyond a politics based on state-approved paths to citizenship is needed. Addressing these concerns moves us far beyond rights politics to address the construction of border regimes beyond the geographical border. This includes not only interactions between the police and border security, but denial of social assistance and health services to people without status, as well as the normalisation of queer migrants to 'work them up' as proper LGBT refugees, which is also part of 'border work' in a broad sense. An analytical approach is needed that addresses bordering practices and learns from boundary struggles (Mezzadra and Neilson, 2013). Such a perspective involves the interruption of regimes of detention, deportation, surveillance *and* normalisation.

My perspective is also informed by No One Is Illegal (NOII) activism. Emerging from the struggles for migrant justice and global justice, the NOII approach calls for the elimination of borders and for status for all. In this view, people have the need for and right to full status since they are people in a global community. From this viewpoint, it has been a mistake for rights to social access and status to reside only in the nation state; this approach moves beyond the nation state, and the derivation of rights from citizenship (Walia, 2013; NOII – Toronto, 2015; NOII – Vancouver, 2015; Anderson et al., 2012). In this view, people need freedom to move, to stay, and to return. It recognises that people need to move because of displacement, misery, poverty, underdevelopment, war, the closing of the global commons and forced eviction from the land as more commodification of social life takes place (McNally, 2006), and climate change among others. People from the Global South follow wealth to more affluent countries like Canada that have been overdeveloped through imperialism and exploitation. Some also flee sexual and gender oppression, although this may be only part of their overall social experience.

Some of these people are classified as migrants, while others are categorised as refugees. It is important not to separate the latter as a class of people distinct from others who are crossing borders. One way to escape persecution and to improve situations is to move and to claim refugee status. This approach views migrants and refugees as negotiating and sometimes defying and resisting border regimes (Nyers, 2015; Hardt and Negri, 2000, pp. 210–14). Migrants are putting borders in question as tens of thousands have hit the borders of 'fortress Europe' engaging in mass direct action with local activists' assistance to

---

6   It is unfortunate in this regard that Envisioning could not, in its interviews and focus groups, gather information from those denied status.

push through fences, across frontiers, and on to trains, to try to build new lives.

In bringing together what has been learned from Envisioning's Canada research team with NOII perspectives, this chapter also draws upon the work of Himani Bannerji (1995) on the mediation of social relations and social differences. Bannerji views different social experiences as having their own moment of autonomy, or specificity, but at the same time they are also mutually constructed through other social relations. There is a need, as Envisioning research has done, to focus on sexuality and gender identification as one important moment of analysis, since these are not the same as other social experiences. But at the same time, sexuality/gender is also mutually constructed through race, class and state relations. Envisioning began to undertake a wider approach with its adoption of an intersectional analysis where all forms of oppression intersect[7] but a social mediational approach pushes this analysis further. Asylum seekers' experiences of sexuality and gender identifications/practices must be addressed, but that stance must include the broader social context of state formation and border regimes. If the focus is on sexuality/gender identifications only, it will not be possible to fully grasp where border problems originate. There must therefore be movement beyond a limited LGBT rights framework. There is a need to expand upon the insights gained from Envisioning research to address racism much more centrally as recommended in the Envisioning report (2015). The specificity of sexual and gender oppression must be focused on, but it must also be placed in the context of racialisation and the transformation of border regimes more generally. This requires making it easier for all asylum seekers and migrants to cross borders, which involves reducing administrative obstacles and substantive barriers to movement and status.

Despite these substantial barriers, and escalating numbers of deportations, Canadian officials have presented themselves on the global stage as being more 'civilised' on LGBT questions than countries in the Global South, by using the figure of the 'gay refugee'. For instance, in the fall of 2012, drawing on a form of orientalist homonationalism (Gentile and Kinsman, 2015; Puar, 2007), immigration minister Kenney sent an email to representatives of Canada's LGBT networks heralding the Conservative government's attempts to make Canada 'a safe haven for Iran's persecuted gay community' (Wright, 2017, p. 250). Here the figure of the gay refugee as passive victim of the Iranian regime was mobilised, ripped out of the context of gender and sexual life in Iranian society. At the same time some people in that country are experiencing major problems, with some needing to flee. In response, some 50 activists wrote an open letter that criticised this attempt to use LGBT people and refugees to buttress Canadian state moves against the Iranian government, given that this

---

7   This is in the Guiding Principles document which all Envisioning research teams adopted (Envisioning, 2012).

came shortly after Canada closed its embassy in Tehran and sent home Iranian diplomats based in Canada. The letter went on to recall those queer refugee claimants who had been denied asylum because of the IRB's heterosexist and anti-trans assumptions and decisions. This exposed Kenney's hypocrisy (Wright, 2017; Envisioning, 2014). Under the Liberal government the contradiction has intensified, because their emphasis on refugees from Syria has led to Iranian LGBT refugees in Turkey being told to apply to go to the US instead. They are now caught up in the Trump administration's 'Muslim ban' and other immigration measures which, if successful, could prevent people from Iran being accepted in the US (Robertson, 2017a; 2017b; 2017c).

While migrant justice activists have criticised the Canadian government for using the figure of the gay refugee as a weapon against countries in the Global South – and Arab- and Muslim-identified people, in particular – some in the gay/lesbian community have argued that Canada saves LGBT refugees from their homophobic cultures and societies.[8] Others concede to the Canadian state on these questions. One instance was the very different responses of EGALE (a cross-country LGBT rights group) and NOII to the revelation that Kenney had made a request in 2009 to delete references to same-sex marriage from a citizenship guide. Whereas EGALE adopted a conciliatory approach to the government, NOII led demonstrations and a broader critique of the heterosexist, racist and sexist policies of the Canadian government. And when Bill C-31 was introduced, EGALE offered a limited critique, while NOII's much deeper and broad-ranging critique moved far beyond queer-related questions (Trevenen and Degagne, 2015, pp. 102–7). Despite the useful work of the Rainbow Railroad in assisting people from around the world to get into Canada, there is a problem with the assumptions its name is based on. As Dryden and Lenon (2015, pp. 10–11; authors' emphases) point out:

> The deployment of racial analogies, in which discrimination against same-sex couples is *now* like oppression faced by African Americans *then,* evokes an 'earlier' politics of race as the precedent for a 'later' gay rights struggle. Such an analogy enables the privilege of forgetting race, with the result that there is little or no accountability to historical and contemporary anti-racist struggles.

In response to those within LGBT communities who argue that 'we' are saving LGBT refugees from the Global South, the actual record of the Canadian state needs to be made clear.

The rest of this chapter will examine the textual practices of refugee construction and the refugee work of LGBT asylum seekers. It will then outline the impact of capitalism, borders and racialised class relations; neoliberal border regimes and what neoliberalism is, including the transformation of queer/LGBT politics with the emergence of the neoliberal queer; and it will examine Bill C-31

---

8   For instance, see the framing in Caryle-Gordge (2012).

and changes in the continuing neoliberal transformation of immigration and refugee policy. The conclusion will include suggestions for a broader no-one-is-illegal approach that centrally addresses sexual/gender experiences.

Before this investigation of the impacts of neoliberalism on border regimes continues, it is important to understand more about the textual practices through which the successful LGBT refugee is produced, and also how textual regulations are used to coordinate the unpaid refugee work that prospective refugees need to engage in.

The textual practices of refugee construction

The determinations of border regimes on whether individuals fit into the 'refugee' category are not simply the results of bad or good individuals, or bad or good decisions. These determinations are coordinated through text-mediated social relations (Smith, 1990) and it is important to map out how textual regulations are organised against most migrants and asylum seekers. Although only a preliminary sketch can be provided here, to be textually constituted as an LGBT 'refugee' in the Canadian context, it is necessary to demonstrate that the applicant is a member of a particular social group, in this case LGBT,[9] and is fleeing persecution on that basis.

The official process of refugee determination can be understood as one of inscription (Smith, 1990) in which certain aspects of people's experiences are lifted out of the context of their broader social experiences and relations and placed into official categorisations like 'LGBT' and 'refugee'. As mentioned, there are two moments in this text-mediated process of being inscribed successfully into the category of 'refugee', which shapes the work in which they engage. In the IRB process, the Basis of Claim form is key to this inscription. It must detail a narrative of being LGBT and of having experienced persecution on this basis in the home country (Murray, 2016, pp. 46–8). As Murray points out: 'Claimants learned that the personal narrative was not simply a matter of telling their "life story" as they saw fit – there was a particular structure or framework for the narrative and it had to include important features . . . that addressed the jurisprudential objective of determining credibility of a refugee claim' (ibid., p. 47).

People who become 'refugees' can be moving for a whole series of reasons, but this needs to be textually inscribed and regulated through official texts and discourse if the applicant is to become a 'refugee'. Asylum seekers are never simply queer or LGBT. Out of the diversity of their experiences they must construct a narrative – often modelled on a coming-out story – based on essentialist theories of sexuality and gender. It may not mesh with their experiences. Central to this successful inscription is the 'credibility' and

9   Sometimes this can also be that others perceive a person to be LGBT, and sometimes this can also be applied for on multiple grounds.

'consistency' of the narrative (Sevigny, 2011; 2012).

Asylum seekers must be able to get themselves inscribed into the list of enumerated groups and demonstrate that they have experienced persecution on this basis. Both elements must be established for the applicant to become a textually constituted refugee. This helps to coordinate the work that asylum seekers and their lawyers and advocates have to do in order for them to be accepted as refugees. This is how the latter are constructed, and this is why the person quoted at the beginning of this chapter wanted to learn who the 'real gay' refugees are. That individual was not looking at this question from the social locations of people needing to move, but from the position of being enmeshed within these state-defined administrative practices that include identification of LGBTs as central to refugee sponsorship. In this case, identification, which can also have the more empowering connotation of claiming or making an identity (Bannerji, 1995), is coded with relations of social power, and freezes people in an essentialist fashion so they can be dealt with administratively (Holloway, 2005).

The refugee work of LGBT asylum seekers

These textual practices coordinate the work that refugees must engage in. Here, I draw upon Dorothy Smith's (2005, pp. 151–2) broader notion of work as 'anything done by people that takes time and effort'.[10] Later this process was extended to the 'hooking up' efforts made by people living with AIDS/HIV (PLWA/HIVs) to access social assistance (Mykhalovskiy and Smith, 1994) and the unpaid 'health work' of PLWA/HIVs and others (Mykhalovskiy and McCoy, 2002). Christophe Sevigny (2011, 2012) extends this approach to refugee work, especially the remembering work required of refugees during interviews and when filling in forms (including retelling the story of traumatic events), and the exceptionally long wait they have to endure in refugee camps while decisions are made about their resettlement. Sevigny describes this as 'waiting work'. Refugee work takes multiple forms.

The work of LGBT refugees also involves constructing a 'credible' and 'convincing' personal narrative for the IRB, sponsoring groups and others. Whereas most refugees do not sufficiently develop their 'organizational literacy' (Darville, 1995) to fully grasp the textual practices that shape their social experiences, their work can entail learning about the refugee determination process. This can include: locating and talking to lawyers; going to support groups (whose letters are often now crucial in refugee determination); attending appointments; filling in the Basis of Claim form (which becomes a central text

10 This approach was influenced by the feminist domestic labour debates and the theoretical work leading up to Wages for Housework that focused on the centrality of unpaid domestic and reproductive labour in the production of capitalist social relations.

for IRB procedures) and constructing a personal narrative (Murray, 2016, pp. 45–9); collecting letters and other documentation (where possible); talking to others from the same area; preparing for IRB hearings; and the everyday work of survival. This survival work includes: securing housing in shelters or low-cost apartments;[11] applying for financial assistance from Ontario Works and staying on it; registering for a temporary social insurance number (Murray, 2016, p. 43); gaining legal employment if they have a work permit and 'illegal' work if they do not; accessing healthcare; and much more. This work is often done while experiencing poverty, lack of support, racialisation and stigmatisation. Refugees are highly active in this process (Sevigny, 2011, 2012). LGBT refugee work is an active attempt to be inscribed successfully into the categories of 'refugee' and 'LGBT' – into a certain way of working up sexualities and genders. This work can have a very performative character in the construction and repetition of a personal narrative about being LGBT and facing persecution in the country from which they have fled.

This work, articulated to the legal regime that governs refugee determination (Murray, 2011, p. 133; 2014, 2016), becomes normalised through filling in forms and learning from lawyers and support groups how to perform themselves as a Western LGBT person would (Murray, 2016). Through his involvement with LGBT refugee claimants and newcomer groups in Toronto, Murray (2011, p. 127) describes this work in terms of formal and informal integration and adaptation as they 'learn about the Canadian nation-state, citizenship, and queer identities and communities and in so doing enter a space/moment of becoming "refugee" as they learn the social, cultural, and bureaucratic processes and norms of the Canadian refugee apparatus'. In other words the 'refugee' emerges only as an official categorisation in this set of relations. Murray (2014, p. 21) describes how, 'despite the deeply diverse social, sexual and migration experiences of these individuals, an already existing set of socio-sexual-political classifications of the destination state forces closure of potential through its commensuration with existing norms'. At the same time, even though these claimants may learn to perform themselves as LGBT in a Western sense in order to become accepted as 'refugees', this does not mean that they subscribe to these identifications, and they may resist, holding on to aspects of their indigenous sexual/gender practices or producing more hybrid forms, merging aspects of their indigenous and more Western practices.

History, capitalism, sexuality/gender, borders and racialised class relations

To place this investigation in a broader historical and social context requires a shift from the standpoint of state regulations, to look at the world from the

11 On the difficulties of finding affordable and adequate housing for Syrian refugees, see Cross (2016).

social locations of migrants and asylum seekers, thus presenting a different and far-sighted perspective (Smith, 1987; Bannerji, 1995). It is necessary to start with the needs of migrants and asylum seekers, which entail a critique of racialised immigration and refugee practices and of neoliberalism (NOII – Vancouver and Toronto, 2015; Walia, 2013).

Capitalism, as a social relation between workers and those who own the means of production broadly defined – based on the exploitation of waged and unwaged labour – is also a bordering practice. This is given its continuing organisation through nation states and citizenship, but also its 'multiplication' of labour with citizen-labour, as well as precarious, temporary, illegal and unpaid forms of labour (Mezzadra and Neilson, 2013). As already mentioned, neoliberal capitalism leads to a growing displacement of people in the Global South. People are also fleeing civil wars and conflicts produced largely or partially through Northern and Western interventions in countries like Iraq and Syria. As I write this, hundreds of thousands of people have fled the civil war in Syria, and within that the forces of the Islamic State (IS). The roots of IS lie in the US-led invasion of Iraq and the militarisation by Western powers and the Assad regime of the initial Syrian conflict, which emerged from the Arab Spring-inspired revolts (Hanieh, 2015). At the same time as its move towards accepting more refugees from Syria, the Canadian state was still in the process of deporting people back to that country (Behrens, 2015, p. 14). The recent waves of refugees from Syria and other countries, and the hardships they have endured, have opened a humanitarian and sponsorship focus on refugees from that region which, although crucial, has tended to eclipse the needs of people fleeing from other areas.[12]

Simultaneously, as mentioned, neoliberalism leads to reorganisation of border regimes, making it more difficult for poorer people of colour from the Global South to legally enter Western countries with long-term status. This leads to construction of growing pools of precarious, temporary and sometimes illegal labour, through immigration policies, alongside the more 'traditional' citizen labourer (Mezzadra and Neilson, 2013). This has a major impact on asylum seekers and helps to account for their growing numbers on a global scale but, as Rohan Sajnani puts it: 'While refugee numbers globally continue to climb, Canada's claim and grant rates have sharply declined relative to other host similarly situated receiving states' (Envisioning, 2014, p. 5).

---

12 The Liberal government taking in close to 40,000 Syrian refugees, mostly from the camps in Lebanon and Jordan, is largely beyond the scope of this chapter. The proposal was based on past practices of family reunification, with a focus on women and children. Initial proposals would have entirely excluded 'single' men on 'security' grounds, which could mean the exclusion of many 'men' involved in gender and sexual diversity. In response to criticism, the government clarified that single 'gay men' could still apply.

Capitalism as a globalising force has also been unevenly imposing Western-defined sexual and gender binaries on the rest of the world, shaped in part by the forms of resistance they encounter. Clearly, sexual and gender formation has taken on a more global character since capitalist relations emerged, especially through colonialism, imperialism and Western-imposed forms of 'development'. In many parts of the Global South the criminalisation of same-gender sexualities is rooted in colonialism and imperialism (Lennox and Waites, 2013) and some nationalist forces in postcolonial states took it up as part of the defence of national tradition. The Western-imposed mode of development on the Global South included the construction of patriarchal relations and the imposition of institutionalised heterosexuality. This helped to create the social basis for the emergence of a naturalised majority 'heterosexuality' and a minoritised 'homosexuality' in parts of the Global South. Neocolonial and 'development' strategies initially reinforced tendencies to impose heterosexuality in the Global South. Later, they also opened spaces for some nationalist forces and morally conservative strands of neoliberalism to mobilise against queers, and gender and sexual diversity – in Africa and elsewhere – in the context of the displacements and disruptions of people's lives through neoliberal capitalism (Rao, 2015). In Russia, the attacks on 'promoting homosexuality' are linked to attacks on the social position of women, including their reproductive rights under cover of defending 'traditional values' in an attempt to undermine the limited gains women won in the former Soviet Union (Erofeeva, 2013).

Capitalist globalisation is now exporting the hetero/homo and male/female binaries around the globe, where they have an impact on other erotic and gender practices that cannot simply be understood through these binaries, for instance, where more than two gender groupings exist (Drucker, 2000, 2015; Massad, 2007; Altman, 2001). Drucker describes this as a process of uneven and combined social construction of sexualities.[13] This approach makes it clear that no single monolithic process is going on across the entire Global South, rather, what can be called 'indigenous erotic and gender practices' are being supplanted in some places by the hetero/homo distinction, while in others there are combinations of Western and other forms. The social transformations of capitalist globalisation are altering social relations in many countries, opening up possibilities for the emergence of both heterosexuality and homosexuality (Drucker, 2015), while affecting people in diverse ways. Now some people in the Global South identify (at least in part) through these initially Western-defined constructs of homosexual, gay, lesbian, bisexual,

---

13 Despite major insights, Drucker's (2015) work is limited in arguing largely that 'economic' regimes of capital accumulation determine forms of sexual formation and in often obscuring the importance of class and social struggles (including gender and sexual) in bringing about these sexual formations and their transformation. Also see my review essay (2017b) on this book.

trans*[14] (Tompkins, 2014) and queer. Often these are people who have more access to Western popular culture and the money to purchase Western lifestyle commodities (Drucker, 2015). At the same time, others continue to participate in practices of eroticism and gender that may not cohere in a distinct social identity. Others have made hybrid forms, mixing elements of Western constructions with more indigenous practices. In these societies a social organisation of eroticism in relation to families and communities often exists which is different from that in the West. To address this diversity of experience, gender and sexual formations, an internationalist critical sexual and gender politics is required that resists Western classifications.

In this global context, the refugee regime becomes part of the construction of these asylum seekers as proper LGBT residents of Canada, imposing these classifications on their experiences. This regime can impose essentialist sexual definitions and gender identification as the 'truth' of people's beings (Foucault, 1980). In this way the refugee determination process becomes part of the imposition of these binaries on people moving around the globe.

These border struggles must be placed in the context of the history of immigration in a racialised capitalist society built on indigenous land. Immigration policies helped to produce a racial division of labour in Canada, with white persons generally at the top and people of colour and indigenous people generally at the bottom. This division was accomplished in part by bringing in poorly paid people of colour when there was need for cheap labour (Bannerji, 1995; Thobani, 2007). This produced a racialised, classed and gendered social formation. Until the late 1960s immigration policy was explicitly racist, with white people preferred. This racialisation was continued less overtly with the introduction of the point system (Thobani, 2007, pp. 96–7). Now the focus on work permits continues racialisation with the temporariness of work and denial of rights and benefits. This is the racialised division of labour that the border regime is built upon and continues, even if no longer in an explicitly racist fashion, and it shapes the experiences of migrants of colour. It is crucial to note that formally weakened racialisation continues in practice and has a major impact on LGBT asylum seekers and migrants of colour.

From the 1950s on, with pressures from the national security regime, immigration policy also came to be explicitly heterosexist. The other side of this exclusion was the construction of heterosexual hegemony, which established heterosexuality as the 'safe' and 'secure' type of sexuality (Kinsman and Gentile, 2010). There were also heteronormative relations constructed in immigrant communities through the family class system, which normalised a male-dominated heterosexuality. The family class was based historically on constituting the proper heterosexual couple in racialised communities

---

14 Includes all transgender, non-binary, and gender non-conforming identities.

(Wright, 2017).[15] The family class was certainly heteronormative and was part of the construction of these relations in immigrant communities, but it also allowed some families from the Global South to gain status. It is now being slashed, and sponsorship of family members has been made more difficult for those without higher incomes.

A new situation was created when the Canadian state became willing to accept LGBT refugees into Canada officially. This new position is in marked contrast to the complete official exclusion of queers from immigrating into Canada, stemming from the early 1950s, and officially ended in 1977 as one of the first human rights victories of the early gay and lesbian movement (Kinsman and Gentile, 2010, p. 252; Kinsman, 1996, p. 170; Girard, 1987).

The shifting figure of the refugee

There has been a shift in the character of the refugee that includes the racialisation and problematisation of the refugee (Wright, 2017). Their image has been generally recast from 'good refugee/bad economic migrant of the past to bad asylum seeker/good economic migrant' – with the partial exception of the recent focus on Syrian refugees. Refugees have until recently been cast by politicians and the mainstream media as bogus, arriving through criminal means and therefore warranting more stringent regulation. The refugee claimant is often still portrayed as illegitimate, and this view was one of the main motivators for Bill C-31, which will be examined later. In her writings on the social construction of immigrant women, Roxana Ng (1996) showed how this category was racialised, as it is now with the refugee. More recently this racialisation has intensified in respect of those coming from Muslim-identified countries and the Islamophobic[16] responses that this has generated. In Canada this has included the massacre at the Québec City Mosque and the organising by far right groups against Muslims (Hussan, 2017).

The figure of the gay refugee is deployed in this context. As Reddy (2011, pp. 163–4) argues, this figure is 'formed in the contradiction between heteronormative social relations mandated for immigrants of colour by the state's policies and the liberal state's ideology of universal sexual freedom as a mask for growing these social relations'. This can allow for them to be posed in a more homonationalist light, but asylum seekers of colour also face this racialisation.

15 There remains a continuing need to question and challenge 'the family' in immigration policy. It is always important to emphasise that this family is not 'natural' but is socially made, in part through immigration policies.
16 Islamophobia has become an organising term describing anti-Muslim mobilisation. At the same time as accepting this term for organising purposes, I question the phobia part of the term, since this can carry with it the individualist and psychological connotations of psychological discourse which obscure how this practice is coordinated through social relation and practices.

As already suggested, neoliberalism has a major impact on immigration and refugee polices. But what exactly is it?

What is neoliberalism?

Understanding neoliberalism requires an analysis anchored in class and social struggles.[17] Neoliberalism emerged as a distinct capitalist perspective in the mid to late 1970s through the articulation into a distinct project of several currents of economic and moral conservatism. The concept was introduced in Canada unevenly, and not until the 1980s did it begin to centrally inform state policies.

Neoliberalism is often understood simply as opposition to earlier Keynesian perspectives, which focused on social funding and the welfare state. Instead, neoliberalism concentrates on cutting back social programmes and expanding private capitalist relations. However, placed in the context of social struggles, Keynesian approaches were rooted in a wave of class and social struggles in the West during and following the Great Depression. In the post-war years in the Global North, this wave of struggle won greater access to social programmes and more rights for workers. In response to this composition of class struggle,[18] Keynesianism attempted to save capitalist relations through limited concessions to workers and people living in poverty. At the same time, however, these concessions continued exclusions and differential inclusions that affected the lives of women, people of colour, indigenous people, queers and non-citizens, and included the building of national security relations. These regulations included restrictive but also somewhat 'liberalised' border regimes, which admitted more people of colour as cheap labour, both as temporary workers (like domestic workers) and as immigrants, who were often constructed in a heterosexual fashion through the family class system (Wright, 2017). This loosening provided more openings for asylum seekers of colour from the Global South, but racist practices continued.

In the 1960s and early 1970s, there was another global cycle of class and social insurgency – of which feminist and gay revolts and Third World national and social liberation movements were a part – that called colonialism, along with capitalist social relations, into question. In response to these struggles, Keynesianism was now seen in capitalist and state circles as giving too much social power to workers and people living in poverty. Conversely, neoliberalism aimed to restore profitability and capitalist relations through undermining this composition of struggle by dismantling social programmes, targeting the social wage, and attacking workers and the poor around the world (Drucker, 2015, pp. 220–8). These cuts to social programmes also led to intensified

17 I use a wider autonomist Marxist analysis of class and class struggle. On this see Kinsman (2005, pp. 41–50), Cleaver (2000) and Dyer-Witheford (1999).

18 On composition of class struggle, see Cleaver (2000) and Dyer-Witheford (1999).

reproductive and domestic labour assigned largely to women and have had a major impact on gender relations. Neoliberalism also laid the basis for new waves of capitalist globalisation through free trade and other regional and international agreements.[19] This expansion of neoliberalism also relates to strategies of development through international financial institutions that initially were part of the imposition of heterosexuality on societies in the Global South (Rao, 2015). This 'development' causes many to be displaced from the land – as it is privatised and commodified – and leads to impoverishment, forcing many people to migrate.

Despite weakening state formation regarding social programme funding, disciplinary forms of state formation were intensified, including campaigns against unions, for 'law and order', against immigrants, and the tightening of borders against poor people of colour from the Global South.

Especially in the 1970s and 1980s, neoliberalism exhibited a moral conservatism in Western countries, focusing on disciplining workers and the poor, including attacks on feminism and gay and lesbian liberation, in order to defend the heterosexual and patriarchal family coded as white and middle class (Gordon and Hunter, 1979). Neoliberalism in much of the world maintains a moral conservative approach to women, gender and sexual diversity. In Uganda, anti-LGBT initiatives are supported by moral conservative Christian forces from the United States, but the ravages of neoliberalism and capitalist globalisation open up a space – for some nationalist forces and moral conservatives – where 'homosexuals' can be scapegoated (as 'foreign' in character) as causing the social problems in these societies (Rao, 2015).[20]

But moral conservatism was not the only form of neoliberalism to emerge. Non-moral conservative forms based on limited moral deregulation of queers (Sears, 2005) emerged in the later 1970s in countries like Canada, to allow for a privatised homosexuality and community and a consumer-focused form of citizenship (Kinsman, 2013). In part, the non-moral conservative strands of neoliberalism appeared in response to the resistance to moral conservatism by feminists, gays and others. The struggles of queer movements and the space opened up by the Charter of Rights led to growing equality rights for LGBT people, including in immigration. These led to the emergence of the neoliberal queer and the homonationalist use of the gay refugee, so that Canada could play a part in 'saving' gay refugees. But although there are major sources of tension between these forms of neoliberalism, they are united in support for tightened borders against most people of colour from the Global South.

19 On this see Cleaver (2000), Dyer-Witheford (1999) and McNally (2006).
20 For an examination of the relationship between moral conservatives, national forces, neoliberalism and the assault on civil liberties in Africa, see in this volume: Jjuuko and Tabengwa, ch. 2; Jjuuko and Mutesi, ch. 10; Lusimbo and Bryan, ch. 12.

Neoliberal border regimes

There are at least three major moments of neoliberal impact on border regimes. First, there is the tightening of boundaries against immigrants, migrants and asylum seekers of colour from the Global South that prevents them from getting into Canada with permanent status (Goldring and Landolt, 2013). Such restrictions exclude people but also create a pool of illegal labour and of precarious workers without status who are denied rights and benefits, and who can be deported at any time. Bill C-31, which will be examined later, intensified these practices.

Second, there is the shift towards and a greater use of temporary migrant workers, who have few rights or social supports (Sharma, 2006). They only have temporary work permits and can be brought in when needed and ejected easily, as they are denied the regular rights that most Canadian workers have. There is a direct connection here to the neoliberal reorganisation of labour, including flexible/lean/agile (Sears, 2003) and just-in-time production. These capitalist management strategies lead to mass production being torn apart, which leads to massive layoffs and forms of production in which workers can be transferred and shifted as needed. These temporary workers face major forms of exploitation and oppression.

Third, there is the downloading of state responsibilities and funding for the services and support available to those who do get in to the country to community networks and organisations via sponsorship programmes. This includes the transfer of integration and normalisation work for LGBT refugees to sponsoring groups and agency-based newcomer groups. Health support to refugees was cut by the Conservative government and was also part of a broader privatisation agenda.

The neoliberal queer and homonationalism

Some currents within gay/lesbian community formation participate in homonationalism, neglecting the practical difficulties that queers of colour face in getting into and staying in this country, and the pervasive racialisation they face in Canada. How did this come about? First, by the mid 1970s, the broader liberationist approaches of the early 1970s had shifted to a more limited strategy based on human rights. Consequently, political organising focused on struggles to gain formal legal equality with heterosexuals. Fighting for sexual citizenship (Evans, 1993) began with the protection of sexual orientation in human rights legislation. There followed a trajectory of struggle for inclusion within the legal and social forms of: spouse, family, marriage, the military, national security, immigrant and refugee. The moment of possible radical transformation of these social forms instead gets subordinated to the moment of simply being included within these heterosexual-dominated, gendered, racialised and classed social forms. Major gains and important victories were won through these struggles, but they also reshaped lesbian, gay and eventually queer movements (Kinsman, 1996; Warner, 2002). By the mid 1980s, Section 15 (the equality rights section) of the 1982 Canadian Charter of Rights and Freedoms (from here on, the Charter)[21] allowed lesbians and gay men to push forward on formal equality rights but did not provide for substantive social equality.

In a critical examination of sexual citizenship struggles, the question should be asked: 'Citizens of what?' This insight also clarifies that state formation and nationalism was clearly gendered, classed and racialised. Indeed, the citizenship articulated in these Charter-based legal struggles is connected to a growing incorporation into Canadian nation-state formation of social layers within LGBT community formation, and to an identification of this colonial settler-state form as the road to equal rights (Kinsman, 2001). The impact of the Charter and the struggle for sexual citizenship rights were central to this transition.

Participation in homonationalist practices by people from queer communities did not happen overnight but came about through social transitions in movements, communities and struggles, as well as the legal and social victories of gay and lesbian movements. Together, these social transitions and legal victories transformed a radical, transgressive social movement into a largely accommodationist project (which is still contested). These shifts occurred within a settler homonationalist context, where an earlier opposition to Canadian national security and sexual policing grew to identify with Canadian nation-state formation based on the colonisation of indigenous peoples. For many, the Canadian state form became the vehicle for rights and liberation. Later more Orientalist or 'Islamophobic' forms of homonationalism were built on this settler homonationalism (Gentile and Kinsman, 2015).

Through these struggles and transitions, a largely white, middle-class and male class layer rose to the top within LGBT community formation and established its hegemony. It developed its own class project (which was never named as such) and presented it as the perspective of the community. This reshaped LGBT community formation and accommodated queers with neoliberal class relations (Duggan, 2003). This group argues for formal equality, including within the categories of immigrant and refugee, but moves away from challenging racism and other forms of oppression beyond narrowly defined LGBT concerns. The rights of LGBT people came to be defined in a limited fashion abstracted from class, poverty and often racialisation. This social/class layer provides the basis for the emergence of homonationalism and for what I describe as the neoliberal queer (Kinsman, 2016; 2017a). The homonationalism based on this class layer presents major obstacles to the development of a radical queer anti-border politics.

21 See http://laws-lois.justice.gc.ca/eng/Const/page-15.html (accessed 13 Mar. 2018).

Bill C-31 and continuing neoliberal transformations

Bill C-31 is one recent central facilitator of neoliberalism on immigrant and refugee policy, one that affects LGBT asylum seekers in important ways. Having been built on earlier neoliberal transformations of immigration and refugee policies, this legislation needs to be analysed in more detail.

Proposed by the Conservative government, Bill C-31 (Protecting Canada's Immigration System Act) was passed in June 2012[22] and came into effect the following December. As stated in the Envisioning report on which this section is based, we understand 'the new regime as decidedly anti-immigrant and anti-refugee' (2014, p. 4). This legislation had a neoliberal character, making life more difficult for people of colour from the Global South and creating more difficulties for LGBT asylum seekers. The main features of this further neoliberal shift in immigration and refugee policy are summarised below.

Under this law people can now be detained for mere criminality, which can include suspicion of having engaged in low-level offences, such as traffic offences. They are no longer required to be a danger to the public to be detained (ibid., p. 14). This is especially a problem where widespread criminalisation exists in the countries of origin from which asylum seekers flee.

'Irregular arrivals' who enter Canada via boats or other non-legal means, and are deemed to have not crossed borders properly, are now defined as designated foreign nationals (DFNs). Although this designation is intended to target smugglers, it instead attacks asylum seekers, who are punished for their means of arrival, regardless of the merit of their claim, and covers 'smugglers' who have acted for humanitarian reasons. If this criterion was used against the thousands of Syrian refugees arriving in Europe, most would be defined as irregular arrivals. Currently those attempting to gain refugee status in Canada, who are fleeing the restrictions and bans imposed by the Trump administration in the US, are arriving by irregular means so that they will not be trapped by the Safe Third Country Agreement between the Canadian and US governments. This means that many of them will not be allowed to claim refugee status in Canada (Canadian Council for Refugees, 2017a, 2017b). This provision is directed specifically against the resistance in which people have engaged to bypass the legal procedures that prevent people from gaining status in this border regime.

This legislation includes the expansion of discretionary ministerial power, which leads to increased use of detention for irregular arrivals (Envisioning, 2014, p. 13). Such persons are subject to mandatory detention and are denied the right to apply for permanent refugee status until five years after

---

22 An act to amend the Immigration and Refugee Protection Act, the Balanced Refugee Reform Act, the Marine Transportation Security Act and the Department of Citizenship and Immigration Act. See www.parl.ca/DocumentViewer/en/41-1/bill/C-31/royal-assent (accessed 13 Mar. 2018).

a successful refugee claim or a determination of protection to a Pre-Removal Risk Assessment, whichever is later (ibid., p. 15). Successful claimants are denied access to refugee travel documents for five years and cannot sponsor family members. They are denied the right to appeal to the Refugee Appeal Division (RAD). They are also denied access to relief based on humanitarian and compassionate grounds and temporary work permits (ibid.). This approach is clearly intended to deter those using irregular means of arrival. Detention has become a major problem for asylum seekers and migrants. It is also a part of constructing 'bad' versus 'good' refugee applicants. Bad asylum seekers arrive through irregular means, while good asylum seekers follow proper procedures, although being 'good' is no guarantee that they will get into the country or be allowed to stay.

Furthermore, a new category has been introduced: designated country of origin (DCO). Countries on this list are designated by the immigration, refugees and citizenship minister as being respecters of human rights and the rule of law, and therefore as being generally 'safe' (ibid.). Countries like Mexico are included in this group. The assumption is that applicants coming from these countries have less chance of making a valid claim, and thus face accelerated timelines for their hearings, and fast removal without the opportunity to have a negative decision reviewed (ibid., p. 16). Until July 2015 people from DCOs were denied the right to appeal through the RAD. Three gay applicants challenged this denial in federal court and won (Envisioning, 2015, p. 20).

The DCO classification affects people fleeing sexual and gender oppression, since there can still be high levels of anti-queer and anti-trans violence and discrimination in 'safe' countries, in familial and other relations, as well as in the continuing criminalisation of same-gender sexual acts. It is important to understand the specificity of sexual/gender oppression rather than to perceive it as simply rooted in state practices.

More generally, Bill C-31 imposed accelerated timelines for all refugee claimants, and even shorter ones for those from DCOs. This can make it difficult for claimants to prepare their applications and secure the necessary documents and support letters. They intensify the refugee work in which asylum seekers must engage (Envisioning, 2014, pp. 17–18). More time is needed for refugee work – in order to contact lawyers, obtain evidence and construct a personal narrative – especially for queer claimants many of whom were not 'out' in their country of origin and have had little time or documentation to demonstrate persecution. Since applicants have little opportunity for community involvement, refugee determination gives special weight to letters from community organisations – such as newcomer support groups – which the applicants have to procure.

A new RAD has been established that can review IRB decisions. It allows for limited appeals of decisions, with major time constraints. In the legislation, DCO claimants and irregular arrivals were denied access to these appeals and were therefore vulnerable to removal orders (ibid., p. 20). The previously mentioned court decision overturned this denial for DCO claimants.

Provisions for humanitarian and compassionate grounds allowing permanent residency to be granted to people who may not meet the strict definition of a refugee, but who would face undue hardship if returned, were made more restrictive. Under Bill C-31 people can no longer seek refugee and humanitarian and compassionate protection at the same time, and rejected refugee claimants are barred from applying on humanitarian and compassionate grounds for one year after their rejection. This ban was also applied to irregular arrivals. Since they cannot apply from overseas, claimants must go underground until they can start the application process. A recent legal decision clarified that this provision must be applied in a flexible and responsive fashion (Canadian Council for Refugees, 2015).

'Pre-removal risk assessments' apply when those removed from Canada may face torture or risk to their life if deported to their country of origin. Under Bill C-31 people can be removed without this assessment and non-DCO claimants are banned for one year from applying for it, while DCO claimants are subject to a three-year ban. The same restrictions apply to those who have arrived via the United States or those found to be 'convention refugees' in another country.

While these processes are being sped up, decision-makers often rely more on stereotypes and credibility assessment. Questioning is more extensive and intensive than under the older system and can last several hours, again imposing more work on those trying to gain refugee status, and requiring them to recall often-traumatic events. Many of the decision-makers lack training generally, and on sexual and gender experiences specifically, so they often rely on Western-derived theories of sexual and gender identification that have almost become common-sense. Those not legible to them as LGBT in these frameworks may appear to lack credibility, especially given the difficulty of securing documents that establish their status. As a result, some claims have been denied because claimants had children or had been in a heterosexual relationship – which in the view of the adjudicator rendered their claim as lacking credibility. Some of these decisions have later been overturned upon appeal. Particular problems are posed for bisexual and trans asylum seekers, and those who do not easily fit into LGBT definitions.

Other changes, not directly related to Bill C-31, also reflect this neoliberal shift. As mentioned previously, an important part of refugee work is contacting and procuring legal advice and lawyers, a crucial service for those who know little about the refugee determination process. Programmes, such as Legal Aid Ontario, which assist in contracting the services of lawyers, have been severely undermined (Envisioning, 2014, p. 23). But legal representation is often necessary, and most asylum seekers have no financial resources. These factors make refugee work much more difficult and the chances of rejection higher.

In 2012, cuts to health coverage for asylum seekers removed vision, dental and medication coverage for all refugees – aside from the few who receive state sponsorship for resettlement. Claimants in the DCO category now had no access to this funding at all (ibid., p. 29). Refugees who are largely from racialised communities already suffer from problems in accessing healthcare. These cuts fit into a neoliberal logic of reducing social expenditure and privatising social services. Following major protests from refugee groups and healthcare providers, courts reversed these decisions and in February 2016 the Liberal government restored this funding.

The significant shift to downloading support for refugees on to community organisations and non-state agencies, including churches, has already been noted above. This approach is also informed by the neoliberal imperative to reduce state expenditures for social services and to involve community groups and agencies in doing and funding this work, including that of regulating asylum seekers.

These changes have pushed Canadian immigration and refugee policies further in a neoliberal direction. Although some of the more extreme aspects of this transformation may be addressed by the Liberal government, the basic neoliberal orientation of Canadian immigration and refugee policies continues and should be challenged.

Some conclusions: No One Is Illegal while addressing sexual/gender oppression

In critically exploring the contradiction between formal LGBT rights for asylum seekers and their denial in practice, this chapter has aimed to provide a social and historical contextualisation for this process, and to suggest ways of organising to improve the situations for queer asylum seekers and all refugees and migrants. An approach is needed that does not focus solely on narrow LGBT issues. This investigation has combined Envisioning insights with NOII activism and research in order to deal with the specificity of sexual and gender oppression while also viewing it through the mutual construction of class, race and state relations. In particular, following the 2015 Envisioning report, there needs to be a focus on challenging racism. This analysis also takes up Holloway's formulation (2005, 2016) of acting simultaneously *within, against and beyond* ruling relations. It is important to operate within existing regulations to use and expand them, to organise against their limitations and to move beyond their restrictions. Here, the NOII approach usefully combines direct action support work against deportations with campaigns against specific regulations in the context of an overall perspective that looks beyond border regimes to status for all. To organise simply within these regulations would mean no major challenge to racism, neoliberalism and border regimes more generally could be mounted.

In struggling *within* these regulations, we can argue for better training for people in the IRB on LGBT and other concerns, and for more time for people to do their refugee work and to collect the documents and 'evidence' they need.[23] We can fight to expand the right of people to appeal decisions made against them. As Gitari (2014) suggested, we can argue that any country with laws criminalising same-gender sex like Kenya cannot be considered 'safe'. In this sense, as Envisioning (2015) suggests, the weight in hearings needs to be far less on proving one is LGBT and much more on demonstrating persecution. At the same time, there are major problems with how 'persecution' has been defined in refugee determinations. Although these important changes will have consequences in many people's lives, they only scratch the surface of what is needed and will do nothing for those denied status or those who cannot get to Canada.

In struggling *against* these regulations, we need to argue for the repeal of Bill C-31. In particular, the DFN and DCO categories need to be abolished so that how people arrive and what countries they come from do not invalidate or weaken their claims. The Safe Third Country Agreement with the US should be abolished to allow refugee claimants to apply safely for refugee status when they cross into Canada from the US (Canadian Council for Refugees, 2017a). Restrictive immigration and refugee policies should be eliminated so that more people can be accepted as refugees. But getting rid of these barriers and restrictions does not in itself provide for access and status for all who need it.

The important changes resulting from organising *within* and *against* these regulations would still leave many people with denied applications – or unable to get to Canada – living without status. Racialisation and stigmatisation of refugees would still continue. This is where the NOII perspective helps us to push *beyond* the limitations of border regimes to put them in question. It includes addressing the survival work of asylum seekers by building alliances with others fighting poverty and striving for better social assistance and supports, housing, healthcare and employment opportunities, and against racism. This NOII-influenced approach includes a focus on surveillance, detention, deportation and normalising regimes, while rejecting the distinction between 'deserving/ undeserving' refugees and migrants. It means not focusing only on asylum seekers who have 'good citizenship' characteristics but also rejecting the notion of the citizen as the only person who should be accorded rights.

One important line of action that grows out of this perspective is the Sanctuary City movement (NOII – Toronto, 2015; Nail et al., 2010), which

23 In 2017, the IRB in Canada asked agencies serving immigrants, asylum seekers and refugees; various experts in the field; and the Envisioning team and its research partners to give recommendations and feedback on their draft new guidelines on SOGI claims. These guidelines, which addressed a number of our concerns, were released on 1 May 2017 and are available at: www.irb-cisr.gc.ca/Eng/BoaCom/references/pol/GuiDir/Pages/GuideDir09.aspx (accessed 7 May 2018).

allows access to services irrespective of status and declares areas of social life off-limits to Canada Border Services Agency officers. This can be expanded along provincial and other lines as well, an approach that begins to erode the distinction between those with status and those without. At the same time, in some municipalities that have declared themselves to be Sanctuary Cities there is still cooperation with Canadian Border Services, and refugees/asylum seekers still have problems accessing services, which undermines any sanctuary that these cities are providing. Real sanctuary cities therefore need to be established (Goffin, 2017). This can be a useful way of pushing towards a status-for-all perspective and needs to be actively taken up in queer communities. For instance, queer community spaces should be a no-go area for Canadian Border Service agents.

Within queer communities and movements, this means that activists need to reject homonationalist influences. We need to reject Canada's 'posturing' that it is civilised in terms of LGBT rights, including refugee rights. We need to support refugees and migrants coming into Canada without thinking we are 'saving' them from their 'bad' cultures. Instead, we need to respect and support people's agency and the refugee work they do. We need to refuse to impose on people the categories of the West and the North.

We need queer refugee, migrant and anti-border struggles that are firmly rooted in anti-colonial, anti-racist, anti-capitalist and feminist perspectives which challenge the border policies of Canada and other nation states. This is what is required to meet the needs of queer migrants and asylum seekers and all those forced to move to try to better their lives. Can we dream of – and organise for – a queer offensive against racism and border regimes?

References

Altman, D. (2001) *Global Sex* (Chicago, IL: University of Chicago Press).

Anderson, B., N. Sharma and C. Wright (2012) '"We are all foreigners": no borders as a practical political project', in P. Nyers and K. Rygiel, (eds.) *Citizenship, Migrant Activism and the Politics of Movement* (London: Routledge), pp. 73–91.

Balibar, E. (2004) *We, the People of Europe? Reflections on Transnational Citizenship* (Princeton, NJ: Princeton University Press).

Bannerji, H. (1995) *Thinking Through: Essays on Feminism, Marxism and Anti-Racism* (Toronto, ON: Women's Press).

Behrens, M. (2015) 'Harper's sorry Syria shift', *NOW (Toronto)*, 10–16 Sep., p. 14.

Canadian Council for Refugees (2015) 'Supreme Court decision on humanitarian decisions welcomed', available at: http://ccrweb.ca/en/ supreme-court-decision-humanitarian-decisions-welcomed (accessed 6 Mar. 2018).

— (2017a) 'Refugees entering from US and Third Safe Country: FAQ', available at: http://ccrweb.ca/en/refugees-entering-us-and-safe-third-country-faq (accessed 6 Mar. 2018).

— (2017b) 'Welcoming refugees at our border: a moral and legal imperative', 9 Mar., available at: http://ccrweb.ca/en/welcoming-refugees-our-borders (accessed 6 Mar. 2018).

Caryle-Gordge, P. (2012) 'Sponsor a GBLT refugee and save a life', *Outwords* (Winnipeg, MB), 190 (2): 16–17.

Cleaver, H. (2000) *Reading Capital Politically* (Oakland, MD: AK Press/ Antithesis).

Corrigan, P. and D. Sayer (1985) *The Great Arch: English State Formation as Cultural Revolution* (Oxford: Basil Blackwell).

Cross, J.S. (2016) 'Fed money needed to house T.O refugees', *Metro* (Toronto), 27 Jan., p. 1.

Darville, R. (1995) 'Literacy, experience, power', in M. Campbell and A. Manicom (eds.) *Knowledge, Experience and Ruling Relations: Studies in the Social Organization of Knowledge* (Toronto, ON: University of Toronto Press), pp. 249–61.

Drucker, P. (ed.) (2000) *Different Rainbows* (London: Gay Men's Press).

— (2015) *Warped: Gay Normality and Queer Anticapitalism* (Chicago, IL: Haymarket/Brill).

Dryden, O.H. and S. Lenon (eds.) (2015) *Disrupting Queer Inclusion, Canadian Homonationalism and the Politics of Belonging* (Vancouver, BC: UBC Press).

Duggan, L. (2003) *The Twilight of Equality? Neoliberalism, Cultural Politics and the Attack on Democracy* (Boston, MA: Beacon Press).

Dyer-Witheford, N. (1999) *Cyber-Marx, Circuits and Cycles of Struggle in High Technology Marxism* (Chicago, IL: University of Illinois Press).

Erofeeva, L. V. (2013) 'Traditional Christian values and women's reproductive rights in Modern Russia – is a consensus ever possible?', *American Journal of Public Health*, 103 (11): 1931–4.

Envisioning Global LGBT Human Rights (2012) 'Envisioning LGBT refugee rights in Canada: exploring asylum issues', available at: http://envisioninglgbt.blogspot.com/p/publicationsresources.html (accessed 25 May 2018).

— (2014) 'Envisioning LGBT refugee rights in Canada: the impact of Canada's new immigration regime', available at: http://envisioninglgbt.blogspot.com/p/publicationsresources.html (accessed 25 May 2018).

— (2015) 'Envisioning LGBT refugee rights in Canada: is Canada a safe haven?', available at: http://envisioninglgbt.blogspot.com/p/publicationsresources.html (accessed 25 May 2018).

Evans, D. (1993) *Sexual Citizenship: the Material Construction of Sexualities* (London: Routledge).

Foucault, M. (1980) *The History of Sexuality: Vol. 1, an Introduction* (New York, NY: Vintage).

Gentile, P. and G. Kinsman (2015) 'National security and homonationalism: the QuAIA wars and the making of the neo-liberal queer', in O.H. Dryden and S. Lenon (eds.) *Disrupting Queer Inclusion, Canadian Homonationalism and the Politics of Belonging* (Vancouver, BC: UBC Press), pp. 133–49.

Girard, P. (1987) 'From subversion to liberation: homosexuals and the Immigration Act, 1952–1977', *Canadian Journal of Law and Society*, 2 (1): 1–27.

Gitari, E. (2014) 'Is Canada a safe haven for refugees?', Envisioning panel, World Pride Human Rights Conference, Toronto.

Goffin, P. (2017) 'Toronto not really a "Sanctuary City", report says', *Toronto Star*, 17 Feb., available at: https://www.thestar.com/news/gta/2017/02/17/toronto-not-truly-a-sanctuary-city-report-says.html (accessed 6 Mar. 2018).

Goldring, L. and P. Landolt (eds.) (2013) *Producing and Negotiating Non-Citizenship: Precarious Legal Status in Canada* (Toronto, ON: University of Toronto Press).

Gordon, L. and A. Hunter (1979) *Sex, Family and the New Right: Anti-Feminism as a Political Force* (Somerville, MA: New England Free Press).

Hanieh, A. (2105) 'A brief history of ISIS: ISIS emerged out of the dashed hopes of the Arab Spring', *Jacobin*, 12 Mar., available at: https://www.jacobinmag.com/2015/12/isis-syria-iraq-war-al-qaeda-arab-spring/?utm_campaign=shareaholic&utm_medium=twitter&utm_source=socialnetwork (accessed 6 Mar. 2018).

Hardt, M. and A. Negri (2000) *Empire* (Cambridge, MA: Harvard University Press).

Holloway, J. (2005) *How to Change the World Without Taking Power: the Meaning of Revolution Today* (London: Pluto Press).

— (2016) *In, Against and Beyond Capitalism, The San Francisco Lectures* (Oakland, CA: PM Press).

Hussan, S.K. (2017) 'Becoming enemies: on Islamophobia, deportations, #Muslim Ban #QuebecShooting', 4 Feb., available at: https://medium.com/@hussansk/becoming-enemies-on-islamophobia-deportations-muslimban-quebecshooting-e9c13c819a1e#.ydvj5ijew (accessed 12 Mar. 2018).

Kinsman, G. (1996) *The Regulation of Desire: Homo and Hetero Sexualities* (Montréal, PQ: Black Rose).

— (2001) 'Challenging Canadian and queer nationalisms', in T. Goldie (ed.) *In a Queer Country: Gay and Lesbian Studies in the Canadian Context* (Vancouver, BC: Arsenal Pulp Press), pp. 209–34.

— (2003) 'Queerness is not in our genes: biological determinism versus social liberation', in D. Brock (ed.) *Making Normal: Social Regulation in Canada* (Toronto, ON: Thomson/Nelson), pp. 262–84.

— (2005) 'The politics of revolution: learning from autonomist Marxism', *Upping the Anti*, 1 (1): 41–50.

— (2013) 'Wolfenden in Canada: within and beyond official discourse in law reform struggles', in C. Lennox and M. Waites (eds.) *Human Rights, Sexual Orientation and Gender Identity in the Commonwealth, Struggles for Decriminalization and Change* (London: Human Rights Consortium, Institute of Commonwealth Studies), pp. 183–205.

— (2016) 'From resisting police raids to charter rights: queer and AIDS organizing in the 1980s', in W.K. Carroll and K. Sarker (eds.) *A World to Win: Contemporary Social Movements and Counter-Hegemony* (Winnipeg, MB: ARP Books), pp. 209–32.

— (2017a) 'Queer resistance and regulation in the 1970s: from liberation to rights', in P. Gentile, G. Kinsman and P. Rankin (eds.) *We Still Demand! Redefining Resistance in Sex and Gender Struggles* (Vancouver, BC: UBC Press), pp. 137–62.

— (2017b) 'Queered Marxism and the making of the neo-liberal queer reviews # 1', *Radical Noise*, 22 Apr., available at: http://radicalnoise. ca/2017/04/22/queered-marxism-and-the-making-of-the-neo-liberal-queer-reviews-1/ (accessed 12 Mar. 2018).

Kinsman, G. and P. Gentile (2010) *The Canadian War on Queers: National Security as Sexual Regulation* (Vancouver, BC: UBC Press).

Lennox, C. and M. Waites (eds.) (2013) *Human Rights, Sexual Orientation and Gender Identity in the Commonwealth, Struggles for Decriminalization and Change* (London: Human Rights Consortium, Institute of Commonwealth Studies).

Luibhéid, E. (2008) 'Queer/migration: an unruly body of scholarship', *GLQ: a Journal of Lesbian and Gay Studies*, 14 (2–3): 169–90.

Luibhéid, E. and L. Cantú Jr (eds.) (2005) *Queer Migrations: Sexuality, U.S. Citizenship and Border Crossings* (Minneapolis, MN: University of Minnesota Press).

Massad, J. (2007) *Desiring Arabs* (Chicago, IL: University of Chicago Press).

McNally, D. (2006) *Another World is Possible: Globalization and Anti-Capitalism*, 2nd edn. (Monmouth, Wales and Winnipeg, MB: Merlin Press/Arbeiter Ring).

Mezzadra, S. and B. Neilson (2013) *Border as Method, or the Multiplication of Labor* (Durham, NC: Duke University Press).

Murray, D.A.B. (2011) 'Becoming queer here: integration and adaptation work experiences of sexual minority refugees in Toronto', *Refuge*, 28 (2): 127–35.

— (2014) 'Real queer: "authentic" LGBT refugee claimants and homonationalism in the Canadian refugee system', *Anthropolica*, 56 (1): 21–32.

— (2016) *Real Queer? Sexual Orientation and Gender Identity Refugees in the Canadian Refugee Apparatus* (London: Rowan and Littlefield).

Mykhalovskiy, E. and L. McCoy (2002) 'Troubling ruling discourses of health: using institutional ethnography in community-based research', *Critical Public Health*, 12 (1): 17–37.

Mykhalovskiy, E. and G.W. Smith (1994) *Getting Hooked Up: a report on the barriers people living with HIV/AIDS face assessing social services* (Toronto, ON: Ontario Institute for Studies in Education/CATIE).

Nail, T., F. Kamai and S. Hussan (2010) 'Building Sanctuary City: NOII-Toronto on non-status migrant justice organizing', *Upping the Anti* (Toronto), 11, http://uppingtheanti.org/journal/article/11-noii-sanctuary-city/ (accessed 12 Mar. 2018).

Nerenberg, K. (2016) 'Liberals boost immigration. Now they must tackle Harper's unfair refugee rules', *Rabble*, 9 Mar., available at: http://rabble.ca/blogs/bloggers/karl-nerenberg/2016/03/liberals-boost-immigration-now-they-must-tackle-harpers-unfair (accessed 12 Mar. 2018).

Ng, R. (1996) *The Politics of Community Services, Immigrant Women, Class and the State* (Toronto, ON: Fernwood).

No One Is Illegal (NOII) – Toronto (2015), available at: http://toronto.nooneisillegal.org/ (accessed 20 Dec. 2015).

No One Is Illegal (NOII) – Vancouver, unceded Coast Salish territories (2015) Never Home: Legislating Discrimination in Canadian Immigration project, available at: https://noii-van.resist.ca (accessed 12 Mar. 2018).

Nyers, P. (2015) 'Migrant citizenships and autonomous mobilities', *Migration, Mobility and Displacement*, 1 (1): 23–39.

Nyers, P. and K. Rygiel (eds.) (2012) *Citizenship, Migrant Activism and the Politics of Movement* (London: Routledge).

Puar, J.K. (2007) *Terrorist Assemblages, Homonationalism in Queer Times* (Durham, NC: Duke University Press).

Rao, R. (2015) 'Global homocapitalism', *Radical Philosophy*, 194 (11–12): 38–49.

Reddy, C. (2011) *Freedom with Violence: Race, Sexuality, and the US State* (Durham, NC: Duke University Press).

Rehaag, S. (2008) 'Patrolling the borders of sexual orientation: bisexual refugee claims in Toronto', *McGill Law Journal*, 53 (59): 59–102.

Robertson, D. (2017a) 'Trudeau government under fire for ending LGBT Iranian refugee program', *Daily Xtra!* 10 Feb., available at: www.dailyxtra.com/canada/news-and-ideas/news/trudeau-government-fire-ending-lgbt-iranian-refugee-program-214979 (accessed 13 Mar. 2018).

— (2017b) '"There is no door open, no hope". The gay Iranian refugee that Canada abandoned', *Daily Xtra!*, 15 Feb., available at: www.dailyxtra. com/canada/news-and-ideas/news/door-open-hope%E2%80%99-the-gay-iranian-refugee-canada-abandoned-215222 (accessed 13 Mar. 2018).

— (2017c) 'Canada's immigration department acknowledges drop in LGBT refugees from Iran', *Daily Xtra!* 2 Mar., available at: www.dailyxtra. com/canada/news-and-ideas/news/canada%E2%80%99s-immigration-department-acknowledges-drop-in-lgbt-refugees-from-iran-216185 (accessed 13 Mar. 2018).

Said, E. (1979) *Orientalism* (New York, NY: Vintage).

Sears, A. (2003) *Retooling the Mind Factory: Education in a Lean State* (Aurora, ON: Garamond Press).

— (2005) 'Queer anti-capitalism: what's left of lesbian and gay liberation?', *Science and Society*, 69 (1): 92–112.

Sevigny, C.A. (2011) *Starting from Refugees Themselves: a Study on the Resettlement of Government-Assisted Refugees in Gatineau, Quebec*, MA thesis, Carleton University.

— (2012) 'Starting from refugees themselves: towards an institutional ethnography of resettlement', *New Issues in Refugee Research*, research paper no. 247 (Geneva: UN Refugee Agency, Policy Development and Evaluation Service).

Sharma, N. (2006) *Home Economics: Nationalism and the Making of 'Migrant' Workers in Canada* (Toronto, ON: University of Toronto Press).

Smith, D. (1987). *The Everyday World as Problematic: a Feminist Sociology* (Toronto, ON: University of Toronto Press).

— (1990) *Texts, Facts and Femininity: Exploring the Relations of Ruling* (London: Routledge).

— (2005) *Institutional Ethnography: A Sociology for People* (Lanham, MD: Rowman and Littlefield).

Smith, D. and S. Turner (eds.) (2014) *Incorporating Texts into Institutional Ethnography* (Toronto, ON: University of Toronto Press).

Spade, D. (2011) *Normal Life, Administrative Violence, Critical Trans Politics, and the Limits of Law* (Brooklyn, NY: South End Press).

Thobani, S. (2007) *Exalted Subjects: Studies in the Making of Race and Nation in Canada* (Toronto, ON: University of Toronto Press).

Tompkins, A. (2014) 'Asterisk', *TSQ: Transgender Studies Quarterly*, 1 (1–2): 26–7, available at: https://read.dukeupress.edu/tsq/article/1/1-2/26/91872/Asterisk (accessed 13 Mar. 2018).

Trevenen, K. and A. Degagne (2015) 'Homonationalism at the border and in the streets: organizing against exclusion and incorporation', in O.H. Dryden and S. Lenon (eds.) *Disrupting Queer Inclusion, Canadian Homonationalism and the Politics of Belonging* (Vancouver, BC: UBC Press), pp. 100–15.

UN Refugee Agency (UNHCR) (2015) 'Asylum trends 2014, levels and trends in industrialized countries', available at: www.unhcr.org/statistics/unhcrstats/551128679/asylum-levels-trends-industrialized-countries-2014.html (accessed 30 Nov. 2017).

Walia, H. (2013) *Undoing Border Imperialism* (Oakland, MD: AK Press and the Institute of Anarchist Studies).

Warner, T. (2002) *Never Going Back: a History of Queer Activism in Canada* (Toronto, ON: University of Toronto Press).

Wright, C. (2006) 'Against illegality: new directions in organizing by and with non-status people in Canada', in C. Frampton, G. Kinsman, A. Thompson and K. Tilleczek (eds.) *Sociology for Changing the World: Social Movements/Social Research* (Halifax, NS: Fernwood), pp. 189–208.

— (2017) 'Nationalism, sexuality and the politics of anti-citizenship', in P. Gentile, G. Kinsman and P. Rankin (eds.) *We Still Demand! Redefining Resistance in Sex and Gender Struggles* (Vancouver, BC: UBC Press), pp. 250–69.

4

Queer affirmations: negotiating the possibilities and limits of sexual citizenship in Saint Lucia

Amar Wahab

Between 2012 and 2013 the Envisioning Global LGBT Human Rights (hereafter Envisioning) Caribbean team conducted 33 semi-structured interviews with members of Saint Lucia's lesbian, gay, bisexual, transgender (LGBT) community. Their experiences, which are examined in this chapter, constitute an archive of LGBT lives, which counters the Saint Lucian nationalist heteronormative archive, as well as the epistemological hegemony of the Global North.

Although the different forms of anti-queer animus in the small-island state should be borne in mind, my analysis also pushes for a wider understanding of the production and regularised disposal of marginal populations in Saint Lucia as part of a complex global phenomenon. As such, I draw on the interview data to open up the messiness of truth-making, suggesting that discourses about 'state-sponsored homophobia', 'LGBT identity' and 'human rights' must incorporate a deeper understanding of the ways in which queer Saint Lucians critically respond to multiple vulnerabilities under global neoliberalism. The chapter begins by considering three contextual strands: the impacts of global neoliberalism in Saint Lucia, the state-sponsored production of legal homophobia and the 'queerness' of the island state as it manages its sovereignty in tension with global discourses of 'homophobic Saint Lucia'. It continues with an examination of the interview data that register the impact of anti-same-sex sentiment on queer Saint Lucians. At the same time, the data open up interesting opportunities for thinking beyond dominant constructions of 'homophobic Saint Lucia'. As such, the final section draws on the epistemological richness of the interviews to productively challenge the discursive frames of both Saint Lucian nationalism and global LGBT human rights projects, while recognising that the agency of researchers and interviewees is also deeply conditioned through the very discourses that organise such projects.

A. Wahab (2018) 'Queer affirmations: negotiating the possibilities and limits of sexual citizenship in Saint Lucia', in N. Nicol et al. (eds.) *Envisioning Global LGBT Human Rights: (Neo) colonialism, Neoliberalism, Resistance and Hope* (London: Human Rights Consortium, Institute of Commonwealth Studies), pp. 131–56.

Producing vulnerability: Saint Lucia and neoliberal globalisation

As a small island nation state that emerged from the gripping force of colonialism in 1979 – more than a decade after many other Anglo-Caribbean states achieved independence – Saint Lucia was thrust into a new era of vulnerability and precariousness within a moment of accelerated global capitalism, while at the same time struggling to determine the terms and conditions of national selfhood. As such, the context in which we can make sense of non-normative gender and sexual citizenship, 'homophobia' and 'human rights' cannot be divorced from the wider tensions that characterise the struggle between self-determination and neoliberal globalisation for Saint Lucia. While much of the discourse around the vulnerability of small island states has tended to focus on issues such as climate change and economic precariousness, little scholarship focuses on the impact of both nationalism and globalisation on the creation, intensification and normalisation of social vulnerability in Saint Lucia.

In this regard, Tennyson Joseph's (2011) careful and insightful analysis demonstrates how Saint Lucia's post-independence project, increasingly affected by the forces of global neoliberalism, can be characterised as one of 'tentative anti-colonialism', resulting in the 'limited sovereignty' of the nation state. According to Joseph (ibid., p. 187):

> The exploration of the independence experience of Saint Lucia reveals that much of the politics revolved around tensions between the local demand for sustaining the economic and political objectives that had given rise to nationalism, on the one hand, and the imperative of adjustment to the largely external demands for adjustment of neoliberal capitalist hegemony, on the other.

Joseph's investigation of each epoch of post-independence political rule shows the constantly shifting and at times contradictory allegiances to 'the global' and 'the national' that make economic and political vulnerability a constant. Whereas Joseph does not undertake a deep investigation of the social implications of the numerous vacillations that occur as a result of this struggle, urgent questions need to be asked about how the vulnerabilities produced from this struggle are distributed across the national population through a neoliberal ideological calculus of determining social assets and liabilities. What Joseph's work allows us to rethink is the limiting discourse suggesting that sexual citizenship and 'homophobia' are state-sponsored affairs, for his analysis of the increasing shift from the welfarist to a managerialist approach by the state reflects the terms and conditions under which the small island nation state is limited in its capacity to respond to the pressures of global neoliberal capital. In fact, Joseph claims that 'under neoliberal globalisation the state has been reconfigured through ideological, economic and political (including military) means to serve as a facilitator of the interests of what William Robinson (2006, p. 10) calls a "transnationalist capitalist class, overturning the previous Keynesianism that had facilitated a more equitable distributive and social function for the state."'

Even more interesting is that Joseph shows that even under leftist governments (for example, by the Saint Lucia Labour Party between 1997 and 2006) which developed 'socialist alternatives', the Saint Lucian state could do only so much to buffer itself from its expectant role as a 'facilitator of global capital' (2011, p. 7) within the context of 'deepening globalization' (ibid., p. 188). Focusing on the debilitating transitions of the island's once-dominant banana monoindustry to the more recent diversification into tourism and service-sector industries, Joseph shows how the state's more managerialist approach has opened up Saint Lucia's 'sovereignty for sale' (ibid., p. 167). Such neoliberal deresponsibilising of the state has also entrenched and normalised precariousness in highly material ways. In fact, in their final report Kairi Consultants (2007) found that poverty had increased to 28.8 per cent of the population, with 40.3 per cent deemed economically vulnerable (especially in the more rural sections of society). Moreover, the process of deepening globalisation in Saint Lucia (from the 1990s onwards, through to the 2008 global economic crisis) has produced an increasing disconnect 'between the interests of the weaker sections of rural society and the broader goal of the economic development of the state', that has resulted in increasing 'popular disillusionment' (Joseph, 2011, p. 189). Further, there has been a widening and normalisation of marginality – under global neoliberal control – that has reframed citizenship as intensely competitive and treated vulnerability through a neoliberal logic of disposability.

The seminal work of M. Jacqui Alexander (1994) in the context of Trinidad and Tobago and the Bahamas is quite instructive in this regard, as it links the governance of sexuality (especially the naturalisation and renationalisation of heterosexuality) to the social implications of recalibrating the postcolonial condition under structural adjustment (an earlier incarnation of neoliberal global control) in the Anglo-Caribbean. For Alexander (ibid., p. 16), structural adjustment policies aimed:

> to impose a set of lending arrangements that would ostensibly reduce the foreign debt through a combination of economic measures to accelerate foreign investment, boost foreign-exchange earnings through export, and reduce government deficits through cuts in spending (McAfee, 1991, pp. 67–79). In particular, the programmes have been organised to reduce local consumption by devaluing currency, increasing personal taxes and reducing wages. The economy becomes privatised through state subsidies to private vendors, lowering taxes and providing tax holidays for foreign multinational corporations, expanding investments in tourism, dismantling state-owned enterprises, and curtailing the scope of state bureaucratic power by reducing the workforce and reducing the social wage – those expenditures for a range of social services for which the state had previously assumed some responsibility.

Alexander has demonstrated how the shifts to private capital accumulation, the increasing economic control by global capital and the resulting 'superexploitation' of the proletariat – under structural adjustment – have created a crisis of state legitimacy. In the Saint Lucian context, Kairi Consultants Limited (2007) found that with growing vulnerability, poverty and indigence, especially in rural society, family dynamics were often negatively affected in ways that severely strained heteronormative gendered expectations and relations. The study claims that 'there is a link between poverty and the inability of males and females to perform adequately their gender roles assigned them by their society' (ibid., p. xxii). Whereas this analysis reiterates a cis-normative logic of neoliberal productivity, it does point to the need to consider the intricate connection between class, geopolitics and gender in mapping out the terrain of vulnerability. Moreover, the report also cites high unemployment among Saint Lucian youth, the socioeconomic degeneration of rural society and the emergence of an informal income-generating sector, including an underground drug-trafficking and crime-based economy, as factors leading to vulnerability. The report claims that Saint Lucia, 'like the rest of the Commonwealth Caribbean, is only slowly adjusting to the reality of radical changes in external conditions, which make it imperative to organise its work-force for as orderly a withdrawal as possible from declining actors and for a shift to new activities' (ibid., p. xxxi). As a result, 'there is evidence of conditions of anomie in some of the marginalised urban communities. All of this has exacerbated other socio-cultural problems: there is segmentation of labour markets that exclude women, including single mothers as heads of households, and the decline of the extended family has left many of the elderly living alone' (ibid., p. xxx). Although the report cites the impact of globalisation on the creation of marginality within Saint Lucia, it constructs the nation state – not global neoliberal capital – as the problem, for which the only response is for Saint Lucia to 'shift to a higher productive platform' (ibid., p. xxxi).

The inability to self-discipline under global conditions has also had implications for rising violence as a way of addressing vulnerability, whereby violence has become a survivalist mechanism of social control between different marginalised populations. In a Transnational Institute study on drug markets, youth and crime in Saint Lucia, Marcus Day (2014, p. 5) claims that

> there is a distinction between violent behaviour that is deemed morally repulsive and punishable by the state, such as murder and rape, and behaviour that, while criminalised, enjoys the approval of large sections of the population. Examples of the latter include most extrajudicial killings of 'bad boys', homophobic violence, corporeal punishment of children and domestic and gender-based violence.

Day's report also provides glimpses into the rise of a neoliberal police state in Saint Lucia where the state has increasingly resorted to 'extreme use of force' to control drug-related gang wars. What both of the above studies highlight, despite their inattention to sexuality per se, is that the highly precarious socioeconomic context of Saint Lucia is a result of global and transnational phenomena. Although much more research is needed to understand how these vulnerabilities are translated, transferred and addressed through prevailing discourses of gender and sexuality, the above analyses push us to rethink 'homophobia' or anti-queer animus as informed by and formulated in response to this complex and globally manufactured context.

State-sponsored legal 'homophobia'

Many of the legal codes that organise and discipline national-normative sociality in postcolonial Saint Lucia have been inherited and revamped from the very same British laws that governed the plantation colony before political independence. In fact, Lennox and Waites (2013, p. 5) have pointed out that a significant number of postcolonial states, once under British rule, continue to criminalise same-sex behaviour between consenting adults. According to United and Strong (2011): 'The legal structure of St Lucia has been inherited from British colonialism and although our constitution has enshrined within it the principles of equality and non-discrimination of all persons, it is not the reality. St Lucia stands as one of the many countries in the world today which still criminalises same-sex acts between consenting male adults.' Legal homophobia in the island state is anchored in a wider context of state-sponsored homophobia that is fundamentally tied to Saint Lucia's Constitution (1979, revised 2006), which deliberately excludes gender and sexuality in all of its clauses, including those regarding 'fundamental rights and freedoms' and 'protection from discrimination'. Moreover, Saint Lucia's Criminal Code[1] (Act 9 of 2004, effective 1 January 2005) explicitly criminalises 'homosexual' conduct under Chapter 2, Part 1 ('Offences against the Person'), Sub-Part C ('Sexual Offences'). Section 133 of the Code on 'Buggery' states:

> (1) A person who commits buggery commits an offence and is liable on conviction on indictment to imprisonment for – (a) life, if committed with force and without the consent of the other person; (b) ten years, in any other case. (2) Any person who attempts to commit buggery, or commits an assault with intent to commit buggery, commits an offence and is liable to imprisonment for five years. (3) In this section 'buggery' means sexual intercourse per anus by a male person with another male person. (p. 95)

Whereas this definition of buggery appears to target only same-sex anal acts between males, the previous section (132) on 'Gross Indecency' implicitly criminalises same-sex acts between women.

Across the Anglo-Caribbean, the legalisation of homophobia continues to be institutionalised as part of postcolonial moral governance through national constitutions and more recent revisions of the British legal codes contained

---

1   Government of Saint Lucia's 2005 Criminal Code is available at: www.govt.lc/ media.govt.lc/www/legislation/Criminal%20Code.pdf (accessed 7 Mar. 2018).

in the Offences against the Person Act (1861). Even more problematic is the selective revising of this act in the postcolonial context, which has hypervisibilised homosexuality as a priority criminal offence (in some cases equating same-sex activity with rape and thus refusing to recognise same-sex subjects as capable of rationalising consent). At the same time other forms of sexual behaviour originally criminalised in the act were deprioritised – especially those linked to heteropatriarchal privilege (see Alexander, 1994; Tambiah, 2009; Robinson, 2009; Wahab, 2012). This postcolonial project of recalibrating and legislating social norms in the interest of national solidarity does not relate only to the explicit recriminalisation of homosexuality, but also involves an overhauling of several legal codes related to the governance of intimacy, social and biological reproduction, and therefore the widening legitimacy of various forms of heterosexual conduct and heteronormative relations. In fact, Tracy Robinson (2009, p. 4) claims that 'the region-wide overhauling of laws dealing with violence against women and the family over the last 25 years revised the focus and boundaries of authorised sex and sharpened the notion and danger of the homosexual *other* . . . The spectre of "the homosexual" is, legally speaking, a relatively modern one.' While Robinson here seems to rely on one of poststructuralist scholar Michel Foucault's major contributions to the history of sexuality,[2] in the postcolonial context it also takes on a different nuancing. Robinson investigates the ways in which sexual offences laws and family law reforms have attempted to redistribute justice by recognising categories such as 'common law unions' and 'visiting relationships' (that were previously positioned as racialised threats to the moral integrity of colonies) as a reflection of the seemingly progressive character of postcolonial modernity. This has had the effect of not only reinstating heterosexuality as the norm, but also legitimising a range of kinship forms that were previously marginalised under colonial rule (and remain somewhat stigmatised).

In this regard, heterosexuality has been increasingly mobilised by the postcolonial state, especially as a discourse with the potential to collectivise and nationalise diverse forms of kinship and intimacy, with a view to widening the terrain from which to responsibilise citizens. This logic presents heterosexuality as crucial to both national solidarity and a sense of sovereignty that is decidedly anti-colonial. Interestingly, Robinson (2009, pp. 4–5) recognises in post-1980s legal reforms in the Anglo-Caribbean a more complicated recalibration of gender and sexuality as postcolonial disciplinary and biopolitical mechanisms:

> This specialized vocabulary of Caribbean conjugality, valorizing heterosexual reproductive intimacy, becomes a signifier of Caribbean authenticity. One consequence of this is that the homosexual is now more discernible as the counterpoint to the reproducing heterosexual citizen. These law-reform initiatives in criminal and family law

2   In his four-volume lifework *Histoire de la sexualité*, begun in 1976.

professed to have the improvement of the status of women as their focus. They, unfortunately, demonstrate how impoverished notions of gender equality have become a modern mechanism for 'redrafting morality' and re-entrenching erotic autonomy.

Although these legal changes are calibrated in various ways by different nation states, it is important to recognise that they do not necessarily reflect the autonomy of postcolonial nation states to draft and enact them. We must enquire about the ways in which global neoliberal politics have affected postcolonial nation-state making and have redrafted/redirected their own biopolitical projects in problematic ways. For example, it is important to situate critically the 'wave' of legal reforms around sexuality, conjugality and kinship – which Robinson identifies as beginning since 1980, within the period of IMF/ World Bank-orchestrated structural adjustment – that revised the conditions of self-governance within the region. Jacqui Alexander has attended to the complexities of this kind of contrapuntal questioning in her exploration of sexual citizenship in Trinidad and the Bahamas, linking the legal revisions around gender and sexuality to wider considerations/currents/shifts in the political, social and cultural arenas as a result of the accelerated globalisation of neoliberal governance.

'Our destination will not tolerate it': queering Saint Lucia

While the above discussion depicts the Saint Lucian state as actively engaged in straightening (that is, heteronationalising) its citizenry, the increasing importance of tourism to the small island economy has reimaged the postcolonial state as a queer(ed) figure under the forces of global capital. For instance, whereas the Saint Lucian government has been reluctant to investigate the murders of several of the island's gay-identified men, the state has paradoxically become responsibilised to publicly address homophobic violence when the targets are legal non-citizens, especially white gay male tourists. This raises the question: Under what national and global conditions is the state responsibilised to address homophobia at the same time as it institutionalises the silencing of homophobic violence as a form of national responsibility?

In March 2011, three white gay American men from Atlanta were robbed and allegedly beaten in the rural town of Soufriere. Within days, news of the incident went into global circulation on LGBT websites such as Advocate.com (linked to 'the oldest and largest gay magazine in the United States') and Pink News.com (touted as 'Europe's largest gay news service'). The news was also spotlighted in some of the regional newspapers, such as the *Jamaica Observer*. The article from Advocate.com Editors (2011) reads: 'According to the victim's account, Michael Baker and his boyfriend Nick Smith were in the shower in the evening when they heard their friend Todd Wiggins scream in another part of the house. Baker emerged to find masked men beating Wiggins, and he and Smith eventually were tied up and beaten, too. The men hiked down a mountain barefoot to escape after their attackers left'. As a result of this public outing and shaming of Saint Lucia as homophobic – by LGBT watchdogs in the Global North – the Saint Lucian government was forced to respond publicly and officially to an issue that it has historically tried to silence or stymie any legitimate public discussion about. This led to an official apology – circulated through social media – made by St Lucia's tourism minister, Allen Chastanet, to the three men. The apology also included the government's claim that 'the attack on three gay visitors to the island appeared to be perpetrated by individuals whose views do not reflect the sentiments of the majority of law abiding citizens' (*Jamaica Observer*, 2011b). The tourism minister further insisted that 'the southern Caribbean island is safe for gay visitors' (ibid.).

These remarks made by the state suggest that it recognises homophobic violence – in the global arena – only when it does not implicate the national consensus (that is, the perpetrators are a few bad individuals) and when the targets of homophobic violence are white tourists. Even more, the claim that the island is 'safe for gay visitors' represents a form of global image management by the government of Saint Lucia, which has become increasingly dependent on tourism. Indeed, one *Jamaica Observer* article (2011a) reported that 'tourism officials are this week arranging meetings with the visitors to do some *damage control*'. In this move to avoid damage to its respectability on the international scene, the small island state constructed the three white gay American men not only as the 'real' victims of homophobic violence, but as benevolent subjects undeserving of such violence. Tourism minister Chastanet remarked that 'one of the men who had become very attached to Saint Lucia was in the process of raising funds to help slow learners in the various schools on the island' (ibid.). In addition, the Saint Lucian police informed the public that some of the perpetrators were arrested and the stolen items recovered – a move which contrasts sharply with the state's silence around violence against Saint Lucian LGBT persons.

The Saint Lucian government's official statement continues: 'Whether or not this crime was motivated by anti-gay sentiment, or during the course of robbery, it is nonetheless unacceptable behaviour and *our destination will not tolerate it. Our enforcement authorities are pursuing this matter relentlessly*' (Geen, 2011; emphasis added). This statement is particularly interesting as it represents the double consciousness of the postcolonial state. While the Saint Lucian state is invested in conditioning the impossibility of same-sex sexuality, intimacy and relationality within the nation, it must simultaneously learn to see and conduct itself through a white Western self-disciplinary gaze, that is, as the object of intervention. It is significant that the tourism minister refers to the island as 'our destination' – not 'our country' – which signals the limits of self-definition and state legitimacy conditioned through the touristic gaze. As such, the 'queerness' of the Saint Lucian state – represented by its paradoxical permissiveness and prohibition of homosexuality/homophobia – cannot be assessed as only a product of the state's autonomy and agency. Across the many reports of the incident in regional and international online media, no mention was made of how Saint Lucia and other small island states are situated by hegemonic touristic discourse, let alone the links to global and transnational circuits of neoliberal governance that unevenly distribute risks and vulnerabilities – only to code them as intrinsic properties of the postcolonial condition. This is not to suggest the false consciousness of Saint Lucians, but the need to scrutinise the renaturalised imperial relations of tourism as something that small island states – such as Saint Lucia – cannot refuse. It is this tentativeness of the nation state – one that selectively hypervisibilises and invisibilises homophobic violence and calculates which kind of violence is worthy of national justice – that suggests the need to rethink 'homophobia' in Saint Lucia as informed by discursive currents operating within and beyond national borders.

The archive of experience: LGBT Saint Lucians speak out

To suggest that the rich and complex testimonies provided by interview participants constitute a kind of queer/LGBT archive is both encouraging and problematic. What these testimonies make possible is an incitement to discourse, as a way of contesting and remembering the official story of Saint Lucian nationhood. From a feminist and queer perspective, which views the experiences and voices of the marginalised as a unique political vantage point from which to critique hegemonic norms, the research participants are engaged in 'turning history upside down'. This is not just because they are telling their stories, but because, in doing so, they unsettle, question and reframe the problem space of public political life in the Saint Lucian polity. Across most of the interviews, participants spoke strongly and passionately about their experiences of discrimination and stigma and in some cases, violence, either because they were queer-identified or suspected of not conforming to normative codes of gender and sexuality. In many cases, bodies read as gender non-conforming were automatically presumed to be sexual outlaws and therefore marked for various forms of disciplining. While the discussion below is representative of a range of homophobic experiences of participants, it is worth noting that they cannot be made meaningful only within Western conceptions of 'homophobia' – as my later discussion will reveal. It is important to recognise these testimonies as belonging not only to a 'Saint Lucian LGBT archive' but to a global archive of the conditions of (im)possibility of certain bodies/subjects and relations.

Many of the participants[3] recounted experiences of homophobic insults

3 The participants named in this chapter provided signed consent for their given names to be used in any publication or distribution of the interview. In instances where they chose to remain anonymous, or in cases where the author felt that revealing their names could perhaps expose participants to certain risks, the code

and discrimination in public (including shared family spaces and situations), implying that these occurrences are not isolated, but have become a normalised feature of queer habitus within Saint Lucia. One of them, Vincent McDoom[4] – a gay-identified man – demonstrates how homophobia has been an integral part of the socialisation process:

> My abuse started . . . as a child because I was very different and very unique the way I was. You know? And society was very abusive . . . in name calling, in bashing. You know? And it's not easy to be a child when you're different and you're at school. I was abused already by the school children . . . I was also abused verbally at home, I was also abused verbally, you know, by society.

Additionally, he recounts how his father forced him to 'walk like a man' – a form of gender disciplining that was aimed at enforcing reputational heteronormative masculinity:

> I remember once . . . my dad he looked at me and he said: 'Could you come here?' And I came to him and he was like: 'No! Go back and come'. And I was like going, 'What for?' And he was like, 'I asked you to walk, come here!' And I said, 'I am walking to you . . . ' He tell me, 'Well, I don't like the way you're walking. You know you're walking like a woman'. You know, so walking like a woman or walking like a man, it gets you from point A to point . . . it gets you from point B from point A. You know, for me as a child that's what was important. It was not the way I got there. It's the fact that I got there, you know what I mean?

In addition, McDoom recounted how gender-based policing is attached to non-normative bodies as a way of orienting such bodies as proper objects of knowledge and control. In doing so, he seems to suggest that the regulation of bodily conduct is routinely expressed through an aversion to 'the feminine'. The following narrative is instructive in this regard, as it demonstrates the power of gender policing to stymie the agency of other orientations of knowledge and desire that are projected as threatening to normative gender logics:

> When I was a child my grandmother, she used to be a seamstress and . . . she went to see a friend of hers, who was another seamstress and she would go to see her to ask for advice on certain things she was doing that she could not complete and this lady's name was Ms X . . . I accompanied her to . . . see this woman and what happened was . . . when I stepped into this lady's, you know, I discovered my vocation. In fact, you know, and I knew that was the job I wanted to do, but as a child . . . I did not know the terminology of this job, and this job was a designer in fact that as a child I knew I wanted to be . . . ; but Christmastime comes around, you know, and the family gathers and

---

'Anonymous#' is used for their interview data.

4   Interviewed on 31 Dec. 2012 by Maria Fontenelle, United and Strong and Envisioning. An excerpt is included in the Saint Lucia Portraits section of the *Telling Our Stories* (2014) documentary series.

. . . start asking questions and saying, you know, 'What would you like to do or what would you like to be when you get older?' I was very happy, you know, I was just waiting my turn for me to say what I wanted to be when I get older and it was very funny . . . my brothers wanted to be a mechanic like my dad, my cousins wanted to be, you know, a nurse or a fireman or a mason and when it was my turn I was so happy – I just blurted out I wanted to be Ms X . . . I was not saying that I wanted to be a woman, I was saying I wanted to do the job she was doing, but unfortunately my family . . . thought that I wanted to be gay.

Another participant, Jessica St. Rose,[5] expressed experiences of homophobic discrimination in public:

I have never been really stigmatised or discriminated . . . at my workplace. But in the public I have been. People have threw remarks at me, call me names, especially when, well I would take part in living singing. And take part of the carnival activities and whatnot, and I would be on the stage. People would be standing and while calling me names and whatnot . . . but that didn't really deter me . . . because I was kind of used to that already.

Yet, she continued, it became clear that the stigma of non-normativity had negatively affected her work and career as a public performance artist:

I had a situation where once I got into this commotion, this fight, and it was opening night for my calypso tent. And the tent leader, he didn't want me to perform. He felt that, me performing onstage would be a bad thing, because of my image and like how people look at me out there. He thought that it, I would be causing a scene onstage, since we want some people would throw bottles at me. I guess he was trying to protect me maybe. But then 'some people pretending', he said. But I felt that wrong thing and I was like: 'No'.

Not only is this testimony reflective of the homophobia she faced in her performance work, but it indicates how non-normative bodies are constructed as liabilities and threats to cultural capital.

A range of respondents also claimed that they chose not to 'come out' because they experienced pervasive levels of homophobia and they did not want to jeopardise the respectability of their family members (despite the fact that some of these same relations had at times been the perpetrators of homophobic discrimination). Yet many of these respondents also gestured to the ways in which their non-normative gender and sexual identity became an open secret. One of them, Anonymous1,[6] illustrated well how social associations can generate stigma and surveillance in the public sphere:

5   Interviewed on 16 Jan. 2013 by Maria Fontenelle, United and Strong and Envisioning.
6   Interviewed on 4 Feb. 2013 by Maria Fontenelle, as above.

I remember a sister in the church calling me. We were very, very close, and she told me that she heard something in a store, and it seems like I had just passed by, and two people saw me passing, and she was also in the car . . . they started a conversation about me saying, you know: 'That girl is a lesbian, that she's with that butch girl'. And then she called me to find out whether it was true. So of course back then I denied it because I was on the down low I guess at that time, I denied it and that's how I started to know, you know, people were talking. My mother used to hear things, I used to reach places that I have never been, you know, did things that I have never done. My sister, of course, have asked the question, the fellas in the CDC [Castries Development Council, Saint Lucia] used to ask, you know, or call me names, and my sister would deny it because I am denying it, so everybody denied it back then.

Whereas these testimonies represent highly material expressions of gender surveillance and punishment, some respondents interestingly claimed that homophobia is a more recent phenomenon in Saint Lucia. For example, Damon O'Donnell[7] observed: 'What I do remember . . . that there wasn't any violence . . . what we now call homophobia . . . it was really a kind of curiosity of people not understanding what was it about . . . having a real negative connotation, which it does today'. Another interviewee, Dr Marie Gradison Didier[8] – a medical professional working in the field of sexually transmitted diseases for over 20 years – also remarked: 'When I first came to Saint Lucia I didn't sense that level of homophobia . . . I didn't sense that anger and then I began to sense a deep anger . . . I found there was a shift'. Not only do these testimonies contest essentialist constructions of Saint Lucia as transhistorically homophobic, but the shift identified is curious, as it implies the need to consider the context in which the discourse of homophobia became viable and mobilised. Such a discussion is beyond the scope of this chapter, but it is important to ask what types of vulnerabilities emerged in this moment to make the discourse of homophobia ideologically and materially feasible as a national-normative mechanism of social control.

Beyond the search for 'tolerance'

Within Western homonationalist discourses, Global South nation states, such as Saint Lucia, have been projected as spaces saturated by homophobia, requiring urgent Western LGBT human rights intervention because they supposedly do not possess the capacity for tolerance. The discourse of tolerance is not only a national fiction in Western nation states, but it also masks a wider discussion about the conditions under which queer subaltern subjects and populations exercise agency within more complicated social structures. Much scholarship

7   Interviewed on 27 Nov. 2012 by Maria Fontenelle, as above.
8   Interviewed on 21 Jan. 2013 by Maria Fontenelle, as above.

has emphasised the reputation/respectability paradigm as a central analytic in understanding moral governance within the Anglo-Caribbean. Whereas reputational discourses – resisting the Eurocentricity of respectability – were mobilised and capitalised on at the time of independence across the region, many postcolonial nation states, under the control of a 'nationalist-modern middle class' (Scott, 1999, p. 93), paradoxically reimagined their futures through the lens of respectability. As such, the national-normative referent of respectability has predominantly conditioned all official norms, including those attached to discourses of gender and sexuality. Although little scholarship on the region has attended to the importance of the reputation/respectability paradigm in organising sexual conduct, the LGBT subjects interviewed in Saint Lucia suggest that this discourse operates simultaneously as a conditioning aspect of *both* homophobia *and* tolerance of gender/sexual non-normativity. This is distinct from the way in which tolerance is conceptualised in the Global North where LGBT-tolerant nation states are projected as exceptional spaces where structures of homophobic hate are categorically absent. Instead, the Saint Lucian interviews suggest the need for a more complicated discourse about the conditions of tolerance that structure both the liveability and vulnerability of queer Saint Lucian subjects. The point here is not a culturalist (racialised) argument about the radical difference of 'Saint Lucian tolerance' but that tolerance is not unproblematic, as it is projected within Western discourses.

Many of the interviewees highlighted the disciplinary effects of public respectability – as a vector of nation-state homophobic governance – but they also pointed to ways in which self-surveillance in the service of public respectability averted their being categorically marked as non-citizens. For example, Anonymous1[9] emphasised the importance of safeguarding family respectability: 'So, you could pretty much say that because of the fact that I was on the down low, I had to pay that money 'cause I would have been outed, I would have been put out of the religion and my mother would have been put to shame, so she had to pay it'.

Another respondent, Anonymous2,[10] emphasised respectable self-conduct in public as a way of averting hypervisibility and violence: 'They [society] accept me because I behave myself . . . I have no problem. I just drive through society, I don't go where I don't belong to it, that people disrespect me because people are very, very ignorant, especially uneducated one; you don't belong there – don't go there!'. Whereas this respondent stressed the importance of the spatial conditions of self-regulation, another interviewee, Anonymous3[11] emphasised the labour of self-conduct along norms of gender/sexuality, although he pointed out that this is no guarantee of averting scrutiny:

9   Interviewed on 4 Feb. 2013 by Maria Fontenelle, as above.
10 Interviewed on 10 Jan. 2013 by Maria Fontenelle, as above.
11 Interviewed on 16 Dec. 2012 by Maria Fontenelle, as above.

> I believe, as a gay man, even in public there is a way to conduct
> you[rself]. You can't . . . believe that you are more woman then man
> and you[r] gay don't impose on people, although you are gay, but still it
> gets bullied or so on. I believe it have to do with how you carry yourself
> and how you see yourself . . . you don't just push onto the people faces,
> and if you gay, you need to be careful and do not let your family to hate
> other person because they will hate you . . . It's not really easy for us,
> in order to survive it, mentally you have to be strong, you have to be
> strong with your head. It's difficult on day-to-day basis for most person,
> even for me to some extent, because you get bullied. People don't use
> buses because you are gay, people cast remarks, persons looking down
> on you. It's disheartening sometimes. So you just have to [do] what you
> have to do; you have to live, no matter what!

Some respondents also claimed that their status as a contributing member of
society helped to avert homophobic scrutiny and foster their acceptance in
society, reflecting the point of many scholars that discourses of respectability
are deeply structured by class and status. Vincent McDoom,[12] for example,
identified how market-based status could become a vehicle for tolerance:

> Homosexuals are creative, you know? So, if you are creative with
> yourself, put that creative aspect into something that is tangible and
> make it work for you and make it allow others to accept you. One
> of the reasons why women accepted me, and the Saint Lucian public
> accepted me beforehand in Saint Lucia, was because I was talented;
> because I was a very, very good dressmaker. And what did I do? I
> dressed the most prominent men and women in society.

Anonymous2[13] – an upstanding public figure – also spoke about his financial
investments in the wider community: 'I have no problem . . . I know I have
the privilege to do things for people . . . now, I am . . . gay but I sponsor . . .
football, I am the one who sponsors football. When I came here, and they have
big football matches and so forth . . . I saw the condition the fellas was playing
in . . . piece of trousers and I said no, no, no, no, no, I sponsor over $40,000
worth.'

   Although the homonationalist resonance of this claim seems evident,
especially as these testimonies seem to suggest that acceptance/liveability
requires tangible investments in normative society, they also provoke questions
of how the forces of capitalism have served to structure respectability. This
structuring requires the bordering of those who are not only undeserving of
tolerance and acceptance, but for whom vulnerability is naturalised because
they are multiply marked as insurgent. Interestingly, some of the same voices
quoted above, reproduced 'the homophobe' as belonging to 'the ghetto'. One
respondent, Anonymous1, claimed that the 'majority of the gay community

---

12 Interviewed on 31 Dec. 2012 by Maria Fontenelle, as above.
13 Interviewed on 10 Jan. 2013 by Maria Fontenelle, as above.

. . . avoid the ghetto areas . . . that's where the bad boys are . . . so to avoid discrimination to avoid any confrontation people stay off those streets'.[14] Similarly, Anonymous4 remarked: 'Especially if you're in a street event, you get different persons from different class, and you get persons from the ghetto, who believes that this song[15] is actually telling them what to do'.[16] Anonymous5[17] also raised the issue of class when identifying the perpetrators of both homophobia and misogyny:

> There are some men. I would call them . . . I could just call them men that don't have class . . . Don't have anything to do but just to smoke and do whatever it is. These kind of men will see me places and call me zami . . . and lesbian, and I'll be like, yo, I could put a bread on my mother's table, I know every month I getting a salary . . . So don't try to go and call me lesbian . . . at the end of the day when I passing in the corner, I'll see you're bending over for another fella, just for what? A dollar?

Although these voices might be read as belonging to the archive of 'Saint Lucian homophobia', they also signal the ways in which queer Saint Lucian subjects perform and contest respectability, thereby complicating any singular reading of national-normative citizenship. In doing so, they activate, mobilise and complicate the class-based structure of respectability and become participant to the remaking and redistribution of vulnerability. This is obviously problematic, since these testimonies reproduce the cisgendered, class-centric and heteronormative conditions of national belonging, but at the same time these testimonies provoke a conceptual shift from assessing subjects within the limited frame of 'tolerance/non-tolerance' to a more complicated understanding of how agency is conceptualised within the context of vulnerabilities.

Tacit recognition

One of the primary epistemological features of global LGBT human rights discourse is the presumption that the freedom of LGBT subjects depends on the legalised public visibility of non-normative sexual identities. This legalistic condition has grave implications for how we think about the archive of queer history in the Global South. Nation states marked by legal homophobia are often misrecognised as excessively heteronormative/homophobic and, by default, without histories of non-normative sexualities, intimacies, desires and so on. In fact, both postcolonial nation states *and* global LGBT human rights advocates sometimes paradoxically help to construct queerness as outside the boundaries of the nation state, as such effacing the possibilities of non-

---

14 Interviewed on 4 Feb. 2013 by Maria Fontenelle, as above.
15 Referring to Caribbean music with homophobic lyrics.
16 Interviewed on 4 Dec. 2012 by Maria Fontenelle, as above.
17 Interviewed on 9 Jan. 2013 by Maria Fontenelle, as above.

Western practices of recognition (of non-normative sexualities). Additionally, if both sets of discourses reiterate the need for a fixed subject – identifying as LGBT – the possibility exists that they do not recognise more complex forms of relationality and intimacy related to sexuality and desire, which are not only about 'sexuality' per se. The work of Carlos Decena is quite instructive in this regard. In *Tacit Subjects* (2011), Decena's analysis of the lives of gay Dominican men in New York demonstrates that their families have a tacit understanding of the sexuality of these men, and, as such, they do not necessarily have to conform to a Western LGBT subjectivity which is crucially hinged on coming out. Decena does not read this uncategorical response by gay Dominican men as false consciousness or evidence of 'Dominican homophobia', but as a more complicated and strategic negotiation of a range of relations related to minimising vulnerability. According to Decena (ibid., back cover), an explicit coming out by these men would jeopardise the crucial bonds with family and community they depend on to buffer the vulnerabilities of migration to New York (especially racism). In addition, Decena does not romanticise these subjects as outside of power and politics. Instead, he analyses these subjects as situated within the contrapuntal politics of transnational relations, suggesting that these tacit subjects 'contest, reproduce, and reformulate Dominican identity in New York' (ibid., back cover). Decena's work shifts the analysis away from fixed identity claims and 'coming out' to the possibilities of different forms/practices of same-sex recognition.

What was immediately apparent in many of the Saint Lucia interview transcripts was the tacit refusal of respondents to reproduce a simplistic story of same-sex animus in the island state. In fact, some responses suggest there is a publicly acknowledged history of same-sex intimacy and relations (despite being officially unacknowledged). Anonymous2[18] claimed, 'When I was growing up, they had stigma, but it wasn't something that was embarrassing, and you grew in it . . . and the elderly person that was gay, they knew how to carry on themselves'. Another interviewee, Anonymous1,[19] recounted: 'My mother used to send comments . . . "not because I'm not speaking doesn't mean I don't know what's going on"'. Both these quotes not only acknowledge the existence of social practices of tacit recognition, but also respond critically to Western discursive presumptions about the ultra-heteropatriarchy of the Global South. They also contest Western hegemonic constructions of 'the postcolonial homophobe' as operating under false consciousness. In addition, some responses resonate with Walcott's 'queer poetics' (2009), suggesting an epistemological shift away from dominant Western identity categories and away from the disciplinary pressure to self-name. For example, Kenita Placide[20]

18 Interviewed on 10 Jan. 2013 by Maria Fontenelle, as above.
19 Interviewed on 4 Feb. 2013 by Maria Fontenelle, as above.
20 Interviewed on 5 Dec. 2012 by Maria Fontenelle, as above.

remarked that people would say 'she is that way' – gesturing to an orientation instead of an identity. She also sidestepped the identity trap to reference herself through her practices (that is, doing, not being): 'I do not call myself a lesbian. I say that I love differently'. These comments are not about making the case for cultural exceptionalism (that is, Saint Lucian sexuality as radically different), but they provoke a need to understand the more complex historically and socially constructed practices of selfhood and community in Saint Lucia.

Moreover, as opposed to the common perception that same-sex sexualities are oppressed in Global South countries (see Pew Research Center, 2014) and any possibility of agency is denied, some respondents spoke about the ways in which they resist and contest the authority of national heteronormative discourse. For instance, Anonymous1[21] recounted how she refuses to play 'the truth game' with her mother, who has repeatedly questioned her about her sexuality: 'I don't want the effort. So I, I think I will continue deny, not deny, but I'll continue not answering her when she asks the question, where my sister has stopped completely'. Not only is her refusal to respond a refusal of the heteropatriarchal call to self, but the silence that is returned and imposed opens up a space of ambivalence that can be counter-disciplinary and counter-pedagogical. Whereas this and many other responses demonstrate that same-sex subjects are aware of the possibilities of multiple forms of resistance, it is also evident that normative society has strategically managed the tacit recognition of non-normative gender and sexual identities. For example, related to claims of some upper-class gay men in Saint Lucia, that their status as contributing members of society helped them avert homophobia, some entrepreneurs have also seen the value of queerness in terms of capital accumulation. Vincent McDoom[22] recounted how his non-normative gender performance was not solely a liability, but spectacularised as an asset to his employer: '[The business owner] understood what was happening . . . he understood that a feminine-boy attract women. And because a feminine-boy attract women, what he did was he gave me a job trying on shoes you know which girls came into the shop and they did a fabulous job you know buying the shoes that I was wearing . . . I felt like I was the attraction at the circus'. These testaments open up a messier picture of sociality involving non-normative subjects, beyond the dominant discourses of legal-categorical recognition and tolerance.

'Small places, big lessons': returning the gaze

The final section of this chapter focuses more directly on the epistemological reorientation begun in the prior two sections – a return of the gaze northwards from the Global South. This reorientation is located within a wider political project concerned with decolonising queer studies, especially questioning the

21 Interviewed on 4 Feb. 2013 by Maria Fontenelle, as above.
22 Interviewed on 31 Dec. 2012 by Maria Fontenelle, as above.

cross-cultural translatability of Western-centric understandings of sexuality and gender. Critical of the limitations of both postcolonial and queer studies, William Spurlin (2001, p. 200) suggests that 'transnational, queer inquiry should enable Western queer studies to radically interrogate and transform the lenses through which it reads and appropriates desire, queer identity, and sexual difference, and to self-reflexively examine its own imperialist and homogenizing impulses made possible through globalization'. I suggest that undoing the coloniality of queer studies also entails speaking back to centres of queerness by those in the Global South who simultaneously dis/identify with Western conceptions of queerness. As many scholars have pointed out, global LGBT human rights discourses that emerge predominantly within the West not only universalise its epistemology about sexuality and sexual freedom (for example, through discursive constructs such as 'the homosexual', 'coming out' and 'discrimination') but, in doing so, they effectively rationalise an imperialist drive to civilise the Global South (imagined as essentially repressed and therefore incapable of rationalising sexual freedom). Joseph Massad (2002) sees this as the work of what he calls 'the gay international' – a group of LGBT activists/organisations in the Global North, acting in conjunction with conservative governments to save helpless queers, victimised by their own national communities in the Global South. In a similar vein, Bacchetta and Haritaworn (2011) – building on Jasbir Puar's concept of homonationalism (2007)[23] – also discuss homotransnationalism as a form of global governmentality. These scholars scrutinise the epistemological frames that organise global LGBT human rights discourse (as homonationalism goes global) and demonstrate how even racialised others within the Global North are called into homonationalist projects. Yet, very little work has focused on the complicated agency of sexual and gender minorities within the Global South, who cannot be viewed simplistically as 'victims' of global homonationalism, but subjects who simultaneously identify and disidentify with the Western-centric rubric of gender and sexual liberation. Along this line of critique, I am interested in scrutinising the Envisioning interviews to think critically about the questions asked (developed by Envisioning participants in Saint Lucia and Canada); the epistemological premises; how they frame the truth of inquiry (that is, about both homosexuality and homophobia in Saint Lucia); and how they constitute the subjects we come to know and recognise as authentic – who, in turn, cannot refuse the call to authorise certain truths and their presuppositions. My interest comes from the work of Michel Foucault, for whom all methods of inquiry – with their own conventions for knowledge production – legitimise the legibility of their speaking subjects and truth effects. The discussion below reflects the complex agency of those in the Global South

---

23 Homonationalism refers to the assimilation and subsequent depoliticisation of gays and lesbians into national-normative machineries within the Global North.

who are always already interpellated into global homonationalist projects to simultaneously reinforce and contest Western-centric framings of gender and sexuality.

As discussed above, the determination of whether or not Saint Lucia is tolerant of LGBT persons frames a highly limited understanding of same-sex relationality and desire in postcolonial nation states. Whereas the discourse of tolerance – as a gauge of modernity – has been framed in the West through decriminalisation, anti-discrimination legislation, rights to same-sex marriage and the recognition of coupled same-sex unions, the interviewees' responses above demonstrate the need to historicise Western discourses of tolerance at the same time as they call for a more historically nuanced and contrapuntal analysis of vulnerability in a global context. In other words, this question must be asked: How does the postcolonial condition, continuously being remade within and responding to the context of global neoliberalism, allow us to reconceptualise the im/possibilities of certain forms of social relations and politics? In posing this question, we might not only situate the 'discourse of tolerance' as a Western disciplinary mechanism, but also open up the possibilities of understanding queer Saint Lucians and normative Saint Lucians as having parallel and shared vulnerabilities under global neoliberal hegemony. For example, what might it mean to recognise queer Saint Lucians as having a shared political itinerary with working-class Saint Lucians – who, in many cases, are projected as the authentic homophobes? If we continue to investigate the Western-centric single-issue politic of 'sexuality' through the human rights rubric, how would these seemingly distinct populations arrive at a more complex and shared understanding of the conditions under which they are denied citizenship? These are not only difficult questions to attend to in concrete ways, but are methodologically challenging, since they require an epistemological shift that transcends the blueprint of rights-based discourses.

Throughout most of the interviews, respondents were asked about one of the most powerful features anchoring the global LGBT human rights discourse: coming out. Although many of them spoke about this experience – whether or not they chose to come out, whether they navigated coming out in particular scenarios, how they came out, how they were outed, and so on – some of the responses were ambivalent about this demand for knowledge and its authorising subject. For instance, Anonymous4[24] was asked, 'How it was for you as a young person, coming to the knowledge that you represented something that the rest of society did not accept?' Responding with a sense of disorientation and as such, disorienting the interviewer's frame of questioning, the interviewee replied: 'How will I answer this question? How do I go about this? . . . I wouldn't say that I had the opportunity to come out, because I haven't really thought of me as being different from anybody. I live my life openly, I

24 Interviewed on 4 Dec. 2012 by Maria Fontenelle, as above.

do not answer to anybody as to my sexuality or what it is. So, basically there's not a coming out, or if you want to say that I have been out, then maybe I have been out – all my life'. If 'coming out' is one of the central tenets of gauging tolerance, then this response not only opens up a great ambivalence about the traction of such a discursive logic, but it also refuses the binary distinction between public and private that is heavily embedded in the coming out narrative and the discourse of tolerance that this narrative supposedly anchors. The response does not fall into the seductive trap of matching a predetermined answer to the question (thereby validating the question), but it almost makes a mockery of the question as a viable technique of truth-seeking.

On another occasion, Vincent McDoom[25] – an expat who lives in Saint Lucia and France – reproduced the idea that the island lags behind the Western world in LGBT human rights:

> Saint Lucia is no longer Saint Lucia. Saint Lucia is part of the growing world. You know? And Saint Lucia has to keep up with what's going on, and you know somehow Saint Lucia must keep up with what's going on if Saint Lucia wants to be part of the future, you know, in this world . . . When I left Saint Lucia, you know, France gave me something that Saint Lucia never gave me: France gave me a voice. You know? Not only did France give me a voice, France gave me visibility, and that visibility somehow or the other you know we must bring it back.

While this comment seeks to locate Saint Lucia (through the culturalist discourse of 'Saint Lucian homophobia') in global disciplinary time, it is necessary to inquire critically into the power of such a construct to make Saint Lucia legible. In other words, is this teleological narrative of coming out (in France instead of Saint Lucia) reflective, more so, of the dominant discursive practice of 'locating homophobia' (Rao, 2014), or is this a powerful discursive prompt that queer subjects, desiring legibility, cannot refuse?

In addition to questioning the saliency of the coming-out narrative, some participants also opened up ambiguity about self-identification and self-naming, especially in terms of categories based on sexual object choice. For example, instead of referring to persons as partners or as girlfriend/boyfriend, responses such as that of Anonymous4:[26] 'I just used to talk about friends' or Anonymous1's 'we are friends'[27] not only represent a hesitation to self-name through Western categories, but also articulate a refusal to distinguish sexuality from sociality. The following excerpt from an interview with Kenita Placide[28] also registers a meaningful apprehension about uncritically adopting Western-generated categories and, even more, the need to think of self through predetermined categories:

25 Interviewed on 31 Dec. 2012 by Maria Fontenelle, as above.
26 Interviewed on 4 Dec. 2012 by Maria Fontenelle, as above.
27 Interviewed on 4 Feb. 2013 by Maria Fontenelle, as above.
28 Interviewed on 5 Dec. 2012 by Maria Fontenelle, as above.

MARIA FONTENELLE: And are you a lesbian?

KENITA PLACIDE: Funny, your question asked by many but answered to few. I don't believe I carry a label, nor do I identify as . . . I just love differently to what cultural norms accept.

MF: What . . . do you think it is restricted to have a label?

KP: I think basically labels just bracket persons, box them, and I think that basically to accept or to wear a label is to allow yourself to be defined by other persons and not necessarily by yourself, and it is one that I always dared to be different, so why do I definitely need to put a tag as to who or what I am? It doesn't matter.

In addition, although some participants did self-identify as gay or lesbian, they also queered these categories in terms of how they predominantly align gender with sexuality and desire. This creative, yet still problematic, thwarting of the gender/sexuality logic is illustrated in this statement by Vincent McDoom,[29] who identifies as 'gay':

I am a boy and I look like a girl, and many of the men who are interested in me are straight men. The majority of them . . . because the normal homosexual man does not want to be with me, he's interested in another man. You know? He does not want anything feminine about the man that he's going out with. You know, you have to put things back into context, and that's why I say in Saint Lucia we have it all confused. You know what I mean? So, because you are a feminite, the normal homosexual guy who is enjoying the image of hetero-normal looking man, even if he's gay . . . he does not even want to be seen with somebody like me.

The respondent's claim about the confusion of gender/sexual desire in Saint Lucia prompts the need for more ethnographic investigation into the ways in which bodies and their relationalities – through desire – do not necessarily conform to the categories and conventions of global LGBT human rights logic. For although Western categories such as 'gay' and 'lesbian' have appeal in the Saint Lucian context, they may have localised inflections of meaning.

If some of the responses either refused the demand for self-categorisation or troubled the discursive meanings attached to identity categories, then others equally questioned the analytic of homophobia. For example, Anonymous4[30] recounted that when she came out to her family, they reacted with: 'We knew that already'. As already discussed above, this tacit public knowledge and permissiveness of non-normativity troubles culturalist discourses about the ultra-homophobia that is not only attached to non-Western nation states, but especially racialised populations. This race thinking, under the banner of 'culture' – the racialisation of homophobia – is evident in one interviewer's

29 Interviewed on 31 Dec. 2012 by Maria Fontenelle, as above.
30 Interviewed on 4 Dec. 2012 by Maria Fontenelle, as above.

questions:[31] 'How much do you think our culture has been an African-based community? How much do you think that has to do with the attitude towards LGBT in Saint Lucia?' One might argue that this question – posed by one queer Saint Lucian to another – is an attempt to open up a space of critical contemplation about the complicatedness of queer agency within postcolonial Saint Lucia that requires further investigation. Some interviews entailed a parallel move to authenticate the subject of homophobia through the lens of gender. For example, Anonymous1 was asked: 'Do they [lesbians] have it easier than the gay men, or do they have it just generally easy? And why is that?'[32] The presumption that gay men are the true targets of homophobia not only reflects the problematic homopatriarchal preoccupations of global LGBT human rights discourse in general, but it also presumes that there is a fixed/authentic public knowledge and recognition of 'homophobia'. The response below is quite instructive, as it highlights how same-sex animus and misogyny are mutually constitutive, yet naturalised for non-normative women. Anonymous1 recounts her experience trying to obtain help from policemen to remove her belongings from a dwelling she had shared with her 'ex':

> My ex and I was going through some problems, and I needed to get my stuff out of the house. And we went to the police station and, you know, there's this back and forth, and the police just laughed. And, you know, it was like a joke, what was going on 'cause I was declaring all I want is my stuff, and she was declaring the stuff is hers, so we went . . . we had that back and forth. And the police just sat down laughing, you know, taking the situation as, you know, nothing. And, until to the end of it we . . . the police came to a decision that they will help me go and get the stuff out of the house 'cause she agreed to it. So they escorted me to the house. And while they were driving they said, 'But why are you going to take your stuff out of the house? You know, you're a lesbian and will go back anyway, so I don't see the point. You know, today or tomorrow you're going to be back.' And I was like: 'But, you know, that's what I want. Whether I go back or not has nothing to do with you. At this . . . present time, this is what I want to do. I want to take my stuff.' Later on they, that, the same two guys who saw me, you know, they came out and said, you know, he says: 'So what happened?' And he's laughing, you know. 'So, did you go back?' you know. I said, 'No. Whether I go back has nothing to do with you.' You know, every time he sees me, you know, he says so . . . he always asks, 'So where're you at now?' You know, so it's like it was never taken seriously what happened. It's like two women just fighting, you know, this is what's going to happen, rather than if it was a woman and a man, you know, there would be some, I think, I can be wrong, but I think they would have taken it a little more seriously than two women.

31 Maria Fontenelle in her interview with Anonymous4 on 4 Dec. 2012, as above.
32 Interviewed on 4 Feb. 2013 by Maria Fontenelle, as above.

The response suggests that the multiple meanings of same-sex animus from different intersecting positions of gender, sexuality, class and so on need to be considered, as opposed to re-anchoring the privileged optic of 'homophobia' through which mainly gay men emerge as subjects deserving justice. Maya Mikdashi's (2011; her italics) critique of the Western discourse of homophobia is compelling in this regard: 'The experience of homophobia as the *primary discrimination* one faces in life is usually the mark of an otherwise privileged existence. For the majority of people in the world, oppression, to paraphrase Edward Said on culture, is contrapuntal. It moves, is multi-directional, it is adaptive, and it forms a terrain of interconnected injustices.' If injustices are interconnected, then the global discourse of sexual freedom would do well to think more widely about the sources and vectors of oppression.

In addition, the limiting presumption that legal justice is the answer to sexual oppression was implicit in some of the interview questions, such as: 'Do you think that the laws currently on the books in Saint Lucia impact on the attitude and the behaviour of the police force towards LGBT people?'[33] The testimony excerpt above not only sheds light on the oppressive effects of social laws (that is, patriarchy), but it also comments critically on the limited capacity of legal reason to calibrate and deliver social justice. Rather than prioritising a legalistic rights-based approach to social justice, it might be useful for global LGBT human rights discourses to demand that postcolonial justice be recognised as a core principle of its political itinerary. This could open up a more meaningful discussion of justice beyond the currently prioritised legal domain. In doing so, homonationalist Western nation states would also be challenged to rethink the terms and conditions under which some in the LGBT community claim sexual freedom. Similarly, in postcolonial states, such as Saint Lucia, a more meaningful conception of oppression and justice would require rethinking the complexities around Western-generated LGBT human rights discourses such as 'state-sponsored homophobia' and 'religious homophobia'. In this vein, many of the interviewees were asked about or themselves identified religious homophobia as a primary vehicle of repression. For instance, Anonymous4 was asked: 'Do you think that religion has a role in actively promoting stigma and discrimination?' Another question posed, to McDoom, was: 'How much do you think your views are shaped by the fact that you grew up in Saint Lucia, in our very Catholic society?'[34] Although homophobic religious discourse, without a doubt, wields a powerful influence on the production of injustice, there is also a need for a more meaningful understanding about the role of religion in Saint Lucia as a way of complicating what we mean by the word 'homophobia'. This is not a call to romanticise or endorse religion, but more a concern about how a focus on the repressive force of religion (and this is a highly racialised

33 Maria Fontanelle in her interview with Anonymous4 on 4 Dec. 2012, as above.
34 Interviewed on 31 Dec. 2012 by Maria Fontenelle, as above.

discourse) masks the violent, debilitating, restructuring and destroying effects of neoliberalism. Perhaps, as a way of rethinking the im/possibilities of sexual freedom, more complicated questions should be asked about the historically nuanced contracting between state and religion in postcolonial Saint Lucia, and the ways in which this contract has predetermined the conditions of normative citizenship and national consensus. This would not only shed light on why anti-same-sex animus has gained traction as a mode of control over certain bodies and relationalities, but might also push us to complicate this contracting between state and religion within a context of globally and locally produced vulnerabilities. This might lead to a shift in thinking from the 'perpetrator/victim' binary that structures global human rights discourses to looking at sexual oppression as inextricably linked to the very neoliberal modernity from which global LGBT human rights have emerged.

While I have offered two distinct and seemingly opposing discursive strands of homophobia above – one that mirrors 'homophobia' as a Western truth effect and another that contests this impetus to signify the Global South in the homonationalist Western imagination – my aim in doing so is to push for a constant questioning of what constitutes the archive of same-sex experience. I would hope that the evidence of homophobic experience would not be prioritised as the only authentic archive or conveniently slotted into 'country profiles' by mechanisms of homo-transnationalist governance (for example, immigration and refugee boards) in the Global North, but instead be held in tension with a constant scrutiny of the governing epistemological frames of the latter. It is by negotiating across this tension that the archive of non-normative Saint Lucian experiences around gender, sexuality and so on can remain politicised and become a vital tool for decolonising dominant ways of understanding gender and sexuality within and across the Global North and South.

References

Advocate.com Editors (2011) 'St Lucia sorry to gay tourists', Advocate.com, 15 Mar., available at: www.advocate.com/news/daily-news/2011/03/15/ st-lucia-apologizes-gay-tourists (accessed 7 Mar. 2018).

Alexander, M.J. (1994) 'Not just (any) body can be a citizen: the politics of law, sexuality and postcoloniality in Trinidad and Tobago and the Bahamas', *Feminist Review*, 48 (1): 5–23.

Bacchetta, P. and J. Haritaworn (2011) 'There are many transatlantics: homonationalism, homotransnationalism and feminist-queer-trans of color theories and practices', in K. Davis and M. Evans (eds.) *Transatlantic Conversations: Feminism as Travelling Theory* (Aldershot: Ashgate Publishing), pp. 127–43.

Day, M. (2014) 'Making a mountain out of a molehill: myths on crime and youth in St Lucia', Transnational Institute, available at: https://www.tni.org/files/download/dmv3-e.pdf (accessed 7 Mar. 2018).

Decena, C.U. (2011) *Tacit Subjects: Belonging and Same-Sex Desire among Dominican Immigrant Men* (Durham, NC: Duke University Press).

Geen, J. (2011) 'Caribbean island St Lucia apologises for attack on gay tourists', *Pink News*, 2 Mar., available at: www.pinknews.co.uk/2011/03/21/caribbean-island-st-lucia-apologises-for-attack-on-gay-tourists/ (accessed 7 Mar. 2018).

Jamaica Observer (2011a) 'St Lucia braces for gay attack', 13 Mar., available at: www.jamaicaobserver.com/news/St-Lucia-braces-for-gay-attack#poll (accessed 7 Mar. 2018).

— (2011b) 'St Lucia defends hospitality after gays attacked', 14 Mar., available at: www.jamaicaobserver.com/news/St-Lucia-defends-hospitality-after-gays-attacked (accessed 7 Mar. 2018).

Joseph, T.S. (2011) *Decolonization in St Lucia: Politics and Global Neoliberalism, 1945–2010* (Jackson, MS: University Press of Mississippi).

Kairi Consultants Limited (2007) *Trade Adjustment and Poverty in St. Lucia – 2005/06*, vol. 1 (main report), available at: www.caribank.org/uploads/2012/03/SLUCPAMainReport.pdf (accessed 7 Mar. 2018).

Lennox, C. and M. Waites (2013) 'Human rights, sexual orientation and gender identity in the Commonwealth: from history and law to developing activism and transnational dialogues', in C. Lennox and M. Waites (eds.) *Human Rights, Sexual Orientation and Gender Identity in the Commonwealth: Struggles for Decriminalisation and Change* (London: Human Rights Consortium, Institute of Commonwealth Studies), pp. 1–59.

Massad, J.A. (2002) 'Re-orienting desire: the gay international and the Arab world', *Public Culture*, 14 (2): 361–85.

McAfee, K. (1991) *Storm Signals: Structural Adjustment and Development Alternatives in the Caribbean* (London: Zed Books).

Mikdashi, M. (2011) 'Gay rights as human rights: pinkwashing homonationalism', *Jadaliyya*, 16 Dec., available at: https://www.europe-solidaire.org/spip.php?article23813 (accessed 7 Mar. 2018).

Pew Research Center (2014) ;The global divide on homosexuality: greater acceptance in more secular and affluent countries', available at: www.pewglobal.org/files/2014/05/Pew-Global-Attitudes-Homosexuality-Report-REVISED-MAY-27-2014.pdf (accessed 7 Mar. 2018).

Puar, J. (2007) *Terrorist Assemblages: Homonationalism in Queer Times* (Durham, NC: Duke University Press).

Rao, R. (2014) 'The locations of homophobia', *London Review of International Law*, 2 (2): 169–99.

Robinson, T.S. (2009) 'Authorized sex: same-sex sexuality and law in the Caribbean', in C. Barrow (ed.) *Sexuality, Social Exclusion and Human Rights: Vulnerability in the Context of HIV* (Kingston, JA: Ian Randle Publishers), pp. 3–22.

Robinson, W.I. (2006) 'Critical globalization studies', in J. Blau and K.E.I. Smith (eds.) *Public Sociologies Reader* (Lanham, MD: Rowman and Littlefield Publishers), pp. 21–36.

Scott, D. (1999) *Refashioning Futures: Criticism after Postcoloniality* (Princeton, NJ: Princeton University Press).

Spurlin, W.J. (2001) 'Broadening postcolonial studies/decolonizing queer studies: emerging "queer" identities and cultures in Southern Africa', in J. Hawley (ed.) *Postcolonial, Queer: Theoretical Intersection* (Albany, NY: State University of New York Press), pp. 185–205.

Tambiah, Y. (2009) 'Creating (im)moral citizens: gender, sexuality and lawmaking in Trinidad and Tobago', *Caribbean Review of Gender Studies*, 3:1–19.

United and Strong (2011) Report on the status of LGBT people in Saint Lucia, 25 Jan., available at: http://lib.ohchr.org/HRBodies/UPR/Documents/Session10/LC/USI_UnitedandStrongInc_eng.pdf (accessed 7 Mar. 2018).

Wahab, A. (2012) 'Homophobia as the state of reason: the case of postcolonial Trinidad and Tobago', *GLQ: A Journal of Lesbian and Gay Studies*, 18 (4): 481–505.

Walcott, R. (2009) 'Queer returns: human rights, the Anglo-Caribbean and diaspora politics', *Caribbean Review of Gender Studies*, 3: 1–19.

Documentary film

Telling Our Stories (Saint Lucia Portraits section) (2014) (Saint Lucia and Canada: United and Strong Inc. Saint Lucia and Envisioning Global LGBT Human Rights), available at: http://envisioning-tellingourstories.blogspot.com (accessed 12 Apr. 2018).

Extracts are cited from interviews with: Vincent McDoom, Jessica St. Rose, Kenita Placide, Damon O'Donnell, Marie Gradison Didier, Anonymous1, Anonymous2, Anonymous3, Anonymous4 and Anonymous5.

5

Violence and LGBT human rights in Guyana

Pere DeRoy with Namela Baynes Henry

> *Once the law's there, still on the book – nobody would feel comfortable*
> Quincy 'Gulliver' McEwan (2012)[1]

Same-sex intercourse, sodomy and cross-dressing have been illegal or prohibited in Guyana since the beginning of the country's colonial era to the present. Laws against sodomy were introduced as part of Roman Dutch legislation during the Dutch colonial era and were continued under British common law during the British colonial era (Carrico, 2012, p. 8). Guyana inherited its legal structure from European colonial powers and maintained many of these laws after gaining independence in 1966, and well after the past government (under the administration of the People's Progressive Party/Civic) initiated a constitutional reform between 2000 and 2001, which shaped the current 2003 Constitution of Guyana. Emerging from this legal backdrop are mechanisms for shaping and monitoring social norms regulating sexuality in Guyana. The parameters of the legal structure in Guyana additionally shape the construction of the current cultural, socioeconomic and political landscapes of the country. Moreover, this inherited legal structure allows us to understand: 1) how social structures[2] create degrees of vulnerabilities and marginalisation for lesbian, gay,

---

1   Quincy 'Gulliver' McEwan, director of Guyana Trans United, is a transgender activist in the country and a plaintiff in a case, *McEwan, Clarke, Fraser, Persaud and SASOD v. attorney general of Guyana* that challenged the law that bans cross-dressing in Guyana. McEwan was interviewed on 27 Nov. 2012 by Namela Baynes Henry, SASOD and Envisioning. An excerpt is included in the Guyana Portraits section of the *Telling Our Stories* (2014) documentary series.

2   Social structure is the organised pattern of social relationships/institutions that together compose society. These structures are not immediately visible to the untrained observer; however, they are present and affect all dimensions of human experience in society.

P. DeRoy with N.B. Henry (2018) 'Violence and LGBT human rights in Guyana', in N. Nicol et al. (eds.) *Envisioning Global LGBT Human Rights: (Neo)colonialism, Neoliberalism, Resistance and Hope* (London: Human Rights Consortium, Institute of Commonwealth Studies), pp. 157–75.

bisexual, transgender (LGBT) persons; and 2) how these same structures have the potential to activate positive change in the lives of people who identify as LGBT in Guyana.

This chapter provides an analysis of how current criminal law acts in Guyana have affected the wellbeing[3] of its citizens who identify as LGBT, in an effort to advocate for conditions that ensure their human rights and security. In addition, it presents a picture to help the government clearly grasp how these laws have played a major role in the formation and maintenance of social norms that stigmatise and discriminate against LGBT persons in all areas of Guyanese society. To inform its analysis, the chapter draws on 25 face-to-face interviews conducted in the country in 2012 by the Envisioning Global LGBT Human Rights team (Envisioning) in partnership with the Society Against Sexual Orientation Discrimination (SASOD). The interviews recount the daily experiences and opinions of LGBT Guyanese mobilised across varied backgrounds related to race, gender, sexual orientation, economic situation, locale and education. It is written from the perspective of a young Guyanese student pursuing graduate studies at York University with support from a grassroots human rights activist and Envisioning community researcher. The latter has been organising in Guyana on behalf of LGBT persons for more than 20 years, and has also mobilised at the local, regional and international levels, to challenge laws and sociocultural values that have been marginalising and oppressing the LGBT community, and disciplining people's sexuality and identity.

Context

The Co-operative Republic of Guyana is a multicultural postcolonial society with a population of 746,955, comprising an indigenous population, descendants of people who came to Guyana primarily as slaves or indentured labourers, and others. Thus, as well as its original inhabitants, the backgrounds of its people range from Europe/Portugal and Africa (referred to as Afro-Guyanese) to China and India (referred to as Indo-Guyanese). These diverse groups are fused together by the English language, although indigenous languages are also spoken.[4]

Guyana is an English-speaking country on the Northeast coast of South America. It shares borders with Suriname, Venezuela and Brazil, and covers nearly 215,000 square kilometres. Its capital, Georgetown, is located on the Atlantic coast. Although Guyana is geographically located in South America,

---

3   Wellbeing is a good or satisfactory condition of existence; a state characterised by health, happiness and prosperity; welfare. Also see Michaelson et al. (2009).
4   Statistics obtained from the Bureau of Statistics – Guyana website, Population & Housing Census Final at: https://www.statisticsguyana.gov.gy/census.html (accessed 20 Jan. 2018).

its plantation history and shared cultural history of British colonialism situates it within the English-speaking Caribbean community (Caricom, which stands for the Caribbean Community and Common Market). The plantation history of Caricom is largely responsible for shared social, cultural, economic and political relations, and institutions that shape the realities of those living in Caricom's member countries. A former colony of the French, Dutch and British, Guyana is one of the 11 countries[5] (Carrico, 2012, p. 6) in this region where British colonialism introduced laws criminalising same-sex relationships and cross-dressing, and it is the only country in South America that criminalises sex between men (Glickhouse and Keller, 2012). Breaching these laws has a range of penalties, for example, in Guyana two years to life imprisonment, and in Barbados life imprisonment for 'buggery', and up to ten years for 'serious indecency' (Jones, 2013).

Criminal laws – discriminatory laws

According to Melinda Jankie:[6]

> Guyana has a very good Constitution, and we have incorporated many human rights conventions, human rights treaties, [for example] conventions of all forms of racial discrimination, elimination [of] discrimination against women, the international convention of civil rights. So [the] basic framework is ... there.

> I think the main challenge here is out-of-date legislation and out-of-date attitudes, based on ignorance, fear of other, [and a] combination of other [issues that] led to actions and activities that are totally unacceptable and discriminate against people who are LGBT.

LGBT individuals living in Guyana have had a long struggle for equal rights and acceptance. Two illustrations of this struggle (Kissoon, 2013) date back to 1959 (when Guyana was still a British colony referred to as British Guiana) and 1968 (after the country had gained independence and was renamed the Cooperative Republic of Guyana). In the first situation, two gay men were arrested and charged for attempting to marry. Interestingly, in their later attempt at a public wedding, the police did not intervene. In 1968 a young person – who would have been considered male at birth – was arrested for

5   These former British colonies in the West Indies are: Antigua and Barbuda, Barbados, Belize, Dominica, Grenada, Guyana, Jamaica, Saint Kitts and Nevis, Saint Lucia, Saint Vincent and the Grenadines, and Trinidad and Tobago. Recently, these laws have been successfully challenged in the courts, in Belize in 2016 and in Trinidad and Tobago in 2018. For more on the Belize case see Orozco, ch. 9.
6   Melinda Jankie, an attorney-at-law and executive director of the Justice Institute Guyana Inc., interviewed on 27 Nov. 2012 by Namela Baynes Henry, SASOD and Envisioning. An excerpt is included in the Guyana Portraits section of the *Telling Our Stories* (2014) documentary series.

wearing a miniskirt (Kissoon, 2013). In both cases, these individuals challenged the heteronormative codes of sexual orientation and gender identity, including gender expression (SOGIE). They were arrested and charged, and the legal structure and medical system perceived them as – and treated them as – either criminals or mentally ill; indeed, the court sent the young cross-dresser for psychiatric treatment (ibid.). These cases demonstrate how identification outside of heterosexuality was regarded as deviant, and behaviour aligning with this deviation warranted a criminal law response. Similar struggles may have occurred prior to 1959, but there is no record of them.

In attempting to understand why these individuals were viewed in this way and subjected to such treatment, it is important to recognise the perceptions of cross-dressing and same-sex relations that were prevalent during this period, and how they affected the lives of persons who identify outside of the acceptable heterosexuality norm. Although Kissoon recognises that several cultural and social factors influence homophobia and transphobia – such as religious conservatism, mainstream media, normative family structures and culture – he argues that laws are primarily responsible for the formation and maintenance of social norms in all areas of society, at the individual, organisational and institutional levels.

Guyana has laws against 'buggery/sodomy', 'gross indecency' and homosexual behaviour, which profoundly influence discourses about sexuality in private and public spheres of social life. They particularly discourage any acceptance of and/or tolerance for diverse sexual orientations and gender identities, regarding them as a threat to deep-rooted social norms of heterosexism and heteronormativity as the social fabric of Guyanese society. Inherited from the colonial era, 'sodomy laws' (using the term 'buggery') were included in Guyana's Criminal Law (Offences) Act (8:01) of 1893, and have remained unchanged. Sections 352 to 354 of that act criminalise consensual intimacy between men in private. The first of those sections penalises acts of 'gross indecency' between men in these terms: 'any male person who, in public or private, commits, or is a party to the commission, or procures or attempts to procure the commission, by any male person, of any act of gross indecency with any other male person shall be guilty of misdemeanour and liable to imprisonment for two years' (Caricco, 2012, p. 8). Section 353 states that 'everyone who (a) attempts to commit buggery; or (b) assaults anyone with intent to commit buggery; or (c) being a male, indecently assaults any other male person, shall be guilty of felony and liable to imprisonment for ten years' (ibid.). This section refers to both consensual and non-consensual homosexual acts between males, as well as attempts at 'buggery' between homosexuals and heterosexuals, regardless of consent. Section 354 of the act reads: 'Everyone who commits buggery, either with a human being or with any other living creature, shall be guilty of felony and liable to imprisonment for life' (ibid.). Since the laws specifically speak to the illegality of same-sex relations between men, one could argue that same-sex relations between women are legal in

Guyana. However, Christopher Carrico argues that, in more recent years, sexual offences laws have more clearly identified men having sex with men *and* women having sex with women as the subjects of these laws designed to deal with 'unnatural offence', buggery, sodomy and 'indecency' (ibid., p. 1).

Unlike these laws, under the Criminal Law (Offences) Act, cross-dressing is listed as a minor offence in the Summary Jurisdiction (Offences) Act (8:02). Section 153 (1) (xlvii) states that a man wearing 'female attire' or a woman wearing 'male attire' in public may face prosecution and conviction – or they may be fined by the court (SASOD, 2014, p. 3). These laws seem to punish those who threaten gender norms, such as feminine-presenting men and masculine-presenting women.

According to the report prepared by SASOD for the 21st Round of the Universal Periodic Review (UPR):

> Despite having the constitutional right to the freedom of expression (Article 146), LGBT persons oftentimes choose not to express their orientations and identities because they are threatened, discriminated against and victimised. Transgender persons are expressly forbidden from expressing their gender identity because of Section 153 (1) (xlvii) of the Summary Jurisdiction (Offences) Act, which makes it an offence of cross-gender dressing. This violates rights to human dignity, freedom of expression and protection from discrimination based on gender.
>
> As a result of this law, transgender persons face high levels of direct discrimination and targeted violence from both the police and private actors (citizens). (p. 6)

The report then gives an example of this discrimination by drawing on a case from April 2014:

> Two transgender sex workers were injured in a drive-by shooting by assailants using pellet guns. Even though the victims have reported the matter to the police and they have provided vital information which helps to identity the assailants, the police took over a month to charge the perpetrators. (ibid.)

Moreover, on September 6 2013, Chief Justice Ian Chang issuing his ruling in the case of *Quincy McEwan, Seon Clarke, Joseph Fraser, Seyon Persaud and the Society Against Sexual Orientation Discrimination (SASOD) vs. Attorney General of Guyana* on Section 153(1) (xlvii) of the Summary Jurisdiction (Offences) Chapter 8:02 which stated that cross-dressing in a public place is an offence only if it is done for an improper purpose. This ruling while seen as a minor victory for the transgender Guyanese, as the Chief Justice states that cross-dressing to express sexual orientation or gender identity could never be an offense, it is still very unclear as he did not say what the term 'improper purpose' means.[7]

---

7   *McEwan, Clarke, Fraser, Persaud and SASOD v. attorney general of Guyana* was filed

This partial victory has not been accompanied with sensitisation to counter prejudice and discrimination perpetrated in Guyana, and basically undermines the freedom of expression of certain groups of people. Two short films, *Sade's Story* and *Selina's Voice*, created by SASOD and Envisioning, capture the impact of the cross-dressing law and the challenges visited upon individuals who cross-dress as an aspect of their gender identity.

Sade's Story looks at the Constitutional Court ruling banning cross-dressing and the impact of the law, through the eyes of Sade Richardson, a transgender fashion designer. The film also explores how the cross-dressing law created conditions conducive to the violation of Sade's basic human rights. Violence often occurs when individuals recognise or perceive that the person before them is a man dressed effeminately or in female attire. Sade relates experiencing violence when using public transport to go to work, and facing cultural and structural violence when trying to access healthcare and advocating for fair treatment in the workplace. Sade says, 'Honestly, I would not be surprised if tomorrow somebody kills me and my body's found somewhere' and recounts an experience one morning while waiting for a minibus to travel to work:

> There were two [men]. One said to the other, 'That's the anti-man. You see how she's dressing? I told you, let's beat her, let's beat her'. The other man replied, 'That's not a woman! That's a man! Let's beat him'. Then one came over to me and said they must never see me at night, because they would make sure they kill me. Nobody can do anything about it, police or nobody can do anything about it. And that's the thing that stayed in my mind. He is right! They can beat me and kill me or do me whatever, and police and nobody can do anything about it. That's the mentality most of them have. It's OK to throw things at me. It's OK for buses to kick me out. It's OK to make me feel fucked up every day, because there is nothing anybody can do about it.

In *Selina's Voice*, Selina Maria Perez, a transgender woman, reflects on growing up and being singled out for not behaving like most of her peers (boys), and 'feeling like a freak', especially as it was impossible to find information that would help her to better understand herself.[8] As a result, she became very shy and introverted, because she felt that expressing herself in the way she wished to would probably get her into trouble as such behaviour was not encouraged.

---

in Feb. 2010 by four of seven trans persons convicted under the cross-dressing law, and SASOD, which was also an applicant in the proceedings. The court's ruling upheld the law as consistent with constitutional rights and did not define 'improper purpose'. The litigants appealed the ruling, however the Court of Appeal upheld the prior ruling. The appellants have appealed the case to the Caribbean Court of Justice (CCJ) where the case was heard on 28 June 2018. For details see: www.u-rap.org/web2/index.php/component/k2/item/64-press-release-mcewan-et-al-v-attorney-general-of-guyana-court-of-appeal-decision (accessed 18 Apr. 2018).

8   Interviewed on 15 Oct. 2012 by Namela Baynes Henry, SASOD and Envisioning. An excerpt is included in the documentary *Selina's Voice* (2013).

She reflects on how family and neighbours would say 'speak up like a man', when she was merely speaking in her natural voice. Her experience of being silenced as a youth encouraged her to study and to engage in advocacy work for people like herself and others in vulnerable positions. Selina then goes on to chronicle the direct violence she experienced as she engaged in LGBT advocacy work. One incident made her feel 'like a dog knocked down on the road and left to die' after being attacked by a group of men for refusing to engage in sexual relations, and being refused services by police and healthcare workers at a public hospital in Georgetown.

These laws undermine the constitutional goal to ensure the fundamental rights and freedoms of citizens. 'Fundamental rights' are enshrined in the Guyanese Constitution and protect its citizens from discrimination and unfair conduct by the executive, judicial and legislative branches of the state, so they can live freely. The state is expected to perform the 'duty of protecting every member of society from injustice or oppression' (Heilbroner, 1992, p. 53), and ensuring an individual's fundamental rights are not violated. But they cannot be enforced between private citizens or members of the private sector (Guyana Association of Women Lawyers, 2011). Enshrined in Article 149 of the fundamental rights section of the 1980 Constitution, is the constitutional goal to protect Guyanese citizens from discrimination 'on the grounds of race, place of origin, political opinion, colour, creed, age, disability, marital status (whether single or married), sex, gender, language, birth, social class, pregnancy, religion, conscience, belief or culture' (ibid.). However, discrimination 'on the grounds of sexual orientation' or gender identity/expression has not been included as a fundamental right in Guyana's Constitution (Kissoon, 2013), even though protection of the individual's right to life is enshrined in its fundamental rights section (Article 138), as well as protection from slavery or forced labour (Article 140); protection from torture, inhuman or degrading or other treatment (Article 141); protection against arbitrary search or entry (Article 143); and the right to a healthy environment (Article 149). With the protection of these rights, one might assume that an environment would be facilitated where all Guyanese citizens could secure their wellbeing.

Laws against sodomy and cross-dressing, and the exclusion of protection of an individual's right to engage in homosexual acts, stigmatise, discriminate against and criminalise that person and deny them their fundamental human rights. These laws contradict or undermine a basic principle of human rights, which is to ensure all people are equal in dignity and entitled to the same fundamental rights, and that no one is expected to have more rights than another person, especially on the grounds enumerated in the Constitution of Guyana. In addition, these laws and the omission of SOGIE signal a prejudice against and exclusion of some groups of people, and imply that the unfair treatment of certain groups of people is constitutional.

This conflicting dynamic is heightened by the fact that Guyana is a signatory to several international human rights instruments, seven[9] of which enshrine the basic principles of human rights (SASOD, 2014, p. 2). More specifically, these laws undermine fundamental rights and basic human rights principles and result directly in significant levels of direct, cultural and structural violence, and the automatic configuration of a group of people as criminals and outsiders on the basis of their SOGIE.

Discriminatory laws and violence in Guyana

According to one respondent, Leon I. Allen,[10]

> You have to not just be mentally strong but physically strong to deal with society when you decide to be yourself, because then you'll be bullied, and then if you can't handle that and they realise that you're not equipped to deal with that, then it moves from just discrimination and stigma and it goes all the way to violence.

Violence can take many forms. Simply put, it 'is any physical, emotional, verbal, institutional, structural or spiritual behaviour, attitude, policy or condition that diminishes, dominates or destroys others and ourselves' (Bobichand 2012, p. 1). Johan Galtung, a renowned scholar of peace and conflict studies, sees such behaviour as the 'avoidable impairment of fundamental human needs or, to put it in more general terms, the impairment of human life, which lowers the actual degree to which someone is able to meet their needs below that which would otherwise be possible. The threat of violence is also violence' (1990, p. 292). Galtung describes three typologies of the phenomenon: direct, structural and cultural, none of which can manifest without the existence of the others (ibid.). Based on interviews with 25 people who identify as LGBT, and representatives of advocacy organisations that work to eliminate discrimination on the basis of human rights and SOGIE, this chapter illustrates how the laws mentioned above facilitate violence, and – more importantly – how people's lives are affected within the context of anti-sodomy and cross-dressing laws.

9   The seven are listed in the Fourth Schedule of the Guyana Constitution: International Covenant on Civil and Political Rights; International Covenant on Economic, Social and Cultural Rights; Convention on the Rights of the Child; Convention on the Elimination of All Forms of Discrimination Against Women; Convention on the Elimination of All Forms of Racial Discrimination; Convention Against Torture and Other Inhumane or Degrading Treatment or Punishment; and the Inter-American Convention on the Prevention, Punishment and Eradication of Violence Against Women.
10   Interviewed on 13 Oct. 2012 by Namela Baynes Henry, SASOD and Envisioning.

Direct violence

Direct violence is an event. It 'represents behaviours that serve to threaten life itself and/or to diminish one's capacity to meet basic human needs. Examples include killing, maiming, bullying, sexual assault, and emotional manipulation' (Harvard Divinity School, 2016). Verbal violence, such as humiliation or put-downs, is also recognised as a form of direct violence. One interviewee, Juanita Burrowes,[11] describes a brutal act perpetrated on a person who identifies as a gay man:

> Well because he is gay and [a] person did not appreciate him in the community, he was in a party, and after leaving the party he was standing in the road waiting for the car or vehicle to go home, and a guy just ride up to him and said: 'Bun a batty boy must dead' [a gay person must die] … and just draw a cutlass from his waist and with one chop, opened his head and shoulder … dead. His head fling clean off.

All interviewees recounted experiences of violence at the hands of law-enforcement officers, both in public locations and at police stations. They also suffered attacks from citizens when using public and private modes of transport or walking in Georgetown's public spaces. In extreme cases LGBT persons had been sexually assaulted (raped or groped) and/or murdered.

In cases of direct violence, an individual's gender identity and gender expression are intertwined with sexual orientation as a basis for policing. Law-enforcement officers and citizens often respond to individuals on the basis of perceptions of how the male-female binary should be expressed. If someone's gender expression does not meet cisnormative expectations, it is concluded that such a person's sexual orientation is homosexual and he therefore warrants having bottles thrown at him, being attacked with weapons and being denied access to public transport. Arbitrary arrests and in some cases extortion by police officers may result, as well as general public humiliation through being stripped and heckled. Dorian Obermuller recalled an experience with the police:[12]

> I was liming with some friends as we would say 'liming' in the Caribbean, which basically means 'hanging out' and 'chilling'. We were hanging out. The police passed, they saw us, picked us up. Well, I was the very flamboyant one in the crowd.
>
> Like, 'What are you all doing here?' and stuff like that. 'You're soliciting and … and … and looking for men', and so on.
>
> We went, 'No we're not. No we're not.'
>
> 'Well, we're taking you down to the police station. That's what you're all doing out here. We're taking you all down to the police station.'

11 Interviewed on 31 Oct. 2012 by Namela Baynes Henry, SASOD and Envisioning.
12 Interviewed on 13 Oct. 2012 by Namela Baynes Henry, SASOD and Envisioning.

We went to the police station. They made a total mockery of us, blah, blah, blah, took statements, laughed, 'Everybody bring their buddies,' [meaning] the fellow police … policemen. They laughed, made jokes of us, and then sent us away.

Experiences of structural violence: varying degrees of access to social services and governance systems

Structural violence represents the 'systematic ways in which some groups are hindered from equal access to opportunities, goods and services that enable the fulfilment of basic human needs. These can be formal, as in legal structures that enforce marginalisation, or they could be culturally functional but without legal mandate – such as limited access to education or healthcare for marginalised groups' (Harvard Divinity School, 2016). Johan Galtung (1990) notes that structural violence exists when some groups, classes, genders, nationalities and so on are assumed to have, and in fact do have, more access to goods, resources and opportunities than others in these categories, and this unequal advantage is built into the very social, political and economic systems that govern societies, nation states and the world. These inequalities may be overt, such as apartheid, or more subtly naturalised through traditions whereby some groups are awarded privileges over others. Structural violence is built into the social system and expresses itself in the unequal distribution of power and unequal opportunities (that is, inequality in the distribution of income, education, opportunities and so on). Galtung equates structural violence with 'social injustice', and concludes that it results in a permanent involuntary state of poverty and exclusion from systems of governance in certain communities (ibid., p. 171).

All interviewees agreed that their LGBT sexual orientation and/or gender identity situated them in disadvantaged positions where they had limited, less or no access to goods, resources and opportunities as a result of the embedded stigmas that shape local social, political and economic institutions in Guyana. While acknowledging that SOGIE are indicators for discrimination, factors that determine the degree of individuals' marginalisation include class, location (urban, rural or interior), race and religion.

Any individuals who seek to express their sexuality outside of the heterosexual norm can experience the disadvantages embedded in the social, political and economic systems that govern the interaction, livelihoods, power and wellbeing of Guyanese people. More specifically, people who identify as LGBT (or are perceived as such) are denied or have less access to goods, resources and opportunities than heterosexual individuals of the same racial, economic or religious backgrounds. Structural violence is subtle, often invisible, and no specific person can (or will) be held responsible. While social services are provided in Guyana, sexual orientation, gender identity and gender expression determine an individual's access to such services, and in turn this determines the wellbeing and health of the people these services are expected to care for.

Cultural violence: reinforcing homophobia and transphobia

Cultural violence is rooted in the prevailing or prominent social norms that make direct and structural violence seem 'natural' or 'right', or at least acceptable. Galtung (1990) notes that cultural violence helps explain how prominent beliefs can become so embedded in societies that they function as absolute and inevitable, and are reproduced uncritically across generations. It speaks to those aspects of culture, the symbolic sphere of our existence – exemplified by religion, ideology, language, laws and art – that can be used to justify or legitimise direct or structural violence (ibid., p. 291). Cultural violence makes direct and structural violence look and even feel right – or at least not wrong – to people living within that culture.

The relationships between these types of violence are powerful. Opinions around heterosexuality and homosexuality emerging from religion and religious myths are retold through the acceptance of jokes and musical lyrics. According to interviewees, prejudices such as homophobia and transphobia, which are prevalent in Guyanese society, are largely the result of religion and law, which are the basis for how individuals are expected to act. Religion has a strong influence on people's morals – whether they are seen as good or bad. Certain religious groups are more sympathetic to the issues raised by LGBT people. For instance, some respondents reported that some Catholic churches provide welcoming spaces that are based on non-discrimination, while other Catholics recounted that they had to leave because the sermon was about sexuality, eternal hell and an indirect message that they did not belong to the congregation. Other Christian, Islamic and Hindu groups make the same argument, as Ram Anthony Paul noted: 'I was brought up in a Christian home. And being in a Christian home, and knowing the books, the words from Christianity, they already tell you … homosexuality is against God's creation. So there and then, discrimination is there.'[13]

Sade Richardson[14] described how, when his family found out he was gay, they claimed he had a demon inside him that needed to come out. He said that according to the church no one is born gay and its members explained to him that, as we grow, evil spirits get into our bodies, but that if he kept going to church, the demons would come out:

13 In a group interview on 9 Oct. 2012 conducted by Namela Baynes Henry, SASOD and Envisioning.

14 Interviewed on 28 Nov. 2013 by Namela Baynes Henry, SASOD and Envisioning. An excerpt is included in the documentary *Sade's Story* (2013). In the film, Sade self-identifies both as 'trans' and 'gay'. Here the pronouns 'he' and 'him' are used in describing Sade's early life.

> It was dramatic: they put their hands on my head, and holy water. It was ridiculous, it was very very ridiculous. Of course by then I was 16 or 17 and getting rebellious and stuff, and mother was reacting, so I go to church. I felt really bad. I believe in Jesus Christ and everything, but I believe that I didn't choose that lifestyle.

Religious institutions wield huge influence on social norms, consequently affecting the attitudes, feelings and behaviours of those living in Guyana. Once religious leaders and institutions in the country decide on an issue, it is highly probable that the rest of society will follow the decision. Karen De Souza,[15] an activist from a local women's advocacy organisation, indicated that in Guyana:

> The church, for me, creates that schism in terms of people's public expressions and private expressions. I don't know how you get past that, and this is why the role of government is so critical, because, the reality is, if the law is passed, then you do the public education after the law is passed. You don't want to pass the law, so you pretend to be consulting with people, and the law never gets passed, and nothing ever moves forward, and that's a really sad situation.

She continued that religious groups do not take a reasonable position, in that:

> [they make] convenient use of their religious books. So there are some sections that you will interpret literally, and some sections that you will not interpret literally. But the thing is that the population of Guyana is a church-going population. And in many ways, the contradiction is, I would say, that the majority of the population would … have no issue at all with passing the laws and so forth, but they don't want to talk about it. You know? Let people live, let be.

The individuals interviewed came from groups with diverse religious affiliations, class, race, location and SOGIE. When asked whether these factors affect how LGBT persons are treated, many noted that an LGBT person's social class affects the privileges they have in society and the level of violence visited upon them. To some extent, access to resources dictates how a person is treated, in terms of the quality of justice and opportunities granted.

The following three respondents spoke of how class affects the violence that LGBT persons face:

> To some extent definitely, I have a colleague, a gay man who … I remember him saying to me 'Col, I am professional, and people at my workplace know of my sexuality, but I am not disrespected'.[16]

> According to your class, I say persons who are at the higher class in society may have the privilege because they have their families who are educated sometimes because of the fact that they have money and they're rich. They buy themselves out of situations … Or the fact that they're rich, nobody can do them anything. But if you are poor, if you

---

15 Interviewed on 5 Oct. 2012 by Namela Baynes Henry, SASOD and Envisioning.
16 Colleen McEwan interviewed on 27 Nov. 2012 by Namela Baynes Henry, as above.

are living in a lower class in the economic crisis that we're in, you're definitely going to be stigmatised, people are going to talk and do things and even try to harm you.[17]

I am very concerned about many other persons who don't have financial means … Yes, I believe that maybe if I was from an affluent family, actions would have been taken. I called the police almost every day, and it felt like I was villain rather than victim of gay bashing; because I have to be calling them. And up to this day, nothing happen. I think police tend to take action depending upon if you are affluent. I am not certain. Definitely once you have position in society you get more attention, and they want to ensure that you get justice. But being a gay person, not an affluent person, it's not of importance.[18]

Akin to the basis of class, many interviewees expressed that the level of violence an LGBT person experiences may vary according to their race and location. There are several ethnic groups from diverse backgrounds in Guyana. Drawing from interviews conducted in rural and urban locations, it is possible to highlight nuances of stigma and discrimination. Three interviewees spoke of how race and social location affect the stigma LGBT persons experience:

In Guyana … being a black person is the most difficult thing in your life. Because you are black, you have to be a man, you have to be masculine, you have to mature. You can't be a black and a gay. That is like a sin or scorn … You're supposed to do this, you should do farming. Farming is not for me. I tried it before. I can't do simple tasks involved in farming. It was too hard. So being a black person in Guyana is very difficult for gays, especially if you are criticised by everybody else.[19]

At the hospital, I don't … for me, I don't think it's with the ethnicity. I think it's with the sexuality at the hospital. Because you gay, you gotta be last.[20]

I know personally an Indian man, he can go anywhere in the black community. I am black man and I am not welcome in my community, and he [the Indian] is welcomed in the black community. He has money, he is comfortable, but I can't.[21]

Moreover, although all LGBT persons stand to be affected by stigma and discrimination, there can be differences and nuances based on whether they are gay, lesbian, bisexual or trans, as well as the extent to which they conform to norms of femininity and/or masculinity on the sexuality spectrum. Given the intersection of gender-based oppression and sexual orientation, violence

17 AnonymousA interviewed on 30 Oct. 2012 by Namela Baynes Henry, as above.
18 Selina Maria Perez, interviewed on 15 Oct. 2012 by Namela Baynes Henry, as above.
19 Alex Fraser interviewed on 28 Nov. 2012 by Namela Baynes Henry, as above.
20 Group interview with Ram Paul and Yadunauth Singh on 9 Oct. 2012 conducted by Namela Baynes Henry, as above.
21 Eon Wilson interviewed on 5 Dec. 2012 by Namela Baynes Henry, as above.

against lesbians may be less understood or documented. For instance, it can be hidden in the private domestic realm and less obvious in the street/public realm.

These excerpts illustrate that not everyone who identifies as LGBT has the same experiences of violence and that social status can affect the degree of violence and how it occurs.

Human rights and the impact of violence on LGBT identities

The challenges faced from their early years by individuals identifying as LGBT and the impact violence has on them are highlighted by this respondent: 'Growing up being homosexual was very, very, very difficult. All the abuse, all the trauma, all the hurt – physically, emotionally – that I went through I don't think we should be, anyone should be, going through that.[22] As religious groups normalise homophobia, people who identify as LGBT are denied their rights to live with dignity, free from violence, stigma and discrimination. Violence – direct, structural and cultural – against such individuals perpetuates their exploitation and dehumanisation. Death, mental illness, a life of secrecy – these are among the challenges faced by LGBT persons living in Guyana.

Individuals identifying as LGBT, regardless of sexuality, race, class, citizenship or gender, are unlikely to receive treatment for traumatic experiences, because no formal systems are in place to provide support. Interviewees reported that homophobia, stigma and discrimination against them have affected their income, in the sense that they were not able to keep a job, and not having a job blocked their access to state benefits such as insurance. Other impacts include limited access to high-quality healthcare and social services – such as education, employment, housing and security – and inadequate responses to mental health issues, resulting in poor coping skills, which can lead to suicides, suicide attempts, use of illegal drugs and depression.

Furthermore, many interviewees reported that homophobia has affected their schooling and housing. As a result of constant bullying at school and being rejected by the family, they dropped out of school and left home. In many cases these actions resulted in homelessness. Additionally, access to information about sexual reproductive health became less accessible, and they got involved in risky sexual behaviour, which increased their chances of contracting HIV/AIDS and other sexually transmitted diseases. Because they have to live a life of secrecy, the ability of many LGBT people to maintain long and healthy relationships is adversely affected, resulting in increased stress levels, decreased social involvement, and deteriorating mental and physical health. Finally, many of the interviewees indicated they would like to migrate or seek asylum in other countries such as the United States or Canada rather than stay in Guyana to champion LGBT causes.

22 AnonymousB, interviewed on 31 Oct. 2012 by Namela Baynes Henry, as above.

Development and the way forward for persons who identify as LGBT

This chapter does not merely protest the conditions LGBT persons are living under, but also advocates for their human rights to be respected and protected. When the government, policymakers, religious groups and citizens speak about development, it is in terms of processes 'of expanding the freedoms that people enjoy' (Iles, 2001, p.1). Amartya Sen indicated that 'development requires the removing of major sources of unfreedom: poverty as well as tyranny, poor economic opportunities as well as social deprivation, neglect of public facilities as well as intolerance. The world has unprecedented opulence and yet denies freedoms to vast numbers of people' (ibid.).

What is it like to speak of social mobility, development, betterment and individual self-actualisation when a percentage of the population is living unfree? Who will answer this question? Who can we/they turn to? The people themselves are the source of this knowledge. Persons who identify as LGBT and representatives of organisations who witness stigma and discrimination in Guyana are equipped to identify what can be or should be done to facilitate development for LGBT persons. When asked what should be done to change the violent landscape Guyanese LGBT people are living in, interviewees made three recommendations:

1. Respect individuals' human rights and repeal buggery laws and the cross-dressing law:

> We need to look at our laws, we need to repeal our buggery laws ...
> At present we have in our High Court the matter of the cross-dressing
> law. We need to address that our laws should be there to protect us, our
> laws should be there to create employment for us, our laws should be
> there to give us the opportunities, whether it's a secular environment,
> whether it's our choices of employment. Our laws should be there to
> protect us in the health sector, our laws should be there to protect us
> when we go on recreations, our laws should be there to protect us in
> terms of giving us pre-retirement, a retirement package, whatever![23]

This recommendation to repeal laws discriminating against LGBT persons was the one that most respondents put first. Such legislative reforms could then also effect systemic change. For instance, employment and housing policies would be adapted so that LGBT people could become visible and be given equal job and housing opportunities; healthcare practice would change for the better if services became more accessible; and school curricula would be modified to reflect diverse SOGIE. Changed laws can also translate into altered societal and cultural views, which could potentially expand the discourse on gender and sexuality in Guyana.

---

23 Cracey Annatola Fernandes interviewed on 7 Oct. 2012 by Namela Baynes Henry, as above.

2. Increase social safety networks. Interviewees are here referring to safe spaces that provide LGBT persons with a place (tangible or intangible) to 'relax and be able to fully express, without fear of being made to feel uncomfortable, unwelcome, or unsafe on account of biological sex, race/ethnicity, sexual orientation, gender identity or expression, cultural background, religious affiliation, age, or physical or mental ability'.[24] Safe spaces in Guyana, according to some interviewees, allow them to recover from traumatic experiences resulting from homophobia and/or transphobia. Organisations and individuals work together to provide training for LGBT individuals and social service agencies, host pageants and parties, and advocate on behalf of the rights of LGBT persons at the local, national, regional or international level:

> Our social networking also comes through ERT [Equal Rights Trust]. We have been liaising with SASOD, GUYBOW [Guyana Rainbow Coalition], the Caribbean Sex-Workers Coalition, United Nations, USAIDS ... UNFPA [United Nations Population Fund] as a matter of fact with UNAIDS as a whole. We have been liaising with GNSWP [Global Network of Sex Work Projects], we have been liaising with Women of Worth in Grenada, we have been doing work with persons in Suriname, we have been doing work across the Caribbean ... We are also doing work with the US Embassy, in terms of trafficking persons, the Human Services and Social Security, which is a ministry within our country here. And we also are doing work with organizations such as Help and Shelter, GUYBOW, and the Red Thread organization we would normally collaborate with.[25]

3. Increase political activism for the rights of LGBT persons. Many of the respondents claimed that deaths of LGBT persons often went unsolved *because* they were either transgender sex workers and/or gay men. If political activism increases, then more people – especially LGBT persons – will become watchdogs over the government, parliamentary processes and any activities that are pro-heterosexuality and anti-homosexuality. One action the Guyanan government can take is to have continuous conversations or consultations with LGBT communities as they plan, implement and evaluate national development goals. In this way, LGBT people are included and involved in the governance of their wellbeing and development. Furthermore, processes for accessing and implementing justice to combat direct and structural violence can be monitored on a closer basis.

24 See 'What is a safe space?' on the Safe Space Network website at: http://safespacenetwork.tumblr.com/Safespace (accessed 12 Mar. 2018).
25 Cracey Annatola Fernandes interviewed on 7 Oct. 2012 by Namela Baynes Henry, as above.

Conclusion

This chapter has provided an overview of the violence LGBT people experience in Guyana and shown what measures should be taken to make their lives safe, supported and visible while upholding their right to dignity. The violence they encounter is rooted in the colonial legislation the country still enforces, a legacy that is backed up by religious beliefs and laws. Consideration and deconstruction of direct, structural and cultural violence – and not heteronormative concepts – need to determine the way in which laws are created and transformed. Laws should be based on protection of their citizens, not on the moral policing that emerges from religion or other cultural factors. The laws that govern the country's citizens who identify as, or are perceived as, LGBT are inconsistent with international human rights conventions, and with the fundamental goal of the Constitution of Guyana. These laws are at the root of inequalities in Guyana. This chapter argues that legal structures influence cultural behaviours. Anti-LGBT sentiment that is expressed culturally is rooted in the law. Guyana's laws against cross-dressing and same-sex relations create a system of structural violence, which is linked to cultural and direct violence. These laws thus embody systematic violence against a group of people and need to be changed in order to bring it to an end.

When seeking to eliminate structural violence, methods that centre on the lived experiences of LGBT people must be used. Methodologically speaking, using the interview as a tool to collect data illustrates the importance of people's narratives, which should be believed and respected (Koirala-Azad and Fuentes, 2009–10, pp. 1–3). Narratives of self-identity should be regarded as legitimate, just as the expression of self should be regarded as a fundamental right. The kind of violence that the interviewees referenced here have experienced should be taken seriously, and steps must be taken to change the structures that have created this heterosexist system. Taking a qualitative participatory approach to documentation and consultation enhances forward movement. Change can take place only when citizens and government commit to eliminating structural violence, and if the narratives of those that it affects are used as a baseline for enacting such change.

References

Bobichand, R. (2012) 'Understanding violence triangle and structural violence', *Kangla Online*, 30 Jul., available at: http://kanglaonline. com/2012/07/understanding-violence-triangle-and-structural-violence-by-rajkumar-bobichand/ (accessed 12 Mar. 2018).

Galtung, J. (1990) 'Cultural violence', *Journal of Peace Research*, 27 (3): 291–305.

Glickhouse, R. and M. Keller (2012) 'Explainer: LGBT rights in Latin America and the Caribbean', *Americas Society/Council of the Americas*,

24 May, available at: www.as-coa.org/articles/explainer-lgbt-rights-latin-america-and-caribbean (accessed 12 Mar. 2018).

Guyana Association of Women Lawyers (2011) 'Constitution of Guyana' booklet, available at: www.guyanaassociationofwomenlawyersonline.org/GAWL/images/pdf/constitutionofguyana.pdf (accessed 10 Sep. 2017).

Harvard Divinity School (2016) 'Typologies of violence and peace', Religious Literacy Project, available at: http://rlp.hds.harvard.edu/typologies-violence-and-peace (accessed 12 Mar. 2018).

Heilbroner, R. (1992) *Twenty-first Century Capitalism* (Toronto, ON: House of Anansi Press).

Iles, V. (2001) Summary of Amartya Sen's *Development as Freedom*, available at: www.reallylearning.com/wp-content/uploads/2013/09/development-as-freedom1.pdf (accessed 12 Mar. 2018).

Jones, S. (2013) '76 countries where anti-gay laws are as bad as or worse than Russia's', available at: https://www.buzzfeed.com/saeedjones/76-countries-where-anti-gay-laws-are-as-bad-as-or-worse-than?utm_term=.vva14VMPr#.bcBaLXEWP (accessed 12 Mar. 2018).

Kissoon, V. (2013) 'From madness to mainstream – "Gay rights" in Guyana, Part I', *Stabroek News*, 24 Jun., available at: www.stabroeknews.com/2013/features/06/24/from-madness-to-mainstream-gay-rights-in-guyana-part-i/ (accessed 12 Mar. 2018).

Koirala-Azad, S. and E. Fuentes (2009–10) 'Introduction. Activist scholarship – possibilities and constraints of participatory action research', *Social Justice*, 36 (4): 1–5.

Michaelson, J., S. Abdallah, N. Steuer, S. Thompson and N. Marks (2009) 'National accounts of well-being: bringing real wealth onto the balance sheet', New Economics Foundation (nef), available at: www.nationalaccountsofwellbeing.org/public-data/files/national-accounts-of-well-being-report.pdf (accessed 12 Mar. 2018).

Society Against Sexual Orientation Discrimination (SASOD) Guyana (2014) 'On Devil's Island: a UPR submission on LGBT human rights in Guyana', Sexual Rights Initiatives, available at: www.sasod.org.gy/sites/default/files/resources/SASOD_SRI_UPR_Guyana_July2014FINAL3.pdf (accessed 12 Mar. 2018).

Documentary films

Sade's Story (2013) dir. N.B. Henry and U. Verbeek (Guyana and Canada: Society Against Sexual Orientation Discrimination and Envisioning Global LGBT Human Rights), available at: http://envisioninglgbtourwork.blogspot.com/p/caribbean.html (accessed 12 Mar. 2018).

Selina's Voice (2013) dir. N.B. Henry and U. Verbeek (Guyana and Canada: Society Against Sexual Orientation Discrimination and Envisioning Global LGBT Human Rights), available at: http:// envisioninglgbtourwork.blogspot.com/p/caribbean.html (accessed 12 Mar. 2018)

Telling Our Stories (Guyana Portraits section) (2014) (Guyana and Canada: Society Against Sexual Orientation Discrimination and Envisioning Global LGBT Human Rights), available at: http://envisioning-tellingourstories.blogspot.com (accessed 12 Mar. 2018). Extracts are cited from interviews with: Melinda Jankie, Selina Maria Perez and Cracey Annatola Fernandes.

6

Cultural discourse in Africa and the promise of human rights based on non-normative sexuality and/or gender expression: exploring the intersections, challenges and opportunities

Monica Mbaru, Monica Tabengwa and Kim Vance

Culture is generally understood to mean the ways that societies conduct and express themselves in time and space. Cultural literacy is created through the understanding of different factors such as history, language, rituals, traditions, music and art, and dress code of different groups. Culture is not static but is constantly influenced by shifting environment, and socioeconomic and political conditions. It has different manifestations, which are influenced by race, ethnicity, age, class and – for the purposes of this chapter – sexual orientation and gender identity (SOGI).

Same-sex sexuality and gender diversity have existed in African cultures for centuries. It is promising that many books and articles have begun to document this reality. For example, Ugandan academic and human rights activist Dr Sylvia Tamale discusses a practice among the Shangani of Southern Africa where men married other men, noting that this was part of their culture and everyday life known as *ngochani* [male wife].[1] Other examples she cites include woman-to-woman marriages among the Kisii in Kenya, among the Igbo in Nigeria, and the Nuer in Sudan.

There is also proof in many African languages that sexual and gender diversity has been known to exist in various African cultures, even if that language strongly suggests social disapproval or stigma. Nevertheless, some gay rights activists in recent years have adopted them to describe themselves with a touch of pride. They say the mere fact that such words exist in African languages is proof that people like them have always been known in traditional culture (Gays and Lesbians of Zimbabwe, 2008).

---

1   Interviewed on 20 Nov. 2014 by Richard Lusimbo, SMUG and Envisioning. An excerpt is included in the documentary *And Still We Rise* (2015).

M. Mbaru, M. Tabengwa and K. Vance (2018) 'Cultural discourse in Africa and the promise of human rights based on non-normative sexuality and/or gender expression', in N. Nicol et al. (eds.) *Envisioning Global LGBT Human Rights: (Neo)colonialism, Neoliberalism, Resistance and Hope* (London: Human Rights Consortium, Institute of Commonwealth Studies), pp. 177–204.

It is also promising that almost all African constitutions have a bill of rights that defines fundamental human rights as universal. However, none of them, with the exception of South Africa, mention SOGI as a protected ground for non-discrimination. Nevertheless, even as South Africa is about to mark the 20th anniversary of the world's first constitution to include specific wording which will protect people from discrimination on the grounds of sexual orientation, the reality on the streets for lesbian, gay, bisexual, transgender (LGBT) people differs from what the legal framework would suggest. Human rights abuses on the basis of SOGI occur daily, including reported cases of lesbian, bisexual and transgender women being murdered, raped and subjected to violence. Furthermore, in the regional and international arena, South Africa has failed to demonstrate consistent and reliable leadership in human rights for LGBT persons.

The absence of specificity in constitutional frameworks has been deliberately used by powerful religious and traditional fundamentalists to generate and perpetuate a cultural discourse that non-normative gender expressions or sexualities are 'foreign'. For instance, organisations working on LGBT rights in these countries have been denied registration on the grounds that they will be promoting an illegal activity that is considered to be 'un-African' and against African culture and tradition (Tamale, 2014).

It is no wonder then, as many reports have suggested, that sexuality and gender have become a cultural and religious battleground in Africa, being fought at the national, regional and international level. This is a common thread that emerges in the Human Rights Watch (HRW) report (2009), 'Together, apart: organizing around sexual orientation and gender identity worldwide':

> Culture – a supposedly monolithic realm of civilizational values – becomes the zone where political rhetoric and religious intolerance combine. Sexual or gender nonconformity is painted as 'un-African', its agents symbolically – and actually – expelled from the community.
> (p. 11)

Same-sex sexual acts are outlawed in some 32 African countries (Carroll and Mendos, 2017), and the majority of these countries have maintained laws inherited from their colonial histories. Many legal scholars and authors have traced the legacy of the current criminal sanctions in many African countries to their colonial roots. Despite the fact that England and Wales decriminalised most consensual homosexual conduct in 1967, this came too late for most of Britain's colonies, many of which won independence in the 1950s and 1960s. Therefore, they won these victories with colonial sodomy laws still in place (Gupta, 2008).

Despite this colonial history and the desire of many African nations to shed these legacies, many leaders invoke the values contained in these outdated and discriminatory laws as 'traditionally African':

> Yet the wealth of data that is available clearly demonstrates that the homophobia of such African presidents as Moi (Kenya), Mugabe (Zimbabwe) and Nujoma (Namibia) who maintain that 'homosexuality is a western perversion, alien to Africans', is not based on African culture and history. In fact, homophobia is an idea introduced by missionaries and colonial administrators (Kendall 1999; Wieringa 2002) and copied by post-colonial leaders. (Morgan and Wieringa, 2005, p. 281)

While positive aspects of diverse cultural and historical backgrounds could contribute to the promotion and protection of human rights and human dignity, culture and traditions comprise a mixed set of views and practices that are often used to legitimise human rights violations. Africa is vast and diverse, composed of many different societies and cultures. And yet, in more recent years, African religious and traditional fundamentalists have come together to defend a shared goal, even building the most unlikely alliances. For example, Christian and Islamic fundamentalists, and traditionalists have formed unions to defend nationalism, religion and so-called traditional values. They see the claim of human rights to universalism, women's reproductive freedom and SOGI rights as a direct attack on the traditional values, cultures and religious beliefs of the majority of the people: 'Fundamentalisms weave together elements from religion, nationalism, and other ideologies and traditions to invent a cultural authenticity that is fixed, unalterable, and monolithic – but threatened by the supposedly corrosive influences of human rights' (HRW, 2009, p. 3).

The protection of traditional values and culture has become a rallying cry in almost all human rights discourses among African states, from national dialogues and parliaments, to the African Commission on Human and Peoples' Rights (ACHPR). Within international spaces, such as the United Nations (UN), African states commonly share and maintain a group position. Even though the common 'values of humankind' are underpinned in national, regional and international human rights law, cultural practices and traditional values that are inconsistent with human rights are frequently invoked to justify human rights violations. This chapter will discuss examples of where the actions of these political bodies contribute to a cultural dialogue in which LGBT Africans are relegated to a social class that operates outside of what it means to be 'African' (and in some cases, 'human'), and therefore deems them ineligible for the protections of international, regional and national institutions.

Alliances with other civil society movements to fight this culture war have not been easy. Although these alliances have been particularly effective in regions such as Latin America, in Africa, even among the mainstream women's movement, there has been some hesitation, if not outright hostility. For example, when South Africa hosted the 2008 Association for Women's Rights in Development (AWID) conference, a panel hosted by the Coalition of African Lesbians (CAL) became the site of a religious and cultural battle, even among feminist allies.

Also, in Latin America, as opposed to Africa, religious forces have not generally aligned themselves with secular, cultural nationalism to create a complex dynamic of cultural authenticity. Secular groups in Latin America that claim to advance cultural rights and the preservation of tradition do not necessarily align themselves with religious forces like the Catholic Church, for example, to attempt to create a monolithic ideology of what it means to be an authentic 'Latin American'. These practices are more common in Africa, where alliances attempt to promote authenticity of what it means to be 'African'. Anyone outside of that scheme, therefore, gets labelled as 'un-African'. This difference in reality may mean that some of the best practices utilised by civil society in Latin America have limited applicability in Africa.

Nevertheless, not all public and political discourses on LGBT rights at the international, regional and national levels are monolithic. The visibility of African scholars, activists and human rights defenders has greatly contributed to dispelling the perception that non-normative gender expression and/or same-sex behaviour is 'un-African'. Powerful religious and state actors have also contributed positively to the discussion and taken concrete action that will broaden the discourse and affect the daily lives of African LGBT citizens. This chapter will also highlight some of those progressive measures at all levels.

The UN framework

The promotion and protection of universally recognised human rights constitutes one of the fundamental pillars of the UN's work. International standards have been affirmed by UN member states in carefully negotiated instruments such as the Universal Declaration of Human Rights, the Millennium Declaration and the World Summit Outcome. Additional instruments and a number of resolutions and declarations recognise the following key principles:

- while cultural, traditional and regional specificities must be borne in mind, states have an obligation to promote and protect all human rights and fundamental freedoms, regardless of their political, economic and cultural systems (UN General Assembly (UNGA), 1993).[2]

---

2   UNGA, 1993, Vienna Declaration and Programme of Action, A/CONF.157/23, World Conference on Human Rights, 12 Jul., available at: www.refworld.org/docid/3ae6b39ec.html (accessed 12 Dec. 2017). The Vienna Declaration and Programme of Action (VDPA) states: 'All human rights are universal, indivisible and interdependent and interrelated . . . While the significance of national and regional particularities and various historical, cultural and religious backgrounds must be borne in mind, it is the duty of States, regardless of their political, economic and cultural systems, to promote and protect all human rights and fundamental freedoms' (para. 5).

- tradition and culture may not be invoked to violate human rights nor to limit their scope (UN Human Rights Council (UNHRC), 2009).[3]
- states have a positive obligation to work towards the elimination of harmful traditional or cultural beliefs, values, stereotypes or practices that are inconsistent with human rights (UNGA, 1993).[4]

Inserting undefined concepts of 'tradition' into this framework risks upsetting the careful balance found in existing instruments and subordinating the universality of human rights to cultural relativism. Following are some recent examples of activity at the UN level on concepts of tradition and culture in relation to SOGI. These examples are not meant to be exhaustive, but rather to provide readers with a flavour of the activity and discourse happening in some UN spaces, with a focus on the African region.

Developments at the Human Rights Council (HRC)

The HRC, located in Geneva, is 'responsible for promoting universal respect of all human rights and fundamental freedoms for all, without distinction of any kind and in a fair and equal manner'.[5] This body has made some significant progress on SOGI issues in recent years.

In June 2011, South Africa tabled a resolution at the HRC that expressed 'grave concern at acts of violence and discrimination, in all regions of the world, committed against individuals because of their sexual orientation and gender identity'.[6] This historic resolution was the first passed in the HRC explicitly on these issues. Only one African country (Mauritius), out of the 13 who were at that time council members, supported it (South Africa was not a voting member then).[7]

3   UNHRC Resolution 10/23, independent expert in the field of cultural rights, A_HRC_RES_10_23' 43rd meeting', 26 Mar. 2009, available at: http://ap.ohchr. org/documents/E/HRC/resolutions/A_HRC_RES_10_23.pdf (accessed 12 Dec. 2017). It affirms: 'No one may invoke cultural diversity to infringe upon human rights guaranteed by international law, nor to limit their scope' (para. 4).
4   The VDPA also calls upon states to work towards the elimination of 'the harmful effects of certain traditional or customary practices, cultural prejudices and religious extremism' (para. 38).
5   UNHRC, Resolution adopted by the General Assembly [without reference to a Main Committee (A/60/L.48)] 60/251 Human Rights Council, 3 Apr. 2006, available at: www.refworld.org/docid/4537814814.html (accessed 12 Dec. 2017).
6   UNHRC, 'Human rights, sexual orientation and gender identity', HRC 17th session, 17 Jun. 2011, available at: www.ohchr.org/EN/Issues/Discrimination/ Pages/LGBTUNResolutions.aspx (accessed 24 May 2018).
7   To read about the journey and development of this resolution, please consult ARC International, 17th session of the HRC, available at: http://arc-international.net/ global-advocacy/human-rights-council/hrc17/ (accessed 11 Dec. 2017).

Despite a well-articulated – though unsuccessful – process outlined by South Africa for follow-up to the 2011 SOGI resolution, it was another three years before this resolution came before the council again.[8] This time, the leadership had shifted to Latin America. Another successful vote took place, which garnered more support than in 2011 and from a wider diversity of regions. Unfortunately, only one voting member from Africa (out of a possible 12) supported it. This time South Africa, which now had council membership, used their vote to back it. Disappointingly, however, they were able to leverage a weakening of the resolution's proposed language before the vote.

Two years later in September 2016, the HRC appointed Professor Vitit Muntarbhorn as the first UN independent expert on SOGI. This followed the successful adoption of the HRC's Resolution 32/2 in June of 2016.[9]

The fight for the establishment of the independent expert on SOGI was uniquely difficult, spanning over five key votes in 2016. South Africa had a key vote on this resolution and regressed in its position from sponsoring the SOGI resolution in 2011 and voting in favour of the next resolution in 2014, to abstaining on the vote at the HRC in 2016.

Other African states such as Botswana, Namibia and Ghana also abstained, but these can be viewed more positively because none of these countries has a domestic constitutional or policy framework that is unequivocally supportive of SOGI issues. It was interesting to note that in spite of not having a specific constitutional provision on SOGI, all three countries referenced the framework of universal human rights as constitutionally prohibiting discrimination. Ghana went one step further and also referenced the 2014 resolution at the ACHPR.[10]

At around the same time as these explicit gains were being made around SOGI, new initiatives on 'traditional values' and 'protection of the family' were also gaining traction within the HRC – despite massive criticism from a range of countries, civil society representatives, and critical input from UN special rapporteurs and other human rights mandate holders and treaty bodies.

---

8   UNHRC 'Human rights, sexual orientation and gender identity', HRC 27th session, 26 Sept. 2014, available at: http://www.ohchr.org/EN/Issues/Discrimination/Pages/LGBTUNResolutions.aspx (accessed 24 May 2018).

9   HRC, Resolution 32/2, Protection Against Violence and Discrimination based on Sexual Orientation and Gender Identity, 32nd session, Agenda item 3, adopted 30 Jun. 2016, see www.ohchr.org/EN/Issues/Discrimination/Pages/LGBTUNResolutions.aspx (accessed 24 May 2018).

10 ACHPR, Resolution 275: Resolution on Protection against Violence and Other Human Rights Violations against Persons on the Basis of Their Real or Imputed Sexual Orientation or Gender Identity, 55th ordinary session in Luanda, Angola, 28 Apr.–12 May 2014, available at: www.achpr.org/sessions/55th/resolutions/275 (accessed 24 Jul. 2017).

The goal of the states proposing and supporting these initiatives was clearly to establish new norms of international law that would undermine the principle of universality of human rights and result in a misleading interpretation of human rights norms.

In 2012, during the HRC's vote on a resolution on so-called 'traditional values', 25 states voted in favour, 15 against, while 7 abstained. Russia, who led this initiative, gathered substantial support, including from many African countries. Significantly, these initiatives fail to acknowledge the positive obligation of states to eliminate traditional attitudes, values and practices that are inconsistent with human rights, as required by the Convention on the Elimination of All Forms of Discrimination against Women (CEDAW) 1979, and the Protocol to the African Charter on Human and Peoples' Rights on the Rights of Women in Africa in 2003 (from here on referred to as African Women's Protocol).

In June 2014, despite the efforts of civil society and supportive states, the Human Rights Council also adopted a harmful resolution on 'protection of the family'.[11] Led by Egypt, the resolution failed to acknowledge violations that occur within family structures, and did not include agreed language on diverse family forms. During the voting stage the council shamefully voted to censor a discussion on whether to include this language.[12] As recently as 2017, this resolution still failed to recognise that various forms of family exist and also stated that 'the family plays a crucial role in the preservation of cultural identity, traditions, morals, heritage and the values system of society' (para. 11), without recognising that families can perpetuate discriminatory and harmful values and traditions.[13]

11 UNHRC, 'Protection of the family', HRC 26th session, 25 Jun. 2014, available at: http://ap.ohchr.org/documents/dpage_e.aspx?si=A/HRC/26/L.20/Rev.1   (accessed 24 May 2018).

12 The resolution was widely viewed by a number of states and NGOs as an initiative to preemptively respond to a potential follow-up SOGI resolution in either the June or September Council session. States like the United Kingdom, member states of the European Union, Chile, Argentina and others voted against the resolution, indicating that the HRC did not recognise diverse family forms or address violations that occur within family units, and therefore failed to uphold human rights principles. Shockingly, Russia called a 'no-action motion' in relation to an amendment to insert this type of language, a tool that had been used only twice before in the HRC, and which censors any possible discussion of the issue whatsoever.

13 UNHRC, 'Protection of the family: role of the family in supporting the protection and promotion of human rights of older persons', HRC, 35th session, 19 Jun. 2017, available at: http://ap.ohchr.org/documents/dpage_e.aspx?si=A/HRC/35/L.21 (accessed 24 May 2018).

Developments at the General Assembly (GA)

The GA, located in New York, is the UN's main deliberative, policymaking and representative organ. Comprising all 193 UN members, it provides a unique forum for multilateral discussion of the full spectrum of international issues covered by the UN Charter, including human rights.

In 2008, signifying a powerful victory for the principles of the Universal Declaration of Human Rights, 66 nations at the UNGA supported a groundbreaking statement confirming that international human rights protections include SOGI. It was the first time that a statement condemning rights abuses against LGBT people had been presented to the GA. It drew unprecedented support from five continents, including six African nations (ARC International, 2008). To many human rights advocates, this statement signified a hopeful shift in UN politics, specifically within the African group.

Nevertheless, two years later, in 2010, the GA was in the spotlight because of a crucial resolution on extrajudicial executions and other unlawful killings (from here on referred to as EJE resolution). Since 2003, this resolution had urged states 'to investigate promptly and thoroughly all killings, including . . . all killings committed for any discriminatory reason, including sexual orientation' (p. 2).[14] It was the first UN resolution ever to include an explicit reference to sexual orientation.

However, later that year on behalf of the African group, Benin sponsored an amendment to delete the reference to sexual orientation in this resolution. Shockingly, this amendment passed. Disappointingly, not one African nation voted to maintain the reference, not even the handful of African states that had signed on to the joint statement at the general assembly in 2008.

This reversal sparked a huge outcry around the world from governments and civil society. The Associated Press commented that 'the battle underscores the divide between U.N. members with their diverse religious and cultural sensibilities on gay rights issues and sparked something of a culture war at the international body' (2010).

On 21 December 2010, the UNGA voted 93–55 to reintroduce the sexual orientation language into the EJE resolution, marking a gain of 23 states in favour. Several swing states indicated a change from their votes a month earlier. One, South Africa, stated that they were 'guided by our Constitution that guarantees the right to life' and that 'no killing of human beings can be justified whatsoever' (International Gay and Lesbian Human Rights Commission (IGLHRC), 2010).

---

14 Resolution adopted by the General Assembly [on the report of the Third Committee (A/57/566/Add.2 and Corr.1-3)] 57/214. Extrajudicial, summary or arbitrary executions, 25 Feb. 2003, available at: www.un.org/en/ga/search/view_doc.asp?symbol=A/RES/57/214 (accessed 14 Sep. 2017).

Although several countries claimed a lack of definition of sexual orientation in international law as a reason for their opposition, countries such as Rwanda firmly rejected this as follows:

> Take my word, a human group need not be legally defined to be the victim of executions and massacres as those that target their members have [already] previously defined [them]. Rwanda has also had this bitter experience sixteen years ago. It is for this that the Delegation of Rwanda will vote for this amendment and calls on other delegations to do likewise. (ibid.)

Unfortunately in 2014, four years after that compelling speech, Rwanda could not be counted on to support the addition of gender identity to this same resolution. During that landmark vote for the trans community, only two African countries supported the expanded language of SOGI, South Africa and Mauritius.

More recently (2016), the African Group led an unprecedented initiative in the GA's 71st session, which attempted to challenge the independent expert mandate on SOGI, established by the HRC earlier in the year. In what is generally perceived as a procedural formality, the GA usually endorses the HRC report. During this GA session, Botswana, who abstained on the vote on the independent expert at the HRC, led the charge on behalf of the African Group to disrupt this formality. The reason for the African position was not phrased in terms of 'African values' or sensitivities but mainly in procedural terms.

Of major significance was South Africa's shift in position in just a matter of months. In the HRC, not only did South Africa abstain but also delivered a statement expressing its opposition to the initiative to establish an independent expert. Months later in the GA, South Africa supported the appointment of the independent expert, and its statement was perhaps one of the most important and powerful to be delivered in the GA's Third Committee. Rwanda, Cabo Verde and Seychelles also joined South Africa in dissenting from the African Group's efforts to derail the mandate of the independent expert on SOGI.

UN Economic and Social Council (ECOSOC) accreditation

LGBT groups began seeking official consultative status with the UN in 1993. Official consultative status is granted by the UN ECOSOC, after reviewing recommendations from its subsidiary body – the Committee on Non-Governmental Organizations (NGOs). This status enables groups to deliver oral and written statements, and attend and organise events, on UN premises.

At the time of writing, no African LGBT groups have UN ECOSOC accreditation. In 2006, Gays and Lesbians of Zimbabwe (GALZ) applied for status but ultimately did not pursue their application. Concerns about igniting African opposition within the ECOSOC were part of the decision to withdraw the GALZ application, especially as it was early days in a campaign encouraging LGBT NGOs to seek accreditation.

The NGO Committee, in particular, has been a fierce battleground for LGBT groups. It wasn't until 2008 that an LGBT group achieved accreditation without deferral and initial rejection by the NGO Committee, often led by or at least with the support of the committee's African members. Both the International Lesbian, Gay, Bisexual, Trans and Intersex Association (ILGA) and OutRight Action International have been granted ECOSOC status and, although based in Europe and the United States, these accredited LGBT organisations both have regional offices in Africa.

The African framework

The legal systems of sub-Saharan African states only exceptionally provide for specific protection of sexual minorities. The South African Constitution of 1996, which guarantees non-discrimination on the basis of sexual orientation, has set the tone for far-reaching legal reforms in that country. More recently, Benin, Madagascar, Mauritius and Mozambique have also adopted laws providing explicit protection on the basis of sexual orientation. Besides any specific form of protection, sexual minorities remain entitled to all constitutional rights and are able to invoke the protection of the law. A majority of states still criminalise consensual same-sex activities between adults based on criminal codes inherited from colonial times.

The African Charter on Human and Peoples' Rights (usually referred to as the African Charter)[15] is the treaty responsible for promotion and protection of human rights and freedoms in Africa. It provides rights defenders with values that can be used to advance efforts to strengthen the HRC. Significantly, the African Charter was ratified by 53 of the 54 members of the African Union (AU) – South Sudan being the exception. This almost universal ratification by AU member states makes the Charter an important tool for the development of human rights values and protection mechanisms. In particular, it has provided a clear opportunity for NGOs and rights defenders working on minority rights to engage and organise.

Article 28 is the bedrock of the Charter's commitment to respect for diversity. It states: 'Every individual shall have the duty to respect and consider his fellow beings without discrimination and to maintain relations aimed at promoting, safeguarding and reinforcing mutual respect and tolerance'.

It is important to be mindful that tradition and culture, and other social and value systems, have frequently been organised to restrict human rights, especially women's sexual and reproductive health rights – in particular, female genital cutting and marital rape. In these circumstances, claims for cultural diversity often challenge the very idea of human rights by asserting the privilege

15 ACHPR (1981) African Charter on Human and Peoples' Rights. Adopted 27 Jun. 1981 OAU Doc. CAB/LEG/67/3rev.5211.LM.58 (1982), entered into force 21 Oct. 1986, available at: www.achpr.org/instruments/achpr (accessed 25 Jul. 2017)·

of culture or national sovereignty over recognition of each person as human. We must therefore be willing to engage in critical discussions around cultural diversity without allowing such discussions to detract from our overarching commitment to universal human rights for all.

The African Union

The African Charter draws inspiration from international law on human rights, particularly from the provisions of African instruments on human and peoples' rights, the UN Charter, the Organization of African Unity Charter, the Universal Declaration of Human Rights and other instruments adopted by UN and African countries. This is in addition to drawing from the provisions of instruments adopted within the UN's specialised agencies of which the parties to the present Charter are members.

Under the AU's political arm, the Strategic Plan 2009–12 gives the African Union Commission (AUC) a mandate

> to achieve good governance, democracy, human rights, and rights-based approaches to development, including social, economic, cultural and environmental rights. In this regard, based on existing institutions and organs, the Commission will promote and facilitate the establishment of appropriate architecture for the promotion of good governance. (para. 97)

In 2011, the AUC was developing a human rights strategy for Africa, which aimed to provide a basis for the collective reflection on shared values – the third pillar of the AUC Strategic Plan 2009–12. It was seen as a progressive document with its focus on good governance, democracy, respect for human rights, accountability and transparency. However, the human rights strategy has remained a draft, and the AUC 2014–17 plan, adopted in June 2013 at the AU 50-year celebrations, deliberately seems to move away from the previous focus to 'economic growth'. There is an intentional silence on human rights, and the current plan is focused on *Agenda 2063*,[16] which channels the AUC's energy into institutional strengthening/growth and human rights framed as 'aspirations' under the third pillar of this new agenda.

LGBT human rights advocates must understand this context and the need to engage the AU in this initiative of developing a strategy for Africa. An analysis of the construction of rights in the area of sexuality for African women demonstrates the value-laden nature of what pass as 'rights'. Most of what is portrayed as 'culture' in contemporary Africa is largely a product of constructions and (re)interpretations of universally recognised principles.

16 For more information on Agenda 2063 see African Agenda 2063: African Union documents, available at: www.au.int/en/agenda2063/about (accessed 11 Dec. 2017).

The African Charter on Human and Peoples' Rights

The African Charter differs from the regional human rights instruments that precede it (for example, its European and American counterparts) as it is highly inspired by African traditions and values (Mutua, 1992). African culture is normatively associated with women as both its custodian and conduit. Article 18.2 of the Charter maintains that 'the State shall have the duty to assist the family which is the custodian of morals and traditional values recognised by the community' (Organisation of African Unity, 1981).

These provisions, assisted by patriarchal morals and traditional values, have been used to justify and sanction repressive structures such as women's oppression. When 'rights' and 'culture' are constructed as conflicting parallel systems, the points of contact between gender, rights and culture become extremely foggy. Culture should not be used to negate human rights for women, diverse African peoples, or on any grounds.

In *Zimbabwe Human Rights NGO Forum v. Zimbabwe*,[17] the ACHPR observed:

> Together with equality before the law and equal protection of the law, the principle of non-discrimination provided under Article 2 of the Charter provides the foundation for the enjoyment of all human rights . . . The aim of this principle is to ensure equality of treatment for individuals irrespective of nationality, sex, racial or ethnic origin, political opinion, religion or belief, disability, age or sexual orientation (2006, para. 169).

The African Women's Protocol was adopted on 11 July 2003 in Maputo, Mozambique, and entered into force on 25 November 2005.[18] The protocol provides a continental legal framework for addressing gender inequality and the underlying aspects of society's arrangement that perpetuates women's subordination and contributes to their marginalisation and their occupation of the lower strata in all spheres of life. It requires states to 'eradicate elements in traditional and cultural beliefs, practices and stereotypes which legitimise and exacerbate the persistence and tolerance of violence against women' (ACHPR, 2005, Article 4d).[19]

---

17 ACHPR, *Zimbabwe Human Rights NGO Forum v. Zimbabwe*, ACHPR39_245, 2 May 2006, available at: www.achpr.org/communications/decision/245.02/ (accessed 25 Jul. 2017).

18 ACHPR, Protocol to the African Charter on Human and Peoples' Rights on the Rights of Women in Africa (Maputo Protocol), 25 Nov. 2005, available at: www.achpr.org/files/instruments/women-protocol/achpr_instr_proto_women_eng.pdf (accessed 25 Jul. 2017).

19 Decision on the ACHPR's 38th Activity Report, DOC.EX.CL/Dec 887 (XXVII), 25 Nov., Banjul, the Gambia.

Recent developments at the African Union Summit and the African Commission

The AU Summit brings together the Union's highest organs. It's a meeting of heads of states and governments that is preceded by the executive council meeting with permanent AU representatives. The executive council implements AU decisions in conjunction with the permanent ministers who work closely with the AUC.

The AU's 15th Assembly, held in Kampala in July 2010, reaffirmed its commitment 'to the universal values and principles of Rule of Law, Democracy and Human Rights', but in the same breath went on to negate that same principle by making a decision based on a resolution submitted by the Egyptian government, which

> strongly rejects any attempt to undermine the international human rights system by seeking to impose concepts or notions pertaining to social matters, including private individual conduct, that fall outside the internationally agreed human rights legal framework, taking into account that such attempts constitute an expression of disregard for the universality of human rights.[20]

Suspiciously, this decision came very soon after the African Commission's 47th session, which had deferred their decision on the application by the Coalition of Africa Lesbians (CAL) for observer status. The AU Summit's decision was therefore instrumental at the ACHPR's subsequent session, where CAL's application was rejected.

The Coalition had applied for this status in 2008, and exactly four years after LGBT rights activists and groups started organising and advocating for rights at the AUC, was denied it at the 48th ordinary session in September 2010. Many of the concerns raised were related to 'family and African values', and the argument that same-sex sexual conduct contradicts what the African Charter has inspired. At the ACHPR session – responding on why the CAL application was rejected – the AUC said that 'CAL objectives do not promote the rights enshrined under the African Charter' (para. 33),[21] a position that negates the very principles that all human rights are interdependent, interrelated and universal. In light of this decision, the outcome of the next AU summit on 'shared values' will be most telling. What are these 'shared values', and why separate people on the basis of their SOGI? The comments of one commissioner (in closing remarks during the 48th ordinary session) demonstrate the uphill battle for LGBT NGOs at the ACHPR (2014):

20 Decision on the promotion of cooperation, dialogue and respect for diversity in the field of human rights. Doc.Assembly/AU/17(XV) Add.9. Egypt had submitted an agenda item for the Assembly on 'Promotion of cooperation, dialogue and respect for diversity in the field of human rights'.
21 28th Activity Report of the ACHPR, para. 33, available at: www.achpr.org/files/activity-reports/28/ (accessed 24 May 2018).

> Their human rights activism around various human rights themes within the framework of the African Charter, taking into account positive aspects of African values and traditions has been highly impressive. The challenge for human rights activists and NGOs on these issues is to maintain the momentum of human rights activism in order to create, foster and nurture a culture of observance of human rights, a climate of legality and infusion of human rights and traditional African and moral values into their human rights advocacy.[22]

The refusal of CAL's application for observer status seemed to bolster the advocacy efforts of NGOs and human rights defenders working on the rights of LGBT persons who believed that the ACHPR was the ideal space to advocate for the equal protection and promotion of the human rights of LGBT persons in Africa. However, as the visibility and presence of LGBT NGOs and activists at each ACHPR session increased, a change in approach was in order. While the ACHPR remained engaged in the inclusion of reports on human rights violations (including murder, rape, sexual and physical assault), acts of persecution, imprisonment, displacement and discrimination aimed at individuals based on their actual or perceived SOGI were becoming increasingly common – thereby warranting more urgent attention.

The use of ACHPR mechanisms such as African peer review, through the submission of shadow reports, became a possible avenue for raising these immediate concerns. The availability of alternative reports highlighting human rights violations based on SOGI resulted in the ACHPR being able to issue concluding observations to countries under review to promote and protect the rights of LGBT persons equally without discrimination. For example, an alternative report on human rights violations (Heartland Alliance, 2014) submitted by a consortium of Liberian NGOs at the ACHPR's 55th session in Luanda, Angola, prompted commissioners to question the Liberian government concerning their intention to introduce a new law and sanctions against same-sex conduct.

In addition to providing shadow reports, NGOs attending the sessions presented draft resolutions for adoption by the ACHPR. These usually asked the ACHPR to condemn all forms of violence and discrimination against persons because of their SOGI. The ACHPR regularly rejected the resolutions. The engagement at the ACHPR continued, and with each session more reports highlighting the violence, discrimination and persecution of people based on their SOGI were submitted.

The increased visibility and sustained engagement of human rights defenders at the sessions finally bore positive results in 2014 when, at its 55th session in Luanda, the ACHPR adopted the Resolution on Protection against Violence and Other Human Rights Violations against Persons on

22 Statement by Vice-Chairperson Commissioner Malila, 48th ordinary session, Jan. 2014 (Banjul, the Gambia).

the Basis of Their Real or Imputed Sexual Orientation or Gender Identity.[23] The resolution is a significant success for all civil society organisations and activists working at the ACHPR sessions, as well as for all LGBT communities who are continuously subjected to violence, discrimination and persecution based on SOGI. It condemned, inter alia, 'increasing incidence of violence and other human rights violations, including murder, rape, assault, arbitrary imprisonment and other forms of persecution of persons on the basis of their imputed or real sexual orientation or gender identity', and urged member states 'to end all acts of violence and abuse, whether committed by state or non-state actors' (para. 1).

This was a significant outcome coming from a human rights body whose members still maintain laws that criminalise same-sex conduct. Moreover, it demonstrates the ACHPR's final acknowledgement that the reports of continuing violence and human rights violations against LGBT persons deserve attention, and that member states have a responsibility to protect LGBT persons equally.

Encouraged by the success of Resolution 275, CAL reapplied for observer status, and this was presented at the ACHPR's 56th session, in April 2015. Observer status was finally granted, recognising CAL's right to appear before the ACHPR and make statements on any of the issues within its mandate. This was a historic development, because being acknowledged by the regional human rights body means that violations against LGBT persons will remain on the ACHPR's agenda and that LGBT organisations and activists can legitimately engage in this space.

National frameworks and judicial pronouncements: impact of litigation

Legal recognition of same-sex relations in the majority of African countries has remained a mirage, in part because sodomy laws, which were largely inherited from colonial laws, remain in the statute books. Such laws prevent LGBT persons from enjoying rights on an equal basis, despite the legal changes that have realised new constitutions[24] and laws. Where concerns are raised about the rights of persons on the ground of SOGI, there is resistance to and failure in applying laws equally and without discrimination.

---

23 ACHPR, Resolution 275: Resolution on Protection against Violence and Other Human Rights Violations against Persons on the Basis of their Real or Imputed Sexual Orientation or Gender Identity, 55th ordinary session in Luanda, Angola, 28 Apr.–12 May 2014, available at: www.achpr.org/sessions/55th/resolutions/275 (accessed 24 Jul. 2017).

24 Such as Uganda's 2006 Constitution, Kenya's 2010 Constitution, and Zimbabwe's 2013 Constitution.

National parliaments have also passed laws to further marginalise sexual minorities by failing to ensure the protection and respect of their fundamental rights. The executive branches of many of these governments have failed to promote and protect the rights of all in situations where state and non-state actors have perpetrated abuses and human rights violations. Public pronouncements by heads of state and presidents from the Africa region have not helped the pursuit of justice when they contain derogatory statements which do not promote the equal protection of all citizens, and when they condemn same-sex relations.[25] In these circumstances, only judicial authority has asserted the equality of rights to all and the need to promote constitutional morality.

The enforcement of rights through courts has now removed the debate on same-sex relations from parliaments, where elected leaders have stifled rights, and governments' executive branches have failed to secure rights guaranteed under the constitutions. Courts are emerging as the sole authority where individual rights and group rights can be effectively enforced. This has not always been easy to do, although efforts so far have borne fruit. There is need to ensure that gains made in courts are not just realised on paper but can be enforced by the governments' executive branches, and that parliaments can amend legislation that criminalises same-sex relations. Taking the lead from Ugandan Members of Parliament (MPs) who passed the anti-homosexuality law, Kenyan MPs formed a parliamentary caucus to agitate for a constitutional amendment of Article 45(2) of the Constitution on the right to family, and proposed in parliament that 'homosexuality is threatening the family union, which is envisaged in Article 45(2) of the Constitution, which provides for the right to form families by persons of the opposite sex' (Wafula, 2014).[26]

A summary follows of cases that have successfully gone through court and affirmed the protection of all persons irrespective of their gender identity and association.

25 On 25 Jul. 2015, a statement from a press conference held by US President Barack Obama and Uhuru Kenyatta, the president of Kenya, said: 'Gay rights is a non-issue in Kenya' (Essa, 2015). On 24 February 2014, president Museveni of Uganda signed the Anti-Homosexuality Bill into law and on 4 July, referring to countries that had frozen foreign aid to Uganda after the bill had been passed, he stated: 'It is "unreligious" and "sinful" for other countries to provide aid on the condition that his people are given the freedom to express their sexuality' (Molloy, 2014).

26 See also: Government statements before the UN Human Rights Committee - Replies from the Government of Kenya to the list of issues (CCPR/C/KEN/Q/3) to be taken up in connection with the consideration of its third periodic report before the HRC (CCPR/C/KEN/3), UN Human Rights Committee, CCPR/C/KEN/Q/3/Add.1, 30 May 2012, para. 116, p. 20.

Kenya

In 2014, a local transgender organisation filed a petition at the High Court of Kenya for judicial review against the Kenya Non-Governmental Organisation Coordination Board (NGO Board) because the latter had refused to register the proposed organisation since applicants did not have the same names on their identity documents as in the application.[27] One of those affected was Audrey Mbugua, who identified as a transgender person, and had a different name on her identity card. The court held that the NGO Board's consideration of the applicants' gender was irrelevant and directed it to register the organisation. Riding on this success, the same Audrey Mbugua, a transgender activist, successfully had the gender marker removed from her academic certificates.[28]

These were landmark decisions from the High Court of Kenya, based on constitutional protections that guarantee rights and freedoms to all citizens. In these two cases it had recognised the need to protect minority rights, as the violation of individual rights had a negative impact on constitutional rights guaranteed under the constitution.

Learning from the Botswana case (discussed later), a similar case was filed in Kenya.[29] Here, Eric Gitari tried to register an NGO, the National Gay and Lesbian Human Rights Commission, with the NGO Board, but his application was rejected. He sought protection of his rights to register his organisation as a 'person' protected in Article 36 of the Constitution who had a right to freedom of association. The NGO Board contested the petition on the grounds that allowing registration of the organisation would promote criminalised conduct of 'homosexual intercourse', contrary to the penal code. The court allowed registration holding: 'We hereby declare that the words "Every person" in Article 36 of the Constitution includes all persons living within the republic of Kenya despite their sexual orientation'.[30]

Uganda

In the case of *Kasha Jacqueline, David Kato Kisule and Onziema Patience v. Rolling Stone Ltd and Giles Muhame*, the High Court of Uganda held that

---

27 *Republic v. Non-Governmental Organization Co-ordination Board and another ex-parte Transgender Education and Advocacy and three others* (2014) eKLR. JR misc. appln. 308A of 2013, available at: http://kenyalaw.org/caselaw/cases/view/100341/ (accessed 31 Jul. 2017).

28 *Republic v. Kenya National Examinations Council and another ex-parte Audrey Mbugua Ithibu*, available at: http://kenyalaw.org/caselaw/cases/view/101979/ (accessed 1 Nov. 2017).

29 *Eric Gitari v. Non-Governmental Organisations Co-ordination Board and four others* [2015] eKLR. Petition 440 of 2013, available at: http://kenyalaw.org/caselaw/cases/view/108412/ (accessed 31 Jul. 2017).

30 Ibid. para. 29.1.

'Section 145 of the Penal Code Act [does not] render every person who is gay a criminal under that section of the Penal Code Act. The scope of Section 145 is narrower than gayism generally. One has to commit an act prohibited under Section 145 in order to be regarded as a criminal'.[31]

However, the small gains the *Kasha* case made were not translated in a subsequent freedom of association case in 2012 that challenged the actions of the ethics and integrity minister when he broke up a workshop that had been organised to discuss LGBT issues.[32] The High Court in Uganda held that the minister's actions were justified, as holding such a workshop amounted to a criminal offence. In its view, discussing LGBT issues amounted to inciting the offence provided for under Section 145 of the Penal Code Act, which defines 'unnatural offences'. An appeal against this decision is still pending.

Then on 1 August 2014 the Constitutional Court annulled the Anti-Homosexuality Act (AHA) on the grounds that it had been passed without following constitutional requirements for the Parliamentary Rules of Procedure on quorum. Unfortunately, the court did not go into the merits of the case (which challenged the constitutionality of the AHA) after making a finding on the technical issue of parliament's non-compliance with procedures.

A further challenge to the enactment of the AHA, was filed before the East Africa Court of Justice (EACJ) by the Human Rights Awareness and Promotion Forum (HRAPF),[33] on the grounds that the act violated the principles that partner states are enjoined to follow under the Treaty for the Establishment of the East African Court of Justice.[34]

31 *Kasha Jacqueline, David Kato Kisule and Onziema Patience v. Rolling Stone Ltd and Giles Muhame*, 2010, p. 9. Miscellaneous Cause no. 163 of 2010, available at: https://www.icj.org/wp-content/uploads/2012/07/Kasha-Jacqueline-David-Kato-Kisule-and-Onziema-Patience-v.-Rolling-Stone-Ltd-and-Giles-Muhame-High-Court-of-Uganda-at-Kampala.pdf (accessed 1 Aug. 2017).

32 *Jacqueline Kasha Nabagesera, Frank Mugisha, Julian Pepe Onziema, Geofrey Ogwaro v. attorney general and Rev. Fr. Simon Lokodo*, available at: https://globalfreedomofexpression.columbia.edu/wp-content/uploads/2015/06/Judgment.pdf (accessed 24 Oct. 2017).

33 *HRAPF v. attorney general of Uganda*. In the EACJ at Arusha First Instance Division, ref. no. 6 of 2014, available at: http://eacj.org/wp-content/uploads/2016/09/Ref.-No.6-of-2014.pdf (accessed 1 Aug. 2017).

34 The Treaty for the Establishment of the East African Community (EAC) in arts. 6(d), 7(2) and 8(1)(c) enjoins partner states [Kenya, Uganda, Tanzania, Rwanda and Burundi] to govern their populace according to the principles of good governance, democracy, the rule of law, social justice, and the maintenance of universally accepted standards of human rights, which include, inter alia, provision of equal opportunities and gender equality as well as the recognition, promotion and protection of human and peoples' rights in accordance with the provisions of the African Charter on Human and Peoples' Rights. The Treaty for the Establishment of the EAC, 1999, available at: www.jus.uio.no/english/services/

As a subregional court, the EACJ has a limited mandate, but has interpreted its role in addressing democratic and matters of rule of law to include the protection of human rights, having interpreted the link between economic development, business and human rights. Citizens resident in East Africa are yet to exploit the full potential of this court.

Botswana

In December 1994, an adult male citizen of Botswana, Utjiwa Kanane, was charged with engaging in unnatural acts and indecent practices between males. A constitutional challenge against the penal code provision criminalising sexual conduct between male persons was launched in his defence on the basis that the law was not only discriminatory on the basis of gender, but that it violated Kanane's fundamental rights and freedoms.[35]

The High Court, in denying the application, held that the 'provisions of the Botswana Constitution that protect rights to privacy, association, and freedom of expression could be curtailed by legislation enacted to support "public morality"' (ibid.).

The applicant appealed this decision and the Court of Appeal rightfully found that the Botswana Constitution did not prevent people identifying as gay, lesbian or any other form of sexual orientation, nor did it stop them from associating with each other 'within the confines of and subject to the law' (ibid.). However, the court also stated that the time had not yet arrived to decriminalise homosexual practices between consenting adults in private. This decision purported to be in the public interest, which it said 'must always be a factor in the court's consideration of legislation' (ibid.).[36]

In 1998, the Botswana government had an opportunity to make things right by decriminalising same-sex sexual conduct when revising provisions for sexual offences in the penal code. However, political and religious forces intervened. Politicians in Botswana defended the laws in the belief that homosexuality represents the antithesis of the Botswana culture and also reflects Western influence. Religious leaders in the country are also opposed to same-sex sexual conduct. Leading the religious opposition is the Evangelical Fellowship of Botswana, a coalition of evangelical churches, which launched a 'crusade' against homosexuality, calling 'all Christians and all morally upright persons within the four corners of Botswana to reject, resist, denounce, expose, demolish and totally frustrate any effort by whoever to infiltrate such foreign cultures of moral decay and shame into our respectable, blessed, and peaceful country' (HRW and IGLHRC, 2003).

---

library/treaties/09/9-05/east_africa_economic.xml#treaty-header1-6 (accessed 1 Aug. 2017).

35 *Kanane v. state* 1995 BLR 94.

36 For further information, see also Tabengwa and Nicol (2013).

As a result of these political and religious influences, Botswana has not only retained the criminalisation of same-sex sexual acts between men but, in 1998, expanded its laws to criminalise sexual conduct between women.

Notwithstanding the criminal laws against same-sex conduct in Botswana, LGBT individuals and organisations have gained publicity and operated without interference from the government and the general community. This is largely attributable to Botswana society's inherent belief in the principle of *botho*, also popularly known as *ubuntu*. Botho is a Setswana word referring to a popular cultural principle, '*Motho ke motho ka batho*' which – loosely translated – means 'I am because we are'. Its importance is emphasised by its inclusion as part of *Botswana Vision* (2016), a national development concept encapsulating the country's aspirations, and serving as a guiding framework for national development programmes and policies. The document describes the concept thus:

> Botho defines a process for earning respect by first giving it, and to gain empowerment by empowering others. It encourages people to applaud rather than resent those who succeed. It disapproves of anti-social, disgraceful, inhuman and criminal behaviour, and encourages social justice for all. It means above all things to base your thoughts, actions and expectations for human interaction on the principles of Love, Respect and Empathy.

This cultural practice of the botho principle has played a hand in shaping the discourse on the universality of human rights, especially those of LGBT persons. There are divergent views on decriminalising same-sex conduct, but the country is mostly agreed that nobody deserves to be discriminated against, subjected to violence, or have their basic rights violated. In 2010, the government of Botswana amended the Employment Act to include 'sexual orientation' as a ground for non-discrimination in employment. This directly acknowledged the vulnerability of LGBT people in terms of employment discrimination.

However, in spite of this relatively liberal attitude, Botswana's Penal Code Sections 162–4, which criminalise same-sex conduct, remain intact. Like all other countries where that conduct is criminalised, the right to associate freely and form organisations that advocate for the human rights of LGBT people has been limited or denied. This has the effect of forcing such groups or organisations to work underground, where they are unable to freely and publicly advocate and represent their constituents' rights. For example, Lesbians, Gays and Bisexuals of Botswana (LeGaBiBo), an organisation representing the rights of LGBT people, has been repeatedly denied the right to register as an association by the Registrar of Societies, which claims it would not be in the public interest.

Opposition to decriminalisation has prompted other approaches generally, and government reluctance to challenge populist views that render other forms

Figure 10. Demonstration by Rainbow Identity Association and Lesbians, Gays and Bisexuals of Botswana, Gaborone, Botswana, 2013. Photo credit: *Botho: LGBT Lives in Botswana,* LeGaBiBo and Envisioning Global LGBT Human Rights.

of sexuality as 'un-African' and against African tradition and values, as well as foreign notions introduced through Western influence. Judicial reluctance to order criminalisation of same-sex conduct as unconstitutional in the *Kanane* case, and the general politicisation of this issue, forced LeGaBiBo and other rights activists to consider other advocacy tactics.

The incremental approach diverts pressure from contentious decriminalisation, and directs focus to other legislation, policies and practices that discriminate on the basis of SOGI. LeGaBiBo adopted the incremental approach and chose not to further challenge penal code provisions criminalising same-sex conduct.

The Registrar of Societies' rejection of LeGaBiBo's registration presented a perfect opportunity to test the judiciary again. Strategic litigation proceeded on the basis of 'violation of the freedom of association', which is guaranteed by Section 13 of the Constitution of Botswana. The application said that by denying lesbians, gays and bisexuals the right to register their association, the government had denied them the ability to associate amongst themselves and/or with other persons wishing to associate with them.

The LeGaBiBo application was upheld in November 2014, when the court ruled that denial to register violated freedom of association. In distinguishing the issues of the LeGaBiBo application from the *Kanane* case, the court said of LeGaBiBo's objectives that 'carrying out political lobbying for equal rights and decriminalization of same sex relationships is not a crime. Lobbying for legislative reforms is not per se a crime. It is also not a crime to be a homosexual.'[37] This was a milestone for LeGaBiBo, an organisation that had existed for over two decades without legal recognition. The state appealed the judgment and, on 16 March 2016, a full bench of the Botswana Court of Appeal upheld the High Court's decision and ordered the Botswana government to register the organisation as a society in terms of the Societies Act. LeGaBiBo was duly registered on 29 April 2016.[38]

The above cases demonstrate that the law can be used to assert rights and, in the right environment before the courts, rights can be enforced and guaranteed for all. The incremental gains realised through litigation cannot be over-emphasised but the importance of broader civil society work in the process should not be overlooked. Much of the background work has been done by community members, rights awareness and policy change campaigns working towards the protection of LGBT people's human rights; they have striven to guarantee and protect the rights to association, registration and enjoyment that already exist under the Constitutions of Botswana, Uganda, Kenya and South Africa.

Once moved by an aggrieved party, such as LGBT individuals seeking rights protection, the judiciary, unlike parliament, has the mandate to interpret and apply rights guaranteed under the constitution. The emerging jurisprudence and pronouncements from the judiciaries are affirmations that well-utilised litigation can realise major protections.

Not all judiciaries are progressive, as noted above; some remain conservative, with an approach to and application of legal technicalities, among other considerations, bordering on conservatism or political propaganda. Recourse to the use of legal procedures, so as not to address the substantive issues at hand is one way of using an 'avoidance approach', especially where political or 'social mood', 'traditional values' and 'culture' are used as a means to avoid addressing human rights abuses and violations against LGBT people.

Mozambique

Mozambique was a Portuguese colony; accordingly, it was spared the British colonial legacy of criminalising 'carnal knowledge against the order of nature'. Instead the law was ambiguous, providing only for 'practices against nature', without defining what those practices were. This law could have been interpreted to include same-sex conduct, as in other Southern-African countries that inherited similar provisions from British colonialism, but the laws remained

---

37 *Thuto Rammoge and others v. attorney general of Botswana*, MAHGB-000 175-13.
38 *Attorney general of Botswana v. Thuto Rammoge and others*, Court of Appeal Civil Appeal no. CACGB-128-14, available at: www.humandignitytrust.org/pages/ LIBRARY?searchTags=The%20Attorney%20General%20of%20Botswana%20 and%20Thuto%20Rammoge%20&%2019%20others (accessed 24 May 2018).

inactive and unenforced, including against LGBT individuals. However, the presence of this provision, even in its ambiguous state, and the overriding social and religiously driven intolerances against same-sex conduct, has meant that LGBT individuals and groups continued to experience discrimination and violation of their rights. Therefore, LGBT activists and rights defenders carried on advocating and lobbying the government to completely repeal these provisions and decriminalise homosexuality. The government responded swiftly by enacting a new Penal Code in December 2014 that did not reference same-sex conduct as an offence, directly or indirectly. This law came into effect on 30 June 2015, effectively decriminalising homosexuality or same-sex conduct in Mozambique.

This decriminalisation was expected, especially as Mozambique is one of few countries in Africa to tolerate same-sex conduct. In fact, it is one of the three countries, including South Africa and Botswana, that provides protection against discrimination based on sexual orientation. Botswana has prohibited employment discrimination on the basis of sexual orientation since 2010[39] and Mozambique since 2007.[40] Section 9 of the South Africa Constitution prohibits all forms of discrimination including on the basis of sexual orientation, in addition, the Employment Equity Act (Sections 5 and 6) also prohibits unfair discrimination on that basis.[41]

While promulgation of laws does not eradicate homophobia and social intolerances, it does indicate leadership that adheres to universal human rights and standards of equality for all. Mozambique is providing a good example to its African counterparts that states are responsible for protecting, respecting and fulfilling the human rights of all people equally, without discrimination.

Joachim Chissano, the former president, has spoken out to other African leaders about the continuing discrimination against LGBT persons, encouraging them to decriminalise same-sex conduct. He is one of the few political leaders in Africa to have provided leadership in the development of human rights protections for LGBT persons. In an open letter to African leaders, he wrote: 'We can no longer afford to discriminate against people on the basis of age, sex, ethnicity, migrant status, sexual orientation and gender identity, or any other basis – we need to unleash the full potential of everyone' (2014).

Conclusion

The challenge for LGBT human rights defenders in Africa is that human rights are inherently forward-looking and visionary. Tradition, on the other hand, is intrinsically rooted in the past and fixed. Obviously, not all forward-looking initiatives are positive for LGBT communities, and not all traditions

39 Botswana Employment Amendment, 2010.
40 Mozambique Labour Law, 2007.
41 The Constitution of the Republic of South Africa, 1996.

are negative for LGBT communities. However, these realities create particular tensions for those who try to engage with both concepts at the same time. All members of marginalised groups know that states often seek to justify human rights violations on the basis that it has 'always been this way'. These so-called 'traditional values' are frequently invoked to justify maintaining the status quo, whereas a human rights-based approach often requires changes in order to ensure compliance with regional and international standards.

Although it is important to challenge assumptions that tradition and culture make only a positive contribution to society, it is also crucial to confront the traditions and culture that are presented on behalf of African societies, where sexuality and gender diversity were, and are, celebrated. Research on African same-sex sexualities and gender identities also needs to demonstrate that many practices claiming to be traditional are in fact of recent origin, and that all African cultures contain diverse or contradictory traditions. Most importantly, it must be emphasised that many traditional values are inconsistent with international human rights.

The appropriate standard in this area was articulated by Navi Pillay from South Africa, the former UN High Commissioner for Human Rights:

> If we are all entitled to the full range of human rights and to equal protection of the law then, I believe, it can never be acceptable to deprive certain individuals of their rights, indeed to impose criminal sanctions on those individuals, not because they have inflicted harm on others or pose a threat to the well-being of others, but simply for being who they are, for being born with a particular sexual orientation or gender identity. To do so is deliberately to exclude a whole lot of people from the protection of international human rights law. It is, in short, an affront to the very principles of human rights and non-discrimination. (UN News Centre, 2010)

Africa, of course, is not the only world region rooted in strong traditional values that might pose challenges to the advancement of human rights for LGBT persons. It is important that other regions, especially those in the Global South, who have overcome some of the challenges, demonstrate strong leadership and guidance. A recent example of such leadership was the convening of a joint dialogue of the ACHPR, the Inter-American Commission on Human Rights, and the UN in November 2015. The report noted that:

> Key principles relating to the pre-eminence of human rights norms and principles in the interpretation and application of cultural and traditional values were highlighted as relevant in the context of sexual orientation and gender identity . . . [M]oreover, many traditional, cultural and religious values, including in Africa and the Americas, are based on the same principles that underpin human rights, including love, respect for others and for their human dignity. (Centre for Human Rights, University of Pretoria, 2016)

This was not only a South-South dialogue, but also involved UN infrastructure such as the Office of the UN High Commissioner for Human Rights (OHCHR). The increase in leadership that has emerged from UN agencies is partly due to the growing support displayed within UN political arenas. ARC International, which tracks UN voting and support for statements on SOGI, documented a steady increase in support for LGBT issues within the UN, despite setbacks and backlash. Although the African region remains largely opposed to the advancement of human rights based on SOGI, no longer is there an African group that can truthfully purport to represent the entire region on these issues. This is an incredible opportunity, but building upon these small, but historic victories, will require a concerted and ongoing advocacy effort.

Having LGBT African voices speaking at the UN during side events and panels has helped to dispel the arguments that being LGBT is culturally 'un-African'. LGBT Africans have delivered powerful speeches at high-level UN events in Geneva and New York which, combined with the presence of African LGBT human rights defenders in UN spaces, have had great impact. Indeed, the comments of former Secretary-General Ban Ki-Moon (2010) illustrate this point:

> Yesterday evening, I spoke to a Human Rights Day event at the Ford Foundation. It was called 'Speak Up', a conversation with human rights defenders. One of my fellow speakers was a young activist from Uganda. Frank Mugisha has been working with a variety of civil society groups to stop legislation that institutionalizes discrimination against gay and lesbian people. With extraordinary eloquence, he appealed to us, the United Nations, for help. He asked us to rally support for the decriminalization of homosexuality everywhere in the world. And that is what we will do. We have been called upon, and we will answer.

The decision to accredit CAL at the African Commission allows LGBT African civil society to fully engage in regional processes. Along with having African LGBT voices speaking and participating in regional and international spaces, it is equally important to support LGBT organisations, groups and individuals in writing shadow reports to help maintain state accountability and ensure that recommendations made by the UN and regional bodies are implemented at the national level. Engaging in documentation and reporting is a crucial component of the functioning of the UN and African regional mechanisms, and its importance cannot be underestimated for advancing a human rights agenda that includes LGBT persons.

Exposing injustices through the courts has brought hope to parts of Africa, especially in stemming state-sponsored homophobia. Through litigation the AHA in Uganda was defeated and declared unconstitutional in 2014. However, NGOs must be careful not to take litigation as an end in itself but rather ensure it is made part of the campaign to generate more visibility and broader systemic change.

Finally, the authors of this chapter believe strongly that respecting the universality of human rights and respect for diversity are not mutually exclusive concepts. In fact, they are mutually reinforcing. A group of UN experts expressed this concept eloquently in their statement for the World Day on Cultural Diversity for Dialogue and Development:

> Cultural diversity, however, can only thrive in an environment that safeguards fundamental freedoms and human rights, which are universal, indivisible, interconnected and interdependent. No one may invoke cultural diversity as an excuse to infringe on human rights guaranteed by international law or limit their scope, nor should cultural diversity be taken to support segregation and harmful traditional practices which, in the name of culture, seek to sanctify differences that run counter to the universality, indivisibility and interdependence of human rights. (OHCHR, 2010)

References

African Union (2014) 'The AU Commission Strategic Plan 2014–2017', available at: https://au.int/en/auc/strategic-plan-2014-2017 (accessed 24 May 2018).

African Union Commission (2009) 'Strategic Plan 2009–2012', 19 May, available at: https://au.int/en/about/vision (accessed 24 May 2018).

ARC International (2008) 'United Nations General Assembly joint statement: NGO press release', available at: http://arc-international.net/global-advocacy/general-assembly/general-assembly-resolutions-and-statements-on-sogi/ga-joint-statement-ngo-press-release/ (accessed 11 Dec. 2017).

Associated Press (2010) 'UN restores gay reference in anti-violence resolution', *Associated Press*, 21 Dec., available at: www.rawstory.com/2010/12/un-restores-gay-reference/ (accessed 12 Dec. 2017).

Ban, K.-M. (2010) 'Remarks at event on ending violence and criminal sanctions based on sexual orientation and gender identity', 10 Dec., available at: www.iglhrc.org/binary-data/ATTACHMENT/file/000/000/459-2.pdf (accessed 11 Dec. 2017).

Botswana Vision (2016), available at: http://unpan1.un.org/intradoc/groups/public/documents/cpsi/unpan033260.pdf (accessed 11 Dec. 2017).

Carroll, A. and L.R. Mendos (2017) *State-Sponsored Homophobia*, 12th edn. (International Lesbian, Gay, Bisexual, Transgender and Intersex Association), May, available at: http://ilga.org/downloads/2017/ILGA_State_Sponsored_Homophobia_2017_WEB.pdf (accessed 21 Feb. 2018).

Centre for Human Rights, University of Pretoria (2016) *Ending Violence and Other Human Rights Violations based on Sexual Orientation and Gender Identity: a joint dialogue of the African Commission on Human and Peoples Rights* (Pretoria University Law Press, available at: www.pulp.up.ac.za/

legal-dialogues/ending-violence-and-other-human-rights-violations-based-on-sexual-orientation-and-gender-identity-a-joint-dialogue-of-the-african-commission-on-human-and-peoples-rights-inter-american-commission-on-human-rights-and-united-nations (accessed 11 Dec. 2017).

Chissano, J. (2014) 'An open letter to Africa's leaders – Joaquim Chissano, former President of Mozambique', *The Africa Report*, 14 Jan. available at: www.theafricareport.com/Soapbox/an-open-letter-to-africas-leaders-joaquim-chissano-former-president-of-mozambique.html (accessed 1 Aug. 2017).

Essa, A. (2015) 'Kenyatta: gay rights is a non-issue for Kenya', *Aljazeera*, 25 Jul., available at: www.aljazeera.com/news/2015/07/kenyatta-gay-rights-issue-kenya-150725182756519.html (accessed 31 Jul. 2017).

Gays and Lesbians of Zimbabwe (2008) *Unspoken Facts: a History of Homosexualities in Africa* (Gays and Lesbians of Zimbabwe, Harare).

Gupta, A. (2008) *This Alien Legacy: the Origins of "Sodomy" Laws in British Colonialism* (New York, NY: Human Rights Watch), available at: https://www.hrw.org/report/2008/12/17/alien-legacy/origins-sodomy-laws-british-colonialism (accessed 11 Dec. 2017).

Heartland Alliance (2014) 'Human rights violations against lesbian, gay, bisexual, and transgender (LGBT) people in Liberia: shadow report on Liberia's compliance with the African Charter on Human and Peoples' Rights', available at: https://www.heartlandalliance.org/gihr/wp-content/uploads/sites/12/2016/07/ACHPR-Liberia-Alternative-Report-2014.pdf (accessed 24 Jul. 2017).

Human Rights Watch (HRW) and International Gay and Lesbian Human Rights Commission (IGLHRC) (2003) 'More than a name: state-sponsored homophobia and its consequences in Southern Africa', available at: http://hrw.org/reports/2003/safrica/ (accessed 24 March 2016).

Human Rights Watch (S. Long) (2009) 'Together, apart: organizing around sexual orientation and gender identity worldwide', 11 Jun., available at: https://www.hrw.org/report/2009/06/11/together-apart/organizing-around-sexual-orientation-and-gender-identity-worldwide (accessed 12 Dec. 2017).

International Gay and Lesbian Human Rights Commission (2010) 'Civil society pressures governments to successfully reverse discriminatory vote at the UN', available at: www.outrightinternational.org/content/civil-society-pressures-governments-successfully-reverse-discriminatory-vote-un (accessed 12 Dec. 2017).

Molloy, A. (2014) 'Ugandan President Yoweri Museveni says gay rights demands attached to western aid are "sinful"', *Independent*, 4 Jul., available at: www.independent.co.uk/news/world/africa/ugandan-president-yoweri-museveni-says-gay-rights-demands-attached-to-western-aid-are-sinful-9584440.html (accessed 12 Dec. 2017).

Morgan, R. and S. Wieringa (2005) *Tommy Boys, Lesbian Men and Ancestral Wives: Female Same-Sex Practices in Africa* (Johannesburg: Jacana Media).

Mutua, M. (1992) 'The Africa human rights system in a comparative perspective: the need for urgent reformation', *Nairobi Law Monthly,* 44: 27–30.

Office of the United Nations High Commission for Human Rights (2010) 'Human rights are essential tools for an effective intercultural dialogue', 21 May, cached at: www.ohchr.org/Documents.

Tabengwa, M., and N. Nicol (2013) 'The development of sexual rights and the LGBT movement in Botswana', in C. Lennox and M. Waites (eds.) *Human Rights, Sexual Orientation and Gender Identity in the Commonwealth: Struggles for Decriminalisation and Change* (London: Human Rights Consortium, Institute of Commonwealth Studies), pp. 339–58.

Tamale, S. (2014) 'Homosexuality is not un-African: it is legalized homophobia, not same-sex relations, that is alien to Africa', *Aljazeera America*, 26 Apr., available at: http://america.aljazeera.com/opinions/2014/4/homosexuality-africamuseveniugandanigeriaethiopia.html (accessed 4 Jul. 2017).

UN News Centre (2010) 'UN officials urge countries to remove criminal sanctions based on sexual orientation', 17 Sep., available at: www.un.org/apps/news/story.asp?NewsID=35976#.V1iHjcagwUU (accessed 12 Dec. 2017).

Wafula, C. (2014) 'MPs to fight homosexuality', *Daily Nation*, 18 Feb., available at: http://mobile.nation.co.ke/news/MPs-to-fight-homosexuality/1950946-2212146-format-xhtml-9uirgo/ (accessed 24 Oct. 2017).

Documentary film

And Still We Rise (2015) dir. R. Lusimbo and N. Nicol (Uganda and Canada: Sexual Minorities Uganda and Envisioning Global LGBT Human Rights), available at: https://vimeo.com/178217397.

7

Haven or precarity? The mental health of LGBT asylum seekers and refugees in Canada

Nick J. Mulé and Kathleen Gamble

Mental health challenges are an important concern for many lesbian, gay, bisexual, transgender (LGBT) asylum seekers and refugees in Canada.[1] The processes of leaving their country of origin, applying for refugee status and settling in Canada often affect the mental wellbeing of many LGBT asylum-seekers and refugees. These experiences have helped to inform this examination of Canadian policies regarding asylum seekers and refugees, raising the question whether or not they effectively address mental health concerns in these populations. Canada is one of 42 countries in the world that has granted asylum to individuals on the basis of persecution due to sexual orientation or gender identity/expression (SOGIE),[2] but can it be considered a haven or a place of precarity? Insights into this can be gained by looking at the mental health of LGBT asylum seekers and refugees who choose to settle there and how Canada addresses the issue through its procedures and responses to needs.

This chapter investigates and considers how homo-bi-transphobia is represented and reflected in Canadian social, political and legal structures – including the healthcare system. Moreover, homo-bi-transphobia intersects with discrimination on the basis of different categories of identity (race, gender,

---

1   Asylum seekers are defined here as persons fleeing persecution and seeking protection, regardless of their desire, eligibility, or attainment of a particular status within the refugee system. Refugees are individuals seeking protection who have obtained refugee status. Claimants are individuals seeking refugee status, but who have not yet attained it.

2   UNGA, 2015, 'Annual report of the United Nations High Commissioner for Human Rights and reports of the Office of the High Commission and the Secretary-General. Follow-up to and implementation of the Vienna Declaration and Programme of Action', A/HRC/29/23, HRC, 29th session agenda items 2 and 8, 4 May.

N. J. Mulé and K. Gamble (2018) 'Haven or precarity? The mental health of LGBT asylum seekers and refugees in Canada', in N. Nicol et al. (eds.) *Envisioning Global LGBT Human Rights: (Neo)colonialism, Neoliberalism, Resistance and Hope* (London: Human Rights Consortium, Institute of Commonwealth Studies), pp. 205–20.

Figure 11. Asylum seekers, Toronto, Canada. Photo credit: Ulelli Verbeke, 2014, Society Against Sexual Orientation Discrimination and Envisioning Global LGBT Human Rights.

class, ability, religion and others) to create deeply personalised and complex experiences. Thus any consideration or discussion about how to improve LGBT asylum seekers and refugees' access to healthcare services (including mental healthcare) must be done within an anti-racist and anti-oppressive framework that acknowledges the intersectional nature of the identities of many LGBT asylum seekers, refugee claimants and refugees. Working towards improvement through anti-oppressive practices specific to LGBTs must include a focus on diverse sexual orientations and gender identities and expressions.

We drew from data specific to the experiences of LGBT asylum seekers and refugees in Canada as well as data about sexual and gender minorities in India, Africa and the Caribbean gathered by Envisioning Global LGBT Human Rights (Envisioning). The Canadian analysis was conducted through focus groups with LGBT asylum seekers and refugees, organised in collaboration with community partners within the Greater Toronto Area (GTA). Our research findings correlate with trends in the broader literature regarding this population's common stressors and the resulting mental health challenges.

The World Health Organization (WHO) defines mental health as 'a state of well-being in which every individual realises his or her own potential, can cope with the normal stresses of life, can work productively and fruitfully, and is able to make a contribution to her or his community' (2014). Likewise, the mental health of LGBT asylum seekers, refugee claimants and refugees relies upon a sense of self-worth and belonging, stress management and coping strategies, available resources in their new country of residence, accessibility of these services, and overall acceptance in their communities among other factors (Envisioning, 2014b). LGBT people face increased mental health stress compared to people who fit within more normative categories of sexual and gender identity (that is, straight and cis-gender people). Social stigma also leads to a chronic psychological strain, expectations of rejection and discrimination, decisions about disclosure of identity, and the internalisation of homo-bi-transphobia (ibid.).

Mental health in Canada

According to the Canadian Mental Health Association (CMHA), mental illness is a major health issue for society and for government (2015). In any given year, one in five Canadians experience a mental health or addiction issue (ibid.). The onset of 70 per cent of mental health problems occurs during childhood or adolescence, and people with a mental illness are twice as likely to have a substance use problem. Canadians in the lowest income group are three to four times more likely than those in the highest income group to report poor to fair mental health, and mental illness is a leading cause of disability in Canada.

Yet discrimination persists in the organisation and provision of hospital care and community healthcare for people with mental illness. Improvements in this area are needed in all ten provinces and three territories to ensure that Canada's healthcare system reflects and upholds the principles of universal access, comprehensiveness, portability and public administration enshrined in the Canada Health Act (ibid.).

Moreover, the stigma associated with mental illness needs to be challenged. According to a 2008 survey, just 50 per cent of Canadians would tell friends or co-workers that they have a family member with a mental illness. As a result, while mental illness accounts for about ten per cent of the burden of disease in Ontario alone, it receives just seven per cent of healthcare dollars and/or reflects an underfunding of about 1.5 billion Canadian dollars (ibid.).

Mental health and wellbeing are largely recognised as important indicators in the measurement of an individual's overall health status. However, funding and service provision are greatly lacking in this area, a gap which can be addressed by developing a mental health policy that reflects the distinct and unique needs of various members of Canadian society. Social support for mental health services for asylum seekers and refugee claimants is limited and usually falls under the umbrella of larger resettlement organisations, which are already under-funded and under-resourced in their capacity to support this community (Envisioning, 2015).

Mental health challenges of LGBT asylum seekers and refugees

The challenges many LGBT asylum seekers and refugees face reflect their experience of high levels of stress and isolation in their countries of origin, in their early years in Canada, and as a result of the refugee claim process itself. In the absence of a safe environment and often facing social isolation, many LGBT asylum seekers are unable to process trauma and mental health issues in both the country of origin and Canada. These asylum seekers have often faced trauma and/or persecution in their country of origin, which may include isolated or repeated physical, mental, emotional and/or sexual violence. Homo-bi-transphobia leads to experiences of discrimination, social stigma and alienation from friends, family and co-workers (ibid.).

As well, LGBT asylum seekers inhabit multiple categories of identity when migrating to Canada, with the result that discrimination and stigma may be compounded. Systemic racism can have a pervasive and devastating impact on their health and wellbeing. For many LGBT refugee claimants, experiences of homo-bi-transphobia intersect with experiences of racism and lead to further marginalisation and social isolation. Additionally, LGBT asylum seekers, refugee claimants and refugees may not have the support of their country-of-origin community in Canada (ibid.).

Discrimination within these communities can trigger memories of abuse in the country of origin, create new psychological trauma and contribute to isolation. LGBT asylum seekers and refugee claimants may feel shame and fear when discussing their sexual orientation and/or gender identity (SOGI), because of the intimate and/or taboo nature of these topics in their home countries. The imperative to disclose, both socially and in certain official contexts (including the refugee process), can be extremely stressful and may cause individuals to avoid accessing support services.

Finally, mental health services for asylum seekers, refugee claimants and refugees are limited and not usually covered by federal and/or provincial healthcare financing models. Knowledge of LGBT people's lives and health needs varies considerably among professionals working in these services. Finding a provider who is sensitive to the specific requirements of LGBT asylum seekers can be difficult, particularly outside major urban centres. Even if services are available, many LGBT asylum seekers may fear being 'outed' following disclosure of their sexual orientation or gender identity to healthcare providers. They may decline support from these services due to fear, guilt, and shame, as well as cultural, religious and language barriers. Mental illness itself is stigmatised in Canada and also elsewhere, so those suffering from such issues may resist seeking help for fear of being labelled themselves.

Haven or precarity?

In this project we operate from the premise that mental health is a key factor in determining the wellbeing of asylum seekers, refugee claimants and refugees. Recognising that the very experience of seeking asylum or applying for refugee status presents emotional and psychosocial challenges, it is anticipated that their mental health will be compromised. Hence, it is important that a host country is perceived as offering a safe haven, an escape from persecution. For the purposes of this research, haven is linked to the LGBT asylum seeker or refugee's perception of safety, inclusion and protection, which is not necessarily the state's perspective. It is the state that can influence policy, often to the detriment of those seeking asylum or refugee status (Sales, 2005). Yet, the very social location of individuals seeking asylum or refugee status based on SOGIE can add an additional layer of precarity due to concerns about heteronormativity, cisnormativity, and racialisation (Ou Jin Lee and Brotman, 2013). Such forms of oppression can be perpetrated systemically in the host country via Westernised notions that are at dissonance with the cultural beliefs and socialisation of asylum seekers and refugee claimants. Our research reveals a multilevel understanding of what is involved in creating a haven or perpetrating precarity.

Factors shaping the mental health and wellbeing of LGBT asylum seekers, refugee claimants and refugees

This section focuses on three factors that directly impact on the mental health of LGBT asylum seekers, refugee claimants and refugees: escaping violence, the refugee determination process in Canada, and resettlement. Our research findings indicate that these factors and how they played out for our participants had deep implications for their mental health and sense of wellbeing. Although this section deals with each factor in turn, it is worth noting that any of them can affect the others, since some of our participants experienced them intersectionally.

Stress and trauma underscored these experiences. Again, it must be acknowledged that LGBT asylum seekers and refugee claimants commonly suffer from either or both of these, whether due to direct persecution, threats or perceived endangerment in their country of origin, the process of escaping persecution, or their heightened vulnerability to stress and trauma as a result of Canada's determination process (Nicholson, 1997). Trauma is generally understood as experiencing a negative encounter that can have a lasting imprint on an individual to the point of producing future stress. Stress can be broadly defined as pronounced pressures, whether mental, physical or psychological, and may intersect with trauma. Whether combined or separated, experiences of both are distressing, with implications for the mental health and wellbeing of newly arrived refugees (Shannon, Vinson et al., 2015). Expressing such stressors and trauma can strengthen the mental health of such individuals under the guidance of prepared and properly trained professionals (Shannon, Wieling et al., 2015).

Escaping violence

Many LGBT refugee claimants in Canada seek asylum under conditions of considerable distress. According to a 2009 study, 45 per cent of lesbians and 24 per cent of gay men reported experiences of physical and/or sexual violence and assault in their refugee claim (Envisioning, 2014a). Similarly, the majority of participants in this study spoke openly about the persecution and violence they had experienced and/or witnessed in their homeland and how this had contributed to their decision to flee their home: 'I'm aware of members who have been beaten, who have been stabbed, whose hands have been cut, who are currently dead . . . some situations you can see it point blank, the brutality of the beating, of the violence involved' (Envisioning, 2015, p. 24).

Not only did many participants experience physical brutality, many had also undergone structural forms of violence which contributed to their decision to seek asylum: 'I've known people who have lost their jobs when it was discovered that they're gay' (ibid., p. 24).

The process of claiming refugee protection, particularly on the basis of the deeply personal and sensitive topics of sexual orientation and gender identity, can be a major source of stress. Coupled with past trauma and future uncertainty, this places LGBT asylum seekers at increased mental health risk. Having to prove one's sexual orientation or gender identity, which the asylum process demands, can cause intense shame and embarrassment. It may also be impossible for some asylum seekers to prove their sexual orientation, due to deeply entrenched survival strategies, such as hiding their identity, that were necessary in their country of origin (Envisioning, 2014b).

Canada's refugee-determination process

Canada acknowledges persecution on the grounds of SOGI as warranting refugee protection. Envisioning's research was conducted at the same time as significant changes were being implemented in Canada's asylum and refugee-determination process. Bill C-31 took effect in December 2012 and is now enforced as the Protecting Canada's Immigration Systems Act.[3] The act

---

3   Government of Canada Bill C-31, 2012: Act to amend the Immigration and Refugee Protection Act, the Balanced Refugee Reform Act, the Marine Transportation Security Act and the Department of Citizenship and Immigration Act,' c17 (60–1), available at: www.parl.ca/Legisinfo/BillDetails.aspx?Language=E&billid=538349 (accessed 2 Aug. 2017).

resulted in a number of changes with significant negative effects on refugees and immigrants – including a disproportionately negative impact on LGBT claimants. These changes included:

- a two-tiered system based on a Designated Country of Origin (DCO) list
- significantly shortened timelines for the refugee-determination process
- restriction on Pre-Removal Risk Assessment (PRRA), and Humanitarian and Compassionate Consideration

Prior to the implementation of the act, refugee claimants had 28 days from making a claim at a port of entry to submit their Personal Information Form (PIF). As well, during this same timeframe, refugee claimants needed to find a lawyer, secure financial assistance and gather the required documentation and evidence to support their claim. Claimants now have only 15 days to submit their statement, renamed Basis of Claim (BOC), and for claimants making inland claims this timeframe can be even shorter.

Although the Canadian government recognises persecution based on SOGI, it also demands that LGBT refugees provide documentation not only of persecution but also 'proof' of their SOGI. Not all refugee claimants have access to this kind of information (that is, police reports, medical files, other forms of testimonies). This is highly inequitable and creates an additional burden for claimants that can often have an adverse effect on their mental health. The experience of 'proving' one's identity can be highly traumatising and may trigger painful memories. As one participant stated, 'To write up your story . . . it's very painful and someone said you're . . . I think you're supposed to have more time to fill out your PIF . . . it's very painful because you have to try to live it over' (Envisioning, 2015, p. 21).

Prior to their arrival in Canada, many LGBT refugee claimants live lives of silence and social isolation due to discrimination and fear of persecution. Canada's immigration and refugee regime throws newcomers grappling with identity issues into highly stressful situations where identity must be demonstrated. As one participant noted,

> You're still traumatised ... You're still worried, where do I go from here? You know no one, and nothing, then you have this officer right in front of you . . . and you're still traumatised about everything that happened. I think I can say what I am running away from . . . but it won't be as clear as when I am talking to someone . . . that I trust. (ibid., p. 21)

As a result, the claims process itself can have a significant and negative impact on the mental health of LGBT refugee claimants who are seeking an escape from social pressure, stigma and violence. As several service providers who participated in this research noted, the claim process itself can make LGBT refugees feel persecuted and/or threatened: 'You feel like you are being persecuted, proving yourself. But there's a constant fear that once it gets rejected you have openly declared as LGBT and you will be deported back to your country' (ibid., p. 3).

For many refugee claimants the process is a major source of anxiety and fear: 'Even the morning of the hearing I swear in my head I used the bathroom like 20 times and I haven't been there, I was just so nervous . . . because you're hearing all these remarks about the new system because it gives you less time for preparation' (ibid., p. 23).

LGBT asylum seekers are often forced to relive past trauma throughout the process. Discussing past trauma and fear of future persecution with strangers such as legal counsel, asylum officers and immigration adjudicators may contribute to retraumatisation, particularly since asylum seekers may harbour mistrust towards government officials/authoritarian figures who are often the perpetrators of persecution in their country of origin.

Resettlement

As refugees navigate a highly stressful claims process, they also face the challenges and struggles of settling in a new country. These include accessing suitable housing services and basic social services (like healthcare) and finding employment. Some participants felt that being identified as a member of the LGBT community, a refugee, or a person receiving social assistance had an impact on their ability to access basic services: 'It's very hard to find housing in terms of being an immigrant or refugee claimant, because of the discrimination when it comes to those things' (ibid., p. 28).

Many LGBT people seek asylum without support from family, extended family or their community as the result of homo-bi-transphobia. Building and maintaining new social support networks takes considerable energy and time for many refugees and immigrant groups.

Moreover, in 2012, the Canadian federal government introduced cuts to the Interim Federal Health Program (IFHP), which provides health coverage for immigrants seeking refuge in the country. The changes barred all refugees, excluding government-assisted refugees, from accessing medication, vision and dental coverage (Canadian Doctors for Refugee Care, 2014). For refugee claimants who participated in our study, these changes made it extremely complicated and difficult to access basic healthcare services, for example: 'The government basically [gave] you this paper . . . it entitles [you] to have healthcare or what not . . . most health institutions [do] not recognise this piece of paper' (ibid., p. 30) and 'I had challenges finding an immigration doctor . . . [or] the doctor doesn't practise immigration medicine anymore . . . it is hard to get a family doctor' (ibid.).

In 2013, six Canadian provinces introduced individual programmes to supplement coverage. The Ontario Temporary Health Program (OTHP) came into effect in January 2014 and provides short-term and urgent health coverage to refugees and asylum seekers. However, provisions for mental health services are still lacking. As previously noted, the challenges faced by many LGBT refugees reflect high levels of stress and isolation, such as those experienced in their country of origin, the refugee claims process itself, and problems related to resettlement in Canada. In one positive development the newly elected federal government, under the Liberal party that came into power in late 2015, fully restored the IFHP in April 2016. However, much work remains to be done to address the mental health needs of LGBT asylum seekers, refugee claimants and refugees.

Many LGBT refugee claimants are unable to process trauma and mental health issues or access services and support in the country of origin and during the refugee process in Canada:

> I got so depressed. I mean it was awhile, like when I came up here, I just tried to forget everything that happened to me . . . so when I had to fill my PIF, to write my story I would cry every day. I was even thinking about committing suicide. I got to the point where I was like, I couldn't deal with it any more . . . and I had no one to talk to and it was very stressful. (ibid., p. 31)

LGBT refugee claimants face difficulties accessing safe housing, finding reliable employment and navigating the refugee claims process – all of which can have a significant impact on their mental health. As one service provider noted, 'The process, even while they are here, compiling this documentation and they don't have money . . . the impact on their health, their stress levels and then all kinds of health issues come up as a result. So many of them are depressed, some have PTSD because of their background' (ibid.).

As noted in Envisioning's 2014 information sheet 'Mental health challenges for LGBT asylum seekers in Canada', supportive environments are extremely important, as research has shown that resilience and self-efficacy flourish in places where there are others who openly share their experiences and where there is social support. Such individuals require access to legal, health and social service professionals experienced in LGBT matters as well as asylum and settlement issues. Mental health professionals need to be conscious of the effects of stress. Moreover, there are cultural differences in how people experience and express stress and illness and how they deal with these feelings.

For example, refugee claimants in this study used various methods to cope with their depression and/or anxiety: 'I always prayed that night wouldn't come . . . when I am alone, I feel cramped. I have to take medication, a sleeping pill . . . sleep is hard because of the agony I passed through back home. It's like they are coming after me all the time' (ibid.).

The Minority Stress Model (Meyer, 2003) describes a state of chronic psychological strain resulting from stigma that can lead LGBT refugees to turn to external coping and numbing mechanisms such as alcohol, drugs or tobacco

(Hatzenbuehier et al., 2009; Envisioning, 2014b, p. 2). Access to appropriate mental health services can make a substantial difference to the mental wellbeing of LGBT asylum seekers, refugee claimants and refugees. Professionals working in these areas can assist these persons by working with them on their trauma. They can advocate for changes in the refugee-determination process to be more informed, enlightened and sensitised to the needs of LGBT asylum seekers and refugee claimants, which in turn may reduce the possibility of retraumatisation. In the meantime, as several refugee claimants noted, being able to access counselling services before, during and after the claims process would be extremely helpful: 'I think there needs to be some counselling like from a psychologist or like from an actual counsellor . . . counselling can actually help you in a lot of ways' (Envisioning 2015, p. 31).

However, service providers participating in this study repeatedly noted that such services are not widely available. Many challenges that LGBT refugees face in accessing services like trauma counselling are an extension of the hurdles that workers in mainstream services come up against in their work with these populations. Some service providers also grapple with developing services to meet the needs of LGBT refugees and acknowledge that more training on LGBT issues needs to occur at all levels of these organisations. In Ontario, small training projects and schemes have been introduced such as the Positive Space Initiative run by the Ontario Council of Agencies Serving Immigrants, Rainbow Health Ontario's Training Program, and Planned Parenthood Toronto's youth-facilitated TEACH Program. Nevertheless, mental health issues and services continue to be overlooked and underfinanced.

How can policy address these issues?

During the period the Envisioning study was being carried out, the aforementioned Bill C-31 came into effect (see Kinsman, chapter 3 for details of the act). Its impact was felt to a significant degree not only by those seeking asylum or refugee status, but also systemically in how this policy reframed refugee and immigration processes, recasting them as a burden on the nation. For example, by reducing timelines for the refugee claims process, in conjunction with budget cuts and strained resources, the government simultaneously increased stresses experienced by asylum seekers and refugees and service providers in this sector (Canadian Bar Association, 2012).

Most service providers participating in the Envisioning study criticised the impact of Bill C-31, questioning whether its intent is to actually assist asylum seekers, refugee claimants and refugees or to create a punitive environment within which to weed out 'bogus refugees' (Speaking Notes, 2012). Beneath the federal rhetoric of cost saving, many identified the hidden agenda to determine who is 'legitimate' and who is 'illegitimate':

I am talking about IFH. I am talking about the C-31 . . . the government has been using . . . the language of entitlements – that folks who are coming from outside are getting what Canadians don't have . . . it's pitting those who are deemed as a legitimate against those who are deemed as illegitimate. So it's also impacting not just . . . refugee claims but also . . . migrant work and work permits . . . the whole language around 'the people who are coming in to take our jobs' . . . it's a scapegoat to use the language of cost savings for Canadians. (Envisioning, 2015, p. 39)

Although at the time of writing the federal Liberal government has done much to redress many of the damaging components of Bill C-31, much still remains for it to do particularly in relation to LGBT asylum seekers and refugees. The current asylum-seeking and refugee claims processes demonstrate the ways in which heterosexuality, Eurocentrism and whiteness are intrinsically privileged within the social structures of Canada, as reflected in refugee and immigration policy. For many LGBT refugees, violence does not necessarily end upon their arrival in Canada, as they may experience violence, such as homo-, bi-, and/or transphobia, within their culture of origin in Canada or racism within Canadian LGBT communities. A determination process with restrictive timelines, forcing refugee applicants to relive traumatic life experiences during their initial arrival, as well as having to prove their SOGI status are examples of a systemic process that is highly Westernised and as such insensitive to the intrinsic mental, emotional and cultural implications. These circumstances can harm LGBTs attempting to resettle in Canada, where basic needs such as housing, employment and support services (health and social) are not easily found or accessed, yet must be addressed.

The Liberal government had to backtrack quickly early in its Syrian refugee crisis intervention in 2015 when it attempted to limit those permitted to enter Canada to women, children and families, initially completely overlooking the plight of gay and bisexual male Syrians by excluding single men (Lum, 2015). Driven by a precautionary security-based agenda intended to contain terrorism, such exclusionary policies risk overlooking the persecution faced by members of that population being targeted due to their SOGIE. This task calls for intricate and sensitised work in separating out security measures that may pose threats to the country and those suitable for individuals who face personal threats based on their social location during highly vulnerable circumstances. It is important for the Canadian federal government to take into serious consideration the everyday experiences of the material realities of asylum seekers, refugee claimants and refugees and the service providers who work with them, in its legal and political practices, as they in turn reflect the values of the Canadian nation state.

A further test of enacting Canadian values are laws and policy that recognise and address the inequities that operate along intersectional asymmetries of geopolitics, class, race, gender, sexuality and ability. Such laws and policies contribute to structural elements that directly affect applicants' capacity to access travel documents, cross borders, sustain themselves and gain access to permanent status. In essence, policy must be cognisant of the fact that for many LGBT refugees, and especially those who are racialised (the case for the majority of participants in the Envisioning study), attempts to resettle in Canada often occur in precarious economic social environments that are highly racialised, gendered, sexualised and classed, with direct and negative implications on their mental health. Their endeavours to attain asylum or refugee status become an additional burden within a tightly administered system, compounding any of the above social locations. The Canadian system, which our research indicates is based on cisgendered, heteronormative, white, Eurocentric values, inevitably creates its own forms of violence sometimes blatant and other times subtle. The determination process forces LGBTs to seek documentation that is hard to obtain, not to mention the direct challenge it poses for any who have to assume a sexual or gender identity they are not culturally socialised to do. Those responsible for service provision and operation should acknowledge and factor in the unique and sensitive needs of LGBT asylum seekers and refugee claimants, as the mainstream resettlement sector lacks the knowledge, training and hence capacity to address such issues.

Discussion and analysis

The requirement for asylum seekers and refugee claimants to prove their sexual orientation/gender identity/expression is a unique challenge. The implications this burden has on mental health cannot be underestimated. What is particularly disturbing about such processes being imposed by the state is its homonationalistic tendency to frame and define such characteristics in terms of Westernised notions, with little or no respect for the international diaspora. This adds to the anxiety felt by LGBT asylum seekers and refugee claimants upon their arrival in Canada, a process that does not accommodate these populations well in general, let alone the gender and sexually diverse. An astonishing number of participants in the Envisioning study spoke of being assisted by total strangers with good hearts, rather than by a formalised systemic response which left them to their own devices.

The normative experience of seeking asylum or refugee status is psychosocially and emotionally fraught, as it is based on the very mixed feelings of having or choosing to leave one's country of origin and all that goes with it (family, friends, career, culture, life). Such normative experiences become exacerbated by sweeping and overly simplistic structural and systemic processes such as determining designated countries of origin, having to prove one's sexual or gender identity and accelerating the timelines of applications and processing. The state's lack of a nuanced approach to these procedures causes the stress levels of all stakeholders to increase and challenges the mental wellbeing of asylum seekers and refugee claimants, particularly LGBTs. The state, lawmakers and policymakers would do well to listen to the voices of LGBT asylum seekers and refugee claimants as well as their service providers – such as those who participated in the Envisioning study. This would help these bodies address the settlement experiences of these individuals in Canada, including their housing, employment, general healthcare and mental health needs.

Mental health service provision to the asylum-seeking and refugee populations is a given need. Yet, sensitively and effectively meeting those needs require collaboration between the state, service providers, and most importantly asylum seekers, refugee claimants and refugees. To underscore such cooperation, a nuanced understanding is required of the many needs these populations have and how best to address them, keeping their mental health foremost. Regardless of their immediate need, such as housing, food, employment and social support, their mental health is being affected. It is crucial then that the desperately needed systemic changes take into consideration the nuances of sexuality, gender identity/expression, race, ethnicity, abilities, age, class and so on, respecting the realities and experiences of these people in their countries of origin and the opportunities that can be provided to them as they resettle in Canada.

Recommendations

The results of Envisioning's study 'Is Canada a safe haven?' clearly demonstrate the need for systemic change that will swiftly address the requirements of LGBT asylum seekers, refugee claimants and refugees and their particular mental health issues. Hence, we reiterate recommendations here that would more sensitively address those needs.

First, LGBT refugees who arrive in Canada navigate and negotiate a complex claims process within a limited time which severely limits their ability to produce the documentation that supports their claim. Not all refugee claimants have access to the information necessary to prove their SOGI as the result of persecution in their home country, lack of a supportive community and lack of access to resources. A disproportionate emphasis on 'credibility' in the claims process forces LGBT refugees to produce highly personal evidence to prove their SOGI, a major source of anxiety and stress for many of them. As a result, the claims process can be a major contributor to retraumatisation. Therefore, we recommend that decision makers focus on proving the threat of persecution as a result of SOGI and not on SOGI as an identity. Although practical challenges can arise when such a principle is implemented, it nevertheless should be the central focus, as it is not possible to attempt a fair assessment of the SOGI of claimants during a refugee proceeding.

It is worth noting here that the Immigration and Refugee Board (IRB) of Canada, charged with determining landed immigrant and refugee status, undertook a review of its SOGI guidelines towards the end of the work carried out by Envisioning. The latter participated in the consultations process providing feedback and policy recommendations based on project findings. The new IRB Chairperson's Guideline 9 regarding SOGI (IRB of Canada, 2017) do take into account a number of recommendations from Envisioning and other specialists in the field, including recognition of mental health concerns based on SOGI and utilisation of procedural accommodations as per the IRB's Chairperson Guideline 8 (IRB of Canada, 2012). Nevertheless, our recommendation that proof of SOGI be dropped in favour of pursuing proof of persecution based on SOGI was rejected. This thus remains an ongoing concern regarding the refugee-determination process.

Secondly, significant gaps in settlement and support services for LGBT refugees make it difficult for claimants to access mental health services. In order to address these gaps, the Envisioning report recommended that the federal government reinstate the IFHP, in keeping with the federal court judgment. As mentioned above, this was done in 2016.

Next, provincial governments must also increase resource allocations to counselling and mental health support services that are sensitive to and aware of LGBT refugee issues. Before, during and after the BOC process is a time of particularly high stress and often traumatises LGBT asylum seekers. Adequate support mechanisms would address their mental health needs during this vulnerable time.

Finally, mental health information on LGBT refugees made available at points of entry would improve access to services for LGBT refugees and claimants. For most of these individuals, arrival and claiming asylum are shaped by incidents of homo-bi-transphobia and racism. Any mental health strategies designed for this community must incorporate a critical race perspective on LGBT asylum that considers how racialised identities intersect with LGBT issues.

Conclusion

This chapter has drawn from the extensive data gathered for this segment of the Envisioning research study to focus in particular on the mental health of the LGBT asylum seeker/refugee claimant/refugee populations in the GTA, It has provided a contextual backdrop for mental health issues in Canada in general and outlined many specific and unique mental health concerns of these LGBT populations. Our data illustrated how escape from violence, the refugee-determination process, and resettlement in Canada have a direct impact on the mental health and wellbeing of our participants. This chapter has also provided a specific critical examination of how policy can address these issues and a broader analysis and discussion highlighting the multilevel nature of many of these concerns. Mental health in and of itself is a highly complex state of being that is always in flux. Our study indicated that the quality of this state is easily and directly affected by the experiences of being an LGBT asylum seeker, refugee claimant or refugee. To this end, we believe the system needs to better accommodate LGBTs who are fleeing from persecution, and that sensitised mental health services are greatly needed.

References

Canadian Bar Association, National Immigration Law Section (2012) 'Submission on Bill C-31: Protecting Canada's Immigration System Act', available at: www.cba.org/CMSPages/GetFile.aspx?guid=293bebf9-5237-4106-a26a-7d4241501a38 (accessed 5 Mar. 2018).

Canadian Doctors for Refugee Care (2014) 'Federal Government sabotaging efforts to provide care for refugees under Ontario Temporary Health Program', available at: www.doctorsforrefugeecare.ca (accessed 12 Dec. 2017).

Canadian Mental Health Association (2015) 'Fast facts about mental illness', available at: www.cmha.ca/media/fast-facts-about-mental-illness/#.VqBHAiorLIU (accessed 12 Dec. 2017).

Envisioning Global LGBT Human Rights (2014a) 'Envisioning LGBT refugee rights in Canada: the impact of Canada's new immigration regime', available at: http://envisioninglgbt.blogspot.com/p/publicationsresources.html (accessed 25 May 2018).

— (2014b) 'Mental health challenges for LGBT asylum seekers in Canada' information sheet, available at: http://envisioninglgbt.blogspot.com/p/resources.html (accessed 25 May 2018).

— (2015) 'Envisioning LGBT refugee rights in Canada: is Canada a safe haven?', available at: http://envisioninglgbt.blogspot.com/p/publicationsresources.html (accessed 25 May 2018).

Government of Canada (2012) 'Speaking notes for the Honourable Jason Kenney, PC, MP, Minister of Citizenship, Immigration and Multiculturalism' for news conference in Ottawa, 16 Feb., available at: www.canada.ca/en/immigration-refugees-citizenship/news/archives/speeches-2012/jason-kenney-minister-2012-02-16.html (accessed 12 Dec. 2017).

Hatzenbuehler, M., S. Nole-Hoeksma and J. Dovidio (2009) 'How does sexual minority stigma "get under the skin"? A psychological mediation framework', *Psychological Bulletin*, 135 (5): 707–30.

Immigration and Refugee Board of Canada (2012) 'Chairperson Guideline 8: procedures with respect to vulnerable persons appearing before the IRB',

available at: www.irb-cisr.gc.ca/Eng/BoaCom/references/pol/guidir/Pages/
GuideDir08.aspx (accessed 12 Dec. 2017).
— (2017) 'Chairperson's Guideline 9: proceedings before the IRB involving
sexual orientation and gender identity and expression', available at: www.
irb-cisr.gc.ca/Eng/BoaCom/references/pol/GuiDir/Pages/GuideDir09.
aspx#note5 (accessed 6 Mar. 2018).
Lum, Zi-Ann (2015) 'How Canada will screen gay Syrian refugee
men', *Huffington Post*, 25 Nov., available at: www.huffingtonpost.
ca/2015/11/25/syrian-refugees-canada-gay_n_8650582.html (accessed 5
Mar. 2018).
Meyer I. (2003) 'Prejudice, social stress and mental health in lesbian, gay
and bisexual populations: conceptual issues and research evidence',
Psychological Bulletin, 129 (5): 647–97.
Nicholson, B.L. (1997) 'The influence of pre-emigration and post-emigration
stressors on mental health: a study of Southeast Asian refugees', *Social
Work Research*, 21 (1): 19–31.
Ou Jin Lee, E. and S. Brotman (2013) 'Structural intersectionality and anti-
oppressive practice with LGBTQ refugees in Canada', *Canadian Social
Work Review*, 30 (2): 157–83.
Sales, R. (2005) 'Secure borders, safe haven: a contradiction in terms?', *Ethnic
and Racial Studies*, 28 (3): 445–62.
Shannon, P.J., G.A. Vinson, E. Wieling, T. Cook and J. Letts (2015) 'Torture,
war trauma, and mental health symptoms of newly arrived Karen
refugees', *Journal of Loss and Trauma*, 20 (6): 577–90.
Shannon, P.J., E. Wieling, J.S. McCleary and E. Becher (2015) 'Exploring
the mental health effects of political trauma with newly arrived
refugees', *Qualitative Health Research*, 25 (4): 443–57.
World Health Organization (2014) 'Mental health: a state of well-being',
www.who.int/features/factfiles/mental_health/en/ (accessed 12 Dec.
2017).

PART 2
Resilience, resistance and hope: organising for social change

Ten years ago, I set out on the path to achieve equality in my country – to bring down Belize's sodomy law – and this year, I won. The news of this victory has reverberated throughout the Caribbean and been a beacon of hope for many ... The best thing I see across the Caribbean today is that we are building an LGBT movement. We are not waiting. We're leading and insisting on a better quality of life for ourselves. (Caleb Orozco, speaking on 21 Sep. 2016)[1]

Figure 12. First Pride march in Uganda, Kampala, Uganda, 6 August 2012. Photo credit: *And Still We Rise*, Sexual Minorities Uganda and Envisioning Global LGBT Human Rights.

1   See: 'At historic UN event, presidents and prime ministers push to LGBT equality', OutRight Action International, https://www.outrightinternational.org/content/historic-un-event-presidents-and-prime-ministers-push-lgbt-equality (accessed 10 Apr. 2018).

8

The rise of SOGI: human rights for LGBT people at the United Nations

Kim Vance, Nick J. Mulé, Maryam Khan and Cameron McKenzie

Three major factors of the Envisioning Global LGBT Human Rights study (Envisioning) are addressed in this chapter: the continuing criminalisation of lesbian, gay, bisexual, transsexual, transgender (LGBT) individuals internationally, including many in the Commonwealth; the extent to which criminalisation and persecution of people based on their sexual orientation and/or gender identity (SOGI) is being taken up and addressed in policy and law in international human rights arenas, in particular the United Nations (UN); and the courage and resolve of LGBT human rights defenders.

Seventy-one countries criminalise consensual same-sex acts. The death penalty can be imposed in eight UN states, with four implementing it (Iran, Saudi Arabia, Sudan and Yemen). It is also enacted in 12 states of Nigeria[1] and Southern parts of Somalia[2] and is implemented without codification in Iraq and Daesh (Carroll and Mendos, 2017, p. 40). The persecution faced by LGBT people includes such human rights violations as extrajudicial killings, torture and ill-treatment, sexual assault and rape, invasions of privacy, arbitrary detention, and denial of employment and education opportunities (Amnesty International Canada, 2015).

Because criminalisation of LGBT people has been instigated by colonial laws, the theoretical premise of this chapter is postcolonial and pro-LGBT, in that we urge a modernised, more nuanced understanding of human rights that broadens and creates a more inclusive scope, namely that of SOGI. Universalist

---

1 The death penalty for homosexuality is not national law in Nigeria, yet 12 of its Northern states where sharia law is followed do impose that penalty for same-sex acts between men.

2 The death penalty for homosexuality is not national law in Somalia, yet their Southern parts have imposed sharia law through their Islamic court rulings, punishing homosexuality with flogging or the death penalty.

K. Vance, N. J. Mulé, M. Khan and C. McKenzie (2018) 'The rise of SOGI: human rights for LGBT people at the United Nations', in N. Nicol et al. (eds.) *Envisioning Global LGBT Human Rights: (Neo)colonialism, Neoliberalism, Resistance and Hope* (London: Human Rights Consortium, Institute of Commonwealth Studies), pp. 223–45.

notions of human rights are deconstructed by Lau (2004), pointing to the challenge presented by the cultural relativist stance of non-Western countries and how sexual orientation is implicated in international human rights law debates. This increasing presence in the international arena, has usually been via a universalist approach to human rights law, which argues that all internationally recognised documents and covenants cover it. Yet numerous nation states will reject sexual orientation on the basis of cultural relativist positions that uphold their cultural sovereignty (p. 1689). This approach has since played out in gender identity/expression and intersex issues, with states contesting notions of gender and sex and attempting to limit and narrow interpretations of them. The pursuit of human rights strictly from a legal rights framework risks reconstituting the status quo, rather than transforming it, thereby failing to achieve social justice (LaViolette and Whitworth, 1994). Legal rights are important for protecting LGBT persons from persecution, but constitute just one component of the larger goal of social construction recognising gender and sexual diversity. Such diversity is made up of the intersection of social locations such as gender, sexuality, culture, class, age, (dis)ability, religion, health and wellbeing and self-determination (Human Rights Watch, 2009; Saiz, 2004; Sauer and Podhora, 2013; Tiefer, 2002). The recognition of such conjunctions represents the core of intersectionality theory.

Puar (2007) has extended intersectionality theory with the notion of 'assemblage', 'a series of dispersed but mutually implicated and messy networks, draw[ing] together enunciation and dissolution, causality and effect, organic and nonorganic forces' (p. 211). Puar proposes looking at the intersections of race, gender, sexuality, nation and class as assemblages – as concepts that are linked, are constantly evolving and 'always in the state of becoming' (p. 194). She urges us to think prior to and beyond the positionality and its intersectional coordinates to account for their fluid movement. Although the concept of assemblages is recognised increasingly in the academic arena and in the literature (Mepschen et al., 2010; Shannahan, 2010), in the work of international human rights circles, including our study, concepts of intersectionality are far more common, and thus this chapter will focus solely on intersectionality.

Envisioning's work was carefully carried out so as not to replicate colonialist actions. For instance, this requires being cognitive of and sensitive to the voices of LGBT human rights defenders in the countries which were cooperating with us. Working in such a manner kept us in check in terms of avoiding falling into Westernised notions of homonormativity (see Duggan, 1995; 2003) or homonationalism and queer liberalism (Puar, 2007). More broadly, imperial and colonial expansion projects have had powerful influences on worldviews with detrimental effects on the marginalised, such as LGBT people (Said, 1994; Wane, 2008). Yet the LGBT movement has evolved in the public arena and internally to take a decidedly postcolonial perspective, one example being increased recognition of gender expression,[3] in addition to gender identity and sexual orientation (SOGIE) (Saiz, 2004; Swiebel, 2009).

This chapter examines how SOGI matters came to be taken up as human rights issues at the UN. While acknowledging the role HIV movements played in this process (see, for example, Joint UN Programme on HIV/ AIDS (UNAIDS), 2008; 2011), our study focused on decriminalisation. This summary begins with the role that civil society played in introducing and advocating attention to SOGI concerns, what the UN response has been over time and the role the Yogyakarta Principles[4] continue to play in guiding the issues. The study's methodology is described and findings are shared from interviews with UN representatives and LGBT human rights defenders. A critical analysis is then provided of the decolonising process, the implications

Figure 13. Dialogue 2012: Focus on Strengthening Caribbean Response and Linking Regional and International Advocacy around the World, Saint Lucia, 6 February 2012. Photo credit: ARC International and Envisioning Global LGBT Human Rights.

3 'Gender expression' refers to how a person presents their gender through their physical appearance – including dress, hairstyles, accessories, cosmetics – and mannerisms, speech, behavioural patterns, names and personal references. This may or may not conform to their gender identity.

4 In 2006, in response to well-documented patterns of abuse, a group of distinguished international human rights experts met in Yogyakarta, Indonesia, to outline a set of international principles on SOGI affirming binding international legal standards with which all states must comply. The result was the Yogyakarta Principles, International Commission of Jurists, 2007, see www.yogyakartaprinciples.org (accessed 5 Oct. 2017).

of SOGI being addressed in the international human rights arena, and the courage and resiliency of the LGBT human rights defenders.

Civil society engagement in UN fora

One of the first opportunities for global engagement on sexuality was the 1975 UN Conference in Mexico to mark International Women's Year. This pivotal moment brought together lesbians from the North and South, who engaged with the feminist movement on sexuality and fostered development of networks that were to play a key role throughout the UN International Women's Decade to follow. Around the same time (1978), the European-based International Gay Association (now known as the International Lesbian, Gay, Bisexual, Trans and Intersex Association, or ILGA) was founded. One of its aims was to maximise the effectiveness of gay organisations by coordinating political action on an international level, in particular applying concerted pressure on governments and international institutions.

As in Mexico in 1975, the UN Women's Conference in Nairobi in 1985 provided a forum for the first public discussion of lesbianism in Kenya. Self-identified lesbians from all regions spoke at a press conference and issued a 'Third World lesbian statement' that challenged the notion that this was a 'white, western' matter (ARC International, 2009, p. 1). By the time of the UN World Conference on Human Rights in Vienna in 1993, global women's networks and activism had developed into coordinated movements to bring women's and lesbian perspectives into mainstream UN activities. Three non-governmental organisations (NGOs) working on lesbian and gay issues (ILGA, the Australian Council for Lesbian and Gay Rights, and EGALE-Canada) were accredited to the World Conference, marking the first time that NGOs working on these issues had been recognised at a UN event. In addition, ILGA was to secure formal UN Economic and Social Council (ECOSOC) accreditation in 1993, but this was revoked in 1994 and not reinstated again until 17 years later in 2011 (ILGA, 2013).

All of these developments set the stage for the Fourth World Conference on Women in Beijing in September 1995 – widely considered a watershed moment in international lesbian visibility. Eleven explicitly lesbian or lesbian and gay organisations were accredited to that conference, and two Canadian lesbian activists unfurled a banner in the main plenary saying 'Lesbian rights are human rights'.

While the world conferences have served as an invaluable forum for sexual and gender minorities, activists working on these issues have increasingly engaged with other UN human rights mechanisms. A turning point came in 2003 when Brazil introduced a resolution on sexual orientation and human rights at the UN Commission on Human Rights in Geneva. Prior to this point, there was little consistent LGBT organising around this particular UN body. Brazil's initiative, although not initially motivated by strong civil society engagement, served as a focal point and mobilising tool for NGOs around the world. An NGO strategy meeting was held in Brazil in December 2003, which was attended by a diverse cross-regional group of activists who engaged with and lent support to Brazilian government representatives responsible for crafting and guiding the resolution (ARC International, 2003).

As a result of that meeting, and similar coordinated organising efforts, the commission's 2004 session saw more than 50 LGBT activists from all regions of the world gather to support the resolution. A global listserv (the 'SOGI list') was initiated by ARC International, a newly launched Canadian-based NGO, to facilitate this worldwide momentum. That listserv now has more than 1500 subscribers who regularly engage in strategic discussions about advocacy in spaces of regional and global politics. Indeed, those debates and the strategic North-South organising that has flowed out of them, have been largely responsible for securing state support for three successful resolutions on SOGI (discussed later) at the UN Human Rights Council (UNHRC) in Geneva (formerly the UN Commission on Human Rights).

Movements of trans and intersex persons have recently started to mobilise in global politics spaces. Like lesbian women who have always been part of the women's/feminist movement, trans people in particular have been part of LBGT movements since their inception. Despite the fact that they often face the most severe human rights abuses and form the basis of some of the earliest documentation from UN experts, it has not been until this decade (from 2010) that they have begun to mobilise more visibly at the regional and international levels, and sometimes from their own separate platforms. Global Action for Trans*[5] Equality (GATE), the first independent trans organisation focused on political engagement at worldwide level, was founded in 2010.

The Organization Intersex International (OII) was founded in Québec in 2004 and has branches on six continents. However, although the consistent engagement of intersex activists in UN spaces has been very recent, it is quite successful in terms of significant victories within the UN treaty body system, for instance.

The international trade union movement has also been an important site for global politics and organising. Two such unions, Public Services International (PSI) and Education International (EI), representing over 50 million workers in 950 trade unions around the world, organised a historic joint LGBT forum in 2004 (see Education International, 2015),[6] which generated important recommendations for the International Labour Organization (ILO), the UN Educational Scientific and Cultural Organisation (UNESCO), UNAIDS and other groups.

5   Includes all transgender, non-binary, and gender non-conforming identities.
6   Subsequent reports on the site reveal that follow-up activities have been conducted within international fora in the wake of these recommendations.

As mentioned above, beginning in 1993, LGBT-identified groups (such as ILGA) began seeking official consultative status with the UN. That status is granted by the ECOSOC, after reviewing recommendations from its subsidiary body – the Committee on NGOs. This committee has rejected more than ten applications submitted by NGOs working on SOGI. In 2006, 2007, 2008, 2009 and 2010, the ECOSOC has had to overturn these recommendations in order to uphold the principle of non-discrimination underpinning the UN Charter. While some recent success has been achieved in this area, civil society groups have resiliently and persistently engaged with international fora.

Sexual and gender minorities have increasingly sought to organise in important regional politics sites as well. A coalition of LGBT organisations began work in 2006 on the inclusion of SOGIE in the draft Inter-American Convention against Racism and All Forms of Discrimination and Intolerance. Its membership has since expanded and it now works more generally on ensuring these issues are included when the Organization of American States (OAS) meets (OutRight Action International, 2015). This coalition has advocated successfully for SOGI resolutions at the OAS every year since 2009.

In addition, since 2004, sexual and gender minorities in Africa have worked in coalition to engage with the African Commission on Human and Peoples' Rights (ACHPR). In 2009, they secured a SOGI resolution from the NGO forum, solidifying strong support from allied civil society groups. Despite groups like the Coalition of African Lesbians (CAL) having their applications for accreditation to this body rejected and then accepted, the coalition work has endured, and in 2014 the ACHPR adopted a resolution on violence and other human rights violations on the basis of real or imputed SOGI.

The UN response

All of this international advocacy, beginning with the efforts of lesbian women in the 1970s and 1980s, led to UN bodies and experts starting to devote attention to these issues in the 1990s and early 2000s. In 1994, the UN Human Rights Committee became the first UN body to acknowledge that human rights encompass sexual orientation (Gerber and Gory, 2014). The human rights complaint that precipitated this acknowledgment was known as the *Toonen v. Australia* case.[7] The UN Human Rights Committee emphasised that discrimination based on sexual orientation was being employed for discrimination on the foundation of sex (Sanders, 1996). The UN recognised in section 6.2 that Toonen was a 'victim of arbitrary interferences with his privacy' and should have had 'a right to freedom from arbitrary or unlawful interference with privacy'.

---

7   *Toonen v. Australia*, CCPR/C/50/D/488/1992, UNHRC, 4 Apr. 1994, available at: www.refworld.org/cases,HRC,48298b8d2.html.html (accessed 4 Mar. 2018).

A review of the reporting indicates that it grew from two Special Procedures addressing these issues specifically in 1998, to five in 2002, building to more than a dozen in 2006. This reporting reflects the commitment of the experts, but also increasing documentation and reporting from the civil society groups who engage with the experts. The special rapporteur on violence against women, its causes and consequences has been critical in documenting and highlighting violence against women based on their SOGI within the UN system. Radhika Coomaraswamy's report (1997) first opened the door for women's sexuality to be regulated by state and non-state actors.[8] Although it did not mention lesbians or trans women specifically, it did highlight family and community violence, including killings, and spoke of the risks facing women who live their lives outside of heterosexuality.

Furthermore, around this time the special rapporteur on extrajudicial, summary or arbitrary executions drew attention to killings of transgender women. Ironically, the Executions resolution[9] adopted by the UN General Assembly (UNGA) in 2003, was the first UN resolution to specifically name these kinds of violations, but it referred only to sexual orientation (gender identity was not added until 2012).

The UN Secretary-General's Study on Violence against Women was also extremely important in documenting violations based on SOGI. Section IV.B.5 in the report, entitled 'Violence against women and multiple discrimination', includes references to SOGI (2006). The US-based International Gay and Lesbian Human Rights Commission (IGLHRC) contributed a powerful input memo to the study (2006), which no doubt shaped some of the references, along with the work of the special rapporteur.

The current and former UN High Commissioners for Human Rights (Zeid Ra'ad Al Hussein and Navi Pillay, respectively) and former UN Secretary-General Ban Ki-moon, have arguably been more vocal on violations based on SOGI than any of their predecessors. In January 2011, a special sitting of the UNHRC was convened to hear remarks from Ban Ki-moon. In a strong statement, he called for an end to human rights violations based on SOGI:

> We must reject persecution of people because of their sexual orientation or gender identity, who may be arrested, detained or executed for being lesbian, gay, bisexual or transgender. They may not have popular or political support, but they deserve our support in safeguarding their fundamental human rights. I understand that sexual orientation and gender identity raise sensitive cultural issues. But cultural practice cannot

8   'Report of the special rapporteur on violence against women, its causes and consequences', no. E/CN.4/1997/47, UN ECOSOC, 1997, available at: www.ohchr.org/EN/Issues/Women/SRWomen/Pages/SRWomenIndex.aspx (accessed 18 Dec. 2017).

9   UNGA: Resolution adopted by the General Assembly 57th session, 57/214, 'Extrajudicial, summary or arbitrary executions', 25 Feb. 2003 (accessed 3 Aug. 2017).

justify any violation of human rights. Women's treatment as second-class citizens has been justified, at times, as a 'cultural practice'. So has institutional racism and other forms of inhuman punishment. But that is merely an excuse. When our fellow humans are persecuted because of their sexual orientation or gender identity, we must speak out.

In September 2016, history was made at the UNHRC in Geneva when it appointed the first ever independent expert on protection against violence and discrimination based on SOGI. Despite a process of amendments to the resolution creating the mandate, a close vote on the resolution itself, and an attempt to undermine the entire appointment during the UNGA meeting in New York, the first appointed independent expert, Vitit Muntarbhorn began work on his mandate in November 2016 and delivered his first reports to the UNHRC in June 2017 and UNGA in October 2017.

Table 8.1 is a timeline of UN resolutions, joint statements and reports. Even though advocacy efforts and evidence from reports began with articulating violations against groups and individuals (that is, lesbians, trans women, gay men and so on), once the UN response began to take shape, the emergence of the concepts of sexual orientation and, later, gender identity in the language of these resolutions and statements could be observed. This has remained the consistent default language, despite some efforts to advocate for specificity in certain resolutions. The next section uses the development and terminology of the Yogyakarta Principles as a case study to further elaborate on the context of SOGI language within the UN.

Table 1. Timeline of UN resolutions, joint statements and reports

2002	Resolution 2002/77 on the question of the death penalty calls on governments to ensure that the death penalty is not imposed for non-violent acts such as sexual relations between consenting adults – adopted (25 in favour, 20 against, 8 abstentions) by the Commission on Human Rights, Geneva. Resolution A/RES/57/214 on extrajudicial, summary and arbitrary executions calls on governments to investigate promptly and thoroughly all killings because of sexual orientation – adopted (130 in favour, 0 against, 49 abstentions) by the General Assembly, New York
2003	Resolution on sexual orientation and human rights, introduced, deferred and then withdrawn in 2004, at the Commission on Human Rights, Geneva (often referred to as the 'Brazilian Resolution')
2005	Joint statement on sexual orientation and human rights, delivered by New Zealand on behalf of 32 states at the Commission on Human Rights, Geneva

2006	Joint statement on SOGI and human rights, delivered by Norway on behalf of 54 states at the Human Rights Council, Geneva
2008	Joint statement on SOGI and human rights, delivered by Argentina on behalf of 67 states at the General Assembly, New York
2011	Joint statement on SOGI and human rights, delivered by Colombia on behalf of 85 states at the Human Rights Council, Geneva
2011	Resolution A/HRC/17/L.9/Rev.1 on human rights and SOGI – adopted (23 in favour, 19 against, 3 abstentions) by the Human Rights Council, Geneva (often referred to as the 'South African Resolution'). As a result of this resolution, a high-level panel on SOGI was held during the Human Rights Council's 19th session
2011	Report of the UN High Commissioner for Human Rights on violence and discrimination based on SOGI (A/HRC/19/41)
2012	Resolution A/RES/67/168 on extrajudicial, summary and arbitrary executions calls on governments to investigate promptly and thoroughly all killings because of SOGI – adopted without a vote by the General Assembly, New York
2014	Resolution A/HRC/27/32 on human rights and SOGI – adopted (25 in favour, 14 against, 7 abstentions) by the Human Rights Council, Geneva (often referred to as the 'LAC4 Resolution')
2015	Report of the UN High Commissioner for Human Rights on discrimination and violence against individuals based on their SOGI A/HRC/29/23
2016	Resolution A/HRC/32/2 on protection against violence and discrimination based on SOGI – adopted (23 in favour, 18 against, 6 abstentions) by the Human Rights Council, Geneva (often referred to as the 'LAC7 Resolution')

The UN and SOGI language: case study on the Yogyakarta Principles

In 2006, the then UN high commissioner for human rights, Louise Arbour, expressed concern about the inconsistency of approach in law and practice on sexual orientation and gender identity. In an address to an LGBT conference held in Montréal, she suggested that although the principles of universality and non-discrimination apply to the grounds of SOGI, a more comprehensive articulation of these rights in international law is needed, 'It is precisely in this meeting between the normative work of States and the interpretive functions of international expert bodies that a common ground can begin to emerge' (Arbour, 2006).

Furthermore, international practice was demonstrating a wide variety of approaches to addressing the human rights situation of lesbian, gay, bisexual, transgender, intersex (LGBTI) people. Although some UN Special Procedures, treaty bodies, and states preferred to speak of 'sexual orientation' or 'gender identity', others spoke of 'lesbians', 'gays', 'transgender', or 'transsexual' people and still others spoke of 'sexual preference' or used the language of 'sexual minorities'. In addition, gender identity was little understood, with some mechanisms and states referencing transsexuality as a 'sexual orientation' and others frankly acknowledging that they do not understand the term at all.

It is in this context of such diverse approaches, inconsistency, gaps and opportunities that the Yogyakarta Principles on the application of international human rights law in relation to SOGI were conceived. The proposal to develop the Principles originated in 2005, led by a coalition of mainstream human rights and LGBT-specific NGOs subsequently facilitated by the International Service for Human Rights and the International Commission of Jurists.

Twenty-nine experts were invited to draft the principles. Coming from 25 countries representing all geographic regions, they included one former UN high commissioner for human rights, 13 current or former UN human rights special mechanism office holders or treaty body members, two serving judges of domestic courts, and a number of academics and LGBTI activists.

Launched in 2007, the principles are a coherent and comprehensive identification of the obligation of states to respect, protect and fulfil the human rights of all persons, regardless of their SOGI. The experts chose this terminology to unify the language and avoid the critique that not all cultures and identities embrace the 'LGBTI' label, as some view it as a 'Western' concept.

Since their launch, the principles have attracted considerable attention from states, UN actors and civil society. They have played a significant role within advocacy efforts and, whether directly or otherwise, in normative and jurisprudential development.

In 2016, the International Service for Human Rights (ISHR) and ARC International launched the YP+10 process to review and update the Principles, taking into account significant developments in international law and gaps in the original document that had been identified. Involving an open call for submissions and a number of consultations, the process ultimately concluded with a second expert's meeting in Geneva in September 2017. These experts produced nine Additional Principles and more than 100 Additional State Obligations with a new list of expert signatories. The new document also expands the 'SOGI' terminology from the original Principles, to 'SOGIESC' (sexual orientation, gender identity, gender expression and sex characteristics).

Methodology

Envisioning's methodological approach included examination of SOGI as a human rights issue addressed at the UN. A critical structural framework encompassing culture, discourses, institutions, legal framework, political systems and socioeconomic infrastructures was deployed. The research partnership with ARC International allowed security clearance to the research team and granted it access to the New York UN offices, and grey literature at the UN library. The researchers analysed data on UN SOGI voting records from 2006 to 2014 via the ARC International website. The records on states involved in the votes were compiled into two categories: potential supporters or non-supporters. The team also conducted online research through UN online databases alongside archival explorations at the New York Central Library, where its members also attended the 'Daily Beast Quorum LGBT Voices' forum with international human rights defenders during the Human Rights Day celebration on 10 December 2014. It should be noted that the researchers contacted all five institutions through ongoing email, social media and cold-calling from September 2014 until June 2015. Snowball sampling was also used. The team went to great lengths to secure interviews with potential participants. All those agreeing to be interviewed did so on condition of anonymity and full confidentiality. Purposive research was conducted at four UN institutions: the UNHRC, the UN High Commission on Refugees (UNHCR), the United Nations Development Programme (UNDP), and UN Women. Special rapporteurs were also contacted and interviewed. Individuals were emailed and phoned to schedule interviews, having been identified as holding positions at the UN concerned with LGBT issues.

The qualitative and semi-structured interviews (Patton, 1990; Wilson, 1996) lasted between 30 and 120 minutes, allowing participants to elaborate on their responses. Non-participatory observation was employed at the Daily Beast Quorum LGBT Voices Forum, an event that provided insights into the lives and experiences of LGBT human rights defenders across the globe. Interview questions focused on four themes under investigation by the Envisioning project: criminalisation of LGBT people; flight from violence and persecution; resistance to criminalisation; and the interaction between international treaty body human rights mechanisms and LGBT rights initiatives. The questions were derived from a literature review and feedback from co-applicants and partners of Envisioning, including ARC International. The interviews, digitally recorded and transcribed for analysis, were conducted in person, over the phone and via Skype from October 2014 to June 2015. Interviewers made every attempt to clarify comments in order to enhance participants' understanding of the research objectives (Glesne, 2011).

The macrosociological discourse analysis perspective (van Dijk 1985a; 1985b) and the qualitative data analytical instrument (Ritchie and Spencer,

1994) provided tools to address institutional influences (hegemonic norms), existing ideologies (how policy is developed and at whom it is directed), and cultural perspectives (perceived cultural clashes between LGBT and other cultural groups). By undertaking a qualitative perspective that captures participants' linguistics (words chosen) and, more importantly, the meaning and values associated with the words they use to express thoughts, this 'meaning-making' could then be attached to the themes identified by our study. Such discourses provide important information on world views, decision-making and knowledge associated with the subject matter, in this case LGBT human rights.

This study received approval from the Ethics Board at York University. Consent forms were sent to participants electronically. Their consent was also obtained orally prior to interviews being recorded. To ensure their anonymity, numerical coding was deployed (P1–12). Participants disclosed only the name of, but not their position at, the UN affiliated body for which they work. This chapter's findings were sent to them prior to publication. Only Quorum human rights defenders were identified, since the event was hosted and publicly broadcasted online and through social media.

Interview data

The following results were derived from the above-described interviews and the presentations given by human rights defenders. Transcripts revealed six broad themes and their sub-themes: 1) language and terminology; 2) reports and guidelines; 3) UN staff internal issues and dynamics; (4) member states' strategies to achieve/put forward LGBT rights on the agenda; 5) relations with the LGBT community; and 6) LGBT issues at the UN. Additionally, UN SOGI voting records (2006–14), provided by ARC International, were reviewed to offer the context of member states' voting on SOGI matters.

Language and terminology

The use of language and identity in the research data is the focus of this theme. All participants had unique understandings of LGBT-related terminology, from which the researchers were able to create nine sub-themes: gender identity, sexual orientation, trans, intersex, lesbian, gay, bisexual, sexual orientation and gender identity. Furthermore, the 'SOGI' term captures regions and countries that may not deploy LGBT categories as identity markers or use UN terminology.

The UN participants P1–P8 and P10–P12 demonstrated a keen awareness of gender and sexual identity. None of them identified a uniform language for discussion of SOGI identity categories. For example, P3, observed,

> We have this imaginary LGBTQ community that, you know, only exists because we imagine it to be so. You know, and yet we are

enormously different, and I don't think that we're always fully aware of our differences. I think that we don't have intersectional analyses. We think because we are LGBTQ, we are therefore not responsible for having a real political analysis. I think that's been a huge issue, actually, and I think that LGBT groups have been taken to task for that.

On a macro level, P9 and P11 expressed their concerns about oppressive member states that do not recognise LGBT persons or terminology. As P11 proffered, 'If you are also an LGBTI individual in a country that is not open to sexual orientation, gender identity, then you . . . the problems that you already are facing as an asylum seeker or refugee will even . . . will be much larger because of your sexual orientation and or, gender identity.'

The individuals P4, P5, P8 and P10 also confirmed the premise about regressive policies whereby LGBT individuals face persecution. Finally, in some of the interviews, the terminology around sexual and gender identity were conflated, and sexual orientation was sometimes used as an umbrella term to discuss gender identities.

Reports and guidelines

This theme explored references to reports and guidelines that UN staff and other affiliates use in responding to and treating LGBT persons and communities. Furthermore, training emerged as a sub-theme, which encapsulated the LGBT sensitivity trainings of UN staff.

Issues related to SOGI have recently gained momentum on UN policy fronts, as highlighted by P4, 'It's only in the last two or three years I'm starting to see more attention to LGBT issues in policy and programming.' Participant P12 from UN Women asserted that they are developing LGBT-related policy and have appointed a lead person in the department.

The importance of developing training modules when working with LGBT refugees and asylum seekers was reported by P11 from the UNHCR:

> UNHCR has developed a training package with several modules for staff and their operational partners who work with [on] refugees and asylum seekers on how to engage with LGBTI individuals. Not just engage, but how to treat them, how to identify, how to make them feel comfortable, how to open up. So, a wide range of issues: how to assist their cases, how to conduct interviews, how to address them and so forth. It has been rolled out in a couple of countries already. There is training for a number of days... training will be assembled according to the profile of the training participants.

Moreover, P8 explained how the UNHRC has prioritised LGBT matters/rights at a policy level:

> We support the work of the UN Special Procedures, the special rapporteurs whose job it is to investigate and report and raise concerns with governments. So we feed a lot of information through to the

special rapporteurs, and a lot of those concerns have been taken up and turned into official communication that is sent to governments asking them to . . . essentially expressing our concerns about facts that they've been reporting to us, and asking them to respond . . . We also, of course, do a huge amount of advocacy, so a lot of that goes on behind the scenes . . . We do a lot of public education, public information work trying to kind of put the UN brand behind a message of equality for everyone, including LGBT people.

UN staff internal issues and dynamics

This theme identified UN internal politics, which play a role in how LGBT issues and rights are discussed and addressed. The UN staff interviewed had extensive experience and expertise in their various roles. As a result, all of them commented on the UN's internal mechanisms and dynamics, which can hinder and/or promote change on LGBT issues and rights. On the subject of employee benefits for same-sex couples, P9 highlighted the progress made and the internal conflicts it has led to among staff members:

> I think the Secretary General has really taken quite an important leadership role here in acknowledging the rights of LGBT staff members ... bitter staff members would say to you, 'Well, the Secretary-General has only engaged on this initiative in order to get re-elected two years ago' ... but nevertheless, it is a good development, and we take it for what it's worth.

P12 asserted that existing politics guide discussions on SOGI concerns. For instance, at UN Women, some staff 'are very keen on looking at the gender binary as a discourse between men and women because they feel that any kind of expansion of that . . . nuancing of that takes away from the focus on the women's movement. As you know, with many movements there is this whole thing about you protecting your constituency'.

The respondents P3 and P8 discussed how at times internal mechanisms can interfere with competing ideas and can lead to departmental power struggles. For instance, when staff members have differing agendas and belief systems, they may end up working in silos, as stated by P3:

> But we don't control what our colleagues in countries do . . . They are independent of us, whereas our regional colleagues and we are part of the same team. So there are some real differences there, and hence we are not uncommonly called out by local LGBT folks for the lack of support they get in their countries. You know? And we say, 'Yes, you know, we work with our country office colleagues as much as we can, but we can't control what they do.'

Other challenges can arise at the regional level as stated by P1: 'At the country level, well, you know, a lot of UN staff won't necessarily be aware or understand some of the challenges faced by LGBT persons. They may not have the training to understand human rights violations that they've faced.'

Similar insights were shared by P1, P6, P8 and P10 about how internal dynamics can affect interactions and working relationships within UN departments and their affiliated agencies.

Member states' strategies to get LGBT rights on the agenda

States' use of strategies to get LGBT rights included on the agenda demonstrates how they employ diplomacy, political tactics, and bargaining to advocate and/or block LGBT issues and concerns. The sub-theme of voting practices emerged, which discusses references to member states and their voting strategies.

The tension and struggles of working with UN member states were highlighted by P1–P12. For instance, P4 asserted, 'We're now under the microscope with member states, who ultimately control the entire UN system and expect us not to meddle in their business because it's their business.'

The challenges in countries where LGBT rights are prohibited were discussed by P1–P3, P6 and P11 while P9 commented on the power dynamics inherent in working collaboratively with member states, such as the lengths to which some of them will go in attempting to block procedures: 'They would allow or ascertain some reference to LGBT rights in return for other favours . . . they all want something from each other . . . there's many small elephants in the room that we don't see.' Similar situations with member states and the UN's focus on LGBT issues were echoed by P1: 'Member states have expressed that they do not believe that the Office should be dedicating attention and resources on this issue.' Additional tension and struggles when working with member states were disclosed by P4 and P7, the latter recounting, 'We don't want homosexuality imposed on this country, and we don't want the international community and the European Union to impose any strange values on our country.' P2 stipulated that even 'progressive member states', such as the United States' current Obama administration (at the time of the study), had prioritised 'reproductive health, women's issues, gay rights', unlike their Republican counterparts.

Further, P8 and P9 maintained that some member states' actions on LGBT issues can be politically motivated or interfered with. As P9 illustrated, 'The American ambassador was going to have a cup of coffee with the Iraqi ambassador at the time of the voting, so Iraq was not present when the voting was taken . . . things like this happen all the time in the UN . . . it's become a bit of a bargaining chip.'

The special rapporteur, P6, expressed the importance of NGOs providing information on the activities in various member states. This can be a delicate matter since special rapporteurs cannot be seen to favour NGOs over governments. 'We receive some official information from the government but very embarrassing stuff comes from the NGOs . . . But we can't be seen as being associated with the NGOs.' Hence, inherent biases within the UN system itself that favour special rapporteur relations between states over NGOs can in its own way contribute to blockages or slowed progress at best.

Relations with the LGBT community

The UN has taken steps to establish trust with LGBT NGOs, persons and communities. Four sub-themes emerged while conducting the analysis. 'Treatment of LGBT persons' looks at how they are treated across the globe, positively and negatively. 'Disclosure' considers when LGBT individuals have disclosed SOGI to human right defenders, UN officials and staff. 'Negative relations with LGBTs' underscores actions at the UN that can create barriers for LGBT NGOs, persons and communities. Lastly, 'Relationship building and advocacy with LGBTs' examines the efforts of UN staff members and human right defenders to support LGBT rights, persons and communities.

Many participants discussed the treatment of LGBT persons and communities in their work with UN departments and affiliated bodies. For example, P1 recollected the criminalisation of sexual and gender expression: 'We've had allegations of killings, of mob attacks, of torture, of discrimination in health, housing, employment; sexual violence and rape . . . restrictions on freedom of expression, freedom of association and assembly, or attacks on human rights defenders'.

Another respondent, P2, identified the myth of LGBT identities as Western inventions that can make promoting LGBT rights highly problematic, 'when people say, "It's western values", they say, "You know, we have nothing against homosexuals because there are none in our country"'.

Participants used a range of theoretical perspectives to guide their work. Many (P3–P8, P11, P12) deployed an intersectional analysis when discussing identities. For example, according to P12,

> At UN Women, it has to be seen as a multiplicity of strategies around intersectionality . . . the issues of somebody working in Malawi on these issues is very different from somebody who will work on this in Turkey and who will work on this in India and who will work on this in Pakistan, where there is a recognition, for example, of a third gender. So all of those multiple strategies need to be considered and brought into place for this work to move forward.

Many of those taking part engaged in LGBT advocacy. Some were creating awareness of LGBT issues and rights (P1–P5, P8, P10). Establishing trust with the LGBT community was also deemed important (P2, P8, P11, P12). Other participants relied on internal influence and support, sometimes covertly during a less supportive time.

Overall, UN departments, member states and countries differ to a certain extent in their interpretations of SOGI. A plethora of issues still need to be addressed in Europe and North America on LGBT human right violations. In most of the interviews, participants alluded to gains that need to be made in African, Middle Eastern and Caribbean regions, which in certain ways mitigate advancements made in these contexts.

LGBT issues at the UN

This last theme captures discussions of how LGBT gains are being made, especially when the term 'progressive' is applied. It also captures the shifts in attitudes, beliefs and values surrounding LGBT matters.

The policy level, according to P7 and P12, can benefit immensely from advocacy for changes to protect sexual and gender expression. As stated earlier, P12 from UN Women noted that the organisation is developing an LGBTI-specific policy, which has been part of the department's vision while P7 highlighted the need for intersectional advocacy and the development of allies: 'I would always go for forming alliances, maybe often new alliances, maybe surprising alliances. So in order, also, to overcome single issue advocacy. I mean, sometimes, of course, we have to also have single issue advocacy. It's legitimate'.

International coalitional organisations like ARC International, as P9 reported, have provided space and access to non-status LGBT groups at the UN while P8 noted that visibility of LGBT matters at the UN has increased in recent years: 'The fact that you have the issues aired so regularly at such a senior level by UN leadership, . . . big high-profile UN public information campaign, Free and Equal, all of that is giving the issue much more visibility, and in the end additional legitimacy and validity'. In addition, as P6 asserted, 'The Office of the High Commissioner for Human Rights in Geneva has worked on LGBTI issues for the past 10 years'. Furthermore, P2, P4, P5 and P10 mentioned that gains have been made, but P3–P8 and P10–P12 were of the opinion that there is need for further work.

In summary, the findings provide insight on how human rights violations experienced by LGBT populations are being addressed by the UN and its organs.

UN SOGI voting record

The researchers analysed data on UN SOGI voting records from 2006 to 2014 via the ARC International website. Votes were divided into two categories: supporters and non-supporters. Progress represents support for SOGI resolutions. Advocacy and education by LGBT human rights defenders has had an increasingly positive influence. Over the last eight years, some states have made advances towards supporting SOGI resolutions, as their voting records demonstrate. African regions (Liberia and Mozambique) and Asian regions (the Philippines, Singapore, Sri Lanka and Vietnam) also appear to be making some progress. Most notably, in the fall of 2014, Vietnam and the Philippines supported the SOGI HRC resolution on combating violence and discrimination. In Central and Eastern Europe, the Republic of Moldova has made some headway; however, it did vote against a SOGI HRC resolution in 2011. Lastly, Latin American and Caribbean countries showing some improvements are Antigua and Barbuda, Bahamas, Barbados, Belize, Grenada, Peru, Saint Kitts and Nevis, and Trinidad and Tobago. Peru also supported the 2014 SOGI HRC resolution on combating violence and discrimination. In the Western European and North American context, voting in favour of SOGI has been consistent.

Discussion

How SOGI is challenging traditional notions of human rights

The concept of human rights has developed as society has become sensitised to the experiences and realities of varying groups of people. The conceptualisation of sexual orientation and gender identity was not initially recognised as a categorical human right in the Universal Declaration of Human Rights[10] at the UN's founding in 1948, reflecting mainstream society's general lacunae on the subject at the time. Nevertheless, and thanks to the brave and courageous work of SOGI human rights defenders, it has gained gradual recognition at the UN through its bodies including the UNHRC, UNHCR and ECOSOC. However, this acceptance remains a work in progress, partly due to the sheer size of the UN and the number of actors to be educated on these populations, and partly due to the fluidity of SOGI and people's subjective experiences of it. Some UN bodies are more progressive than others and the level of knowledge about SOGI varies across the UN's bureaucratic system. Additionally, for some the aspect of their SOGI identity may be closely tied to other intersecting ones such as race, ethnicity, religion, age, class, abilities, a concept some within the UN understand, others less so. How nation states assemble social locations to target particular groups is a macro form of policymaking and criminalising that can target assemblages such as SOGI (Puar, 2007).

Yet this recognition is hard fought. Although SOGI issues and legal means of addressing them have been documented in the Yogyakarta Principles of 2007, same-sex desires remain criminalised in 72 countries (Carroll and Mendos, 2017). Nation states are also arguing for narrow definitions and family values, and advocating against what they view as the promotion of homosexuality, and for protection for their sovereign right to discriminate. Shifting such penalising views of SOGI to ones in favour of human rights is further complicated by the political dynamics among UN state representatives as well as its staff. Within this large bureaucratic structure, intense discussions, some formal and others

---

10 See www.un.org/en/universal-declaration-human-rights/ (accessed 18 Dec. 2017).

informal, involving negotiations, trade-offs and favours, are common. Also UN staff may not be familiar with SOGI matters or how they are being handled in the nation states they deal with. Moreover, sociopolitical entanglements need to be disentangled and carefully addressed, such as UN Women grappling with the issue of trans women as part of its mandate. This group traditionally has located itself socially on the basis of biomedical notions of gender in the binary of female and male, focusing on the former. Nevertheless, the Convention on the Elimination of all forms of Discrimination Against Women (CEDAW) needs to acknowledge and address diverse gender forms within itself, such as trans bodies, in which gender identity and expression intersect (ibid., p. 22) with traditional notions of gender.

Critical analysis of colonial laws criminalising LGBTs and the implications of their existence, whether or not acted upon

What underscores the findings are the lingering effects of colonial laws criminalising LGBT persons in the countries reviewed in this study. Despite their UN membership, these countries maintain British colonialist laws along with their associated sociocultural and world-view implications. Whether sanctioned through state actors, such as law enforcement or through the social prescriptions of non-state actors, LGBT people are victimised by discrimination arising from colonisation. In turn, these disparities are then demonstrated at the UN in voting trends and the degree of support for LGBT initiatives. Actors within the UN must then grapple with increased recognition of LGBTs in policies, treaties and positions, while simultaneously being confronted with far less accommodating colonial positions. This raises serious questions regarding governments that claim to be against colonialism, but which continue to retain colonial-era laws and in some cases to even strengthen them.

The agency and resilience of LGBT defenders undertaking critical human rights work in the international arena

States commonly assert their right to abuse the human rights of LGBT people. In this hostile climate, the personal safety of LGBT human rights defenders is jeopardised, especially when they come from the countries that maintain such penalties. Similarly, the very mandates and skills of UN special rapporteurs have been challenged publicly because of their work on sexuality and gender. For example, during the second session of the UNHRC in September 2006, the special rapporteur on extrajudicial, summary, or arbitrary executions expressed concern that Nigeria retains the death penalty for homosexuality. In response,

> The Nigerian delegation criticised Mr Alston for exceeding his mandate by addressing the issue of the continued imposition of the death penalty on lesbians, gays, bisexuals or transgender people (LGBT people), and used the opportunity to comment that death by stoning could be

considered 'appropriate and fair' in the circumstances (International
Service for Human Rights, 2006, p. 6).

Such reactions continue to occur despite the HRC's adoption of the UN
resolutions on SOGI in Geneva in 2011 (ARC International, 2011).

Defenders (and staff/experts) must remain resilient in the face of such
hostility. Despite many obstacles, the last three decades have seen an enormous
increase in the visibility and influence of LGBT human rights defenders within
the international arena. For instance, not having (or losing) UN accreditation
has not prevented groups from engaging with UN bodies. Many ECOSOC-
accredited allied groups working on sexual and reproductive rights, women's
rights, HIV/AIDS and general human rights have been extremely helpful in
accrediting representatives from LGBT organisations to attend meetings and
assist with sponsorship of workshops and parallel events.

As SOGI issues gather traction and state support, the ability of groups to
gain access to UN spaces and speak in their own name has increased. With
larger numbers and a greater diversity of LGBT engagement facilitating access
for LGBT human rights defenders of the Global South and trans and intersex
groups, state and agency support becomes more compelling and a positive
reinforcement cycle is created. Interviewee P8 acknowledges the importance
of LGBT civil society organisations: 'There are many positive examples where
we engage on the ground with civil society in countries, and it's crucial to our
work'.

LGBT human rights defenders have used global platforms (such as the
SOGI listserv) to participate in enhanced reflection and analysis about best
practice and successful engagement. They have built their capacity and are
aware that human rights are routinely negotiated in spaces of global politics for
broader interests, such as trade, conflict and aid, and that it is highly important
to understand and gauge the impact of these realities.

Defenders have also engaged in routine documentation and reporting and
are responsible for a growing body of evidence on human rights violations. UN
Special Procedures regularly document violations based on SOGI, and states
are informed how extensive these violations are. This cannot happen without
strong community relations and trust.

Conclusion

This chapter has used a postcolonial, critical, structural and intersectional
framework to present our work and analyses, and has outlined the growing
activism of LGBT human rights defenders at the UN, and how the latter
is responding. The analysis has delved into the challenges associated with
language and labels for LGBT people and how relevant they are to a multitude
of cultures internationally. Data were shared and assessed using qualitative
semi-structured interviews as a basis, revealing progress made on LGBT issues,

yet also the amount of work that still remains to be done. The increasingly favourable voting record of UN nation states must be balanced against challenges facing the aforementioned defenders at home, and by nation states that oppose such issues. Given that numerous states continue to criminalise LGBTs, the work of these defenders is relevant and warranted so that globally these populations will one day have the rights and protections they need, in line with the mandate of the UN itself.

References

Amnesty International Canada (2015) 'LGBTI rights', available at: www. amnesty.ca/our-work/issues/lgbti-rights (accessed 18 Dec. 2017).

Arbour, L. (2006) 'Louise Arbour: keynote address', International Conference on LGBT Human Rights, available at: http://montreal2006.info/en_ louise_arbour.html (accessed 18 Dec. 2017).

ARC International (2003) 'International dialogue on gender, sexuality and human rights: an overview', available at: http://arc-international.net/wp-content/uploads/2011/08/international-dialogue-report-brazil2003.pdf (accessed 18 Dec. 2017).

— (2009) 'UN General Assembly joint statement on sexual ordination and gender identity: building on the past looking to the future', available at: www.sxpolitics.org/wp-content/uploads/2009/03/unga-statement-backgrounder.pdf (accessed 18 Dec. 2017).

— (2011) '17th session of the Human Rights Council', http://arc-international.net/global-advocacy/human-rights-council/hrc17/ (accessed 18 Dec. 2017).

Ban K., statement SG/SM/13366-HRC/12, 25 Jan. 2011, available at: https://www.un.org/press/en/2011/sgsm13366.doc.htm (accessed 11 July 2018).

Carroll, A. and L. R. Mendos (2017) 'State-sponsored homophobia: a world survey of sexual orientation laws: criminalisation, protection and recognition', ILGA, available at: http://ilga.org/downloads/2017/ILGA_ State_Sponsored_Homophobia_2017_WEB.pdf (accessed 5 Oct. 2017).

Duggan, L. (1995) 'Queering the state', in L. Duggan and N. Hunter (eds.) *Sex Wars: Sexual Dissent and Political Culture* (London: Routledge), pp. 179–93.

— (2003) *The Twilight of Equality? Neoliberalism, Cultural Politics, and the Attack on Democracy* (Boston, MA: Beacon Press).

Education International (2015) 'Resolution on LGBTI rights', available at: https://ei-ie.org/en/detail/14752/resolution-on-lgbti-rights (accessed 18 Dec. 2017).

Gerber, P. and J. Gory (2014) 'The UN Human Rights Committee and LGBT rights: what is it doing? What could it be doing?', *Human Rights*

Law Review, 14 (3): 403–39, available at: https://aademic.oup.com/hrlr/
article-abstract/14/3/403/644285 (accessed 18 Dec. 2017).

Glesne, C. (2011) *Becoming Qualitative Researchers: an introduction*, fourth
edn. (Boston, MA: Pearson).

Human Rights Watch (2009) 'Together, apart: organizing around sexual
orientation and gender identity worldwide', available at: www.hrw.org/en/
reports/2009/06/10/together-apart (accessed 18 Dec. 2017).

International Gay and Lesbian Human Rights Commission (IGLHRC)
(2006) 'International Gay and Lesbian Human Rights Commission
input memo to the UN Secretary-General's study on violence against
women', available at: www.un.org/womenwatch/daw/vaw/ngocontribute/
International%20Gay%20and%20Lesbian%20Human%20Rights%20
Commission.pdf (accessed 18 Dec. 2017).

International Lesbian, Gay, Bisexual, Trans and Intersex Association (2013)
'ECOSOC: LGBT voices at the United Nations/ECOSOC Council vote
grants consultative status to ILGA', available at: http://ilga.org/ecosoc-
lgbt-voices-at-the-united-nations-ecosoc-council-vote-grants-consultative-
status-to-ilga/ (accessed 18 Dec. 2017).

International Service for Human Rights (2006) Human Rights Council,
2nd session preliminary overview, available at: http://olddoc.ishr.ch/hrm/
council/cmreports/sessionoverviews/second/OverviewSecondSession.pdf
(accessed 18 Dec. 2017).

Lau, H. (2004) 'Sexual orientation: testing the universality of international
human rights law', *University of Chicago Law Review*, 71: 1689–720.

LaViolette, N. and S. Whitworth (1994) 'No safe haven: sexuality as a
universal human right and gay and lesbian activism in international
politics', *Millennium Journal of International Studies*, 23: 563–88.

Mepschen, P., J.W. Duyvendak and E.H. Tonkens (2010) 'Sexual politics,
orientalism and multicultural citizenship in the Netherlands, *Sociology*,
44: 962–79.

OutRight Action International (2015) 'Activists address LGBTTTI issues at
OAS in Lima, Peru', available at: https://www.outrightinternational.org/
content/activists-address-lgbttti-issues-oas-lima-peru (accessed 18 Dec.
2017).

Patton, M.Q. (1990) *Qualitative Evaluation and Research Methods.*, 2nd edn.
(Newbury Park, CA: Sage Publications).

Puar, J.K. (2007) *Terrorist Assemblages: Homonationalism in Queer Times*
(Durham, NC: Duke University Press).

Ritchie, J. and L. Spencer (1994). 'Qualitative data analysis for applied policy
research', in A. Bryman and R.G. Burgess (eds.) *Analysing Qualitative
Data* (London: Routledge), pp. 173–94.

Said, E.W. (1994) *Culture and Imperialism* (New York, NY: Vintage Books).

Saiz, I. (2004) 'Bracketing sexuality: human rights and sexual orientation. A decade of development and denial at the UN', *Health and Human Rights*, 7: 48–80; doi:10.2307/4065348.

Sanders, D. (1996) 'Getting lesbian and gay issues on the international human rights agenda', *Human Rights Quarterly*, 18, 1: 67–106.

Sauer, A.T. and A. Podhora (2013) 'Sexual orientation and gender identity in human rights impact assessment', *Impact Assessment and Project Appraisal*, 31: 135–45, available at: www.tandfonline.com/doi:10.1080/14615517.2 013.791416 (accessed 18 Dec. 2018).

Shannahan, D.S. (2010) 'Some queer questions from a Muslim faith perspective', *Sexualities*, 13 (6): 671–84.

Swiebel, J. (2009) 'Lesbian, gay, bisexual and transgender human rights: the search for an international strategy', *Contemporary Politics*, 15 (1): 19–35.

Tiefer, L. (2002) 'The emerging global discourse of sexual rights', *Journal of Sex and Marital Therapy*, 28: 439–44.

UN Secretary-General (2006) 'In-depth study on all forms of violence against women', A/61/122/Add.1 UN General Assembly, 61st session, available at: www.un.org/womenwatch/daw/vaw/violenceagainstwomenstudydoc.pdf (accessed 12 Dec. 2017).

— (2011) 'Secretary-General's remarks to the Human Rights Council', available at: www.un.org/sg/STATEMENTS/index.asp?nid=5051 (accessed 12 Dec. 2017).

UNAIDS (2008) *UNAIDS: the first 10 years* (UNAIDS).

— (2011) *Outlook 30*, available at: www.unaids.org/sites/default/files/media_asset/20110607_JC2069_30Outlook_en_0.pdf (accessed 18 Dec. 2017).

van Dijk, T.A. (ed.) (1985a) *Handbook of Discourse Analysis, Vol. II, Dimensions of Discourse* (London: Academic Press).

— (1985b) 'Introduction: the role of discourse analysis in society', in T.A. van Dijk (ed.) Handbook of Discourse Analysis, Vol. IV, Discourse Analysis in Society (London: Academic Press), pp. 1–8.

Wane, N.N. (2008) 'Mapping the field of Indigenous knowledges in anticolonial discourse: a transformative journey in education', *Race Ethnicity and Education*, 11: 183–97.

Wilson, M. (1996) 'Asking questions', in R. Sapsford and V. Jupp (eds.) *Data Collection and Analysis* (London: Sage Publications), pp. 94–120.

9

Resistance to criminalisation, and social movement organising to advance LGBT rights in Belize

Caleb Orozco

The United Belize Advocacy Movement (UNIBAM) received non-governmental organisation (NGO) status on 4 May 2006, an achievement, it might be argued, that marked the beginning of the lesbian, gay, bisexual, transgender (LGBT) rights movement in Belize. It was subsequently involved in launching a constitutional challenge on 24 September 2010 against Section 53 of Belize's Criminal Code,[1] a colonial-era law that criminalises 'carnal intercourse against the order of nature'.[2] Filing the case became the most important event in the effort to advance LGBT civil rights in Belize, and needs to be examined in the context of UNIBAM's development and the environment in which it works.

The founding of UNIBAM was inspired by the implementation of the 2005 multicentric study supported by the US Agency for International Aid (USAID) that examined conditions faced by sex workers, people living with HIV, and men who have sex with men (MSM). Although the study was never completed, it inspired UNIBAM's first situational analysis on MSM and HIV/AIDS in 2006, along with community conversations. At the time I worked as a health educator for the Pan American Social Marketing Organization (PASMO) with

1   *Caleb Orozco v. attorney general of Belize.* Caleb Orozco, executive director of UNIBAM, was the sole applicant litigant. In Dec. 2012, Madam Justice Arana struck out UNIBAM as an applicant to the litigation. Thereafter it joined the litigation as an 'interested party'. The overall responsibility for the case rested with the University of West Indies Faculty of Law Rights Advocacy Project (U-RAP), see: http://u-rap.org/web2/index.php/2015-09-29-00-40-03/orozco-v-attorney-general-of-belize/item/2-caleb-orozco-v-attorney-general-of-belize-and-others (accessed 17 Feb. 2018).

2   Section 53 states that 'every person who has carnal intercourse against the order of nature with any person or animal shall be liable to imprisonment for ten years.' The offence does not require lack of consent.

C. Orozco (2018) 'Resistance to criminalisation, and social movement organising to advance LGBT rights in Belize', in N. Nicol et al. (eds.) *Envisioning Global LGBT Human Rights: (Neo) colonialism, Neoliberalism, Resistance and Hope* (London: Human Rights Consortium, Institute of Commonwealth Studies), pp. 247–68.

support from the Organization of Petroleum Exporting Countries' (OPEC) project of the United Nations Population Fund (UNFPA). I implemented group sessions to further the vision of LGBT community leadership in Orange Walk, a northern district of Belize. This was important because there had been no direct representation or political voice for the population since the HIV epidemic started in the country in 1986, despite the fact that gay men were disproportionately affected by the outbreak. As well, UNIBAM could not have existed had the basic framework for an LGBT rights movement in Belize not been created by organisations such as the Alliance Against AIDS (AAA), which responded to the HIV epidemic during the 1980s. The Alliance offered community training on HIV prevention, stigma and discrimination, as well as male sexual health. In addition, OPEC's Fund for International Development supported work with marginalised groups including sex workers and MSM populations through UNFPA. The HIV prevention work with MSM, carried out by PASMO, along with the health ministry's multicentric 2005 study, set the gears in motion for LGBT community representatives to engage with policy and health spaces, advance data structures and institutional representation, and build relationships with international allies. In essence, the formation of UNIBAM was inspired by the Ministry of Health's study.

On 16 February 2006, ten people from Belize City and Orange Walk met to come up with a name that could reflect Belize's cultural diversity. Although English is the country's official language, people speak Spanish in the North, indigenous languages like Mopan, Ketchi and Garifuna in the South, and Creole English in Belize District – and it is also home to various other ethnic groups from around the world. Members of the LGBT community at the meeting strove to ensure that communication could be sustained across linguistic and ethnic lines. Initially we invested our own funds and, with help from supporters, were able to register UNIBAM as an NGO. Five months later, in October 2006, we received our first grant from the HIV Collaborative Fund, Tides Foundation for the Caribbean – and we have never looked back.

Launching the constitutional challenge

The year 2007 was one of opportunities. We participated in a human rights meeting in Santo Domingo, sponsored by the United Nations Development Programme (UNDP), that had invited Simeon Sampson, a leading human rights lawyer in Belize, to participate. That meeting marked the beginning of UNIBAM's relationship with the University of the West Indies. Tracy Robinson, professor of law, spoke to me about the goals of the University of West Indies Rights Advocacy Project (U-RAP) and their legal research on member states of the Caribbean Community and Common Market (Caricom). There, I learned about U-RAP's efforts in legal mapping, and the need to identify a claimant for a legal challenge to Section 53, Belize's sodomy law.[3] I quickly raised my hand and said: 'I was ready yesterday!' Professionally, I felt that the need for a claimant synergised with UNIBAM's mission statement, which declares us as an advocacy organisation using rights-based approaches to reduce stigma and discrimination. On a personal level, I had experienced physical assault, homophobic slurs, mockery and threats of violence for two decades. I felt that if I was going to experience discrimination and violence for doing nothing, I would rather be mistreated for doing something that I believe in passionately.

I met with Professor Robinson and Arif Bulkan, a lawyer from Guyana, to talk about the legal framework for a constitutional challenge to Section 53 of the Belize Criminal Code, and to prepare for the case. In 2009, Lisa Shoman[4] became senior counsel for the case and filed it in 2010 as well as providing advice about the process. Another lawyer, Westmin James, took on court procedure. Public education and advocacy, and community engagement and mobilisation were UNIBAM's domain. In 2011, Human Dignity Trust, the Commonwealth Lawyers Association and the International Commission of Jurists (ICJ) submitted an application to become interested parties in the case, in support of rescinding Section 53. The Catholic and Anglican churches and the Belize Evangelical Association of Churches submitted applications to become interested parties on the side of the Belize government defending the provision.

To prepare a knowledge mobilisation strategy, UNIBAM commissioned the first LGBT legal review in Belize in 2010, in partnership with Northwestern University, Illinois. Completed in 2014, the review looked at the Belize Constitution and subsidiary laws to examine gaps in legal protections affecting the socioeconomic and civil rights of LGBT citizens. With regard to litigation to decriminalise same-sex intimacy, the review revealed systematic exclusion from legal protections, despite the existence of a liberal constitution (Northwestern University, 2014). We circulated the review and a summary of its findings to cabinet. The Michigan Law Clinic also assisted in building our knowledge of legal protections or gaps. As a result, we were able to develop our capacity on how to advance legal reform.

The Section 53 case was strategically timed. It built on a 2008 legal review by the National AIDS Commission (NAC) that called for the repeal of Section 53; the Organization of American States' (OAS) resolutions on human rights

3   U-RAP identified Belize and Guyana as strategic sites for litigation and subsequently initiated two cases: *Caleb Orozco v. attorney general of Belize*, which challenges Section 53 of the Criminal Code of Belize, and *McEwan et al. v. attorney general of Guyana*, which challenges Section 153(1)(xlvii) of the Summary Jurisdiction (Offences) Act that makes it an offence for a man to wear 'female attire' and for a woman to wear 'male attire' in public for an 'improper purpose'. For more on the Guyana case, also see: DeRoy and Henry, ch. 5, this volume.

4   Lisa Shoman, a lawyer, was Belize's foreign minister from 2007 to 2008.

in terms of sexual orientation and gender identity (SOGI), which had been supportive since 2008; and the 2009 UN Universal Periodic Review (UPR) which, while not directly supportive, recognised the rights and freedoms of all Belizeans as enshrined under Section 3 of the Belize Constitution. Furthermore, it was important for us to treat the litigation as a mapping exercise to expose our opponents and profile their public statements as evidence of discrimination and psychological violence, as well as to inspire and mobilise the LGBT community. The controversy surrounding the case fostered public debate with members of the public and church leaders who were encouraged to consider their position on LGBT rights and reflect on whether the dignity of the person was important.

As the claimant, I played a role both as an advocate and political strategist, with the support of Belizeans for the Constitutional Challenge, a group created to advance the Section 53 case and to assess and report community communication. They also monitored news outside of Belize and channelled information to amplify our message and challenge opponents. Allies and community members effectively countered the arguments of opponents of decriminalisation on social media platforms like 'Se La vee' – a virtual forum for general discussion with a membership of over 2,000 – as well as engaging with our opponents, such as Belize Action, on their Facebook page. Still more LGBT community members developed additional virtual spaces for engagement, analysis and concerns.

Building regional and international alliances

Regional and international networking was critical to develop strategic alliances, build capacity, and take advantage of knowledge mobilisation opportunities. Use of international spaces was important, particularly given that the Belize government did not provide any financial support to build capacity for LGBT rights organising. Two grants were secured by UNIBAM to build internal capacity and invest in a small building for the organisation. The Collaborative Fund for the Caribbean and the American Foundation for AIDS Research (amfAR) were UNIBAM's first funders. Without their support, we would not have been able to advance our advocacy work in Belize.[5]

---

5   In addition, The American Foundation for AIDS Research, the Center for Constitutional Rights, the Southern Poverty Law Center, Heartland International, the International Treatment Preparedness Coalition, ARC International, SOGI (sexual orientation and gender identity) listserv, and Envisioning Global LGBT Human Rights (Envisioning) all helped to expand our knowledge, develop resources, conduct research, and raise awareness of our concerns regionally and internationally.

Regionally, UNIBAM was able to network with the Caribbean Vulnerable Communities Coalition (CVC),[6] and became a peer member of the Caribbean Treatment Action Group (CTAG), and of Heartland International (which led an LGBT coalition to advance the SOGI resolution at the OAS in 2008). Our partners were: the Heartland Alliance for Human Needs and Human Rights, the Sexual Rights Initiative (SRI), the Caribbean Forum for Liberation and Acceptance of Genders and Sexualities (CariFLAGS) and the Kaleidoscope Trust, among others, to leverage political spaces, raise awareness and improve our ability to communicate our concerns.

Nationally, UNIBAM was appointed as a NAC commissioner, and became a member of the Women's Issues Network of Belize (WIN-Belize).[7] In 2010, recognising the value of enhancing community capacity, UNIBAM also supported the development of transgender leadership by acting as a fiscal sponsor to support efforts to build a regional network for transgender people, called Caribbean Regional Trans in Action (CRTA). In turn, this led to the first research on self-perception and rights awareness for transgender people in Belize, and created the framework for the legal incorporation of TIABelize, a transgender-focused organisation founded in the country in 2015.

Our international work started in 2007 at a regional meeting which brought together activists from across the Caribbean to revitalise CariFLAGS, in Ocho Rios, Jamaica.[8] The vision for the region was ambitious. A CariFLAGS listserv was created to act as a clearing house of news and support resource mobilisation and knowledge engagement that affected MSM populations. These efforts were enhanced by the OAS meeting in Panama in 2007, where LGBT activists from across Latin American and the Caribbean region intervened for the first time. We stayed up until 3 am to draft our first declaration as a coalition – which condemned violence against persons based on SOGI – and called on the OAS system to set up structures to investigate and address these concerns. In 2008 CariFLAGS, with the help of CVC, held a meeting in Barbados to develop a plan of action for the region. During that meeting, as alternative speaker, I drafted a two-minute presentation that was used at the UN high-level neeting on AIDS in New York. Seeing Belize's health minister, the chair of NAC, the head of the national AIDS programme, and a Permanent Mission representative together in the session, I realised for the first time that international spaces could be leveraged for advocacy work at the country level.

6   The CVC brings together community leaders and NGOs working with marginalised at-risk Caribbean populations who are especially vulnerable to HIV infection. See: http://cvccoalition.org (accessed 22 Feb. 2018).

7   WIN-Belize is an umbrella organisation of NGOs that work in the area of women and children's issues, including raising awareness about gender-based violence and HIV/AIDS.

8   CariFLAGS dated back to 1997 as a concept, and had its foundation in Caricom's need to engage MSM communities in its HIV/AIDS response.

Figure 14. Left to right: Namela Baynes Henry (SASOD) and Caleb Orozco (UNIBAM), Emancipation Park, Kingston, Jamaica, 10 July 2013. Photo credit: Ulelli Verbeke, SASOD and Envisioning.

Our first attempt at UNIBAM to get the state to issue a formal position on its LGBT citizens came in an unpublished shadow report, developed in partnership with the SRI for the 2009 UPR. Through this process we learned of the Belize government's response to recommendation 9 of the United Nations Human Rights Council (UNHRC) UPR, which addresses decriminalisation of sodomy. Their statement read: 'The Government of Belize has considered this recommendation and is of the view that any legislative changes in this regard would require extensive national consultations given the nature of the issues involved. The Government does not yet have a mandate to effect these changes' (para. 6).[9]

Further, in response to recommendation 28, regarding discrimination on the grounds of sexual orientation and reviewing discriminatory legislation, the Belizean government said: 'While there is no political mandate at this time to amend the relevant legislation, the Government is nonetheless committed to protecting all members of society from discrimination. Indeed protection from

9   UNHRC, Universal Periodic Review: Report of the Working Group on the Universal Periodic Review Belize, Addendum, Views on Conclusions and/or Recommendations, voluntary commitments and replies presented by the State under review', 12th session, 18 Sep. 2009, available at: https://documents-dds-ny.un.org/doc/UNDOC/GEN/G09/156/96/PDF/G0915696.pdf?OpenElement (accessed 17 Feb. 2018).

discrimination is protected by the Belize Constitution' (para. 28). This was the first time since 1981 that the Belizean government had given an official position on its LGBT citizens.

In 2010, we attended a meeting on HIV and the law, in Port of Spain, Trinidad and Tobago, supported by the UNDP. A Belizean who had been invited to the meeting, Mia Quetzal (regional coordinator, Caribbean Regional Trans in Action), was subjected to transphobic behaviour by an immigration officer upon arriving at Port of Spain. The incident was covered by the media (*Daily Express*, 2011) and an investigation was launched. Mia Quetzal's experience offered an important lesson on the need to raise the profile of the LGBT community in Belize.

Inspired by the Port of Spain regional meeting, and with help from the UNDP, resources were found to organise a national dialogue in Belize, attended by more than a hundred Belizeans and featuring the visible engagement of LGBT participants.

Engaging with international human rights mechanisms

In 2013, UNIBAM and the Heartland Alliance submitted a shadow report as part of the country review for the International Covenant on Civil and Political Rights (ICCPR) for consideration at the United Nations Human Rights Committee's 107th session. It was entitled 'Human rights violations of Lesbian, Gay, Bisexual, and Transgender (LGBT) people in Belize'. Significantly, the foreign affairs ministry had invited a UNIBAM representative to its consultation for both the UPR and its national report for ICCPR. Religious opponents from Belize's Evangelical Association were also at the table. In its response to the UPR, the Belize government noted all 14 LGBT-specific recommendations referencing SOGI.[10] While the government did not move to act on any of the recommendations, it did not directly oppose them either.

Over the years, we learned that sustaining national efforts requires strong international partnerships. Working in coalition with the coordinators of Heartland Alliance from 2008 to 2015 gave UNIBAM access to national leaders regionally, which was helpful for political engagement and gaining knowledge. For six years we worked to engage Caribbean ambassadors on the OAS resolutions on human rights in terms of SOGI. The resolutions called for investment and action to be taken by the OAS system, condemned acts of violence, and called for annual progress reviews. We learned quickly that

10 UNHRC, 'Compilation prepared by the Office of the High Commissioner for Human Rights in accordance with paragraph 15 (b) of the annex to Human Rights Council Resolution 5/1 and paragraph 5 of the annex to Council resolution 16/21 Belize', A/HRC/WG.6/17/BLZ/2, 7 Aug. 2013, available at: www.refworld.org/pdfid/5268e33f4.pdf (accessed 17 Feb. 2018).

there was a regional profile of Caribbean politics and value in using social media to document the presence of opponents in these political spaces. We learned that regional leaders were making decisions based on values rather than policy and rights obligations, and that they knew little about the application of fundamental rights in relation to LGBT citizens.

At the 2013 OAS General Assembly in Guatemala, and again in 2014, we witnessed Belize adding reservations to SOGI resolutions, while encouraging the adoption of all other resolutions.[11] Interestingly, the reservations have no legal value and can be deemed only as a political statement. Such reservations are usually raised to highlight a country's political concern without derailing the resolutions. They can be used to weaken the commitment of states to respond to the resolution nationally, or to support political positions that are irrelevant to the substance of the resolution itself. On the other hand, UNIBAM engaged discussions on Caribbean support and perception in relation to LGBT issues. The Latin American and Caribbean Coalition of lesbian, gay, bisexual, transvestite, transgender, transsexual and intersex organisations (LGBTTTI Coalition), working within the OAS, gained political momentum and shifted the political tone from indifference to building support systems such as the LGBT Unit.[12]

In 2013 the far right began to show up at the OAS in greater numbers. It was a time of turmoil in Belize, as the case against Section 53 was heard, and the Belize Gender Policy – which included sexual orientation – was introduced to cabinet, and the religious right held protests, which they called 'constitutional marches'. Personal security became a concern after I filed the constitutional challenge in 2010, indeed security became a big part of the advocacy process, as the people around me were also affected, particularly at the UNIBAM office. Harassment was ever present. We discovered how fragile our security was. In the context of protests against the case, I was assaulted and lost two teeth. The UN Special Rapporteur on the promotion and protection of freedom of expression and on the situation of human rights defenders wrote to the government in 2012 about my safety. Against this backdrop, the OAS approved precautionary measures for me.[13] These are requests made by the

11 OAS, 'Human rights, sexual orientation, and gender identity and expression', Inter-American Commission on Human Rights, General Assembly resolution, fourth plenary session, 5 Jun., see www.oas.org/en/iachr/lgtbi/docs/AG-RES2863-XLIV-O-14eng.pdf (accessed 22 Feb. 2018).

12 The LGBTTTI coalition is a partnership of organisations, whose strategic goal is political visibility, advocacy and mobilising, to ensure the full and systematic commitment of the OAS and its regional human rights protection system, to advocate for and defend LGBTI human rights in the Americas. The first meeting took place in Panama City in May 2007, during the OAS's 37th General Assembly. Today the coalition involves more than 27 activists from 23 countries of the region.

13 See PM 155/13 – Caleb Orozco, Belize, 29 May 2013, available at: www.oas.org/en/iachr/lgtbi/protection/precautionary.asp (accessed 20 Mar. 2018).

OAS's Inter-American Commission on Human Rights (IAHCR) that looks into the security of human rights defenders after receiving reports of violence. They can call for a state to prevent irreparable harm to the person or the organisation of concern.[14]

My family, who were on the frontline of maintaining my safety, ensured that my doors were locked and that I did not walk long distances. Behind the scenes, community members provided support. I learned to drive at the age of 39, I stayed away from crowds and minimised my travel at night. During the 2013 hearings, four security officers accompanied me to and from court. These efforts were complemented by security support from two regional programmes that lasted for approximately three years.

Four years of engagement with the OAS system led to an invitation in 2012 for me to meet the foreign minister at his office in Belize. We built on that invitation and sought a thematic hearing on discrimination and violence against LGBT persons with the IAHCR. The hearing took place on 28 March 2014. Stephen Diaz and I spoke on behalf of UNIBAM; it was the first time that LGBT Belizeans had presented their concerns about discrimination and violence to the IAHCR. The government of Belize sent its ambassador, Nestor Mendez, to present on their behalf.[15]

In 2015, the LGBTTTI Coalition saw approximately 30 fundamentalists – numbers equal to our own representatives – at the OAS General Assembly in Washington DC. There, I met Helene Coley Nicholson, president of the Lawyers Christian Fellowship. A news report from July 2014 gives insight into her perspectives and professional background:

> . . . according to Helene Coley Nicholson, a member of the Jamaica CAUSE Secretariat, the group finds the agenda of the Lesbian, Gay, Bisexual, Transgender and Intersex, LGBTI community, to be a cause for concern.

> Nicholson further stated that Jamaica CAUSE stood to oppose said agenda which, according to her, seeks to foster a society where all sexual expression is free and those in opposition are punished. (Collom, 2014)

In a letter to the editor of the *Jamaica Gleaner* on 15 November 2013, Philippa Davies of Jamaica wrote: '. . . isn't forcing unwanted laws and behaviour on the majority of a population an act of oppression? Where is the justice in that move, Minister Golding?'. She was referring to discussions by Mark Golding, the then justice minister, about efforts under way to review laws pertaining to sexual conduct.

---

14 For general information about precautionary measures, see: http://oas.org/en/iachr/decisions/about-precautionary.asp (accessed 20 Mar. 2018).

15 OAS, 'Human rights situation of LGBTI persons in Belize', Inter-American Commission on Human Rights [hearing] 28 Mar., see www.oas.org/es/cidh/audiencias/advanced.aspx?lang=en (accessed 22 Feb. 2018).

At the OAS General Assembly in Washington in 2015, it was quid pro quo between the religious right's opposition to LGBT rights and the LGBT coalition. When a diplomat spoke in support of their rights, the LGBT coalition clapped and the right-wing groups responded. When fundamentalists' issues were backed, the LGBT coalition held up protest signs, written in Spanish, that covered such concerns as US visa restrictions (which had prevented some coalition members from arriving in Washington), and laws affecting transgender populations, reproductive rights, rights without homophobia, diverse families and equal treatment. We carried out research on religious fundamentalist opposition in Latin America and the Caribbean and reported events as they transpired through social media, creating our own alternative news stream designed to educate people about the political process at the OAS and the presence and statements of the opposition. We were able to reach 879 members on CariFLAGS' Facebook page and 300 Belizean members on the UNIBAM Facebook page. Belizean activists joined the coalition in protest against the position of fundamentalists, and used the opportunity to arrange meetings at the Belize mission with our foreign minister. They also engaged USAID representatives on work being done in the country. Visibility at the OAS and engagement with Belizean diplomats and political leaders allowed us to document and record the experience for institutional memory.

The legal case, the gender policy, our community and our allies

During 2013 UNIBAM conducted interviews with 39 LGBT individuals and allies in Belize as part of the work carried out by the Envisioning Global LGBT Human Rights team (Envisioning), a process that gave us insights into issues affecting LGBT people. We discovered incidents of unreported violence and discrimination, and failure by state officials to document violence and discrimination experienced by LGBT individuals. Mia Quetzal,[16] a participant in the study, highlighted the reasons why data on violence was so limited:

> There's two older persons who are gay, one is 40, one is close to being 40 and the story they've been telling me is that they had to fight their way out of the situations that got them discriminated [against]. And the story that this other 20 year-old one tells me is that some of them got raped, two of them got raped by different persons. They couldn't tell their parents. They were shy, they were scared to tell anybody or even go to the police and report what was happening to them. So they just kept it to themselves ...

> The Criminal Code ... has been used as a tool for police to discriminate and not hear our reports. Or if we go to the police station and try to

16 Interviewed on 16 Jul. 2013 by Caleb Orozco, UNIBAM and Envisioning. An excerpt is included in the Belize Portraits section of the *Telling Our Stories* (2014) documentary series.

make a report, the only thing they will do to us is mock us, laugh at us, and we feel intimidated. We won't continue on to the report.

The research taught us that we needed to better understand the requirements for structural interventions, including: the need to establish rights enforcement and protection mechanisms; increase our knowledge about subsidiary laws; refine our monitoring and evaluation strategies; and build our political capacity to address protection from violence concerns. Interviews with community members and allies highlighted the challenges faced by LGBT people, as well as revealing the impact of UNIBAM's advocacy. Inspiring methods of resilience were also revealed:

> [I've been] living here in my village for about ten years now . . . A lot of the village persons look for me to cut hair, the makeup, the nails . . . We have another transgender person in the village, that her earnings come from working with her dad at the bush farm. She goes, she plants crop, she brings in firewood, and she does all the field work with her dad.[17]

> I am a lesbian mother living in the community of San Pedro town . . . I've had a partner now for the past three years, but I've been with women for the past ten years . . . I can say that I was very much sheltered . . . living in San Pedro, on the whole it's very much open here, where the gay community is allowed a little bit more freedom to be who they are; and that's what I grew up seeing.[18]

> Not so far from me, like an arm length, there were like three guys and two ladies, and they were talking in Spanish: 'Sodom and Gomorrah, and this UNIBAM, and Belize, and my children' . . . and this guy came in front of me and said, 'Sodom and Gomorrah'. I spoke my mind . . . I looked at him and I said, 'Not today. You never bring me down today. No way, 'cause God loves me'.[19]

Although the case had been filed on 24 September 2010, it was not until February 2011 that it drew media interest. Recognising the need for broader support, UNIBAM joined WIN-Belize. It was our belief that should women's rights be eroded, LGBT issues would also be open to attack. We began by collecting information on the anti-abortion group, Voices for Life. In 2010, they joined a group led by right-wing pastor, Scott Stirm (Jubilee Ministries/ Belize Action), to oppose sexual and reproductive rights and LGBT rights. They started a petition that sought to roll back the current abortion law. The National Advocacy Working Group (NAWG) worked to find out the nature of the petition, while the LGBT community monitored efforts by Voices for Life in the Cayo and Belize districts. In 2010, NAWG developed a brief that provided data and policy recommendations on women's health, which was

17 Ibid.
18 Kainie Manuel interviewed on 3 Sep. 2013 by Caleb Orozco, UNIBAM and Envisioning.
19 Estrellita Reyes interviewed on 8 Sept. 2013 by Caleb Orozco, as above.

submitted to the prime minister's office. Subsequently, the prime minister called WIN's executive director and made a commitment to not change the abortion law. It was our first success using a coalition strategy against religious-right members, a strategy that we would continue to build on.

In 2013 Belize's cabinet approved the gender policy as a framework to look at the needs of men and women. The policy addressed health, education, wealth and employment, gender-based violence, power and decision-making. It had five priority areas guided by principles. One of these – which spoke of 'respect for diversity' – included sexual orientation in its definition. The response of many in the LGBT movement to this was expressed best by Dennis Craft:[20] 'the recent gender policy, the inclusion of sexual orientation into that policy was like a huge, huge, huge win, it's a big thing . . . So, even though there's a law that says that we can't be gay, there is a policy that . . . gives us equal rights'.

The gender policy ignited protests organised by religious fundamentalists. Opposition to the policy was based on the belief that it was supporting the 'gay agenda'. There were also efforts to derail a teacher's manual that spoke of comprehensive sexuality education.[21] One WIN-Belize organisation reported that it had lost donations from a church group who disagreed with its support of the gender policy.

As one of WIN's members, UNIBAM worked to define a common position on the gender policy and issued a media statement in the midst of the protests against the gender policy. One of our partners, Tikkun Olam Belize, an NGO that advocates for sex workers' rights, organised a protest to support the gender policy (Channel5Belize.com, 2013b). An interview conducted with one of the organisers, Elisa Castellanos,[22] for Envisioning reveals how significant that experience was:

> We went to all the media houses in Orange Walk and we were on radio shows and talk shows, so we did as much promotion as we could ... We took all the parts of the gender policy and wrote it on Bristol board, and then Aaron [a UNIBAM member] and his group stood in the middle . . . We made straight people hold the flag along with Aaron to show that unity, and there were people just looking. And I felt in that instant that it was worth it ... Somebody called me and said, 'oh but you have the LGBT flag and it's sending a wrong message', and I said, I will not tell people to bring down their flags because that is a representation of who they are and ... they have every right to fly the flag that they want and I will hold it along with them.

With assistance from NAC, the creation of Generation Zero, a coalition of like-minded organisations and individuals concerned about human rights and discrimination, took place during a conference on vulnerable groups. The

20 Interviewed on 25 Aug. 2013 by Caleb Orozco, as above.
21 For more information see Channel5Belize.com (2012).
22 Interviewed on 2 Aug. 2013 by Caleb Orozco, as above.

NAC was able to offer us a long-term base for policy and advocacy engagement, which facilitated institutional backing for the challenge against Section 53. Prior to these efforts, community meetings were held at the NAC secretariat to map out a communication plan that eventually led to the creation of virtual communities. It was the first time I had seen upper-middle-class people expressing an interest or concern about opposition to Section 53. We created a 'war room' where we plotted strategies to counter our opponents. The NAC supported our knowledge mobilisation strategy and assisted us in mapping legislative opportunities. It helped us identify allies and opponents within governing bodies, gain access to new research, and advocate for research on violence and discrimination against MSM. The NAC also backed UNIBAM's evolution at the policy table not just as a commissioner but as an executive member of the Country Coordinating Mechanism (CCM), and a member of the wider CCM representing MSM. It facilitated access to the UN Special Envoy for HIV in the Caribbean and gave us a map of the political directorate who make decisions in cabinet.

Our supporters documented religious extremists' comments about the gender policy and our members were able to meet with the leader of the opposition, Francis Fonseca, in 2013, after he had previously met with evangelical opponents. We participated in private sessions with evangelicals to engage them on their position, including a meeting of the Belize Chamber of Commerce, which included presentations from Pastors Scott Stirm and Louis Wade Jr (talk show host and Christian youth motivational speaker), and one with Judith Alpuche, chief executive of the human development and social transformation ministry. Others debated the position of gender policy opponents on the aforementioned Se La vee social media site. We wrote to the prime minister's office asking for a meeting, and later documented every comment he made regarding the gender policy. Our conclusion was that he would support the gender policy and would not remove the principle that called for respect for diversity. Ultimately, most of the gender policy's content was preserved.

The opposition – culture wars

Opposition to the gender policy and to decriminalisation of same-sex intimacy and the constitutional challenge to Section 53 came from the media, particularly *The Amandala*, the largest independent newspaper in Belize, and PlusTV in Belmopan. The newspaper published an online poll on the Section 53 case saying that people could vote several times a day (the result in 2011 led to claims that 78 per cent of Belizeans did not support changing the law). Opposition also came from religious institutions, including a mass against UNIBAM organised by the Catholic Church in 2013.

The mobilisation of Christian fundamentalists had particular impact. The case against Section 53 rendered our opponents visible for the first time including: Pastor Scott Stirm (Jubilee Ministries/Belize Action); Maria Zabaneh (Voices for Life/Belize Action);[23] Pastor Eugene Crawford (Belize Association of Evangelical Churches); Patrick Andrews Jones (Peoples United Party [PUP] and co-host of a popular TV show *Rise and Shine*); Pastor Louis Wade Jr (also co-host of *Rise and Shine* and Christian youth motivational speaker); Simeon Lopez, then Mayor of Belmopan; minister of public works (2008–12), Anthony 'Boots' Martinez (2011); and Julius Espat, then campaign manager for the opposition party People's United Party (PUP), to name just a few. It was Scott Stirm's Belize Action, among others, who led the way in ensuring Catholic, Evangelical and Anglican churches joined together as interested parties on the side of the government in the case to oppose the challenge to Section 53.

When Belize's Evangelical Association, through Belize Action, started to organise protests against the gender policy and the Section 53 case, we monitored social media. In their first 'constitutional march' in the district of Punta Gorda, one of our supporters filmed an effigy at the front of the march, a cardboard figure of a hanging man labelled UNIBAM. Allies posted the video clip on the virtual group Se La vee, which has over 2,000 members. Members of the LGBT community, frustrated by the social message of Belizean church groups, showed that they were prepared to resist their efforts to perpetuate discrimination. Speaking about the constitutional marches in 2013, Aaron Mai[24] stated:

> If the march ever comes to my region of the country, then I would be out there with my gay flag and I would take a stand against the church. And so on the day of the march, I decided to get on my scooter and I put on my gay flag and I went out there and I followed the march . . . And I was so stirred up that (when) I was asked by the media to have an interview, and I decided to go on national TV and to express my frustration and my story against the church and their movement . . . There was a lot on my heart that needed to come out and I released what was in me to the religious media that came to march in my region.

Eventually, Minister Allamila spoke out and condemned the effigy as dangerous (Jones, 2013). Our allies pounced on this issue on Facebook, documenting our opponents' comments and storing them on file for future use. This work effectively held our opponents accountable and called on them to retract their incendiary language.

---

23 Maria Zabaneh (2011) speaking at 'Take a Stand Rally', Dec. 2011, stated: 'The body of Christ today in Belize is united on the issues that threaten the divine laws of God.' See: https://www.youtube.com/watch?v=CEVBEl6eNBs (accessed 22 Feb. 2018).

24 Interviewed on 16 Jul. 2013 by Caleb Orozco, UNIBAM and Envisioning. An excerpt is included in the Belize section of the *Telling Our Stories* (2014) documentary series.

It also became clear that fundamentalist opposition came from the 'dominionist' movement. Scott Stirm, who was born in Texas and moved to Belize as a young adult, demonstrated his views when he posted a reply to a thread started by Nefretery Nancy Marin on Facebook:[25]

> I am grateful for the truths we were taught in Youth With A Mission about the '7 influencing areas of society', once called the 'Mind Moulders' that shape society, now also called, 'The 7 Mountains'. Church, Education, Family, Gov't, Business & Commerce, Media, Arts & Entertainment. Loren Cunningham taught us that when the Church pulls back from any of these areas, then darkness takes over!

Dominionist theology is a term developed by sociologist Sara Diamond (1990, 1995) to describe a growing political tendency in the US Christian right that encourages Christians, as mandated by God, to be active in civil society to dominate the political process and to occupy secular institutions (see also, Theocracy Watch, 2006). Professor Didi Herman (1997) examines the history of US-based white Christian extremism, including the Moral Majority founded by Jerry Falwell, and traces a shift to active political engagement as a response to, and opposition to, the social and civil rights movements of the 1950s and 1960s which sought to advance rights for women, racialised people and lesbians and gays.

The incendiary narrative stemming from the Christian fundamentalist opposition in Belize did not slow down until a report, published by the Southern Poverty Law Centre (2013), exposed their links to the US-based fundamentalist Christian right. The report, which identified Stirm as associated with dominionist theology, was covered by a national newscast in July 2013, which claimed 'that there were extremist right wing religious groups who were influencing the local Christian organisations in their campaign to resist what has been called the "homosexual agenda"' (7NewsBelize.com, 2013d). The newscast also reported on Stirm's response, in his own press release, that the report was a weak attempt timed to attempt to distract the nation from a month of constitutional marches across Belize. Stirm commented further that the marches 'mobilized almost 10,000[26] Belizeans to stand for constitutional values and [were] opposed to the 2013 Gender Policy in its present form' (ibid.). Stirm also restated that his organisation is a wholly funded by Belizeans who stand for strong family values. He did, however, admit that the US-based Alliance Defending Freedom (ADF) and Centre for Family and Human Rights

---

25 To Marin's question 'If God fearing men walk away from politics and leave it to corrupt and sinful men to lead us [. . .]', Scott Cheryl Stirm posted the first reply on 17 Jun. 2014. The page can no longer be accessed. However, UNIBAM documented the exchange on their blog, see: http://unitedbelizeadvocacymovement.blogspot.com/2014/06/a-review-of-lies-of-our-belizean.html.

26 Stirm's numbers may not be reliable, others estimated approximately 4,000 people participated nationwide.

(C-FAM) provided advice, legal assistance and strategy, and he noted that: 'they are assisting in cases all over the world in the homosexual global attack on morality & family values' (ibid.).

The revelation of ADF's support of Belize Action was a sign that the culture wars had arrived in the country and that US-based Christian fundamentalists were intervening to stop the 'homosexual agenda'. The ADF was founded in 1994 by 30 prominent Christian leaders in response to what they believed were increasing attacks on religious freedom, and the destruction of the institution of marriage. 'This vicious propaganda, born and bred by American ideologues, has found fertile soil across the globe' (Southern Poverty Law Centre, 2013, p. 6). This is significant, especially when we take into consideration influence or links to conservative US-based fundamentalists of additional groups such as Christian Fellowship Lawyers and the Jamaican Coalition for a Healthy Society (JCHS) who are actively opposing decriminalisation across the Caribbean. A JCHS petition against the 'Justice for All roadmap' (the anti-discrimination programme of the Pan Caribbean Partnership Against HIV/AIDS) influenced Caricom political leaders' response to decriminalisation in 11 countries with similar laws across the region. The results of their effort led to a call for the roadmap to be refined to make decriminalisation a long-term goal in the region, in essence derailing its commitment to decriminalisation.

National strategy: 'We are one! In dignity and rights!'

The case was heard from 7 to 10 May 2013. We in UNIBAM fought back against the right-wing opposition with our own daily news coverage. We rallied supporters to vote in our own poll with a differently worded question, and the results showed that over 49 per cent backed changing the law. Our goal was to show our opponents that they did not control the public narrative. UNIBAM had exposed homophobia through media coverage that documented rallies against LGBT rights and decriminalisation at Battlefield Park in 2011, and constitutional marches organised by the religious right around the country in 2013. Never before had a litigation case resulted in prayer meetings across the country, including in front of the Belize Supreme Court.

The LGBT community responded to the right-wing fundamentalists' campaigns, organising pride parties and pageants, even under severe threat of opposition. Allies joined in TV advertisements, and 1,800 people wore wristbands that read, 'We are one! In dignity and rights!', as a symbolic response of resistance. We witnessed protest threats in Orange Walk in 2013 by evangelical groups against the Miss Gay Goddess Pageant:

> On Saturday, protestors in favor of the existing laws of Belize took to the streets of Corozal Town in demonstration against the content of the Revised Gender Policy 2013, as well as a constitutional challenge brought against the government by Caleb Orosco [sic], who is seeking

to have repealed Section Fifty-three of the Criminal Code. While that religious crusade winded down after several weeks of touring the country, a group of openly gay men was making final preparations for Miss Gay Goddess Belize 2013 later that night. Amid the controversy surrounding the pageant, many have expressed disdain over such flamboyant display of homosexuality, despite the fact that it was being held privately in Belize City (Channel5Belize.com, 2013a)

We produced advertisements with the 'We are one! In dignity and rights!' headline, and we created short documentaries on the issue of faith and rights. We participated in talk shows and used our virtual room to plan talking points for public communications. In addition, during the visit of Dr Edward Greene, the UN Special Envoy for HIV and AIDS in the Caribbean, we took advantage of the dialogue initiated by Caricom to revisit the abovementioned Justice for All roadmap. Dr Greene informed us that faith-based leaders were ready to talk. Later, in March 2015, we met the head of the Evangelical Association of Churches, the Methodists and the Anglican canon, Leroy Flowers – a past president of the Belize Council of Churches – to discuss our concerns about discrimination and violence.

The LGBT community and allies joined the fightback with an effective social media strategy, creating virtual rooms like BCC (Belizeans for the Constitutional Challenge), a community education group which monitored the media and opponents' comments on Facebook prior to, during and after the trial. This helped us to profile our opponents' comments which in turn informed the 'We are one! In dignity and rights!' campaign. When Belize presented its national report for the UN's UPR, it was also shared directly with an audience of 800 people on BCC. However, our group's comments were infiltrated and showed up on opponents' sites, so we were forced to cut all 800 names from the list and begin again, ending up with 320 people in the community education group. By 2014, the e-library had collected 8,000 articles from around the world that anyone in the group could access. We created a group called BCC Planning, which linked allies from across sectors, and together we divided up the tasks and countered Belize Action's opposition.

Individuals provided technical support, negotiated language on sexuality, and provided information that helped to discredit our opponents. A healthy debate ensued between opponents and supporters, and LGBT issues became the hot topic in a Facebook group and generated more than 1,200 comments. Supporters monitored Facebook, identifying any libellous statements or any engaged in hate propagation. If any threatening statements were encountered, Facebook would be asked to shut down the account or remove the comment. This monitoring and evaluation was never more effective than when we identified some comments in the international media (chiefly *The Guardian*) that Boots Martinez, the minister of works, had made in 2011 (they had previously been reported in the national media):

> My position is that God never placed anything on me for me to look at a man and jump on a man. I'll be clear on it . . . How would you decriminalise that, I am sorry, but that is law. Not only is the law made by man, that is a law made from the Bible. Why you think God made a man and a woman, man has what woman wants, and woman has what man wants, it's as simple as that. I'll fight tooth and nail to keep that law. (Williams, 2011)

The intense media attention raised the profile of the case and the work of UNIBAM. Kathleen Esquivel,[27] NAC chair, underlined this point: 'Ten years ago, very few people outside the NGO community even knew that UNIBAM existed. I don't think there's anyone in Belize now that doesn't know (of it now).' Another interviewee referred to the way that 'UNIBAM' was being used as another word for 'gay':

> I wore my skinny jeans with my biker boots and y'know a tight top . . . So I was there taking photos and then there was this young woman . . . and she just kinda like looked at me ... and she's like, 'So, what, you're UNIBAM too?' Y'know and I looked at her and I was like, 'Do you even know what that word means?'[28]

Others spoke about the impact on public discourse of the debate and discussion about the case:

> It's been three years [since the case was filed]? Wow! It's hard to imagine that it's been three years, first of all. My understanding has grown tremendously, and I think, so too has the national consciousness, the discourse. It's not always been intellectual or healthy, but there's a discussion occurring that has never occurred before.[29]

There were requests for interviews from international media as well as speaking engagements in Washington DC, which were supported by the Human Rights Campaign and the Swiss ambassador to Mexico.

Moving forward

The work of UNIBAM succeeded in winning political support from both Prime Minister Barrow and the leader of the opposition, Francis Fonseca. This is a milestone in Belize's public discourse and, indeed, for any Caribbean leader. In a media interview, Prime Minister Barrow said:

> There can be no discrimination in terms of employment opportunities, in terms of access to healthcare, in terms of the services that the society offers. This administration certainly is not concerned about what happens in the bedrooms of the employees of the government, there are constitutional protections for public officers, properly appointed, and even with respect to open vote workers there can never be any kind

27 Interviewed on 28 Aug. 2013 by Caleb Orozco, UNIBAM and Envisioning.
28 Dennis Craft interviewed on 25 Aug. 2013 by Caleb Orozco, as above.
29 Imani Fairweather-Morrison interviewed on 30 Aug. 2013 by Caleb Orozco, as above.

of interference, any kind of surveillance, any kind of concern about
the sexual orientation of the employees of government. (7NewsBelize.
com, 2013b)

Four months later, on Independence Day, Prime Minister Barrow followed up
with: 'Government will . . . fully respect the right of the churches to propagate
their understanding of the morality, or immorality, of homosexuality. But what
Government cannot do is to shirk its duty to ensure that all citizens, without
exception, enjoy the full protection of the law' (7NewsBelize.com, 2013e).

The leader of the opposition, Francis Fonseca, also offered his thoughts
when interviewed a week before the 2013 OAS General Assembly: 'I am the
leader of a political party that embraces all Belizeans. I have Belizeans in my
party who are homosexuals, and we embrace all Belizeans' (7NewsBelize.com,
2013a). This led to UNIBAM engaging with the foreign minister, and indirectly
engaging with the Council of Churches and the IACHR, developments which
opened up discussions on policy development which adheres to the principle
of respect for diversity.

Unfortunately, we were unable to turn the political tone of 2013 into
substantive legislative change in 2015 that would address discrimination and
violence, or enforce rights and protection for all citizens. Gaining substantial
recognition/awareness in a country of 370,300 people (Statistical Institute of
Belize, 2015) with unknown quantifiable LGBT citizens, remains a challenge.
In conclusion, as I write, a court decision is still pending on the Section 53
constitutional challenge. Filed in 2010, the case was finally heard between
7 and 10 May 2013. Three years later, there has been no decision from the
Supreme Court. In the meantime, the environment is changing as people
reflect more on the prejudice and the propaganda they hear. We at UNIBAM
continue to lead the way, with actions like our 2015 conference which looked
at the intersection of rights for the first time.

Editors' update:

On 10 August 2016, after this chapter was written, the Supreme Court released
its decision. The Hon. Chief Justice Kenneth Benjamin accepted all grounds
claimed in the constitutional case *Caleb Orozco v. attorney general of Belize*.
He ruled that Section 53 violated Orozco's rights under the constitution
and ordered it to be 'read down', thus legalising same-sex intimacy between
consenting adults in private. He also added that constitutional protection on
the basis of 'sex' includes 'sexual orientation'. This historic decision has been
widely celebrated, and has significant implications for similar legal challenges
across the region.

Orozco's response to the decision points to the progress made through
activism: 'Our judicial system has been proven to be robust and unprejudiced.
This judgment should give other oppressed groups the confidence to speak up

and stand up for themselves in situations of human rights abuses in the way I have' (GLAAD, 2016).

However, after initially stating that it would not appeal the decision, the Belize government reversed its position following a meeting with church leaders. On 16 September 2016, it filed an appeal[30] narrowly based on two parts of the decision: against inclusion of 'sexual orientation' under 'sex'; and against the judge's finding that Section 53 was inconsistent with the right to freedom of expression. Religious bodies also appealed, including an appeal by the Roman Catholic Church of Belize that challenged all grounds of the decision including privacy, dignity and equality. However the religious groups dropped their appeal and in March 2018, the Roman Catholic Church withdrew their appeal and removed itself from the case. The Belize government then also dropped its appeal – and the judgment stands.[31]

References

Collom, K. (2014) '25,000 protest in Jamaica against "homosexual agenda"', *China Topix*, 16 Jun., available at: www.chinatopix.com/articles/3612/20140701/25–000-protest-jamaica-against-homosexual-agenda.htm#ixzz3w8EZARXx (accessed 17 Feb. 2018).

Daily Express (2011) 'Transgender Belizean cries discrimination', 14 Apr. www.trinidadexpress.com/news/Transgender_Belizean_cries_discrimination-119892154.html (accessed 22 Feb. 2018).

Diamond, S. (1990) *Spiritual Warfare* (Montréal, PQ: Black Rose Books).

— (1995) *Roads to Dominion: Right-Wing Movements and Political Power in the United States* (New York, NY: Guilford Publishing).

GLAAD (2016) 'In historic step, Belize court scraps law targeting gay and bisexual men', 10 Aug., available at: www.glaad.org/blog/historic-step-belize-court-scraps-law-targeting-gay-and-bisexual-men (accessed 17 Feb. 2018).

Herman, D. (1997) *The Anti-Gay Agenda, Orthodox Vision and the Christian Right* (Chicago, IL: University of Chicago Press).

Jamaica Gleaner (2013) 'Where is the justice, Mr Golding?', letter to the editor, 15 Nov., available at: http://jamaica-gleaner.com/gleaner/20131115/letters/letters5.html (accessed 17 Feb. 2018).

Jones, P.E. (2013) 'Minister Lisel Alamilla expresses grave concerns', *West Vision*, 11 Jul., available at: www.westvision.bz/minister-lisel-alamilla-expresses-grave-concerns/ (accessed 22 Feb. 2018).

30 *Attorney general of Belize v. Caleb Orozco.*
31 Chief Justice Benjamin shares his overview of the case at a forum, LGBT + Equality and the Rule of Law organised by Kaleidoscope Trust 2018 on 12 June 2018. Available at: www.blackrock.com/investing/search/video-feature-results?videoId=20180517_LGBT (accessed 10 July 2018).

Northwestern University (2014) 'Belize's responsibility to its LGBT citizens: an assessment of the treatment of the lesbian gay bisexual and transgender community in Belize and laws inhibiting equal rights', 10 Dec.

Southern Poverty Law Center (2013) 'Dangerous liaisons: the American religious right and the criminalisation of homosexuality in Belize', available at: https://www.splcenter.org/20130709/dangerous-liaisons (accessed 22 Feb. 2018).

Statistical Institute of Belize (2015) 'Annual Report 2015', available at: http://sib.org.bz/publications/annual-reports/ (accessed 22 Feb. 2018).

Theocracy Watch (2006) 'Dominionism and dominion theology', available at: www.theocracywatch.org/dominionism.htm (accessed 22 Feb. 2018).

United Belize Advocacy Movement and Heartland Alliance for Human Needs and Human Rights (2013) 'Human rights violations of Lesbian, Gay, Bisexual, and Transgender (LGBT) people in Belize', submitted to the 107th session of the United Nations Human Rights Committee, Geneva, available at: http://tbinternet.ohchr.org/Treaties/CCPR/Shared%20Documents/BLZ/INT_CCPR_IFS_BLZ_14350_E.pdf (accessed 22 Feb. 2018).

Williams, Zoe (2011) 'Gay rights: A world of inequality', *The Guardian*, 13 Sep., available at: www.theguardian.com/world/2011/sep/13/gay-rights-world-of-inequality (accessed 17 Feb. 2018).

Television news reports

Caricom.org (2014) 'Regional news, Belize observes World AIDS Day with goal of getting to ZeroHIV', 5 Dec., available at: http://caricom.org/communications/view/belize-observes-world-aids-day-with-goal-of-getting-to-zerohiv (accessed 13 Feb. 2018).

Channel5Belize.com (2011) 'Minister Boots Martinez catfight "tooth and nail" with UNIBAM', 14 Sep., available at: http://edition.channel5belize.com/archives/60793 (accessed 17 Feb. 2018).

— (2012) 'Ministry of Education recalls manual that had pro-gay remarks', 13 Sep., available at: http://edition.channel5belize.com/archives/75834 (accessed 17 Feb. 2018).

— (2013a) 'Miss Gay Goddess Belize 2013', 22 Jul., available at: http://edition.channel5belize.com/archives/88350 (accessed 17 Feb. 2018).

— (2013b) 'Pro-gay protest to be held in the north', 1 Aug., available at: http://edition.channel5belize.com/archives/88790 (accessed 17 Feb. 2018).

7NewsBelize.com (2013a) 'Opp. leader Fonseca doesn't expect Guats to hold referendum in 2014', 29 May, available at: www.7newsbelize.com/sstory.php?nid=25639 (accessed 13 Feb. 2018).

— (2013b) 'PM says gender policy not law', 30 May, available at:

www.7newsbelize.com/sstory.php?nid=25663&frmsrch=1 (accessed 17 Feb. 2018).

— (2013c) 'Pastor Stirm: We don't need those types of allies', 27 Jun., available at: www.7newsbelize.com/sstory.php?nid=25903 (accessed 17 Feb. 2018).

— (2013d) 'Stirm strikes back at SPLC', 29 Jul., available at: www.7newsbelize.com/sstory.php?nid=26163 (accessed 17 Feb. 2018).

— (2013e) 'PM Barrow uses Independence Day platform to support equal treatment for all, gays included', 23 Sep., available at: www.7newsbelize.com/sstory.php?nid=26598&frmsrch=1 (accessed 17 Feb. 2018).

Documentary film

Telling Our Stories (Belize Portraits section) (2014) (Belize and Canada: United Belize Advocacy Movement and Envisioning Global LGBT Human Rights), available at: http://envisioning-tellingourstories.blogspot. com (accessed 17 Feb. 2018). Extracts are cited from interviews with Mia Quetzal, Kainie Manuel, Estrellita Reyes, Dennis Craft, Aaron Mai, Elisa Castellanos, Kathleen Esquivel and Imani Fairweather-Morrison.

10

The multifaceted struggle against the Anti-Homosexuality Act in Uganda

Adrian Jjuuko and Fridah Mutesi

On 1 August 2014, the Constitutional Court of Uganda – in a unanimous judgment – nullified the hugely popular Anti-Homosexuality Act (AHA).[1] The annulment was on the grounds that the Parliament of Uganda had passed the law without the requisite quorum as provided for by the country's constitution.[2] This was one of the most memorable moments in the history of lesbian, gay, bisexual, transgender, intersex (LGBTI) organising in Uganda; people wept, shouted, and danced, and the rainbow flag was waved triumphantly in the courtroom.

This momentous event was in sharp contrast to the incident witnessed only five months earlier, on 24 February 2014, when Uganda's President Yoweri Museveni, in a telecast aired live on national television and in front of local and international press, unexpectedly signed the AHA. That moment was the epitome of all the efforts to ensure that the Anti-Homosexuality Bill (AHB) became law, which had begun when the latter was first tabled before parliament by the MP for Ndorwa West, David Bahati in October 2009.[3] The signing of the law and its subsequent coming into force on 10 March 2014 – just a

1 For the 2014 AHA see: www.refworld.org/pdfid/530c4bc64.pdf (accessed 11 Feb. 2017). For the court case that resulted in its nullification, see: *Oloka-Onyango and nine others v. attorney general* (Constitutional Petition no. 8 of 2014) [2014] UGCC 14 (1 Aug. 2014), available at: www.ulii.org/ug/judgment/constitutional-court/2014/14/ (accessed 11 Feb. 2017).

2 The bill was passed following a session that fewer MPs had attended than the third required to pass a law. Two members including the then prime minister raised the issue of quorum on the parliament floor, but were overruled by the speaker who did not follow the procedure laid down for such cases (see Parliament of Uganda, 2013).

3 The full text of the 2009 AHB may be found at: http://hrapf.org/laws/ (accessed 20 Mar. 2018).

A. Jjuuko and F. Mutesi (2018) 'The multifaceted struggle against the Anti-Homosexuality Act in Uganda', in N. Nicol et al. (eds.) *Envisioning Global LGBT Human Rights: (Neo) colonialism, Neoliberalism, Resistance and Hope* (London: Human Rights Consortium, Institute of Commonwealth Studies), pp. 269–306.

day before the landmark petition that nullified it was filed – had a chilling effect on LGBTI organising in the country. The AHA, in the hands of anti-gay groups, was the ultimate weapon for subjugating pro-gay arguments and sentiments. The original AHB's notorious provision for the death penalty had been removed. However, the AHA still contained most of the AHB's other draconian provisions, such as: broadly defining homosexuality to include acts like 'touching with the intent' (Section 2, subject to life imprisonment); and granting immunity to anyone who committed 'any crime … as a direct result of his or her involvement in homosexuality' (Section 5(1)).[4] Additional provisions addressed the aiding and abetting of homosexuality (Section 7), and a sweeping one prohibited 'promotion' of homosexuality (Section 13). Some included pejorative language such as referring to the houses of LGBTI persons or the hotels which accommodated them as 'brothels' (Section 11).

Parliament's passing of the AHA on 20 December 2013, and indeed its coming into force in March 2014, saw a spike in the number of cases documented involving LGBTI persons, including arrests, prosecutions for 'carnal knowledge against the order of nature', landlords and local authorities throwing people out of their rented accommodation, and cases of threatened and actual violence, including mob violence. The Human Rights Awareness and Promotion Forum (HRAPF) and the Consortium on Monitoring Violations Based on Sex Determination, Gender Identity and Sexual Orientation (hereafter, Consortium) recorded 89 cases of violations against LGBTI persons in 2014 (Consortium, 2015). Of these cases, 48 (47 per cent) were by non-state actors (ibid.). Contrasting this with the 13.7 per cent recorded for 2013 and before reveal a large increase in violations by non-state actors, a growth which could be due to the passing of the AHA. Frank Mugisha, executive director of Sexual Minorities Uganda (SMUG), describes the situation thus:

> We saw this very harsh reaction from not only law enforcers, but including our fellow Ugandans. People started being evicted, people started being thrown out of their homes, being thrown out of school. And the reference was always this law, the president signed the law . . . We received very many cases of violence, discrimination towards LGBT persons, and we wrote it exactly as it was and published a report (SMUG and the National LGBTI Security Team, 2014). Within the period of the passing of the law and the period of our report, that was only a period of four months, we had documented about 164 cases and these were individuals coming to us and telling us this happened to me

4 This provision effectively allowed immunity to anyone who committed a crime, including murder, against a person with whom they had been engaged in homosexual acts. In such a case, the defendant would allege that the victim of the violent crime tried to involve them in homosexuality through romantic and sexual advances, a move so offensive and frightening to the defendant that it brought on a psychotic state characterised by unusual violence.

because of the law.[5]

Another effect of the law was the emigration of ordinary LGBTI persons from Uganda. Many ended up in neighbouring Kenya, where they were subjected to more violations,[6] while some were resettled outside Africa. The UN High Commissioner for Refugees recorded 363 Ugandans who had sought asylum in Kenya on grounds of persecution based on sexual orientation and gender identity (SOGI) (Zomorodi, 2015). Fifty per cent of these arrived in 2014, while the rest arrived in early 2015 (ibid., pp. 12–13). Prior to the passing of the act, only 20 cases had been registered (ibid., pp. 25–6). Some organisations temporarily closed and key leaders left the country.[7] The LGBTI community's main allies were raided by the police and others were ordered to stop providing services.

Although many people were arrested during this period, none, surprisingly, were charged under the new law, but rather under the colonial Penal Code Act. Its Section 145(a) is considered to be the main provision criminalising same-sex relations in Uganda using this terminology: 'carnal knowledge against the order of nature', a concept derived from the British anti-sodomy provisions that were imported into the colonies. People were also charged under the Penal Code's vague and sweeping provisions on 'idle and disorderly persons' (Section 167) and 'rogues and vagabonds' (Section 168).[8] The increased clampdown on service provision and the increased violations were based on the new law, but without any resultant prosecution this created uncertainty and apprehension, as no one knew what to expect.

After the law had been nullified, the number of reported violations appeared to have dropped, before increasing again. Legally speaking, however, for many individuals and organisations, the nullification of the law lifted a yoke from their necks.[9] Nevertheless, LGBTI individuals continued to face violations,

---

5   Interviewed on 26 Nov. 2014 by Richard Lusimbo, SMUG and Envisioning. An excerpt is included in the documentary *And Still We Rise* (2015).

6   Court record of David Malombe's affidavit filed in support of HRAPF's filed reference challenging the AHA at the EACJ, May 2015.

7   Among the leading activists forced to leave at the time were Nikilas Mawanda (then executive director of Trans Support Initiative Uganda), John Wambere alias Long John (member of Spectrum Uganda), Junic Wambya (executive director of Freedom and Roam Uganda), and Robert Karemire (member of Frank and Candy and chair of the LGBTI security committee).

8   The Uganda Penal Code was introduced in 1930 as the Penal Code Ordinance no. 7 of 1930. It became Cap 128 when the laws were compiled. Few amendments have been made to the Penal Code, and provisions intended for use during the colonial times are still present. For a more detailed discussion of its origins, see Jjuuko (2013).

9   Other laws exist that the state could still use to restrict the work of LGBTI organisations. For example, the Non-Governmental Organizations (NGO) Act,

especially from non-state actors. One Ugandan activist (Zomorodi, 2015, pp. 11–12) stated:

> Even though they struck down the law, the general public has been poisoned. It's not the law people are afraid of – it's their very neighbors, their friends, their relatives. When you hear about violations, it's not done by the law. The police arrest you and parade you, but then they release you because they have nothing to charge you with. Once you go back to the community, you are at the mercy of the people you live with.

Nullification of the AHA was the result of deliberate and painstaking planning and lobbying. This chapter documents its defeat. The authors were at the centre of the struggle, from October 2009 when the bill was tabled through to its nullification in August 2014, as they both worked at HRAPF which coordinated the legal efforts of the Civil Society Coalition on Human Rights and Constitutional Law (CSCHRCL, or simply Coalition). The chapter opens with a background on the AHA, from the time it was tabled as a bill in Uganda's parliament to when it came into force, including civil society efforts to organise against it.[10] It then discusses the aftermath, the violations and the impact on LGBTI persons. It delves into the legal challenge made to the AHA and the process: building a group of petitioners and legal teams, analysing the issues, drafting the constitutional petition, the hearing, the application by the anti-gay groups to join the petition as parties, and the outcome. It also documents the case at the East African Court of Justice (EACJ),[11] which was filed at almost the same time as the Constitutional Court case. Finally, it discusses the advocacy strategies of the struggle against the AHA and the aftermath of its nullification.

The long road: the making of the AHA, 2014

Hugely popular from the time of its tabling in parliament by the Hon. David Bahati, the Ndorwa West MP, in October 2009,[12] the AHB appeared poised

---

2016 contains provisions that deny registration to organisations whose objectives 'contravene the law'. It also imposes special obligations that could be used against LGBTI groups, including doing nothing to prejudice the security interests and laws of Uganda, or the dignity of the people of Uganda. For a detailed analysis of the bill from which it emerged, see HRAPF (2015b). For the NGO Act, 2016, Republic of Uganda, see https://www.ulii.org/node/25931 (accessed 9 Sep. 2017).

10 See also 'Kuchu resilience and resistance in Uganda: a history', ch. 12, this volume.

11 *Human Rights Awareness and Promotion Forum v. attorney general of Uganda*, available at: http://hrapf.org/?mdocs-file=9243&mdocs-url=false (accessed 17 Feb. 2017).

12 David Bahati is now minister of state for finance, planning and economic development. He was reelected unopposed in 2011 after tabling the bill and retained his seat in 2016. He had become the vice chair of the parliamentary caucus of the National Resistance Movement (NRM, the ruling party) by the time of his

to sail through. This was never to be easy, however, for it took the bill five turbulent years to go through the legislative process. Touted as the perfect solution to the 'problem' of homosexuality, the bill was supported by most religious leaders – the most outspoken of whom was evangelical pastor, Martin Ssempa; political leaders led by the then minister of ethics and integrity, Nsaba Buturo and his successor Rev. Fr Simon Lokodo; parliamentarians led by its sponsor, the Hon. David Bahati, and later the parliament speaker, Rebecca Kadaga; and the majority of the population.

The bill was promoted as a way of protecting the 'traditional family' and children and young people from homosexuality, as well as safeguarding culture and traditional values.[13] However, its extreme provisions led to an outcry from civil society and development partners. Those who opposed it pointed out that the bill was too draconian and if passed into law would violate the rights not only of LGBTI persons but also of others (Coalition, 2011). They also pointed out that its provisions could not address the problems it was intended to solve. In addition, it was not possible to clearly identify the traditional family as such extended families were dying out, afflicted by so many things extraneous to homosexuality, including increased economic hardship, domestic violence and alcoholism (Tamale, 2009). As for children and young people, the Penal Code Act had been amended in 2007 to protect boys and girls from sexual exploitation.[14] And the right to culture was clearly protected in the Uganda Constitution (Article 37), and recognised as a source of law, although there is a proviso that subjects customary law to natural justice, good conscience and the law.[15] Again, even if homosexuality were indeed a threat, the existing law on 'unnatural offences' would have curtailed any threatening homosexual practices. Significantly, not a single conviction has been recorded under the Penal Code in Uganda's postcolonial legal history (Coalition and HRAPF, 2013, pp. 35–56).

The bill did not seek to repeal the Penal Code provisions, but instead sought to supplement them by creating the new offence of 'homosexuality',

---

appointment as minister.

13 See generally, Memorandum to the Anti-Homosexuality Bill, 2009, in Human Dignity Trust (2014), p. 1.

14 Penal Code (Amendment) Act 2007, Section 2, which replaced Section 129 of the Penal Code Act Cap 120, accords protection to both boys and girls in cases of defilement, unlike the previous section, which only protected girls. The protection is valid regardless of whether the sexual exploitation occasioned is hetero- or homosexual in nature.

15 Section 15(1) of the Judicature Act Cap 13 provides that 'Nothing in this Act shall deprive the High Court of the right to observe or enforce the observance of, or shall deprive any person of the benefit of, any existing custom, which is not repugnant to natural justice, equity and good conscience and not incompatible either directly or by necessary implication with any written law'.

defining it as an act rather than an orientation. It included touching with the intent to commit homosexuality among the more usual acts relating to carnal knowledge. Punishment for this new offence was life imprisonment.[16] The AHB also sought to create the offence of 'aggravated homosexuality', punishable by death (Clause 3(2)). Clause 3(1) stated that this had been committed when any listed aggravating factor was involved, such as the accused being a 'serial offender', the 'victim' being a child aged under 18, the victim having a disability, or the offender being HIV positive. The provision on children (Clause 3(1)) was unnecessary, since the Penal Code already provided for it with the same punishment (Penal Code Amendment 2007, Section 2). The provision on persons living with HIV/AIDS (Clause 3(1)(b)) would have had a negative effect, as it would further fuel the stigmatisation of people living with HIV/AIDS. The new offence also portrayed people with disabilities (Clause 3(1)(e)) as lacking the capacity to consent to same-sex relations. It then provided for protection of 'victims' by making those who had been 'coerced' into homosexuality immune to prosecution for crimes committed while involved in homosexual acts (Clause 5(1)). Aiding and abetting homosexuality was another controversial provision, which could include anything done for or about a homosexual (Clause 7). Promotion of homosexuality, covering a wide range of acts, could make NGOs, as well as individuals, criminally liable simply for advocating for equal rights or providing services to LGBTI people (Clause 13). In one of its most infamous provisions, the bill sought to oblige all 'persons in authority' to report any homosexual they were aware of within 24 hours. Failure to do so would be a crime (Clause 14). This meant that parents would be obligated to turn in their children, teachers their students, and lawyers and doctors their clients, regardless of any professional oaths. It made all the offences extraditable (Clause 17) and provided for the nullification of international instruments that were inconsistent with the spirit and provisions of the bill (Clause 18(1)). The bill was passed with all these provisions intact, except that it replaced the death penalty for 'aggravated homosexuality' with life imprisonment, removed the obligation to report, and deleted the nullification of international instruments.

Despite its huge popularity, the bill met its match in civil society organising. Bodies working on behalf of women's and refugee rights, LGBTI people and sex workers, alongside religious organisations and legal aid service providers, among others, formed an alliance of 50 members to oppose the Bill. This was the aforementioned Coalition, which sought to oppose the bill on the grounds of defending LGBTI rights but also because of the implications of the bill

---

16 Curiously, this is the same punishment as under Section 145 of the Penal Code for 'carnal knowledge against the order of nature', and so apart from clearly defining the acts that could be regarded as homosexual, it did not seek to enhance the punishment.

for civil society rights. As Professor Joe Oloka-Onyango,[17] a key Coalition member, argued:

> The idea behind the coalition was that, yes, the Anti-Homosexuality Act was focused against LGBTI people, but it also had implications beyond that community. And we were very concerned that those implications as well undermined the observation of rights: for example, freedom of association, freedom of assembly, freedom of speech, even what people could talk about.

The Coalition immediately set about creating awareness of the law and lobbying the Ugandan government and others to oppose the bill. But they had limited success, since the main modes of creating awareness, such as the mass media, were not readily available. Print media humiliated and routinely exposed the personal details and addresses of people perceived to be LGBTI. This increased the violence and threats perpetrated against community members. Television and radio stations rarely hosted LGBTI people or activists.[18] The leading media house in Uganda, the Vision Group, had (and still has) an editorial policy that prevents the publication or broadcasting of content including advertisements, that 'propagates' homosexuality and instead can publish only content from the president, parliament, or courts (Vision Group, 2014).

Nevertheless, advocacy worked quite well. Members of Parliament (MPs) were approached, and influential thinkers like Professors Makau Mutua of the State University of New York, Sylvia Tamale from the law faculty at Makerere University in Kampala, Uganda, and Joe Oloka-Onyango at Makerere's Human Rights and Peace Centre, held public talks which targeted MPs. The Coalition brought the bill to international attention. As a result, Uganda and its stance on the AHB became a key feature of foreign policy in many countries, particularly the United States, the United Kingdom, Sweden and the Netherlands. Many other countries in the Global North spoke out against the bill. It was debated in the international press, and indeed at one point, the Ugandan president had to warn MPs to go slow on the bill, as it had become a foreign policy issue (*New Vision*, 2010).

The bill then became a tool for concealing scandals and corruption, for as soon as any erupted, moves were made to reintroduce the bill, and local and international attention was diverted back to that. Moreover, the AHB needs to be seen in the context of several pieces of legislation introduced to regulate civil society. Nicholas Opiyo,[19] one of the lawyers in the Constitutional Court challenge against the AHA, observed,

17 Interviewed on 3 Dec. 2014 by Richard Lusimbo, SMUG and Envisioning. An excerpt is included in the documentary *And Still We Rise* (2015).

18 This was partly due to a fine imposed on a media personality for hosting a person who identified as lesbian. See Mugisa (2007).

19 Interviewed on 21 Nov. 2014 by Richard Lusimbo, SMUG and Envisioning. An excerpt is included in the documentary *And Still We Rise* (2015).

> You have several legislations now emerging that seek to constrict the
> space, not just for LGBTI but for everybody else who is involved
> in activism – the NGO Amendment Bill . . . and the NGO laws in
> practice now seek to limit civil liberties. The Public Order Management
> Act seeks to limit people who want to challenge government. So there's
> an emergence of legislation that seeks to eat away, to eat at the edges of
> civil liberties across the board.

The Coalition continued to guide international attention to all the violations
and scandals going on in the country, since at one time the focus on the AHB
had threatened to render other violations largely invisible.

The bill came close to being passed in 2011, just before parliament closed
but, in the absence of a quorum, the speaker, Edward Ssekandi ruled that
there could be no vote. Increasingly the bill came to be used for political ends,
sacrificing the human rights of a small minority to political ambitions. Under
the stewardship of Rebecca Kadaga, the deputy speaker, the Ninth Parliament
raised the stakes once more. The bill continued to be used as a tool for political
aggrandisement as she made it her personal mission to get it passed. On 29
October 2011, she led parliament in saving all the bills that had been tabled
in the Eighth Parliament, including the AHB. As Nicholas Opiyo explained,

> As opposed to being a law that sought to make an act criminal, the law
> was then being used for meeting people's own political ends, namely
> the Speaker of Parliament who at the time was said to be angling
> to contest for the presidency. When she realised that the law was so
> famous amongst people here in the country, she took it upon herself, it
> became her own personal crusade, and she then promised the country
> the law as a Christmas gift; and promised to pass it.

In October 2012 Kadaga told John Baird, Canada's foreign minister,
to back off on Ugandan issues (Mugerwa, 2012). She was then treated to a
hero's welcome on her return, and promised to give the bill to Ugandans as
a Christmas gift by the end of the year (Naturinda, 2012). And she actually
delivered that gift, albeit one year later than planned, when the AHA was
passed on 20 December 2013. In a heated session discussing the bill, the
speaker brushed aside the prime minister's caution that a quorum was needed.
This later proved to be the chink in the armour of the crusade to pass the
law, for even though Kadaga had achieved what she wanted, this was the
ground upon which the Constitutional Court later nullified the AHA.[20] The
recommendations of the legal and parliamentary affairs committee to remove
redundant and anti-human rights provisions (Parliament of Uganda, 2012)
were largely ignored, and most provisions remained. The minority report by
four MPs was completely rejected, and the law was passed.

After the bill had been passed, the president sent a letter to the speaker

20 *Professor Oloka-Onyango and nine others v. attorney general*, Constitutional Petition
no. 8 of 2014.

and MPs saying there was no need for homosexuality to be criminalised for in his view homosexuals were 'abnormal persons' who needed help. He appeared to indicate that the bill had been passed without adequate consultation and that the government did not support it. Indeed many interpreted this as the president's veto of the bill (Mugerwa, 2014).

Although the president had indicated that he fundamentally disagreed with the law and would not sign it, nonetheless, according to Opiyo, [21]

> Certain geo-political events happened in the region that forced the hand of the president. Uganda was heavily involved in the conflict in the Sudan. There was a public fallout between the US and Uganda, in which the head of state of the United States asked President Museveni publicly to withdraw from Sudan. That in many ways angered President Museveni, and in so doing, he found recourse in the AHA as a way of getting back at the American head of state for his public rebuke for Museveni's role in South Sudan. Nationally, the president went on a countrywide ... Christmas tour ... And every place the president went he was being told by religious leaders, by ordinary people, to sign the law. His own political party, in a party caucus retreat, made a public plea to the president to sign this law in exchange for the party declaring him as a sole candidate in the forthcoming election.

Further, in a strange twist, the president stated that his signing would depend on the opinion of scientists on whether homosexuality was caused by nature or nurture. He interpreted their largely inconclusive report as concluding that it was a nurture issue rather than a nature one. He thus called a press conference and signed the bill into law on 24 February 2014 amidst fanfare and before local and international media. He blasted the West for interfering in governance issues and for directing African countries on how they should conduct their affairs. He asserted Uganda's sovereignty and capacity to pass any laws it wished (BBC News, 2014a; Kasasira, 2014). Following Museveni's assent to the bill, the AHA came into force on 10 March 2014.

Immediate effects of the AHA

As soon as parliament passed the AHA on 20 December 2013, violations against LGBTI people increased. This trend continued until the president signed the bill into law, after which they surprisingly became less frequent. The following analysis of the effects covers the time after it was passed and the period when the AHA was in force.

This section on the immediate effects, broadly categorised into violations by state actors and non-state actors, relies primarily on data collected by HRAPF and the Consortium, which is chaired by HRAPF. The latter operates

---

21 Interviewed on 21 Nov. 2014 by Richard Lusimbo, SMUG and Envisioning. An excerpt is included in the documentary *And Still We Rise* (2015).

the only specialised legal aid clinic for LGBTI people in Uganda. It records and documents violations against such individuals, and produces periodic reports on this issue. The organisation chairs the Coalition's legal committee and was responsible for coordinating the legal and advocacy efforts involved in challenging the AHB and the AHA.

Violations by state actors

Most rights violations that occurred when the law was in force were committed by state actors. The main perpetrators were members of the Uganda Police Force (Consortium, 2015, p. 21).

In the aftermath of the act being passed, many LGBTI people were subjected to **arbitrary arrests** – that is, arrests not based on reasonable suspicion that a crime had been committed. They began three days after the AHA became law – HRAPF recorded eight arrests of LGBTI persons (involving ten people in total) between 20 December 2013 and 13 March 2014.[22] According to HRAPF's records relating to time-spans of less than three months, this period saw the largest number of LGBTI people taken into custody.[23] In contrast, at the same stage of the previous year, HRAPF recorded only five arbitrary arrests, where those apprehended had either been found walking on the streets (especially transgender persons) or had been detained following tip-offs from hostile members of the public.

On 20 December 2013, police arrested a transgender woman while she was walking on the street, held her overnight for 'impersonation', and released her next day without charge. On 27 January, four people were taken into custody, two of them men found watching a movie, whose crime was 'possession of pornographic materials'. The third person was a transgender woman, apprehended as she was about to board a taxi after being attacked by a mob. The fourth was a transgender woman, arrested after escaping from a mob which had raided the house where she was spending the night with a colleague. The next day, 28 January, a man reported assault after being beaten by a mob and thrown out of his house by local leaders who suspected him of being gay and of housing gay people. He was apprehended, along with a transgender woman who had escaped the mob violence. The two were later charged together under the Penal Code provision of having carnal knowledge against the order of nature. On 10 February, a transgender man was apprehended for impersonation while visiting a colleague who had previously been arrested. Private guards seized another person on 5 March when he was at a friend's gate

22 Data provided by Patricia Kimera, who was interviewed on 15 Sep. 2015 by Adrian Jjuuko, Envisioning. She was a legal officer at HRAPF in charge of receiving and handling cases relating to LGBTI people.

23 Para. 15(a), court record of Adrian Jjuuko's affidavit filed in support of HRAPF's case challenging the AHA at the EACJ, 23 Apr. 2014.

and later took him to the police station. Yet another was arrested after sending a text message. On 13 March, a man suspected of being gay was apprehended after police received a complaint that he had touched another man with the intent to commit a homosexual activity.[24]

Of the ten people arrested, only four were formally charged with an offence, and of those only two made it to court.[25] In both instances, the charges were dismissed for want of prosecution (*Yahoo News*, 2014), demonstrating that the arrests were not based on real evidence but instead constituted persecution, and revealing a connection between the passing of the act and the arrests. There was an increase in the latter soon after the AHA was passed, and a reduction when the act was nullified.[26] It is interesting that none of those apprehended were charged under the act, but the spike in numbers clearly shows that the passing of the act inspired the police to perform these actions. It is important to note that the police usually act on tip-offs from members of the public and usually make an arrest before carrying out investigations.

After the above individuals had been apprehended, other rights besides the right to liberty were violated. These **violations during arrest** (multiple in the majority of cases) were:

1. Lengthy pre-trial detentions without charges. The Consortium reported that in 2014, out of the 36 persons arbitrarily arrested, 18 spent more than the constitutional 48 hours in police detention without being formally charged (Consortium, 2015, p. 25). In three of these cases, the individuals were taken to court only after HRAPF had submitted complaint letters to the Inspector General of Police and the Uganda Human Rights Commission.[27]

2. Denial of access to lawyers. None of the detainees were informed of their right to a lawyer as prescribed by Article 23(3) of the Uganda Constitution (Consortium, 2015, pp. 26–7). Sometimes, when HRAPF lawyers went to the police stations to meet with clients, the officers there were hostile and sometimes refused to grant them access to their clients, claiming that the cases were 'very serious' and that they were still being investigated.[28]

3. Forced medical anal examination. The police subjected three of the 32 people arrested in 2014 to anal exams (Consortium, 2015, p. 29). Such exams have been discredited as a way of proving whether sexual acts have taken place, and are invasive violations of privacy – constituting inhumane

---

24 Patricia Kimera, interviewed on 15 Sep. 2015 by Adrian Jjuuko, Envisioning.
25 Kim Mukisa and Jackson Mukasa were charged with carnal knowledge against the order of nature.
26 Patricia Kimera, interviewed on 15 Sep. 2015 by Adrian Jjuuko, Envisioning.
27 Ibid.
28 Ibid.

and degrading treatment. The results were never used as medical evidence during trials. Indeed no full trial concerning consensual same-sex relations has taken place in Uganda (Coalition and HRAPF, 2013, pp. 35–6).

4. Forced HIV tests and revelation of results. The police disregarded the requirement of consent before subjecting the suspects to HIV/AIDS tests. Four detainees were subjected to these tests without their consent and without being counselled (Consortium, 2015, p. 29). The results of one case were declared to the media, which later led to publication of disparaging stories about the suspect. For example, the Kampala tabloid *Red Pepper* published an article called 'HORRIBLE: city sodomite infects 17 boys with HIV' (2014).

5. Parading the suspects before the media. Eleven of those arrested in 2014 were presented before the media as if they had already been found guilty of the offences (Consortium, 2015, p. 30). This is a common but illegal, cruel, inhumane and degrading practice going against the spirit of the constitution, which is underpinned by the presumption of innocence. When the LGBTI suspects were arrested, whether or not evidence warranted their charges, they were exposed to the media as homosexuals or 'wrong persons' attempting to con the public. In most cases they became the laughing stock of police officers, who in turn notified the press. A transgender woman reported, 'I became like a cartoon for the police. They would call the press, every five minutes I was in and out of the cell. They would call the press and make me sit there and ask me embarrassing questions, some of which were difficult to answer.'[29]

6. Threats and abuse from prison authorities. Those who ended up in prison faced abuse. Sam Ganafa,[30] executive director of Spectrum Uganda Initiative, was arrested along with three others, paraded before the press, and subjected to abuse and threats from the prison authorities. As he recounts his experience,

> The deputy himself was insulting us, even told other prisoners on morning parade . . . he was alerting other inmates, 'Be very careful with these people, these are homosexuals, they can rape you, they are rapists, they can rape you in the cells, so be very, very careful with them.' So when he came to me he says, 'This one is accused of homosexuality.' And the guy who was receiving us boxed me in the back, saying, 'You man, if you do those things here, we are going to kill you.'

29 Brenda Kiiza, interviewed on 4 Apr. 2014 by Richard Lusimbo, SMUG and Envisioning.
30 Interviewed on 29 Nov. 2014 by Richard Lusimbo, SMUG and Envisioning. An excerpt is included in the documentary *And Still We Rise* (2015).

Kim Mukisa and Jackson Mukasa,[31] who were also arrested, recollected their prison experience:

> MUKASA: We felt so scared when we reached in prison. Things were not so easy. The place was so disgusting. Even, they told me, 'That is your food.' Do you know maize bran? They brought for me maize bran.
>
> MUKISA: It's food for the pigs.
>
> MUKASA: For real! I just touched the food. I felt like I want to vomit. The plate – since you are gay – the plate you have to use is different. The food you eat, it's also different. The bathrooms you have to use, they're different. You have to sleep on the floor. You understand? On the floor, since you are gay!
>
> MUKISA: When they get to know that you're gay, you have to sleep in the bathroom.
>
> MUKASA: Take these gays to the toilet.

The overall effect of all the abuses listed here is that many LGBTI persons are afraid of reporting cases of violations to the police for fear of being arrested instead of the perpetrator(s). Moreover, out of all those reported to the police, only one has been resolved – and that not fully, as some of the perpetrators were never apprehended.

During the period that the act was in force, direct **attacks on service providers** and institutions that include LGBTI persons in their provision of service, were made. Examples that stood out were the raid on the Makerere University Walter Reed Project (MUWRP) and the suspension of the Refugee Law Project (RLP), part of Makerere University's School of Law. On 4 April 2014, the Ugandan police raided MUWRP, a US-funded HIV research and treatment centre that also provides health information and services to LGBTI people as part of its studies (Kafeero and Ayebazibwe, 2014). The raid took place after allegations that the project was 'recruiting' people into homosexuality. The police took away files and HIV/AIDS-prevention materials, including lubricants and condoms, and arrested a member of staff. As a result of this raid, the US embassy directed the centre to close, and consequently service provision for LGBTI persons came to an immediate halt.

In the second case, the RLP, the host and a key member of the Coalition, had its services in refugee camps suspended by the minister of relief, disaster preparedness and refugees, in the Office of the Prime Minister, over allegations of 'promoting homosexuality'. This was later extended to shutting down the Kampala office completely (Feder, 2014). The suspension was eventually lifted. As the RLP was a leading service provider, its suspension had a huge effect on service provision and also on other organisations, which resorted to stopping their services or disguising them for fear of being closed.

---

31 Interviewed on 26 Nov. 2014 by Richard Lusimbo, SMUG and Envisioning. An excerpt is included in the documentary *And Still We Rise* (2015).

Violations by non-state actors

Following the passing of the act, violations by non-state actors included **evictions of LGBTI persons from rented premises**. Some were evicted after being arrested, others after being outed in the media or merely because their landlords suspected them of being LGBT. The Consortium and HRAPF documented 20 evictions during this period (2015, pp. 32–4) while SMUG and the LGBTI security committee recorded 68 examples of people being expelled from their homes (2014, p. 7). The expulsions were illegal, as the tenants had not been given the requisite notice. Some were also violent and people lost their property. In three cases documented by HRAPF,[32] evictions were perpetrated by local council leaders who worked with the landlords to turn out suspected LGBTI persons. In the first, the local council chairperson actually led the team carrying out the eviction. In the second, on the day the bill was assented to, the landlord complained to local leaders about a tenant he suspected of being a homosexual and evicted him for no clear reason. He did not wish to reveal his real motive to the HRAPF lawyers who intervened, although he did admit the individual had been a good tenant. In the third example, a trans man was given 48 hours to vacate the house in a letter signed by the landlord and stamped by the local area chairperson.

Another consequence of the act being in force was **mob justice**. At this time HRAPF registered its first two cases of mob justice against LGBTI people in Uganda. One was incited by the area's local council chairperson who stormed the house of a suspected gay man at 6 am and ordered him and his visitor to leave. This attracted a mob which started beating the suspects until they managed to escape with significant physical injuries. When they reported what had happened, the police completely ignored their allegations of mob justice and arrested them on charges of having carnal knowledge against the order of nature (Consortium, 2015 p. 26). In the second case, a transgender woman and a gay man were separately tricked into a house by unknown persons who had tracked them on Facebook. They were then beaten and forced to confess their homosexuality. One of them was released and called HRAPF lawyers, who involved police leaders who then rescued the second person. One attacker was arrested and later convicted only of robbery (ibid., p. 23).

Effects on LGBTI organising

Passage of the act also led to the weakening of the Coalition and LGBTI organisations. Leading LGBTI activists were forced to seek asylum in other countries following persecution and threats of violence. They joined many others who had left when the bill was before parliament. Several LGBTI organisations operated on a much smaller scale and disguised their activities,

32 Patricia Kimera, interviewed on 15 Sep. 2015 by Adrian Jjuuko, Envisioning.

some turning their offices into bedrooms to avoid being questioned. Many Coalition members also reduced their activity in the Coalition and others suffered a loss of morale. The few that remained in operation continued with their activism, albeit at a more cautious level.

The multipronged approach: how the AHA was finally defeated

Coalition activists created a strategy on how they would react to the bill should it be passed by parliament. It began with lobbying the president not to sign the bill into law, guiding and controlling international response to the passage of the bill, and creating awareness of the negative provisions of the law in the general population. If the bill was enacted into law, the plan was to focus on litigation, challenging the law before the Constitutional Court as being inconsistent with the constitution. It was the success of this multipronged approach that finally got rid of the AHA.

Litigation: building the case

Challenging the law had always been part of the Coalition's strategy since the anti-gay groups first decided to use the law-making process to forward their agenda. The Ugandan Constitution is the country's supreme law, and all laws inconsistent with it are null and void to the extent of their inconsistency (Article 2). Article 137(3) allows any person to challenge any act or action of any organ if they feel the act or action is inconsistent with or is in contravention of the constitution. It was strongly believed that the AHA was in contravention. Indeed, the Coalition in its submissions to the legal and parliamentary affairs committee in 2011 had clearly indicated that the only way parliament would legally pass the bill with such provisions would be by amending the constitution first (Coalition, 2011).

As soon as the bill was passed, preparations began for the legal challenge that would become the case, *Professor J. Oloka-Onyango and nine others v. attorney general of Uganda*, spearheaded by the Coalition's legal committee, which was chaired by HRAPF and composed of key lawyers and representative organisations which work on legal issues.[33] Nothing was left to chance. The legal committee resolved that the act should be challenged in the Constitutional Court. This was approved by the steering committee,[34] and all that remained were the practicalities.

33 The legal committee was composed of Adrian Jjuuko and Fridah Mutesi (HRAPF); Kim Mukasa (RLP); Stella Murungi, Tabitha Netuwa and Rosette Arinaitwe (East and Horn of Africa Human Rights Defenders Project – EHAHRDP); Professor Joe Oloka-Onyango (individual capacity); Professor Sylvia Tamale (individual capacity); and Sarah Kihika (individual capacity).

34 The steering committee was responsible for the Coalition's day-to-day work. It was made up of the host organisation (RLP), represented by Dr Chris Dolan as chair with Walter Aliker as the alternate; LGBTI community members (SMUG) represented by Dr Frank Mugisha with Pepe Julian Onziema as the alternate;

Laying down the strategy

A two-day strategising workshop, held in Kampala on 11 and 12 February 2014, was attended by more than 30 people including activists and lawyers and some participants from other East African countries. All attendees were familiar with the AHA's provisions.[35]

The workshop studied the AHA, provision by provision, to identify inconsistencies with the constitution. Almost every provision violated a constitutional provision, except for the clause under 'aggravated homosexuality' which criminalised same-sex relations with children.[36] It was thus decided that all provisions of the law should be challenged that could be said to contravene the constitution. The Constitutional Court was identified as the best avenue for carrying this out.

It was feared the case would be delayed at the Constitutional Court, as had happened with earlier filed cases,[37] so the decision was made to explore alternative international and regional mechanisms. In light of the requirement to exhaust local remedies, which was a precondition before going to the African Commission on Human and Peoples' Rights (ACHPR), other options had to be investigated. The EACJ was the best alternative. Although it does not have a human rights jurisdiction, Articles 6(d), 7(2) and 8(1)(c) of the Treaty for the Establishment of the East African Community (EAC Treaty) enjoin partner states to govern their populace on the principles of good governance, democracy, the rule of law, social justice and the maintenance of universally accepted standards of human rights. Treaty provisions include inter alia, provision of equal opportunities and gender equality as well as the recognition, promotion and protection of human and peoples' rights in accordance with the provisions of the African Charter on Human and Peoples' Rights. Cases have been brought to and entertained by the court before through this avenue. As such, it was also decided to go to the EACJ and because this court had a

---

Freedom and Roam Uganda (FARUG) represented by Jacqueline Kasha Nabagesera with Ssenfuka Warry (Biggie) as the alternate; Strategic Initiatives for People with Congenital Disorders (SIPD), represented by Julius Kaggwa, with Tom Makumbi as the alternate; mainstream organisations represented by HRAPF with Adrian Jjuuko, representative, and Flavia Zalwango, alternate; organisations working on defenders' security, represented by EHAHRDP with Hassan Shire Sheikh, representative, and Nora Rehmer, alternate; and Geoffrey Ogwaro and Clare Byarugaba, the co-coordinators, who were ex officio members.

35 Almost all had been with the Coalition since its formation in October 2009.

36 This provision protected children; however, it was simply a repetition of Section 129 of the Penal Code Act as amended by the Penal Code Amendment Act 2007 and was therefore unnecessary.

37 For example, *Jjuuko Adrian v. attorney general*, Constitutional Petition no. 1 of 2009, which was filed to challenge the Equal Opportunities Commission Act and had been pending in the court since Jan. 2009.

time limitation of two months from the date of the law's enactment and was the court of first instance in the treaty's interpretation, the cases would be filed almost simultaneously. The legal committee was instructed to prepare to file in both courts but first priority was given to the Constitutional Court case.

Building the legal team

The legal committee's first task was to engage the lawyers who would work on the case. The Coalition had suggested names of senior lawyers who would be willing to handle procedures jointly with lawyers previously used by the Coalition. Five lawyers were thus approached and all five rejected the instructions. Most of them refused outright to take on the case on the basis of not seeing anything wrong with the law. Those who were at least willing to engage stated that they could not take instructions for fear of losing their other clients and also for fear of the security implications of handling the case. The legal committee sat again and suggested other individuals, who were also approached but only one, Caleb Alaka, agreed to join the legal team. The Coalition thus had to rely mainly on the lawyers it had worked with previously. The most senior was Dr Henry Onoria, who was lead counsel in *Kasha Jacqueline, David Kato Kisuule and Pepe Julian Onziema v. the Rolling Stone Ltd* (the *Rolling Stone* case),[38] which successfully challenged the Ugandan tabloid's publication of pictures, names and addresses of suspected gay persons and its call for them to be hanged. The third lawyer in the team was Ladislaus Kiiza Rwakafuuzi, who has handled many human rights cases in Uganda, including the first civil case concerning LGBTI rights: *Victor Mukasa and Yvonne Oyo v. attorney general* (*Victor Mukasa* case).[39] The fourth was Francis Onyango, co-counsel in the *Rolling Stone* case, and lead counsel in *Jacqueline Kasha Nabagesera, Frank Mugisha, Julian Pepe Onziema, and Geoffrey Ogwaro v. attorney general and Hon. Rev. Fr Simon Lokodo* (*Lokodo* case),[40] which challenged the stopping of an LGBTI skills-training workshop by minister of ethics and integrity, Simon Lokodo. The fifth lawyer was Nicholas Opiyo of Chapter 4 Uganda, a civil liberties organisation, who was at the time secretary general of the Uganda Law Society (ULS). The sixth was Fridah Mutesi, head of HRAPF's access to justice department. And the seventh lawyer was Adrian Jjuuko, HRAPF's executive director, who was the team's Coalition representative liaising between the lawyers and the Coalition's legal committee. This legal team, put in place within a very short period, prepared the petition and handled the case in court. Each member was brought on board on different terms, taking on separate tasks and foci.

38 Misc. cause no. 163 of 2010.
39 High Court misc. cause no 247 of 2006.
40 High Court misc. cause no. 33 of 2012.

For the EACJ case, Ladislaus Kiiiza Rwakafuuzi was given instructions to represent the applicants. He was supported by Fridah Mutesi from HRAPF.

Engaging the lawyers also entailed fundraising for them, a task that was taken on by UHAI-the East African Sexual Health and Rights Initiative (UHAI-EASHRI), which paid the lawyers' fees for both cases at the Constitutional Court and at the EACJ. The lawyers were duly instructed to begin work.

The lawyers who agreed to challenge this popular law risked their careers to stand up for what they believed in. Those in private practice, especially those handling their first LGBTI-related case, reported that their more religiously inclined clients had withdrawn instructions. Others lost their positions on the boards of legal bodies. Nicholas Opiyo, who was the ULS secretary general, intended to stand for the same post again. However, a Christian organisation sent an email to some members of the ULS body that has the mandate to elect executive members. Arriving just in time for their annual general meeting (AGM), it stated in part that 'some of those vying for major positions are people who petitioned against the Anti homosexual Act 2014 (sic). In that regard, your presence is called for to safeguard the legal profession leadership against such candidates.'[41] At the AGM on 22 March 2014, Opiyo contested for the position, but lost. Another member of the legal team also reported losing his position on a board in his home area because of his involvement in the case.

The choice of petitioners

There were ten petitioners:

1. Professor Joe Oloka-Onyango, a constitutional law professor who was director of the Human Rights and Peace Centre, Makerere University, and is widely published in the areas of human rights, constitutional law and the history of Uganda. His experience includes being a member of the UN Sub-Commission on the Promotion and Protection of Human Rights, and UN Special Rapporteur on Globalisation and Human Rights.

2. Fox Odoi-Owyelowo, a lawyer and a member of the Ninth Parliament, representing West Budama County North, Tororo District, chairperson of the Rules and Privileges Committee of the Ninth Parliament, and member of the Ninth Parliament's legal and parliamentary affairs committee. He is an author of the minority report on the AHB.

3. Andrew Mwenda, journalist of global repute, founder and owner of the *Independent*, a current affairs news magazine, a John S. Knight Journalism Fellow at Stanford University and an advocate of freedom

---

41 Email dated 20 Mar. 2014 forwarded to the authors which indicated that it was from the Administration of the Uganda Christian Lawyers Fraternity (UCLF).

of expression. He was a petitioner in the second constitutional appeal (2002) that challenged the constitutionality of the publication of the offence false news, which was a provision in the Penal Code Act.

4. Professor Morris Ogenga-Latigo, former MP and leader of the opposition in the Eighth Parliament, and former associate professor of entomology and ecology, Makerere University.

5. Dr Paul Semugoma, medical doctor, who offers medical treatment to gay persons in Uganda. He is also a global activist on HIV/AIDS prevention and non-discrimination of sexual minorities in provision of health services.

6. Kasha Jacqueline Nabagesera, an LGBTI rights activist and recipient of the Martin Ennals award for human rights defenders. She is founder and former executive director of Freedom & Roam Uganda.

7. Pepe Julian Onziema, a transgender man, activist and recipient of the 2012 Clinton Global Citizen award. He is SMUG's programmes director and advocacy officer.

8. Frank Mugisha, activist and recipient of the 2011 Robert F. Kennedy human rights award and the 2011 Thorolf Rafto prize. He is SMUG's executive director.

9. The organisation, HRAPF, which works to achieve equality, non-discrimination and equal access to justice for marginalised groups in Uganda. It operates a specialised legal aid clinic for LGBTI persons.

10. Centre for Health, Human Rights and Development (CEHURD), an organisation working towards an effective, equitable, people-centred health system and ensuring the full realisation of the right to health and the promotion of human rights.

This was a diverse line-up of petitioners, far broader than had been anticipated. The petition brought together people who belonged to different political camps, people who did not identify as LGBTI and those who did, and people who had been on the front lines in opposition to the AHB. It was an impressive collection, which demonstrated support for the human rights of LGBTI people and also showed that the act not only violated their rights but was also an unprecedented abuse of the rule of law and constitutionalism.

This line-up did not come about by accident; rather, it was built and organised after thorough consideration. Each petitioner had something to add to the petition and each affidavit was unique. Professor J. Oloka-Onyango's affidavit focused on the unconstitutionality of the AHA in light of the constitutional provisions, including those on quorum and substantive human rights. The Hon. Fox Odoi-Oywelowo's affidavit focused on what happened in parliament, and on its procedures, on the day the bill was passed, in his capacity as the chairperson of the parliamentary rules and privileges committee. Andrew

Mwenda's was on the act's effect on freedom of expression. The Hon. Ogenga-Latigo's was on parliamentary procedures and the effect of the law. Dr Paul Semugoma's affadavit was on the act's effect on HIV service provision. Kasha Jacqueline Nabagesera's was on the act's effect on LGBTI organising and on LGBTI individuals. Pepe Julian Onziema's was on the act's effect on transgender people. That of Frank Mugisha was on LGBTI organising generally. The focus of HRAPF's affidavit was the impact on legal aid service providers and on LGBTI persons generally, based on the cases it had so far received. Finally, that of the Centre for Health, Human Rights and Development concentrated on how access to health services had been affected.

Having approached all potential petitioners, the legal team ended up being spoilt for choice as there were far more people willing to join the petition than could be included. This was a really humbling moment because the petitioners were taking on a popular law, and had more to lose than to gain. Indeed, the decision to be petitioners cost some of them dearly, especially those with political ambitions. The Hon. Fox Odoi-Owyelowo faced hostility in his constituency because of his stand (*The Observer*, 2014a), and eventually lost his position in the 2016 elections.

Preparing the petition

Preparation of the petition took a long time, with the legal team working in concert to classify the violations in accordance with the constitutional provisions they violated, then producing a working draft.

The first draft was submitted to a team of lawyers and advisers, composed of professors of law, legal practitioners and key activists, for comment on its suitability. They suggested improvements and also advised on the strategic implications of filing the draft as it was. The Coalition then submitted the draft for input to more than 20 lawyers from jurisdictions all over the world. Contributions were received from organisations and lawyers in Kenya, South Africa, the US, Canada and the UK. These contributions were considered by the legal team and the Coalition's legal committee, and a final draft agreed upon with the Coalition's steering committee, which is responsible for strategic decisions. Fourteen issues were identified:

> 1. Enactment of the AHA, 2014, by the Ninth Parliament on 20 December 2013 was without quorum, in contravention of Constitution Articles 79(1) and (3), 88 and 94(1) and Rule 23 of the rules of procedure which enjoin parliament to respect the constitution and to pass laws with the quorum stipulated in those rules.

> 2. Sections 1, 2 and 4 criminalised consensual same-sex relations among adults, in contravention of the right to equality before the law without discrimination and the right to privacy guaranteed under the Constitution – 21(1), (2) and (4) and 27.

3. Section 2(1)(c) criminalised touching by persons of the same sex, which created an offence that was overly broad and in contravention of the principle of legality under the Constitution – 28(1), (3b), (12), 42 and 44(c).

4. The penalty for homosexuality was life imprisonment, a disproportionate punishment for the offence and thus in contravention of the right to equality and freedom from cruel, inhumane and degrading punishment guaranteed under Constitution Articles 21, 24 and 44(a).

5. Section 3(1)(b) criminalised consensual same-sex/gender sexual activity among adults one of which is a person living with HIV, in contravention of the freedom from discrimination guaranteed under Constitution Articles 21(1) and (2).

6. Section 3(1)(e) criminalised consensual same-sex/gender sexual activity among adults one of which is a person with disability, in contravention of the right to freedom from discrimination and the right to dignity of persons with disabilities guaranteed under Constitution Articles 21(1), (2) and (4c) and 35.

7. Section 3(3) subjected persons charged with 'aggravated homosexuality' to a compulsory HIV test, in contravention of the freedom from discrimination, the right to privacy, freedom from cruel, inhumane and degrading treatment, and the right to the presumption of innocence guaranteed under Constitution Articles 21, 27, 24, and 28, 44 and 45 respectively.

8. Section 4(2) imposed a maximum life sentence for attempted aggravated homosexuality, providing a disproportionate punishment for the offence in contravention of the right to equality, and the freedom from cruel, inhuman and degrading punishment guaranteed under Constitution Articles 21, 24 and 44(a) respectively.

9. Sections 7 and 13(1) criminalised aiding, abetting, counselling, procuring and promotion of homosexuality; created offences that were overly broad; and penalised legitimate debate, professional counsel, HIV-related service provision and access to health services, all in contravention of the principle of legality, the freedoms of expression, thought, assembly and association, and the right to civic participation guaranteed under principle XIV of the National Objectives and Directive Principles of State Policy, and Constitution Articles 8A, 28(1), (3b), and (12), 29(1), 36, 38(2), 42 and 44(c).

10. Section 8 criminalised conspiracy by any means of false pretence or other fraudulent means, and its provision was vague, uncertain, ambiguous

and in contravention of the principle of legality under Constitution Articles 28(1) and (3b), 42, 44(c), 28(12).

11. Section 11 classified houses or rooms as brothels merely on the basis of occupation by homosexuals, creating an offence that was overly broad and in contravention of the principle of legality guaranteed under Constitution Article 28(12) and the rights to property and privacy guaranteed under Constitution Articles 21, 26 and 27.

12. The spirit of the AHA, 2014, promoted and encouraged homophobia, amounting to institutionalised promotion of a culture of hatred and constituting a contravention of the right to dignity protected under Constitution Articles 24 and 44(c) and the National Objectives and Directive Principles of State Policy, especially objective no. III, V, VI and XIV

13. The AHA 2014, by encouraging homophobia and stigmatisation, was in contravention of the duty of the government to respect, protect and promote the rights and freedoms of persons likely to be affected by the act as stipulated under Constitution Articles 20(2), 21(1), 32(1) and (2).

14. The AHA, 2014, in criminalising consensual same-sex/gender sexual activity among adults, was in contravention of obligations with regards to the rights guaranteed under international human rights instruments ratified or acceded to by Uganda, including the African Charter on Human and Peoples' Rights; the Protocol to the African Charter on Human and Peoples' Rights on the Rights of Women in Africa; the UN Covenant on Civil and Political Rights; and the UN Covenant on Economic, Social, and Cultural Rights; and in contravention of Objectives XIV, XXXVIII(i)(b) of the National Objectives and Directive Principles of State Policy, Constitution Articles 2(1) and (2), 8A, 20, 45 and 287.

Controversial issues arose during the preparation of the petition. One was whether to include the issue of a quorum, and another was whether to use this opportunity to challenge Section 145 of the Penal Code. On the matter of a quorum, all members agreed that the law had been passed without the requisite quorum, and this ground had previously been used to nullify a controversial law. The point of contention was more strategic; it was on whether or not to include it in light of the fact that the judges might use it as a quick way out and nullify the act on this basis, without looking at the grounds based on equality and non-discrimination. Some members did not see this as a bad thing and argued that if the judges relied on quorum alone to nullify the act, this would result in it no longer being on the law books and, moreover, was the only ground that could lead to it being totally nullified. Including it was therefore the best course of action. The second school of thought held the view that if the judges nullified the act on this basis, then the rights-based arguments would not be considered, and this would leave all parties involved without a decision on whether consensual same-sex relations were unconstitutional. The former view carried the day, and quorum indeed became the deciding feature of the petition.

The issue of challenging Section 145 and the AHA together had proponents who argued that the Coalition should seize this opportunity to challenge laws criminalising same-sex conduct. This way the court would pronounce itself once and for all on the constitutionality of such laws, and if the legal team were successful, there would be no need to bring another suit specifically on Section 145. Opponents of this view argued that since the whole structure of the AHA went beyond same-sex sexual relations into matters like promotion and aiding and abetting, it would be more strategic to limit the petition to the AHA and address all the issues it raises, dwelling on consensual same-sex relations only in sections that specifically addressed it. And if the court declared the provisions on same-sex relations unconstitutional, Section 145 would falter too, since a precedent had been set. Putting emphasis and focus on the laws criminalising consensual same-sex sexual relations would alienate some petitioners who were interested in the broader scheme. The Coalition was firmly of the latter view since, strategically, decriminalisation was planned through an incremental approach, and Section 145 had been deliberately left unchallenged, despite pressures from many quarters to challenge it. The Coalition's view won the day, and Section 145 was left to rest, at least for the moment.

The petition and the accompanying affidavits and their attachments spanned more than 200 pages, and 12 volumes were prepared and bound. Each affidavit had to be commissioned by a commissioner for oaths, who would also mark and verify each attachment. Putting the documents together alone took three days. In addition to the petition, there were two applications from the same parties, each with their own supporting affidavits. One was for an interim injunction and the other for interim orders. Aimed at obtaining a temporary injunction or interim orders to stop the implementation of the law, they were applied for by notice of motion and chamber summons respectively. All documents were prepared at the same time.

Filing the petition

Usually filing court cases is a simple matter of paying the requisite fees and getting the documents stamped by the court registry. This was essentially what happened with the AHA on 11 March 2014, but it was accompanied by more pomp and publicity. The filing was planned for 2 pm at the Constitutional Court, at Twed Towers, Nakasero, Kampala. Of the petitioners, the Hon. Fox Odoi-Owyelowo, Professor Ogenga Latigo, Pepe Julian Onziema, and HRAPF were expected to be present and to hold a press conference nearby afterwards.

The media had been alerted and were there in droves, long before the lawyers arrived with the petition.

At 2 pm, final touches were still being put to the petition at the HRAPF offices, which are about eight kilometres from the court. The vehicle carrying it had to negotiate rush-hour traffic with double indicators flashing in an attempt to make up time. Thirty minutes later, the documents were at court. Adrian Jjuuko, the HRAPF executive director and chair of the Coalition's legal committee, and his HRAPF colleague, Fridah Mutesi, led the team carrying the petition. They joined Counsel Ladislaus Kiiza Rwakafuuzi and Nicholas Opiyo, who were waiting at the court premises, and then the Hon. Fox Odoi and Professor Ogenga Latigo. Followed by flashing cameras, the group strode to the Office of the Registrar, where the documents were received, stamped and the petition was allocated the number '8 of 2014' and filed.

The petitioners and lawyers led the group of journalists and activists to the press conference, where they were addressed by the Hon. Fox Odoi-Owyelowo, the Hon. Ogenga Latigo, Adrian Jjuuko and Nicholas Opiyo. When asked whether this would not affect his re-election to parliament, the Hon. Odoi's response that all he cared for was justice and equality for all, and not just his re-election, stood out. The Hon. Ogenga Latigo stated that the passing of this law had brought him out of semi-retirement because he strongly believed that consensual same-sex relations should not be criminalised. Adrian Jjuuko recounted the number of cases of human rights violations against LGBTI persons that HRAPF had recorded since the law was passed. Nicholas Opiyo emphasised that this was a struggle for justice and equality for all. The press conference was a resounding success and many newspapers, radio stations, and TV stations locally and internationally carried the news (BBC News, 2014b). It was clear that this group of individuals and organisations including prominent Ugandans had decided to stand up for what was right.

The hearing

The hearing of the petition came as a surprise to many, including the petitioners and the attorney general. The date of 25 June was fixed for conferencing. On that date, counsel for both sides appeared in court but Justice Kiryabwire, who was to handle the conferencing, was indisposed and the parties instead appeared before Deo Nzeyimana, the registrar, who adjourned it to 10 September. However, on 25 July, in a surprising and unusual twist, the Constitutional Court served the parties with notices of the hearings of the constitutional petition and the two applications, which were scheduled to start on 30 July at 9.30am. In spite of this change of date, the Coalition's legal team was prepared and only had final touches to make. At the hearing, the attorney general's legal team applied for an adjournment, which the court denied. They then asked the court to start with the applications rather than the main petition, but the judges informed them the petition was to be heard first.

The justices asked the petitioners to address the first issue, that of the lack of a quorum. The petitioners' lawyers argued there had been no quorum in parliament when the law was passed and the speaker had disregarded the rules of procedure when the matter of quorum was raised. The attorney general's legal team did not deny the allegations but insisted that the petitioners had to adduce evidence showing there was no quorum in the house when the law was passed. The evidence provided included an affidavit by the Hon. Fox Odoi, one of the petitioners and a member of the Ninth Parliament, and copies of Hansard reporting its proceedings the day the act was passed.[42] The attorney general insisted that this was insufficient proof and that the petitioners needed to adduce more evidence. The justices took time off to give their ruling on the issue of quorum.

The anti-LGBT-rights lobby and its attempt to join the case

The hearings took place over two days. On day one, three anti-gay organisations filed an application to be joined as parties through Miscellaneous Constitutional Application no. 23 of 2014. They were the Inter Religious Council of Uganda, the Family Life Network (FLN) and the Uganda Centre for Law and Transformation and they cited the attorney general and the ten petitioners as respondents. The application was by notice of motion supported by affidavits filed by Bishop Joseph Serwadda of Victory Christian Centre and Stephen Langa of the FLN. The application was filed after the petition hearing had already commenced, and it was never fixed for hearing. They had aimed to become petition respondents in order to 'effectively oppose' the petitioners as they believed the attorney general did not seem ready to do so.

The decision

The unanimous decision of five justices of appeal sitting as a Constitutional Court was delivered by the deputy chief justice on 1 August 2014. The court held that the AHA had been passed without the requisite quorum: that during the session the prime minister and leader of government business had raised the issue of the lack of a quorum, which the speaker Rebecca Alitwala Kadaga brushed off. The justices pointed out that he who alleges must prove, and to that end the petitioners had backed up their allegation that there was no quorum with sworn affidavits. The court further noted that in reply to the attorney general's petition, the attorney general had not specifically denied that there was no quorum, and a general rule existed that where the respondents do not deny the allegations, they are considered to have conceded on that point.

42 Parliament of Uganda Hansard, parliamentary official report, 3rd session, 2nd meeting, 20 Dec. 2013.

The justices further noted that this was a civil case where the standard of proof was on a balance of probabilities, and the evidence of the Hon. Fox Odoi's affidavit and the Hansard records were sufficient to prove lack of a quorum in parliament. They also noted that the speaker has a constitutional duty to observe a quorum and this time, although she was prompted three times on the issue, she had failed to perform her duty, as mandated under the law. They therefore held that on the evidence adduced, and the failure of the attorney general to specifically deny the allegations, the act had been passed without a quorum and was declared null and void. That was it. The hugely popular AHA was no more!

The surprise nullification of the AHA by Uganda's Constitutional Court within months of the petition being filed was quite simply unprecedented. No other petition had been heard so quickly since the court's formation in 2005. The court did not state what prompted them to decide the case in such record time, and so the real reason is subject to speculation, but it was quite clear that political forces beyond the judicial process were also at play.

The continued pursuance of the case at the EACJ

The Consitutional Court's surprisingly quick and decisive decision had implications for the case that had been filed at the EACJ.[43] As previously mentioned, this reference was filed at almost the same time as the one at the Constitutional Court in order to beat the two-month time limitation imposed by the EACJ. It had been expected that the EACJ would deliver its judgment ahead of the Constitutional Court.

Since the two cases were almost the same, the determination of the constitutional petition clearly made the one at the EACJ moot and academic. A decision thus had to be made whether to proceed with the case or to withdraw it.

Originally, the case had challenged the AHA as being contrary to the rule of law and good governance principles enshrined in the EAC Treaty. It also challenged the resultant violations, which saw a marked increase in abuses of the human rights of LGBTI people.

The EACJ case had implications for other East African countries beyond Uganda since a decision made by that court affects them all. An East African Convening was therefore organised in Kampala which brought together activists and lawyers from across the region to discuss what to do in relation to the EACJ case. It was decided to proceed with it, albeit in an amended form, in order to avoid the 'mootness' barrier. The reasons for this decision were both legal and strategic. Legally, it could be argued that the case was not moot since

43 The case had been filed in April 2014 as *Human Rights Awareness and Promotion Forum (HRAPF) (applicant) v. attorney general of Uganda (respondent) and the Secretariat of the Joint United Nations Programme on HIV/AIDS (UNAIDS) amicus curiae)*, ref. no. 6 of 2014.

Article 1(2)) of the EAC Treaty also included repealed laws in its definition of laws, and as such they could arguably be challenged. Moreover, the EACJ has on various occasions ruled that correcting wrongdoing does not take away the fact that the violation occurred. As such, nullification of the law did not remove the fact that its enactment violated EAC Treaty provisions. Finally, it could be argued that the subject matter of the reference differed from the Constitutional Court of Uganda's decision, which focused on the constitutionality of the act, as the case was concerned with whether or not its passing had violated EAC Treaty provisions. The strategic reasons were: the need to proactively test the extent to which the treaty's provisions have meaning for the wellbeing of all citizens of the East African region, and to forestall the process of having a new bill passed by the Parliament of Uganda or by any of the other East African countries.

Soon after the AHA had been nullified, government officials attempted to have the act brought back before parliament to be passed again, this time with a quorum. To forestall this, the Coalition wrote to the speaker informing her of the existence of the case that had been filed before the EACJ. According to the rules of procedure, this fact would stop parliament from retabling the bill until those proceedings terminated.

Having been amended to reflect the fact that the AHA had been nullified in Uganda, the reference was thus limited to the fact that the AHA had been passed with particular provisions that were in violation of the fundamental principles of good governance, rule of law and human rights, as enshrined in the EAC Treaty. The selected provisions were: Section 5(1) on the immunity of 'victims' of homosexuality from being tried for any offence committed when involving themselves in homosexuality; Section 7 on aiding and abetting homosexuality; and Section 13 (1)(b) (c) (d) and (e) concerning promotion of homosexuality.

The Coalition encouraged different groups to join the reference as amicus curiae. Health Development Initiative Rwanda (HDI Rwanda), UHAI-EASHRI, Dr Ally Possi and the Centre for Human Rights, University of Pretoria, and UNAIDS responded to this call and filed amicus applications. Of these, only the one from UNAIDS was accepted.

Before the case was heard, the attorney general objected to the amendment on the basis that it went beyond the fact that the AHA had been nullified. They also raised the issue of mootness: the fact that since the act's nullification by a competent court of an EAC member state, the other points due to be raised during the case had ceased to exist so it was now moot. To this, HRAPF responded that the matter was still live, for the act's nullification did not take away the fact that it had been passed with provisions that violated the EAC Treaty, and that during the period when it was in force, violations were committed under these specific provisions. In addition, the MPs who had sponsored the original bill had been given leave of parliament to allow them preparation time for retabling the bill.

The court delivered its judgment on 27 September 2016. It decided that the case was moot since the reference challenged a law that had been nullified by the court. It considered the public interest exception to the general rule and found there was insufficient evidence to 'establish the degree of public importance attached to the practice of homosexuality in Uganda.'[44] Although the case had been lost, this was the first time an international tribunal in Africa had heard a case concerning laws primarily affecting LGBTI persons. It galvanised Ugandan, East African and African activists into taking their destiny in their own hands and challenge the passing of laws threatening the rights of LGBTI individuals. According to the chief executive officer of the Pan African Lawyers Union (PALU), Donald Deya,

> The Applicant has shown that African citizens – through their civil society formations – have the knowledge, skills, experience and courage to challenge in international courts any legislation or policy that they feel may infringe upon the human or peoples' rights of LGBTI and PLHIV.[45] The States have been put to sufficient notice, and we believe that they will be much more circumspect when formulating law or policy in future (HRAPF and the Coalition, 2016).

Advocacy

Courts do not operate in a vacuum, so the hearing of the petition at that particular time was perhaps the result of advocacy rather than the mere fact that a petition had been filed. National and international partners supported the move to challenge the act. Advocacy began as soon as the law had been passed, aimed at the president, the Ugandan population and the international community.

Advocacy directed towards the president

Parliament's passing of the AHA drew significant attention to the president, since after the former had played its part, it was legally the latter's call from then on. The president has the power to sign any law passed by parliament. There are three options: to sign, to refuse to sign, or to ask for the law to be amended. The last was crucial in stalling the bill, since it would mean that parliament would have to pass the law again, and if the president again refused to sign, it would have to pass it one last time with a two-thirds majority. This process would have considerably delayed the passing of the law.

The president could refuse to sign such a law because he had a constitutional duty to uphold the constitution. Signing a law that was passed without a quorum and one with provisions that clearly violated the constitutional

44 *HRAPF (applicant) v. attorney general of Uganda (respondent) and UNAIDS (amicus curiae)*, ref. no.6 of 2014.
45 People living with HIV/AIDS.

protections of human rights would not be the right thing for the president to do. The only problem was how to get to the president in order to convey this viewpoint. No Coalition member had access to the president, so indirect routes would have to be taken.

The only effective route was to engage diplomatic community members who were already concerned about the law. Coalition members met with representatives of several countries and asked them to request their governments to engage the president on this issue through diplomatic channels. In some cases the Coalition advised on public statements, especially those from world opinion leaders. Indeed, some governments like that of the United States did so more publicly, and then US President Barack Obama warned of effects on the relationships between Uganda and the US (Arinaitwe and Mulondo, 2014).

However, using foreign governments to deliver the message has always been a double-edged sword because it is common for Western governments to be willing to speak out and this feeds the perception among many leading figures in Africa that a Western agenda exists which aims to make homosexuality acceptable in the continent. This attitude was evident during the president's public signing of the law.

The president's reaction did not necessarily favour the Coalition's position. He began by writing to the speaker of parliament, criticising the way the bill had been passed into law, and stated that criminalisation would not in general be the best way of approaching the matter. He promised to handle it through parliament's ruling party caucus. Many thought this meant that he had vetoed the law (Mugerwa, 2014). However, legally speaking, he could only veto by clearly stating so. What he did do was bring the matter before the caucus and seek the advice of scientists in Uganda on whether homosexuality is a matter of nurture or nature (Tugume, 2014).

Coalition members used this opportunity to ask partners for a scientific opinion to present to the president. An open letter signed by more than 200 international leading scientists was sent to him and published in Ugandan newspapers (Throckmorton, 2014). The internationally accepted scientific position was that no known gene caused homosexuality, but that a combination of natural and environmental factors contributed to sexual orientation. The Ugandan scientists' report came to the same conclusion, but the president chose to dwell on the point that no single gene had been identified as causing homosexuality, and he interpreted that to mean that scientists had found it is nurture – and not nature – that causes homosexuality (Republic of Uganda, State House, 2014).

His delay in signing the law was greeted with substantial opposition. Nevertheless, he finally signed it on 24 February 2014, in the presence of local and international media at a function which was televised live (BBC News, 2014a; Kasasira, 2014). He blasted the approach of Western governments on this issue, especially the statement on aid conditionalities, but also blamed the scientists, who in his opinion had concluded homosexuality was largely due to nurture rather than nature, and even those who had proposed the bill in the first place. The president did not discuss the constitutionality of the process through which the law had been passed or that of the law's provisions, though they were brought to his attention.

Signing the law was not the president's last action on it, since he went out of his way to warn against enacting another law. Soon after it had been nullified by the Constitutional Court, he warned parliament that such a law was not good for Uganda's economic growth, since international organisations and investors would cut ties with the country (*New Vision*, 2014). This perhaps demonstrates he had after all understood the message from foreign governments and international organisations about the effects of signing the law but he had done so for domestic political reasons, since elections were just two years away. Indeed some commentators suggested that he signed the law knowing that it could not survive Constitutional Court scrutiny (*The Observer*, 2014b). Via these means he balanced demands within the country while the Constitutional Court satisfied those of the international community.

Efforts directed towards the president continued, both before and after the law had been nullified in August 2014. Demonstrations took place against him when he visited London in May that same year. The tabloid, *Sunday Pepper*, ran an article on 10 May called, 'Homos attack M7 with rotten eggs' (Special Forces Command, 2014). The Coalition did not necessarily support or call for these actions, but they were done to show solidarity with the Ugandan LGBTI community.

Advocacy directed at the international community

The AHB had attracted attention from governments, human rights bodies, organised groups and individuals in other countries, especially in the US, Canada, Australia and almost all Western European countries. Most of them were also opposed to the AHA. In this international interest lay the real challenge: how could these groups be of help without awakening the feeling that a 'western agenda' existed to promote homosexuality in Uganda, and Africa at large? The silence from African countries – including those, like South Africa, that had decriminalised homosexuality and had extensively inclusive laws – was loud. No African leader spoke against the bill. Instead, Kenya (KenyaNews247. com, 2014) and Tanzania (Muga, 2014) seemed to be preparing similar laws. It was the activists in these countries who stood in solidarity with the Ugandan LGBTI community and its allies.

The Coalition advised the international community on moves that would be helpful[46] after the law had been passed, especially encouraging public statements and actions directed towards the president.

46 For a more detailed discussion, see Jjuuko (2016).

Amnesty International with Human Rights Watch (2014) and many other organisations condemned passage of the act and revealed its violations. They relied on information provided by individual bodies like HRAPF and the Coalition.

The Coalition also reached out to UN agencies, including the Office of the High Commissioner for Human Rights (OHCHR) and special rapporteurs. Partly as a result of this, the UN Secretary General roundly condemned the law (*NDTV*, 2014) as did the OHCHR (2014a). Moreover, a joint communication from UN special rapporteurs was produced, including one on human rights defenders[47] (UN OHCHR, 2014b). Specialised agencies from the UN also spoke out, especially UNAIDS (2014).

The World Bank also reacted, postponing the US$90 million due to Uganda, and reached out to activists, seeking their views (*New York Daily News*, 2014). As a result, the minister of health issued a directive for the non-discriminatory provision of health services (Republic of Uganda, Ministry of Health, 2014).[48]

The Coalition also made it clear that it did not support aid cuts (aid conditionality), since they affected ordinary Ugandans, including LGBTI Ugandans. However, the Coalition respected the decisions of states to cut aid. Countries such as Sweden (Croome, 2014) and Norway (Butagira, 2014a) did so immediately. The US started a review of its relationship with Uganda, which led to an examination of military support and the imposition of travel restrictions (Butagira, 2014b). The US also severed its aid to some agencies which supported the act, like the Inter Religious Council of Uganda (Tajuba and Ssenkabirwa, 2014). The general national mood may thus also have affected the court, leading to the expedited hearing of the petition and the law's later nullification.

In effect, during the few months that the AHA was in force, Uganda had become a pariah state and the fact that it had been ostracised may have contributed to the law being nullified.

Advocacy directed at the Ugandan public

Efforts were also made to target the Ugandan population, though this proved increasingly difficult, especially when the law was in force. The raid on the US Department of Defence-funded Makerere University Walter Reed Project, which was conducting HIV/AIDS research; the suspension of the organisation hosting the Coalition; and escalated arrests of LGBTI persons were clear blows that made every other organisation fear for its own survival. This also affected the activists, and few dared to speak out; indeed, many of the leading voices had left the country and sought asylum elsewhere. The Vision Group (2014),

---

47 Margaret Sekaggya, who was Uganda's special rapporteur on the situation of human rights defenders at the time, contributed to the report.

48 See also DeBarros (2014).

which is partly owned by the government, banned publication of homosexuality issues, and other media houses feared speaking out. Nevertheless, social media were rife with stories of violations and efforts were made to protect and defend LGBTI persons. Indeed, virulent comments on social media were not as frequent as before.[49]

Publications offered another available avenue. Professor J. Oloka-Onyango (2014) published an excellent analysis of the laws that had been passed within the period that the AHA was in effect. It showed that it was part of a broader agenda to narrow political and civic space. A volume of HRAPF's *Human Rights Advocate Magazine*, which was dedicated to the AHA, included articles by Professor Oloka-Onyango, Dr Stella Nyanzi, Linnette Du Toit, Francis Tumwesige, Joaninne Nanyange, Jenevieve Discar, Edward Mwebaza, Asia Russell and Adrian Jjuuko (2015a). HRAPF also initiated a public dialogue on the act's effects and published statements on the case challenging the AHA filed at the EACJ. A report of violations that had occurred since the AHA had been passed was published by SMUG, and it made many similar attempts to demonstrate the effects of this law to the public (SMUG and the National LGBTI Security Team, 2014).

Although the impact of such efforts may be difficult to measure, it was clear that the message was getting out. Indeed, articles by opinion leaders began to appear in the press which criticized the AHA. These two factors may also have contributed to the Constitutional Court's decision to expedite the hearing.

Many more factors besides litigation therefore played a part in the fight against the AHA.

The aftermath: the AHA's legacy

The decision to nullify the act was a great relief and excellent news to the LGBTI community and their allies. A seemingly popular law had been short-lived. This was a huge win, one we should continue to celebrate, despite the looming threat of yet another long battle with a new anti-gay law.[50]

The attorney general immediately filed notice of appeal, which remains in court records, and the appeal could be instigated at any time. As soon as parliament reconvened, members expressed their intention to reintroduce the law after it had been nullified by the Constitutional Court. Signatures began to be collected almost immediately to show how popular the law was, and within one week of the decision, more than 200 MPs had signed a petition to return the law to parliament. Unfortunately for them, a collection of signatures was of no legal consequence in legislative procedures.

49 Patricia Kimera interviewed on 15 Sep. 2015 by Adrian Jjuuko, Envisioning.
50 Shortly after the AHA's nullification, MPs threatened to retable the bill and the government established a committee to look into a new law. Soon, an alleged bill surfaced, called 'The prohibition of promotion of unnatural sexual practices bill, 2014'. However, no one acknowledged ownership of it and it was never tabled.

Despite the act's nullification, its effects endure; the most important being the chilling effect on LGBTI organising. The significant number of leaders who had already left could not be brought back nor could organisations be revitalised. It may thus take a long time for this trend to be reversed or even for the movement to return to where it was pre-AHA. Although the Walter Reed Project has been reopened and the RLP started operating again, the Coalition has no physical and fiscal host, and morale among LGBTI movement allies is generally low.

What stands out is the resilience of the Ugandan LGBTI community and its allies. Despite continued threats and intimidation, it held a successful Pride event on 9 August 2014, and has continued to push boundaries and beat odds to hold Pride annually.[51] Members of the LGBTI community stood strong against attacks and violations. Although many activists left the country, others, like Frank Mugisha, Pepe Julian Onziema and Kasha Jacqueline Nabagesera, stayed and were all petitioners in the case. These individuals and many others have proved that although the law was passed against them, they could not remain seated. During the hearing, the Constitutional Court was full of activists who never shied away from raising the rainbow flag in court. Envisioning Global LGBT Human Rights (Envisioning) documented these successes in *And Still We Rise*,[52] a moving 70-minute documentary. It reveals the LGBTI community's resistance and resilience against the AHA, until it was finally nullified. The court process would not have been successful without the dedication and determination of these LGBTI people. In them, the lawyers had a firm client.

Conclusion

Efforts to nullify the AHA were much broader than litigation. It was a multi pronged approach with the judiciary as the last resort. The executive and the legislature had been adequately engaged and the bill had not become law for five years, despite the overwhelming support in parliament and among the general population. Advocacy was the main tool keeping the bill at bay for that whole time; but ultimately, it was litigation that finally defeated the law. The judiciary was the only governmental organ that had not yet expressed an opinion. The courts were under great pressure to pronounce themselves, as parliament and the executive had done. Luckily for the LGBT movement, the judiciary overruled the other two organs (executive and legislature) of government – albeit on an issue of parliamentary procedure in passing the law. Efforts to have a new law retabled were countered through maintaining the case at the EACJ. Even though it was lost on the ground of mootness, it

51 In 2016, and again in 2017, organisers were forced to cancel the Pride parade because of police raids and threats from the ethics minister.
52 For more on *And Still We Rise*, see 'Telling Our Stories: Envisioning participatory documentary', ch. 14, this volume.

had helped to show that LGBTI persons and human rights defenders will not simply remain passive when basic rights are violated through oppressive laws. Despite all the movement's gains against the AHA, parliament is committed to bringing back provisions of the nullified act; if not as it was, then in piecemeal form in subsequent legislation such as the NGO Act 2016.[53] Therefore, all this has been just one battle in an ongoing war.

References

Arinaitwe, S. and E. Mulondo (2014) 'Obama warns Museveni on anti-gays bill', *Daily Monitor,* 18 Feb., available at: www.monitor.co.ug/News/ National/Obama-warns-Museveni-on-anti-gays-Bill/688334-2210616-td3mr6z/ (accessed 11 Aug. 2017).

BBC News (2014a) 'Ugandan president Yoweri Museveni signs anti-gay bill', 24 Feb., available at: www.bbc.com/news/world-africa-26320102 (accessed 28 Oct. 2017).

— (2014b) 'Uganda anti-homosexuality law challenged in court', 11 Mar., available at: www.bbc.com/news/world-africa-26532705 (accessed 28 Oct. 2017).

Butagira, T. (2014a) 'Norway cuts $8.3m aid to Uganda over anti-gay law', *The East African,* 26 Feb., available at: www.theeastafrican.co.ke/news/ Norway-cuts--8-3m-aid-to-Uganda-over-anti-gay-law/-/2558/2222782/-/ dewf1f/-/ (accessed 9 Sep. 2017).

— (2014b) 'US punishes Uganda for anti-gay law: withdraws support to police, UPDF and health', *Saturday Monitor,* 20 Jun., available at: www. monitor.co.ug/News/National/-US-cancels-exercise-with-UPDF--withdraws-support-to-police/688334-2355208-k8qa0t/ (accessed 9 Sep. 2017).

Civil Society Coalition on Human Rights and Constitutional Law (2011) 'Statement on the Anti-Homosexuality Bill, 2009, submitted to the Legal and Parliamentary Committee of Parliament', 9 May, available at: www.ugandans4rights.org/attachments/article/404/11_05_09_Final_ Coalition_submission_to_Legal_committee_of_parliament.pdf (accessed 9 Sep. 2017).

Civil Society Coalition on Human Rights and Constitutional Law and Human Rights Awareness and Promotion Forum (2013) 'Protecting morals by dehumanizing suspected LGBTI persons? A critique of the enforcement of the laws criminalizing same sex conduct in Uganda', available at: www.lgbtnet.dk/component/docman/doc_details/230-a-critique-of-the-enforcement-of-the-laws-criminalising-same-sex-conduct-in-uganda?tmpl=component&Itemid=273 (accessed 9 Sep. 2017).

---

53 Non-Governmental Organizations Act, 2016, Republic of Uganda, available at: https://www.ulii.org/node/25931 (accessed 9 Sep. 2017).

Consortium on Monitoring Violations Based on Sex Determination, Gender Identity and Sexual Orientation (2015) 'Uganda report of violations based on sex determination, gender identity and sexual orientation', available at: https://www.outrightinternational.org/sites/default/files/15_02_22_lgbt_violations_report_2015_final.pdf (accessed 25 Jul. 2017).

Croome, P. (2014) 'Sweden suspends some aid to Uganda over anti-gay law', *Reuters,* 6 Mar., available at: www.reuters.com/article/us-uganda-aid-sweden/sweden-suspends-some-aid-to-uganda-over-anti-gay-law-idUSBREA2509720140306 (accessed 9 Sep. 2017).

DeBarros, L. (2014) 'Uganda health ministry rejects gay discrimination', *Mamba Online,* 16 Jul., available at: www.mambaonline.com/2014/07/16/uganda-health-ministry-rejects-gay-discrimination/ (accessed 9 Sep. 2017).

Feder, J,L. (2014) 'Ugandan government launches investigation of leading NGO for "promoting homosexuality"', *BuzzFeed News,* 5 Jun., available at: www.buzzfeed.com/lesterfeder/ugandan-government-launches-investigation-of-leading-ngo-for#.fjLpvP3Dd. (accessed 3 Aug. 2017).

Human Dignity Trust (2014) 'Uganda: Anti-Homosexuality Act 2014', available at: www.humandignitytrust.org/uploaded/Library/Other_Material/Briefing_on_Anti-Homosexuality_Act_2014_final.pdf (accessed 17 Feb. 2018).

Human Rights Awareness and Promotion Forum (HRAPF) (2015a) 'Beyond quorum: why the Anti-Homosexuality Act 2014 was unconstitutional', *Human Rights Advocate,* 2, Mar., available at: hrapf.org/wp-content/uploads/2016/08/SECOND-ISSUE-OF-THE-HUMAN-RIGHTS-ADVOCATE.pdf (accessed 9 Sep. 2017).

— (2015b) 'The NGO Bill 2015 and its practical and human rights implications on organisations working on the rights of marginalised persons', 15 May, available at: http://hrapf.org/?mdocs-file=1586&mdocs-url=false (accessed 9 Sep. 2017).

HRAPF and Civil Society Coalition on Human Rights and Constitutional Law (2016) 'East African Court of Justice decides case challenging the enactment of Uganda's Anti-Homosexuality Act 2014', press release, 29 Sep., available at: http://hrapf.org/hrapf-eacj-case-press-statement/ (accessed 1 Oct. 2017).

Human Rights Watch and Amnesty International (2014) 'Uganda: Anti-Homosexuality Act's heavy toll: discriminatory laws prompt arrests, attacks, evictions, fright', 14 May, available at: https://www.hrw.org/news/2014/05/14/uganda-anti-homosexuality-acts-heavy-toll (accessed 9 Sep. 2017).

Jjuuko, A. (2013) 'The incremental approach: Uganda's struggle for the decriminalisation of homosexuality', in C. Lennox and M. Waites (eds.) *Human Rights, Sexual Orientation and Gender Identity in the*

Commonwealth: Struggles for Decriminalisation and Change (London: Human Rights Consortium, Institute of Commonwealth Studies), pp. 381–408.

— (2016) 'International solidarity and its role in the fight against Uganda's Anti-Homosexuality Bill', in K. Lalor, E. Mills, A. Sánchez García and P. Haste (eds.) '*Gender, Sexuality and Social Justice: What's Law Got to Do with It?*' (Brighton: Institute of Development Studies), pp. 126–35, available at: https://www.ids.ac.uk/publication/gender-sexuality-and-social-justice-what-s-law-got-to-do-with-it (accessed 10 Jan. 2018).

Kafeero, S. and A. Ayebazibwe (2014) 'Makerere project recruited gays – police', *Daily Monitor*, 9 Apr., available at: www.monitor.co.ug/News/National/Makerere-project--recruited-gays---police/688334-2272794-tol72cz/ (accessed 24 Jul. 2017).

Kasasira, R. (2014) 'Joy, anger as Museveni signs law against gays', *Daily Monitor*, 24 Feb., available at: www.monitor.co.ug/News/National/Joy--anger-as-Museveni-signs-law-against-gays/688334-2220400-lbtu35/ (accessed 25 Jul. 2017).

KenyaNews247.com (2014) 'After Uganda, Kenya gears up for anti gay law', 5 Mar., available at: www.kenyanews247.com/news/after-uganda-kenya-gears-up-for-gay-rights-debate#.U1wnFMduH9I (accessed 8 Sep. 2017).

Muga, E. (2014) 'Dar plans to introduce tougher anti-gay bill', *East African*, 29 Mar., available at: www.theeastafrican.co.ke/news/Dar-plans-to-introduce-tougher-anti-gay-Bill--/2558-2262374-pxd14jz/ (accessed 8 Sep. 2017).

Mugerwa, Y. (2012) 'Kadaga, Canadian minister in gay row', *Daily Monitor*, 25 Oct., available at: www.monitor.co.ug/News/National/Kadaga--Canadian-minister-in-gay-row/688334-1594430-t0reff/ (accessed 24 Jul. 2017).

— (2014) 'Museveni blocks Anti-Homosexuality Bill', *Daily Monitor*, 17 Jan., available at: www.monitor.co.ug/News/National/Museveni-blocks-Anti-Homosexuality-Bill/688334-2148760-lq03yn/ (accessed 24 Jul. 2017).

Mugisa, A. (2007) 'DJ suspended over homo talk show', *New Vision*, 29 Aug., available at: www.newvision.co.ug/new_vision/news/1158013/dj-suspended-homo-talkshow (accessed 24 Jul. 2017).

Naturinda, S. (2012) 'Kadaga wants anti-gay bill tabled', *Daily Monitor*, 16 Nov., available at: www.monitor.co.ug/News/National/Kadaga-wants-anti-gay-Bill-tabled/688334-1621218-8qyfc/ (accessed 10 Jan. 2018).

NDTV (2014c) 'United Nations chief urges Uganda to repeal anti-gay law', 26 Feb., available at: www.ndtv.com/world-news/united-nations-chief-urges-uganda-to-repeal-anti-gay-law-552018 (accessed 8 Sep. 2017).

New Vision (2010) 'Museveni warns NRM on Homosexuality Bill', 12 Jan., available at: www.newvision.co.ug/new_vision/news/1298014/museveni-warns-nrm-homo (accessed 9 Sep. 2017).

— (2014) 'Gay bill: Museveni warns MPs', 12 Aug., available at: www.newvision.co.ug/new_vision/news/1306786/gay-museveni-warns-mps (accessed 11 Aug. 2017).

New York Daily News (2014) 'World bank freezes $90 million Ugandan loan over anti-gay law', 28 Feb., available at: http://m.nydailynews.com/news/world/world-bank-freezes-90-million-ugandan-loan-anti-gay-law-article-1.1706385 (accessed 9 Sep. 2017).

Observer, The (2014a) 'Pro gay MP Fox Odoi booed at Oketcho burial', 28 Apr., available at: www.observer.ug/news-headlines/31466-fox-odoi-booed-at-oketcho-burial- (accessed 11 Aug. 2017).

— (2014b) 'Museveni behind gay law victory?', 4 Aug., available at: http://en.africatime.com/ouganda/articles/museveni-behind-gay-law-victory (accessed 9 Sep. 2017).

Red Pepper (2014a) 'HORRIBLE: city sodomite infects 17 boys with HIV', 29 Jan., no longer available.

Republic of Uganda, Ministry of Health (2014) 'Ministerial directive on access to health services without discrimination', Jun., available at: https://www.scribd.com/document/233209149/MoH-Ministerial-Directive-on-Access-to-Health-Services-Without-Discrimination-19-June-14 (accessed 8 Sep. 2017).

Republic of Uganda, State House (2014) 'President to sign anti-gay Bill after experts prove there is no connection between biology and being gay', 15 Feb., available at: www.patheos.com/blogs/warrenthrockmorton/2014/02/15/report-on-homosexuality-by-ugandas-ministry-of-health/ (accessed 17 Aug. 2017).

Sexual Minorities Uganda and the National LGBTI Security Team (2014) 'From torment to tyranny: enhanced persecution in Uganda following the passage of the Anti-Homosexuality Act 2014', 20 Dec. 2013–1 May 2014, available at: http://sexualminoritiesuganda.com/wp-content/uploads/2014/11/SMUG-From-Torment-to-Tyranny.pdf (accessed 3 Aug. 2017).

Special Forces Command (2014) 'Museveni's UK visit was peaceful', available at: http://specialforcescommand.go.ug/musevenis-uk-visit-was-peaceful-2/ (accessed 11 Aug. 2017).

Tajuba, P. and A. Ssenkabirwa (2014) 'US cuts aid to religious council over anti-gay law', *Saturday Monitor*, 4 Jul., available at: www.monitor.co.ug/News/National/US-cuts-aid-to-religious-council-over-anti-gay-law/688334-2371374-n4cs03/ (accessed 9 Sep. 2017).

Tamale, S. (2009) 'A human rights impact assessment of the Anti-Homosexuality Bill 2009', *Equal Rights Review*, 4: 49–57.

Throckmorton, W. (2014) 'Over 200 scientists and mental health professionals respond to President Museveni regarding Ugandan's anti-gay Bill', *patheos.com*, 13 Feb., available at: www.patheos.com/blogs/warrenthrockmorton/2014/02/13/over-200-scientists-and-mental-health-professionals-respond-to-president-museveni-regarding-uga (accessed 11 Feb. 2018).

Tusume, J. (2014) 'Museveni now takes gays bill to scientists', *Daily Monitor*, 6 Jan., available at: www.monitor.co.ug/News/National/Museveni-now-takes-gays-Bill-to-scientists/688334-2160114-lixnflz/ (accessed 11 Aug. 2017).

UNAIDS (2014) 'UNAIDS expresses deep concern over impact of Ugandan bill on the rights of gay men', 18 Feb., available at: www.unaids.org/en/resources/presscentre/pressreleaseandstatementarchive/2014/february/20140218psuganda (accessed 9 Sep. 2017).

United Nations, Office of the High Commissioner on Human Rights (UN OHCHR) (2014a) 'Anti-homosexuality law in Uganda violates human rights and endangers LGBT people – Pillay', 24 Feb., available at: www.ohchr.org/EN/NewsEvents/Pages/DisplayNews.aspx?NewsID=14275&LangID=E#sthash.87F4r4sR.dpuf (accessed 8 Sep. 2017).

— (2014b) Mandates of the Working Group on Arbitrary Detention et al., 'Joint communication on the alleged passing of the Anti-Homosexuality Act', ref: AL G/SO 218/2 G/SO 214 (67-17) Assembly & Association (2010-1) Health (2002-7) G/SO 214 (107-9) UGA 1/2014.

Vision Group (2014) 'Editorial policy', available at: https://issuu.com/newvisionpolicy/docs/243661083-editorial-policy-complete (accessed 24 Jul. 2017).

Yahoo News (2014) 'Uganda "gay" trial dismissed due to lack of evidence', *Agence France-Presse (AFP)*, 22 Oct., available at: https://www.yahoo.com/news/uganda-gay-trial-dismissed-due-lack-evidence-103542367.html?ref=gs (accessed 25 Jul. 2017).

Zomorodi, G. (2015) 'SOGI-related migration in East Africa: fleeing Uganda after the passage of the Anti-Homosexuality Act', Global Philanthropy Project, Jul., available at: https://globalphilanthropyproject.org/2016/03/15/sogi-related-forced-migration-in-east-africa-fleeing-uganda-after-the-passage-of-the-anti-homosexuality-act/ (accessed 3 Nov. 2017).

Documentary film

And Still We Rise (2015) dir. R. Lusimbo and N. Nicol (Uganda and Canada: Sexual Minorities Uganda and Envisioning Global LGBT Human Rights), available at: https://vimeo.com/178217397. Extracts are cited from interviews with: Frank Mugisha, Joe Oloka-Onyango, Kim Mukisa, Jackson Mukasa, Sam Ganafa, and Nicholas Opiyo.

11

Emergent momentum for equality: LGBT visibility and organising in Kenya

Jane Wothaya Thirikwa

In Kenya, lesbian, gay, bisexual, transgender (LGBT) and queer identifying persons have at one point or another endured violent attacks, lived in fear, or been at the receiving end of crimes targeted at them due to their sexual orientation and/or gender identity and gender expression (SOGIE). This state of being is mainly the result of legal interpretations and perceptions of legislation based upon colonial anti-sodomy laws promulgated by the British Empire to control social and sexual conduct. Kenya is among the 36 (of 53) Commonwealth member countries still criminalising same-sex conduct.

Consensual adult same-sex conduct is criminalised under sections 162(a), 163 and 165 of the Kenya Penal Code, which punishes contravention with imprisonment of up to 14 years.[1] These sections criminalise 'carnal knowledge against the order of nature', widely interpreted as anal intercourse between men. This criminalisation of consensual sex between adult males has been used to legitimise discrimination and stigmatisation. People who identify as LGBT are isolated by the burden of stigma and are often ostracised by family members, religious formations and society at large. They are also constantly exposed to shame through the media and self-appointed moral policing. Socially, culturally and politically, their rights of expression have been almost non-existent. Because of the legal implications of their homosexuality, they are unable to obtain protection from the state.

This criminalisation of homosexual conduct in Kenya provides a legal basis for, and thus largely contributes to, the appalling obstacles faced by sexual minority populations in securing non-discriminatory access to healthcare, livelihoods, education, justice mechanisms and other vital services. Although Kenyan authorities rarely enforce the anti-sodomy laws, the practical effects of

---

1 Penal Code, revd. edn., 2014, available at: www.kenyalaw.org/lex/actview. xql?actid=CAP.%2063 (accessed 1 Nov. 2017).

J. W. Thirikwa (2018) 'Emergent momentum for equality: LGBT visibility and organising in Kenya', in N. Nicol et al. (eds.) *Envisioning Global LGBT Human Rights: (Neo)colonialism, Neoliberalism, Resistance and Hope* (London: Human Rights Consortium, Institute of Commonwealth Studies), pp. 307–21.

criminal sanction include widespread discrimination in education, healthcare and employment. Criminalisation is also instrumental in inciting threats, abuse and other violations against actual and perceived LGBT people because perpetrators may believe that the state would be less inclined to bring full justice to those who pursue violence against these groups.

It also exacerbates blackmail and extortion, more so for those living closeted or double lives. These manipulative tactics take advantage of the vulnerability of those LGB people, for instance, who are in heterosexual relationships or marriages. Some may be blackmailed by their heterosexual partners, while others may even be forced to give up their children and asked to part with exorbitant sums for their maintenance. Criminal elements have also taken to social media and LGB dating sites, luring victims and setting them up for blackmail. Moreover, governmental recognition of anti-sodomy laws – as well as the homophobic rhetoric of state officials – contributes to prejudiced and hateful attitudes that spur violence against LGBT individuals.

Visibility through LGBT organising

In Kenya, the use of and representation of appropriate, accurate and inclusive terminology to describe and classify individuals and groups on the basis of SOGIE varies. Some organisations restrict themselves to a discourse on LGBT rights, while other focus on intersex, transgender and gender non-conforming (ITGNC) individuals.

Introducing diversity, and in particular sexual and gender diversity, into public discourse has been an extremely challenging task for organisations across Africa, partly because most LGBT people are closeted, and groups representing them are hampered by legal obstacles and non-existence of visibility channels. Kenya's pioneer LGBT coalition – the Gay and Lesbian Coalition of Kenya (GALCK) – was created in 2006, to bring together small, isolated LGBT groups and to defend the rights of the LGBT community as a collective. Besides the absence of a platform to address SOGIE, GALCK also faced the lack of a visibility breakthrough, the consequence of media bias and negative public discourse. Other external factors included disassociation from the wider civil society movement and the security risks the organisation's staff were exposed to due to their line of work. However, the movement gained momentum after the seventh World Social Forum (WSF) in Nairobi (2007), where activists aimed at educating and changing perceptions on homosexuality, and integrating SOGI and gender expression issues in the wider social justice movement.

The conference brought together more than 60,000 delegates from all over the world. Amid participants denouncing injustices of all kinds, the issues of homophobia and transphobia were raised by the collective of lesbian, gay, bisexual, transgender, intersex (LGBTI) organisations, which, besides GALCK, included the Coalition of African Lesbians (CAL) and Sexual Minorities Uganda

(SMUG). However, this was met with hostility. Some delegates heckled Kasha Jacqueline Nabagasera, a prominent human rights activist from Uganda, who is also an out lesbian, during her presentation. As well, LGBT community members suffered a backlash after they were featured in local news coverage. Nevertheless, the Nairobi WSF opened up spaces for activists in Kenya to speak up more boldly about homophobia and transphobia. It also strengthened regional LGBT organising, specifically in the East African and Southern African regions.

With continuing advocacy and emphasis on creating allies within the wider social justice efforts, the LGBT movement in Kenya is constantly reviewing its strategies to incorporate a multifaceted advocacy approach that is based on the intersectionality of social justice struggles. As a result, the multi-tier route to achieving equality and non-discrimination, spearheaded by GALCK, has since been adopted. This approach has brought together a network of GALCK's partners and stakeholders which focuses on legal and non-legal strategies for decriminalisation of same-sex conduct between consenting adults. It has also widened the scope of social justice issues to include other concerns including health, security, an enabling legal environment and quality citizenship. The decriminalisation approach emphasises changing the narrative of the movement from sexuality and identity politics only to quality citizenship. This strategy is envisioned to link with and inform advocacy on other human rights clusters such as legal, health and sociopolitical contexts.

Although the consideration of ITGNC persons often intersects with sexual orientation, these communities are gender minorities, not necessarily sexual ones. However, a general lack of understanding of SOGIE concepts exists in Kenya, leading to ITGNC persons being treated in the same way as sexual minorities. In order to meet their specific needs, organisations such as Jinsiangu and Transgender Education and Advocacy (TEA) cater for the human rights and social wellbeing of ITGNC individuals. Their vulnerabilities include being subjected to bullying, the legal hurdles to be surmounted to get names and gender markers changed on documents, psychosocial challenges, and inadequate or complete lack of medical/health services. In a 2012 interview with Envisioning Global LGBT Human Rights (Envisioning), Jinsiangu co-founder Guillit Amakobe[2] said that the organisation 'helps intersex and transgender people with information and resources regarding transitioning, counselling and complexities of psychosocial challenges for ITGNC people'. The organisation also facilitates safe spaces and support specific to members' needs. Jinsiangu targets the psychosocial challenges faced by ITGNC individuals, while TEA focuses on such legal issues as name changes, procurement of identification documents and advocacy for legislation that protects transgender and intersex persons.

---

2   Interviewed on 26 Aug. 2012 by Immah Reid, GALCK and Envisioning. An excerpt is included in the Kenya Portraits section of the *Telling Our Stories* (2014) documentary series.

Correlation between criminalisation and violence

Criminalisation of same-sex conduct gives a pretext for stigmatising and discriminatory attitudes, and it radically undermines human rights efforts for sexual minorities. It also creates structural barriers for persons perceived to be and/or who are LGBT or queer when they try to access and enjoy fundamental human rights such as privacy, health and sociopolitical participation. As with much patriarchal socialisation, most of the evidence of the effects of this criminalisation has primarily cited gay and bisexual males and other men who have sex with men (MSM). Though the criminal law against homosexual conduct in Kenya does not explicitly reference lesbian, bisexual and other women who have sex with women (WSW), the fundamental stigmatisation of same-sex relations has also had an adverse effect on transgender women and those who identify as gender non-conforming.

Lesbian, bisexual and transgender women and gender non-conforming individuals suffer persecution as a direct result of the broad interpretation of the criminalisation of homosexuality. They are also subjected to physical and mental abuse for what is seen as undermining heterosexual masculinity. Notably, women who have sex with women routinely suffer egregious affronts to their human dignity and endure distinct forms of discrimination because of their status as both women and sexual minorities. The United Nations Development Programme's (UNDP) 2012 Gender Inequality Index (GII), for example, ranked Kenya 130th out of 148 countries. The GII demonstrates gender inequality in relation to reproductive health, empowerment (in the form of parliamentary representation as well as attainment in secondary education) and labour force participation. While Kenyan women in general struggle to achieve full equality in these dimensions, WSW face extraordinary obstacles in accessing sexual and reproductive health services, education and employment. Gendered stereotypes coupled with moral imperatives often justify the discrimination and abuse of women, particularly those who do not visibly conform to prevailing gender norms and expressions.

There is no hate crime legislation in Kenya, and incitement to violence on account of SOGIE is not considered hate speech under the National Cohesion and Integration Act of Kenya.[3] Targeted violence on the basis of real or perceived SOGIE is common, though many of these crimes go unreported by victims for myriad reasons. Many are shamed and accused of provoking perpetrators because of their identity and gender expression. Others have described being sexually assaulted by the very law enforcement agents to which they have reported cases, while others fear that the resulting court proceedings would expose and out them.

---

3   National Cohesion and Integration Act, 2008, available at: http://kenyalaw.org/kl/fileadmin/pdfdownloads/Acts/NationalCohesionandIntegrationAct_No12of2008.pdf (accessed 1 Nov. 2017).

According to statistical analysis of violence patterns between 2012 and April 2014, conducted by the National Gay and Lesbian Human Rights Commission (NGLHRC),[4] 12 lesbian women stated they had been raped on account of their sexual and gender non-conformity. None of these survivors of sexual violence reported the attack to the police for fear of stigma and ridicule from immediate family members and law enforcement agents. In February 2014 mobs in Nairobi stripped two lesbians naked. Ten lesbian women and gay men reported they had been beaten in their own homes and their property vandalised on account of their perceived sexual orientation. Verbal violence and threats were reported by 95 per cent of respondents.[5] Most victims stated that this abuse had begun with family members or guardians feeling obliged to punish them for abdicating their feminine or masculine roles in society.

Targeted violence is also perpetrated by outlawed militia and vigilante groups in different parts of the country, such as the Mungiki, Sungu Sungu and Taliban Boys. These militant gangs and so-called vigilante movements are widespread throughout Kenya, particularly in urban environments and in low-income areas of major cities. They operate outside the law, mostly in poor, crime-infested neighbourhoods where the police have little authority or influence. To fund their activities, the gangs extort protection money from businesses and residents, public transport operators and any other opportunistic 'soft spots' such as real or suspected gays and lesbians. The militia gangs terrorise and blackmail them, threatening them by leaving pamphlets at their homes and residences, warning them to vacate or face dire consequences. Such activities have been supported, albeit unobtrusively, by unscrupulous politicians seeking to take advantage of divide-and-rule ethnic politics as they vie for political supremacy. In a country riddled with economic privation and suffering from government failure to quell criminal insurgents, the groups' impunity has been emboldened by politically driven unrest.

Another population at risk within the LGBT cluster – the sex workers – also face the ever-present threat of violence. All sex workers are at risk, but those who identify as LGBT are susceptible to greater degrees of assault. Mobs attack some and others are murdered on the streets. Yet more are constantly subjected to the brutality of City Council *askaris* [officers] and the police during night patrols, who arrest them and in some cases sexually assault them. GALCK as a coalition is making a resolute effort to document these incidents, along with its member groups and other LGBT partner organisations such as NGLHRC, the Nyanza, Rift Valley and Western Kenya Coalition, Persons Marginalized and Aggrieved (PEMA Kenya) and Health Options for Young Men on AIDS and STIs (sexually transmitted infections). These will not only form vital evidence

4 Obtained by author from the unpublished NGLHRC report 'Legal Aid Clinic summary report 2012–14'.
5 Ibid.

to support cases filed against perpetrators, but also build precedents in the eventual pursuit of decriminalisation.

Organised religion, hate campaigns and impunity

Organised religion, both Christian and Muslim, is extremely hostile to homosexuality in terms of its preaching and its lobbying of the government to further criminalise gay and lesbian people. An influx of mostly American evangelists who have imported anti-gay bigotry and policies in the name of morality has exacerbated homophobia in the region.

A network of heavily funded American Christian evangelists are spreading noxious rhetoric and using discredited science to skew public opinion. Their organisations include the American Center for Law and Justice (ACLJ), which has offices around the world, including its East African Centre for Law and Justice office in Kenya. According to the ACLJ, these affiliate offices 'engage in domestic and international litigation, provide legal services, advise individuals and government agencies, and counsel clients on human rights issues' (2016). Another is Family Watch International (FWI), which has also set up a base in Kenya. Led by Sharon Slater, it has continuously lobbied African governments 'to withstand the anti-family agenda' (Kaoma, 2012, p. 16). Slater addressed legislators, policymakers and religious leaders in the country, and even coordinated a 'pro-family' conference in Nairobi 2002. It also supported the Kenya Christian Professionals Forum in organising the National Family Conference in May 2015 where Slater was one of the main speakers.

Through a network of religious formations in the country such as the Kenya Christian Lawyers Fellowship and right-wing politicians, the churches continue to instigate violence and discrimination against LGBT people. They promulgate that homosexuality is taboo, ungodly, 'un-African' and a threat to the 'normal' family unit. Often they portray homosexuality as sexual abuse, equating it to paedophilia and bestiality. They promote beliefs that to engage in it is a mortal sin, one that society should control. The pictures they paint tend to portray homosexuality as a threat to humanity. These religious organisations sometimes brand themselves as a 'traditional values movement' and are usually protected by the conservative global machinery of religious institutions.

Kenya's human rights record was reviewed at the United Nations Universal Periodic Review (UPR) in January 2015. One key recommendation presented by a collective of LGBT and partnering civil society organisations was the development and enforcement of protective laws for LGBT persons, including anti-discrimination and hate crime legislation that forbids violence or incitement on all grounds, including SOGIE. The existence of regressive laws and policies has resulted in state-sponsored homophobia and impunity in cases of public incitement to violence against LGBT people.

Often spearheaded by pockets of religious clergy and conservative, and sometimes fringe, political affiliations, hate campaigns propagate targeted violence against perceived or actual LGBT people. In 2010, unsubstantiated rumours about a planned 'gay wedding' circulated in Mtwapa, in Kilifi. Local radio stations in Mombasa picked up the unconfirmed story. The Council of Imams, Preachers of Kenya and the National Council of Churches of Kenya called a news conference and demanded the closure of the Kenya Medical Research Institute (KEMRI), a government health centre that provides HIV/AIDS services to the community, accusing it of 'providing services to criminals'. Later, several imams and muftis (Islamic scholars) told their congregations during Friday prayers to be vigilant and to expose the homosexuals via a campaign called 'Operation Gays Out'. An armed mob surrounded the KEMRI health centre and police took several staff members and clients into custody, allegedly to protect them from the mob. However, one of the men taken 'to safety' was severely beaten and almost lynched. None of the attackers or the religious clergy who incited the violence have ever been arrested.

Some of the most violent religiously instigated persecutions of LGBT people have taken place in the coastal region, including Mombasa and Malindi. The main LGBT organisations there, PEMA Kenya and Tamba Pwani, attribute this to the complex sociocultural and religious conditions that exist in the region. Culturally, the Swahili people who inhabit the coast of East Africa have maintained a social order of very close-knit families. Since Islam was introduced in the seventh to tenth centuries, its followers have maintained a consistent conservatism, while tolerating traditional customs such as polygamy and close family relations. This combination presents challenges for sexual and gender minorities in the region. The upsurge of international terrorism, especially after the war on Iraq, also saw radicalised and extremist factions emerge within Islam all over the world. A similar form of fundamentalism within evangelical Christianity, combined with international global politics, has led to the strengthening of conservative teachings and tendencies, especially the targeting of homosexuality. These extremist religious movements have backed the wave of anti-homosexuality and the introduction of even more punitive legislation across African countries, including a failed attempt in Kenya.

Religion and politics

Hate speech against LGBT persons is rampant in Kenya, including from high-ranking government officials and politicians. William Ruto, the deputy president since 2013, has been consistently homophobic, often chastising gays and lesbians from church pulpits. In February 2013, during a televised debate on Capital FM Kenya, he equated homosexuals to dogs. In May 2015 he cited religious beliefs to denounce homosexuals, stating that they are unwelcome and should not be part of Kenyan society (*Daily Nation Kenya*, 2015). Daniel

Arap Moi also condemned homosexuality during his presidency claiming that it was 'un-African' and un-Christian (BBC News, 1999).

Since 2009 when Ugandan MP David Bahati first proposed the Anti-Homosexuality Bill (AHB), a clampdown on LGBT people's rights has spread into Kenya. Morality dogmas and political innuendos fuelled the ensuing upsurge of homophobia and transphobia, particularly those put about by right-wing legislators seeking political mileage. In March 2014, the AHB (now Act) became law in Uganda.[6]

Fuelling the anti-homosexuality rhetoric, in July 2012, the Anglican Bishop Julius Kalu of Mombasa told a congregation that Christians are confronted by 'the enemies of the Church', mainly homosexuals and lesbians, and that terrorism is a lesser threat (Beja, 2012). Building further upon this negative perception, Aden Duale, the majority leader, stated during a news conference in March 2014 that there was 'need to go and address the issue the way we want to address terrorism. It is as serious as terrorism and as any other social evil' (Ngirachu, 2014). Instigators who use extremist religiosity and conservative interpretations of religious doctrines contribute immensely to the use of violence and discrimination against sexual and gender minorities.

A group of Kenyan members of parliament (MPs), led by Irungu Kang'ata, launched a parliamentary caucus against homosexuality in February 2014. This was during a period of intense international debate over whether the Ugandan president should sign the AHA. The caucus lobbied for stricter enforcement of sodomy laws, including calls for citizens to arrest suspected gays and lesbians where police had failed to act. Further, a 2014 Facebook post by I. Kang'ata[7] also incited negative public opinion and violence. This hate campaign was followed in the same month by an anti-homosexuality protest in Nairobi. Its leader said that homosexuality 'is an affront to nature, religious and biological norms. It is a disgrace to the men and women victims who are supposed to be role models with upright morals in society' (Agoya, 2014).

Backed by the MP caucus against homosexuality, a fringe political party, the Republican Liberty Party, proposed and presented an anti-homosexuality bill to the Kenyan parliamentary committee on justice and legal affairs. It prescribed, among other penalties, stoning to death as a punishment for foreigners engaging in homosexuality and life imprisonment for Kenyan lesbian and gay individuals. The bill's proposal was aimed at strengthening the nation's capacity to deal with internal and external threats to the traditional heterosexual family. The bill did not reach parliament, though the petitioners

6   The Anti-Homosexuality Act (AHA) was nullified by Uganda's Constitutional Court on 1 Aug. 2014. For the history of its defeat, see 'The multifaceted struggle against the Anti-Homosexuality Act in Uganda', ch. 10, this volume.

7   On 24 Feb. 2014. See: https://m.facebook.com/irungu.kangata/posts/10152237181040853?stream_ref=10 (accessed 20 Mar. 2018).

continued to lobby the parliamentary committee to present the bill for debate there.

Faith, identity and family

For most LGBT people, finding the balance between their faith, their identities and relationships with their families is extremely challenging. The centrality of the family is founded on religion, marriage and procreation, which are not seen as individual choices, but instead as social obligations. People who come out to their relations or are unwillingly outed are burdened with the guilt of shaming their family. Social disapproval of these individuals extends beyond them to their immediate relatives. In many instances, their families disown them and their social support is cut off.

'My mother had me arrested and locked up for a week. We had a serious argument and she told me to pack my things and leave her house', said Brian Macharia in 2012,[8] a volunteer at GALCK. His mother did not want to be associated with the shame, stigma and social isolation that would result when the news spread that her son was gay. I experienced the same conflicts once I came out to my family as a lesbian. The socialisation around family is that everyone is expected to do them proud in every way, including avoiding scandal or inappropriate behaviour that would shame and tarnish the family name.

This narrative is experienced by many LGBT people, when their relations are concerned about their social reputation, disapproval and potential backlash. Where both the immediate and external family members are verbally abused, humiliated, ostracised or condemned within their religious affiliations because of being related to LGBT people, some members resort to inhumane treatment, which they justify as preserving the honour of the family, including 'corrective rape' of lesbians by male relatives, disownment and forced marriage. Few of these violations are reported and, if they are, victims get little or no redress.

Health implications

Criminalisation of same-sex sexual conduct among consenting adults has led to their increased vulnerability to HIV/AIDS and those who are under care being unable to access sexual reproductive health services and treatment (National AIDS Control Council and National AIDS and STI Control Programme, 2014). Persons infected by HIV are still stigmatised in Kenya and other parts of the world. The burden of this stigma is doubled by the shaming of, and discrimination against, persons suspected of engaging in same-sex conduct. Criminalisation obstructs access to information, support structures, care and treatment of persons affected by HIV/AIDS. According to the 2014 report cited

8   Interviewed on 30 Jul. 2012 by Immah Reid, GALCK and Envisioning. An excerpt is included in the documentary *A Short Film on Kenyan LGBTI Stories* (2014).

above, HIV prevalence among MSM was 18.2 per cent. Yet this population also experiences lack of – or disproportionate interruptions to – treatment, caused largely by attempts to arrest and hold people suspected of engaging in consensual same-sex conduct (Mbote/Gay Kenya Trust, 2011).

Exceptional challenges are also faced by WSW, especially inadequate sexual reproductive and mental healthcare services. According to a study conducted by Minority Women in Action (2013) – a constituent member organisation of GALCK – one out of four respondents had never visited a physician, for reasons that included fear of being outed to their relations by family doctors, or being turned away altogether on account of their SOGIE. In other cases, healthcare providers are insensitive to the needs of WSW and may be prejudiced by personal beliefs.

Legal reform and decriminalisation

Legal reform is one pragmatic strategy in the fight to decriminalise same-sex conduct. Spearheaded by GALCK's legal advisory team, the movement began exploring possible approaches toward decriminalisation and legal reform. This endeavour faces stiff challenges, such as legislative delay, emotional public debate, backlash on the LGBT community and heightened social stigma.

The existence of the criminal law contributes to the wider climate of discrimination and encourages the sense of impunity for acts of violence, as perpetrators assume that their actions are justified because same-sex conduct is illegal.

In a 2012 interview with the Envisioning research team in Kenya, Anthony Oluoch, GALCK's former legal officer pointed out that the movement had consulted other LGBT movements from India and South Africa at a Nairobi workshop in 2011, to identify the most effective strategies for decriminalisation, borrowing from the experiences in both countries. Delhi's High Court had decriminalised consensual same-sex conduct in July 2009, but the Supreme Court reversed the judgment in December 2013, recriminalising it. Of interest in the deliberations with activists from India and South Africa was the incorporation of evidence and documentation to create precedents for arguments against the criminal law in Kenya. The strategy includes challenging sections of the Penal Code on the basis of the Kenyan Constitution, which includes a non-discrimination clause. 'We want the courts to determine if this law is conducive with the constitution, that states that every Kenyan is entitled to equal treatment before the law. To question if these laws infringe on people's rights, which they do', said Oluoch.[9]

9   Interviewed on 1 Aug. 2012 by Immah Reid, GALCK and Envisioning. An excerpt is included in for the documentary *A Short Film on Kenyan LGBTI Stories* (2013).

The LGBT movement and its partners are cognisant of the fact that for legal reform to be actualised, a variety of gradual legal processes must be conducted, because constitutional reform can take years. Combined with a vigorous social change campaign, it can gain public support, benchmarked on constitutional provisions for basic human rights for all. Judicial review of the Penal Code sections is also a strategy, with the ultimate objective being to offer protection to vulnerable minorities.

As a result of criminalisation, LGBT organisations have been denied legal registration, forcing the majority of them to register as community-based bodies and/or under pseudonyms, including GALCK and almost all of its constituent member institutions. Non-profit bodies are registered and governed by the National Non-Governmental Organisations Board (NGO Board), under the Office of the Attorney General. The NGO Board has occasionally justified refusal to register these LGBT groups, citing their use of names including words like 'gay' and 'lesbian', and suggesting that the existence of such bodies is against the public interest. The emergence of independent movement partners, such as the NGLHRC, increased the legal reform momentum through increased legal discourse on SOGIE. Indeed in 2013, the NGLHRC sued the NGO Board and the attorney general for the former's refusal to register the organisation.

In April 2015, the Kenya High Court ruled in NGLHRC's favour, stating that LGBTI persons can formally register their organisations.[10] The bench also found that the NGO Board had violated Article 36 of the Constitution (freedom of association), when they consistently refused NGLHRC's registration application. The Constitutional Court further held that morality should not be justification for limiting rights in an open and democratic society, under Article 24 of the Constitution of Kenya, and further ordered the NGO Board to comply and register the NGLHRC.

Although this judgment was groundbreaking, it also fuelled a national anti-homosexuality movement, led by conservative religious formations and the anti-homosexuality caucus of MPs led by former Kiharu MP, Irungu Kang'ata. The consistently homophobic Deputy President William Ruto also weighed in on the judgment, saying at a church service that Kenya had no room for homosexuals. Kenya's attorney general, Githu Muigai, has since filed a notice of appeal against the ruling for the registration of NGLHRC.[11]

In July 2014, the High Court compelled the NGO Coordination Board to register a transgender organisation, TEA, after it had refused to do so.[12] In

10 *Eric Gitari v. Non-Governmental Organisations Co-ordination Board and four others*, 2015, available at: http://kenyalaw.org/caselaw/cases/view/108412/ (accessed 1 Nov. 2017).

11 For an overview of the case and the appeal, see Gaballa (2017).

12 *Republic v. Non-Governmental Organizations Co-ordination Board and another ex-parte transgender education and advocacy and three others*, available at: http://kenyalaw.org/caselaw/cases/view/100341/ (accessed 1 Nov. 2017).

another landmark case, in October 2014, the High Court ordered the Kenya National Examinations Council (KNEC) to change the names of a transgender woman's academic certificates and remove the male gender index. The High Court judge ruled that KNEC should recall Audrey Mbugua's national examination certificate and replace it with one in her name, which should be without a gender mark.[13] This ruling was a big win for the transgender community, who face immense challenges when applying for name changes on their identification and academic documents. It also indicated what can be achieved through the judicial system in Kenya for minority groups.

Rising visibility

Sexual and gender minority persons do not enjoy protections under Kenyan law. The result of this criminalisation of consensual same-sex conduct has entrenched stigma and discrimination and other human rights violations, including deprivation of life. However, the LGBT movement has remained steadfast and continues to grow. The GALCK coalition, which comprises more than 15 member organisations from across the country, is also supporting and building the capacity of grassroots LGBT groups, to activate and strengthen their engagement within the human rights networks.

Collectives of human rights defenders continue to urge the state to decriminalise sexual relations between consenting adults of the same sex in order to bring its legislation in line with the Constitution of Kenya, which guarantees equal rights for all citizens. In order for all Kenyans, including sexual minority persons, to enjoy quality citizenship, the government has also been urged to end the social stigmatisation of homosexuality and send a clear message that it does not tolerate any form of harassment, discrimination, or violence against persons based on their sexual orientation. By various means including the United Nations UPR of Kenya in 2010, and most recently in January 2015, these recommendations have been made clear to the government.

Concurrently, the LGBT movement continues to partner with a widening base of partners and stakeholders who are amplifying their voices and incorporating LGBT issues into wider social justice efforts. These include the Kenya Human Rights Commission (KHRC), which in 2011 published a report titled, 'The outlawed amongst us: a study of the LGBTI community's search for equality and non-discrimination in Kenya' (KHRC, 2011). Sexual orientation and gender identity/expression as protected grounds anchored in human rights have also been incorporated by other partners such as the Kenya

---

13 *Republic v. Kenya National Examinations Council and another ex-parte Audrey Mbugua Ithibu*, available at: http://kenyalaw.org/caselaw/cases/view/101979/ (accessed 1 Nov. 2017).

National Commission on Human Rights (KNCHR).[14] Collaborations with KNCHR have informed advocacy through the UN UPR, as well as through political and democratisation processes.

Other human rights organisations, responsible for issues such as LGBT refugee rights, health, religion, economic development and sociopolitical causes of action, have strengthened the network. These collaborations have enabled a home-grown approach to LGBT activism and movement building. The support of civil society continues to encourage meaningful participation in a wide range of public actions. These struggles' intersectionalities have contributed to the amplification of the LGBT community's voice in calling for freedom of expression, opinion, assembly and association. Key attention has also been paid to the legal environment, and there is tremendous support from both local and international partners.

Stakeholders and partners have exposed and called for sweeping changes to the state's inadequate protection of human rights defenders as well as to its efforts to introduce legislation to shrink civil society spaces.

The LGBT movement in Kenya continues to grow, braving the odds and being resiliently steadfast in the struggle for equality. Its partners and allies are injecting much-needed support and using their strengths to catalyse activists' efforts. The repeal of legal provisions that punish sexual relations between consenting same-sex individuals is a key item still remaining, a platform that will provide protection for and equal treatment of LGBT persons.[15]

References

Agoya, V. (2014) 'Lobby plans anti-gay protest', *Daily Nation Kenya*, 18 Feb., available at: www.nation.co.ke/news/homosexuality-President-Barrack-Obama-Uganda/-/1056/2211834/-/bryhf3/-/ (accessed 20 Mar. 2018).

American Center for Law and Justice (2016) 'About the American Center for Law and Justice', available at: http://aclj.org/our-mission/about-aclj (accessed 20 Mar. 2018).

Beja, P. (2012) 'Bishop: gays dangerous than terrorists (sic)', *Standard Media Kenya*, 23 Jul., available at: www.standardmedia.co.ke/article/2000062448/bishop-gays-dangerous-than-terrorists (accessed 20 Mar. 2018).

14 KNCHR is a public human rights institution established through a government act, while the KHRC is a non-profit organisation.

15 On 15 Apr. 2016 Eric Gitari filed a decriminalisation case. The petition requests that the 'Honourable Court declare Sections 162 and 165 of the Penal Code, CAP 63 (disputed provisions) to be unconstitutional, and accordingly void and/or invalid to the extent that they purport to criminalise private consensual sexual conduct between adult persons of the same sex'. See *Eric Gitari v. attorney general and another*, available at: http://kenyalaw.org/caselaw/cases/view/122862/ (accessed 1 Nov. 2017).

BBC News (1999) 'Moi condemns gays', 30 Sep., available at: http://news. bbc.co.uk/2/hi/africa/461626.stm (accessed 20 Mar. 2018).

Capital FM Kenya (2013) 'Kenya deputy presidential debate (part 1)', YouTube video, 14 Feb., available at: www.youtube.com/ watch?feature=player_embedded&v=OU7neGAvmAc (accessed 20 Mar. 2018).

Daily Nation Kenya (2015) 'There is no room for gays, warns Ruto', 3 May, available at: www.nation.co.ke/news/There-is-no-room-for-gays-warns-Ruto/-/1056/2705458/-/36g1obz/-/ (accessed 20 Mar. 2018).

Gaballa, S. (2017) 'A crucial case on freedom of association in Kenya', *The Star Kenya,* 4 Mar., available at: https://www.the-star.co.ke/ news/2017/03/04/a-crucial-case-on-freedom-of-association-in-kenya_ c1516295 (accessed 1 Nov. 2017).

Kaoma, K.J. (2012) 'Colonizing African values: how the U.S. Christian right is transforming sexual politics in Africa', *Political Research Associates,* available at: www.sxpolitics.org/wp-content/uploads/2012/08/ colonizingafricanvaluespra.pdf (accessed 8 Nov. 2017).

Kenya Human Rights Commission (2011) 'The outlawed amongst us: a study of the LGBTI community's search for equality and non-discrimination in Kenya', available at: www.khrc.or.ke/mobile-publications/equality-and-anti-discrimination/70-the-outlawed-amongst-us/file.html (accessed 20 Mar. 2018).

Mbote, D.K./Gay Kenya Trust (2011) 'Breaking the walls of criminalization', Storymoja Africa, Nairobi, available at: www.gkenyatrust.org/wp-content/ uploads/2012/03/Breaking-the-Wall-of-Criminalization-Business-Case. pdf (accessed 9 Nov. 2017).

Minority Women in Action (2013) 'Breaking the silence: the status of women who have sex with women in Kenya', available at: https://www.galck.org/ wp-content/uploads/2017/01/Breaking-the-Silence-Status-of-Kenyan-WSW-2013-first-version.pdf (accessed 9 Nov. 2017).

National AIDS Control Council (2009) 'Kenya national AIDS strategic plan 2009/10–2012/13', available at: http://siteresources.worldbank.org/ INTHIVAIDS/Resources/375798-1151090631807/ 2693180-1151090665111/2693181-1155742859198/ KenyaNationalStrategy.pdf (accessed 31 Oct. 2017).

National AIDS Control Council and National AIDS and STI Control Programme (2014), 'Kenya HIV prevention revolution road map', available at: www.lvcthealth.org/ onlinelibrary?format=raw&task=download&fid=17 (accessed 31 Oct. 2017).

Ngirachu, J. (2014) 'Homosexuality a serious problem as terrorism, says Duale', *Daily Nation Kenya,* 26 Mar., available at: www.nation.co.ke/

news/politics/Homosexuality-a-serious-problem-as-terrorism--says-
Duale/-/1064/2258336/-/kgxersz/-/ (accessed 20 Mar. 2018).
United Nations Development Programme (2013) 'Human development
report 2013', available at: http://hdr.undp.org/sites/default/files/Country-
Profiles/KEN.pdf (accessed 8 Nov. 2017).

Documentary films

A Short Film on Kenyan LGBTI Stories (2013) dir. C. Kaara, J. Muthuri and
I. Reid (Kenya and Canada: Gay and Lesbian Coalition of Kenya and
Envisioning Global LGBT Human Rights), available at: https://vimeo.com/
73786260. Extracts are cited from interviews with Anthony Oluoch and
Brian Macharia.
Telling Our Stories (Kenya Portraits section) (2014) (Kenya and Canada: Gay
and Lesbian Coalition of Kenya and Envisioning Global LGBT Human
Rights), available at: http://envisioning-tellingourstories.blogspot.com
(accessed 16 April 2018). Extracts are cited from the interview with
Guillit Amakobe.

12

Kuchu resilience and resistance in Uganda: a history

Richard Lusimbo and Austin Bryan

Uganda has been called 'the world's worst place to be gay' (Mills, 2011), but this has not always been the case, nor does it reflect the current situation for lesbian, gay, bisexual, transgender, intersex (LGBTI) people and the work to advance their rights in the country. Prior to the Anti-Homosexuality Bill's (AHB) introduction into the Ugandan Parliament in 2009,[1] the LGBTI community was already pushing back against the anti-homosexuality movement. Although LGBTI people are persecuted by some religious groups and traditional leaders who argue that homosexuality is 'un-African' and immoral, a plethora of historical and anthropological evidence debunks this claim (see, for example: Murray and Roscoe, 1998; Epprecht, 2004, 2008; Van Zyl, 2011; Cheney, 2012; Nyanzi, 2013). What is actually 'un-African' is homophobia not homosexuality.

As early as 1999, in response to growing societal discrimination, Ugandan LGBTI people, locally known as kuchus,[2] began organising formally and informally. But it was not until 2002 that Ugandan LGBTI activists started a campaign to raise awareness about their community, their experiences and the difficulties they face in daily life, following a statement by the country's President Museveni. In March 2002, while accepting an award for Uganda's HIV/AIDS prevention programmes, Museveni stated, 'We don't have homosexuals in Uganda' (*New Vision*, 2002; Human Rights Watch and IGLHRC, 2003, p.

1   The Anti-Homosexuality Bill, no. 18, 2009, Bills Supplement to the *Uganda Gazette* no. 47 vol. CII, 25th Sep. For an analysis of the bill's implications, see Jjuuko and Tumwesige (2013).

2   The term 'kuchu' is derived from Swahili, spoken largely in coastal East Africa, where it means 'same'. Later it was adopted by Ugandan LGBTI people as a term for sexual and gender minorities. Kuchu is used in many ways including as a password in public spaces allowing Ugandan LGBTI persons to identify one another and speak freely without other members of wider society being aware of the situation.

R. Lusimbo and A. Bryan (2018) '*Kuchu* resilience and resistance in Uganda: a history', in N. Nicol et al. (eds.) *Envisioning Global LGBT Human Rights: (Neo)colonialism, Neoliberalism, Resistance and Hope* (London: Human Rights Consortium, Institute of Commonwealth Studies), pp. 323–45.

51). The growing visibility of kuchus in the country seemed to anger many traditional leaders and religious groups, including US-based evangelicals from the Christian right such as the Family Research Council[3] and The Family (also known as the Fellowship).[4] Many activists believe this helped to create a moral panic in Uganda in which local leaders began openly demonising homosexuality and seeking to increase criminal penalties against it and its 'promotion'.[5]

Perhaps the most infamous example of the influence of US-based evangelicals is Scott Lively, a pastor from Springfield, Massachusetts. Lively came to Kampala in 2009 and addressed hundreds of Ugandan religious leaders, teachers and social workers to brainstorm anti-gay efforts at a conference entitled, 'Seminar on Exposing the Homosexual Agenda'.[6] Afterwards, Lively was invited to private briefings with political and religious leaders, and addressed the Ugandan Parliament for four hours. His speech at the seminar conflated homophobic rhetoric and holocaust revisionism as follows:

> The gay movement is an evil institution thats [sic] goal is to defeat the marriage-based society and replace it with a culture of promiscuity. [There is] a dark and powerful homosexual presence in other historical periods: the Spanish Inquisition, the French 'Reign of Terror', the era of South African apartheid, and the two centuries of American slavery. This is the kind of person it takes to run a gas chamber or to do a mass murder ... the Rwandan stuff probably involved these guys.

Just a few days later, as a consequence of the Family Life Network conference, the National Anti-Gay Task Force,[7] whose mission is to wipe out gay practices

3   In 2010, the Family Research Council spent over $25,000 on US congressional lobbyists to advocate for US support and promotion of the AHB in Uganda (what they described as 'Res. 1064 Ugandan Resolution Pro-Homosexual Promotion'). See Weigel (2010).

4   In 2009, David Bahati cited a conversation with members of the Family in 2008 as having inspired his anti-homosexuality legislation. Bahati first floated the idea of executing gays during the Family's Uganda National Prayer Breakfast in 2008, as reported by NPR in Nov. 2009. Also see Kaoma (2010).

5   Sylvia Tamale and Joe Oloka-Onyango, interviewed on 29 Nov. 2014 and 3 Dec. respectively, by Richard Lusimbo, SMUG and Envisioning. Excerpts are included in the documentary *And Still We Rise* (2015).

6   This seminar at the Anti-Homosexuality Conference 2009 was filmed by Political Research Associates senior researcher, Revd Dr Kapya Kaoma. It is available at: https://www.youtube.com/watch?v=e9F9k4guN3M (accessed 20 Mar. 2018).

7   The National Anti-Gay Task Force was chaired by Martin Ssempa, one of Uganda's strongest AHB advocates. Ssempa is perhaps best known for championing the bill by showing explicit gay pornography in his church and asking, 'As Africans, we want to ask Barack Obama to explain to us: is this what he wants to bring to Africa as a human right – to eat da poo poo?' His statements subsequently circulated the internet as a viral video. The task force he led was made up of the National Fellowship of Born Again Churches, the Seventh Day Adventist Church, the

in Uganda, was formed and the Ugandan MP David Bahati unveiled his AHB. The bill included the death penalty and other severe punishments for consensual same-sex acts. The international Western media called it the 'Kill the Gays Bill'.[8]

Uganda's President Museveni signed the AHB into law on 24 February 2014, when it became known as the Anti-Homosexuality Act (AHA).[9] Although the death penalty had been removed, many other provisions remained the same as in the original bill. After the AHA came into effect, Ugandan human rights activists reported an increase in anti-gay harassment, detailing evictions, threats of violence and death, unlawful raids, arrests and 'corrective rape'. A Sexual Minorities Uganda (SMUG) Report (2014) documented 162 cases of human rights abuses based on sexual orientation or gender identity during a period of just four months following the passage of the law. An additional 89 cases of human rights abuses were verified in a report released by the Consortium on Monitoring Violations Based on Sex Determination, Gender Identity and Sexual Orientation – violations that went unprosecuted (Consortium, 2015).

Almost overnight, the introduction of the AHB focused an international spotlight on Uganda. Many in the West inaccurately thought that this was when the LGBTI movement started in the country. However, Uganda's resistance to the anti-homosexuality movement began before the bill's introduction, and has been characterised by much more than the single tragic story concerning Uganda often presented by Western mainstream media, with headlines such as: 'They want to cut my throat' (Hamrud, 2015), and 'Uganda's anti-gay witch hunt has officially begun' (Markham, 2014). Kuchus across the country have resisted the anti-homosexuality movement propagated by Westerners and sustained by local religious and political leaders. Kuchus have thrived against all odds, creating a community of sexual and gender minorities and developing a systematic method of fighting for inclusive government – a significant and unique resistance movement against oppression.

This chapter draws on the testimonies of individual activists and LGBTI persons, gathered from a rich body of empirical data that includes 50 semi-structured interviews conducted between May 2012 and December 2015 by a team of one researcher and two videographers as part of the Envisioning Global LGBT Human Rights project (Envisioning) with SMUG. After gaining informed consent from all participants, interviews were video-recorded,

---

Uganda Joint Christian Council (which also represented the Orthodox Church in Uganda), the Roman Catholic Church in Uganda, the Islamic Office of Social Welfare in Uganda, and the Born Again Faith Federation.

8   The full text of the 2009 AHB may be found at: http://hrapf.org/laws/ (accessed 20 Mar. 2018). For a discussion of the AHB and the AHA, see also Jjuuko and Mutesi, ch. 10, this volume.

9   AHA, 2014, available at: www.refworld.org/pdfid/530c4bc64.pdf (accessed 11 Feb. 2017).

transcribed and added to a password-protected online database. The research and documentation also resulted in the production of a number of video shorts and the feature documentary film, *And Still We Rise* (2015).[10]

The history of homosexuality in Uganda is also explored in this chapter, and the influence of Western stakeholders in the anti-homosexuality movement, alongside evidence that a thriving community of kuchus exists in the country which is developing its own initiatives for Africans by Africans, and is leading the fight for the human rights of LGBTI Ugandans.

Western influence, persecution

Contemporary African opponents to homosexuality continuously cite it as 'un-African', even though this claim has been repeatedly debunked through historical and anthropological evidence demonstrating that homosexuality existed on the continent prior to colonisation (Murray and Roscoe, 1998; Epprecht, 2004, 2008; Van Zyl, 2011; Cheney, 2012; Nyanzi, 2013). Moreover, early 20th-century ethnographies contain brief and subtle accounts of same-sex activity or gender non-conformity across the African continent (although such reports are often problematic because of their historical utility in justifying racism while propping up colonisation).

Jack Driberg (albeit from his Western imperialist perspective) observed that some males among a group of agriculturalists north of Lake Kwania in Uganda were called *mudoko daka* and 'treated as women' but 'could carry as men' (Murray and Roscoe, 1998). Although Driberg thought this was rare, Lango people informed him that the behaviour was quite common and also practised among other pastoralist people to the East, including the Iteso (Teso) of Eastern Uganda and Western Kenya and the Karamojan (Karamojong) of Northwestern Kenya and Northeastern Uganda (Driberg, 1923). Similarly, some among the Nkole, in what is now Southwestern Uganda told Mushanga (1973) that the Bahima of Western Uganda and Northern Rwanda also engaged in same-sex practices.

In Uganda, Kabaka Mwanga, the king of Buganda who ruled from 1884 to 1897, is infamously known as the ruler who killed 45 of the pages from his royal court who had converted to Christianity (now called the Ugandan Martyrs). The group is widely commemorated across the country through memorials, schools, a national holiday, and notably, a papal visit. However, accounts of Mwanga's life largely gloss over the specifics behind why these Christian converts were killed. Prior to converting, the pages had engaged in some form of pederasty with Kabaka Mwanga (Faupel, 1962). According to Faupel, the king viewed them as property and expected them to be sexually submissive. The homosexuality of Kabaka Mwanga is still a taboo subject in

---

10 *And Still We Rise* (2015) premiered in Kampala, Uganda, on 26 Jan. 2016. For more on the documentary see Nicol, ch. 14, this volume.

Uganda; however, some historians and scholars in the region have tried to address it. One notable example is a popular biography of Mwanga's life by Ugandan scholar Sawmill Lwanga-Lunyiigo (2011), who wrote:

> There were also accusations that Mwanga was addicted to the weed and practised unnatural acts. Let us look at the unnatural acts. Surely the British could not have been shocked if Mwanga, indeed performed unnatural acts. Paxman writes that the English refer to homosexuality as the usual thing and some British contemporaries of Mwanga were greatly addicted to it namely General Gordon of Khartoum, and the famous poet and dramatist Oscar Wilde who was romantically linked to a fellow poet, Lord Alfred Douglas 'who became the love of the author's life'.
>
> To the Baganda homosexuality was unheard of and was therefore bound to shock them, isolate and alienate whoever was accused of practising it. This accusation was leveled against the Kabaka simply because he surrounded himself with many unmarried young men. Mwanga had no shortage of buxom girls from Buganda and Busagala (Nkore). In Buganda the beauty of Basagala women was legendary and powerful men such as Mwanga had a bevy of belles from there. So, homosexuality was used to make him appear despicable to the Buganda. The missionaries who rejected his requests to be baptized refused to grant him the sacrament on the account of his polygamy! (p. 83)

Lwanga-Lunyiigo's implication that homosexuality is somehow Western is neither subtle nor surprising. Likewise, the sexualisation and objectification of the female body as evidence for Mwanga's heterosexuality is extremely problematic. The passage exemplifies the way that opponents of homosexuality struggle to find actual evidence for their claim that it is 'un-African', relying on hyperbole, myths and scriptural references. Continuing to deny Mwanga's homosexuality, as Lwanga-Lunyiigo does, supports the claim that homosexuality is 'un-African', and works to prop up the anti-homosexuality movement.

It is important to note that prior to colonialism same-sex sexual expression was never criminalised in what is present-day Uganda. Originating in British colonial law, Sections 145–7 of the Penal Code of Uganda criminalise 'carnal knowledge of any person against the order of nature', which has been interpreted as criminalising homosexuality.[11] Since that time this vague language has been used to justify human rights abuses against sexual and gender minorities, including arrests and torture by state actors. Criminalisation might never have happened if colonisation had never occurred. The regulation of sexuality became a pressing issue for the colonial administration largely due to Victorian

---

11 Ugandan Penal Code, introduced in 1930 and updated in 1950, Chapter XIV Offences Against Morality, Sections 145–7. For more on the origins of Penal Code law and the AHB see: Jjuuko (2013) and Jjuuko and Mutesi ch. 10, this volume.

Britain's conservative and conventional views on sexuality and the family.[12] Western interference was thus actively involved historically in the repression of homosexuality, and remains a dominant force shaping the loud homophobic discourse that has arisen in the past decade.

'Let Us Live in Peace': the beginning of a visible movement

In 2007, for the first time in Uganda's history, LGBTI activists stepped out of the shadows and into a room full of international and local media representatives. Disguised by hand-made manila masks, four LGBTI activists sat at the front of a conference room in Speke Hotel in Kampala, waiting to give their testimonies. The tension in the air was thick. The first masked activist said:

> No person should be deprived of their constitutional rights, and homosexuals and transgender people are no exception. All people are equal under the law. Therefore, we step into the public today to give a face to the many who are discriminated against every day in our country. Some of us have brought our faces before you for you to know us. But many of us come before you today with masks to represent the fact that you see homosexuals and transgender people every day without realising that it is what we are. We do not harm anyone. We are your doctor, your teacher, your best friend, your sister, maybe even your father or son.[13]

And so began the 45-day media campaign, called 'Let Us Live in Peace', fighting for the rights of LGBTI Ugandans. The audience began shouting out questions: 'Why would you decide to speak now?' 'Aren't you scared of being attacked?' 'Who is making you do this?' But the testimonies continued:

> Across East Africa, we are many who were born like this. We are lesbians, gays, bisexuals, transgender, and intersex Africans who come from villages that are very far, who come from trading centres, and some who even come from large cities like Kampala, Dar es Salaam, and Nairobi.
>
> But our traditions of loving each other come from very far back in our African history, before the colonialists ever entered our land. Many of our ancestors in our tribes across East Africa were the way we are. They were born like this. We were accepted in our communities before the colonialists came, and we come before you today to ask you for that same acceptance that was part of our African culture before we were destroyed by laws from the west. Because of the prejudice brought by the west, we have been threatened, intimidated, and harassed.

12 This history is deconstructed in Michel Foucault's *The History of Sexuality* (1976).
13 This testimony and the following one are by two unknown masked activists in Kampala, Uganda, Aug. 2007. Transcript made available by Human Rights House (2007).

I stand today from Kenya in solidarity with the LGBTI people in East
Africa to proclaim that these human rights violations are completely
unacceptable. We have had enough of the abuse, neglect, and
violence. In fact, our leaders have recognised this and made our East
African countries signatories of international agreements to end such
discrimination.

There is need for liberation in East Africa as a whole. Just as if people
were starving in Kenya, but had plenty to eat here, we would still fight
against poverty in our region.

In the years before the media campaign began, activists mostly did their work
behind closed doors and out of the spotlight. Several activists wrote opinion
columns in local newspapers to spark discussion about homosexuality. To
protect their identities, they used pseudonyms. But slowly the movement
became increasingly more visible.

The media campaign 'Let Us Live in Peace' was prompted in part by the
murder of a lesbian student in a Kampala suburb, and a court case brought
by two trans activists, Victor Juliet Mukasa and Yvonne Oyo in 2008.[14]
The police and a local council chairperson forced entry into and ransacked
Mukasa's home, abducted Oyo and forced him to undress at the police
station, and denied him access to toilet facilities (Jjuuko, 2013). The case was
heard by Justice Stella Arach Amoko, who, after referring to international
human rights precedents, found that Mukasa and Oyo's right to privacy had
been violated. The case represented an important victory in fighting for the
rights of sexual and gender minorities and guaranteeing the right to privacy
for all persons.

The campaign attracted much attention both domestically and
internationally – a focus that according to Frank Mugisha, SMUG's executive
director, activists 'did not anticipate'.[15] Newspaper articles, radio talk shows,
and church sermons began responding to this new recognition that human
rights abuses were being perpetrated against sexual and gender minorities.
One of the most high-profile articles published the week following the case
was an interview, in the *Sunday Vision*, with minister for ethics and integrity,
James Nsaba Buturo. To the question 'What about the argument that it
[homosexuality] is one of the fundamental rights'? he replied,

Of course that is the argument that someone should feel free to do
what they choose. Well, clearly, then people will start sleeping with
animals, dogs and of course commit bestiality, which is another crime,
and then they will quote human rights issues. Human rights must have

14 *Victor Juliet Mukasa and Yvonne Oyo v. attorney general of Uganda*, available at:
www.chr.up.ac.za/index.php/browse-by-subject/490-uganda-mukasa-and-another-
v-attorney-general-2008-ahrlr-ughc-2008-.pdf (accessed 11 Feb. 2017).

15 Interviewed on 18 Jun. 2012 by Richard Lusimbo, SMUG and Envisioning. An
excerpt is included in the documentary *And Still We Rise* (2015).

> a limit and it is part of society to decide what its values are and sticking
> to those values strictly. (Tamale, 2007, pp. 35–8).

In response to this, LGBTI activists began to consider strategies to raise awareness and challenge homophobia and transphobia. According to Frank Mugisha:[16]

> We looked at very many strategies. We looked at 'Do we go out on the
> streets and start marching every day?' and 'Do we go and talk to people
> silently?' 'Do we go up to people's offices and talk to them one-on-one?'
> 'How do we get the media?' For us, we are trying everything – because
> we do not have a lot of exposure on advocacy itself. We did not have a
> lot of skills in campaigning, and let alone, we did not know how to go
> about campaigning for LGBT rights. But the process, that was making
> SMUG stronger.

The campaign was a key turning point in what is now one of the most visible LGBT movements in the world. But even in the late 1990s, kuchus had begun informally organising in bars and social settings to meet one another and create a sense of community. From this, the movement grew slowly from strictly social gatherings to peer-to-peer groups that would later become formally organised and politically active. Two of the first groups to grow out of these gatherings were Freedom and Roam Uganda (FARUG), and Spectrum Uganda Initiatives. Founded in 1999, they now operate as two of the oldest LGBT organisations in Africa and the first to exist in the country.

Spectrum Uganda was formed by a group of 40 gay-identifying men who began meeting regularly in local bars to drink and to create a safe space for kuchus. Its purpose was to serve those it was created by: marginalised men who have sex with other men (MSM). Because many of the founding members saw that people in their community were increasingly becoming infected with HIV and were being denied access to health services, Spectrum made it its goal to end this marginalisation. Spectrum Uganda registered as a human rights non-governmental organisation (NGO) in the country without mention of serving LGBT persons. In subsequent years, as other LGBT bodies were founded, Spectrum decided to focus its work on providing services specifically to MSM.

The lesbian community in Uganda also worked to form their own organisation (FARUG), after some felt that kuchu women were being overlooked in LGBT programming. One of the movement's most notable activists, Kasha Jacqueline Nabagesera, says about the founding of the group, 'The issue of some of us has always been feminism. The LGBT organisations we were seeing around the world were being led by men, and we said, "Where are the women's voices?" So we said, "We are women, let's advocate for our own rights."'[17]

---

16 Ibid.
17 Interviewed on 25 May 2012 by Richard Lusimbo, SMUG and Envisioning. An
    excerpt is included in the documentary *And Still We Rise* (2015).

Wearing green or purple to identify one another, FARUG's first members began meeting regularly at a local bar in Kampala. After people in the community heard that women suspected of being lesbians were frequenting the bar, Kasha noticed that people were visiting the bar to 'look at lesbians'. 'After drinking, we would just meet to talk about sex, hang out, smoke, but when we were leaving home, people would attack us'.[18] Unfortunately, even these simple attempts to create meeting places were repressed. Eventually, many of the lesbians frequenting the bar were exposed in the local newspaper as homosexuals and subsequently lost their jobs, family or housing.

In November 2007, a 16-year-old lesbian was killed in Nsambya. There was no coverage of the murder on local or international news outlets. However, many in Uganda actually praised the murder because, as reported in local tabloids, they had got rid of a lesbian. The organisation decided to condemn the action publicly but not all FARUG members were happy with this decision, fearing they would be exposed. Speaking about this critical turning point in FARUG's history, Nabagesera says, 'So we sat down and negotiated and said, those who still want the organisation to be just social can go ahead. But those who want to make a change, should also be allowed'.[19] As a result, FARUG shifted its goals from those of a social group to include activism, and moved on to its current location at the centre of the fight for the human rights of LBTI persons in Uganda, albeit with ongoing challenges.

The movement was expanding and experiencing growing pains. Spectrum and FARUG were still for the most part informal organisations. From the early 2000s until 2005, funding for LGBTI programming was sparse, untransparent and channelled largely through individuals rather than formal bodies. This resulted in a person-centred leadership structure in the community, whereby certain individuals became the face of the movement. This created tension and resulted in a drastic decrease in funding. Because there was lack of transparency, accountability and structure, donor funding for LGBTI programming in Uganda was almost completely cut in 2005. It was not until 2007 that a proper flow of funding and accountability structures returned to Ugandan LGBTI organisations.

Spectrum and FARUG inspired the many other LGBTI organisations that were soon to be created across the country. For example in May 2012, activists opened the first LGBTI-specific health clinic at Ice Breakers Uganda (IBU). Between 2012 and 2015, IBU reached 3,646 clients, both at the clinic and through outreach programmes nationwide. In 2015 alone, they reached 2,179 people and distributed 15,000 lubricants and 23,000 condoms. Similarly, LGBTI organisations began popping up across the country, both formally and informally. A research mapping done by UHAI – East African Sexual Health

18 Ibid.
19 Ibid.

and Rights Initiative – shows that the number of groups working on LGBTI issues in the country increased from two in 1999 to more than 31 in 2013 (Magezi and Nakaweesi-Kimbugwe, 2013).

But the boom of LGBTI organisations in Uganda would not have happened if SMUG had not been developed and founded. In 2004, a pan-African LGBTI meeting was convened in South Africa. Among its goals was to centralise funding for LGBTI programming and to generate a common agenda for LGBTI human rights on the continent. As a result, a resolution to form the African Solidarity Alliance was passed. This alliance connected LGBTI activists and kept them up to date on LGBTI issues occurring on the continent – from human rights abuses to event programmes. While there, the conference participants decided that it would be useful to set up subregional groups and coalitions similar in structure to the African Solidarity Alliance.[20] When the Ugandan delegates returned home, they arrived with the mission to do just that, which led to the founding of SMUG, an umbrella coalition of organisations dedicated to fighting for the liberation of LGBTI persons across Uganda.

Also in 2004, the National AIDS Commission was drafting the national AIDS policy. Dr Sylvia Tamale and Shimsher Reuben Deoprado (the country director of UNAIDS) who were involved in drafting the national policy, realised that for the first time in Ugandan history, MSM had been included in the programming. LGBTI and human rights activists met this news with much shock and surprise. Although including MSM in the national policy was an obvious step in the right direction, local activists knew that there was no actual implementation of HIV funding targeted at sexual minorities. Instead, they surmised that including MSM in the draft policy was meant to appear progressive in order to attract increased funding. This left many in the LGBTI community asking where exactly the money was going, and led to concerns that the funds might lead to the opportunity for government officials to line their pockets. This presented an opportunity for the LGBTI community to raise their voices for the first time and demand accountability for funding. Victor Mukasa,[21] SMUG's founding chairperson, describes this history as follows:

> Once we started concentrating on this, we decided that we are going to write a petition to the Commission and thank them; [and] express our gratitude for remembering MSM but also ask them to include other sexual minorities, like lesbians and bisexuals. But [we asked] 'how were we going to send it?' 'Who was going to send it on behalf of

20 The African Solidarity Alliance was a coalition formed by African LGBTI activists in the early 2000s to fight back against growing homophobia spanning the African continent. This coalition was instrumental in building the spirit of the LGBTI Ugandan activists to self organise.

21 Interviewed on 25 May 2012 by Richard Lusimbo, SMUG and Envisioning. An excerpt is included in the documentary *And Still We Rise* (2015).

the LGBT community?' So that is when we thought, 'Why don't we start a national coalition that involves everybody, and that speaks for everyone?' And then it was agreed upon, there and then at the table. We decided we are going to form a coalition [and] we are all going to be members. But what were we going to call it?

The result was the creation of SMUG in 2004 with ten member organisations. Two representatives from each were on its first board. Victor Mukasa was the first chair, and under his leadership HIV/AIDS programming formed SMUG's backbone. Its first task was to petition the Uganda AIDS Commission to include all other sexual minorities in the national policy, not just MSM. But the petition was unsuccessful; sexual and gender minorities were never included in the final policy and MSM were removed from the draft. The Most at Risk Population Initiative (MARPI) at Mulago Hospital, one of Uganda's national referral hospitals, is one of the only resources in a government health facility in the country to track and provide access to HIV and AIDS treatments to MSM. Even so, MARPI had to develop their own documents to ensure that MSM and other sexual and gender minorities were included as a key sector of the population.

In April 2007 the World Social Forum was held in Nairobi, Kenya, the first time it had taken place in Africa. The event attracted more than 66,000 people from 110 countries and highlighted the continent's many anti-imperialist struggles. It also coincided with the 'coming out' of the LGBTI community in Kenya, when the Gay and Lesbian Coalition of Kenya (GALCK) went public (Ismi and Schwartz, 2007). Representing GALCK, Kasha Nabagesera gave a speech to a crowd of thousands at the closing ceremony leading them in the chant 'Respect for all! Human rights for all!' (Barris, 2009) before continuing with these words: 'I speak in the name of the Gay and Lesbian Coalition of Kenya, the Coalition of African Lesbians, the Sexual Minorities of Uganda, the International Lesbian and Gay Association.' The audience fell silent and fists began to rise, with some people crying out, 'No! No! No!'. But Kasha continued, even when the presenter tried to take the microphone from her: 'People, people, if you do not agree, if you do not understand homosexuality, you have to at least agree with me on one principle: we have to learn to live together. Gays and lesbians also have the right to live in peace in Africa!' Kasha then fell to her knees, crying, 'I beg you, tolerate us!' before leaving the stage chased by two men with raised fists, who shouted 'Fire! fire on homosexuals!' (ibid.). It was clear the LGBTI community was not wanted – yet activists like Kasha Nabagesera were not going to sit back and let their human rights be stripped away.

Not long after, in November 2007, the Commonwealth Heads of Government Meeting (CHOGM) took place in Kampala, Uganda, to focus on the year-long theme 'Respecting difference, promoting understanding'.

The British Council invited activists, like Pepe Julian Onziema,[22] to represent SMUG in the 'Commonwealth Peoples' Space', a CHOGM event designed to provide opportunities to share Commonwealth populations' diversity and richness. Further, it was designated specifically as a space open to all people allowing them to interact and create social change. However, LGBTI activists were met with much hostility at the event. Pepe Julian describes the experience:

> As we walked to claim safe space, we ran into a prominent anti-gay pastor, Martin Ssempa, who heads the Inter-Faith Rainbow Coalition against Homosexuality. He said 'hello' and hell broke loose. In less than five minutes we were surrounded by people who shouted and ridiculed us as cameras flickered and recorders pointed at us. An elderly woman asked, 'Would you be here today had your mother been a lesbian?' Pastor Ssempa gave a devilish smile as other twenty-somethings of his brigade from Makerere University yelled and shouted, 'You don't deserve to be on earth, not here! Lesbians, lesbians – where is security? Police! Security take them away and lock them up!' (2007, p. 3)

Six members of the Ugandan police forced Pepe, along with other activists, outside the gates of the event venue, where they remained for seven hours waiting to be let back inside. They had not come to the event that day to start a protest; they came to participate. The altercation led to a shift in the Ugandan LGBTI movement. Being publicly excluded from international events and the ensuing media campaign made it clear that LGBTI people were now out and visible, like their Kenyan counterparts (Ekine, 2007). They continued fighting for inclusion in health programming, cultural events and equal protection under the law. For the next year-and-a-half Ugandan activists made progress, generated dialogue, and sensitised communities – until the AHB's introduction forced their advocacy to take a new direction: ensuring that LGBTI people would not face the death penalty.

Criminalised lives

When the AHB was introduced in the Ugandan Parliament in 2009, it became clear that the LGBTI movement had to adjust its strategies in order to support its rights. Now, instead of focusing on HIV/AIDS programming and creating family support groups and social spaces, members had to prioritise the fight to prevent the AHB becoming law. But the LGBTI movement was not alone. Even before the original draft of the bill was introduced in parliament, civil society members became aware of it and began organising. The Civil Society Coalition on Human Rights and Constitutional Law (the Coalition) was founded, comprising more than 50 organisations ranging from women's groups to sex worker associations. The coalition met to plan how, together, they would

---

22 Pepe Julian Onziema, cited as Pepe Julian, is a leading transgender activist, and SMUG's programmes director and advocacy officer.

fight the bill. Leading Ugandan intersex activist, Julius Kaggwa, became the coalition's first coordinator and made LGBTI rights the focus. Daily activities included producing research and documentation on LGBTI rights in Uganda, identifying which MPs supported the AHB, and lobbying them to oppose it.

The AHB was introduced, tabled and reintroduced in parliament several times, and the process of lobbying government officials became quite difficult. Often MPs would recognise co-coordinators Geoffrey Ogwaro or Clare Byarugaba from the coalition, and would try to kick them out. Ogwaro says, 'When they realise you're LGBTI activists and they see you in the lobby, they begin telling the security to kick you out of parliament. They are that intimidating – but of course we counter them, and tell them, "we know our rights, this is public space, you cannot just kick us out of here like that"'.[23]

Religious leaders were perhaps among the most influential people to lobby government officials in support of the AHB. It was important, however, according to Ogwaro, that religious leaders be part of the coalition in order to really create change. He added, 'We do have a few religious leaders, or clergymen, who quietly tell us that they are in support, but ... they cannot come out and say it because they will be defrocked, or they will be excommunicated from their churches'.[24] Without religious institutions in Ugandan civil society lending support, full equality for LGBTI persons will be difficult to achieve.

At the end of 2010, Frank Mugisha began a tour in the United States to meet human rights defender partners, including the Center for Constitutional Rights (CCR) in New York. Mugisha also did research on the American Christian right in an endeavour to understand what would come next in Uganda, and the best way to fight the influence of the US-based anti-homosexuality agenda in country. As a result of this work, CCR came on board to represent SMUG in the US court in a civil lawsuit against Scott Lively for 'crimes against humanity', for his role in fomenting hatred against LGBTI people in Uganda (Kilborne, 2016).[25]

But in January 2011, while still on tour, Mugisha received devastating news: his friend and fellow activist David Kato had been found murdered in his home in Mukono. Many considered Kato to be the father of the Ugandan LGBTI movement because of his activist work on its behalf and his status as one of the first openly gay people in the country. For local activists and the international community there was reason to suspect that Kato was killed because of his sexual orientation and activism. Three weeks prior to his murder,

23 Interviewed on 8 Jun. 2012 by Richard Lusimbo, SMUG and Envisioning. An excerpt is included in the documentary *And Still We Rise* (2015).

24 Ibid.

25 *SMUG v. Lively* was heard in the US federal court. The case sought to prosecute Scott Lively for persecution, a crime against humanity under international law. For background on the case see the Center for Constitutional Rights website: http://ccrjustice.org/home/what-we-do/active-cases (accessed 11 Feb. 2017).

he had won a right to privacy case in Uganda, which he had filed with Kasha Nabagesera and Pepe Julian Onziema against the notorious Ugandan tabloid, the *Rolling Stone*.[26] In October 2010, it had printed the names, addresses and photographs of hundreds of people 'suspected of being homosexuals'. The front page featured David Kato with the headline, '100 pictures of Uganda's top homos leak' with a banner declaring 'Hang them'. He received many death threats after the article was published.

The persecution continued. In February 2012, just a week after David Bahati reintroduced the AHB in parliament, Ugandan police raided a training and skills-building workshop hosted by FARUG and SMUG. The workshop, which had taken place annually since 2010, was hosting LGBTI activists from Uganda, Kenya, Tanzania and Rwanda. The minister of state for ethics and integrity, Simon Lokodo, came personally with police escorts to shut down the event in Entebbe, and 35 participants were threatened with arrest (Human Rights Watch, 2012). In June, activists challenged this raid in the Uganda High Court, arguing that in no way had they violated the law, and that shutting down the workshop was a clear violation of their constitutional right to freedom of assembly.[27]

But on 18 June, just days after bringing the case to court, another workshop was arbitrarily shut down because of its focus on LGBTI rights. In an attempt to identify and detain its participants, police held them, as well as other guests and staff, hostage for more than three hours. Hassan Shire Sheikh, executive director of East and Horn of Africa Human Rights Defenders Project, which hosted the event, commented, 'This arbitrary closure confirms a pattern of behavior by the authorities, that LGBTI people, and those working on LGBTI issues, will not be afforded the same protections as other people in this country' (Freedom House, 2012).

In July 2014, the Uganda High Court finally made its judgment in the case. The judge ruled that the workshop participants were promoting or inciting same-sex acts, essentially maintaining that human rights training on LGBT rights is itself a form of incitement to engage in prohibited same-sex practices, and is in contravention of the law. The case was a setback for freedom of expression and association. According to Adrian Jjuuko,[28] the founder of the Human Rights Awareness and Promotion Forum (HRAPF):

26 *Kasha Jacqueline, David Kato Kisuule & Pepe Julian Onziema v. Rolling Stone Ltd*, case no. 163 of 2010, High Court of Uganda, 30 Dec., available at: https://globalequality.files.wordpress.com/2011/01/uganda-high-court-ruling_rs.pdf (accessed 13 Feb. 2017).

27 *Jacqueline Kasha Nabagesera, Frank Mugisha, Julian Pepe Onziema, and Geoffrey Ogwaro v. attorney general and Hon. Rev. Fr Simon Lokodo*, available at: https://globalfreedomofexpression.columbia.edu/wp-content/uploads/2015/06/Judgment.pdf (accessed 13 Feb. 2017).

28 Interviewed on 21 Jan. 2014 by Richard Lusimbo, SMUG and Envisioning. An excerpt is included in the documentary *And Still We Rise* (2015).

We were surprised when the judge, instead of enforcing the right, rather applied the limitation of the right ... though the applicants enjoy the right to freedom of expression and the other rights, these are limited under the constitution. One of the limitations would be if the penal law provided for it. And therefore in his view, the scope of Section 145 exceeded beyond the sexual act ... organising meetings and talks ... may be included under the scope of [Section] 145 [of the Uganda Penal Code]. I think that's the widest interpretation of that section ever given.

Although at times painfully slow for those whose human rights are violated daily, there has been progress for LGBTI persons in Uganda. Perhaps these advances have been slowest for transgender persons. According to Beyonce Karungi, a trans woman living in Uganda, and the founder and director of Transgender Equality Uganda, when the LGBTI movement started in the country, both the wider Ugandan society and members of the kuchu community itself discriminated against transgender people: '[We] were discriminated [against] by the LGB ... the LGB doesn't understand transgender people while the trans men were empowering themselves and leaving us out. And yet we are the people who were visible, and we have a lot of challenges'.[29] Karungi had experienced these violations personally: 'People in clubs would always abuse me and beat me up, pour beer on me and burn me with cigarettes'.[30] It was clear to her that trans women specifically needed a safe space – which is why she created Transgender Equality Uganda in 2011.

Similarly, Nikki Mawanda, a trans man and human rights defender for transgender and intersex rights, co-founded the Trans-Support Initiative Uganda in 2007 (originally known as Transgenders, Intersex and Transexuals Uganda). As with Karungi's organisation, the Trans-Support Initiative's goal was to create a support network for transgender persons. Like many other LGBTI groups, it began informally, but grew into an NGO legally registered in the country. Speaking on its goals, Mawanda says:

What we are doing is we are creating awareness, because if someone lacks self-esteem they will not be able to address those issues. If you are not yourself, believing in yourself, you will not tackle other issues. So creating a safe space for them to know, Yes I'm trans. I accept I'm trans, and what are the challenges ... and how can I live in this hostile environment as a trans person and survive?[31]

Transgender Equality Uganda and Trans-Support Initiative Uganda are also working to create small-scale skills-building initiatives for transgender people because many of them drop out of school or are limited in their higher education options because of social stigma or family banishment. According to

29 Interviewed on 8 Jun. 2012 by Richard Lusimbo, SMUG and Envisioning.
30 Ibid.
31 Interviewed on 30 May 2012 by Richard Lusimbo, as above.

Karungi, 'The challenge I'm getting is trans women never go to school because of their lives – eviction from homes, their family's rejection from homes, they are on their own when they find out who they are. They have family members reject them, so they never go to school'.[32] It is exactly this type of systematic discrimination that makes the work of Karungi and Mawanda so difficult. Not surprisingly, Mawanda explains that challenges will persist without large-scale change:

> One of the big challenges is we struggle as human beings, but also we struggle because we are different. People don't understand. You try to fight as a person and then somebody who you think will understand, brings a big barrier – and these are people we trust. So many trans people today can't find good partners just because they are different. You start seeing someone, she is a lesbian, you propose – but because you are different they start to say, 'I can't be with a man.' … The support systems that we are having, even if it's the government, even if it's within the LGBT movement that we call our own, they do not cater for us. Today, we will find most of the messages we print, even if somebody is talking, we are talking so much of only 'lesbian [and] gay.[33]

But kuchus like Karungi and Mawanda have never stopped their battle before, during, or after the AHB became law. As a result, Uganda's response to the anti-homosexuality movement has been one of the strongest when compared to that of other African countries. It has gained in strength by fighting the notion that kuchus are at the mercy of their oppressors or dependent on Western intervention to 'save them', while concurrently establishing one of the most organised communities of LGBTI people on the African continent.

A thriving community

Uganda's resistance to homo/transphobia, and particularly to the AHA, has often been presented as a single tragic story. Journalists, writers, scholars and visitors are almost always shocked to learn that the country has a community of LGBTI-identifying persons and strong organisations working to advance their rights. Many even continue to claim that this does not exist. For example, in a recent interview, Isobel Yeung, who filmed the 2015 VICE documentary, A Prayer for Uganda, said, 'There's not much of a homosexual community in Uganda, apart from advocates who are a whole other level of brave. But people who live with others of the same sex or who live a different lifestyle to what's considered normal are all under threat' (Mwaluko, 2016). The lack of acknowledgement that there is an LGBTI sector in Ugandan society is common among journalists, writers and visitors alike, who often unknowingly

---

32 Interviewed on 8 Jun. 2012 by Richard Lusimbo, as above.
33 Interviewed on 30 May 2012 by Richard Lusimbo, as above.

perpetuate the notion that Ugandan LGBTI persons live in constant fear and need the West to 'save them'.

Although it is extremely important to understand the human rights abuses that form part of the lived experience of many LGBTI Ugandans, it is equally imperative to recognise the successes that they have experienced. Many of the country's LGBTI activists feel that the rhetoric of tragedy holds back the movement for change. A 25-year-old member of the LGBTI community living in Kampala, told us: 'On Google they say Uganda is the worst place to live if you're gay. But even me, I put on micro-shorts and walk around and I am OK. I even go to the beach in micro-shorts. People turn to look sometimes, but nothing else. And saying Uganda is the worst place to be gay isn't changing anything'.[34]

The daily work of activists and LGBTI persons in Uganda is building an LGBTI community across the region, which is perhaps what makes the movement unique. It has a strong sense of organisation, mobilisation and vocalisation that continues to resonate. One key example is the way that Ugandan LGBTI activists successfully organised a Pride event in the country for four consecutive years. Uganda, Mauritius and South Africa are the only three countries in the continent ever to have held such an event. In August 2012, the first Ugandan Pride parade was held in Entebbe to protest about the AHB and the government's treatment of kuchus. However, the event ended in the arrest of several participants and the next day local tabloids printed the names and photos of participants, exposing them as homosexuals. Despite the societal backlash, Pride Uganda continued to be held in Entebbe annually, but state repression of such events continued. In August 2016, police raided the celebrations and the planned parade was cancelled, and, in 2017, Pride organisers were once again forced to cancel it due to the ethics minister threatening police raids and violence.

In the face of tremendous challenges, the movement has created a community of LGBTI people, not just in Kampala but across the country, such as Rainbow Health in Mbarara and GEHO Uganda in Jinja. In regions without organisations, activists utilise upcountry (rural-based) focal points or non-discriminatory partner bodies to do outreach sessions with LGBTI people. The movement has also opened one of Africa's only LGBTI-specific health clinics at Ice Breakers Uganda. The country can also lay claim to having the first LGBTI media house, Kuchu Times, which publishes an annual publication called Bombastic.

Although many LGBTI refugees fled the country after the AHB was passed, many key activists have stayed (Senzee, 2014). The international community has celebrated the deep conviction and leadership of Ugandan kuchus. Several activists were awarded international human rights awards, including: intersex

---

34 Anonymous person interviewed on 16 Sep. 2015 by Austin Bryan.

Figure 15. Opening of the first Pride in Kampala, Uganda, 6 August 2012. Left to right: Richard Lusimbo (research and documentation officer, SMUG), Dr Frank Mugisha (executive director, SMUG), Bishop Christopher Senyonjo and Kasha Jacqueline Nabagesera (founder, Freedom and Roam Uganda). Photo credit: *And Still We Rise* (2015), SMUG and Envisioning.

activist Julius Kaggwa[35] (Human Rights First Award, 2010); Kasha Jacqueline Nabagesera (Martin Ennals Award for Human Rights Defenders, 2011); Frank Mugisha (the Thorolf Rafto Prize for Human Rights and the Robert F. Kennedy Award for Human Rights, 2011); and Pepe Julian Onziema (Clinton Global Citizen award, 2012). This has brought international recognition to the movement and worked to further establish a community of LGBTI Ugandans.

Lastly, the Coalition brought together LGBTI community members and representatives from many sectors of civil society. For the first time, Ugandan LGBTI activists were able to stand up for their rights with support from organisations and groups that understood both their struggle and how the assault on LGBTI rights could undermine civil liberties for the wider Ugandan society. Through the Coalition, LGBTI groups in the country have shared ties with many members of civil society organisations and can work together to advocate for inclusiveness in national and international policies. The work of the Coalition's legal group and the broader movement against the AHA resulted in its annulment in 2014.[36] And since March 2015, because of the Coalition,

35 Julius Kaggwa is the executive director of Support Initiative for People with Atypical Sex Development. He was the Coalition's first coordinator.
36 *Oloka-Onyango and nine others v. attorney general,* Constitutional Petition no. 8 of 2014), UGCC 14, 1 Aug. 2014, available at: www.ulii.org/ug/judgment/

Ugandan LGBTI people have been represented by Kikonyogo Kivumbi on the Country Coordinating Mechanism for Global Fund, a seat that LGBTI advocates have been seeking since 2010.

Pawns of Western influence?

Many, particularly in the West, believe that locally led LGBTI initiatives by Africans for Africans have never existed. But this is simply not true. Although LGBTI movements in African countries still sometimes focus on HIV or only on health, Ugandan activists have been able to use this as an entry point for the movement, expanding its scope to include LGBTI persons' rights within the broader human rights agenda. This has included programming to address the specific needs of sexual and gender minorities in relation to family banishment, eviction and workplace rights; and the development of LGBTI groups and coalitions and their inclusion in broader civil society organisations defending civil liberties.

A *New York Times* article of 20 December 2015 claimed that US funding intended to challenge institutionalised homophobia in Nigeria actually had a negative impact on LGBTI persons' rights and freedoms there. It said that the US had 'spent more than $41 million specifically to promote gay rights globally, along with a portion of $700 million earmarked for marginalized groups to support gay communities and causes' (Onishi, 2015, p. A1). However, according to Andrew Park of the Williams Institute in a Huffington Post article a week later, this figure is highly inflated and, moreover, was quoted widely by anti-gay groups including the Family Research Council. Park writes, 'While the US government funds HIV programs for vulnerable and marginalized populations in Africa, very little of that funding goes to advocacy for LGBT human rights ... the US government probably spends less than $7 million of its own dollars per year on global LGBT issues'.[37] Park further notes that such reporting perpetuates the 'myth of affluence' that hinders the work of LGBTI activists around the world, and in countries that receive foreign aid, like Uganda, local and international leaders perpetuate that myth to support statements by African leaders and conservative evangelicals, such as Ugandan President Museveni and Scott Lively, about homosexuality, money and the 'recruitment' of children. But, as Frank Mugisha wrote in his letter of 29 December to the New York Times in response to the first of these articles, 'LGBTI Africans are more than just "pawns of western interests"', adding the comment, 'Is there more violence now that L.G.B.T.I. people are more visible in Nigeria and elsewhere? Maybe, but it is homophobia, not funding, that is

---

constitutional-court/2014/14/. See also Jjuuko and Mutesi, ch. 10, this volume.

37   After Park's article, *The New York Times* issued a correction on 15 Jan. 2016, saying that the figure for global US funding in support of gay rights was at least US$41 million, not over US$700 million (yet still well over Park's figure of US$7 million).

at fault' (p. A18).

It has long been recognised by LGBTI Ugandans that they are up against a competing stream of support from sources such as US-based evangelical Christian groups which have put political and economic weight behind initiatives like the AHA. Yet one thing is clear: Ugandan kuchus are not just sitting back waiting for the rest of the world to step in and save them. Instead, they have organised, mobilised and led the international community to fight, support and one day liberate the kuchus of Uganda. It is exactly this resistance and resilience that is essential to fight the battle to advance LGBTI rights in the country, and the rest of the world can learn from this history of organising.

References

Amnesty International (2001a) 'Uganda: criminalizing homosexuality – a license to torture', 27 Jun.

— (2001b) 'Crimes of hate, conspiracy of silence: torture and ill-treatment based on sexual identity', ACT40/016.

Barris, S. (2009) 'World Social Forum Nairobi 2007: Respect for All! Another world is possible for African LGBT people, too', International Lesbian, Gay, Bisexual, Trans and Intersex Association Pan Africa ILGA, 1 Oct., available at: http://ilga.org/world-social-forum-nairobi-2007/ (accessed 8 Sep. 2017).

Cheney, K. (2012) 'Locating neocolonialism, "tradition", and human rights in Uganda's "Gay Death Penalty"', *African Studies Review*, Cambridge University Press, 55: 2.

Civil Society Coalition on Human Rights and Constitutional Law (2013) 'Uganda's Anti-Homosexuality Bill: the great divide'.

Consortium on Monitoring Violations Based on Sex Determination, Gender Identity and Sexual Orientation (2015) 'Uganda report of violations based on gender identity and sexual orientation'.

Driberg, J.H. (1923) *The Lango, A Nilotic Tribe of Uganda* (London: Thorner Coryndon).

Ekine, S. (2007) 'LGBTs evicted from the People's Forum in Kampala', *Black Looks*, 24 Nov., available at: www.blacklooks.org/2007/11/lgbts_evicted_from_the_peoples_forum_in_kampala/ (accessed 20 Sep. 2017)

Epprecht, M. (2004) *Hungonchani: the History of a Dissident Sexuality in Southern Africa* (Montréal and Kingston: McGill-Queen's University Press).

— (2008) *Heterosexual Africa? The History of an Idea from the Age of Exploration to the Age of AIDS* (Athens and Scottsville, OH: University of KwaZulu-Natal Press and Ohio University Press).

Faupel, J.F. (1962) *African Holocaust: the Story of the Uganda Martyrs* (New York, NY: P.J. Kennedy).

Foucault, M. (1976) *The History of Sexuality*, vol. 1 (Paris: Éditions Gallimard).

Freedom House (2012) 'Uganda: police raid on LGBT activists workshop in Kampala condemned', available at: https://freedomhouse.org/article/uganda-police-raid-lgbti-activists-workshop-kampala-condemned (accessed 12 Jan. 2018).

Hamrud, A. (2015) 'They say they want to cut my throat', *Ottar*, 27 Nov., available at: www.ottar.se/artiklar/they-say-they-want-cut-my-throat (accessed 4 Oct. 2017).

Human Rights House (2007) 'Ugandan homosexuals launch media campaign: let us live in peace', available at: http://humanrightshouse.org/noop/page.php?p=Articles/8169.html&d=1 (accessed 12 Jan. 2018).

Human Rights Watch (2012) 'Uganda: Minister shuts down rights workshop: LGBT group denied freedom of assembly, expression', available at: https://www.hrw.org/news/2012/02/16/uganda-minister-shuts-down-rights-workshop (accessed 12 Jan. 2018).

Human Rights Watch and International Gay and Lesbian Human Rights Commission (2003) 'More than a name: state-sponsored homophobia and its consequences in southern Africa', available at: https://www.hrw.org/report/2003/05/13/more-name/state-sponsored-homophobia-and-its-consequences-southern-africa (accessed 12 Jan. 2018).

Ismi, A. and K. Schwartz (2007) 'The World Social Forum in Nairobi African activists lead resistance to western plundering and imperialism', Canadian Centre for Policy Alternatives, 1 Apr., available at: https://www.policyalternatives.ca/publications/monitor/april-2007-world-social-forum-nairobi (accessed 8 Sep. 2017).

Jjuuko, A. (2013) 'The incremental approach: Uganda's struggle for the decriminalization of homosexuality', in C. Lennox and M. Waites (eds.) *Human Rights, Sexual Orientation and Gender Identity in the Commonwealth: Struggles for Decriminalisation and Change* (London: Human Rights Consortium, Institute of Commonwealth Studies), pp. 381–408.

Jjuuko, A. and F. Tumwesige (2013) 'The implications of the Anti-Homosexuality Bill 2009 on Uganda's legal system', Institute of Development Studies (IDS) Evidence Report, no. 44, Brighton, and Human Rights Awareness and Promotion Forum (HRAPF), Nov., available at: https://opendocs.ids.ac.uk/opendocs/handle/123456789/3224 (accessed 8 Sep. 2017).

Julian, P. (2007) 'Commonwealth peoples' space, Kampala 2007 report', Sexual Minorities Uganda.

Kaoma, K. (2010) 'The US Christian right and the attack on gays in Africa', *PublicEye*, winter 09/spring 10, available at: www.publiceye.org/magazine/

v24n4/us-christian-right-attack-on-gays-in-africa.html (accessed 8 Sep. 2017).

Kilborne S. (2016) 'Will hate go to trial? Following the case against anti-gay extremist Scott Lively', *Huffington Post*, 6 Dec., available at: www.huffingtonpost.com/sarah-s-kilborne/will-hate-go-to-trial-fol_b_13136066.html (accessed 20 Sep. 2017).

Lwanga-Lunyiigo, S. (2011) *Mwanga II: Resistance to Imposition of British Colonial Rule in Buganda 1884–1899* (Kampala: Wavah Books).

Magezi, M. and S. Nakaweesi-Kimbugwe (2013) 'Lived realities, imagined futures: lesbian, gay, bisexual, transgender and intersex Uganda baseline survey', UHAI – East African Sexual Health and Rights Initiative.

Markham, L. (2014) 'Uganda's anti-gay witch hunt has officially begun', *Vice*, 27 Jun., available at: www.vice.com/read/ugandas-anti-gay-witch-hunt-has-officially-begun-627 (accessed 23 Oct. 2017).

Mills, S. (2011) 'The world's worst place to be gay', BBC, 20 Oct., available at: www.bbc.co.uk/programmes/b00yrt1c (accessed 8 Sep. 2017).

Mugisha, F. (2015), 'Support for gay rights in Africa', letter to the editor', *New York Times*, 29 Dec.

Murray, S., and W. Roscoe (eds.) (1998) *Boy Wives and Female Husbands: Studies in African Homosexualities* (New York, NY: St Martin's Press).

Mushanga, M.T. (1973) 'The Nkole of Southwestern Uganda', in A. Molnos (ed.) *Cultural Source Materials for Population Planning in East Africa: Beliefs and Practices* (Nairobi: East African Publishing House), pp. 174–86.

Mwaluko, N.H. (2016) 'The anti-gay movement in Uganda is still alive and kicking', *Vice*, available at: www.vice.com/read/the-anti-gay-movement-in-uganda-is-still-alive-and-kicking (accessed 20 Sep. 2017).

New Vision (2002) 'Commonwealth honors Museveni', 4 Mar.

Nkabahona, A., S. Okuni, and B. Rukooko (2013) 'Homosexuality and human rights in Uganda: summary report', School of Liberal and Performing Arts, Makerere University.

Nyanzi, S. (2013) 'Dismantling reified African culture through localised homosexualities in Uganda', *Culture, Health & Sexuality*, 15 (8): 952–67.

Onishi, N. (2015) 'U.S. support of gay rights in Africa may have done more harm than good', *New York Times*, 20 Dec., available at: https://www.nytimes.com/2015/12/21/world/africa/us-support-of-gay-rights-in-africa-may-have-done-more-harm-than-good.html (accessed 20 Sep. 2017).

Park, A. (2015) 'New York Times fuels myth of gay affluence', *Huffington Post*, 28 Dec., available at: www.huffingtonpost.com/andrew-park/new-york-times-fuels-myth_b_8866334.html (accessed 20 Sep. 2017).

Senzee, T. (2014) 'Activists: hundreds of LGBT refugees have fled Uganda', *Advocate*, 27 Jun., available at: www.advocate.com/world/2014/06/27/activists-hundreds-lgbt-refugees-have-fled-uganda (accessed 20 Sep. 2017).

Sexual Minorities Uganda (2014a) 'Expanded criminalisation of homosexuality in Uganda: flawed narrative; empirical evidence and strategic alternatives from an African perspective'.

— (2014b) 'From torment to tyranny: enhanced persecution in Uganda following the passage of the Anti-Homosexuality Act 2014: 20 December 2013–1 May 2014'.

Stewart, C. (2015) 'Finally, an LGBT voice on Uganda's anti-HIV panel', 76 Crimes blog, 5 Mar., available at: https://76crimes.com/2015/03/05/finally-an-lgbt-voice-on-ugandas-anti-hiv-panel (accessed 20 Sep. 2017).

Tamale, S. (2003) 'Out of the closet: unveiling sexuality discourses in Uganda', *Feminist Africa: Changing Cultures*, Africa Gender Institute, no. 2, available at: https://www.researchgate.net/publication/291173660_Out_of_the_closet_Unveiling_sexuality_discourses_in_Uganda (accessed 8 Jun. 2018).

— (ed.) (2007) *Homosexuality Perspectives from Uganda* (Kampala: Sexual Minorities Uganda).

Van Zyl M. (2011) 'Are same-sex marriages un-African? Same-sex relationships and belonging in post-apartheid South Africa', *Journal of Social Issues*, 67 (2): 335–57.

Weigel, D. (2010) 'Right now, inside the conservative movement and the Republican Party: Family Research Council explains: It lobbied for changes to Uganda resolution', *Washington Post*, 4 Jun., available at: http://voices.washingtonpost.com/right-now/2010/06/family_research_council_explai.html (accessed 8 Sep. 2017).

Documentary film

And Still We Rise (2015) dir. R. Lusimbo and N. Nicol (Uganda and Canada: Sexual Minorities Uganda and Envisioning Global LGBT Human Rights), available at: https://vimeo.com/178217397. Extracts cited from interviews with: Victor Mukasa, Sylvia Tamale, Joe Oloka-Onyango, Kasha Jacqueline Nabagesera, Geoffrey Ogwaro, Adrian Jjuuko and Frank Mugisha.

13

Gender theatre: the politics of exclusion and belonging in Kenya

Guillit Amakobe, Kat Dearham and Po Likimani

Since the creation of Kenya's first lesbian, gay, bisexual, transgender, intersex (LGBTI) organisations in the late 1990s and early 2000s, the movement has employed conventional non-governmental organisations (NGOs) or non-profit structures. Initially these primarily served men who have sex with men (MSM) and, to a lesser extent, lesbians. The focus on a static construction of sexual orientation meant that issues of gender identity and questions of fluidity were largely ignored.

In 2011, Jinsiangu was conceived as a community-based group focused on the provision of psychosocial support for intersex, transgender and gender non-conforming (ITGNC) Kenyans. The group evolved and expanded in ways the founders had not anticipated, and sometimes perpetuated the same issues it had been created to escape.

This chapter is an oral history of the LGBTI movement in Kenya and the process of creating Jinsiangu. Through the reflections of three of Jinsiangu's co-founders, it touches on the intersections between LGBTI and ITGNC organising, money, class, exclusion, community building and the use of art in activism and healing. Its title, 'Gender theatre,' refers to the ways in which gender identity and the role of activist are performed and politicised in the context of LGBTI organising in Kenya. Through our work in Jinsiangu, we have often felt the pressure of observation and the push to conform to roles as if we were actors playing out parts. We explore here the tensions between types of organising – collective and member-driven *v.* professional, hierarchical and donor-driven – and how some balance might be found between them. In documenting Jinsiangu's history, this chapter is a starting point for reflection and discussion on universal themes of LGBTI activism and social justice work.

G. Amakobe, K. Dearham and P. Likimani (2018) 'Gender theatre: the politics of exclusion and belonging in Kenya', in N. Nicol et al. (eds.) *Envisioning Global LGBT Human Rights: (Neo) colonialism, Neoliberalism, Resistance and Hope* (London: Human Rights Consortium, Institute of Commonwealth Studies), pp. 347–70.

Setting the stage: LGBTI organising in Kenya

Po Likimani: I got involved in LGBTI organising around 2005, as a co-founder of Minority Women in Action (MWA). This was the first-ever lesbian, bisexual, transgender and intersex women's organisation in Kenya. And even while it identified as LBTI, it was predominantly a lesbian and bisexual group – mostly cisgender women. So there was little information and little interest in seeking out information for transgender and intersex people and gender non-conforming people.

At the same time that MWA was developed, the Gay and Lesbian Coalition of Kenya (GALCK) was formed. It was a coalition of a half-dozen LGBTI organisations. It was meant to be an umbrella body to support their work, to help mitigate violence and hostility towards gay people and around talk of homosexuality in Kenya. By now information was out that it wasn't wrong to be gay, and a lot of the available information was on sexuality and sexual orientation. There was discussion around how same-sex behaviour is criminalised, but it is not illegal to identify as a gay person. So it was a lot about empowering gays and lesbians.

My engagement was as an activist, as a forefront warrior, as a 'soldier boi'. I was involved in organising community meetings, following up with emails, doing logistics, just trying to keep the energy flowing throughout the year. I would appear in interviews, respond to questions, be the contact person for people who wanted to come out. I would reach out to any space that would work with LGBTI people.

A lot of organisations around this time were very informal. They were support spaces, they were people trying to get together and get social space or recreational space. An HIV-prevention NGO called LVCT Health hosted monthly meetings that included support groups and discussions on how to empower LGBTI people to engage in their own advocacy for health. At this time at LVCT Health we also started a hotline. We did a campaign with material on anal sex and the increased risk of contraction of HIV and AIDS. And that opened up the conversation more. Over time, the Kenya National Commission on Human Rights also got involved. In 2007 the World Social Forum in Nairobi brought us our first international visibility,[1] But World AIDS Day, 1 December 2006, was the first time gays and lesbians gained national visibility.

Throughout this time I also had contact with Oyo, a Kenyan who had sued the Ugandan government, together with Ugandan trans activist Victor Mukasa, after being assaulted by police during a raid on Victor's house.[2] Oyo

---

1   For more information on this event and its impact, see Thirikwa, ch. 11, and Lusimbo and Bryan, ch. 12, this volume.

2   *Mukasa and another v. attorney general*, AHRLR 248 (UgHC 2008), available at: www.chr.up.ac.za/index.php/browse-by-subject/490-uganda-mukasa-and-another-v-attorney-general-2008-ahrlr-ughc-2008-.pdf (accessed 9 Nov. 2017).

identified as a trans person, but there hadn't been any resources in Kenya to support him.

GUILLIT AMAKOBE: The first time I knew that other LGBTI people existed in Kenya was at World AIDS Day in 2006, where there was a tent for LGBTI people. After that, I tried to look for people, but it was difficult because I was not out. At the time I identified as a lesbian.

Later on I met lesbians in Dandora Estate, a slum area in Nairobi where I grew up. They were mostly neighbours that I hadn't interacted much with before because of the fear of being discovered. They introduced me to other lesbians and we hung out together.

It wasn't until 2007 that I first went to GALCK and realised that this was the same group that had the tent at World AIDS Day. There were no trans organisations back then and I joined MWA. I was working full-time so I didn't have much interaction with them. They held movie and social nights, which I sometimes attended, and I was happy that there was a whole new group of people where I could be open and express myself. Through MWA, I started to see how I could fit in and what I could offer.

PO: From 2007 to around 2009, there was a huge wave of gays and lesbians coming out, creating organisations, and engaging in conversation about sexuality. Mainly as a response to the homophobia that existed, to the violence that was ongoing.

By then Transgender Education and Advocacy (TEA) had been hosted by GALCK and had also started growing. It was an organisation predominantly for transgender people. It was led by a trans woman, Audrey Mbugua.

The thing that was important in all this was people's willingness, presence and inspiration. And one thing triggered another. There was the growth of gay and lesbian organising, but also the inspiration of gender non-conforming, transgender and intersex people seeing space to speak about their issues.

GUILLIT: TEA was the first transgender organisation in Kenya. It was formed in 2008, and is still active today, dealing mostly with legal and advocacy issues. That included helping trans people get name changes and navigating systems relating to identity documents. I was introduced to Audrey, the founder and leader of TEA, at a function at GALCK. It was very exciting to meet another trans person and to finally connect with someone who understood what I was going through.

I had also joined Artists for Recognition and Acceptance (AFRA), a group for lesbian and bisexual women which focuses on using art as an advocacy tool. There were a few bi and trans members, but the trans women did not really participate or come to events. Probably they didn't feel welcome or felt that the events were not useful for them. That was common to all of the gay and lesbian organisations. They said that they worked with trans people, but in reality we were not included unless you weren't out as trans. I volunteered for TEA but remained in AFRA because of the focus on art.

KAT DEARHAM: I first became involved in LGBTI work in Kenya in 2010. I'm from Canada and had been coming to Kenya since 2005, first as a student and then working with NGOs. Since I was always in straight environments and had never to my knowledge met any LGBTI Kenyans, I struggled with how to stay in the country while embracing and living my queerness. That was difficult, even with all of my access to privilege that would have allowed many avenues of escape if I had needed them, which most LGBTI Kenyans don't have access to.

I'd read about GALCK in the newspapers, but the reporting at the time was shrouded in religious moralising that made me wonder how anyone was managing to organise in such a hostile atmosphere. Being gay was portrayed as sinful, as an illness, and as 'unnatural' behaviour that had been brought to Africa by Westerners – despite the long history and evidence of same-sex attraction and behaviours across the continent (see Aarmo, 1999; Epprecht, 2004; Epprecht and Clowes, 2008; Hoad, 2007; Morgan and Wieringa, 2005; Murray and Roscoe, 1998). At that time there was little public knowledge or discussion of ITGNC people.

Eventually I actively sought out other queer people. My entry point to LGBTI organising was to carry out research on queer women's activism and identity in Nairobi. MWA generously agreed to host me and take me on as a volunteer while I was doing the research. It was beautiful to finally connect with people I considered family and to see how much important work was being done. Part of my research was to examine the frameworks that queer women in particular were using to carry out their activism, and how this fitted into global understandings and struggles for queer liberation.

At the time most of the LGBTI organisations were operating under GALCK, and TEA was the only transgender-focused organisation. As is the case in most ostensibly 'LGBTI' organisations and communities, the focus of most groups in GALCK was on gay men and MSM. It's troubling that LGBTI is continually conflated with and used to refer to gay people only. Most of the programming at the time was health-focused, which is part of the reason for the emphasis on MSM. HIV/AIDS was a major entry point for activists to have the kind of public conversation that was used to let people know that LGBTI Kenyans actually exist. There was also a lot of work on creating safe social spaces for LGBTI Kenyans, where LGBTI people could organise, discuss and create the networks that are necessary for survival.

MWA was formed partly as a reaction to the male-dominated nature of the LGBTI organisations in the early 2000s. Lesbian and bisexual women struggled with issues that were different from men's issues, partly because women largely carry the burden of domesticity and propagation of the nuclear family. Many queer women are confronted with familial expectations of marriage. Particularly in rural areas it's difficult for women to beat another path for themselves outside of compulsory heterosexual marriage and childbearing.

Women are also much more vulnerable to domestic violence and sexual assault, the latter sometimes being carried out within intimate relationships, and sometimes as a method of 'converting' queer women to heterosexuality. So there are a lot of issues that are specific to women that required a specific space, and MWA was attempting to fill that gap.

Methods and approaches

Po: Initially, organising was very passionate. It was focused on change, on people's lives becoming different. It was thriving because everybody was willing and it was on volunteer terms. People connected the things they loved or were about to the work that was happening.

Then donor funding came in, as well as more hostility from the public, introduction of laws on sexual orientation and gender identity in countries like Uganda, the Gambia and Nigeria, decriminalisation in India and the globalisation of the conversation.[3] Organisations were expected to have structures based on what is acceptable to donors. We have had little time to reflect on and analyse the impact of these actions and newly created structures – about the lives that we're living and the change that we hope to see.

There have also been more frequent meetings, conferences and spaces created specifically for LGBTI issues. A huge number of LGBTI persons are able to be visible online and offline. A lot more events and activities can be tracked down to LGBTI organisations existing and forming. Now more and more people are beginning to work within these organisations, so there is professionalisation of these organisations.

All of this is good news for organisations hoping to be efficient in their systems and procedures, but difficult for a community still ridden with poverty, with self-esteem issues, with lack of information and limited access to resources. Also, these communities are still only visible or accessible or able to know each other within urban areas, with low information within rural areas.

When we also think about the fact that Kenya has had a high rate of internally displaced persons, we also think of the increase of targeted terrorism and militarisation in Kenya. What that means is that with security, with LGBTI

---

3   For more information on the introduction of new laws in Africa, see Jjuuko and Tabengwa, ch. 2, this volume; on decriminalisation in India, see Narrain, ch. 1, this volume; and on globalising the conversation, with emphasis on strategies for decriminalisation in Kenya, see Anthony Oluoch being interviewed on 1 Aug. 2012 by Immah Reid, GALCK and Envisioning. An excerpt is included in the documentary, *A Short Film on Kenyan LGBTI Stories* (2013).

people being a vulnerable population and being also a stigmatised population, these circumstances affect them even more deeply. Organisations are not prepared or thinking through how to deal with the ever-changing political or socioeconomic aspect of the world.

One effect we've seen on ITGNC people, with threats of both domestic and interstate terrorism, is increased surveillance and security all over the country. That means there are more gender-segregated security checkpoints, more scrutiny of state identification, and generally more regulation and restriction of bodies and movement. All of this leaves ITGNC people more vulnerable to state violence.

Guillit: Organising with MWA was difficult. As a new member, I had little information and often didn't know what was going on, as members were often left in the dark. Those of us who came from slum areas especially felt excluded, because we were never selected to represent the group at any meetings. MWA's programmes were offered in English, and because of where I came from I wasn't used to conversing in English. So that meant it was difficult to participate. Many members just came because they were getting paid a stipend if they participated in meetings and events. It's easy to say that they shouldn't have done that, but many needed even that small money to survive.

At the time there were also a lot of physical attacks on gays and lesbians, especially in the slums, because the slums are both densely populated and very community-oriented. Everyone knows everyone else's business and polices their behaviour so it's harder there to have privacy. The norms in these areas are focused on religion and tradition. There isn't as much outreach from LGBTI organisations to these areas, so being gay or lesbian is still seen as being alien. Violence in general was more common in the area where I grew up, so that also applied to LGBTI people. The organisations that existed at the time didn't have any way of dealing with this, or with other issues like being thrown out by family and becoming homeless.

Since then, leadership has changed many times and people are trying to do things differently. But it still always ends up with hierarchy and lack of transparency and communication. This is not just MWA, but most of the LGBTI organisations in Kenya. Staff often become defensive about their position and are unwilling to share with group members. Skills and opportunities are not passed on or shared within the group, so the leaders gain a lot of skills and experience while the members stay the same. I guess you could say that there's a lack of mentorship within organisations.

Kat: The nature of activist work ended up creating problems within organisations, as it meant that those who were most deeply affected by intersectional issues such as poverty, homelessness and lack of access to education and employment were not the ones who decided what programmes to run and how to run them.

Leaders often had access to more formal education. They often ended up in positions of leadership because they had the skills to run the organisation in a fashion similar to a business or corporation. This is not to say that they shouldn't have been in leadership positions, as they were usually very passionate people who dedicated so much of their time, energy and resources to doing this work. But there was little reflection on ways to do the work differently to benefit everyone.

As a result of this configuration there were frequently whispers of classism within organisations, yet these issues were tiptoed around and never clearly addressed or resolved. Oftentimes organisations' relationships with donors would dictate the focus of their work, whether intentionally or not, since groups would need to run programs in a particular way in order to report back effectively.

But not all LGBTI organising happens in such a public fashion. There have always been and will always be LGBTI people organising informally and supporting each other through social networks. People who take in a friend who's been kicked out of their family home, or give food and a couch to crash on to someone who's been assaulted. People providing all kinds of domestic and emotional labour that we don't necessarily see or count as activist work, but is just as valuable as the professional work.

Po: A positive change has been the diversity that has grown within LGBTI organising itself. More trans and intersex people have come out, more organisations are visible and working. Gender non-conforming people are also coming out, and gender non-conforming politics are being put into the conversation. More people are becoming able to access resources because of the awareness that's been created. So there's been a lot of change and a lot of growth.

Largely, LGBTI organising was done in Kenya through the HIV/AIDS avenue, through the public health access avenue. And then over time the human rights-based approach was used, and the engagement of the judiciary, such as in the National Gay and Lesbian Human Rights Commission's case to be registered as an NGO.[4] Organisations, events and activities will be found within the city centre, and mostly within Nairobi, the capital city. But organising also goes on in other cities. And there's a lot of influence from the donor world. A lot of organisations have been formed predominantly because of donors and there is money that can be accessed.

---

4   *Eric Gitari v. Non-Governmental Organisations Co-ordination Board and four others*, eKLR, 2015, see http://kenyalaw.org/caselaw/cases/view/108412 (accessed 8 Feb. 2018).

KAT: Public LGBTI organising is so hierarchical and heavily donor-dependent for a number of reasons. One factor is the huge presence and influence of the development industry in the country. The UN is there, along with all sorts of major international development players. When people are constantly surrounded by this development paradigm of improving lives via time-bound, measurable projects executed by 'experts', it starts to feel like that's just how you organise. It also means that the human rights framework is employed pretty much across the board within LGBTI groups, since it's the framework that people are most familiar with. But this framework doesn't resonate well in many contexts and feels alien to many people.

In my previous research with queer women activists in Nairobi, many activists talked about the pragmatic use of the human rights framework as something that made sense to international donors, and to an extent within the local context. However it did not sit as well in more grassroots contexts away from NGO spaces because of its potential to sound imperialist and donor-driven (Dearham, 2013). This may be so particularly in Kenya where the UN is visibly segregated from grassroots communities. There is a lot of scepticism about the UN, which of course is the originator of many of the human rights instruments, being used to argue for LGBTI rights. Many people are cynical about how the UN's existence benefits impoverished and marginalised communities. So while human rights arguments may play well in certain contexts, for example in the courts or with other agencies and bodies employing the human rights framework, they are not as readily accepted in the village or in urban slums. While the concepts underpinning the human rights framework are universal, the language itself is not and is often perceived as being Western (ibid.).

Considering how much sexual and gender diversity there is within communities across Kenya and the continent, there are many avenues for approaching this in a culturally appropriate way. I think the use of the human rights framework by LGBTI organisations actually makes their work easier to dismiss by folks who think that being LGBTI is an 'un-African' import – even if this is simply a convenient political justification for homophobia. It is important to continue to use rights-based approaches where this is effective, recognising both the utility and the limitations of this framework.

When we're working specifically for 'LGBTI rights' that also means we are often working independently from other movements that we could build stronger alliances with. We are so separate from people working on issues like land rights, labour, economic justice and democracy, for instance. We tend to become focused on building awareness for ourselves without acknowledging the multiplicity of factors that affect all of us. There's a lack of intersectional analysis in that sense, and lack of solidarity with other interconnected movements.

There are more groups now doing outreach work with people from all walks of life, sharing their stories and personalising them in a way that is humanising and approachable. I really love that and think that documentation, storytelling and other forms of art are wonderful ways of connecting with people who mistakenly see us as threatening to their traditions and communities. This is part of the reason why Envisioning's research work and particularly the participatory video-making is so important – because it is using storytelling to explore these complex issues in an accessible and relatable way. In Kenya, other organisations that are using storytelling and documentary-based approaches to reach out and expand the conversation around LGBTI lives and issues include the Nest Collective,[5] None on Record: Stories of Queer Africa,[6] and Artists for Recognition and Acceptance.[7]

GUILLIT: From my own perspective, the reason we organise this way is because of the social and environmental norms in Kenya and in most of Africa. That's the way we were raised, in a patriarchal society where the one person at the head of the household makes all the decisions. Our political structures and schooling are the same, everywhere there is this extreme hierarchy. I think that's how we have been shaped by colonialism.

When the colonisers came, they always had someone within the community who would speak on their behalf, represent their views and carry out their orders within the community. Those people had more power, more money and access to land. And we've been raised to respect people who have power over others. It's very individualistic because it's not about the common good, but about what individuals can gain for themselves.

Reclaiming gender identity and expression

PO: ITGNC organising from the beginning has been left out. The conversation about gender has been solely about women and men. About gender-based violence focusing on cisgender women only. About gender in cisgender terms. But I also want to acknowledge the early solidarity efforts. In 2007 in Uganda, activists collected money to form the country's first transgender and intersex organisation. It was called TITs (Transgender, Intersex and Transsexuals) Uganda. And here in Kenya there's been the formation of TEA in 2008, and then Jinsiangu in 2011.

What that means is that there's been space. Also a lot of people came into contact with the feminist movement. And the feminist movement, knowingly or unknowingly, always brought about these politics of gender non-conformity. It

5 See www.thisisthenest.com (accessed 8 Feb. 2018).
6 See www.noneonrecord.com (accessed 8 Feb. 2018).
7 See https://www.mamacash.org/en/artists-for-recognition-and-acceptance-kenya (accessed 8 Feb. 2018).

was not specifically transinclusive but it did bring about important questioning of women's roles and it broke down barriers. So organising has always been happening. But organisations dealing with ITGNC people have only recently been formed in Kenya.

Also arrests of intersex and trangender people reported in the public news stimulated discussions. In one case the mother of an intersex child, dubbed Baby 'A', sued the registrar of birth and death certificates for refusal to indicate an appropriate gender marker.[8] A question mark was indicated on the register of birth in place of a gender marker, which meant that Baby 'A' never received a birth certificate. This would make it difficult for the child to access public services such as medical care and education, and basic legal rights like voting. The court ruled that Baby 'A' should be issued a birth certificate, though it specified that a third gender category would not be created for intersex people through this ruling. The attorney general was ordered to name a body that would take responsibility for conducting a census of intersex Kenyans and to develop guidelines and policies for their recognition and support.

Richard Muasya, an intersex person, was arrested for criminal activity, but then was really oppressed and violated throughout the detention and throughout the incarceration. Muasya was later awarded damages from the High Court in recognition of this abuse. He also proposed introduction of a third gender in Kenyan legislation, though this was rejected by the court.[9]

As we go on, we see that slowly the language, the people and the presentation are changing. The representation of these issues has continued to grow, and there continue to be spaces where ITGNC people can feel safer and issues can be raised.

I remember how Audrey got space at the GALCK centre, after she said that she as a trans person wanted to organise around trans issues. Then the whole board of GALCK had to sit down because this was so new for them, and they were against the idea of a 'man changing into a woman', as they put it. There were religious reasons, social reasons, just fear in itself. This existed even within the more progressive feminist spaces.

So the place in which ITGNC politics has been, and continues to be, is a very precarious place. It's a struggle to break the norm, to break the binary, to ask people to see beyond or without the binary. And also to struggle to understand how organising will be efficient and effective for ITGNC people.

GUILLIT: Within GALCK there was always some kind of internal conflict between groups. In the office, the space was shared between member organisations and there was a short wall that would partition the space for

8   *Baby 'A' and another v. attorney general and six others*, eKLR, 2014, see http:// kenyalaw.org/caselaw/cases/view/104234 (accessed 8 Feb. 2018).

9   *R.M. v. attorney general and four others*, eKLR, 2010, see http://kenyalaw.org/ caselaw/cases/view/72818 (accessed 8 Feb. 2018).

different groups. So we would always see and interact with one another. But none of the groups worked on intersections – each one focused on its own constituency only, which as I mentioned was mostly gay men and lesbians.

The gay and lesbian organisations did not take ITGNC issues seriously. They understood sexual orientation but didn't understand how gender minorities feel about their own bodies and that some of us want to transition. They would say that this is weird, or wrong, or a mental issue. They didn't understand the conflict of body and mind, which is why they didn't take it seriously, even though TEA made efforts to sensitise GALCK as a whole.

KAT: When I first became involved with GALCK in 2010, it was common to hear transphobic remarks in the office. TEA had a confrontational relationship with GALCK staff as a result, and the atmosphere was hostile to trans people.

GUILLIT: For intersex and gender non-conforming people, it's like they didn't exist. A few intersex people would come into the office, and it was like they were outsiders, like they didn't belong to the same family. It wasn't always said out loud, but someone doesn't need to ridicule you using words. It's just how they treat you. It was not a welcoming environment.

I volunteered for TEA for a few months, but I had to stop as I felt it was too emotionally draining. I also felt that I wasn't moving towards my goal of transition. I had seen videos of top surgery on the internet, but I had no idea of the steps I would have to take to get it myself in Kenya. There were no trans men to guide me, nobody who could say that they had gone through it and how.

PO: In the community there is a lot of observed, if not reported, poverty. There is limited access to education, limited access to healthcare, lack of information or very little information about ITGNC people. Not a huge representation of these people. Thus people still find it a foreign conversation. So there has always been imposed inferiority of ITGNC organising within the larger LGBTI organising or politics.

I want to acknowledge also that the acronyms, the language, the approach, the strategy, and the framework that are being used to raise awareness and to change the lives of people can be very constricting. Using this very limiting and narrow framework requires that every day there's a new name or letter added to the long list. I think we need to rethink how we are organising and what it means to be labelled or to label ourselves with this name.

The creation of Jinsiangu

GUILLIT: After leaving TEA, I was still a member of AFRA. As a member of AFRA, I did a fellowship programme with a pan-African social justice organisation called Fahamu Networks for Social Justice. A friend of mine was urging me to apply, and I liked the fact that they didn't care about your level of education or class. Not having gone to college or university wasn't a big deal. They just cared that you were part of a grassroots organisation. You didn't have to be a chairperson or a secretary or even hold any kind of position. You just had to be a member. I applied, with the help of my friend who also applied, and her girlfriend who helped me with the application. I was selected for an interview and got in.

The fellowship was for one year and it was an intense course. We discussed many things and we were placed in different organisations to learn from their work. That's when I realised that I can do much more than I thought, but there was still this fear, and I still didn't feel like my authentic self. The course gave me the space to explore myself and learn about how society works. They took us through how power can be used by people at a grassroots level if we work towards common goals. We learned how oppression can degrade you and hold you back from achieving your goals.

Through the Fahamu course I realised that my whole life I've been living for others and that I had to make a change. During my last placement in Rwanda, I decided to stop living for others. I'd been exploring the idea of being a trans person since I was young, never really knowing what it meant or why I felt so different. During the placement, I came out as an openly trans person to my friends and colleagues.

I shared this with Kat, who I was dating at the time and who is now my partner. She gave me strength and was a great support when I came out. She shared with me several books about being trans in different parts of the world that made me question a lot. At some point I realised that they all had a chapter describing my life. So at the end of the fellowship, in late 2011, I graduated as a trans person.

The gay and lesbian community didn't take my coming out seriously. I had always been a quiet, introverted person and let fear be my guide, so they didn't think I would have the courage even to transition socially and come out to my family. Some people told me that it was just a phase that I would go through, and others just didn't understand why I would want to transition at all. Other friends were supportive, some of them gay and some straight.

With Kat I started thinking through the idea of creating a group for intersex and trans people. We worked on the initial idea together. We thought of creating another group rather than joining up with an existing organisation, because we wanted to do things differently. Initially we didn't want to create a formal organisation, just an informal group where intersex and trans people could gather and learn from each other's experiences. I had met with a few other trans people, especially trans men, and an intersex person who had been shifted from group to group. They were interested in starting something apart so that they wouldn't get sucked into the politics of the existing LGBTI groups, since they felt it was not healthy for them. We all felt that we needed peer support, someone who would understand what we were going through, not even necessarily providing help.

KAT: I became involved in the creation of Jinsiangu organically, through discussions and brainstorming with Guillit during the final leg of the Fahamu fellowship. We had met a few trans activists in Rwanda and were feeling energised by many of Guillit's colleagues in the fellowship, who were supportive.

To me this work is important, because I feel that it's crucial to deconstruct gender roles and to separate expectations about one's human potential from the gender they were assigned at birth. Of course it was to a degree personal because I could see the toll that transphobia was taking on Guillit's physical and mental health, and on their[10] relationships and the opportunities that were available to them. But if you think about the issues that the ITGNC community are facing, there are so many interconnections with other movements. It's about bodily autonomy, about mental health, about violence from religious institutions, the state and the family. About access to appropriate medical care and being recognised as a member of society and even as a human being. These are issues that we all need to be concerned about, and often ITGNC people are most deeply affected.

GUILLIT: The group started in late 2011. Initially it was called Ushirikiano Panda (UP), which in Swahili means 'climbing together'. Later, our member Barbra Muruga suggested that we change the name to Jinsiangu (a contraction of the words *jinsia yangu*, my gender) since UP was a mouthful. At the beginning we were just targeting intersex and trans people, and later expanded to include gender non-conforming people as time went on. Po really challenged us on GNC inclusion when they came in, which was good for the growth of the group.

PO: I felt the need to organise around ITGNC issues because it's important. And I think it's been wrong that we grow up all our lives, even myself, analysing or seeing life through a cissexist perspective. It's important that we continue to challenge ourselves to accept, include, and build work around people's identities, people's politics, people's realities, people's lives. So that the work that we're doing can respond to the needs of these people. And my engagement with the ITGNC community was really to find a voice that we could all speak in that could begin or continue to articulate our needs. But also to begin to highlight or give direction to the solutions that we require so that we can be whole, healthy people.

---

10 Guillit identifies by the pronouns 'they', 'their' and 'them'.

There has been a lot of focus on transgender, and then over time we realised that intersex and gender non-conforming issues – and gender identity and expression in general – are very important. That they don't have to lie within the prospects of transgender and the narrowness that name or identity might take on. There was already TEA, which had over time decided that it wanted to work only on transgender issues. And it focused mostly on those who were transitioning, especially those going through a physical process of taking hormones, thinking of surgery and so on.

GUILLIT: I think it made sense for us to work with all gender minorities because for me as a trans person, I had felt that my issues were not well articulated within LGBTI groups. It took me a long time to get to where I am now; I understood what it was like to be silenced and ignored, and I didn't want to do that to others working on similar issues. We were all struggling with gender identity issues and non-conforming to gender binaries and norms. I thought that, through the peer groups, all of us ITGNC people could understand each other better and see how our issues are both different and similar. This wasn't always easy, but I think it was important for us not to repeat the same story of exclusion in Jinsiangu.

KAT: The belonging part was also very important to me, as someone who has experienced rejection and stigma within LGBTI spaces. I'm bisexual, which to me means that I have the potential to be attracted to people of my own and other genders. I quickly found that there is little respect for any kind of fluid identity within LGBTI spaces. There's a lot of biphobia that hinges on the fear of something that is not easily defined or pinned down. So it's pretty easy for bi people to fall into the cracks, since you are often ignored and dismissed by the community that you think is yours. This holds true for ITGNC people as well. I think for this reason, there is a potential for a beautiful and affirming alliance between ITGNC and bisexual/queer/fluid people. We are all struggling for self-determination.

The organisation started first as an intersex and transgender organisation, and later there was a lot of discussion around the inclusion of gender non-conforming/genderqueer/gender-fluid people as well. Po was one of the people who was really pushing for inclusion, and I'm so thankful for that. To me the exclusion of gender non-conforming people specifically from trans-focused organisations was analogous to the exclusion of bisexual people from gay and lesbian spaces. There is the fear of something unpin-downable, of an identity that is not so cut and dried and can shift and mutate and trouble categories. There is something so delicious yet vulnerable about being in that position. It scares the shit out of a lot of people who think that if your identity is not static, it is not real or not enough.

This also holds true for intersex people; there is a lot of shame and so many misconceptions about intersex bodies and where or how they fit in. It's interesting because in North America (and probably elsewhere), intersex movements are quite separate from LGBT movements. It's not clear to me how or why they came to be so linked in East and Southern Africa at least, but I would love to learn more about that.

In Kenya, as in so many places, non-consensual and unnecessary genital surgery is often performed on babies who are seen to be ambiguous at birth, primarily in urban areas. This is partly because home deliveries are more common in rural areas, since medical clinics are often inaccessible both in location and expense. In villages, intersex kids are often completely socially isolated and literally shut away from the community, causing immense emotional damage. Violence against intersex people is common.

There is also the question of bureaucratic documentation, since identity documents are important in order to secure employment, housing, travel documents, and to vote. Without identity documents that accurately reflect your gender identity, it's much more difficult to participate in all sorts of social institutions, which puts people in a vulnerable situation. This is common across the ITGNC spectrum. Ultimately I think it did only make sense for intersex and gender non-conforming people to be part of Jinsiangu, partly because they had played an integral role in the formation of the group, but mainly because safety, belonging, bodily autonomy and self-determination are common to all ITGNC people.

Po: Essentially life is understood through the aspect of being male or female, and thus citizenry will be recorded, will be validated, will be acknowledged on the basis of maleness or femaleness. What this means for intersex and gender non-conforming bodies, or trans bodies in general, is that you will forever have to fit, to pass, to change a part of yourself to suit the world that you're living in rather than living your life fully.

Jinsiangu would then be the place where people would feel safe and people would gather as a support group. Where people would think about their lives while doing everything they could to be able to change for the better. To be able to be whole again. What this means is that Jinsiangu was thought of as a collective. It would be a family, a space for members to come back to and feel human. Feel like they didn't need to explain, or be influenced by anything outside themselves. We met in people's houses, we cooked each other food, we cried together, we laughed together.

Jinsiangu envisioned addressing people's lives as we were. We wanted to develop information, data, statistics. We wanted to do work around people getting well enough to be able to do the work they need to do for themselves. For the change they wanted. It was also highly about psychosocial support, recognising the extent to which oppression happens to the bodies of ITGNC people and how few resources there are to seek redress and healing. So Jinsiangu was an important foundation for health. For safety. For wellness. For ensuring that a community was speaking its truth, and was speaking when and how it needed to speak. Jinsiangu envisioned working through our mental illnesses, dealing with our physical bodies. And then using our strength in the change that we wanted to see.

KAT: Psychosocial support was an important starting point for Jinsiangu, partly because of the nature of the group. At the beginning it was totally informal. We just wanted to create a space for people to share their stories, share resources and support each other. And maybe most importantly, to know that they were not alone in their experience. There's something so powerful about meeting others like you that nothing else can replicate. Just that feeling of connection and being recognised can do so much to combat isolation.

We wanted to avoid reproducing the oppression and imbalances of power we had seen in other groups. Initially we saw Jinsiangu as a collective, a group of like-minded people supporting each other however we could. Since at the time I identified as cisgender – and on top of that I was a foreigner – I tried to remain conscious of the fact that I was a guest in a space that was not mine and had more learning to do than anyone. So it was a challenge to navigate giving support and contributing what I could, but not taking up too much space or taking the lead when it wasn't warranted. I don't know that I was always successful, but I tried to remain mindful and also trusted the members to hold me accountable.

GUILLIT: Before Jinsiangu, peer and psychosocial support didn't really exist for us to talk deeply and be vulnerable about what we endure when we're out there alone. It eases you up to know that you're not abnormal. That you are what you are, and you need to be proud of it. It feels good to unload.

Later on, when we had funding, we added one-on-one therapy with a paid counsellor. This was because we found that a big priority for members was to transition physically. When we approached doctors about transitioning, most of them refused outright because they thought that gender transition is not part of 'African tradition' or that it was against the Bible. It was hard to find doctors even willing to work with us at all. When we did find some, they always wanted a letter from a psychologist, which normally would be out of reach, because it's too expensive for most of us. It's not an easy step to be evaluated for who you are, but it's something that was required by the doctors, and eventually many of the members wanted to access counselling for other issues relating to gender identity or their personal struggles. There was a lot of trauma and depression associated with growing up ITGNC.

At first for the peer support groups, we met at people's houses. This was partly just practical, since we had no funding, and we thought that it would be safer to meet in private spaces than in public. But it was also in order to see where each other lived in case of emergency or threats. It was important both to see where people lived physically and also to understand what kind of environment they were living in.

The evolution of Jinsiangu

GUILLIT: Eventually the number of members became too large to meet at people's homes. We were always concerned about safety, and a big crowd of ITGNC people attracted too much attention, so it became unsafe for the person whose home we were visiting. Neighbours ended up asking too many questions. At that time we started to fundraise so that we could meet elsewhere. At some point when the membership grew, and with more demand for funds, members had a vote on whether to make Jinsiangu a registered organisation. Most donors require that a group be registered and have its own bank account and staff to get funding, so that was a big consideration. In the end, the majority voted for registration, so we started that process in 2014 and were registered after a few months. In the registration process we did not mention that we were an ITGNC organisation, but said that we dealt with gender issues, in order to avoid any problems.

Members also wanted to do more than the support groups. The most pressing demand was access to medical services, and there was a lot of advocacy work that needed to be done with medical professionals. We started attending meetings and running trainings with doctors, expanding our networks. When we were forming the organisation we had to create positions and talk more about structures. Members wanted more of a hierarchical structure than the initial flat concept, I think because they had been in organisations before and had seen that's 'how it's done'.

Po: There were huge challenges in being a collective or thinking through being a collective. And so slowly, slowly, by donor expectations, by peer pressure Jinsiangu then became an NGO, using a rights-based approach to focus more on external advocacy like any other LGBTI organisation and moving away from our peer-support roots. It continues to look that way.

KAT: When the group decided to formalise, I had many concerns and I think a number of other members did too. It's one thing to hold peer-support groups in your living room, but creating sustainable programming in a community-led fashion is something else entirely. We held meeting upon meeting, trying to hammer out a structure that would work for us and establish guiding principles. Most of us didn't have much experience in this, so it was slow going – but I was proud that we did the work collaboratively and created all of these guidelines as a group. Later on we also held a strategic mapping with an organisational consultant. I think that this was helpful, but perhaps it was not internalised. The work is ongoing.

GUILLIT: Having a more hierarchical structure also put less pressure on members to be active. Because they weren't expected to be as involved in how things were run, they could participate less. I thought that this was not useful, because in my own experience, if I want transparency and want activities to suit my needs, I need to participate and be deeply involved. In hierarchical structures, you're not able to voice your issues, and your needs will not always be met. I think this is what happened with Jinsiangu.

Most of the members also didn't take up positions, either because they were not willing or not able to commit to the responsibility. I think there were a lot of misconceptions about what being a leader entailed, because of how in other organisations the leaders would always be the ones who are the most educated or most articulate. In Jinsiangu we communicated mostly in Swahili, but members felt that they had to communicate in English for the benefit of donors or in meetings. I think we could have found other ways of making things work.

KAT: Creating staff positions was useful in that it gave us some framework and helped us to divide up the work rather than everyone trying to do everything, which was satisfying but chaotic and ineffective. But once we created the positions and division of responsibility, there was a lot less membership engagement.

I guess we were quite idealistic. Maybe it didn't make sense to ask folks who have grown up in such hierarchical systems to embrace consensus-building. Maybe not everyone had the same vision. Maybe we hadn't built up enough trust. I really don't know the answer.

GUILLIT: Some of the other challenges we faced were financial. There wasn't enough funding to pay staff well or to run sustainable programmes, so that was another challenge in keeping people involved. It was always difficult to get donors to support medical services, since they were more focused on advocacy and training. It was also difficult to get funding for income-generating activities, which could have made us more autonomous. The argument from donors was that advocacy is more cost-effective than directly helping people access medical services, so they wouldn't fund anything related to transition. But advocacy is a slow process. In the meantime our members were struggling with dysphoria and depression.

KAT: We lacked the capacity and resources to actually accomplish everything we wanted to do. Inciting social change is a never-ending task, and change occurs in fits and starts. Once we decided to expand programming, we were so eager to take on so much. Members did step up in many ways. When we did outreach and training, people who had never run workshops were helping to design and facilitate them. Members met with rather intimidating groups of doctors, sharing their experiences and recommendations with people who didn't know the first thing about being an ITGNC person. That had a lot of impact. But still we struggled, in the sense that quite a small number of people ended up doing the bulk of the work and were constantly teetering on the edge of burnout.

It's a challenge in this kind of environment as well to balance the desire to portray some kind of professionalism in order to be taken seriously by our partners and funders with the desire to remain true to our roots and vision of inclusivity. If what we were doing was not useful to the people who were most vulnerable, those who wouldn't normally have access to 'professional' spaces, then what use was it?

It's always tricky to do this kind of work within the capitalist framework. Ultimately, at some point you need money to survive, so there's always tension between being able to do a lot of work without funding, yet needing to be paid to live. So you can either do side work to live, or you could become a 'professional activist' and focus your energies on this work. But the latter means that acquiring funding becomes a necessity and it's something that you end up dedicating a lot of energy to, especially if you're running a number of programmes that need constant support. There must be better ways of doing it, and I would like to learn more from others and explore different ways of organising.

When you have a group with a mix of paid position-holders and volunteers, that creates resentment. And some folks will become involved because it's just a job to them, not something they would be doing of their own volition, and that brings a different kind of energy that is not necessarily community-oriented. You can also accomplish a lot more when you have people who are able to commit a substantial amount of time to the work.

All that said, I am grateful to the funders who understood what we were about and respected Jinsiangu's vision and autonomy. Thanks to them and to the work of our members, we were able to carry out a lot of work that we wouldn't have been able to do otherwise. We established an ITGNC centre in Nairobi, which opened in late 2014. This is the first space in Kenya run by and for ITGNC people, a space where people are free to express themselves without that fear that exists even in LGBTI spaces. It's important not only for safety, but for community building and autonomy.

Jinsiangu also did outreach visits to other parts of Kenya to build up networks and support systems across the country. We created *Resilience*, a resource guide that included information on mental and physical health, legal issues and gender transition alongside personal stories, photos and artwork. And we held the first public ITGNC Day of Remembrance in Kenya. Plus the trainings with medical doctors and the psychosocial support piece. All of this happened within the first two or three years of Jinsiangu's existence, so we were able to accomplish quite a bit with the limited resources available to us.

On art as activism

KAT: Jinsiangu uses art in almost all of its programmes, both as a way of communicating to others and for the members to have another avenue towards wellness. Various forms of art were part of our outreach programmes, part of our research and publications, and part of our events. In November 2015, Jinsiangu held Kenya's first ITGNC-themed art exhibition, Bodies Unbound, where members' artwork was auctioned off to help subsidise medical costs.

To me the use of art was an important component of that drive to make Jinsiangu and its communications as accessible as possible. Even if you don't necessarily understand the terminology or relate to people's stories, you can still gain an understanding of their lives and inner worlds through their art. It allows people to reveal as much or as little as they like; it's visceral and thought-provoking.

PO: From the early onset Jinsiangu tried to engage with popular culture and art. At our first public event, the ITGNC Day of Remembrance in 2013, we had people performing poetry, we had T-shirt making and banner-making. People were very engaged and excited to be able to engage through other forms of expression. And to be able to remain anonymous or to be known, but still be able to do more than write or read or give a formal presentation. Just be. Art is very powerful and has helped a lot of us. Even though we're still struggling with finding a way to locate it within our lives.

KAT: Art is also an incredible tool for healing, as it helps people process and externalise their experiences and identities. Part of wellness is developing self-knowledge and owning your story, seeing how you fit into the world around you. You don't need a particular training or skill. Any form of movement or scribble or doodle is valuable if used as a form of exploration.

GUILLIT: I like to use art for activism, because art makes it easier for people to understand – through art, people can relate to what you've been through. It creates a story that stays in someone's mind much more easily than a report or a paper. Art makes it easier for people to empathise and remember. It creates a history so that in the future people will remember the past struggles. Some of this history has been documented through Envisioning's work.[11]

It also helps you express what you're going through. Putting my thoughts and feelings down in poetry, painting, or drawing helps me to destress and avoid other ways of coping that can drain me emotionally.

Dreaming the future

Po: My relationship with Jinsiangu became strained. There was a lot of conflict and we weren't able to find a way to resolve this conflict in a healthy way. I was part of the advisory board, but I left it because I didn't think the group was being run ethically and staying true to its values.

But I remain committed to the dream of Jinsiangu. I can see the place, I can see the change, I can see the dream turn out. And it's going to be difficult, but it's work that we have to do.

KAT: As a member who identified as cisgender at that time, it was always the plan for me to step back from Jinsiangu once it was up and running. This is because Jinsiangu was always meant to be run by and for ITGNC people. Some cisgender people are members, but the group is careful to ensure that ITGNC people are the decisionmakers, and the cisgender members are there to learn and provide support. So after 2013 I became less involved and eventually moved away entirely. I'm simply cheering Jinsiangu on from afar.

I have faith that community members will make it work and do what makes sense for them. After all, it's their lives at stake. There is great talent and skill within the ITGNC community, and I trust that there will always be members who are committed and invested in making the world safer for themselves and others.

GUILLIT: I was on the advisory board of Jinsiangu for a while, and left it once I felt I couldn't serve anymore. I've relocated to another country, so it's hard to be involved very much. The move wasn't easy because I felt like I was leaving just as Jinsiangu was starting to take baby steps. Members seemed to be participating more, and I miss that community.

KAT: The environment has already changed quite a lot in the past ten years, and I think it will continue to change. Partly this is due to the work of organisations.

11 See www.envisioningLGBT.com (accessed 8 Feb. 2018), which includes research outcomes such as video shorts made by Envisioning in collaboration with its community partners, one of which is GALCK. It also includes *Telling Our Stories*, a series of video portraits of 30 international activists/community members in eight countries. The Kenyan Portraits are available at: http://envisioning-tellingourstories. blogspot.com/p/kenya-2.html (accessed 8 Feb. 2018).

TEA pushing for legal reform and recognition of trans people's names and genders.[12] Audrey telling her story on national television and being unashamed of who she is in the face of public ridicule. Jinsiangu members reaching out to other ITGNC people all over the country, forming bonds, and helping each other through the day. Talking with doctors and judges about their lives and about reframing the way we talk about bodies and sex and gender. There are also ITGNC people working in different industries and movements, which is healthy and helps prevent the ITGNC movement from becoming too narrow and static.

Change is also due in large part to the ITGNC people all over the country who are surviving and thriving in their own environments. Trans sex workers looking out for each other through informal networks. Intersex kids who find support within their communities when their parents are abusive. Genderqueer people finding ways of being in their bodies. It's important for us to recognise that the formation of NGOs is just one way of organising and doesn't necessarily address everyone's needs. We can build community and lift ourselves up in so many ways.

Po: The challenges that we face now are in relationships and leadership, and sustainability of resources and access to those resources. And the equitable sharing of those resources. Also information, research, commitment and consistency.

The fact is that gender itself is a complex issue. Gender identity and expression is an even more complex issue. And gender justice continues to remain a dream. Continues to remain people's destination rather than people's practice. And this is where I always feel that we get caught up.

I see the future of ITGNC organising in Kenya growing and still taking the form and the space of formal NGO structures. But I also see all kinds of people who are working actively towards ensuring that this conversation of gender is going to continue to grow. To be more radical.

So I think that there is a future in organising for ITGNC, and the future comes with a lot of work. Comes with a lot of commitment. Calls each one of us to be alive to how we have been socialised. To how comfortable we've become within the binary. And to begin to challenge ourselves to unlearn the binary. And to accept that gender requires of us to be really present. Present and working at the now.

GUILLIT: Times are changing, in the sense that Jinsiangu has at least had the chance to work with medical doctors and build networks with different activists

---

12 See *Republic v. Kenya National Examinations Council and Audrey Mbugua Ithibu*, eKLR, 2014, available at: http://kenyalaw.org/caselaw/cases/view/101979 (accessed 8 Feb. 2018).

and people on the ground. A lot of Kenyan LGBTI organisations now focus on psychosocial support, and I feel proud that Jinsiangu was a leader in that, as we were one of the first to offer that kind of programming. We really pushed for recognition of how much living with constant discrimination impacts ITGNC people's mental health. The group tried to address that by offering different forms of healing through both peer support and counselling. Maybe now it will be easier for the group to gain allies to support their programming.

Po: An ideal future for ITGNC people would be a future where each and every person has the freedom to be who they are. To live their lives with all the support that they can get. And to be accountable for their actions, and responsible for the lives that they want and the choices that they want to make.

So in essence, even with the struggles, even with the fact that organising continues to be very difficult, especially through the LGBTI and human rights frameworks, there's the importance of people waking up to the connectedness of oppression. To the fact that there's a connection between the rates of poverty, the rates of gender-based violence, the rates of cissexism and the lack of information. And unless we are continually willing to work to teach each other, to share, to learn, to listen, this work will continue to remain very difficult.

GUILLIT: From my experience, if ITGNC people are able to voice their concerns and access services, rates of depression, suicide and substance abuse will go down. People can be themselves and live their lives without feeling like they need to hide who they are. They just need to be.

References

Aarmo, M. (1999) 'How homosexuality became "un-African": the case of Zimbabwe', in E. Blackwell and S.E. Wieringa (eds.) *Female Desires: Same-Sex Relations and Transgender Practices across Cultures* (New York, NY: Columbia University Press), pp. 255–80.

Dearham, K. (2013) 'NGOs and queer women's activism in Nairobi', in S. Ekine and H. Abbas (eds.) *Queer African Reader* (Nairobi: Pambazuka Press), pp. 186–202.

Epprecht, M. (2004) *Hungochani: the History of a Dissident Sexuality in Southern Africa* (Montréal and Kingston: McGill-Queen's University Press).

Epprecht, M. and L. Clowes (2008) *Unspoken Facts: a History of Homosexualities in Africa* (Harare: Gays and Lesbians of Zimbabwe).

Hoad, N. (2007) *African Intimacies: Race, Homosexuality, and Globalization* (Minneapolis, MN: University of Minnesota Press).

Morgan, R. and S. Wieringa (eds.) (2005) *Tommy Boys, Lesbian Men and Ancestral Wives: Female Same-Sex Practices in Africa* (Johannesburg: Jacana).

Murray, S.O. and W. Roscoe (eds.) (1998) *Boy Wives and Female Husbands: Studies of African Homosexualities* (New York, NY: St Martin's Press).

Documentary films
A Short Film on Kenyan LGBTI Stories (2013) dir. C. Kaara, J. Muthuri and I. Reid (Kenya and Canada: Gay and Lesbian Coalition of Kenya and Envisioning Global LGBT Human Rights), available at: https://vimeo.com/73786260. Extract from interview with Anthony Oluoch quoted.
Telling Our Stories (Kenya Portraits section) (2014) (Kenya and Canada: Gay and Lesbian Coalition of Kenya and Envisioning Global LGBT Human Rights).

14

Telling Our Stories: Envisioning participatory documentary

Nancy Nicol

> *For apart from inquiry, apart from the praxis, individuals cannot be truly human.*
> *Knowledge emerges only through invention and re-invention, through the restless,*
> *impatient, continuing, hopeful inquiry human beings pursue in the world, with*
> *the world, and with each other.*
>
> *Paulo Freire (1970)*

Participatory documentary was a key part of the output and methodology of Envisioning Global LGBT Human Rights (Envisioning), working together with community partners and human rights defenders who are engaged in efforts to transform society and advance lesbian, gay, bisexual, transgender and intersex (LGBTI) rights in Africa, the Caribbean and India. In the spirit of Freire, this method of documentary-making involves participants in the process of telling their stories, to engage community, advocate for social justice and transform their lives. It is a powerful and accessible way of investigating human rights violations, and of documenting and celebrating stories of resistance.

Freire's classic text continues to be relevant and increasingly urgent as capitalist crisis and neoliberal policies degrade living standards, deepening exploitation, impoverishment, oppression and conflict. In the Global South this process is often fuelled by neo-colonialist and religious right interventions with particularly negative impacts on sexual minorities. At the same time, LGBTI rights organisations, which have grown significantly in the Global South, are challenging these dehumanising impacts and are engaged in efforts to transform their communities and advance sexual orientation and gender identity (SOGI) rights.

On 9 November 2016, the morning following the election of Donald Trump, I attended a hearing of a US Federal Court case in Springfield, Massachusetts. Together with activists from Sexual Minorities Uganda (SMUG) and their legal representatives from the Center for Constitutional Rights in New York

N. Nicol (2018) 'Telling Our Stories: Envisioning participatory documentary', in N. Nicol et al. (eds.) *Envisioning Global LGBT Human Rights: (Neo)colonialism, Neoliberalism, Resistance and Hope* (London: Human Rights Consortium, Institute of Commonwealth Studies), pp. 371–401.

City, we were attending the proceedings of a precedent-setting case, *Sexual Minorities Uganda v. Scott Lively*. Prominent US anti-gay evangelical extremist Scott Lively was present at the hearing, which was being held in his home state. He sat with his legal counsel and supporters on the opposite side of the court. SMUG and their legal counsel asserted in the case that Lively, through his anti-gay activism in Uganda, bore responsibility for depriving LGBTI Ugandans of their fundamental human rights, based solely on their identity – the definition of persecution under international law. Lawyers for SMUG argued that this effort led to the introduction of the Anti-Homosexuality Bill (AHB), which Lively, in collaboration with Ugandan government officials and religious leaders, helped engineer. SMUG was able to sue Lively under a US law in which a US citizen can be charged for serious human rights violations in other countries. This hearing followed a groundbreaking ruling three years prior, in August 2013, where Judge Michael Ponsor held that, 'Widespread, systematic persecution of LGBTI people constitutes a crime against humanity that unquestionably violates international norms'.[1] The case had significant implications for US-based religious right extremists who have sought to prevent decriminalisation of same-sex intimacy and fostered hatred against sexual minorities in the Global South.

In support of SMUG's case, video interviews gathered by SMUG and Envisioning for the documentary *And Still We Rise* (2015), were submitted as evidence in the case. The material recorded the impact of the Anti-Homosexuality Act (AHA), through interviews with service providers, community members, leaders and human rights defenders in Uganda that spoke to the escalation of human rights violations, arrests and closure of services following parliament passing the AHA in December 2013 and its enactment into law in March 2014.

The impact of Western-based religious right actors, neoliberal policies and local opportunistic political forces on LGBT rights and on civil rights in the Global South is a theme explored by a number of contributions to this anthology,[2] and is examined in the Ugandan context in *And Still We Rise*. Ugandan lawyer Nicholas Opiyo argues in the documentary,[3] that politicians have used the assault on homosexuals as part of a deepening assault on civil liberties and political opposition:

1   *Sexual Minorities Uganda v. Scott Lively*, 960 F. Supp. 2d 304, 316 (D. Mass. 2013). On 5 Jun. 2017, the court affirmed SMUG's charges against Lively; however, it dismissed the case on jurisdictional grounds. For details see: https://ccrjustice.org/home/what-we-do/our-cases/sexual-minorities-uganda-v-scott-lively (accessed 8 Feb. 2018).

2   See for example: Jjuuko and Tabengwa, ch. 2; Mbaru et al., ch. 6; Orozco, ch. 9; and Jjuuko and Mutesi, ch. 10.

3   Interviewed on 21 Nov. 2014 by Richard Lusimbo, SMUG and Envisioning. An excerpt is included in the documentary *And Still We Rise* (2015).

I think for me the defining moment for civil liberties, not just in Uganda but around the world, is 9/11. The unholy alliance between states allegedly to fight terrorism, has provided, in my view, a fertile excuse for the limitation of fundamental rights and freedoms. So, all around the world states are now 'coming together' to fight terrorism; and in doing so have found an excuse for limitation of fundamental liberties and rights. In Uganda, that has been expressed in the enactment of the Anti-Money Laundering Act, in the enactment of the Public Order Management Act, in the enactment of the Phone Tapping Law, the Interception of Communications Act. So there is an onslaught on civil liberties across the world.

And Still We Rise and the interview material from it submitted to the court, is one example of the way in which participatory documentary contributed to the goals of the Envisioning partnership's research, documentation and knowledge mobilisation. This chapter gives an overview and synopsis of the work created through Envisioning, and outlines how the documentaries were made. I hope that Envisioning's experience provides a useful template for others interested in using this type of filming to strengthen and support struggles for social justice and equality.

Research/Creation

Envisioning's methodology sought to synthesise creative practice with participatory action research using participatory documentary. According to Nichols (2010), this mode of documentary is characterised by engagement between the filmmaker and film participants through interviews; and/or where the filmmaker is or becomes part of the events being documented. Such work articulates a 'point of view' rather than a neutral or objective stance as in conventional journalism. Point-of-view documentary is one approach taken by Envisioning; however, participatory documentary may also involve the participant or subject in the filmmaking process itself. Such an approach,pioneered by the Challenge for Change/Société nouvelle documentary programme in Canada in 1967, sought to place the tools of production into the hands of those who were the subject of the film.[4]

In developing Envisioning's approach to participatory documentary, I drew on 30 years' experience of creating documentaries with diverse communities and organisations. As an early member of video-art collectives[5] in Canada, my work was influenced by, and contributed to, creative developments in video art characterised by experimentation, as well as by community-based video that

---

4   Challenge for Change/Société nouvelle was an initiative of the National Film Board (NFB) of Canada,which ran between 1967 and1980. For a history of the programme see: Waugh et al. (2010).

5   For example, Trinity Square Video, one of Canada's first artist-run centres and its oldest media arts centre, founded in Toronto, 1971.

sought to create new approaches to film/video-making and to expose issues and foster social change. Programmes such as the Challenge for Change/Société nouvelle in Canada, as well as efforts to democratise broadcast media, as with Paper Tiger Television's[6] work in the United States, resonated with the social movement politics of the time which sought to challenge corporate control. Feminist, Black feminist, Marxist, new left, and postcolonial perspectives, as well as involvement in struggles for social justice and civil and human rights shaped my formative years, and deepened my understanding of the forces that shape contemporary conflicts and struggles. These influences informed my documentary practice: a commitment to social justice and a participatory approach have remained at the centre of my work. From the mid 1990s to 2005, my research and documentary work increasingly focused on LGBT history and organising. It includes directing a body of work (2002–9) which examines social and legal developments on SOGI issues in Canada spanning 40 years, and examinations through the documentary *One Summer in New Paltz, a Cautionary Tale* (2008) and an article (Nicol and Smith, 2008) of relationship recognition and the campaign for equal marriage in the US and Canada. This work integrated creative practice with extensive research drawing on sociology, legal consciousness literature and sociolegal studies to document and analyse the social movement histories under investigation.

Envisioning brought together community-based researchers, activists, videographers, creative artists, professional legal and human rights experts and academic researchers. It required an open reading of research that was alive to different possible interpretations, rather than a fixed one, and could respond to challenges and change. Envisioning appreciated that communities which are engaged in struggles for human rights or social justice are uniquely positioned to contribute experience, expertise and analysis. It sought to bring people's experience to life, by documenting and examining stories of injustice, resistance and movements for social change from the perspectives of those directly involved – through their voices. Trust, dialogue, exchange, openness, caring and willingness to experiment and to challenge perceived ideas were all part of this process.

The core goals of this work were to put on record human rights violations and the experiences of LGBT people, as well as to document community experiences and organising histories – all needs that Envisioning partners had clearly identified. However, while documentation is an important resource for community mobilising and public education, it can be challenging for grassroots groups that are often under pressure just to respond to immediate conditions. Envisioning sought to fill the gap by providing resources, mentorship and support for documentation by means of participatory documentary. In practice,

---

6   Paper Tiger Televison, a video collective based in New York City, produces public access television, community screenings and media literacy programmes.

depending on the priorities and needs of the community partners, the extent and type of participation varied across the work carried out by Envisioning. I adjusted my approach as necessary, acting as an educator, facilitator, mentor, collaborator, editor or co-editor, and director or co-director, depending on the priorities and needs of the partners. As the project developed, collaboration across the team deepened, resulting in a number of co-directed and/or co-edited projects, such as the aforementioned *And Still We Rise*, co-directed by Richard Lusimbo and me, and *The Time Has Come* (2013), which was shot by community partners from Africa and the Caribbean under the direction of Envisioning partner, ARC International.

Working with community partners, I directed or co-directed three feature-length documentaries: *No Easy Walk to Freedom* (2014), *And Still We Rise* (2015) and *Sangini* (2016). These films are characterised by a multiplicity of voices woven together to create a layered, complex, collective story that probes into shifting societal attitudes, social movement politics, conflicts, challenges, issues and history – a method I have developed in my past works on histories of organising. The contributions made by partners and interviewees were essential to undertaking these documentaries. Partners assisted with research development, facilitated connections with those interviewed, provided outreach to marginalised communities, supported translation, conducted research; and, depending on the partner's priorities and needs, interviewed participants and directed or co-directed documentary outcomes. Dialogue and exchange informed the researchers' and videographers' understanding of local and national histories and issues.

Creating documentaries on social movements is fraught with challenges, including a need for sensitivity to the internal debates characterising such movements. This was particularly challenging, given the complexities of culture, religion and politics in the context of economic 'development' and globalisation and their impact on the diverse and complex societies that made up the Envisioning partnership. The contribution of community partners who were directly involved in organising efforts and community building was essential to the work. *No Easy Walk to Freedom* drew on the experience and advice of these partners, and of participants at the forefront of the struggle to advance LGBT rights in India, and on 55 interviews in four major urban centres in India. Those interviewed included queer community leaders, members and activists; scholars in queer theory and same-sex love in Indian history; HIV/AIDS prevention outreach workers; and lawyers at the forefront of the constitutional challenge to Section 377 of the Indian Penal Code. The interviewees contributed first-hand knowledge, expertise and varied experiences in relation to the issues, communities and histories investigated in the documentary.

Methodologically this 'bottom-up' approach enables content to precipitate from a rich and varied data set. Such flexibility is key when exploring social issues and histories of social movements and using ethnographic data. It facilitates a nuanced intersectional perspective that seeks to bring out internal contradictions and complexities, while maintaining coherence. A similar methodology is used in *Sangini*, created in partnership with the Sangini Trust, an LBT shelter located in Delhi. The documentary is based on interviews I did with Betu Singh[7] and Maya Shankar, who together ran the shelter, as well as with lesbians and transgender people who sought shelter there, Sangini's legal counsel, Shivangi Rai (Lawyers Collective) and two leading activists and feminists, Maya Sharma and Pramada Menon, who address issues facing lesbians and female-to-male (FTM) transgender people. *Sangini* probes into issues of patriarchal dominance, women's oppression, class, rural/urban differences and challenges, family pressures, forced marriage, sexual violence and Sangini's work to educate women on understanding their rights.

A similar approach was taken for *And Still We Rise*, filmed by the SMUG participatory documentary team, which draws on 42 interviews carried out by Richard Lusimbo. The documentary built on three years of collaboration with SMUG and represents a transformative process of creation and learning from each other. I will discuss the content of and the contribution made by *And Still We Rise*, *No Easy Walk to Freedom* and *The Time Has Come* later in this chapter.

Participatory documentary teams

Working with community partners, Envisioning established documentary teams in seven countries in the Caribbean and Africa.[8] They comprised three persons, a researcher and two videographers, positions either designated to existing staff or to people hired by the community partner. Envisioning sought to support capacity enhancement in research methodology and participatory documentary-making for individual team members, and to strengthen the capacity of the community partner.

Envisioning provided equipment, resources and funding to support all aspects of the work, including travel for the purposes of conducting research, documentation and outreach nationally. Using small-format HD cameras, computer-based editing software and dissemination over the internet, the

---

7   An early activist in the Indian lesbian movement, Betu founded Sangini in 1997. Sadly, Betu passed away on 4 Oct. 2013 and Sangini was forced to close. The film is dedicated to Betu and Maya in appreciation of their courageous groundbreaking work.

8   The community partners were: Society Against Sexual Orientation Discrimination (SASOD), Guyana; United and Strong, Saint Lucia; Jamaica Forum for Lesbians, All-Sexuals and Gays (J-FLAG), Jamaica; United Belize Advocacy Movement (UNIBAM), Belize; Lesbians, Gays and Bisexuals of Botswana (LeGaBiBo), Botswana; Gay and Lesbian Coalition of Kenya (GALCK), Kenya; and SMUG, Uganda.

project sought to make the process of creating documentary accessible and useful. The video equipment package was selected to balance ease of use with capacity enhancement, having the dual goals of keeping technical aspects accessible for first-time videographers, while enhancing their skills and experience.[9]

Together with York University research assistants, we ran research and participatory video workshops for the abovementioned teams at the community partners' offices. Workshops covered such technical, creative and research aspects as production planning, camera techniques, sound recording, lighting, location shooting. They also ranged across interview techniques, informed consent, participatory action research and ethical considerations to take into account when making participatory documentary. The workshops were coordinated with local or regional Envisioning research team meetings and often set up to coincide with events that provided an opportunity for community researchers and videographers to develop their video skills, with mentorship and support on hand. For example, in February 2012, the first workshops were held at United and Strong in Saint Lucia in conjunction with the event, International Dialogue: Focus on Strengthening the Caribbean Response.[10] Following the workshop, United and Strong videographers recorded the conference. In May 2012, we did workshops with African partners, starting with Lesbians and Gays of Botswana (LeGaBiBo) in Botswana, and later that month with SMUG, and the Gay and Lesbian Coalition of Kenya (GALCK) at the GALCK centre in Nairobi, Kenya. Following that workshop, participants filmed Nairobi's International Day Against Homophobia (IDAHO) organised by GALCK.

Following production workshops, Envisioning provided video-editing equipment and software,[11] and Kaija Siirala[12] and I led video-editing workshops. We created technical manuals for the documentary teams, and provided

9   The Envisioning video-production package included: a Sony HXRNX70 compact AVCHD HD camcorder, a fluid head tripod, three types of microphone (a unidirectional with boom pole and alternative camera mount, a wireless microphone, a handheld cardioid microphone), a tabletop microphone tripod and a basic light kit. In addition we provided high-capacity rugged hard drives. The camcorder had professional balanced line microphone inputs to support the use of external microphones.

10 The International Dialogue: Focus on Strengthening the Caribbean Response was an international conference organised by ARC International, United and Strong and Envisioning in Saint Lucia.

11 The Envisioning editing package included a Mac Pro laptop, external drives, and software including: Adobe Premiere Pro CS6 editing software, Adobe PhotoShop, Adobe After Effects, and Microsoft Word to support transcription work.

12 Kaija Siirala was an Envisioning staff member who assisted me with the participatory video work. Kaija coordinated the video projects, contributed to the editing, helped liaise with community partners, and gave them support and technical advice.

Figure 16. LeGaBiBo participatory documentary team workshop, Gaborone, Botswana, 1 May 2012. Left to right: Terra Long (MFA, York University), Yoon Jin Jung (MFA), Tuna Mabuza, Phyllis Waugh, and seated in front: Tebogo Motshwane and Nancy Nicol. Photo credit: LeGaBiBo and Envisioning.

ongoing mentorship and support. Seeking ways to enhance connections across the project, Envisioning also developed peer-to-peer training by supporting the travel costs of researchers and videographers who had completed the workshops and gained experience in the field, to enable them to pass on their skills and experience to other partners. This process facilitated exchange on research and participatory documentary, fostered collaboration across differently located partners, and enhanced the teams' skills and confidence.

Creative practice and research: tensions

The Envisioning community partners were grassroots LGBT organisations, working under conditions of criminality. Gathering documentation on issues affecting LGBT persons as well as recording work being done to advance rights based on SOGI were significant needs identified by these partners, which Envisioning sought to address. But in addition to outcomes, process was equally important to the project goals. Participatory documentary involves community members and partners in research, including discussions about content, goals and questions of voice, audience, safety and security and ethical considerations. This collaborative process contributed to knowledge and capacity in research

Figure 17. GALCK and SMUG participatory documentary team workshop, GALCK Centre, Nairobi, Kenya, 16 May 2012. Back left to right: Yoon Jin Jung (MFA, York University), Nancy Nicol (Envisioning PI), Terra Long (MFA) and front left to right: Caroline Kaara (GALCK, videographer), Junic Wambya and Nkyooyo Brian (SMUG, videographers) and Jim Muthuri (GALCK, videographer). Photo credit: Envisioning Global LGBT Human Rights.

methodology, community building/outreach, skills exchange and knowledge mobilisation. We sought to place politics, ethics and creative response at the centre of the work.

Participatory documentary is based on an active engagement with the world and with others that builds context and interpretation through a creative process of interaction and collaboration over time. Creative practice takes a different approach to research and knowledge than conventional approaches to research do. Participatory documentary is not subject to a tightly designed methodology: it must be open-ended and highly creative to respond to the lived experiences of those taking part and the challenges they face. Similar to the intuitive response valued in creative practice, participatory documentary foregrounds experience as a kind of knowledge, one that supports and values a more intuitive approach to research, prioritising the voices of participants who are directly involved in the issues, the struggles or campaign histories being investigated. To be effective, the process must be inclusive and collaborative, engage communities, and respect their leadership and knowledge.

This approach was particularly necessary in the context of documenting the lives and experiences of sexual and gender minorities – experiences that are often denied and repressed, but at the same time are characterised by profoundly creative and courageous acts of resilience in the face of societal exclusion. As one example of this dual aspect of silence and resilience, Maya

Sharma,[13] recounts her work with tribal *Adivasi*[14] groups in rural India:

> Even in places where there are very few amenities or facilities, people
> have carved out their niche. I know nearly five to six women who have
> had breast surgery. They are very poor people. How they must have
> saved money! I know two couples very closely who had operations,
> got married, and have a child through IVF.[15] It's not as if they belong
> to the same caste or religion. They are interreligious and intercaste
> couples. Regardless, there's a lot of tolerance in their families and work
> places. It's very difficult for such people to live their lives. They've faced
> countless hardships and violence. But after all this, it's clear that people
> find a way. They live with courage.

Alongside each team's contributions, participatory documentary also values
those who give their time, knowledge and experiences through interviews and
focus groups. The documentary teams were often moved, at times to tears, by
the resilience and courage demonstrated in the stories the participants shared.
I was also greatly moved by the courage of the teams themselves, as they
negotiated their way through extremely difficult circumstances with profound
care and compassion in order to document the voices of the community.

Given the sensitive nature of working with vulnerable populations,
grassroots partners were best placed to know and understand local conditions
and to safeguard the security of those taking part. In practice this was fraught
with challenges. For example, participants were given the option of being
anonymous or on camera.[16] In all of our locations, community leaders who
were already publicly identified with SOGI issues were confident about being
on screen. From their perspective, their on-camera presence and public voice
was an essential part of movement building, generalising the lessons of the
struggle to advance LGBT rights and furthering public education on SOGI

---

13   Interviewed on 8 Nov. 2011 by author. An excerpt appears in the documentary *No Easy Walk To Freedom* (2014).

14   In India, Adivasis make up a significant minority, 8% of India's population. Land rights – ecological degradation caused by modernisation and development which has pushed indigeous peoples off ancestral lands – is a significant issue. According to the World Directory of Minorities and Indigenous Peoples, 'Adivasis is the collective name used for the many indigenous peoples of India. The term Adivasi derives from the Hindi word "adi" which means of earliest times or from the beginning and "vasi" meaning inhabitant or resident, and it was coined in the 1930s, largely as a consequence of a political movement to forge a sense of identity among the various indigenous peoples of India. Officially Adivasis are termed scheduled tribes, but this is a legal and constitutional term, which differs from state to state and area to area, and therefore excludes some groups who might be considered indigenous'. See http://minorityrights.org/minorities/adivasis-2/ (accessed 20 Sep. 2017).

15   In vitro fertilisation.

16   For anonymous interviews the video teams used backlighting and audio filters to disguise participants' identity; or conducted the interview using audiotape.

issues. However, the teams sought to minimise the risk to those who had not previously been publicly identified with SOGI issues by encouraging them to remain anonymous. Nonetheless, many interviewees opted to waive their right to anonymity. Telling their story on camera was an act of courage in the face of societal exclusion and marginalisation, one that contributed to their sense of self and the importance of their account. To do so represented an act of embodiment and defiance, a way of speaking back, challenging erasure and negation. Being on camera heightened their enthusiasm and connected the project with a spirit of activism. These interconnected tensions and complexities involved in safeguarding participants, while at the same time supporting self-determination, activism and community building, were highly important to the teams' capacity enhancement. They addressed these dilemmas by allowing for different levels of disclosure – from public screenings in local festivals or on community websites, to organising in-house screenings where participants could share their stories in a safe space as part of a community event. Whether the participants opted to be on camera or remain anonymous, their being part of the project helped to overcome isolation and stigma. This connected them to the organisation and to other LGBT people, sometimes for the first time.

Community engagement

The participatory documentary teams in each country videotaped solo interviews and small focus groups as well as documenting community events. By this means partners extended their outreach to involve sections of their community they had not previously accessed, enhancing engagement. The material was edited into documentaries and video portraits for community use and outreach. The video interviews were transcribed to support analysis of the research, development of papers and reports, and publication of the findings. The collected documentation of human rights violations contributed to reports on human rights in different countries, and supported Envisioning and community partner advocacy efforts and public education.

Following editing workshops in Nairobi in November 2012, the LeGaBiBo, GALCK and SMUG teams premiered their first documentaries at a community forum at the GALCK centre in Nairobi. These were: *The Law, Discrimination and the Future* (2012), *A Short Film on Kenyan LGBTI Stories* (2012), and *Life Experience of LGBTI in Botswana* (2013). The room was packed with an engaged audience of community activists and leaders and the challenging and insightful discussion facilitated the connection between the project and the community, and fuelled the teams' commitment and resolve.

Life Experience (2013) documents LeGaBiBo's vision of creating an inclusive environment that protects the rights of LGBT people in terms of health, law and social policy through the voices of members and leaders from four organisations in Botswana: LeGaBiBo, Botswana Network for People

Living with HIV/AIDS, Ditshwanelo (a human rights non-governmental organisation (NGO) based in Gaborone) and Rainbow Identities. A few months later, in February 2013, LeGaBiBo coordinated the first LGBT film festival in Botswana, Batho Ba Lorato (People of Love), which received significant local media coverage. Following that, the LeGaBiBo team toured the country, screening their work to promote outreach and public education opportunities. A second short done with LeGaBiBo, *Botho: LGBT Lives in Botswana* (2013), explores the legal challenge mounted against the colonial-era law of Botswana which criminalises same-sex intimacy. Litigant Caine Kaene Youngman and lawyer Monica Tabengwa speak about LeGaBiBo's constitutional challenge while Alice Mogwe, Ditshwanelo's director, contrasts the colonial-era criminal law with the concept of *botho*, an understanding of human rights that has been part of African tradition for millennia. On the importance of botho in addressing debates on tradition and culture, and issues of homophobia and exclusion, Mogwe notes,[17]

> Starting from the discussion of human rights as a concept, we've focused our attention on our Botswana concept called botho. Botho, [and] the South Africa *ubuntu* concept [is] the idea that, I am because you are, or I am human because you are human, and what I do to dehumanise you effectively dehumanises me as well. And if one uses botho as the basis of the work which we do, we're able to explain to people that human rights did not come in a package on a ship, which came from Europe and docked in Cape Town and then came on horseback or donkeyback to Botswana. It is a concept which has existed amongst peoples from time immemorial.

A Short Film on Kenyan LGBTI Stories (2012) includes interviews with leading LGBT activists in the country. Drawing on 25 interviews done in 2012, the video explores cases of human rights violations, including: suspension from school, imprisonment, family-based violence, workplace harassment. It also examines examples of community building including: lesbian parenting, relationships and same-sex marriage. Participants discuss strategies to decriminalise same-sex intimacy in Kenya and examine the Criminal Code law in light of the provisions of the Kenyan Constitution which guarantee every Kenyan equal rights.

In 2013, at the second Uganda Pride, SMUG premiered their first documentaries: *The Law, Discrimination and The Future* (2012), *Hope for the Future* (2013) and *First Uganda Pride* (2013), a 45-minute video about the first Pride held in the country in 2012. The political, legal and social context and conditions were particularly challenging in Uganda. The introduction of the AHB in parliament in 2009 had forced SMUG to turn much of their

---

17 Interviewed on 4 May 2012 by author and Junior Molefe, LeGaBiBo and Envisioning. An excerpt is included in the documentary *Botho: LGBT Lives in Botswana* (2013).

time and resources to opposing it. Yet, in the face of opposition and violence, SMUG continued to organise: opening Uganda's first and only LGBT clinic (at Icebreakers Uganda), doing outreach to smaller communities and rural areas, and holding and filming the above-mentioned Pride. The films sought to speak directly to fellow Ugandans, to build allies and work together for a better future. They tracked the progress of the AHB from its beginning in 2009, the campaign of media hatred and public outings of LGBTI people unleashed by the Ugandan tabloid *Rolling Stone,* and the murder of SMUG founder, David Kato.

In the Caribbean, Envisioning partners from Belize, Guyana, Jamaica and Saint Lucia met again in Kingston, Jamaica in 2013. The conference focused on development of the research and included a participatory video workshop led by videographers from Guyana and Saint Lucia, who shared their experience with participants from Jamaica and Belize. A community screening was hosted by Jamaica Forum for Lesbians, All-Sexuals and Gays (J-FLAG), which premiered three documentaries: *Our Saint Lucian Experience* by United and Strong, Saint Lucia; *Sade's Story* (2013) by Society Against Sexual Orientation Discrimination (SASOD), Guyana; and *The Time Has Come* (2013),which was filmed by Envisioning videographers from Africa and the Caribbean, and directed by project partner, ARC International.

Figure 18. Kendale Trapp (UNIBAM) and Avellina Stacy Nelson (United and Strong), Caribbean team participatory documentary workshop, Kingston, Jamaica, 9 July 2013. Photo credit: Envisioning Global LGBT Human Rights.

In addition to these works, SASOD created three other video shorts in 2013: *Homophobia in Guyana*, *Selina's Voice* and *Jessica's Journey* – the latter two, together with *Sade's Story*, constituted a series of portraits of transgender people in Guyana. Giving first-hand accounts of profound transphobic violence in public spaces, by police and in healthcare institutions, their voices were particularly significant in the context of the legal challenge to the cross-dressing law in Guyana.[18] The videos were screened at SASOD's LGBT film festival, Painting the Spectrum 10, held in Guyana in June 2014 with *Jessica's Journey* being featured at its opening night. The Caribbean participatory documentaries have been used to build awareness, generate discussion and support outreach.[19]

Video interviews with litigants in criminal code challenges in India, Botswana, Guyana and Jamaica provided a window into their experiences and often exposed how the existence of a law that criminalises consensual same sex-acts contributes to denial of access to justice. For example, in February 2013, a young outreach worker at J-FLAG acted as a litigant in a domestic challenge against the sodomy law of Jamaica, after he was evicted from his home due to his sexual orientation. As an outreach worker, he also testified to the daily reports of violence he heard from poor gay men and transgender persons. According to documentation by J-FLAG at the time, the organisation had received 36 reports of mob violence due to sexual orientation including two murders within the last year. In a video interview with the J-FLAG/ Envisioning team, the litigant[20] shared his reasons for stepping forward as a litigant in the case:

> I recognise that violence is a pretty effective mechanism to keep people silent and invisible ... that if I don't challenge them and challenge their authority to impose silence upon me then they get to win, right? But I do think I have something important to say and I do want to see change in my country because I don't want to feel like a stranger here for the rest of my life ... With regards to my family ... I came out to them years before I actually became a public figure.

In August 2014 the litigant withdrew his case because of threats of violence against him and his family.

18 For more information on the cross-dressing case in Guyana see: DeRoy and Henry, ch. 5.
19 Screenings included: the Urban Justice and Health Initiative/CITIES project in New Amsterdam, Berbice, Guyana; community meetings in Guyana, Saint Kitts and Saint Lucia; stigma and anti-discrimination training with healthcare providers in Saint Lucia; International Women's Day in Saint Lucia; Association for Women's Rights in Development 13th International Forum; OECS Litigation, Advocacy and Education Strategy forum; 11th Caribbean Institute in Gender and Development (CIGAD); Victory Institute political leadership meeting; Caribbean Women and Sexual Diversity conference; and the World Out Games, Human Rights Conference: From Safe Harbours to Equality.
20 J. Jaghai interviewed on 22 Jul. 2013 by B.P. Welsh, J-FLAG and Envisioning.

The Time Has Come

Establishing the Envisioning documentary teams in the Caribbean and Africa also provided a unique opportunity for international collaboration across the partnership. ARC International harnessed this capacity to create *The Time Has Come*, documenting a significant juncture in SOGI issues at the United Nations. Under ARC International's direction, Envisioning videographers from Africa and the Caribbean filmed a series of six state-led and civil society regional seminars held between January and June of 2013 in Paris, Brasilia, New York, Nairobi, Kathmandu and Oslo in the lead up to that year's United Nations Human Rights Council (UNHRC) session in Geneva. The seminars were designed to raise awareness and promote dialogue on SOGI issues. Filming the sessions provided Envisioning videographers with an opportunity to enhance their video skills as well as their knowledge and understanding of UN processes related to SOGI issues.

The Time Has Come captures a critical time in the advancement of SOGI issues at the UN.[21] In 2011, a historic resolution recognising sexual orientation and gender identity as prohibited grounds for discrimination was passed. In March 2012, UN Secretary General Ban Ki-moon delivered a speech asking countries around the world to end discrimination against LGBT people.

Figure 19. GALCK videographer, Caroline Kaara, International Day Against Homophobia, 17 May 2012, Nairobi, Kenya. Photo credit: Envisioning Global LGBT Human Rights.

21 For more on SOGI work at the UN see: Vance et al. and Mbaru et al., this volume, chs. 8 and 6 respectively.

Anticipating a possible follow-up resolution in the 2013 session, ARC sought to document these developments and capture key discussions and experiences of LGBT people, and the aspirations, hopes and strategies of LGBT leaders internationally. The documentary features LGBT human rights defenders from around the world discussing ways of strengthening protections for LGBT people. Subsections of the film address: universality and non-discrimination, security of the person and freedom of association.

Its participants also speak about the challenge to the concept of universal human rights at the UN by the introduction of a resolution on traditional values that would exclude SOGI issues from human rights provisions. Approaching the concept of tradition through a critical lens, the film explores the legacy of colonialism, the repression of sexual and gender diversity and expression, and its impact on indigenous societies worldwide. Elizabeth Kerekere[22] from Tiwhanawhana Trust for Takatapui, New Zealand, says,

> As Maori, we are a colonised people. We share the experience of indigenous people around the world, of loss of land, systematic erosion of our language and our culture – not to mention the suppression of our more fluid forms of sexuality and gender expression. As LGBTIQ we experience the generational trauma of the strict gender roles, homophobia and transphobia, brought to us courtesy of the British Empire, imposed on Maori culture and instilled into the fabric of New Zealand society.

Bolivian speaker and founder of Fundación Diversencia, Ronald Céspedes[23] notes,

> We can't make progress in a lot of countries, especially in Latin America, for these two factors: the first, that it invokes a discourse of traditional values in relation to indigenous people; and the second, which equates traditional values with the Judeo-Christian tradition. And not even Judeo-Christian but secular societies perpetuate ethics and morality that originate from the morals and ethics of Judeo-Christianity.

The Time Has Come concludes with a discussion of next steps at the UN to advance SOGI issues and protect the human rights of LGBT people across the world. The film premiered at a special UNHRC session in Geneva, organised by ARC International in June 2013, and was subsequently screened at the UN in September of that year.

Telling Our Stories

In preparation for World Pride, held in Toronto, Canada in June 2014, Envisioning partners – with editing support from Kaija Siirala – created *Telling Our Stories,* a collection of 30 five-minute video portraits of LGBT

---

22 In the documentary *The Time Has Come* (2013).
23 Ibid.

activists and community members filmed in India, Africa and the Caribbean.[24] It premiered at the Canadian Lesbian and Gay Archives as part of the 2014 World Pride events. The exhibition brought together work by the Envisioning participatory documentary teams, and a photo-and-text essay by the project's Guyanese photographer, Ulelli Verbeke, composed of images of Caribbean LGBT people who have sought asylum in Canada due to discrimination on the basis of SOGI. The event raised significant questions about the meaning of home in a world of homophobic and racist oppression.

The participants in the series speak directly about what continuing with the struggle for LGBT rights means, despite violence and risk. Their stories speak to profound discrimination, violence and loss: random violence

Figure 20. Photo credit: *Telling Our Stories*, Envisioning Global LGBT Human Rights.

24 See http://envisioning-tellingourstories.blogspot.com (accessed 14 Feb. 2018).

in public places; violence and hate by police, church and state; loss of employment, education, friends, family and community. But there are also tales of resistance: stories of family, friends, neighbours and strangers who have acted as allies; organisations developing security plans to protect LGBT persons; positive media opening up discussion; community mobilising; and LGBT people joining legal challenges. Some examples from this collection include the following portraits:

Stosh Jovan Mugisha, a trans man who was then executive director of Kuchus Living with HIV/AIDS (KULHAS) in Uganda, speaks about stigma, sexual violence and rape in relation to being HIV positive, a trans man and gender non-conforming – what he refers to as a sense of 'triple-stigmatisation'.

Kenita Placide, then executive director of United and Strong in Saint Lucia, talks about some of the challenges of highlighting abuse and discrimination. She argues that what is needed in Saint Lucia is for society to see beyond ignorance, and that this will only happen through advocacy and action, not through waiting for society to bestow acceptance and rights.

Maya Sharma, a leading feminist scholar in India, activist and author of *Loving Women: Being Lesbian in Unprivileged India* (2006), speaks about the liberty and freedom she felt when she first began to identify as a woman who loves women at a time when there was no queer movement in India. Her reflections on how silence can speak links her own experience with that of the queer people she works with in rural tribal areas in India.

Tanya Stephens is a Jamaican reggae artist whose repertoire features social commentary hits such as 'What a Day' and 'Turn the Other Cheek'. She speaks about using her talent as a singer and writer to raise awareness about social justice. Her experiences in meeting gay people changed her childhood assumptions that queerness was 'wrong'.

Veena, a Dalit trans woman and a peer support educator with Sangama in Bangalore, speaks about her experiences of discrimination from an early age and how her experience at Sangama became empowering. 'We are all one', Veena says, as she describes a movement that fights for the rights of all minorities and victims of discrimination.

Tshepo Riqu Cosadu, then advocacy officer for Rainbow Identity Association in Botswana, works as an advocate for transgender and intersex rights on health issues, HIV/AIDS prevention, prenatal and postnatal care, transgender parenting, and legal recognition and rights for transgender and intersex people. Tshepo speaks about the strong, culturally embedded gender roles in Botswana, based on a female/male binary, and the issues that this creates for transgender and transsexual individuals.

And Still We Rise

> *Every time I wake up in the morning, pray for a better tomorrow.*
> *Pray to God to really help change things from what they are.*
> *Hoping every morning, hoping every evening, hoping every time.*
> *I'm keeping this hope alive. I'm keeping this hope alive.[25]*
>
> Nkyooyo Brian, composer, 'Hope Alive' (2014)

From 2009 to December 2013, SMUG and the Civil Society Coalition on Human Rights and Constitutional Law (Coalition), combined with international pressure, successfully managed to prevent the AHB from being passed.[26] When the AHA was passed in December 2013 and enacted into law in March 2014, SMUG faced a crisis. The act's passage led to increasing violence towards LGBTI people and many groups and organisations that had supported LGBTI rights were forced to close or suspend their work. Many LGBTI people were thrown out of their apartments by landlords, and subjected to arrest, media outings and mob violence. Several of those affected fled to neighbouring Kenya where many remain to this day in overcrowded and dangerous conditions.

The violence directly impacted members of SMUG and the participatory documentary team based in Uganda. The day after the AHA was passed in December 2013, Richard Lusimbo (Envisioning researcher and SMUG documentation manager) and Junic Wambya (the project's videographer and the then executive director of Freedom and Roam Uganda) were both outed in the Ugandan media. Junic Wambya faced mounting threats and was forced to flee the country.[27]

In this urgent and difficult context, the team discussed the need to document human rights violations as a result of the AHA, while minimising risk in the context of escalating violence. It is a testament to the courage of the SMUG documentary team that they decided to continue the work and to create a film that would focus on the impact of and resistance to the AHA. The result was *And Still We Rise*. I worked closely with the SMUG team and co-directed the film with Richard Lusimbo. Caroline Kaara, an Envisioning videographer in Kenya, replaced Junic as camera operator. Nkyooyo Brian, executive director of Icebreakers Uganda, composed an inspiring music track for the film. And Junic, having relocated to Toronto, was able to work closely with me on editing the documentary.

---

25 A song from *And Still We Rise* (2015) for which Nkyooyo Brian was the composer and lyricist.

26 For more on the impact of, and resistance to, the AHB/AHA see Jjuuko and Mutesi, and Lusimbo and Bryan, this volume, chs. 10 and 12 respectively.

27 My partner and I supported Junic in coming to Canada and settling in Toronto, where she successfully claimed asylum.

I asked Caroline to capture their process including filming Richard as he met with and interviewed the participants. But it was only as I was editing that I realised that the stories of the SMUG documentary team – and how the AHA affected them – would form a core narrative alongside the story of the AHA, as examined through the interviews they had filmed. Caroline's footage following Richard provided the visual thread for this self-reflexive approach, which incorporated the filmmakers' journey into the film narrative.

Tracing the history from 2009, *And Still We Rise* weaves together personal accounts of individuals caught up in the widespread repression that followed passage of the act: media hate, clinic closures, arrests, human rights violations and mob violence. It includes the impact on the filmmakers and activists themselves. In a moving nighttime sequence of a drive through the streets of Kampala, the narrator, Junic Wambya, describes how her landlord forced her out of her apartment because he saw her picture in the newspaper. This is followed by a sequence where the team drove in a heavy rainstorm to Richard's hometown. There they interviewed Richard's cousin and a childhood friend as they grappled with the media outing of Richard as a gay rights activist, and expressed their love and ongoing support for Richard in the face of negative reactions to the news in the town.

The documentary provides an analysis of intersecting domestic and international forces underlying the AHA, and an in-depth look at the resistance to it, led by SMUG and the Coalition, which brought together some 50 civil society organisations to oppose the AHA and other laws that undermine civil liberties in Uganda. Richard's interviews with local legal, academic and community leaders together provide an in-depth analysis of the neocolonial religious right's role in Uganda in fomenting hate, situating the AHA within a broader assault on civil liberties, a context used by opportunistic local politicians to secure and retain power. The executive director of Chapter Four Uganda, Nicholas Opiyo, a lawyer in the constitutional case against the AHA, analyses the act in the context of the post 9/11 assaults on civil liberties under an ageing regime headed by President Museveni. Dr Frank Mugisha, SMUG's executive director, Adrian Jjuuko, executive director of the Human Rights Awareness and Promotion Forum, Kasha Jacqueline Nabagesera, founder of Freedom and Roam Uganda, Sam Ganafa, Spectrum Uganda's executive director and others describe personal and organisational impacts of the act's passage. Dr Sylvia Tamale, dean of Makerere University's law faculty, deconstructs the myth that homosexuality is 'un-African',[28] citing examples of same-sex practices and diverse gender expression across Africa. She also draws out connections to women's oppression, arguing that, 'those same arguments of "un-African" are used to justify women's subordination, especially when we try to assert our rights to sexual autonomy. Then you will hear the same mantra.'

28 Interviewed on 29 Nov. 2014 by Richard Lusimbo, SMUG and Envisioning. An excerpt is included in the documentary *And Still We Rise* (2015).

According to Frank Mugisha, *And Still We Rise* captured SMUG's work and the story of resilience and resistance to the AHA for the first time. Despite the forces of hatred arrayed against SMUG, the AHA met its match in the Coalition and SMUG, who succeeded in getting the law struck down. On 1 August 2014, the Constitutional Court of Uganda nullified the AHA, on the grounds that the Parliament of Uganda had passed the law without quorum.

No Easy Walk to Freedom

This 2014 documentary follows the case against Section 377 of the Indian Penal Code, which criminalises same-sex acts. It probes into contemporary queer organising and the broader social and political context in relation to LGBT rights in India. The research and development for it began in 2009–10 when I travelled to India to develop partnerships. These three key organisations joined Envisioning: Naz Foundation (India) Trust (Naz India), an HIV/AIDS education and prevention NGO based in Delhi; Naz Foundation International (NFI) in conjunction with the Maan AIDS Foundation, an HIV/AIDS education and prevention NGO based in Lucknow; and Sangini, an LBT shelter in Delhi. Naz India and NFI played a key role in the Section 377 struggle. The former, with

Figure 21. *No Easy Walk to Freedom* production team, Delhi, India, 31 October 2011. Left to right: Phyllis Waugh (research), Nancy Nicol (director), Shakeb Ahmed (cinematography), Pratik Biswas (location sound), Pearl Sandhu (line producer), Rhaesh Rajbhar (lighting). Photo credit: Envisioning Global LGBT Human Rights.

the Lawyers Collective in Delhi, filed the case against Section 377 in 2001. Also in 2001, Maan's predecessor, Bharosa Trust, was raided and its health workers were arrested in an incident that was a turning point in the development of the case. In addition to these partners, I also drew on the expertise of the Lawyers Collective in Delhi, the Humsafar Trust in Mumbai, the Alternative Law Forum (ALF) and Sangama in Bangalore, and the coalition Voices Against 377 (Voices). These organisations contributed additional expertise and facilitated networking and access to interview participants.

The approach taken in the documentary is highly intersectional: a reflection of the organising strategies of the movement, queer politics in India, and the intersecting issues at stake in the Section 377 case. Challenging viewers' expectations, *No Easy Walk to Freedom* opens with a sequence of children in an orphanage. Its significance in relation to a narrative on Section 377 of the Indian Penal Code becomes apparent as the film unfolds. The orphanage is run by Naz India, which was founded by Anjali Gopalan, through whose compassionate leadership an orphanage was started for HIV positive children. Naz India did pioneering work in HIV and AIDS prevention and education, sending outreach workers into Delhi's slums to access at-risk populations, including sexual and gender minorities. Naz India also provided meeting space for them, through the Milan Centre, a programme which supported marginalised queer communities. In the documentary, Milan Centre staff member, Shashi Bhushan,[29] speaks about the experiences of transgender people, unpacking intersecting issues of modernisation, loss of traditional practices, employment discrimination and poverty:

> They are not into the traditional jobs, assigned to the transgender people, which is dancing on some auspicious occasions; because now they have very little opportunity to do that as well. On top of that, if they're not given any jobs, they are jobless. So that's why they go to prostitution. Most of them, they don't want to do that, and so that's why we are having these programmes so that we can help them somehow to become economically independent.

Through their pioneering work with at-risk populations in Delhi's slums, Naz India ran afoul of Section 377 of the Indian Penal Code. Police would harass and arrest Naz outreach workers for 'promoting an illegal activity'[30] by distributing condoms to men who have sex with men (MSM). Motivated by a sense of injustice born out of witnessing discrimination against homosexuals as well as the jeopardy to Naz India's HIV/AIDS prevention work – and weary of midnight trips to police headquarters to get Naz outreach workers out of custody – Gopalan approached the Lawyers Collective, and together

29 Interviewed by the author on 29 Oct. 2011 for the documentary *No Easy Walk to Freedom* (2014).
30 Anjali Gopalan interviewed by the author on 28 Oct. 2011 for *No Easy Walk to Freedom* (2014).

Figure 22. Milan Centre, Naz Foundation (India) Trust outreach workers: Prince, Kiran and Bobby, with client, Delhi, India, 29 October 2011. Photo credit: *No Easy Walk to Freedom*, Envisioning Global LGBT Human Rights.

they filed a case challenging the constitutionality of Section 377.[31] There were tensions at the outset of the case. Naz India and the Lawyers Collective came under criticism from activists on various grounds including filing the case without consultation.[32] The result of these debates ultimately strengthened the movement against Section 377 and queer mobilising in India. In response to community concern, regular consultations were held starting in 2003, to discuss all aspects of the case and organising strategy. Queer organising, including within feminist organisations as well as transgender, lesbian, gay and MSM groups, had existed well before the Section 377 case. The documentary probes into some of this work through interviews with leading Indian feminists and with queer and HIV/AIDS activists. As the case went on, the struggle drew in more sectors from across Indian society, which in turn better reflected the diversity and intersections of the issues at stake.

By the 1990s health workers and NGOs recognised that HIV/AIDS prevention was impeded by the presence of Section 377. There were growing numbers of MSM and gay men impacted by HIV who started coming to the Lawyers Collective offices because they were being harassed and blackmailed by police.[33] Lawyers with the Lawyers Collective HIV unit would become key players in the legal challenge to Section 377. In July 2001, police raided the

31 Anjali Gopalan, ibid., and Anand Grover, interviewed on 9 Nov. 2011 by author for
    No Easy Walk to Freedom (2014).
32 For an account of the debates and tensions of that time see Dave (2012).
33 Anand Grover interviewed by author on 9 Nov. 2011, and Vivek Divan interviewed
    by author on 27 Jan. 2014, for *No Easy Walk to Freedom* (2014).

offices of the HIV/AIDS prevention NGOs, Bharosa Trust and NFI, which work with marginalised populations of MSM, *hijras*, *kothis* and others[34] in Lucknow, in the province of Uttar Pradesh. Police seized condoms and lubricants and a dildo used for condom demonstrations, labelling these items as 'obscene materials' and 'sex toys'; and seized books and videos, labelling them as 'pornography'. They arrested the Bharosa Trust's manager and three outreach workers, charging them under Section 377 for promoting and engaging in 'unnatural practices', obscenity and more. In the media, police characterised the Bharosa Trust as a brothel, and justified the raid as necessary to break up a 'sex racket' and stop the 'vice of homosexuality'. In the documentary, three of the men arrested recount their experience. Imprisoned for 47 days, they were subjected to extreme abuse and humiliation by prison authorities.[35]

News of the arrests in Lucknow reached Delhi and galvanised activists who organised protests against the arrests. Indira Jaisingh and Anand Grover, co-founders of the Lawyers Collective, travelled to Lucknow to support the accused and argue for their release. Organisations in the city working in the field of social issues, human rights and women's rights started holding demonstrations outside the jail. Due to this pressure, the men were eventually released and the charges under Section 377 dropped (although the charges for obscenity were not dropped).[36] The Lucknow incident acted as a further catalyst for launching the constitutional challenge to Section 377.[37]

While the colonial roots of Section 377 and the Victorian language of the law – 'carnal intercourse against the order of nature' – provide the connecting narrative line of the documentary, various speakers address the colonial legacy in far-reaching and subtle ways. They speak to the racist assumptions of the British lawmakers; the interconnections between repression of indigenous societies and diverse forms of sexual and gender expression in precolonial India; and the implications of the Section 377 case for constitutional protections of all minorities in India. Saleem Kidwai[38] addresses the suppression of pre-colonial traditions:

34 MSM and transgender people in the Envisioning research study in India identified themselves by sexual practice or gender performance or gender identity as: *hijras, kothis, kinnars, panthis, jogtas, dangas, alis,* double-deckers, *chakkas, dhuranis* and other terms. Lesbian, gay, transgender and bisexual were also used, albeit more with English-speaking participants. Queer is sometimes the preferred term due to these complexities, and because it reflects a nuanced and shifting understanding that does not confine sexual identities to fixed LGBT categories.

35 Sudeesh and Shahid interviewed on 22 Nov. 2011 by author, and Arif Jaffar interviewed on 23 Nov. 2011 by author for *No Easy Walk to Freedom* (2014).

36 Ibid.

37 Anand Grover interviewed on 9 Nov. 2011 by author, and Gautam Bhan interviewed on 7 Oct. 2011 by author for *No Easy Walk to Freedom* (2014).

38 Ruth Vanita and Saleem Kidwai's groundbreaking book, *Same-sex Love in India* (2000) translated texts from 15 languages covering 2000 years to bring to light

Prior to the introduction of Section 377 there is enough evidence to show that homosexuality was prevalent in India ... The idea of the modern family, the Victorian family, with defined roles – not just defined roles, defined behaviour – which is in direct contrast to what the precolonial family and the precolonial traditions were, immediately gets the reformers, who are by definition modernist, seeing themselves as people who need to reform that and get rid of all this old baggage ... Suddenly all this is deemed traditional and therefore seen to be abandoned for Victorian values. It's also a similar thing happening in Europe. It's not as if Victorianism spared anyone. But in India the contrast was far, far greater.

By 2003, the coalition, Voices Against 377, had been formed. In an attempt to ensure that the struggle was not limited to the courts, Voices adopted a broad-based approach, arguing that Section 377 was a social issue 'about all of us'.[39] Its report *Rights for All* (2005) called on a range of organisations to have position statements, and formed alliances with human rights, women's rights, children's rights and labour organisations. Voices coordinated the One Million Voices Campaign to demonstrate to the government that many people were concerned about and affected by the law, and to open up public discussion about sexuality in a broader, political sense.[40] At the core of their efforts was the perspective that engaging public discussion of the issues was essential to raising awareness and advancing greater liberty and freedom in relation to sexuality and gender identities, whatever the outcome of the legal challenge itself.

Others in the film speak to the ways in which LGBTQ people find a way to live their lives regardless of the laws. Deepa[41] who self identifies as she-male, describes her wedding to her boyfriend conducted by a local Hindu priest in Delhi:

On my wedding day I went to Jhandewala temple. A policeman came up to me and said, 'You're not allowed stand here.' I asked, 'Why, sir? Am I assaulting or stealing? Tell me, sir.' He replied, 'You won't go away? I'll get a stick.' He got a stick. When he hit me, I went straight to the police station. Then I returned and got married. The priest guided us through the pujas. We exchanged rings with each other. He gave me this bangle. I gave him a ring and a chain. Then we circled the fire.

---

references to same-sex love in ancient, medieval and modern texts in India, including in the scriptures and Persian and Sufi literary traditions. Kidwai was interviewed on 16 Nov. 2012 by the author for *No Easy Walk to Freedom* (2014).

39 Gautam Bhan interviewed on 7 Oct. 2011 by author for *No Easy Walk to Freedom* (2014).

40 For more on the growth and perspectives of the movement see also the anthology ed. Narrain and Bhan (2005).

41 Interviewed on 2 Nov. 2011 by author for *No Easy Walk to Freedom* (2014).

Figure 23. Nancy Nicol (director) and Shakeb Ahmed (cinematography) filming *No Easy Walk to Freedom* in Delhi, India, 14 November 2011. Photo credit: Envisioning Global LGBT Human Rights.

Another example, recounted by Alok Gupta,[42] describes the 'Bombay solution'. Apartments in Bombay (Mumbai) are governed by cooperative building society rules which, in an effort to prevent illegal subleasing, state clearly that people who are not related to each other cannot live in the same apartment. In effect the rules act as a barrier to a couple living together unless they are married. So Alok Gupta described a 'Bombay solution', which was to buy two adjacent flats and break down the middle wall. He suggested this solution to a gay couple – who loved the idea. About three years later they were able to buy the apartments, but, Alok noted, 'they couldn't find adjacent, they found a top and bottom (laughs). So one is on the top, the other is on the bottom'.[43]

Eventually, Voices also filed a petition against Section 377, represented by the ALF in Bangalore, and worked to gather affidavits – further mobilising participation in the case. Those involved included Sangama, an NGO based in Bangalore which, informed by a social and economic analysis of oppression, works to address issues of poverty, land rights and sex work, as well as discrimination and oppression on the basis of SOGI. It brings together groups

42 Interviewed on 16 Nov. 2011 by author for *No Easy Walk to Freedom* (2014). This story was not included in the film. I am glad to share it with you now.
43 Interviewed on 16 Nov. 2011, as above.

Figure 24. Sangama demonstration, Bangalore, India, 19 November 2011. Photo credit: *No Easy Walk to Freedom*, Envisioning Global LGBT Human Rights.

such as Dalits,[44] Adivasis, sex workers, *hijras, kothis*, and those who identify as third gender or trans, bisexual, lesbian or as gay men. Sangama founder Manohar Elavarthi[45] describes Sangama's politics thus:

> Injustice happens in the name of sexual orientation, gender identity, in the same way it happens in the name of class, caste, gender, disability. So we believe that we need to join hands, there should be solidarity. Only then can we build a society which is based on justice … Marginalised people get their rights as a collective, as a community. Dalits, women, adivasis – without having a strong organisation and being together, constantly demanding things – only then changes happen.

In the documentary, Sangama joins a demonstration for land rights of Dalit and rural Adivasi people, carrying a banner with an image of Dr Ambedkar, a leader of the Dalit movement and an architect of the Indian Constitution. Dr Ambedkar advanced the concept of constitutional morality, which the 2009 Delhi High Court drew on in its decision to read down Section 377.

In December 2013, the Supreme Court of India set aside the 2009 Delhi High Court ruling and upheld Section 377, recriminalising LGBT people in India. Angry demonstrations took place across the country. In a speech to the demonstrators,[46] Voices activist Gautam Bhan declared, 'We will take your law and we will tell you that criminal law never outweighs human truth.' Activists resolved to continue the fight against the 2013 verdict, including filing curative

---

44 Dalit, which means 'oppressed' in Sanskrit is the name popularised by Dalit leader, Dr Ambedkar, for India's so-called 'untouchable' or lower castes.
45 Interviewed on 19 Nov. 2011 by author for *No Easy Walk to Freedom* (2014).
46 Bhan gave his speech in Delhi on 12 Dec. 2013.

petitions against it, which in April 2014, the Indian Supreme Court agreed to consider. In August 2017 in a separate case, a different Supreme Court bench declared that the 2013 Supreme Court had gravely erred in annulling the Delhi High Court verdict. Justice Dhananjay Y. Chandrachud, who authored the lead judgment, held that privacy is a fundamental right:

> Sexual orientation is an essential attribute of privacy. Discrimination against an individual on the basis of sexual orientation is deeply offensive to the dignity and self-worth of the individual. Equality demands that the sexual orientation of each individual in society must be protected on an even platform. The right to privacy and the protection of sexual orientation lie at the core of fundamental rights guaranteed by Articles 14, 15 and 21 of the Constitution.[47]

As of the time of this writing, the Section 377 case is once again under consideration by the Supreme Court of India. Additional petitions have been filed to the court, including a petition from Arif Jaffar, who recounts in the documentary, the abuse he was subjected to when he was arrested in 2001 in Lucknow. The history of the struggle against Section 377 preserved in this documentary is a testament to the resilience of the movement to remove the legacy of the colonial law and advance human rights in India.

Conclusion

Envisioning partners have used the participatory documentaries for public education, legal interventions, community mobilising and as a catalyst for discussion. They have been shown at film festivals and conferences locally, regionally and internationally – and a large number of organisations internationally have used them to support outreach and education. Significantly, appreciation has been expressed by audiences from local, national and international contexts.

What stands out in all of this work is the tremendous resilience of the participants and the documentary teams, who have drawn on community mobilising and activism to document history in the making, and to shed light on the lives and experiences of LGBT people as they struggle to assert and express their identities in the face of persecution, exclusion and repressive laws.

The overall outcome of Envisioning's documentary work is an extensive archive of LGBT experience and social movement histories as told by participants directly involved in these issues in each country involved in the research during the period between 2011 and 2015. The existence of this body of work stands as a testament to the endurance, courage and resilience of those who took part and provides a rich historical record of this period of conflict and change.

47 *Justice K.S. Puttaswamy (retd.) and ANR v. Union of India and ORS*, Judgment 24 Aug. 2017, para 126.

References

Dave, N. (2012) *Queer Activism in India: A Story in the Anthropology of Ethics*, (Durham, NC: Duke University Press).

Freire, Paulo (1970) *Pedagogy of the Oppressed* (London, Sydney, Delhi and New York, NY: Bloomsbury Press).

Narrain, A. and G. Bhan (eds.) (2005) *Because I Have a Voice, Queer Politics in India*, (New Delhi: Yoda Press).

Nichols, B. (2010) *Introduction to Documentary*, 2nd edn. (Bloomington, IN: Indiana University).

Nicol, N. (2008) 'Politics of the heart: recognition of homoparental families', *Florida Philosophical Review: Journal of the Florida Philosophical Association*, University of Central Florida philosophy department, 8 (1).

Nicol, N. and M. Smith (2008) 'Legal struggles and political resistance: same-sex marriage in Canada and the US', *Sexualities*, 11 (6): 667–87.

Sharma, M. (2006) *Loving Women: Being Lesbian in Unprivileged India* (Yoda Press, New Delhi).

Vanita, R. and S. Kidwai (eds.) (2000) *Same-sex Love in India: Readings in Indian Literature* (Basingstoke and New York, NY: Palgrave).

Voices Against 377 (2005) *Rights for All: Ending Discrimination Under Section 377* (Vikas Offset Press: New Delhi), available at: www.unipune. ac.in/snc/cssh/HumanRights/01%20STATE%20DEMOCRACY%20 AND%20LAW/38.%20Voices%20against%20Section%20377%20 Rights%20for%20All%20-%20Ending%20Discrimination%20under%- 20Section%20377,%20New%20Delh.pdf (accessed 15 Feb. 2018).

Waugh, T., M.B. Baker and E. Winton (2010) *Challenge for Change, Activist Documentary at the National Film Board of Canada* (Montréal-Kingston: McGill-Queen's University Press).

Documentary films

And Still We Rise (2015) dir. R. Lusimbo and N. Nicol (Uganda and Canada: Sexual Minorities Uganda and Envisioning Global LGBT Human Rights), available at: https://vimeo.com/178217397. Extracts are cited from interviews with: Dr Sylvia Tamale, Dr Frank Mugisha and Nicolas Opiyo.

A Short Film on Kenyan LGBTI Rights (2012) dir. I. Reid, C. Kaara and J. Muthuri (Canada and Kenya: Gay and Lesbian Coalition of Kenya and Envisioning Global LGBT Human Rights), available at: https://vimeo. com/73786260.

Botho: LGBT Lives in Botswana (2013) dir. N. Nicol (Botswana and Canada: Lesbians, Gays and Bisexuals of Botswana and Envisioning Global LGBT

Human Rights), available at: https://vimeo.com/69577157. Extract from interview with Alice Mogwe.

First Uganda Pride (2013) dir. R. Lusimbo, J. Wambya and B. Nkoyooyo (Uganda and Canada: Sexual Minorities Uganda and Envisioning Global LGBT Human Rights). No online access.

From Criminality to Equality film series (2002–9) dir. N. Nicol, comprising *Stand Together* (2002), *Politics of the Heart* (2005), *The End of Second Class* (2006) and *The Queer Nineties* (2009) (Canada: Intervention Productions). See: www.yorku.ca/nnicol/documentary.html; http://digitalcollections.clga.ca/exhibits/show/nancy-nicol/nn-collection.

Homophobia in Guyana (2013) dir. N.B. Henry, U. Verbeke and J. Grant (Guyana and Canada: Society Against Sexual Orientation Discrimination and Envisioning Global LGBT Human Rights). No online access.

Hope for the Future (2013) dir. R. Lusimbo and P. Onziema (Uganda and Canada: Sexual Minorities Uganda with Voices of the Abasiyazzi and Envisioning Global LGBT Human Rights), available at: https://vimeo.com/73786262.

Jessica's Journey (2013) dir. N.B. Henry, U. Verbeke and J. Grant (Guyana and Canada: Society Against Sexual Orientation Discrimination and Envisioning Global LGBT Human Rights). No online access.

Life Experience of LGBTI in Botswana (2013) dir. T. Motshwane, T. Mabuza and J. Molefe (Botswana and Canada: Lesbians, Gays and Bisexuals of Botswana and Envisioning Global LGBT Human Rights), available at: https://vimeo.com/75420906.

No Easy Walk to Freedom (2014) dir. N. Nicol (India and Canada: Naz Foundation (India) Trust and Envisioning Global LGBT Human Rights), available at: https://vimeo.com/87912192. Extracts are cited from interviews with: Shashi Bhushan, Anjali Gopalan, Anand Grover, Vivek Divan, Gautam Bhan, Saleem Kidwai, Arif Jafar, Maya Sharma, Deepa, Manohar Elavarthi, Alok Gupta, Sudeesh, Shahid and Veena.

One Summer in New Paltz, a Cautionary Tale (2008) dir. N. Nicol (Canada and US: Intervention Productions). See: www.yorku.ca/nnicol/documentary.html; http://digitalcollections.clga.ca/exhibits/show/nancy-nicol/nn-collection.

Our Saint Lucian Experience (2013) dir. M. Fontenelle, K. Placide, M. Danton and S. Nelson (Saint Lucia and Canada: United and Strong and Envisioning Global LGBT Human Rights). No online access.

Sade's Story (2013) dir. N.B. Henry, U. Verbeke and J. Grant (Guyana and Canada: Society Against Sexual Orientation Discrimination and Envisioning Global LGBT Human Rights), available at: https://vimeo.com/75422884.

Sangini (2016) dir. N. Nicol (India and Canada: Sangini Trust and Envisioning Global LGBT Human Rights), available at: https://vimeo.

com/164737117.

Selina's Voice (2013) dir. N.B. Henry, U. Verbeke and J. Grant (Guyana and Canada: Society Against Sexual Orientation Discrimination and Envisioning Global LGBT Human Rights), available at: https://vimeo.com/88493864.

The Law, Discrimination and the Future (2012) dir. R. Lusimbo, J. Wambya and B. Nkoyooyo (Uganda and Canada: Sexual Minorities Uganda and Envisioning Global LGBT Human Rights), available at: https://vimeo.com/73786261.

The Time Has Come (2013) dir. K. Vance, J Fisher and S. Kara (France, Brazil, USA, Kenya, Nepal, Norway, Switzerland and Canada: ARC International and Envisioning Global LGBT Human Rights), available at: http://vimeo.com/67796115. Extracts are cited from statements by Elizabeth Kerekere and Ronald Céspedes.

Appendix: Envisioning Global LGBT Human Rights participatory documentaries

Documentaries as well as video documentation of Envisioning events, conference presentations and public forums are included in this appendix – listed in order of date of completion. Videos are available on the Envisioning Global LGBT Human Rights website and/or on vimeo. To access go to: www. envisioninglgbt.com or to the vimeo link provided for each title.

Sangini (2016) tells the stories of lesbians and transgender people who fled their families and sought sanctuary at Sangini, a shelter for lesbian, bisexual, transgender (LBT) women in Delhi. [Documentary film, 45:19 min.] N. Nicol (director), N. Mor (editor), S. Ahmed (cinematographer), P. Sandhu (line producer). India and Canada: Sangini and Envisioning. See https:// vimeo.com/164737117. For institutional use, please contact the distributor: GIV (www.givideo.org).

And Still We Rise (2015) follows Richard Lusimbo as he documents the impact of, and resistance to, the Anti-Homosexuality Act in Uganda. [Documentary film, 68:35 min.] R. Lusimbo and N. Nicol (directors), N. Nicol and J. Wambya (editors), C. Kaara (director of photography), Nkyooyo B. and Talented Ugandan Kuchus (music). Uganda and Canada: Sexual Minorities Uganda (SMUG) and Envisioning. See https://vimeo.com/178217397. Information and trailer: www.andstillwerise.ca. For institutional use, please contact the distributor: Vtape (www.vtape.org/distribution), or GIV (www. givideo.org).

No Easy Walk to Freedom (2014) examines the struggle to decriminalise homosexuality in contemporary India, as told through the voices of HIV/AIDS workers, queer activists, legal experts and community leaders, filmed in Delhi, Mumbai, Bangalore, Lucknow and rural India. [92 min.] N. Nicol (director), S. Ahmed(cinematographer), P. Sandhu (line producer), K. Siirala (assistant editor). India and Canada: Naz Foundation (India) Trust (Naz India), Naz Foundation International (NFI) and Envisioning. See https://vimeo.com/87912192.

Information and trailer: www.noeasywalktofreedom.com. For institutional use please contact the distributor: Vtape (www.vtape.org/distribution), or GIV (www.givideo.org).

Envisioning Global LGBT Human Rights at World Pride (2014) documents Envisioning team participation in World Pride, Toronto. Canada: Envisioning. [Documentary film, 4.03 min.] K. Chisholm (editor). See http://envisioninglgbt.com.

Telling Our Stories documentary series (2014), created with Envisioning community partners in India, Africa and the Caribbean. LGBT community members and activists share stories of homo-bi-transphobia, violence and discrimination, as well as resilience, resistance and organising histories. [30 five-minute videos]. Series editors: N. Nicol, K. Siirala and K. Chisholm with Envisioning partners. See http://envisioning-tellingourstories.blogspot.com. The series includes the following:

Belize Portraits: C. Orozco (researcher), K. Trapp (videographer). Belize and Canada, United Belize Advocacy Movement (UNIBAM) and Envisioning.
1. Aaron Mai, Norman Bonnell and Abner Recinos, UNIBAM.
2. Mia Quetzal, Caribbean Vulnerable Communities.

Botswana Portraits: J. Molefe (researcher), T. Motshwane and T. Mabuza (videographers). Botswana and Canada, Lesbians Gays and Bisexuals of Botswana (LeGaBiBo) and Envisioning.
3. Caine Kaene Youngman, LeGaBiBo.
4. Manno Setaelo, LeGaBiBo.
5. Tshepo Riqu Cosadu, advocacy officer, Rainbow Identity Association.

Guyana Portraits: N.B. Henry (researcher), U. Verbeke (videographer), J.A. Grant (coordinator). Guyana and Canada: Society Against Sexual Orientation Discrimination (SASOD) and Envisioning.
6. Cracey Annatola Fernandes, Guyana Sex Work Coalition, Global Network of Sex Work Projects and Caribbean Vulnerable Communities.
7. Melinda Jankie, lawyer, Justice Institute.
8. Selina Maria Perez, transgender woman and social worker.

India Portraits: N. Nicol (director), S. Ahmed (cinematographer) and P. Sandhu (line producer). India and Canada: Naz India, NFI and Envisioning.
8. Veena, peer support educator, Sangama.
9. Maya Shanker and Betu Singh, Sangini. In memoriam, Betu passed away 4 October 2013.
10. Gautam Bhan, Voices Against 377, PRISM.
11. Shivananda Khan, founder and chief executive, NFI. In memoriam, Shivananda passed away 20 May 2013.
12. Maya Sharma, scholar, activist, author.

Jamaica Portraits: L. Nugent (researcher), B. Welsh and M. Thompson (videographers). Jamaica and Canada: Jamaica Forum of Lesbians, All-Sexuals and Gays (J-FLAG) and Envisioning.

13. Jalna Broderick, co-founder and director of administration, Quality of Citizenship Jamaica.

14. Tanya Stephens, reggae artist.

15. Anonymous1.

16. Anonymous2.

17. Anonymous3.

18. Anonymous4.

Kenya Portraits: I. Reid (researcher), J. Muthuri and C. Kaara (videographers). Kenya and Canada, Gay and Lesbian Coalition of Kenya (GALCK) and Envisioning.

19. Guillit Amakobe, founding member, Jinsiangu.

20. Douglas Masinde, founder and programme coordinator, Tamba Pwani.

21. Akinyi Margareta Ocholla, founding member and former executive director, Minority Women in Action.

22. Jane Wothaya Thirikwa, then programmes and communications coordinator, Gay Kenya Trust.

Saint Lucia Portraits: M. Fontenelle (researcher), M. Danton and S. Nelson (videographers). Saint Lucia and Canada: United and Strong and Envisioning.

23. Bary Hunte, United and Strong.

24. Vincent McDoom, actor, fashion icon, writer.

25. Kenita Placide, then executive director, United and Strong; Eastern Caribbean coordinator of Caribbean Forum for Liberation and Acceptance of Genders and Sexualities.

Uganda Portraits: R. Lusimbo (researcher), Nkyooyo B. and J. Wambya (videographers). Uganda and Canada: SMUG and Envisioning.

26. Nikki Mawanda Salongo, founder and then executive director, Transgender Support Initiative Uganda.

27. Dr Frank Mugisha, executive director, SMUG.

28. Stosh Jovan Mugisha, Kuchus Living with HIV/AIDS.

29. Geoffrey Ogwaro, co-coordinator, Civil Society Coalition on Human Rights and Constitutional Law.

30. Anonymous.

Kandi's Story (2014) Transgender Jamaican Kandi talks about the persecution she has faced: forced to quit school, fired from work and outed in the newspaper. [Documentary film, 12:38 min.] L. Nugent, B. Welsh and M. Thompson (participatory documentary team). Jamaica and Canada: J-FLAG and Envisioning. See https://vimeo.com/89556756.

No Going Back (2014) captures widespread protests to the recriminalisation of same-sex acts in India, contrasting the voices of celebration when India decriminalised same-sex intimacy in 2009, with voices of anger and resistance when the Supreme Court overturned that historic ruling in 2013. [Documentary film, 17 min.] N. Nicol (director), K. Siirala (editor), S. Ahmed (cinematographer), P. Sandhu (line producer). India and Canada: Naz India, NFI and Envisioning. See https://vimeo.com/85002638.

The Time Has Come (2013, updated 2016) features perspectives of human rights defenders around the world on issues of sexual orientation and gender identity (SOGI). Filmed at regional seminars held in six countries to strategise ways of working with the UN to strengthen SOGI protection. [Documentary film, 30 min.] K. Vance, J. Fisher and S. Kara (directors), N. Nicol and K. Vance (producers), K. Siirala (editor), C. Kaara, T. Mabuza, S. Nelson, Nkyooyo B., U. Verbeke and J. Wambya (videographers). Paris, Brasilia, New York, Nairobi, Kathmandu, Oslo, Geneva and Toronto: ARC International and Envisioning. English: http://vimeo.com/67796115.
French: *Le Moment Est Arrivé*: http://vimeo.com/74709548.
Spanish: *Ha Llegado El Momento*: http://vimeo.com/74625595.

Life Experience of LGBTI in Botswana (2013) presents LeGaBiBo's vision of creating an inclusive environment that protects the rights of the LGBT community in terms of health, law and social policy. [Documentary film, 13:34 min.] T. Motshwana, T. Mabuza and J. Molefe (participatory documentary team), Botswana and Canada: LeGaBiBo and Envisioning. See https://vimeo.com/75420906.

Botho: LGBT Lives in Botswana (2013) discusses gender, sexuality, culture, tradition, family and the Botswanan 'botho' concept in the struggle to challenge Penal Code criminalisation of same-sex conduct in Botswana. [Documentary film, 13:27 min.] N. Nicol (director), Botswana and Canada: LeGaBiBo and Envisioning. See https://vimeo.com/69577157.

Hope for the Future (2013) tracks the progress of, and resistance to, the Anti-Homosexuality Bill, and the campaign of media hatred and public outings of LGBTI people during the period 2009–13. [Documentary film, 7:30 min.] R. Lusimbo and P. Onziema (directors), T. McCarthy (editor), J. Wambya (camera), Nkyooyo B. (sound). Uganda and Canada: SMUG with Voices of the Abasiyazzi[1] and Envisioning. See https://vimeo.com/73786262.

---

1   *Abasiyazzi* is the Ugandan equivalent of the term 'queer'.

Sexuality, Repression and the Law: Resistance and Asylum and book launch of C. Lennox and M. Waites (eds.) *Human Rights, Sexual Orientation and Gender Identity in the Commonwealth: Struggles for Decriminalisation and Change* (2013) Toronto, 26 Jun.

Video documentation divided into the following sections:

- Part One [35 min.]: panel speakers – introduction by Nancy Nicol, Envisioning's principal investigator (PI), Matthew Waites, University of Glasgow, Gary Kinsman, Laurentian University and Canada research team, Debbie Douglas, Ontario Council of Agencies Serving Immigrants. See https://vimeo.com/70217990.

- Part Two [40 min.]: Nancy Nicol, Envisioning's PI, Monica Tabengwa, Africa research team, and screening of video short: *Botho: Lesbians, Gays and Bisexuals of Botswana.* See https://vimeo.com/70371903.

- Part Three [26 min.]: Marcela Romero, regional coordinator for Latin American and Caribbean Network of Transgender People, Nick J. Mulé, Canada research team, and a representative of Pride Uganda Alliance International. See https://vimeo.com/70417403.

One Love (2013) [12 sec.]. Video documentation of Envisioning's Caribbean research team rally in Emancipation Square, Kingston. Jamaica and Canada: J-FLAG and Envisioning. See https://vimeo.com/75420842.

LGBT Equality Litigation in the Caribbean (2013). Video documentation of Envisioning's Caribbean research team public event at Osgoode Hall Law School, York University, Toronto, 21 Nov:

- Part One [22 min.]: Nancy Nicol, Envisioning's PI and Maurice Tomlinson, legal adviser, Marginalized Groups, AIDS-Free World. See https://vimeo.com/80420432.

- Part Two [16:34 min.]: Caleb Orozco, UNIBAM's executive director. See https://vimeo.com/82217139.

- Part Three [27:20 min.]: Brian-Paul Welsh, J-FLAG and CariFLAGS. See https://vimeo.com/82220090.

Alok Gupta (2013) examines the British colonial origins of Section 377 of the Indian Penal Code. [Documentary film, 7 min.] N. Nicol (director), N. Nicol and K. Siirala (editors). India and Canada: Naz India, NFI and Envisioning. See https://vimeo.com/75914791.

Shivananda Khan, In Memoriam: Part One (2013). Khan recalls founding a group for queer Asians in the UK and queer organising during the 1970s. [Documentary film, 11:25 min.] N. Nicol (director), K. Siirala (editor). India and Canada: Naz India, NFI and Envisioning. See https://vimeo. com/75415047.

Shivananda Khan, A Portrait: Part Two (2013). Khan talks about marriage, family, culture, identity, hijras and transgender people in contemporary India. [Documentary film, 10:28 min.] N. Nicol (director), N. Nicol and K. Siirala (editors). India and Canada: Naz India, NFI and Envisioning. See https:// vimeo.com/75407900.

Shivananda Khan, Quote from the Gita (2013) [Documentary film, 42 sec.] N. Nicol (director), K. Siirala (editor). India and Canada: Naz India, NFI and Envisioning. See https://vimeo.com/75419138.

Chief Justice Shah on Naz Foundation v. Govt. of NCT of Delhi (2013). Chief Justice Shah (retired) outlines the constitutional grounds of his historic ruling in 2009 that read down Section 377 of the Indian Penal Code. [Documentary film, 8 min.] N. Nicol (director), N. Nicol and K. Siirala (editor). India and Canada: Naz India, NFI and Envisioning. See https://vimeo.com/75994483.

Sangama: Movement Building (2013). Activists participate in a demonstration for land rights, and talk about their approach to organising, addressing issues that affect sexual minorities, sex workers, and *adivasi* communities. [Documentary film, 10 min.] N. Nicol (director), K. Siirala (editor). India and Canada: Naz India, NFI and Envisioning. See https://vimeo.com/75992346.

Akkai (2013). Akkai sings a song she composed to describe her history and transition from male to female. [Documentary film, 3:49 min.] N. Nicol (director), K. Siirala (editor). India and Canada: Naz India, NFI and Envisioning. See https://vimeo.com/75994482.

Sade's Story (2013). Sade Richardson, a transgender fashion designer, describes violence and discrimination directed against her, in the context of the cross-dressing law in Guyana. [Documentary film, 12 min.] N.B. Henry, U. Verbeke and J.A. Grant (participatory documentary team). Guyana and Canada: SASOD and Envisioning. See https://vimeo.com/75422884.

Jessica's Journey (2013). Jessica, a transgender person from Guyana talks about the impact of transphobia on her life and her hope for the future. [Documentary film, 7:40 min.] N.B. Henry, U. Verbeke and J.A. Grant (participatory documentary team). Guyana and Canada: SASOD and Envisioning. There is no online access for this video.

Selina's Voice (2013). Selina Maria Perez describes violence against transgender persons in Guyana and a near fatal assault that left her permanently scarred. [Documentary film, 11:13 min.] N.B. Henry, U. Verbeke and J.A. Grant (participatory documentary team). Guyana and Canada: SASOD and Envisioning. See https://vimeo.com/88493864.

Homophobia in Guyana (2013) [Documentary film, 11:42] N.B. Henry, U. Verbeke and J.A. Grant (participatory documentary team). Guyana and Canada: SASOD and Envisioning. There is no online access for this video.

Our Saint Lucian Experience (2013) [Documentary film, 5 min.] M. Fontenelle, K. Placide, M. Danton and S. Nelson (participatory documentary team). Saint Lucia and Canada: United and Strong and Envisioning. There is no online access for this video.

Focus on Kenya, Uganda, Botswana (2012). Video documentation of presentation by the Africa research team on their research and screening of their participatory documentary work in progress filmed at Bonham Centre for Sexual Diversity Studies, University of Toronto, 12 Sep.
- Part One [22 min.]: Caroline Kaara, GALCK, speaking on work in Kenya. See https://vimeo.com/73495847.
- Part Two [23 min.]: Junic Wambya, Freedom and Roam Uganda, and Richard Lusimbo, SMUG (via Skype), speaking on work in Uganda. See https://vimeo.com/73502128.
- Part Three [22 min.]: Nancy Nicol, York University, Toronto, describing work in Botswana. See https://vimeo.com/73502816.

The Law, Discrimination and the Future. Activists share stories of how family, employers and society have discriminated against them, and speak of the importance of building community, now and for the future. [Documentary film, 15 min.] R. Lusimbo (research), J. Wambya (camera), Nkoyooyo B. (sound). Uganda and Canada: SMUG and Envisioning. See https://vimeo.com/73786261.

A Short Film on Kenyan LGBTI Stories (2012) discusses strategies for decriminalising same-sex intimacy in Kenya and cases of human rights violation. [Documentary film, 15 min.] I. Reid, C. Kaara and J. Muthuri (participatory documentary team). Kenya and Canada: GALCK and Envisioning. See https://vimeo.com/73786260.

IDAHO (2012). Documentation of the International Day Against Homophobia event organised by GALCK in Nairobi. Dance, spoken word, and song are intercut with speakers who elaborate on ways to eliminate ignorance and achieve equality by way of the law, the Constitution of Kenya, education and social change. [Documentary film, 7:30 min.] N. Nicol, K. Siirala, J. Wambya, C. Kaara, J. Muthuri and Nkoyooyo B., participatory documentary team. Kenya and Canada: GALCK and Envisioning. See https://vimeo.com/46496713.

Why is Documentation Essential to LGBT Movements? (2012). Video documentation of talk by Graeme Reid, Lesbian, Gay, Bisexual and Transgender Rights Program, Human Rights Watch. [8:40 min.] K. Siirala (editor), M. Danton and S. Nelson (videographers). Saint Lucia and Canada: United and Strong and Envisioning. See http://envisioninglgbt.blogspot.com/p/resources.html.

How is Human Rights Documentation Helpful When Combating Violence? (2012). Video documentation of talk by Maurice Tomlinson, legal adviser, Marginalized Groups, AIDS-Free World. [15:47 min.] K. Siirala (editor), M. Danton and S. Nelson (videographers). Saint Lucia and Canada: United and Strong and Envisioning. See http://envisioninglgbt.blogspot.com/p/resources. html.

Sexuality and Queer Politics in India: the Indian Experience (2011). Video documentation of event at Ontario Institute for Studies in Education, University of Toronto, 7 Oct:
- Part 1 [15:27 min.]: Naisargi N. Dave, anthropology department, Centre for South Asian Studies at the Asian Institute, University of Toronto. See https://vimeo.com/76567393.
- Part 2 [24 min.]: Gautam Bhan ed. *Because I Have a Voice: Queer Politics in India.* See https://vimeo.com/76565704.

International Association for the Study of Forced Migration (IASFM) 13 Conference: Governing Migration (2011). Envisioning Global LGBT Human Rights panel: LGBT Identities, Governance, and Asylum. Kampala, Uganda, 3–6 July [Video documentation by Centre for Refugee Studies, York University]:
- 'Uganda's Anti-Homosexuality Bill: its implications for forced migration' by Adrian Jjuuko, Civil Society Coalition on Human Rights and Constitutional Law) [15:20 min.]. See www.youtube.com/watch?v=3iRRPkYlixE.

- 'LGBT "discretion", persecution and self-protection:
  an international comparative analysis of refugee status
  determination' by Robert Lidstone, geography department,
  York University, Toronto [18:42 min.]. See www.youtube.com/
  watch?v=eNKG8cg3Fy8.
- 'Impact of discriminatory legislation on LGBT human rights
  defenders in Uganda' by Hassan Shire, East and Horn of Africa
  Human Rights Defenders Project, Kampala [15:26 min.]. See www.
  youtube.com/watch?v=N95_YGYdeGg.
- 'Envisioning Global LGBT Human Rights: connecting the dots
  across global struggle' by Nancy Nicol, York University, Toronto
  [13:41 min.]. See www.youtube.com/watch?v=L5dUIbhH9ZA.

Index

A.B., S.H. v Jamaica, 15
abnormal/abnormality/normal, 22,
    28, 151, 277, 312, 338, 362
access to justice/access to a lawyer,
    15–16, 277–8, 285–8, 384
activism/advocacy/organizing/
    visibility, 3, 6, 13, 17, 25–9,
    33, 66, 69, 85, 87, 89, 105,
    113, 114, 115, 116–17, 122,
    144–5, 172, 190, 226–7, 243,
    247, 250–253, 257, 260, 262–4,
    269, 274–6, 282–3, 308–9, 319,
    323–4, 328–32, 335, 338, 339,
    347–8, 349, 353, 350–66, 368,
    371, 381, 390, 393, 397
Adivasi, 380, 397
African Charter on Human and
    Peoples' Rights/African Charter,
    76, 183, 186–190, 284, 290
African Commission on Human and
    Peoples' Rights (ACHPR), 76,
    179, 189, 284 (advancement
    of SOGI issues by), 77, 89,
    189–91, 200–1, 228
African Solidarity Alliance, 332
African Union Commission (AUC),
    187, 189
African Union Strategic Plan, 187
African Women's Protocol, 183, 188
aggravated homosexuality, 65, 66,
    274, 284, 289
aid/aid conditionality, 75, 77, 88–9,
    192, 297, 299,
Alaka, Caleb, 285

Alliance Defending Freedom (ADF),
    25, 261
Alternative Law Forum (ALF), 392
Ambedkar, Dr. B. R, 18, 52, 55, 397
anal exam/anal medical exam, 44–7,
    279, 280
Anglican (*see* Church of England)
anti-gay groups, 83, 84, 85, 272,
    341
Anti-Homosexuality Act (AHA)
    Uganda, 65, 80, 83–4, 86,
    269–71, 277–83, 314,
organising against/legal challenge
    to, 21, 27–8, 90, 194, 283–92,
    296–7, 298–300, 301, 325, 338,
    372, 389–91,
nullification, 63, 69, 194, 269,
    271–2, 290, 293–6, 300–2
Anti-Homosexuality Bill (AHB),
    Uganda, 79–80, 83–4, 86, 90,
    269–70, 273–4,
organising against, 27–8, 274–6,
    324–5, 339–41
Anti-promotion laws/anti-
    propaganda laws/morality laws
    (*see also* AHA and AHB), 21, 22,
    28, 65–6, 84–5
Anti-Pornography Act, Uganda, 68,
    86
ARC International, 10, 32, 181,
    201, 227, 232, 233–4, 239, 375,
    383, 385–6
arrests (*see* police/law enforcement/
    arrest(s)/arbitrary arrest)

art (and activism) (*see also* participatory documentary), 347, 349–50, 355, 366–7, 373
asylum/asylum seeker (*see also* refugee and refugee health/ mental health), 24–25, 99, 101–2, 103, 106–8, 112–13, 116, 120–1, 170

Bahati, David, 80, 83, 86, 269, 272, 273, 314, 324–5, 326
Ban Ki-Moon, 201, 229, 385
Belize Criminal Code (Section 53) (*see also Caleb Orozco v. the Attorney General of Belize*), 14, 26, 248
organising against, 27, 249–59, 262–5
Belize Action, 25, 250, 257–62
Belizeans for the Constitutional Challenge, 250, 263
Benegal, Shyam, 54
Bill C-31 (*see* Protecting Canada's Immigration System Act)
bisexual/bisexuality (*see also* LGBT, LGBTI), 120, 215, 310, 332, 349–50, 360
biphobia, 360
blackmail/extortion, 29, 165, 308, 311, 393
botho/ubuntu, 22, 196, 382, 406
border security/policing borders/ border regimes, 7, 11, 23, 24–5, 100, 101–7, 110, 112, 114–16, 118
Botswana Penal Code (Sections 162–4), 20, 63, 72, 88, 135–6, 159–61,
organising against, 196–7
Botswana Vision (2016), 196
breast surgery/top surgery (*see also* surgery/hormone treatment), 357, 380

bully/bullying, 170, 309
buggery/sodomy (laws against), 11–12, 15, 38, 64, 66, 135–6, 157, 160, 161, 163, 164, 171, 178, 191, 249, 252, 271, 307, 308, 314, 384

Caleb Orozco v. the Attorney General of Belize, 14, 15, 247, 248–9, 257, 262, 265
Cameroon, 20, 63, 68, 72
capitalism/capitalist/capitalist globalisation, 7, 11, 22–3, 25, 29, 31–2, 64, 106, 100, 109–16, 132–4, 137, 144–5, 351, 365, 371, 375, 372–3
Caribbean Coalition of lesbian, gay, bisexual, transvestite, transgender, transsexual and intersex organisations (LGBTTTI Coalition), 17, 254, 255
Caribbean Regional Trans in Action (CRTA), 251, 253
Caribbean Vulnerable Communities Coalition (CVC), 251
Caribbean Sex-Workers Coalition, 172
Caricom/Caribbean Community, 13, 159, 248, 262, 263, 266
CariFLAGS, 251, 256
carnal intercourse/knowledge against the order of nature (laws against), *see* criminalisation (colonial laws) and (post-independence laws) and Indian Penal Code (Section 377)
Catholic Church (Roman), 167, 180, 259–60, 324–5
Centre for Family and Human Rights (C-FAM), 261–2
Challenge for Change/Société nouvelle, 373–4

Christian Fellowship Lawyers, 262

Christian fundamentalists/ fundamentalism/evangelical (opposition to SOGI rights), 12–13, 25–7, 28, 78–80, 86–7, 115, 167, 179, 195, 249, 253, 255–63, 264, 273, 286, 293, 312–15, 324–5, 335, 341–2, 362, 372, 386

Church of England (Anglican), 25, 79, 249, 260, 263, 314

cisgender, 145, 216, 348, 355, 362, 376, 397

cissexism/cissexist/cis-normative, 134, 359, 369

citizenship, sexual, 54, 58, 116–17, 132–3, 137, 145, 149, 154, 309, 318

Civil Society Coalition on Human Rights and Constitutional Law (CSCHRCL), 27, 88, 272–3, 274–6, 278, 281, 282–301, 340, 389, 390

civil society/civil society organizations (see also Civil Society Coalition on Human Rights and Constitutional Law), 6, 8, 11, 25, 26, 27, 81, 89–90, 98, 179, 180, 182, 183, 184, 198, 201, 225–9, 232, 249, 261, 308, 312, 319, 341, 385

class/class struggle/classism, 28, 34, 46, 59, 105, 106, 109–13, 114, 115, 116–17, 121, 132–3, 134, 144, 145, 147, 149, 153, 163, 166, 168–9, 170, 205–6, 215–16, 217, 224, 240, 347, 353, 357–8, 376

Coalition of African Lesbians (CAL), 89, 179, 189–91, 201, 228, 308–9, 333

colonial/colonialism/colonisation (see also criminalisation –

colonial law), 2–3, 6, 7, 11, 12, 22, 29, 30, 64, 76, 111, 114, 117, 123, 132, 136, 148, 157, 158–9, 355, 386

Commonwealth Heads of Government Meeting (CHOGM), 334

consent/consensual/consenting adults, 17, 32, 47, 49, 66–7, 135–6, 160, 195, 230, 247, 266, 274, 280, 309, 315, 318, 319

Consortium on Monitoring Violations Based on Sex Determination, Gender Identity and Sexual Orientation (Consortium), Uganda, 270, 277–8, 279–80, 282, 325

[The] Constitution (Amendment) Act (Uganda 2005), 64

constitutional equality/prohibition of discrimination (see also constitutional morality), 14, 16, 17, 19–20, 21, 22, 27, 28, 43, 49, 55, 56, 57, 59, 60–1, 63, 64–5, 81, 82, 135, 157, 161, 162, 163, 178, 182, 186, 188, 193, 194, 195, 197, 201, 247, 248, 249, 264, 269, 287, 284, 288, 291, 309, 316, 317, 318, 328

constitutional right to privacy, 14, 15, 19, 26, 50, 52, 55, 58, 60, 195, 223, 228, 279, 288, 289, 290, 310, 329, 336, 398

constitutional marches (Belize), 27, 254, 260–2

constitutional morality/public morality, 18, 52–3, 55,192, 195, 317, 397

constitutional prohibition of same-sex/equal marriage, 20, 63, 64

constitutional protection on the grounds of SOGIE, 82

constitutionalism in Africa, 76, 80–2

Criminal Tribes Act, India, 59

criminalisation (colonial laws), 5, 9,
11–14, 17, 18, 19, 23, 27, 43–9,
52, 59, 63, 67–8, 72–5, 88, 111,
118, 119, 135–136, 160, 161,
173, 178–9, 186, 191, 194, 197,
223–4, 241, 247, 271, 273, 291,
307–8, 310–11, 318, 327, 382,
394–5

criminalisation (post-independence
laws), 6, 19, 26, 29–30, 63–9,
75–84, 136, 196, 270, 272, 291,
310–11, 318

cross-dressing (laws against) (*see also*
Guyana, *Section 153 Summary
Jurisdiction Offences Act*), 5, 14,
16, 44, 157, 159–60, 161–4,
171, 173, 384

culture/cultural politics, 23–4, 26,
50, 79, 100, 106, 112, 123,
151–2, 153, 160, 163, 167–70,
177, 178–9, 180–1, 186–7, 188,
190, 195, 198, 200, 202, 215,
224, 233, 273, 290, 328, 366,
382, 386, 406

culture wars, 76, 84–5, 184,
259–62, 324

curative petition (against Section
377, India), 19, 60–1

customary law, 65, 74, 273

death penalty, 19, 223, 230, 241–2,
270, 274, 314, 325, 334

Decena, Carlos, 146

decriminalisation, 7, 9, 14, 21, 22,
23, 52, 69, 76, 77, 88, 149,
196–7, 199, 250, 252, 259,
262–4, 291, 309, 316–19

Delhi High Court (Section 377,
2009), 12, 13, 18, 19, 49, 54,
57, 397–8

detention/imprisonment (*see also*
refugee determination, Canada),
24–5, 102, 103, 104, 118–19,
122, 223, 279–81, 356

deviant/deviancy, 71–2, 159–60

dignity (*see* constitutional equality)

disability/(dis)ability, 207, 274, 289

domestic violence, 273, 251

donor dependency/donor funding
(impact on organising), 8, 29,
351, 353–4, 363–4

East African Court of Justice
(EACJ), 65, 194, 195, 271, 272,
284, 286, 294–6, 300–1

education (access to), 16, 166, 170,
223, 307–8, 310, 337–8, 352–3,
356, 357, 388

Egale Canada, 106, 226

Egypt, 21, 183, 189

employment discrimination, 196,
199, 392

*Eric Gitari v Non-Governmental
Organisations Co-ordination
Board & four Others*, 20, 193,
317, 353

*Eric Gitari v. attorney general and
another*, 319

eunuch, 44, 45

evangelical (*see* Christian
fundamentalists/
fundamentalism/evangelical)

Evangelical Association of Belize,
249, 253

Evangelical Fellowship of Botswana,
195

eviction (of LGBTI persons), 104,
282, 341

family/familial/family unit, 18,
23–4, 29, 44, 49, 57, 71, 79,
114–16, 134, 136–7, 139–44,
146, 151, 160, 163, 167, 167,

170, 183, 189, 208, 212, 229, 255, 307, 311, 313, 315–16, 325, 327–8, 331, 334, 337, 338, 341, 350–1, 352, 353, 358, 359, 361, 376, 382, 384, 388, 395

family class (immigration), 103, 110–13, 116, 114, 119

family values/normal family unit/ traditional family/'pro-family', 26, 28, 78, 79, 84–5, 182, 183, 188, 189, 192, 241, 261–2, 273, 312, 314–15

Family Life Network (FLN), 65, 79–80, 293, 324–5

Family Watch International (The Family), 8, 26, 28, 80, 312, 324

Family Research Council (Uganda), 324, 341

feminism/feminists, 98, 108, 114, 115, 123, 139, 180, 226, 227, 330, 356, 374, 376, 388, 393

foreign policy, 78, 275

Freedom and Roam Uganda (FARUG), 271, 283–4, 330, 389, 390

freedom of association/expression, 20, 22, 193–4, 197, 238, 275, 317, 385–6

Freire, Paulo, 371

fundamentalists/fundamentalism opposition to SOGI rights (see Christian fundamentalists/ fundamentalism and Islamic opposition)

gay/gay men/homosexual, (also see refugee determination) 49, 52, 54, 55, 57, 83, 90, 131, 139–42, 143–5, 146–7, 151–3, 159–60, 165–70, 177, 178, 248, 256, 257, 260, 285, 307, 310, 311, 312, 315, 323, 339, 350, 352, 384, 388, 393, 396

'gay agenda', 12, 78, 85, 258, 324

gay wedding (see same-sex marriage/ equal marriage)

Gay and Lesbian Coalition of Kenya (GALCK), 308, 333, 348, 377

Gays and Lesbians of Zimbabwe (GALZ), 178, 185

gay international (see also international/transnational/ global SOGI organizing efforts), 23, 148

gender identity/gender expression, 6, 44–5, 59, 77, 90–1, 99, 159–60, 161, 162, 165, 166, 172, 177, 178, 181, 185, 190–1, 193, 200, 205, 207, 208, 210, 216–17, 224, 229–30, 231, 232, 235, 240–1, 270–1, 307, 325, 347, 355, 360–3, 368

gender fluidity/gender queer/ gender non conforming (see also Intersex, Transgender and gender non-conforming), 8, 13, 347

gender norms, 161, 310

Gender Policy (Belize), 27, 254, 256–9, 260, 261–3

genital cutting (female), 187

Ghana, 72, 76, 81, 88, 182

Global Action for Trans* Equality (GATE), 26, 227

global/globalisation, 7, 22, 23, 31, 64, 111, 115, 132–135, 137, 351, 375

Global North, 1, 5, 12, 25, 75, 85, 100, 114, 131, 138, 143, 148, 154, 275

Global South, 2, 4, 5, 10, 11, 12, 13, 22–3, 24–5, 27, 30–1, 32, 34, 35, 99, 100, 101, 102, 104, 105, 106, 110, 111, 113, 114, 115, 116, 118, 142, 145, 146, 147, 148, 154, 200, 201, 226, 242, 371, 372

gross indecency (criminalisation of),
15, 73–4, 135, 160–1
Gopalan, Anjali (*see also* Naz
Foundation (India) Trust),
392–3
Gupta, Alok, 396, 407
Guyana, 13, 157–75
Guyana, Criminal Law (Offences)
Act (Sections 352 to 354), 160,
164–70, 171
Guyana, Summary Jurisdiction
Offences Act (Section 153)/cross
dressing law, 14, 16, 161, 162–3,
164–70, 250
Guyana Trans United, 157

hate crimes/speech, 80, 86, 310,
313, 314
health (adverse effects due to
discrimination on SOGIE
grounds) (*see also* mental health/
mental illness and refugee health/
mental health), 68, 91, 162, 163,
166, 170, 171, 186, 237, 238,
248, 257, 258, 264, 281, 287,
288, 289, 295, 299, 307, 309,
310, 311, 313, 315–16, 330,
331, 333, 334, 339, 341, 348,
350, 353, 357, 359, 362, 384,
388, 392, 393
Heartland Alliance, 190, 251, 253
heteronormative/heteronormativity,
112, 113, 131, 134, 136, 140,
145, 147, 151, 160, 173, 209,
216
heterosexism/heterosexist, 47, 49,
71, 100, 106, 112, 160, 173
heterosexual/heterosexuality/
heterosexual norms, 7, 23, 29,
71, 73, 82, 111, 112, 114, 115,
116, 120, 133, 136, 160, 166,
167, 172, 215, 229, 308, 310,
314, 327, 351

hijra, 18, 44, 57, 59, 60, 394, 397
Hindu (opposition to SOGIE
rights), 50, 167, 395
HIV testing (forced), 280, 289
HIV/AIDS criminalisation (of
transmission), 69
HIV/AIDS (adverse effects of
criminalization/discrimination
on prevention and healthcare/
police raids on HIV/AIDS
service providers), 49, 50, 67, 68,
69, 76, 82–3, 90, 170, 248, 280,
281, 288, 299, 313, 315–16,
323, 330, 332, 333, 334, 341,
348, 350, 353
HIV/AIDS (people living with/
PLWA), 108, 247, 248, 274,
289, 296
HIV Prevention and Control Act,
Uganda, 68, 69
homonationalism/homonationalist,
23, 100, 105, 113, 116–17, 123,
142, 144, 148, 149, 153, 154,
216, 224
homotransnationalism, 148
homophobia/homophobic/state
sponsored homophobia, 1, 23,
27, 51, 57, 64, 85, 87, 89, 91,
100, 102, 106, 131, 132, 134,
135–9, 140, 141, 142, 143, 144,
145, 146, 147, 148, 150, 151,
152, 153, 154, 160, 167, 170,
172, 179, 199, 201, 249, 256,
262, 290, 308, 309, 312, 313,
314, 317, 323, 324, 328, 330,
341, 349, 354, 382, 386
housing (access to) (*see also* refugee
settlement/services, Canada, 170,
171, 238, 278, 331, 361
housing/poverty/slum conditions (and
SOGI issues), 7, 28–9, 34, 133,
134, 171, 166, 329, 351, 352,
354, 357, 369, 392, 396, 397

Human Dignity Trust, 249
human rights (*see* constitutional equality/prohibition of discrimination)
Human Rights Awareness and Promotion Forum (Uganda), 20, 270, 336
Human Rights Awareness & Promotion Forum (HRAPF) versus The Attorney General of Uganda (East African Court of Justice), 194, 272, 284, 268, 294–6, 301
human rights defenders, 9, 22, 25, 26, 30, 35, 68, 180, 190, 199, 201, 224, 233, 234, 238, 239, 240, 241, 242, 254, 255, 287, 299, 318, 319, 336, 340, 371, 372, 386, 406

Ice Breakers Uganda (IBU), 331, 339
Immigration and Refugee Board (IRB) of Canada (*see* refugee determination, Canada)
imperialism/neo-imperialism, 29, 30, 76, 104, 111
imprisonment (*see* detention/imprisonment)
indecent act/indecency/gross indecency (criminalisation of), 67, 135
Indian Penal Code (Section 377), 11, 43–8, 73, 394, 395
organising against, 18, 19, 49–61, 375, 391, 392, 393, 394, 395, 396, 397, 398
indigenous/pre-colonial sexual, erotic and gender identities/expression, 70–2, 177, 326–8, 380, 386, 394–395
Inter Religious Council of Uganda, 80, 293, 299

Interim Federal Health Program (IFHP), Canada, 212
International Commission of Jurists (ICJ), 19, 225, 232, 249
International Gay and Lesbian Human Rights Commission (IGLHRC), 229
International Lesbian, Gay, Bisexual, Trans and Intersex Association (ILGA), 6, 186, 226, 228
International Labour Organization, 227
intersectional/intersectionality, 8, 27, 28–9, 35, 90–1, 105, 206, 209, 215–16, 224, 234–5, 238, 239, 309, 319, 352–3, 354–5, 392, 395, 397
intersex, 8, 224, 227, 232, 234, 242, 335, 337, 339–40, 347, 348, 349, 353, 355, 356, 357, 358, 359, 360, 361, 368, 388
intersex, transgender and gender non-conforming (ITGNC) (*see also* gender fluidity/gender queer/gender non conforming), 13, 14, 28, 308, 309, 310, 328, 347, 350, 352, 355, 356, 357, 359–63, 365, 366, 367, 368, 369, 394
in vitro fertilization/IVF, 380
irregular arrivals (*see also* borders and asylum), 118–20
Islamic (opposition to SOGIE rights), 167, 179, 223, 313, 325
Islamophobia, 113, 117

Jacqueline Kasha Nabagesera, Frank Mugisha, Julian Pepe Onziema and Geoffrey
Ogwaro v. attorney general and Hon. Rev. Fr Simon Lokodo, Uganda, 20, 69, 194, 285, 336

Jamaican Coalition for a Healthy
Society (JCHS), 262
Jamaica Forum for Lesbians, All-
Sexuals and Gays (J-FLAG), 15,
383
*Javed Jaghai v Attorney General of
Jamaica*, 15, 16, 385
Jinsiangu (Kenya), 8, 28, 309, 347,
355, 357–66, 367, 368, 369
Jjuuko, Adrian, 28, 285, 272, 292,
336
Jjuuko Adrian v. attorney general
(re: Equal Opportunities
Commission Act), 284
Jones, Jason, 17–18
Joseph, Tennyson, 132
*Justice K. S. Puttaswamy (retd.) and
ANR v. Union of India and ORS*,
19, 398
Justice for All roadmap, 262, 263

Kabaka Mwanga (Ugandan martyrs),
326–7
Kadaga, Rebecca, 276
Kaggwa, Julius, 335, 340, 384
Kanane, Utjiwa, 88
Kapya, Kaoma John, 25–6, 78, 79,
80, 324
*Kasha Jacqueline, David Kato Kisuule
and Pepe Julian Onziema v. The
Rolling Stone Newspaper*, 70, 81,
193, 194, 285, 383, 336
Kato, David (*see also Kasha
Jacqueline, David Kato Kisuule
and Pepe Julian Onziema v. The
Rolling Stone Newspaper*), 69,
335, 336, 383
Khairati (*see Queen Empress v
Khairati*)
Kenya Human Rights Commission
(KHRC), 318
Kenya Medical Research Institute
(KEMRI), 313

Kenya National Commission on
Human Rights (KNCHR), 319,
348
Kenyan Penal Code (Section 162,
163 and 165) (*see also Eric Gitari
v. attorney general and another*),
307–8, 319
Keynesianism, 114, 132
Kidwai, Saleem, 29, 394
kuchu, 272, 323, 324, 325, 326,
330, 337, 338, 339, 342
Kuchu Times, 339

Latin America, 7, 17, 19, 179, 180,
182, 240, 251, 256, 386
Latin American and Caribbean
Coalition of lesbian, gay,
bisexual, transvestite,
transgender, transsexual
and intersex organizations
(LGBTTTI Coalition), 17, 254,
255
Lawyers Christian Fellowship, 255
Lawyers Collective, India, 49, 50,
376, 392, 393, 394
legal advocacy/litigation (to advance
SOGI rights/repeal of laws that
criminalise same sex relations),
5, 11, 12, 14, 15, 16, 17–18, 19,
20, 21, 27–28, 49–61, 69, 70,
79, 80, 81, 86, 87, 90, 157, 161,
193, 194, 196–7, 228, 249–59,
262–5, 283–92, 296–7, 298–
300, 301, 317, 318, 319, 324,
325, 336, 338, 341, 353, 368,
372, 385, 385, 389–91, 398
legal protection from discrimination/
non-discrimination (on the
grounds of SOGI), 81, 178, 186,
196
lesbian(s)/lesbianism/queer women
(*see also* women who have sex
with women (WSW), 26, 52,

54, 55, 63, 89, 142, 145, 147, 151, 152, 169–170, 178, 179, 189, 195, 210, 226, 227, 228, 229, 230, 232, 234, 242, 257, 269, 275, 309, 311, 312, 313, 314, 315, 317, 328, 329, 330–1, 332, 333, 334, 338, 347, 348, 349, 350–351, 352, 354, 360, 376, 382, 388

Lesbians, Gays and Bisexuals of Botswana (LeGaBiBo), 20, 22, 196, 197, 198, 377

Lively, Scott (*see Sexual Minorities Uganda v. Scott Lively*)

Lokodo, Hon. Rev. Fr Simon, 273, 285, 336

love, 18, 48, 52, 53, 54, 57, 61, 64, 147, 151, 196, 200, 257, 327, 375, 382, 388, 390

LVCT Health, Kenya, 348

Malawi, 20, 63, 68, 72, 81, 88, 238

Massad, Joseph, 23, 148

Mauritius, 72, 181, 185, 186, 339

Mbugua, Audrey (*see also Republic v Kenya National Examinations Council & Another Ex-Parte Audrey Mbugua Ithibu,* Kenya), 193, 318, 349, 356, 368

McEwan, Clarke, Fraser, Persaud and SASOD v. Attorney General of Guyana, 16, 157, 161, 249

media (*see also* social media)
reporting on SOGI issues, 25, 27, 83, 85, 113, 137–9, 160, 192, 253, 257, 260, 261, 263, 264, 269, 275, 277, 280, 282, 285, 292, 297, 298, 300, 307–9, 313, 314, 325, 329, 331, 334, 336, 339, 350, 383, 389, 390, 394
use of for advocacy, 226, 258, 262, 292, 297, 328–30, 339,

368, 374, 382, 388

medical/medical evidence (*see* anal exam)

men who have sex with men (MSM), 83, 91, 247, 251, 259, 316, 330, 332, 333, 350, 392, 394

mental health/mental illness (*see also* refugee health/mental health)
impact of discrimination on the basis of SOGIE, 170, 207, 208, 218, 316, 359, 362, 369
treatment of homosexuality or transgenderism as illness, 350, 160

Minority Women in Action (MWA) Kenya, 316, 348–52

mobs/mob justice/mob violence, 238, 270, 278, 282, 311, 313, 384, 389, 390

moral panic, 324

moral regulation (*see also* anti-promotion, anti-propaganda laws), 21, 28, 52, 53, 115, 135, 137, 143, 173, 188, 195, 307, 310, 314, 317

moral/immoral, 47, 48, 53, 58, 85, 89, 134, 190, 195, 262, 265, 323, 350

Most At Risk Populations (MARP), 333

Mozambique, 13, 21, 67, 69, 73, 81, 186, 188, 198, 199, 239

MSM (*see* Men who have Sex with Men)

Muasya, Richard, 356

Mugisha, Dr. Frank, 201, 270, 287, 288, 301, 329, 330, 335, 340, 341, 391

Mughal empire, 59

Mukasa, Victor, 329, 332, 333, 348

multi-tiered/multifaceted/ multipronged/incremental

approach (to advocacy) (*see also* intersectional), 20, 27, 197, 198, 283, 291, 269–302, 309

Muntarbhorn, Vitit, 26, 182, 230

Muralidhar, Justice, 52

Museveni, Yoweri, 22, 68, 71, 76, 77, 80, 84, 192, 269, 270, 275–7, 283, 296–8, 323, 325, 341, 390

Muslim(s), 55, 59, 79, 100, 106, 113

Mutesi, Fridah, 28, 272, 285, 292

Mwenda, Andrew, 286, 288

Nabagesera, Kasha Jacqueline, 287, 288, 301, 330, 331, 333, 336, 340

National AIDS Commission (NAC) Belize, 27, 249

National AIDS Control Organization (NACO) India, 50

National Anti-Gay Task Force Uganda, 324

National Coalition for Gay and Lesbian Equality and another v. minister of justice and others, 82

National Gay and Lesbian Human Rights Commission (NGLHRC) Kenya, 20, 193, 311, 353

National Legal Services Authority v Union of India, 18, 44, 58–61

nationalism, 117, 131, 132, 179, 180

Naz Foundation (India) Trust, 49, 50, 54, 391, 392, 393

Naz Foundation International (NFI), 391, 394

Naz Foundation v NCT Delhi, 18, 43, 49–53, 54, 55, 57, 58, 60, 393

neo-colonial/neo-colonialism, 11, 12, 13, 22, 26, 29, 76, 85, 111, 371, 390

neoliberal/neoliberalism, 7, 11, 12, 13, 22–5, 29, 31, 35, 98, 101–3, 106, 107, 110, 111, 114–16, 118, 120, 121, 131–4, 137, 139, 149, 154, 371, 372

neoliberal queer, 25, 101, 106, 115–17

Nehru, Jawaharlal, 55, 56

Nigeria, 20, 22, 63, 66, 70, 72, 81, 86, 89, 177, 223, 241, 341, 351

ngochani, 177

None on Record, 355

normalising, normalised/ normalisation, 24–5, 29, 100, 102, 104, 109, 112, 116, 122, 132, 133, 140, 170

No One Is Illegal (NOII), 103, 104, 105, 106, 121, 122

non-discrimination in employment (on the basis of sexual orientation), 196, 199

Non-Governmental Organizations Act/NGO Act, Uganda, 22, 68, 86, 271, 272, 302

Non-Governmental Organizations (NGOs) (denial of registration of NGOs and organisations / legal challenges to denial) (*see also Eric Gitari v Non-Governmental Organisations Co-ordination Board & four Others; Republic v Kenya National Examinations Council & Another Ex-Parte Audrey Mbugua Ithibu and Thuto Rammoge and others v. attorney general of Botswana*), 20, 22, 66, 68, 69, 89–90, 178, 193, 197–8, 271–2, 317, 354, 363

Nowshirwan v Emperor India, 43, 46, 47, 53

Obama, Barack, 78, 192, 237, 277, 297, 324

Odoi-Owyelowo, Hon. Fox, 287, 288, 292, 293, 294
Offences Against the Person Act Jamaica/offences against the person (legal codes), 14, 135, 136
Ogenga-Latigo, Hon. Morris, 287, 288, 292
Oloka-Onyango, Dr. Joe, 68, 275, 276, 286, 287, 300
Onoria, Dr. Henry, 285
Onyango, Francis, 285
Onziema, Pepe Julian, 287, 288, 301, 334, 336, 340
Opiyo, Nicholas, 275, 276, 277, 285, 286, 292
oppression (*see* discrimination/ persecution)
Organization of American States (OAS), 17, 27, 228, 249, 251, 253–6, 265
Organization Intersex International (OII), 227
Orozco, Caleb, 7, 14, 25, 27, 221, 247, 262, 265
OutRight Action International (formerly, International Gay and Lesbian Human Rights Commission (IGLHRC), 186, 228

paedophilia, 312
Pakistan, 46, 238
Pan-Africanism, 76
participatory research/participatory action research, 1, 3, 32, 373, 377
participatory documentary (Envisioning), 3, 5, 32, 371–98
patriarchal/patriarchy/ heteropatriarchal/ homopatriarchal, 111, 115, 136, 146, 147, 152, 153, 188, 310,

355, 376
persecution (*see* discrimination/ inequality/persecution)
Pillay, Navi, 200, 229
police/law enforcement
    arrest(s)/arbitrary arrest by, 19, 28, 44–8, 49, 57, 59, 63, 68, 88, 90, 98, 134, 138, 153, 159–60, 162, 165, 229, 256, 270, 271, 272, 278–82, 299, 311, 314, 315–16, 325, 327, 336, 339, 356, 372, 389–90, 392, 394, 398
    prosecution/charges, 29, 46, 47, 88, 160–1, 270, 271, 274, 279, 280, 282, 394
    raids by (against LGBTI people or organisations) (*see also* HIV/AIDS (adverse effects of criminalization/discrimination on prevention and healthcare/ police raids on HIV/AIDS service providers), 68, 271, 281, 301, 313, 329, 334, 336, 339, 348, 393–394
    violence and degrading treatment by (*see also* rape (custodial – by police, prison authorities, guards), 16, 44–5, 57, 98, 102, 104, 138, 152, 161, 163, 165, 166, 169, 272, 278, 279, 280, 281, 282, 311, 334, 384, 388, 392, 393, 395
post-colonial/post-independence (re: SOGI issues), 10, 19, 23, 55–6, 63–9, 74–92, 132–7, 142, 143, 157, 179
pornography/pornographic/porn, 68, 86, 278, 324, 394
pre-colonial sexual and gender expression (*see* indigenous/pre- colonial sexual, erotic and gender identities/expression)

Pride, 33, 56, 221, 262, 301, 339, 340, 382, 383, 386–7
privacy (*see* right to privacy)
Professor J. Oloka-Onyango, Hon. Fox Odoi-Owyelowo, Professor Morris Ogenga-Latigo, Andrew M. Mwenda, Dr Paul Semugoma, Jacqueline Kasha Nabagesera, Julian Pepe Onziema, Frank Mugisha, HRAPF and CEHURD v. attorney general, 83, 90, 269, 276, 283–94, 300, 340
Protecting Canada's Immigration System Act, 103, 106, 113, 118–21
protest (*see* activism)
Puar, Jasbir, 23, 148, 224
Public Order Management Act, Uganda, 68, 276, 373

Queen Empress v Khairati, India, 44
queer/queer organising/queer studies, 23, 49, 51, 97, 99, 116, 131, 137, 138, 143, 145, 146, 147, 148, 151, 307, 310, 350, 354, 360, 375, 388, 391, 392
Quincy McEwan, Seon Clarke, Joseph Fraser, Seyon Persaud and the Society Against Sexual Orientation Discrimination (SASOD) vs. Attorney General of Guyana, 161–2, 249

racism/racist/racialisation/anti-racist, 29, 34, 35, 91, 97, 100, 102, 105, 106, 109, 110, 112, 113, 114, 116, 117, 121–3, 136, 143, 146, 148, 151, 153, 158, 159, 163, 166, 168, 169, 170, 172, 177, 188, 205, 206, 208, 209, 215, 216–18, 224, 228, 230, 240, 261, 326, 387, 394
Rainbow Identity Association (Botswana), 197, 388, 404
Rainbow Railroad, 106
rape/sexual assault, 136, 165, 187, 190, 191, 223, 238, 256, 311, 351, 388
rape ('corrective'), 315, 325
rape (custodial – by police, prison authorities, guards), 29, 57, 134, 165, 178, 280
Refugee Appeal Division, Canada, 119
refugee (barriers to claiming asylum), 24, 101–3, 118, 119, 120
refugee camps, 11, 101–103, 108, 271, 281
refugee (conditions facing LGBTIQ), 10, 11, 208, 210, 213, 235, 339
refugee determination, Canada, 24, 97, 98, 99, 100, 105, 106, 110, 111–12, 113, 115, 119, 120, 154, 205, 207, 208, 210–12, 215, 218
Basis of Claim/personal narrative, 107, 108, 211, 218
Designated Country of Origin, 119–21, 122, 211, 216Designated Foreign National/irregular arrival, 118–20, 122
detention/deportation, 24–5, 102–5, 110, 116, 118–19, 120–2, 212
family class system, 103, 112–14
policy/laws/recommendations, 102, 103, 118, 121–3, 214, 216
proving sexual orientation/gender identity, 98, 99, 120, 122, 210, 211, 217
Western and essentialist concepts of sexual orientation/gender identity, 99, 109, 111, 112, 120, 209, 215

refugee health/mental health, Canada 102, 104, 108, 106, 116, 121, 122, 205–19

refugee settlement/services, Canada, 10, 34, 116, 206, 212, 215, 218

refugee sponsorship, Canada, 98, 99, 108, 110, 113, 116

religious right/religious extremism/ religious-based intolerance against LGBTIQ (*see* Christian fundamentalists/ fundamentalism/evangelical (opposition to SOGI rights), Hindu (opposition to SOGIE rights) and Islamic (opposition to SOGIE rights)

Republic v Kenya National Examinations Council & Another Ex-Parte Audrey Mbugua Ithibu, 193, 318, 368

rights (*see* constitutional equality/ prohibition of discrimination/ dignity and constitutional right to privacy)

Robinson, Tracy, 136, 248, 249

Roman Catholic Church (*see* Catholic Church)

Rolling Stone case (*see Kasha Jacqueline, David Kato Kisuule & Pepe Julian Onziema v the Rolling Stone Ltd.*)

Royal Canadian Mounted Police (RCMP) (national security campaigns), 98

Saint Lucia, 7, 10, 13, 23, 131–54, 159

same-sex marriage/equal marriage/ gay wedding, 17, 78, 82, 106, 149, 159, 313, 382, 395

same-sex marriage (legal/ constitutional prohibition), 20, 63, 64, 65, 66, 81, 82, 88–9

Same-Sex Marriage (Prohibition) Act, Nigeria, 20, 66, 89

same-sex relationship/family law, 13, 20, 82, 136, 149, 170

same-sex parental rights/adoption (legal recognition of), 82, 382, 388

sanctuary city, 122

Sangama, 388, 392, 396, 397

Sangini, 375, 376, 391, 400

safe space(s), 172, 309, 330, 334, 337

Safe Third Country Agreement (Canada/USA), 118, 122

Section 377 (*see* India Penal Code Section 377)

Section 145 (*see* Uganda Penal Code Act Section 145)

service provision/providers, 24, 28, 63, 66, 69, 90, 102, 104, 116, 120, 121, 123, 133, 163, 166–7, 170, 171, 172, 206, 207, 208, 211, 212, 213, 214, 215, 216, 217, 218, 264, 271, 274, 281, 288, 289, 299, 307, 309, 310, 313, 315, 316, 330, 356, 363, 364, 369, 372

settler-state, 117

sexual citizenship (*see* citizenship, sexual)

Sexual Minorities Uganda (SMUG), 5, 20, 22, 27–8, 270, 282, 287, 300, 308–9, 325, 328–34, 335, 336, 371–2, 376, 381, 382–3, 389–91

Sexual Minorities Uganda v. Scott Lively, 5, 79, 80, 86, 87, 324, 335, 341, 372, 379

sexual reproductive health/rights, 89, 170, 186, 237, 310, 315

sex work/sex workers, 14, 16, 161, 172, 247, 248, 258, 274, 311, 334, 368, 396–7

Shah, Chief Justice (retd.), 51, 52, 55, 57
scientists' report, Uganda, 297
social imperialism/to impose social values, 77
social media (use of for advocacy), 250, 254, 256, 259, 260, 263, 381
Society Against Sexual Orientation Discrimination (SASOD), 16, 17, 158, 161, 162, 172, 383–4
sodomy/sodomise/sodomite/Sodom (*see also* buggery/sodomy (laws against)), 44, 45, 46, 64, 79, 257, 280
South Africa, 65, 70, 72, 76, 77, 78, 81, 82, 178, 179, 181, 182, 184, 185, 186, 198, 199, 200, 231, 288, 298, 316, 324, 332, 339, 352, 382
Spectrum Uganda Initiative, 280, 330
Ssempa, Pastor Martin, 79, 86, 87, 273, 324, 334
St Lucia (*see* Saint Lucia)
state security/anti-terrorism measures (impact on SOGIE organising), 28, 98, 112, 114, 116, 117, 215, 272, 313, 314, 351–2, 373
Stirm, Scott/ Jubilee Ministries/ Belize Action, 257, 259, 260, 261
structural inequality/inequalities/ structural adjustment, 23, 30, 31, 133, 134, 137
structural violence, 162, 164, 166, 167, 172, 173
Sudan and South Sudan, 70, 72, 177, 186, 223, 277
suicide, 170, 213, 369
Suresh Kumar Koushal and another v Naz Foundation and others, India, 18, 19, 43, 54–8, 60, 61

surgery/hormone treatment, 17, 60, 360, 361

Tamale, Dr. Sylvia, 30, 177, 275, 332, 390
third gender, 5, 60, 238, 256, 297
Third World lesbian statement (UN Women's Conference, Nairobi), 226
Thuto Rammoge and others v. attorney general of Botswana, 20, 197–8
Toonen v. Australia, 81, 228
tourism/gay tourism, 133, 137–9
trade unions/organised labour (and SOGIE rights), 51, 227
tradition/traditional/values/ culture (*see* also family values/ normal family unit/traditional family/'pro-family'), 23, 24, 53, 64, 65, 70, 71, 76, 78, 79, 111, 166, 177, 178, 179, 180, 181, 182, 183, 186, 188, 190, 197, 198, 199, 200, 202, 240, 273, 312, 313, 314, 323, 324, 328, 352, 355, 362, 382, 386, 392, 394, 395
traditional courts, 65
trans/trans men/trans women (*see also* refugee determination), 5, 11, 14, 16, 17, 18–19, 44–5, 52, 54, 55, 57, 58–60, 70, 157, 160–4, 172, 178, 185, 193, 229, 230, 232, 234, 241, 242, 257, 278, 280, 282, 310, 376, 384, 388, 392
Transgender Education and Advocacy (TEA) (Kenya), 193, 309, 355, 317, 349
Transgender Equality Uganda, 337
transgender/trans (community/ organising/advocacy), 26, 161, 193, 227, 251, 254, 287–8, 308, 309, 317, 318, 328, 329, 337,

338, 347–69, 376, 393, 394, 397

Transgender, Intersex and Transsexuals (TITs) (Kenya), 355

Trans-Support Initiative Uganda, 337

Trans Murder Monitoring project/ Transgender Europe, 14

transnational/North-South/South-South (SOGI organising), 1, 2, 3, 5, 30, 31, 148, 153, 154, 201, 227

transphobia, 160, 167–70, 172, 309, 314, 359, 386, 404

transsexual, 57, 232, 254, 355, 388

Uganda Penal Code Act (Section 145), 21, 69, 194, 271, 274, 290, 291, 337

Ugandan Martyrs, see Kabaka Mwanga

'un-African', 24, 26, 28, 85, 178, 180, 197, 201, 312, 314, 323, 326, 327, 354, 391

UNAIDS, 172, 225, 227, 295, 299, 332

United and Strong, 10, 32, 135, 377, 383, 388

United Belize Advocacy Movement (UNIBAM), 7, 247–66

United Nations (advancement of SOGI issues), 172, 223–43, 248, 252, 253, 310, 385

United Nations High Commissioner for Refugees (UNHCR), 98

United Nations Independent Expert on SOGI issues, 6, 26, 181, 182, 185, 230

UN Women, 226, 233, 235, 236, 238, 239, 241

Universal Declaration of Human Rights (1948), 180, 184, 187, 240

Universal Periodic Review (UPR) Guyana, 161
Belize, 250, 252, 253, 263
Kenya, 312, 318

University of West Indies Rights Advocacy Project (U-RAP), 14, 17, 247, 248, 249

unnatural offences/intercourse/ practices (see carnal intercourse/ knowledge against the order of nature)

vagrancy/idle and disorderly (laws against – use re: SOGIE and ITGNC minorities), 13–14, 271

Victor Mukasa and Yvonne Oyo v Attorney General, 81, 285

violence/violations/abuse (on the basis of SOGI) (see also police/ law enforcement), 6, 11, 14, 16, 22, 23–4, 28, 30–1, 63, 88, 89, 90, 102, 119, 134, 136, 137, 138, 139, 142, 143, 161–3, 164–70, 172, 173, 178, 181, 188, 190, 191, 196, 208, 209, 210, 215, 216, 218, 228, 229, 230, 231, 238, 240, 249, 250, 251, 253, 255, 256, 257, 258, 259, 263, 265, 270, 273, 275, 278, 282, 308, 310–13, 314, 316, 318, 325, 329, 339, 341, 348, 349, 351, 352, 355, 359, 361, 369, 376, 380, 382, 383, 384, 387, 388, 389, 390

Voices Against 377/Voices, 4, 50, 54, 392, 395, 396, 397

Walter Reed Project (Makerere University), 281, 299, 301

Warren, Pastor Rick, 87

Western and essentialist concepts of sexual orientation/gender identity (see also refugee determination, Canada), 2, 7, 23, 24, 29, 30, 97, 111, 112, 139, 142, 146–51, 153, 154, 209, 224, 232

West Indies Rights Advocacy Project, 248–249

women (human and reproductive rights)/women's movement/ organising (*see also* UN Women), 23, 25, 27, 29, 50, 70, 85, 90, 111, 113, 114–15, 134, 136–7, 152, 159, 164, 168, 172, 179, 183, 186, 187, 188, 229, 237, 242, 251, 257, 258, 261, 274, 290, 310, 330, 334, 351, 356, 376, 390, 394, 395, 397

women who have sex with women (WSW) (*see also* lesbian(s)/ lesbianism), 310, 316

criminalisation of, 13, 16, 63, 135, 160–1, 196, 241, 310, 330, 331, 348

World AIDS Day, 348, 349

World Social Forum (Nairobi 2007), 308, 333, 348

Yogyakarta Principles/Yogyakarta Principles plus 10, 26, 225, 230, 231–2, 240

Zeid Ra'ad Al Hussein, 229

Zimbabwe, 20, 63, 66, 67, 68, 69, 70, 77, 86, 177, 179, 188

Zimbabwe Human Rights NGO Forum v. Zimbabwe, 188

Lightning Source UK Ltd.
Milton Keynes UK
UKHW05f0242040918
328247UK00010B/130/P